FOUNDATIONAL PSYCHOLOGY
基础心理学

○主编/陈中永

内蒙古科学技术出版社

图书在版编目（CIP）数据

基础心理学：汉、英 / 陈中永主编. —— 赤峰：内蒙古科学技术出版社，2016.12（2020.2重印）
ISBN 978-7-5380-2762-4

Ⅰ. ①基… Ⅱ. ①陈… Ⅲ. ①心理学—双语教学—高等学校—教材—汉、英 Ⅳ. ①B84

中国版本图书馆CIP数据核字（2017）第006456号

基础心理学

主　　编：	陈中永
责任编辑：	张文娟
封面设计：	陈子建
出版发行：	内蒙古科学技术出版社
地　　址：	赤峰市红山区哈达街南一段4号
网　　址：	www.nm-kj.cn
邮购电话：	0476-5888903
排版制作：	赤峰市阿金奈图文制作有限责任公司
印　　刷：	天津兴湘印务有限公司
字　　数：	1005千
开　　本：	787mm×1092mm　1/16
印　　张：	33.5
版　　次：	2016年12月第1版
印　　次：	2020年2月第2次印刷
书　　号：	ISBN 978-7-5380-2762-4
定　　价：	128.00元

编委会

主　编：陈中永
副主编：七十三　钟建军　陈子冰　高喜天
编　委：潘　卓　张　虹　吴柏周　赵子萱
　　　　　李　婷　刘立立　张　琦　窦雪婷
　　　　　李　倩　李　鑫　陈婷丽　贾缨琪
　　　　　月　盈　王　畅　张　丹　刘　旭
　　　　　邰少琦　苏　宁　张金钟

前　言

　　心理学专业的学习者和研究者需要有一个坚实的理论知识框架，这个框架过去一般认为是普通心理学。近年由于教学需要，多把以普通心理学知识为主体，涉及多门心理学分支学科核心概念的教学体系称之为基础心理学。顾名思义，基础心理学就是心理学专业学习者的专业基础知识体系，是学习者的入门课程，是进一步走向专业领域的基石。这门课程也是不断吸纳心理学前沿研究成果，吸纳世界各国不同文化背景下心理学研究优秀成果的动态知识体系。同时，对基础心理学的学习和研究不仅可以不断地完善普通心理学的知识体系，还会不断产生出理论和实践方面的新课题和新的学科生长点。

　　心理学专业外语课程的开设目的，是使学习者掌握文化交流的语言工具，并用这种工具学习国外心理学研究的成果，吸纳其精华，并进而与国际同行展开交流与合作，也将我们的研究成果向世界传播出去。事实证明，那种为学语言而学语言的模式效果不佳，只有为了用语言而学语言才是正确的途径。为此，本书把基础心理学和心理学专业外语（英语）结合为一体，使学习者通过本书，能较全面地掌握一门专业外语，并相应地形成运用外语进行学习和交流的能力。

　　这本书正是基于上述理念编写的。全书一共二十章，内容以普通心理学体系为主线，但增加了西方心理学流派、人类的行为、心理学的生物学基础等内容。在此基础上，涉及了发展心理学、教育心理学、心理测量学、变态心理学、社会心理学等分支学科的重要知识。最后，还为学习者提供了国外心理学学术期刊的投稿要求和论文样例。

本教材的编写，陈中永同志主持了全部工作，编制了体系框架，并对全书进行统稿。七十三、钟建军、陈子冰、高喜天四位同志作为副主编完成了统稿、内容审核、校对工作。潘卓、张虹、吴柏周、赵子萱、李婷、刘立立、张琦、窦雪婷、李倩、李鑫、陈婷丽、贾缨琪、月盈、王畅、张丹、刘旭、郜少琦、苏宁、张金钟完成了一定章节的录入、修改和校对工作。

由于教材内容较多、篇幅较长，编校工作尚不充分，教材中内容编排不当之处、漏校之处还存在很多，有待今后进一步完善。

编者

2016 年 6 月

目 录

第一章 心理学概观 ··· 1
 第一节 心理学的范围：从神经细胞到社会 ····························· 1
 第二节 研究目标 ··· 9
第二章 西方主要心理学流派 ·· 13
 第一节 冯特及其影响 ··· 14
 第二节 格式塔心理学 ··· 14
 第三节 行为主义 ··· 15
 第四节 精神分析 ··· 16
 第五节 认知心理学 ·· 17
 第六节 人本主义心理学 ··· 23
第三章 心理与行为的生物学基础 ··· 29
 第一节 神经系统概述 ··· 30
 第二节 神经系统内的联系 ·· 32
 第三节 神经系统的结构与功能 ·· 38
 第四节 心理的化学过程 ··· 47
 第五节 内分泌系统 ·· 51
 第六节 未来研究趋向 ··· 53
第四章 感觉 ·· 58
 第一节 感觉系统 ··· 59
 第二节 听觉 ·· 62
 第三节 视觉 ·· 68
 第四节 化学性质的感觉：嗅觉和味觉 ······································ 80
 第五节 躯体感觉和前庭系统 ··· 82
 第六节 未来研究趋向 ··· 88
第五章 知觉 ·· 94
 第一节 从感觉到知觉：概述 ··· 96
 第二节 心理物理学 ·· 98
 第三节 组织知觉世界 ··· 109

        第四节　识别知觉世界……………………………………… 121
第六章　注意与意识…………………………………………………… 129
    第一节　什么是意识……………………………………………… 130
    第二节　意识的状态……………………………………………… 132
    第三节　注意与意识……………………………………………… 135
    第四节　特殊的意识状态………………………………………… 141
第七章　记忆…………………………………………………………… 145
    第一节　记忆系统概述…………………………………………… 146
    第二节　感觉记忆………………………………………………… 150
    第三节　短时记忆………………………………………………… 154
    第四节　长时记忆………………………………………………… 162
    第五节　构建着的记忆…………………………………………… 174
    第六节　提高你的记忆…………………………………………… 175
    第七节　未来研究趋向…………………………………………… 179
第八章　思维与语言…………………………………………………… 184
    第一节　概要：从刺激到动作…………………………………… 185
    第二节　思维……………………………………………………… 190
    第三节　问题的解决……………………………………………… 196
    第四节　风险决策………………………………………………… 205
    第五节　语言……………………………………………………… 210
    第六节　未来研究趋向…………………………………………… 218
第九章　思维与教学…………………………………………………… 223
    第一节　思维与理解的重要性…………………………………… 223
    第二节　概念的学习与教学……………………………………… 224
    第三节　学习中问题的解决……………………………………… 227
    第四节　思维的教学与学习……………………………………… 234
    第五节　迁移的教学……………………………………………… 238
第十章　情绪…………………………………………………………… 242
    第一节　情绪类型与诱因………………………………………… 242
    第二节　情绪的表现……………………………………………… 245
    第三节　情绪理论………………………………………………… 248
    第四节　情绪的性别差异………………………………………… 255
第十一章　动机………………………………………………………… 258
    第一节　什么是动机……………………………………………… 258
    第二节　动机理论………………………………………………… 259

第三节　生理性动机：饥与渴 …………………………………………… 261
　　　第四节　性：最隐私的动机 ……………………………………………… 267
　　　第五节　成就、权力、交往：人类特有的动机 ………………………… 273
第十二章　智力 ……………………………………………………………………… 282
　　　第一节　智力的含义 ……………………………………………………… 282
　　　第二节　智力理论 ………………………………………………………… 283
　　　第三节　智力的极端现象 ………………………………………………… 288
第十三章　人格 ……………………………………………………………………… 292
　　　第一节　人格概念 ………………………………………………………… 292
　　　第二节　心理动力论 ……………………………………………………… 294
　　　第三节　特质论 …………………………………………………………… 301
　　　第四节　行为主义观点 …………………………………………………… 306
　　　第五节　人本主义观点 …………………………………………………… 309
　　　第六节　人格特质的测量 ………………………………………………… 313
　　　第七节　探求人格动力：投射测验 ……………………………………… 315
第十四章　人类行为 ………………………………………………………………… 319
　　　第一节　行为 ……………………………………………………………… 320
　　　第二节　组织行为 ………………………………………………………… 320
　　　第三节　行为科学 ………………………………………………………… 321
　　　第四节　人类行为的系统观 ……………………………………………… 322
　　　第五节　天性与教养的争论 ……………………………………………… 324
　　　第六节　行为与环境 ……………………………………………………… 325
　　　第七节　行为态度 ………………………………………………………… 327
　　　第八节　行为与认知过程 ………………………………………………… 330
　　　第九节　行为与动机 ……………………………………………………… 331
第十五章　心理的发展 ……………………………………………………………… 334
　　　第一节　人类发展的概念 ………………………………………………… 334
　　　第二节　发展的规律性 …………………………………………………… 336
　　　第三节　发展的理论 ……………………………………………………… 342
　　　第四节　认知发展 ………………………………………………………… 347
　　　第五节　社会性及情感的发展 …………………………………………… 351
第十六章　学习 ……………………………………………………………………… 358
　　　第一节　行为主义学习观 ………………………………………………… 358
　　　第二节　认知理论学习观 ………………………………………………… 366
　　　第三节　人本主义学习观 ………………………………………………… 372

第十七章 心理测量 385
第一节 测量与评价 385
第二节 测量量表 386
第三节 测量与目标 388
第四节 良好测量工具应具备的特征 391
第五节 标准化测验 394
第六节 教师自编测验 405
第七节 参照标准测验 410

第十八章 心理变态与治疗 415
第一节 心理变态的界定 415
第二节 变态行为的分类 418
第三节 心理障碍的治疗 422

第十九章 社会心理学 427
第一节 概述 427
第二节 态度和态度改变 428
第三节 归因与印象形成 436
第四节 偏见与刻板印象 442
第五节 社会吸引 446
第六节 从众与依从 450
第七节 攻击与利他主义 457

第二十章 心理学研究方法 467
第一节 事件与变量 467
第二节 实验法 469
第三节 观察法 472
第四节 个案研究 473
第五节 调查 474
第六节 现场研究 475
第七节 跨文化研究 476
第八节 相关法研究 477
第九节 研究范式的本质特征 477
第十节 科学、方法论与理论 479

附录 482
附录1：国外心理学文献撰写格式 482
附录2：国外主要心理学期刊及网站 487
附录3：APA格式范文 492

CONTENTS

CHAPTER 1 THE WORLD OF PSYCHOLOGY 1
    FROM CELL TO SOCIETY: THE SCOPE OF PSYCHOLOGY 1
    THE GOALS OF RESEARCH 9

CHAPTER 2 MAIN SCHOOLS OF THE OCCIDENTAL PSYCHOLOGY
.... 13
    WUNDT AND HIS INFLUENCE 14
    GESTALT PSYCHOLOGY 14
    BEHAVIORISM 15
    PSYCHOANALYSIS 16
    COGNITIVE PSYCHOLOGY 17
    HUMANISTIC PSYCHOLOGY 23

CHAPTER 3 BIOLOGICAL BASES OF BEHAVIOR AND PSYCHOLOGY
.... 29
    THE NERVOUS SYSTEM: AN OVERVIEW 30
    COMMUNICATION IN THE NERVOUS SYSTEM 32
    STRUCTURES AND FUNCTIONS OF THE CENTRAL NERVOUS SYSTEM 38
    THE CHEMISTRY OF PSYCHOLOGY 47
    ENDOCRINE SYSTEMS 51
    FUTURE DIRECTIONS 53

CHAPTER 4 SENSATION 58
    SENSORY SYSTEMS 59
    HEARING 62
    VISION 68
    THE CHEMICAL SENSES: SMELL AND TASTE 80
    SOMATIC SENSES AND THE VESTIBULAR SYSTEM 82
    FUTURE DIRECTIONS 88

CHAPTER 5 PERCEPTION 94
    FROM SENSATION TO PERCEPTION: AN OVERVIEW 96
    PSYCHOPHYSICS 98

ORGANIZING THE PERCEPTUAL WORLD ·················· 109
　　　RECOGNIZING THE PERCEPTUAL WORLD ················ 121
CHAPTER 6　ATTENTION AND CONSCIOUSNESS ················ 129
　　　WHAT IS CONSCIOUSNESS ································· 130
　　　STATES OF CONSCIOUSNESS ····························· 132
　　　ATTENTION AND CONSCIOUSNESS ······················· 135
　　　SPECIAL COUSCIOUS STATE ······························ 141
CHAPTER 7　MEMORY ··· 145
　　　THE SCOPE OF THE MEMORY SYSTEM ·················· 146
　　　SENSORY MEMORY ·· 150
　　　SHORT-TERM MEMORY ····································· 154
　　　LONG-TERM MEMORY ······································· 162
　　　CONSTRUCTING MEMORY ··································· 174
　　　IMPROVING YOUR MEMORY ································· 175
　　　FUTURE DIRECTIONS ·· 179
CHAPTER 8　THINKING AND LANGUAGE ·························· 184
　　　FROM STIMULUS TO ACTION: AN OVERVIEW ············ 185
　　　THINKING ·· 190
　　　PROBLEM SOLVING ·· 196
　　　RISKY DECISION MAKING ···································· 205
　　　LANGUAGE ··· 210
　　　FUTURE DIRECTIONS ·· 218
CHAPTER 9　THINKING AND TEACHING ··························· 223
　　　THE IMPORTANCE OF THINKING AND UNDERSTANDING ··· 223
　　　LEARNING AND TEACHING ABOUT CONCEPT ············ 224
　　　PROBLEM SOLVING IN LEARNING ·························· 227
　　　TEACHING AND LEARNING ABOUT THINKING ············ 234
　　　TEACHING FOR TRANSFER ·································· 238
CHAPTER 10　EMOTION ··· 242
　　　EMOTION TYPES AND INCENTIVES ························ 242
　　　EXPRESSION OF EMOTION ·································· 245
　　　THEORIES OF EMOTION ····································· 248
　　　CONTROVERSY: ARE MAN OR WOMAN MORE EMOTIONAL ··· 255
CHAPTER 11　MOTIVATION ·· 258
　　　THE CONCEPT OF MOTIVATION ···························· 258
　　　THEORIES OF MOTIVATION ·································· 259

  HUNGER AND THIRST: MOTIVES WITH A BIOLOGICAL BASIS ··· 261
  HUMAN SEXUALITY: THE MOST INTIMATE MOTIVE ········ 267
  ACHIEVEMENT、POWER、AFFILIATION: SOME UNIQUELY
    HUMAN MOTIVES ·· 273
CHAPTER 12 INTELLIGENCE ·· 282
  WHAT DOES INTELLENCE MEAN ································· 282
  THEORIES ON INTELLIGENCE ······································ 283
  THE EXTREMES OF INTELLIGENCE ······························ 288
CHAPTER 13 PERSONALITY ··· 292
  CONCEPT OF PERSONALITY ·· 292
  THE PSYCHODYNAMIC PERSPECTIVE ·························· 294
  THE TRAIT PERSPECTIVE ·· 301
  THE BEHAVIORAL PERSPECTIVE ·································· 306
  THE HUAMANISTIC PERSPECTIVE ······························· 309
  MEASUTING PERSONALITY TRAIT ······························· 313
  EXPLORING PERSONALITY DYNAMICS: PROJECTIVE TEST ······ 315
CHAPTER 14 HUMAN BEHAVIOR ·· 319
  BEHAVIOR ·· 320
  ORGANIZATIONAL BEHAVIOR ····································· 320
  THE BEHAVIORAL SCIENCES ······································· 321
  HUMAN BEHAVIOR: A SYSTEMS VIEW ························· 322
  THE NATURE-NURTURE CONTROVERSY ······················ 324
  BEHAVIOR AND ENVIRONMENT ·································· 325
  BEHAVIOR AND ATTITUDES ·· 327
  BEHAVIOR AND COGNITIVE PROCESSES ······················ 330
  BEHAVIOR AND MOTIVATION ····································· 331
CHAPTER 15 PSYCHOLOGY DEVELOPMENT ······················ 334
  CONCEPTS IN HUMAN DEVELOPMENT ·························· 334
  PRINCIPLES OF DEVELOPMENT ································· 336
  THEORIES OF DEVELOPMENT ····································· 342
  COGNITIVE DEVELOPMENT ·· 347
  SOCIAL AND EMOTIONAL DEVELOPMENT ···················· 351
CHAPTER 16 LEARNING ··· 358
  BEHAVIORAL VIEWS OF LEARNING ····························· 358
  COGNITIVE VIEWS OF LEARNING ································ 366
  HUMANISTIC VIEWS OF LEAMSING ····························· 372

CHAPTER 17   PSYCHOLOGICAL MEASUREMENT   385
- MEASUREMENT AND EVALUATION   385
- SCALES OF MEASUREMENT   386
- MEASUREMENT AND GOALS   388
- CHARACTERISTICS OF A GOOD MEASURING INSTRUMENT   391
- STANDARDIZED TESTS   394
- TEACHER-MADE TESTS   405
- CRITERION-REFERENCED TESTING   410

CHAPTER 18   MENTAL ABNORMAL AND THERAPY   415
- THE DEFINITION OF ABNORMALITY: WHAT IS ABNORMAL BEHAVIOR   415
- CLASSIFYING ABNORMAL BEHAVIOR   418
- THERAPY FOR PSYCHOLOGICAL DISORDER   422

CHAPTER 19   SOCIAL PSYCHOLOGY   427
- INTRODUCTION   427
- ATTITUDES AND ATTITUDES CHANGE   428
- ATTRIBUTION AND IMPRESSION FORMATION   436
- PREJUDICE AND STEREOTYPES   442
- SOCILA ATTRACTION   446
- CONFORMITY AND COMPLIANCE   450
- AGGRESSION AND ALTRUISM   457

CHAPTER 20   RESEARCH METHODS AND TECHNIQUES OF PSYCHOLOGY   467
- HAPPENING AND VARIABLE   467
- THE EXPERIMENTAL METHOD   469
- OBSERVATION   472
- CASE STUDY   473
- SURVEY   474
- FIELD INVESTIGATION   475
- CROSS-CULTURE INVESTIGATION   476
- CORRELATIONAL STUDY   477
- ESSENTIAL FEATURE OF RESEARCH PARADIGMS   477
- SCIENCE, METHODOLOGY AND THEORY   479

APPENDIX   482

第一章 心理学概观
(THE WORLD OF PSYCHOLOGY)

本章要点(Chapter Outline)
心理学的范围(The Scope of Psychology)
心理学的分支(Subfields of Psychology)
研究心理的多种途径(Psychology Approaches)
研究的目标(The Goals of Research)

在现代社会中,随着人类的物质文明和精神文明的高度发展,心理科学越来越受到人们的高度重视。心理学作为一门独立的科学,已有一百多年的历史,但它的渊源可以追溯到几千年以前,可以说"心理学是一门古老而又年轻的科学"。由于人的心理与行为极其复杂,就需要心理学内部进行分工予以研究。从单个神经细胞的活动到复杂社会中的社会矛盾,从孩童时代的语言发生发展到老年时代应具有的判断力等问题发展出一系列着重于理论研究的分支学科;另一方面,人有无数实践活动的领域都涉及人的心理因素问题,需要应用心理学的理论来解决人们面临的实际问题,这就产生出了很多着重于应用研究的分支学科。据估计,现代心理学已有一百多个分支学科,包括:教育心理学、发展心理学、管理心理学、心理测量学等,它们组成了一个门类繁多且又具有旺盛生命力的心理学世界。

Psychology is the science of behavior and mental processes. This means that psychologists use the methods of science to investigate all kinds of behavior and mental processes, from the activity of a single nerve cell to the social conflicts in a complex society, from the development of language in childhood to the adjustments required in old age. In this chapter, we offer an overview of the field, including a description of what subfields and approaches psychology encompasses, what psychologists do, and how psychologists go about their work. In Later chapters, we will focus on the results of psychological research and how those results are being applied to improve the quality of life for many people.

第一节 心理学的范围:从神经细胞到社会
(FROM CELL TO SOCIETY: THE SCOPE OF PSYCHOLOGY)

As an illustration of the scope of psychology, consider the case of Jack Montgomery. Jack is a

47-year-old father and leader of a youth group at the East Side YMCA. For the last twenty-five years, he has smoked more than two packs of unfiltered cigarettes a day. This pattern of behavior has not been kind to him. Jack has already lost one lung to emphysema, and his doctors have warned him that he will soon die unless he quits smoking. When he brings children from the Y to a day camp and begins chopping firewood, he can make only two or three ax strokes before his breathing becomes heavy wheezes. One of the young campers is naive enough to tell him he should stop smoking. "Son", says Jack, "I've tried to quit, but I would rather die than live without cigarettes."

Is smoking a learned habit, a nicotine addiction maintained by biololgical forces, or a combination of the two? Do different people smoke for different reasons, and do those reasons determine how difficult it will be for them to quit? Why do people start smoking in the first place? Health warnings have dramatically reduced the prevalence of smoking over the last two decades, but nearly one-third of American adults still smoke; some of them began using tobacco before they entered high school (Gallup, 1986). Why don't smokers heed warnings about the grave dangers of smoking? What can be done to motivate smokers to quit? These are just a few of the questions that a psychologist might ask about smoking. There are lists at least as long for other phenomena, which questions particular psychologists choose to address and where they look for the answers depend on their area of specialization and on the psychological approach they prefer.

Subfields of Psychology

In 1879, in Leipzig, Germany, Wilhelm Wundt a physician and physiologist who hoped to identify the basic elements of human consciousness established the first formal psychology laboratory. We will have more to say about the history of psychology in Chapter 2. For now, suffice it to say that psychology has expanded greatly since the founding of Wundt's laboratory. Like other sciences, psychology has developed numerous subfields, or areas of specialization. These subfields approach behavior and mental processes in somewhat different ways.

Biological psychology Psychologists who analyze the biological factors in behavior and mental processes are called **biological** or **physiological psychologists**. They might analyze, for example, the relationship between how a smoker smokes (the rate of puffs) and how much deadly carbon monoxide reaches the brain.

Some biological psychologists explore the chemical interactions within and between nerve cells. especially in the brain and spinal cord. Understanding these interactions is vital to understanding behavior and mental life because experiences, perceptions, actions, and emotions all depend on how nerve cells communicate. Some researchers explore the relationships between brain activity and behavior, for example, they might map the parts of the brain that become activated when people solve problems or confront unexpected events. Other biological psychologists look for clues to how hormones influence emotion and behavior. Still others painstakingly unravel the puzzle of how certain groups of nerve cells allow people to translate energy from the outside world into the experiences of sight and hearing.

Experimental and cognitive psychology Many smokers say that cigarettes help them to concentrate and to perform various mental tasks more efficiently. Is this self-delusion, or does smoking change mental efficiency?

This is the type of question that experimental and cognitive psychologists might ask. They have found, for example, that giving nicotine to rats can impair the rats' ability to recall tasks they learned just twenty-four hours earlier (Gilliam & Schlesinger, 1985). But researchers have also found that male smokers do better at detecting rapidly presented stimuli on a television screen after being allowed to smoke than after twelve hours of cigarette deprivation (Edward et al., 1985).

Experimental psychology once was psychology. This was the area in which Wilhelm Wundt, William James, Edward Titchener, and other early psychologists worked. They used the term experimental to distinguish their experiments on human perception, learning, and memory from the endeavors of philosophers and others who thought hard about such phenomena but performed no experiments. The scientific methods of experimental psychology are now evident in research in every subfield of psychology.

Today, **experimental psychologists** continue to conduct experiments aimed at better understanding learning, memory, and other basic behavioral and mental processes in both animals and humans. Research on human learning has helped curriculum planners and teachers in everything from deciding how much new material should be presented in one lesson to advising students on how to study. You may find some of the research described in Chapter 7, on memory, especially valuable as you prepare for tests.

In recent years, many experimental psychologists have begun to shift their research toward ever more detailed analysis of the mental processes involved in learning, memory, and perception. They explore the processes underlying judgement, decision making, problem solving, imagination, and other aspects of complex human thought, or cognition. Those who focus on these processes have come to be known as **cognitive psychologists**.

Cognitive psychologists also study people with learning problems people like Phil, a grade-school student with the learning disability known as dyslexia. Like other dyslexics, Phil has normal intellectual abilities and a perfect understanding of speech; but somewhere in the process of translating printed symbols into meanings in his head, something goes wrong. When Phil reads, he often leaves out words or confuses the letters b and d ox o and c. Where, why, and how these disruptions occur are some of the questions being asked by psychologists who study how the mind perceives each letter, how letters are grouped into words, how words are grouped into sentences, and how sentences are grouped into ideas. As they find answers to such questions, psychologists and other professionals can begin to correct the problems of dyslexia and other learning disabilities.

One of the many places where cognitive and experimental psychology come together is engineering. For example, the safety of commercial aviation is in part due to psychological studies of how people perceive the world around them and how much information they can handle at once. This research has allowed cognitive psychologists to advise engineers about how to arrange an airliner s vast array of instruments and warning lights so that the pilot can quickly understand and act on them. Engineering psychologists are becoming increasingly prominent in the design of everything from telephone equipment and computer keyboards to control panels for nuclear power plants.

Personality psychology Whereas experimental and cognitive psychologists seek laws that govern the behavior of people in general, **personality psychologists** focus on the characteristics that make us unique. They also try to identify the specific ways in which people differ and to explore the relationships between people's personalities and their tendency to think, act, and feel in certain ways. For example, personality researchers have found that some people tend to at tribute success or failure to external forces, such as good or bad luck, other people believe that success or failure is controlled largely by personal effort, As we will see in chapter 14, on personality, such differences have been linked to a variety of from the tendency to smoke cigarettes to the tendency to become depressed.

Social psychology Junior high school students do not simply wake up one morning and decide to start smoking cigarettes. Social influences over time shape their behavior. They may see their parents, and especially their friends, smoking. They cannot help seeing magazine ads that portray the glamour supposedly associated with smoking. Influences like these are the special interest of **social psychologists**. They study how people influence one another, especially in groups of two or more.

Some social psychology research focuses on how people influence one another's attitudes. For example, studies of prejudice show that children learn negative attitudes and biased behavior toward certain racial or ethnic learn negative attitudes and biased behavior toward certain racial or ethnic groups by listening to bigoted parents or friends. Other research focuses on group behavior—asking, for example, how the personality of a group's leader affects its ability to solve problems, make decisions, or maintain a pleasant social atmosphere. Industrial–organizational psychologists often conduct or apply research on such questions in the business world. They might help select the people most likely to work well in various settings, improve supervisors' leadership skills, create groups that function at maximum efficiency, and suggest other research—based steps to increase both productivity and satisfaction.

Clinical psychology Whereas most psychologists explore normal behavior and mental processes, **clinical psychologists** seek to understand and correct abnormal functioning. Using tests, interviews, and observations, they conduct research on the causes and symptoms of mental disorders. In the consulting room, they use similar methods to pinpoint individuals' problems and offer therapy to help solve those problems.

Preventing disorders is another concern of clinical psychologists, especially those called community psychologists. Their emphasis on prevention has inspired programs to head off psychological problems among teenage parents, people under heavy stress, and others who may be at high risk for developing mental disorders.

Developmental psychology Behavior and mental processes change constantly over the course of a lifetime. **Developmental psychologists** have set themselves the task of describing those changes, trying to understand their causes, and exploring their effects. They have conducted research on the stress of adolescence, the challenges of adulthood, and the changes associated with old age. But because changes in language, thinking, social skills, and personality occur most rapidly and dramatically in infancy and childhood, much developmental research has focused on those early stages of life.

Research by developmental psychologists has increased the understanding of how childhood experiences are related to subsequent behavior and thought. Early work by Rene Spitz showed, for example, that orphaned infants placed in an institution where they had basic care, but no chance to form a close attachment to an adult, typically became socially and emotionally disordered. Orphans placed in homes where conditions were quite bad, but where they could develop a close relationship with a caregiver, did far better emotionally. Other research has helped launch special educational programs for underprivileged preschoolers who appear likely to be at a disadvantage when they start school.

Quantitative psychology   The rules of science require that the topic studied whether chemical reactions, planetary movements, or memory be accurately measured and carefully analyzed so that the results of research will be as free from error as possible. All psychologists therefore face the task of measuring and analyzing the phenomena they choose to study. Many of these phenomena—heart activity, learning, emotions, mental disorders, social development, or any of a thousand other behaviors or mental processes are particularly difficult to translate into quantitative form and are not easy to analyze using conventional mathematical tools.

Suppose, for example, that you want to analyze smoking behavior. You could ask subjects to fill out a questionnaire summarizing their smoking over the past six months, you could ask them to keep track of their smoking over the next two weeks by recording in a daily diary the time and place of each cigarette. You could also observe the subjects as they smoke, recording the number and duration of puffs. Whatever the approach, you need a method of summarizing and analyzing the data you have collected, in order to compare one subject with the next and perhaps even to identify groups of subjects with similar smoking styles.

Quantitative, or measurement, **psychologists** devote much of their energy to developing and applying mathematical methods for summarizing and analyzing data from virtually every area of psychology. For example, they have helped biological psychologists find precise mathematical ways of describing the changes in a subject s heart rate, blood pressure, or brain waves when certain stimuli are presented. Some of these methods, known collectively as statistical analyses, are discussed in the Appendix.

Quantitative psychologists are also involved in constructing and evaluating paper-and-pencil tests used to measure traits, attitudes, mental capacity, and mental disorders. These tests are used every day to help diagnose people's problems and to select individuals for admission to everything from college to jobs in the military and the space program.

In other studies, quantitative psychologists attempt to create mathematical formulas, or models, to describe and even predict such complex behavior as judgment and decision making. In diagnosing a patient's physical problems, for example, doctors use information from physical examinations, medical histories, blood tests, brain scans, and many other sources. How is all this information combined to reach a diagnosis? A quantitative psychologist might try to describe the process in mathematical terms, creating a model to predict other doctors' diagnoses in future experiments and; by implication, in actual medical situations.

Psychological Approaches

Suppose you were a psychologist trying to understand why a certain group of people had failed when they tried to quit smoking. Where would you look for an answer? Would you search for environmental stressors that might have prompted relapse? Would you blame the physical discomfort created by quitting?

Many such approaches are possible and useful. The one you would choose would most likely depend on your assumptions about the most important factors causing, maintaining, and altering behavior and mental processes in general and cigarette smoking in particular. These assumptions would lead you to prefer different theoretical approaches. The most influential approaches in psychology today are generally labeled biological, psychodynamic, behavioral, humanistic, and cognitive.

The biological approach   One way to understand smoking is to explore how and why smokers need or become addicted to nicotine. This reflects the biological approach. It begins with the assumption that biological factors, such as genetics, electrical and chemical activity in the brain, and the actions of hormones are the most important determinants of behavior and mental processes. Those who adopt this approach study emotions, mental disorders, memory, thinking, and other psychological phenomena by seeking out and learning about their biological components.

The psychodynamic approach   The psychodynamic approach was founded by Sigmund Freud, the famous Viennese physician whose interest in "neuroscience" (people with physical symptoms with no physical causes) led him to develop, late in the nineteenth century, a theory of personality, mental disorder, and therapy known as psychoanalysis. The psychodynamic approach presumes that behavior and mental processes reflect constant, dynamic, and often unconscious struggles within each person. These struggles are varied and complex, but they usually involve conflict between the impulse to satisfy instincts or wishes (for food, sex, or aggression, for example) and the restrictions imposed by society.

Viewed from this perspective, abnormal or problematic behavior reflects either an unsatisfactory resolution of conflicts or an outright failure to resolve them. Smoking might thus be but one symptom of an unconscious conflict between wanting to remain a pampered infant and wanting to be an independent adult, inhaling a cigarette might symbolize sucking on a bottle. A psychodynamic psychologist would expect therapy aimed at resolving inner conflicts to greatly enhance a person's ability to quit smoking permanently.

The behavioral approach   At about the same time that Freud was developing his psychodynamic approach, a young American, John Watson, was urging psychologists to study only what they could observe directly, and not unobservable mental events. By focusing on observable actions alone, said Watson, psychologists would not have to rely on people's possibly distorted reports about mental processes and could begin to understand behavior whether it occurs in adults, children, the mentally ill, or animals.

Watson's views gave birth to the behavioral approach to psychology. According to this approach, the pattern of rewards and punishments that each person has experienced determines most behaviors and ways of thinking. Biological factors provide the raw material on which these rewards, punishments, and other learning experiences act to mold each of us.

Few behaviorists endorse a version of the behavioral approach as radical as Watson's, but they do suggest that most problematic behaviors can be changed by helping people to unlearn old habits and develop new and better ones. Thus, smoking might be viewed as a habit learned by watching others and maintained because the smoker associates cigarettes with pleasent serial occasions, relief from stress, or other rewards. People might break the habit if they learn to develop rewarding alternative responses in situations previously associated with smoking.

The humanistic approach   So far, the approaches we have described focus on how a person is acted upon, whether by biological forces, inner conflicts, or environmental stimuli. In contrast, a fundamental assumption of the humanistic approach is that people control themselves. Furthermore, according to this approach, each person has an innate tendency to grow toward his or her own potential, although the environment (including other people) may block this growth.

According to the humanistic perspective, behavior is determined primarily by each person's capacity to choose how to think and act. These choices are dictated, say humanistic psychologists, by each individual's unique perception of the world. If you perceive the world as a supportive, friendly place, you are likely to feel happy and secure. If you view it as dangerous and hostile, you will probably be defensive and anxious. Humanistic psychologists view even severe depression not as mental illness but as a sign of a person's pessimistic perceptions and attitudes. Seen from the humanistic perspective, the decision to smoke or not, or to quit or not, depends primarily on how a person perceives the benefits and the dangers involved. Unless the smoker decides to quit, any effort prompted by someone else is likely to fail.

The cognitive approach   In the last fifteen years or so, another perspective the cognitive approach has become particularly influential. More than any of the other approaches we have discussed, the cognitive approach emphasizes the importance of thoughts and other mental processes. This perspective focuses directly on mental processes that is, on how the brain takes in information, uses its functions of perception, memory, thought, judgment, decision making, and the like to process that information, and generated integrated patterns of behavior.

For example, the cognitive perspective would hold that a person continues to smoke or tries to quit because of what that person recalls about the dangers of smoking, how that person perceives those dangers (are they personally threatening?), and how he or she judges the effects of quitting (would it reduce the risks significantly?). Similarly, since severe behavior disorders reflect some disorganization in the processing of information, effective treatment might range from drugs to training that would help a person think in more organized or rational ways.

The question of which of these approaches is the "right" one can never be answered, simply because "rightness" or "wrongness" is not at issue. Nor does each psychologist have to choose and adhere once and for all to just one approach. In studying smoking, for example, one might want to consider biological, cognitive, and behavioral variables, indeed, this is exactly what many smoking researchers do. Each approach to psychology emphasizes a particular set of factors that tells part of the story of behavior and mental processes. We will see throughout this book that each approach has made its own contribution to psychological theory, research, and applications. A full understanding of psychology is unlikely to develop without appreciating these diverse contributions.

Unity within Diversity

Psychology's many subfields and approaches have led psychologists into a wide variety of interests and activities. These activities include conducting research and applying the results to solve and prevent human problems, as well as teaching and writing about research findings and psychological knowledge. In spite of this diversity, however, at least two factors unify psychologists' varied interests, activities, and values.

First, because they are all interested in behavior and mental processes, psychologists in every subfield constantly draw on and contribute to knowledge from all the other subfields. For example, the biological psychologist's finding that chemical imbalances in the brain can produce disordered thinking may provide the clinical psychologist with clues to the cause of certain mental disorders. Similarly, research in developmental psychology may help the cognitive psychologist better understand how the ability to use language, solve problems, or think logically is built up over time.

Secondly, because psychology is a science, all of its subfields emphasize empirical research the collection and analysis of information about topics of interest. Psychologists not only speculate about certain phenomena, such as smoking behavior, but also gather information, or data, about it. Even psychologists who do not themselves conduct research depend heavily on research discoveries to teach or write knowledgeably, provide up-to-date treatment, and solve the endless variety of problems they confront every day. Indeed, most of the facts, theories, and applications that make up today's psychological knowledge originated in or were stimulated by research.

Without this research base, psychology might merge with philosophy, or psychologists might issue proclamations with no more credibility than those of astrologers or the National Enquirer. To make it easier to appreciate and evaluate the research described in later chapters, we turn now to a general review of the goals of scientific research and of the rules and methods that help psychologists make progress toward those goals. More detailed coverage of data analysis is offered in the Appendix.

第二节 研究目标
(THE GOALS OF RESEARCH)

There is a country and western song called "Can't Stop smoking that Cigarette." On hearing that song over twenty years ago, a psychologist we know became curious about why so many people find it so hard to quit smoking. He has been doing research on smoking ever since. His story is not unusual. The research adventure in psychology, as in all other sciences, often begins simply enough with curiosity.

Curiosity frequently provokes very interesting, very stimulating questions, but often these questions are phrased in terms that are too general to be investigated scientifically. After agonizing over the glacial slowness with which a group of friends chooses a restaurant or movie, for example, you might notice the same phenomenon in other groups and begin to ask such questions as: How do groups make decisions? What would help them work more efficiently? The scientist must be more specific asking: What kinds of groups and what kinds of decision are involved? (The decision-making process among prisoners planning an escape might be different from that used by children choosing a game.) What is meant by efficiency? (Ratings of efficiency by group members and ratings by an outside observer might tell very different stories.)

If you are trained as a psychologist, you would begin to ask these more precise questions. The new questions might be less interesting than those you first posed, but you are more likely to be able to answer them with some confidence. It is only by putting together the answers to many smaller questions that researchers begin to see answers to sonic of the larger ones.

To find these answers, psychologists, like other scientists, depend on the accumulation of knowledge over many years by many people. They also rely on several levels of research guided by four basic goals: description, prediction, control, and explanation.

Description

In order to answer any research question, the scientist must first describe the phenomenon of interest, If, for example, you decided to use jury deliberations at criminal trials as the source of data for studying group decision making, you would first have to gather detailed information about trials and jury deliberations. How are criminal trials conducted? What are the characteristics of the defendants, the witnesses, the attorneys, and the evidence? What do jurors say to each other about the evidence? Do they vote secretly or publicly?

These are just a few of the characteristics of decision making in the courtroom that you would measure and summarize before aiming for more ambitious goals, such as predicting the outcome of a trial. Such descriptive data are usually collected through surveys, case studies, and observations, each of which we will describe shortly.

Prediction

As you examine your data, you would probably begin to see some interesting patterns. It might appear, for example, that six-person juries reach verdicts more slowly than twelve-member juries or that witnesses who wear suits or dresses impress jurors more than those who wear blue jeans. Noticing these apparent relationships, you might aim for a more ambitious research goal: prediction. You might, for example, predict that if defense witnesses are well dressed, then the jury is likely to acquit the defendants. When a prediction is stated as a specific, testable proposition about a phenomenon, it is called a **hypothesis**.

To test your hypothesis, you would gather additional data, looking not only for evidence that supports the hypothesis but also for evidence that refutes it. In research aimed at prediction, one typically tests hypotheses by analyzing descriptive data in order to detect relationships between variables, which are specific factors or characteristics that can vary in some way. witnesses' clothing, for example, can vary from cutoffs to formal wear, and verdicts can vary from guilty to not guilty.

The relationships detected in prediction-oriented research usually appear as correlations. **Correlation** means just what it says: "co-relation," the degree to which one variable is related to another. For example, you could test the hypothesis that small juries make slower decisions than large juries by analyzing descriptive data to see whether jury size and decision time are correlated, or related to one another. If jury size and decision time are related, then knowing the size of the jury in a given trial would allow you to predict something about how long that jury took to reach it verdict.

To confirm a hypothesis, however, you need to know more than the simple fact that two variables are correlated. You also need to know how strong the correlation is and what its direction is . The correlation may be so weak that knowing something about one variable tells you very little about the other. Or the direction of the correlation may differ from the predicted relationship; it may turn out that smaller juries tend to make faster rather than slower decisions.

The strength and direction of correlations can be summarized precisely by calculating a statistic called the **correlation coefficient**. We will not discuss the mathematics of the procedure here, but understanding its underlying logic will clarify the meaning of many research findings.

Control

Suppose that, after observing smokers in many situations, a psychologist finds high positive correlation between the amount of stress in a situation and the number of cigarettes consumed per hour in that situation. The psychologist hypothesizes that smokers use tobacco to cope with stress. This makes intuitive sense, but there are other plausible hypotheses. Perhaps the people in highstress situations all happen to be heavier smokers. Perhaps some of the lowstress observations took place in no-smoking areas. Perhaps some of the smokers observed in low-stress conditions were out of cigarettes or were trying to quit.

A researcher trying to describe or predict smoking, using only correlational methods, might find it difficult to choose among these hypotheses. To rule out rival hypotheses, the psychologist might aim for a more ambitious goal: control. He or she would try to establish a situation in which factors that might interfere with an understanding of the cause-effect relationship are eliminated. Instead of merely observing smokers who happen to come into view, the experimenter might ask some smokers to serve as volunteers for a study in which they perform high or low-stress tasks in the same laboratory setting. The experimenter would be careful to vary the stressfulness of the situation while keeping everything else constant the age, sex, and health history of the smokers, how much they typically smoke per day, and so on. Under these controlled conditions, if more smoking occurred in the high than in the low-stress situations, the researcher would have strong evidence that stress can produce changes in smoking behavior.

When a researcher can manipulate one variable and observe its effect on another variable, we call the result controlled research. Controlled research involves experimental methods, which we will discuss shortly. In our smoking example, the need to exert control over many aspects of the environment forced the experimenter to work in a laboratory setting, but controlled experiments can also be conducted in the "real world" if proper precautions are taken against unwanted external influences.

Explanation

After examining data from descriptive, predictive, or controlled research (usually all three), scientists can begin to suggest-explanations. For example, you might explain the finding that larger juries reach decisions more slowly by suggesting that it takes longer for all members to be heard. Explanations often include or lead to the formation of general rules about certain categories of behavior or mental processes, such as that larger groups take more time to do anything.

Sometimes these general rules are organized into a **theory**, which is an integrated set of principles that can be used to account for, predict, and even control certain phenomena. In devising his theory of evolution, for example, Charles Darwin formed a set of principles that accounts for the development of all life on earth from ancient fossils to living creatures, explains why there is so much variability in animal life, and allows predictions about the future of our planet. Sigmund Freud's theory of psychoanalysis provides an example of a psychological theory whose scope is almost as broad; it seeks to explain virtually all aspects of why people behave as they do. Other psychological theories focus on explaining narrower phenomena, such as color vision, memory, and sleep. Theories are tentative explanations that must be evaluated scientifically.

Predictions flowing from a theory proposed by one psychologist will be tested in correlational and experimental research by many other psychologists. If research supports a theory, that theory usually expands to become a more prominent explanation of some aspect of psychology. If not, the theory is revised or, sometimes, abandoned. Some explanations in science are so well established by constant reconfirmation and fit so consistently and well into everything else we know that they become known as laws.

The constant formulation, evaluation, reformulation, and abandonment of psychological theories results in many explanations of behavior and mental processes. In later chapters, we will present several competing theories for many psychological phenomena which may give you the impression that psychology is in a state of confusion. Actually, ferment is a better word for the situation. The existence of conflicting theories helps motivate psychologists to expand their knowledge through more creative research.

There is no fixed sequence in the relationships among description, prediction, control, and explanation. Sometimes explanatory theories spark the curiosity that begins new research projects and guides researchers in their choice of which variables to explore. Psychoanalytic theory, for example, influences some researchers to look at peopled dreams for clues to the causes of human problems. Sometimes psychological research begins with observation of say children playing together and leads to predictions or explanations that foster the development of a new theory of human relations. as in other sciences, the goals, methods, and data sources of psychology interact constantly. Without descriptive, predictive, and experimental data, there would be nothing to explain; without explanatory theories, the data might never be organized in a coherent and usable way. This continuing interaction of theory and data lies at the heart of the research process that has created the massive amount of knowledge generated in psychology over the past century.

词汇 (Vocabulary)

1. absolue value   n. 绝对值
2. attribute   n. 本性、属性
3. cause-and-effect relationship   n. 因果关系
4. clinical psychology   n. 临床心理学
5. community psychology   n. 大众心理学
6. delusion   n. 错觉
7. dyslexia   n. 诵读困难
8. engineering psychologist   n. 工程心理学家
9. ethical standards for psychologists   n. 心理学家的道德标准
10. ethologist   n. 人种学家
11. experimental and cognitive psychology   n. 实验和认知心理学
12. industrial-organizational psychologist   n. 工业组织心理学家
13. malformation   n. 畸形
14. neuropsychology   n. 神经心理学
15. neurotic   n. 精神神经病患者
16. paper-and-pen test   n. 文字测试
17. personality psychology   n. 人格心理学
18. psysiological psychology   n. 生理心理学
19. psychoanalysis   n. 精神分析方法
20. psychodynamic approach   n. 心理动力疗法
21. psychotherapy   n. 心理疗法
22. subfields of psychology   n. 心理学学科分支
23. statistical analyses   n. 统计分析
24. the behavioral approach   n. 行为趋向
25. the cognitive approach   n. 认知趋向
26. the humanistic approach   n. 人本主义趋向
27. trallma   n. 身体上的外伤或心理上的精神创伤
28. unity within diverisity   n. 多样性的统一
29. variable   n. 变量

第二章 西方主要心理学流派
（MAIN SCHOOLS OF
THE OCCIDENTAL PSYCHOLOGY）

本章要点（Chapter Outline）
冯特及其影响（Wundt and His Influence）
格式塔心理学（Gestalt Psychology）
行为主义（Behaviorism）
精神分析（Psychoanalysis）
认知心理学（Cognitive Psychology）
人本主义心理学（Humanistic Psychology）

1879年，在德国的莱比锡大学，致力于心理学研究的生理学家冯特（W. Wundt, 1832—1920）建立了世界上第一个心理学实验室，并把很多心理学现象都纳入了心理实验室加以研究。现在，世界心理学界都公认1879年是心理学成为一门独立学科的新纪元，公认冯特是实验心理学的主要奠基人。

在冯特之后，西方心理学研究日益繁荣起来，并形成了很多的学派。以冯特为代表的构造主义学派，主张心理学研究意识内容。以华生（J. B. Watson, 1878—1958）为代表的行为主义学派反对研究意识，认为应该以行为作为心理学的研究对象，并把人和动物的行为简化为刺激—反应的组合。格式塔学派的代表人物有惠特海默（M. Wertheimer, 1880—1943）、苛勒（W. Köhler, 1887—1967）、考夫卡（K. Koffka, 1886—1941），他们反对把心理分析成元素，强调心理的整体性。奥地利精神病医生弗洛伊德（S. Freud, 1856—1939）认为人的一切生活行为都受本能冲动，特别是性欲本能冲动所支配，这些本能被压抑于无意识中得不到满足，并在梦境、口误、笔误中表现出来，压抑严重时导致各种神经病和精神病，所以心理学家想了解人们心理的真实情况和精神病形成的原因，就需要通过一定的手段分析人的"无意识"，由此开创了精神分析学派。20世纪50—60年代，以马斯洛（H. Maslow, 1908—1970）、罗杰斯（C. Rogers, 1902—1987）为代表的人本主义学派主张心理学必须说明人的本质特性，研究人的尊严、价值、创造力和自我实现。70年代后成为西方心理学一个主要学派的是认知心理学，它主张用信息加工、整体综合的方法研究人的复杂认知过程。以上诸心理学派各有自己的哲学基础和自然科学依据，都对心理科学的发展做出了贡献，但也都有这样那样的局限性。

第一节 冯特及其影响
(WUNDT AND HIS INFLUENCE)

In 1879 Wundt founded an "institute" for the study of experimental psychology, a few rooms at the university in Leipzig. Prior to this, Wundt had studied medicine and written three major works summarizing the knowledge then available concerning psychology. The most ambitious of these works was **the Principles of Physiological Psychology**, which incorporated much of the information obtained by Wundts predecessors such as Helmholtz and Fechner. Another key work, the **Beiträge**, included an introduction in which Wundt laid out his ideas concerning the nature of a truly experimental psychology. Wundt's general outlook was discussed under six heads: his classification of the sciences, his beliefs as to what constituted laws of psychology, his dissatisfaction with introspection, his voluntarism, his concern about the dangers of dividing the flow of mental experience into elements (despite his own contributions along those lines), and his suggestions about animal psychology, including his remarks on associations, apperception, along with his tridimensional theory of feelings.

At about the same time Ebbinghaus founded a department of psychology at Berlin and G.E.Müller headed a department of psychology at Göttingen. Both of these authors made substantial contributions to psychophysics and, more particulary, to the study of human memory.

These three departments gave doctoral degrees to a number of students who then went on to head departments of their own, including some in the United States. Among Wundt's American students were Stanley Hall, who was involved in the setting up of the American Psychological Association and the **American Journal of Psychology**, and Titchener, who became the chief representaive of the Wundtian tradition in the early twentieth century. Titchener especially favored introspection as a method in psychology, but he also acted as a sounding board for many of the new movements that began in his lifetime. Titchener also played a focal role in a controversy between structuralism and functionalism; many American psychologists in the early twentieth century came to think of themselves as functionalists, despite Titchener's disapproval. One consequence of the functionalist abandonment of Titchener's structuralism was a shift to group testing in the study of human psychology.

第二节 格式塔心理学
(GESTALT PSYCHOLOGY)

Gestalt is the German word for "whole" of "configuration". Several psychologists prior to the beginnings of the Gestalt school had stressed that we perceive and think in terms of integrated units which cannot always be analyzed into smaller units, and that relations between perceptual entities determine how we perceive those entities. Wertheimer, Köhler, and Koffka met at Frankfurt in 1911 and shared a common interest in this point of view. Wertheimer's studies of apparent movemem indicated that one "sees" more than just two elements if one is presented rapidly after the other, and he initiated attempts to specify the brain processes underlying perceptual events. Other studies crucial to the development of the movement followed, including research on figure-ground organization, responses to relationships, the restructuring of the elements in a problem-solving situation (Köhler's apes), the introduction of the terminology of fields and forces, Wertheimer's laws of perceptual organization, and the time error. Köhler's Gestalt Psychology (1929) and Koffka's **Principles of Gestalt Psychology**(1935) were key works in presenting Gestalt psychology as a unified system. Köhler, Koffka, and Wertheimer moved to America in the 1930s and continued their works there; we note particularly Wertheimer's analysis of problem-solving processes in humans and Köhler and Wallach's of problem-solving processes in humans and Köhler and Wallach's analysis of figural aftereffects.

Lewin offered a system in which the individual was seen to be the object of forces acting on him or her to produce particular motives. He inspired a considerable amount of research on motivation and, later, in social psychology.

第三节 行为主义
(BEHAVIORISM)

Two questions that particularly interested psychologists at the turn of the last century were whether the word **consciousness** should be used in describing animal behavior and what role learning as opposed to instinct played in determining animal behavior. Lloyd Morgan insisted that anthropomorphic accounts of animal behavior be avoided. And Loeb and Jennings, in their studies of invertebrates, insisted on mechanistic accounts of their behavior. There was thus a move against the use of the words based on conscious experience. As to the role of learning, several authors stressed that learning was important in infant development and animals; Thorndike, following his studies of cats escaping from boxes, stressed that their behavior should be described as trial and error learning rather than intelligent learning; moreover, successful outcomes were the result of the behaviors' being reinforced by rewards (the Law of Effect). Even so, some authors maintained that animals should be seen as being more intelligent than Thorndike maintained.

Meanwhile, very simple forms of learning were being investigated in Russia. In the nineteenth century Sechenov had argued that even learned behaviors could be described in a language based on reflexes and inhibition; later Pavlov, who had observed psychic reflexes during his studies of digestion, mapped out the course of what is now called classical conditioning. **Conditioning was described in the terminology** of stimulus, response, extinction, generalization, and inhibition. Bekhterev, who had followed Sechenov in his belief that complex human behavior could be reduced to sequences of psycho reflexes, also developed experimental paradigms for studying conditioning.

The person who pulled these various lines of thought together was J.B.Watson. He argued explicitly, in 1913, that a scientific psychology should be based on the observation of behavior only and that it could do without the concept of consciousness. The introspection method was also invalid, he claimed a direct challenge to Titchener and to the Würzburg psychologists. He later investigated conditioned reflexes and claimed that adult personality could be seen as the result of many instances of individual conditioning superimposed on a basic set of innate behavior patterns. Watson propagated his behaviorism for many years, even after leaving the academic world.

In the 1930s a number of learning theorists tried to elaborate on Watson's view and produce systematic accounts of conditioning and higher learning. Thorndike studied his Law of Effect in more detail; Guthrie studied the role of contiguity in learning; Hull constructed a large system based on axioms concerned with stimulus-response events; Skinner explored operant conditioning, where habits are formed after spontaneous actions are systematically rewarded; and Tolman discussed the more cognitive aspects of learning in animals. These authors formed the nucleus of the neobehaviorist movement.

第四节 精神分析
(PSYCHOANALYSIS)

The history of psychiatry is traced from the temple healing in ancient Greece through the witch hunts of the late Middle Ages to the growth of the medical model in the eighteenth and nineteenth centuries. Pinel played a role as scientist and as liberator of the insane. During the nineteenth century, however, studies of hypnosis led some psychologists, such as Charcot and Janet, to realize that some mental illnesses, particularly cases of hysteria, might be the result of psychodynamic forces working on the unconscious in such a way as to cause conflicts which interfered with normal conduct.

The founder of the psychoanalytic school, Sigmund Freud, had studied with Charcot and initially used hypnosis to try to unearth unconscious conflicts in his patients. Gradually, he came to use free association instead. He formulated and elaborated a scheme in whtch he tried to list the unconscious conflict laid down in all of us as the result of experiences in infancy and childhood. These conflicts, argued by Freud, mainly concern the sexual domain: Sexual energy, or libido, is focused on various bodily zones in a fixed order at various stages in development. By the time the child is about five, libido cannot focus on the original love object, the mother, and must be directed elsewhere. Successful behavior in maturity depends on the successful redirection of libido: Hindrances to this can result in conflicts severe enough to cause a clinical neurosis. In later developments of the theory, he argued that there was an instinct towards self-destruction as well as a love instinct; he also conceived of the constructs of id, ego, and superego as conflicting entities, each with unconscious and conscious components. The need to reconcile unconscious desires with conscious moral demands also led to Freud's describing a number of defense mechanisms.

Some colleagues of Freud broke away from the movement in its early years: Adler, for example, laid more stress on conflicts within the family than did Freud, and Jung laid less emphasis on sexuality and more on self-development.

第五节 认知心理学
(COGNITIVE PSYCHOLOGY)

The "cognitive revolution" represented a breakaway from S-R psychology to a psychology of human mental processes that assumed that it was once again acceptable to talk of consciousness (and the unconscious); to do research on images(which many people never doubted existed); and to define human behavior as guided by goals and purposes (as the Gestalt and Würzburg schools had insisted). Moreover, the researchers in the new vein explored tasks such as the identification of verbal material presented tachistoscopically, the memorization of stories rather than lists of non-sense syllables, and the solution of tricky problems of reasoning and calculation that did not lend themselves readily to analysis in S-R terms. And finally, if S-R psychology is one based on the mechanical analogy of a "chain" of conditioned reflexes, the new cognitive psychologists drew their analogies from different types of technological systems, some of which may now be listed.

For example, behavior was seen as "controlled" because if it got out of hand it could be brought back to a stable level much as an automatic pilot brings a ship back on course if it veers too much in one direction. Such a correction involves feedback into the system of information about what the system was doing, and this word was frequently used to refer the fact that subjects monitor own responses and adjust their behavior accordingly. The pioneer of this new view was Wiener (1948), and much of the evidence for feedback came from studies of the skilled behavior of pilots and gunners during World War II.

Or again the human operator was thought of as an active processor of information: A rare event tells you more than something you are expecting. so information can be measured in terms of the probability of the various stimuli you encounter. In the 1950s there was some hope that by measuring human efficiency in terms of how much information could be processed in acts of perception. And memory, new light would be shed on how we operate (Attneave, 1958; Garner,1962). One important discovery that came out of this work was that there is a limit on how many distinct categories of a particular kind of stimulus one can "hold in one's head" at a time: It is very much fewer than the number that can be distinguished by the senses. Another important discovery was that the ability to make discriminations was facilitated if elements in the stimuli were

"redundant" or repeated. But information theory has only been used occasionally since the early 1960s.

A third analogy to come out of the 1950s compared a human mind with a detection system such as a radar network that can discern whether, say, an aircraft enters a particular area. The immediate context of this analogy was psychophysics, where the task of finding an absolute thresh-old, for example, was restated in terms of detection. If a person is in a dark room, fixating a particular spot, and has to detect whether a dim light is present, that person will experience a number of states of consciousness and must determine whether a given state comes from a set of possible states associated with the presence of a stimulus or whether it comes from a set of possible states associated with the absence of a stimulus. This is a decision the observer has to make, and we note immediately the strong contrast here with the vocabulary of S−R theory: S−R theory postulates a response competition in which the stronger response will win, with no need for the word "decision" except to describe what the an S−R account of what occurs (which, by the way, might be possible though as yet unattempted), states that the decision is based on the subject's setting himself a certain standard or criterion: If there are no serious costs to making an error, one may well say "Yes, the stimulus is there" even at the risk of being wrong whereas if one is penalized for error one will adopt a more cautious criterion.

This adoption of a criterion, and the relative weights of the various feeling states associated with "stimulus" and "no stimulus" , can be modeled mathematically. The important outcome for psychologists was the acknowledgment that the old notion of a fixed threshold might have to be reviewed: The "threshold" as measured in different experiments will vary with the observer's sensitivity, certainly, but also with the criterion for responding that the observer adopts. Signal detection theory was extended to cover not only psychophysical problems, but also problems in recognition memory (have you seen this stimulus before, yes or no?) and it is routinely applied to experimental situations where we wish to know the effects of subjects' biases, which will affect the criterion setting. An evaluation of the historical importance of signal detection theory is given by Gigerenzer and Murray (1987); a good representative paper from the early years of this tradition is that of Swets, Tanner, and Birdsall(1961).

The most important analogy of all for the cognitive psychologists was with the computer. Computers have always been of importance to psychologists, at first because they greatly facilitated the computation of statistics such as factor analysis and the analysis of variance. (The latter is a technique introduced in the 1930s for suggesting whether differences between scores obtained under different conditions are greater than chance would lead us to expect.) It was soon discovered, though,that computers could be used to run experiments: They could be turned into high−powered tachistoscopes, for example, that not merely presented verbal material for fractions of a second, but also measured and scored the subject's responses. Many experiments on human memory that had been tedious to carry out by conventional means such as slide presentations now became easy with the aid of a computer screen. A third use of computers was in the simulation of models of human behavior: The idea was that if a given theory was any good, it could be programmed on the computer and the behavior generated would mimic what humans actually do.

A final consequence of the invention of computers was that many psychologists began to wonder if human minds were like computer "minds" and Vice versa, if computers could be deigned to do what human minds could do. These two questions, which should be clearly differentiated, formed the basis for an interest in what became known as artificial intelligence in the 1970s and 1980s. However, the origins of the cognitive revolution have been dated to the year 1956 in the year of the first computer program for solving problems and a year of important progress in understanding memory, language, and thinking.

Since the 1960s the "cognitive revolution" seems to have bifurcated into two groups of researchers. One group consists of experimentalists, the group that originally got the movement going by its new look at problems of memory and word identification; this group remained relatively unified and still publishes research in such journals as Memory and Cognition (founded in 1972). The other group, which has stronger links with computer science and artificial intelligence, tends to have turned its back on what it sees as slowpoke experimentation; this group included many members of the Cognitive Science Society, and some of its goals were outlined in an inaugural address to that society (Simon, 1980). The question is, which group has contributed most to our understanding of psychology in the last twenty years? In the author's view, the experimentalists are making slow and steady steps forward, whereas the artificial intelligent; group produces the occasional flash of insight that deserves further exploration. We shall now examine selected examples of both kinds of contribution.

The study of human memory is now very intensive, and we know much more now than was available to Hull in the 1930s. The major change away from S–R analysis of verbal learning came when Broadbent (1958) suggested that information was received in parallel at the senses, was processed item by item m a short–term memory store that could be seen as having two aspects, sensory and internal speech, and that the result of this processing was that some information was stored in longterm memory. This series of events can be modeled by a flowchart showing separate boxes for flowchart models, an important mathematical version of the sequence was given by Atkinson and Shiffrin (1968). Equally important was the exploration of short–term recognition memory by signal detection methods. Wickelgren and Norman's (1966) model demonstrated how recognition ability was a function both of the attention given to the stimulus as it was encoded and of a weakening of memory for the target item as new items arrived after the target item. The first of these aspects of memorization has received extensive treatment since; Cermak and Craik (1979) have reviewed accumulated evidence that one retains material best that one has encoded into a context provided by previously existing memories ("levels of processing"). There are now several studies showing how retention is poor if the subject is prevented from articulating the material as it is presented ("articulatory suppression," D. J, Murray, 1966). There is less consistent opinion on the nature of forgetting.

Another major contribution to memory theory was the establishment by Tulving and his colleagues that any memory theory as to describe not only the setting up of a trace and its vanishing from consciousness, but also the relationship between a successful retrieval cue and the trace. In a word, the best retrieval cue is one that was associated with the target item at the time the latter was encoded into memory. Tulving's theory had many similarities with a theory put forward by Richard Semon (1859–1918). Semon's theory was neglected partly because it involved an unusual vocabulary, including the word engram to refer to the physiological representation of a memeory, and partly because Semon had no university position in Germany in the first decades of the century. Schacter (1882) has written a biography of Semon that attempts to analyze why some good scientific theories are overlooked in their time. Tulving describes the new work on retrieval in his Elements of Episodic Memory (1983), a book in which he also makes the distinction between memories for events that happened to us and can be located in time (episodic memory), and memory for knowledge in general that seems to form an autonomous system separate from episodic memory (semantic memory).

Finally, there is an ongoing movement, led by Murdock (1982), to pull memory theory together in one comprehensive model that takes as its starting point the notion that items entering memory can be seen as bundles of features and that these bundles become interfused with each other in a particular way. Retrieval involves the "unfusing" of individual bundles of features from these fusions. Because it is not always an accurate replica of the original that is unfused, the observer must make a decision (as in signal detection theory) about whether the retrieval is accurate or not. According to this model, retrieval does not involve a chain of reflexes culminating in a revocation of the original trace; every memory we ever had is fused with all the rest and is "distributed" rather than localized in a particular place in the brain (or in a box in a flowchart). Murdock is making rapid strides in extending this model to the process of learning material over a series of trials; he has made extensive use of computer simulation in testing whether the model is mathematically plausible. In some ways, the model with which this is best contrasted is that of Anderson and Bower (1973), the first major model of memory to be tested by computer simulation. Anderson and Bower's model is essentially an elaboration of S–R association theory with the complication that the model is being applied to propositions. The representation of associations in a proposition is by fanlike structures (several associations lending from a single node) rather than a chainlike structure(association 1 leading to association 2, leading to association 3, and so on), This model was also of historical importance in encouraging the growth of the artificial intelligence movement.

Another task explored by the experimentalists was human problem solving. The two main contributions of the last forty years have both aroused controversy. First, Newell and Simon in their Human Problem Solving(1973) reviewed evidence that certain kinds of problems could be solved by computers. These problems involved algorithms, the routine application of some procedure over and over again until the problem is cracked. Examples are chess problems, proofs of certain propositions in symbolic logic, and cryptarithmetic (e. g, where AB+C = AC, what numbers can replace A, B, C? There are several possible answers, e. g, A= 1, B = 0, and C=2:10 + 2=12). But many problems solved by humans involve the discovery of heuristics, systematized ways of looking at the total problem and seeing the elements in a new light. Newell and Simon discussed how far heuristics can be programmed into computers, and their work was an essential starting point for modern research in which computers are programmed to be "expert systems." Since 1973, however, this work has been mainly carried out in computer science departments or in private industry, which likes to keep its findings secret. At the risk of sounding pessimistic, we must regard progress in this area as slow despite all the publicity surrounding the development of computers that can "think" like humans.

Also controversial were a number of studies, summarized in Kahneman, Slovic, and

Tversky (1982), in which difficult problems involving the calculations of probabilities were given to educated subjects to solve mentally. This work is usually reported as indicating that even highly intelligent subjects are prone to biases that distort their rationality: They are biased, for example, to give responses that come readily to mind (the "availability" bias) or to make judgments depending oil how "representative" a stimulus is of a certain class. For example, if there is a series of coin tosses (heads, H; tails, T), many persons predict that the series HTHTTT is less likely to occur than the series HTHHTT, because the latter corresponds to a stereotype of "randomness." In fact, the two series are equally probable. Nevertheless this work has received some criticism on the grounds that often the problems set were ambiguous and that the evidence for "irrationality" is not so convincing as it seems (see Gigerenzer and Murray, 1987, Chap.5)

Turning to contributions from the artificial intelligence group, we divide the topic into two issues: (1) whether the human mind is like a computer's, and (2) whether computers can do what human minds can do.

1. An enormous amount of heartsearching has resulted from the question of what makes the human mind unique. Brentano's concept of "intentionality" has been revived, although sometimes intentionality in its original meaning the intrinsic property mind has of reflecting external reality—seems to have been stretched to include purposiveness in general. Pylyshyn (1984) has argued that any system, computer of human, consists of a functional architecture that is hardwired in and cannot be altered the human equivalent is the nervous system and an alterable or programmable part. Pylyshyn maintains that many aspects or perception, memory, and thought can only be understood if we include reference to the factors other than the functional architecture. Such factors suggest that a proper explanation of perception, memory, and thought will have to include reference to cognition, so that there is a valid justification for a separate branch of enquiry known as cognitive science.

In this new science, we have to be clear about the way in which the mind "represents" reality, and an issue of some importance is whether we represent reality entirely in systems of words or "propositions," or whether it is also represented by visual and other sensory images. The idea that there is a "dual coding" system, verbal and visual, was first stressed strongly by Paivio (1971), and increasing evidence since then suggests that we do use more visual images in a variety of tasks (for the newer evidence, see paivio, 1986). Pylyshyn, however, though not denying that we do experience images, is skeptical about whether the storage of information is in a "visual" form and thus queries whether our "representations" of reality are encoded in any form other than propositionally.

There are also problems with arguing that human memory is like a computer memory. Among the differences are the following: You can revive a computer's memeory by accessing an address, then revive it again at a later time and get the same "content". But it seems that every revival of a human memory subtly changes the content, as Semon's model and Murdock's model can predict. It is therefore probably wrong to think of a human memory as being a "content" with an "address". Second, access to a computer's memory is probably by a series of switches, whereas access to human memory might be more like a sympathetic resonance: Just as, if you sing to a piano, one piano string will resonate to the frequency you are singing, so one retrieval cue may serve to access one pattern of firing that is distributed throughout the brain. Third, some people believe that human memory is characterized by the fact that being reminded of part of a total scenario that took place in the past is enough to evoke a memory of the total scenario. This part—whole kind of association is not normally built into computers, though I believe that it could be programmed in if it were found useful. Fourth, if x is entered into a computer's memory and the same content x is entered at a later time, the two may be entered into different addresses. But in human memory there is sometimes an association formed between the two automatically: The second x "reminds" you of the first x, Again, even though this could be programmed into a computer, in the human it might be part of the functional architecture for one stimulus to evoke a memory of a similar stimulus that occurred in the past. In general, then, any attempt to show that the human mind is a model of the computer mind will not necessarily fare very well.

2.On the other hand, some progress has been made at programming computers so that they imitate humans. In particular, as Gardner (1985) outlines in detail, progress has been made in the area of modeling visual identification and even the manipulation of visual stimuli. There are programs that can "discriminate" between squares and triangles, and programs that can "pick up" blocks of different shapes and build them into structures. Progress has also been made in modeling human decision making: Programs are currently being used, for example, for selecting medical diagnoses or stock market investments on the basis of evidence fed into the computer. It is trite to say that these programs are only as good as their programmer's minds, but they can work faster than humans and take into account more information and more possibilities than the average human. These are the "expert systems" yielding most easily to investigation. Not so easy to devise are expert systems that will understand, translate, learn, and adapt their reasoning to new problems. There are many collaborations between computer scientists and psychologists working to overcome these problems: I have the impression that the computer scientists are not very impressed with the efforts of psychologists so far to unravel higher-order cognitive processes.

Finally, there has been a general discussion on whether computers can only successfully imitate human minds if a great deal of computation goes on in parallel. Not all cognitive scientists are convinced this is so: Simon (1980) stresses the need for serial processes, for example. Humans can do many things at once, and the process of reading, for example, illustrates just how complex the interaction of sensation with memory and thought can be. A recent book that has attracted much attention is a volume entitled Parallel Distributed Processes (Vol. 1: Rumelhart and McClelland, 1986; Vol 2: McClelland and Rumelhart, 1986). In this book, a number of discrete problems in cognitive psychology are approached via a mix of general principles concerning the activation of large systems of neurons all working in parallel. Such models have been called connectionist, an unfortunate choice of word as it already has been used to refer to seventeenth-century learning theory (p.92) and Thorndike's system (p.304) . The book includes a neurological model of how, from a series of individual exemplars of a concept, we derive a final prototype—for example, from a Cocker spaniel, a Labrador retriever, and a Cairn terrier we can derive a general concept of "dog". It also involves models of speech perception and reading, and includes a neurological model of memory consolidation.

In summary, the cognitive revolution has focused extensively on higher-order human mental processes, is heavy on speculation, and makes use of concepts unwelcome to Skinner and other neobehaviorists, such as images, representations, and goals. It was mentioned earlier that Skinner (1985) himself believes that the cognitive revolution was a backward, rather than a forward, step in the history of psychology. Neisser, the author of the first modern book with the title Cognitive Psychology (1967), is also of the opinion that the contemporary mélange of computer science and psychology is retrogressive, like the theories of neobehavioriszn, it is restricted to the analysis of simple artificial tasks that bear little relation to real life. Instead, Neisser prefers an "ecological" approach, and he himself has contributed to the study of memory in actual life situations by a collection of studies of memory in very gifted persons, memory by professional storytellers, and recall for vivid historical events (Neisser, 1982).

第六节　人本主义心理学
(HUMANISTIC PSYCHOLOGY)

In the 1940s a movement emerged that presented itself as a third force in psychology, an alternative to psychoanalysis and behaviorism. It is now known mainly under the name humanistic psychology and is associated not so much with a type of explanation of human behavior as with the assertion that the task of the psychologist is to encourage the development of a new set of positive outlooks for the individual. In part, this movement had its roots in a disenchantment with the results of traditional psychoanalysis, but it also had origins in the philosophical movement known as existentialism and in the work of Kurt Goldstein (1878–1965), a great neurologist strongly influenced by the Gestalt movement.

The existentialist philosophers ranged from S. A. Kierkegaard(1813–1855), a Christian philosopher who saw a possible escape from a despair at humanity's helplessness in the adoption of a God, to J. P. Sartre (1905–1980), a modern philosopher who claimed in his atheism that one's only escape from the despair at knowing one will eventually be confronted with death—that is, nothingness—was to develop one's own abilities and will power. What they have in common is a concern with how the individual should "face up to" a feelingless universe. These remarks give nothing of the searching detail of the existentialist quest, but they do lead us to note that some psychiatrists, trained in orthodox psychoanalysis, were led by contemporary existentialists to become critical of psychoanalysis, they argued, was too deterministic: It saw the individual as a machine at the mercy of memeories left by childhood fixations. Therefore they argued, therapy aimed simply at revealing the "complexes" was of necessity inadequate if the person were to become a happier and more integrated individual. The word become is significant in existentialist thought: It stresses the notion that a person's goal in life should not be merely to survive in a biological sense but rather to develop a positive attitude to his or her own self and make the best of his or her talents. To use the terminology of the thinker most influential on psychologists, Martin Heidegger, one must establish an authentic "existence" and take reponsibility for achieving this state of being. Heidegger had studied under Husserl (Brentano's student) and in turn influenced the Swiss psychiatrist Medard Boss. In Boss's Psychoanalysis and Daseins—analysis (1963) the contrast is clearly drawn between the therapist who treats a patient's fears and emotions as essentially the negative results of childhood traumata and the more enlightened therapist who sees a patient's symptoms as expressions of the patient's search for a more satisfactory mode of being (Dasein is the German for existence in the positive sense outlined before).

A similar emphasis on the virtues of self—development came from a more unexpected source, in the work of Goldstein. Goldstein had made his reputation with his studies of the effects of brain injuries in World War I, and his contacts with the Gestalt psychologists were strong. His book The Organism (1939) was an attempt to change the way people thought about the brain. In contrast to the view that a reflex was an isolable unit of behavior and that the brain was simply a more complex unit influencing the efficiency of reflex behavior, Goldstein stressed that even reflex affects all parts of the body via the brain. He argued that only a holistic, uestalt like view of the brain's mechanism could explain some of his findings on brain injuries. For example, if movement in the right hand is impaired, the patient can readily learn to use the left hand for tasks previously allotted to the right hand, such as writing. But the left hand does not have to acquire its new capabilities step by step: There seems to be a transference of many modes of use from right to left hand, and this "adjustmental shift," as Goldstein called it, can even be seen In the lower animals after experimental amputation of a limb. The brain has been functioning as a whole, a view then quite in fashion partly because of the research findings of Lashley. But Goldstein noted—almost casually that no "motivated" behavior could be isolated from the total behavior of the organism. Food seeking, maternal behavior, and sexual behavior were all part of a general propensity on the part of the organism not merely to survive but to improve its lot. Goldstein gave the name self—actualization to this general tendency, and the word was readily adopted by other psychologists in such a way as to become the focus of their interests.

Perhaps the best—known of these was Goldstein's student, Abraham H. Maslow (1908–1970). Maslow surveyed not persons who were psychologically depressed or otherwise disturbed, but rather those who were successful and had well—integrated personalities, broad interests, and a realistic view of themselves and others. Such persons, he argued, had achieved self—actualization. they had gone beyond the mere satisfaction of survival needs to the satisfaction of their needs as growing individuals. Often such persons had what Maslow called peak experiences, sensations of joy and completion in their own achievements. The goal for the therapist, he argued, was to help the patients build on their abilities so as to become more satisfied with themselves. His Toward a Psychology of Being (1968) is an account of what it is like to be self—actualized; it generously acknowledges that Goldstein and the existentialists were precursors of this view.

In the early 1960s this new emphasis on the positive role to be played by the therapist—one that, it is fair to add, had been anticipated by others, particularly Adler—led to the mushrooming of many new forms of psychotherapy. What they have in common is the belief that psychotherapy, if properly applied, can help the patient to a more positive and happier outlook on life. Where they differ is in the significance they attribute to individual symptoms. For some, such as A.Ellis, many symptoms are the results of false beliefs, and the aim of the therapy is to change those beliefs to a more rational view of the world. Others believe that the patient needs to be educated in socialization techniques, and they often advocate group therapy as a means for expressing and confronting self-damaging emotions.

An important forerunner of these various therapies stressing the growth of the individual was the "client-centered therapy" of Carl Rogers. As the name suggests, the therapist does not view the patient as another "subject" in a grand experiment where stimuli influence the organism to respond, but rather he tries to help the patient in his or her search for self-respect and self-regard. Like Maslow and Goldstein, Rogers stresses the concept of actualization, but he is also concerned to demonstrate, using scientific methods, that this form of therapy is actually effective. Thus, in both his Client-Centered Therapy (1951) and his The Therapeutic Relationship and Its Impact (1967), he emphasizes statistical evidence showing the improvement of the patients. In the latter work, Rogers repeats that the therapist should always try to understand the client's "selfmeaning" and to communicate to the client the therapist's understanding of that meaning, even with patients as disturbed as schizophrenics.

Useful reviews of the plethora of new psychotherapeutic methods that are challenging psychoanalysis are given by Corsini (1973) and Harper(1975). In 1972 the American psychological Association formed a special division for humanistic psychology. The impact of this movement had been felt mainly by psychologists concerned with counseling and therapy; psychologists concerned with the scientific explanation of behavior have remained relatively untouched by it.

In the above account, we have stressed progress in relation to the evaluation of the various schools of the 1930s and added short accounts of the developments in cognitive and humanistic psychology. But the real progress in psychology has been in the amassing of data concerning behavior, both human and animal. The problem is how—within the span of a few pages—to give a diorama of this data base without tediously listing facts or simply giving a series of useful references. One solution is to stand back from the overview of the history of psychology and ask, "What are the main questions psychologists have posed?" Without doubt, one question that is highly central to the psychological thinking is how information is gathered, stored, and retrieved by an organism that has within it, from the time of its birth, the potential for certain kinds of behavior. The question can be refocused by use of the term tabula rasa a concept that has preoccupied psychologists from the time of Plato: Is the organism indeed a blank tablet from birth, or is there innate knowledge in it? We may give a continuity to the flow of the argument in these last pages by attempting to outline the discoveries of modem psychology that would be of interest to a tabula rasa theorist such as Locke or an empiricist such as Helmholtz.

词汇 (Vocabulary)

1. algorithm   n. 算法、规则系统
2. ambiguous   adj. 含糊的
3. analogy   n. 比喻、相似、类似
4. anthropomorphic   adj. 拟人的
5. articulating   v. 表达、说
6. artificial intelligence   n. 人工智能
7. atheism   n. 无神论
8. axiom   n. 公理
9. bias   n. 倾向、偏好
10. bifurcate   vt vi. 分为两支
11. clinical   adj. 临床的
12. contiguity   n. 接触、相邻、邻近
13. criterion   n. 判断的标准
14. cryptarithmetic   adj. 密码算术的
15. cue   n. 提示、信号
16. culminate   vi. 升到或形成顶点
17. diagnose   vt. 诊断
18. digestion   n. 消化、吸收
19. diorama   n.（小孔窥视的）透明幕上的画面、西洋景
20. disenchantment   n. 使从着魔状态解脱出来的行动
21. dual coding system   n. 双重密码系统
22. encode   vt. 译成密码
23. engram   n. 印迹，一种记忆的痕迹，特指被假定为由于持续记忆而引起的神经组织中的一种原生质的变化。
24. enquiry inguiry   n.（真理、知识等的）探究
25. entity   n. ①存在，实体 ②本质
26. episodic   adj. 一时的、在时间的持续或重要性上只限于某一定时期的
27. equivalent   n. 相当者、对等者
28. fanlike   adj. 扇状的
29. flowchart   n. 流程图、生产过程图
30. generalization   n. 泛化
31. hardwired   adj. 固定电路的
32. heal   v. 治愈、治疗
33. heuristics   n. 启发法
34. holistic   adj. 完整主义的
35. hysteria   n. 癔病、歇斯底里症
36. inaugural address   n. 就职演说
37. intrinsic   adj. 内在的、本质的

38. introspection   n. 内省、反省
39. invertebrate   n. 无脊椎动物
40. mélange   n.（法语）混合物
41. mushroom   vi. 突然或很快地长出、增殖
42. neurosis   n. 神经官能症、精神神经病
43. nonsense syllables   n. 无意义音节
44. nucleus   n. 核心，中心
45. operant conditioning   n. 操作性条件反射,亦称工具性条件作用(instrumental conditioning)、强化条件作用（reinforcement conditioning）
46. orthodox   adj. 正统的
47. paradigm   n. 范例、示例
48. parallel   adj. 平行的
49. penalize   vt. 处罚
50. plethora   n. 大量、过剩
51. postulate   vt. ①假设、假定 ②要求
52. precursor   n. 预兆，征兆
53. prone   adj. 有……倾向的，易于……
54. psychiatry   n. 精神病学、精神病治疗法
55. purposiveness   adj. 有目的或有意图
56. randomness   n. 随机性、随机状态
57. resonance   n. 共振
58. retrieval   n. 重新得到收回、恢复或补救的行为或过程
59. retrogressive   adj. 倒退的、退后的
60. scenario   n. 连续发生的事情
61. schizophrenic   adj. 不可思议的
62. self-actualization   n. 充分发挥自己的潜力
63. slowpoke   n. 慢性子的人   vi. 像慢性子人那样慢性
64. spaniel   n. 狗
65. superego   n. 超我
66. superimpose   v. ①重叠 ②附加、添加
67. tabula   n. 横隔
68. tachistoscopically   adv. 利用速转实体镜
69. tediously   adv. 令人厌烦的
70. terminology   n. 术语、专门名词
71. therapy   n. 治疗、疗法
72. time error   n. 时致误差,比较量值时的一种系统误差,是由于在时间上一个量值紧跟另一个量值而引起的。
73. traumata   n. 创伤、心理精神创伤
74. trial-and-error   n. 试误法

75. tridimentional   adj. 三维的、立体的
76. trite   adj. 陈旧的、使用陈言套语的
77. via   prep. 经由……，通过……的手段
78. vice   prep. 代替、取代
79. voluntarism   n. 唯意志论
80. witch   n. 搜寻、迫害

第三章 心理与行为的生物学基础
(BIOLOGICAL BASES OF BEHAVIOR AND PSYCHOLOGY)

本章要点（Chapter Outline）
神经系统概述（Nervous System: An Overview）
神经系统内的联系（Communication in the Nervous System）
中枢神经系统的结构与功能
（Structures and Functions of the Central Nervous System）
心理的化学过程（The Chemistry of Psychology）
内分泌系统（Endocrine System）

  辩证唯物主义认为：心理是人脑的机能。阐明心理的实质必然要与心理的生理学基础结合。人脑是世界上最复杂的机能组织，人的心理现象的产生与人脑的信息加工活动是与人脑的特殊结构分不开的。

  人脑通过生物化学的、生物物理的复杂机制以一定的物质载体为信息的负载物在不同的神经元内进行信息的接收、处理和传输。神经递质，如乙酰胆碱、去甲肾上腺素、5-羟色胺、钾、钠等离子在信息的传递和处理上负有重要职责。人脑由数以百亿计的具有处理不同信息功能的神经元组成。神经元之间以复杂的方式形成了具有不同功能的结构，又以复杂的信息活动方式形成功能统一的人脑整体。研究神经元、大脑的各皮质分区，皮质下的诸结构等的功能，以及不同结构间活动的联系方式，是从生理层次研究心理必不可少的方面。

  心理的产生与人脑有密切联系，而人脑又是人体不可分割的整体中的一部分，心理与其他生理系统，如内分泌系统也有密切联系。本章对脑这一机能系统就上述问题作一论述并对其他生理系统，如内分泌系统与心理的关系亦作说明。

One evening in 1983, a man we will call MD had a mild stroke. A stroke is a disruption of blood flow to part of the brain; the resulting tissue damage can cause death. If damage is less severe, part of the stroke victim's brain does not work the way it should. Many stroke victims are paralyzed or unable to remember things. Some experience more specific problems, such as inability to recognize faces, name colors, or use numbers. MD was exceptional because his brain damage resulted in a particularly narrow loss, namely, the inability to name fruits and vegetables. His verbal abilities and memory for other things were perfectly normal. In fact, he could name an abacus or a sphinx, objects many normal people might have difficulty identifying, but when presented with an apple or an orange, MD wad dumfounded. On the other hand, he could read the word apple, then pick one out of a group of other objects and describe what it was like. His problem seemed to be only with gaining access to the proper words for fruits and vegetables. MD's condition must have been exasperating, but it was not debilitating, he has returned to work at a federal agency (fortunately, not the Department of Agriculture).

The story of MD vividly illustrates the fact that normal behavior depends on normal brain functioning. Indeed, no behavior or mental process could take place were it not for the many physical structures and biological processes that define our bodies and keep us alive. **Biological,** or **physiological, psychology** takes center stage at this level of cells and organs. Researchers in this area ask questions about the nature and location of the physical and chemical changes that occur when, for example, people learn, forget, see, think, become emotional, or fall asleep. They also try to identify the specific biological mechanisms that cause and are influenced by those changes.

This search for an understanding of biological factors in behavior and mental processes is important to research in virtually every area of psychology, as the Linkages diagram suggests. In fact, a full understanding of psychology demands at least some familiarity with basic biological structures and mechanisms. In this chapter, we provide an introduction to some of the most important of those structures and mechanisms.

But we should begin at the beginning. The development of a human being from a single cell into a complex, functioning individual occurs in part because various cells in the body specialize to become skin, bones, muscles, hair, and so on. For psychology, the most interesting specializations are those that allow cells to communicate with one another. When cells communicate, a body becomes an integrated whole that not only can detect what is in the world but also can respond to that world. The body contains several systems that are specialized for communication. Foremost among them is the nervous system.

第一节 神经系统概述
（THE NERVOUS SYSTEM: AN OVERVIEW）

The nervous system is a complex combination of cells whose primary function is to allow an organism to gain information about what is going on inside and outside the body and to respond appropriately. The parts of the nervous system that provide information about the environment are known as senses, or sensory systems. These include hearing, vision, taste, smell, and touch. Other parts of the nervous system are called **motor systems；** they influence muscles and other organs to respond to the environment in some way.

Figure 3.1 illustrates the three basic functions of the nervous system receiving information, or "input", integrating it with previous information to generate choices And decisions, and guiding actions, or "output". In this example, light reflected from an object stimulates the eyes to communicate signals to the brain by way of nerve cells. Other nerve cells in the brain interpret this input, based on previous experience, as either an appealing snack or a dog treat. The brain decides which it is, then sends signals to the arm and hand muscles to either grasp the object or wave it away.

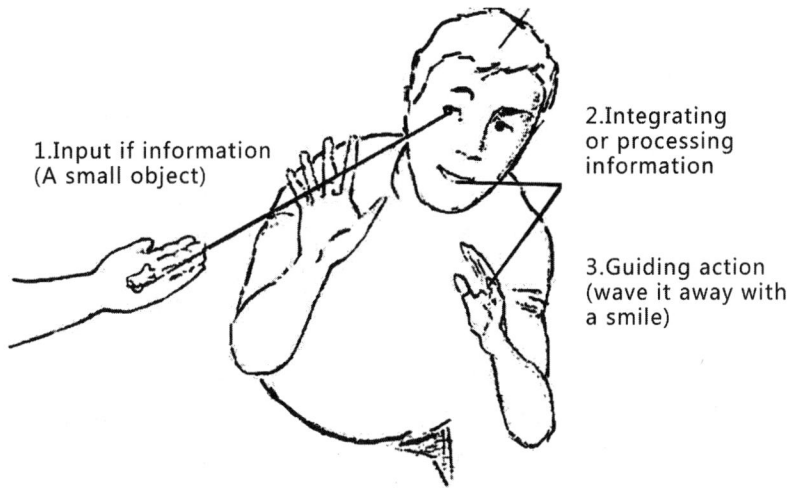

Figure 3.1
Three Functions of the Nervous System
The nervous system's three main functions involve receiving information, integrating or processing that information, and guiding actions. Here, the visual information received a small object offered by a friend is integrated with what the person knows about the appearance of hors d'oeuvres and dog treats and about whether the friend is a practical joker. The result of this information processing will be a decision to either refuse the object or to reach out for it while preparing the mouth and stomach to receive food.

Either way, information has been taken in, processed, and acted on. This sequence might remind you of the functions of a computer, which, like the nervous system, has input and output functions and a central processor. As this and other chapters will show, however, the nervous system not only is much more complex and flexible in its functioning than any computer yet constructed, but also has capacities for creativity, analysis, and judgment that today's computers do not have. The nervous system has two major units: the central nervous system and the peripheral nervous system. All of its parts are connected throughout the body and function together.

The central nervous system (CNS) is the part encased in bone. It includes the brain, which is inside the skull, and the spinal cord, which is in the spinal column (or backbone). The CNS is the central executive of the body; most information about the environment is sent to it to be processed and acted on.

The peripheral nervous system (PNS) includes all of the nervous system that is not housed in bone. It has two main subsystems. The first is the **somatic nervous system**, which transmits information from the senses to the CNS and carries signals from the CNS to the muscles that move the skeleton. The somatic nervous system is involved, for example, in relaying from the hand the sensations of warm sand and in passing on to the arm the brain's message about moving the hand around in that sand. The second subsystem is the **autonomic nervous system (ANS)**; it carries messages back and forth between the CNS and the heart, lungs, and other organs and glands in the body. These messages increase, decrease, or otherwise regulate the activity of these organs and glands to meet varying demands placed on the body and also provide information to the brain about that activity.

The autonomic nervous system itself has two divisions, known as the sympathetic and parasympathetic branches, which often create opposite effects. For example, the sympathetic nervous system can make the heart beat faster, whereas the parasympathetic nervous system can slow it down. For now, we will consider how these and other components of the nervous system communicate with one another and with the rest of the body.

第二节 神经系统内的联系
(COMMUNICATION IN THE NERVOUS SYSTEM)

The hallmark of the nervous system is its role in carrying messages from one part of the body to another. This is possible because the fundamental units of the nervous system are special cells called nerve cells, or neurons, which have the remarkable ability to communicate with one another.

Neurons: The Basic Unit of the Nervous System

Neurons share characteristics with every other kind of cell in the body. First, as Figure 3.2 illustrates, they have a membrane, which, like a fine screen, lets some substances pass in and out while blocking others. Second, each neuron has a cell body, which contains a nucleus.

The nucleus carries the genetic information that determines whether the cell will be a liver cell, a brain cell, or whatever, and acts to direct that cell's functioning. Third, neurons contain structures called mitochondria, which turn oxygen and glucose into usable energy. This process is especially vital to brain cells, because although the brain accounts for only 2 percent of the body's weight, it consumes more than 20 percent of the body's oxygen (Sokoloff, 1981).

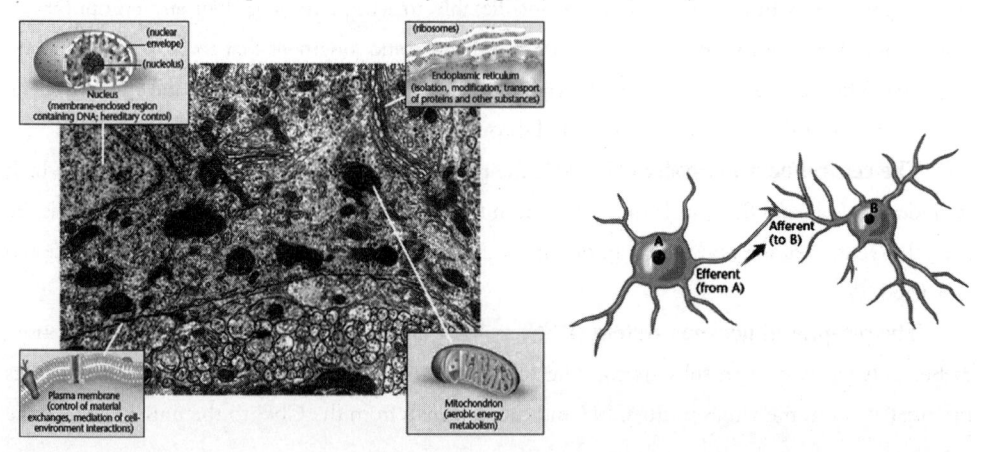

Figure 3.2
图片引自《生物心理学》(第 10 版 p.29 James W. Kalat 著)(Source: Micrograph courtesy of Dennis M. D. Landis)

The Neuron

(a)The cell body of a neuron, enlarged from one of the whole neurons shown in (b). The cell body has typical cell elements, including a membrane and mitochondria, (b) Some of the shapes neurons can take, highlighting the fibers extending outward from each cell body. These fibers, the axons and dendrites, are among the features that make neurons unique.

But the characteristics that make neurons special are even more interesting. Unlike other types of cells, they can transmit signals, both within themselves and to other neurons. Three types of physical specializations enable nerve cells to perform this feat. The first is their structure. Although neurons come in a wide variety of shapes and sizes, all have long, thin fibers that extend outward from the cell body (see Figure 3.3). When these fibers get close to other neurons, communication between the cells can take place. The second specialization is the excitable surface membrane of some of these fibers, which allows a signal to be sent from one end of the neuron to the other. The third specialization involves the minute gaps, or synapses between nerve cells, where one neuron receives signals from another.

The structure of neurons: Axons and dendrites

The fibers extending from a neuron's cell body fall into just two categories: axons and dendrites. **Axons** are the fibers that carry signals from the cell body out to where communication occurs with other nerve cells. Each nerve cell generally has only one axon leaving the cell body, but that one axon may have many branches. Axons can be very short, or like the axon that sends signals from the spinal cord all the way down to the big toe, they can be several feet long. **Dendrites** are the fibers that receive signals from the axons of other neurons and carry those signals to the cell body. A neuron can have dozens, hundreds, or thousands of dendrites. Usually dendrites have many branches (dendrite means literally "of a tree" in Greek).

Occasionally axons carry signals to other axons and to the cell bodies of other neurons. But, as a general rule, the axon delivers these signals from the cell body of one cell to the dendrites of another cell; those dendrites in turn transmit the signal to their cell body, which may relay the signal down its axon and thus on to a third cell, and so on. Thus axons carry signals away from the cell body, whereas dendrites detect those signals.

Axons and dendrites allow neurons to influence anywhere from 1,000 to 100,000 other nerve cells (Guroff, 1980), some of which may be quite far away. These patterns of intercell-ular communication permit the brain to conduct extremely complex information processing. But, like the cables connecting parts of a computer, axons and dendrites are not of much use unless a signal can be sent from one end and received at the other. Such signals can occur in the nervous system thanks to the two other special features of neurons: the membrane of their axons and the synapses between neurons.

Membranes and action potentials

To understand these signals in the nervous system, you first need to know something about cell membranes. The outer membrane of all cells is selectively permeable, which means that it lets some chemical molecules pass through yet blocks others. Some molecules can cross the membrane anytime, anywhere along the membrane. Others must be carried across. Still others can pass only by going through channels, or holes, in the membrane. These channels have gates that can be opened to let certain molecules through.

Many molecules carry a positive or negative electrical charge. If, because of the selective permeability of the membrane, the distribution of positively and negatively chained molecules inside and outside the membrane is uneven, the membrane is said to be polarized. In fact, the inside of the membrane in all body cells is slightly negative compared with the outside. Because molecules with a positive charge are attracted to those with a negative charge, a force (called an electrical potential) drives positively charged molecules toward the inside of the cell, but many of them are kept outside by the membrane.

For communication in the nervous system, the most important of these "excluded" molecules is sodium (the same sodium in table salt); when it is positively charged, sodium is symbolized Na^+. Sodium is highly concentrated on the outside of the cell.

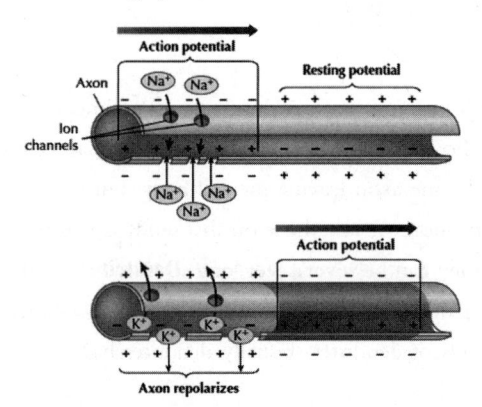

Figure3.3
图片引自《心理学导论》（第 11 版 p.55 John O. Mitterer 著）

Though strongly attracted to negatively charged chlorine molecules inside the cell, it can pass through the membrane only by going through channels, or sodium gates, which are distributed all along the axon. Normally the sodium gates are closed, but sometimes the membrane around a particular sodium gate becomes less polarized, or depolarized, causing the gate to open, as shown in Figure 3.3. Sodium then rushes into the cell through the open gate, changing the potential at a neighboring gate, which causes that gate to open. This sequence continues, and the change in potential spreads like a wild rumor all the way down the axon.

The Beginning of an Action Potential

This very diagrammatic view of a polarized nerve cell axon shows the normally closed sodium gates in the cell membrane. If stimulation of the cell causes depolarization near a particular gate, that gate may swing open allowing sodium to rush into the axon, stimulating the next gate to open, and so on down the axon. This spread of depolarization and the consequent that progressive entry of sodium into the cell is called an action potential; when it occurs, the cell is said to have fired. The action potential fired by one cell may subsequently stimulate other cells f to fire.

This abrupt change in the potential of an axon is called an **action potential**, and its contagious nature is referred to as its self-propagating property. When the neuron shoots an action potential down its axon, the neuron is said to have fired. This kind of nerve communication is of an "all-or none" variety; the cell either fires at full strength or does not fire at all. The speed of the action potential as it moves down an axon is constant for a given cell, but in different cells the speed ranges from 0.2 meters per second to 120 meters per second (about 260 miles per hour; McGeer, Eccles & McGeer, 1978). The speed depends on the diameter of the axon (larger ones are faster) and on whether myelin is present. **Myelin** is a fatty substance that wraps around some axons and speeds action potentials. Larger, meylinated cells are usually found in the parts of the nervous system that carry the most urgently needed information. For example, in the somatic nervous system, fastacting sensory, or afferent, neurons receive information from the environment about onrushing trains, hot irons, and other dangers, whereas high speed motor, or efferent neurons carry messages that prompt immediate protective actions in the appropriate muscles. Afferent means "coming toward" ; efferent means "going away" . Where more and more connecting nerves, called interneurons, come between sensory and motor neurons, the system slows down somewhat.

Although each neuron fires or does not fire, in an "all-or-none" fashion, the neuron's rate of firing varies. It can fire over and over, because the sodium gates open only briefly, allowing polarization to build up again after they close. Between firings, there is a rest, or **refractory period**, while the membrane becomes polarized again. Because the refractory period is quite short, a neuron can send action potentials down its axon at rates of up to one thousand per second. The pattern of repeated action potentials amounts to a coded message.

Synapses and communication between cells

How does the action potential in one neuron have an effect on the next neuron? For communication to occur between cells, the signal must somehow be transferred across the gap, or **synapse**, between neurons, usually between one neuron's axon and the dendrites of another (see Figure 3.4)

The transfer is accomplished by a type of chemical called a **neurotransmitter**, as we shall see; there are many different neurotransmitters, each of which is used by a particular set of neurons. When an action potential reaches a synapse, the axon releases neurotransmitters. These neurotransmitters spread across the synapse to reach the next, or postsynaptic, cell. There the neurotransmitters trigger a change in the membrane potential of the postsynaptic cell, thus creating an electrical signal. This signal is either excitatory, making the postsynaptic cell more likely to fire, or inhibitory, making the cell less likely to fire. If the signal is excitatory, a wave of depolarization in the membrane of the postsynaptic cell's dendrite begins to move toward its cell body. However, unlike the action potential in an axon, which remains at a constant strength, this signal fades as it goes along. Only if the signal is strong enough to begin with will it pass through the next cell body and trigger a new action potential. Because a neuron may have synapses with thousands of other neurons, it may receive a conflicting pattern of excitatory ("fire") and inhibitory("don't fire")signals (see Figure 3.5), Whether or not the neuron fires and how rapidly it fires depend on which kind of signal predominates from moment to moment at the junction of the cell body and the axon.

Communication between Neurons

When a neuron fires, a self-propagating action potential shoots to the end of its axon, it will triggering the release of a neurotransmitter into the synapse. This stimulates neighboring cells. One type of stimulation is excitatory, causing depolarization of the neighboring cells, which may be strong enough to fire their action potentials.

Neurotransmitters and Receptors

The predominating signal itself depends both on the types of neurotransmitters that reach the postsynaptic cell and on where they was ashore.

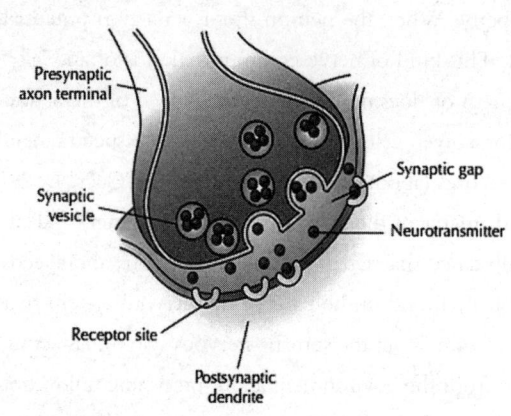

Figure3.4
图片引自《心理学导论》(第 11 版 p.56 John O. Mitterer 著)

The neurotransmitters can stimulate the postsynaptic neuron only at specialized sites, called **receptors**, on the surface of the postsynaptic cell. Receptors are usually located on the dendrites, sometimes on the cell body. These receptors recognize only one type of neurotransmitter. Like a jigsaw puzzle piece fitting perfectly into its proper place, a given neurotransmitter fits snugly into its own receptors but not into receptors for other neurotransmitters (see Figure 3.6). Only when a neurotransmitter fits precisely into a receptor does it trigger the chemical response that changes the membrane potential and passes cm a signal from one neuron to another.

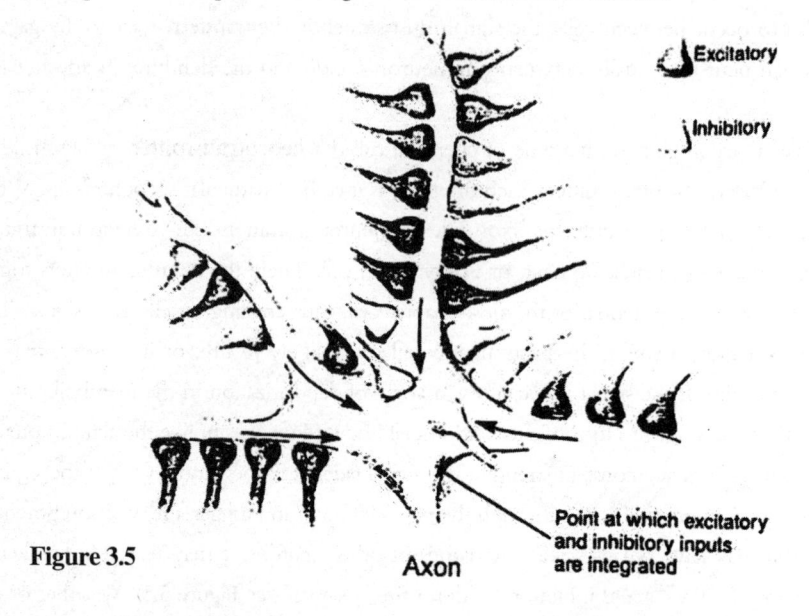

Figure 3.5

Integration of Neural Signals

The signals that a neuron receives can arrive at its dendrites or at its cell body. These signals, which typically come from many neighboring cells, can be conflicting. Some are excitatory, stimulating the cell to fire; other, inhibitory signals tell the cell not to fire. Whether the cell actually fires or not at any given moment depends on a number of factors, including whether excitatory or inhibitory messages predominate at the junction of the cell body and the axon.

What that signal will be depends in part on what type of receptor the neurotransmitter contacts. Stimulation of excitatory receptors makes the cell more likely to fire. Stimulation of inhibitory receptors, on the other hand, makes the cell less likely to fire. Though each receptor recognizes only one type of neurotransmitter, a given neurotransmitter can stimulate both types of receptors. As a result, the same neurotransmitter may produce both excitatory and inhibitory effects in different locations.

The neurotransmitter stays at the receptor site for only a brief time. It must be removed from the synapse after interacting with its receptor, or it will continue to stimulate receptors in definitely. The removal occurs in one of two ways. An enzyme at the synapse can break down the neurotransmitter. Or, more commonly, the neurotransmitter can be transported back into its presynaptic area; this process is called reuptake.

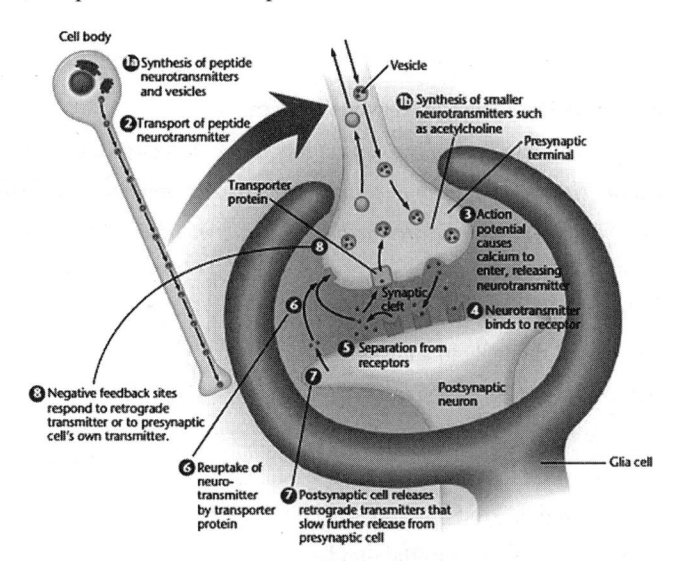

Figure3.6　图片引自《生物心理学》（第 10 版　p.69　James W.Kalat 著）

The Relationship between Neurotransmitters and Receptors

Neurotransmitters influence postsynaptic cells by stimulating special receptors on the surface of those cell's membranes. Each type of receptor receives only one type of neurotransmitter, the two fitting together like puzzle pieces or like a key in a lock. Stimulation of these receptors by their neurotransmitter causes them, in turn, to either help or hinder the generation of a wave of depolarization in their cell's dendrites. As noted earlier, only if this wave is strong enough will it pass through the cell body to trigger an action potential.

Pathways and Nuclei

Nerve cells are not lined up neatly like computer circuits or carefully laid out streets. In fact, the nervous system looks more like Boston, with distinct neighborhoods, winding back streets, and multilane expressways.

The nervous system's "neighborhoods" are collections of cell bodies called nucleic. The nervous system's "highways" are made up of axons that travel together in bundles called **fiber tracts**. The fiber tracts are also known as pathways. Like a freeway ramp, the axon from a cell may merge with and leave fiber tracts, and it may send branches into other tracts.

In learning your way around these structures, there is no substitute for memorizing some descriptive terms. Most of the terms provide a description of the appearance or location of a structure. For example, an area of the brain now known to be important in memory was named the hippocampus. Greek for seahorse, and another area was called the mammillary bodies, because they resemble breasts. Table 3.1 contains translations of some of the directional terms used in anatomy. Like northwest or southeast, these terms can be combined to form words like anteriormedial (the front part of the middle of a structure) or ventromedial (the bottom part of the middle of a structure). In describing pathways in the nervous system, an o is often used to indicate "from this to that". For example, the spinothalamic tract carries information from the spine to the thalamus.

Table 3.1
Directional Terms Used to Describe the Nervous System

The seemingly complex terms used to refer to structures in the nervous system are actually quite informative. As the table shows, each term describes some aspect of where a structure is located. Often these terms are combined, as in ventromedial ("lower middle"), to create more precise designations.

Term	Direction
Ventral	Lower; toward the belly in animals
Dorsal	Upper; toward the back in animals
Anterior	Toward the front
Posterior	Toward the rear
Medial	Toward the middle
Lateral	Toward the side; away from the middle
Basal	Toward the base or bottom
Rostral	Toward the nose
Caudal	Toward the tail

第三节 神经系统的结构与功能
(STRUCTURES AND FUNCTIONS OF THE CENTRAL NERVOUS SYSTEM)

The structure and functioning of these collections of neurons are impressive in themselves, but when they blend into larger, more complex combinations to form the central nervous system their role in human behavior becomes clearest. The central nervous system, or CNS, allows us to walk and talk, to breathe and sigh, to play the piano or the horses, to read books, and best of all, to think about them. The link between the brain and behavior is vital and fragile. A stroke or other malfunction in the central nervous system can leave a person with deficits in sensation, movement, language, recognition of the world, and countless other aspects of behavior and mental processing that most of us take for granted. If the damage or disorder is severe enough, the central nervous system may even lose its ability to maintain breathing, the heartbeat in other words, life itself.

In this section, we review the structures of the central nervous system and consider their role in the creation and coordination of behavior and mental processes. Later we will discuss some of the chemical processes that underlie the functioning of the CNS. Our exploration begins at the spinal cord and progresses upward, toward the skull.

The Spinal Cord

The spinal cord receives signals from peripheral senses, such as touch, and relays them upward to the brain through fibers within the cord. Neurons in the spinal cord also carry signals downward. For example, axons from neurons in the brain stimulate cells in the spinal cord that, in turn, cause muscles to contract and move the body.

Some simple behaviors are organized completely within the spinal cord. These behaveiors are called **reflexes** because the response to an incoming signal is directly "reflected" back out. They are controlled by a reflex pathway (sometimes called a reflex arc), which consists of a sensory, or afferent, neuron; a minimal number of connecting neurons, or interneurons; and a motor, or efferent neuron.

For example, suppose you sleepily reach for a pot of hot water to make your morning coffee and touch the hot burner instead. The incoming nerve impulses from sensory, or afferent, neurons in your hand quickly stimulate the fibers that operate your arm muscles, and you withdraw your hand. This is called the withdrawal reflex, and it occurs entirely within the spinal cord. The pain stimulus does go on to the brain for analysis, but because of the reflex, your muscles respond without waiting for instructions from the brain. Because the brain is not involved in spinal reflexes, they are considered involuntary. They are very fast, because they involve few time-consuming synapses.

Four principles of central nervous system functioning

Although the spinal cord is far simpler than the brain, its functioning demonstrates the principles that govern the whole central nervous system. The first principle of CNS functioning is central coordination of opposing actions. For example, when a simple spinal reflex set off by touching a hot burner causes one set of arm muscles to contract, that contraction causes another reflex that makes an opposing set of muscles relax. If this did not happen, the arm would go rigid. Second, the central nervous system coordinates the creation of complicated behaviors from simpler ones. Thus, the complex movements involved in walking are built up of reflexes that not only prompt repeated contraction-relaxation cycles in the muscles of each arm and leg, but also time these cycles so that the left arm and right leg move forward while the right arm and left leg swing or push backward.

The third principle of CNS activity is that smooth functioning depends on feedback systems. **In a feedback system**, information about the consequences of an action is returned to the source of the action, so that adjustments can be made. A thermostat is the classic example of feedback. You set the thermostat to the desired temperature and the furnace generates heat, while the thermostat monitors the room temperature. When the desired temperature has been reached, the thermostat feeds that information back to the furnace, which turns off. When the temperature drops below the desired level, the furnace goes on again. When feedback keeps a bodily function such as body temperature within a steady range, it is called homeostasis. The spinal cord does not have a thermostat, but muscles have stretch receptors that send impulses to the spinal cord to let it know how extended they are; a reflex pathway then adjusts the muscle contraction. This feedback tends to stabilize the position of the body and allows smooth move ments. This reflexive feedback is also what causes the classic knee—jerk response when the knee is tapped (through a feedback system, the tapping causes the thing muscle to stretch and reflexively contract).

Fourth, normal behavior results from the coordination of several levels of central nervous system organization. Consider again the act of walking. When you walk, the brain directs your movements, but rather than override the reflex connections already present in the spinal cord, it works right along with them.

Studying the Brian

Much of what psychologists have learned about the brain has come from studies with animals. Another major source of knowledge comes from studying deficits in victims of strokes and other localized brain damage. Examining these patterns and sometimes studying their brains after death can reveal a relationship between damage to a specific part of the brain and loss of particular behavior or mental activity.

New technologies have also allowed psychologists to view the brain's functioning more directly; to eavesdrop on and take snapshots of its activity. These techniques have helped reveal that some complex mental functions appear to be handled in one particular area of the brain and that others are not as localized. We will describe some of the details later. However, the brain is so complex that it is difficult to make simple statements about specific regions and kinds of behavior. Damage to one region can lead to malfunctioning of other parts that are far removed.

The Structure of the Brain

The brain has three major subdivisions; the hindbrain, midbrain, and forebrain. On opening the skull one sees the outer surface of part of the forebrain, a wrinkled surface called the cerebral cortex (cortex means "bark").Beneath the forebrain is the midbrain and under that, near the spinal cord, lies the hindbrain, where we begin our exploration.

The hindbrain

The hindbrain is an extension of the spinal cord, but inside the skull. Blood pressure, heart rate, breathing, and many other vital functions are controlled by nuclei in the hindbrain, particularly in an area called the medulla. Reflexes and feedback systems are important to the functioning of the hindbrain. For example, if blood pressure drops, heart action increases reflexively to compensate for that drop. When one stands up very quickly, there is sometimes such a sudden drop in blood pressure that it produces some temporary lightheadedness until the hindbrain reflex "catches up".

The cerebellum

The cerebellum is also part of the hindbrain. Its primary functions are to control finely coordinated movements, such as threading a needle. Recent research has shown that the cerebellum in also a place where certain types of learned associations that involve movement arc stored (McCormick & Thompson, 1984). This appears to be where well-rehearsed movements, such as those associated with ballet, piano playing, and athletics, reside.

The midbrain

As its name implies, the midbrain lies between the hindbrain and the forebrain. It is a small structure in humans, but it serves some very important functions. Information from the eyes, ears, and skin is relayed through the midbrain, and certain types of automatic behaviors are controlled there. For example, when a loud noise causes you to reflexively turn your head and look in the direction of the sound, your midbrain circuits are at work.

One vital midbrain nucleus is the blackish substantia nigra (meaning literally "black stuffs"). This small area is necessary for the smooth initiation of movement. Without it, you would find it difficult, if not impossible, to get up out of a chair or lift your hand to swat a fly.

The reticular formation

Threading throughout the hindbrain and midbrain is a collection of nuclei and fibers composed of cells that are not arranged in any well-defined form. Because they look like a network, they are called the reticular formation (reticular means "netlike"). This network is very important in altering the activity of the rest of the brain. It is involved, for example, in arousal and attention; stimulating an animal's reticular formation will arouse the animal from sleep.

The forebrain

The forebrain is the most highly developed part of the brain. It is responsible for the most complex aspects of behavior and mental life. The forebrain is composed of two main structures; the diencephalon and the telencephalon. Two structures in the diencephalon, the hypothalamus and the thalamus, are involved in emotion, basic drives, and sensation.

Hunger, thirst, and sex drives, for example, are regulated, in part, by the hypothalamus, a structure with many connections to and from the autonomic nervous system, as well as to other parts of the brain. Damage to the hypothalamus can disrupt these drives. Destruction of one section of the hypothalamus results in an overwhelming urge to eat, imbalances in the regulation of blood sugar, and consequent obesity. Damage to another area of the male's hypothalamus causes the sex organs to degenerate and the sex drive to disappear. We will discuss these functions of the hypothalamus in more detail in the chapters on motivation and emotion.

As suggested by its name, the hypothalamus lies underneath the thalamus (hypo-means "under"). The thalamus relays signals from the eyes and other sense organs to upper levels region in the brain, and it plays an important role in processing and making sense out of this information.

The largest part of the forebrain is the telencephalon meaning "front end of the brain," where it is located. It is also called the cerebrum. The outermost part of the cerebrum appears rather round or spherical and has right and left halves that are similar in appearance. These halves are called the cerebral hemispheres.

The striatum is one of several structures in the cerebrum. Its name, which means "striped," comes from the fiber tracts that pass through the structure, giving it a striped appearance. Along with the substantia nigra, the striatum is responsible for smooth initiation of movement. Thus, damage or dysfunction in these areas can keep a person from voluntarily taking a step or beginning some other practiced movement. If someone helps the person get started, however, these movements can be flawlessly coordinated as long as the cerebellum is intact.

The Cerebral Cortex

The outer surface of the cerebral hemispheres, the cerebral cortex, has a surface area of one to two square feet—an area that is larger than it looks because of the folds, or convolution, that allow the cortex to fit compactly inside the skull. The convolutions give the surface of the human brain its wrinkled appearance, its ridges and valleys. The ridges are called gyri and the valleys, sulci or fissures. As you can see in Figure 3.7, several deep sulci divide the cortex into four areas called the frontal, parietal, occipital, and temporal lobes.

The cerebral cortex can also be divided according to the functions its various areas perform. These functions including higher orders thought, complex integration and analysis of information from all the senses, and control of voluntary movements—are performed in areas called motor cortex, sensory cortex, and association cortex. As shown in Figure 3.7, sensory cortex lies in the parietal, occipital, and temporal lobes; motor cortex is in the frontal lobe, and association cortex appears in all the lobes.

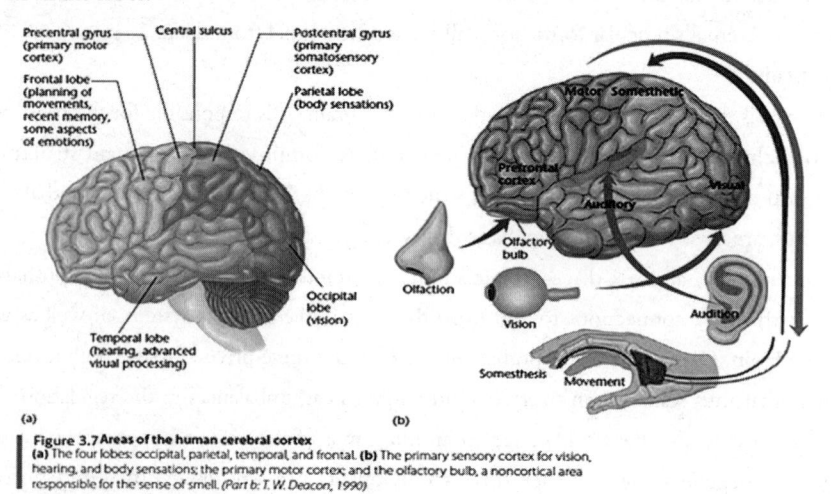

Figure 3.7 Areas of the human cerebral cortex
(a) The four lobes: occipital, parietal, temporal, and frontal. (b) The primary sensory cortex for vision, hearing, and body sensations; the primary motor cortex; and the olfactory bulb, a noncortical area responsible for the sense of smell. (Part b: T. W. Deacon, 1990)

Figure 3.7 图片引自《生物心理学》（第 10 版 p. 101 James W. Kalat 著）

Sensory and motor cortex

Different regions of the sensory cortex receive information about different senses. For example, cells in the parietal lobe take in information from the skin about touch, pain, and temperature, whereas cells in the occipital lobe receive visual information, from the thalamus to analyze what we see. Stimuli from the ears reach cells in the temporal lobe near areas of cortex that are involved in understanding language.

In the somatosensory cortex, skin sensations from neighboring parts of the body are represented in neighboring parts of cortex, as Figure 3.8 illustrates. It is as if the outline of a tiny person, dangling upside down, determined the location of the sensory and motor areas. This pattern is called the homunculus, which means "little man".

The motor cortex follows the same pattern. Neurons in specific areas of the motor cortex initiate voluntary movements in specific parts of the body, some controlling movement of the hand, others stimulating movement of the foot, the knee, the head, and so on. The motor cortex is arranged in a way that mirrors the somatosensory cortex. For example, as you can see in Figure 3.8, the parts of the motor cortex that control the hands are near parts of the sensory cortex that receive sensory information from the hands.

Association cortex

Parts of the cerebral cortex that are not directly involved with receiving specific sensory information or initiating movement are called association cortex. The term association is appropriate because these areas receive information from more than one sense or combine sensory and motor information. These are the areas that perform such complex cognitive tasks as associating words with images and other abstract thinking.

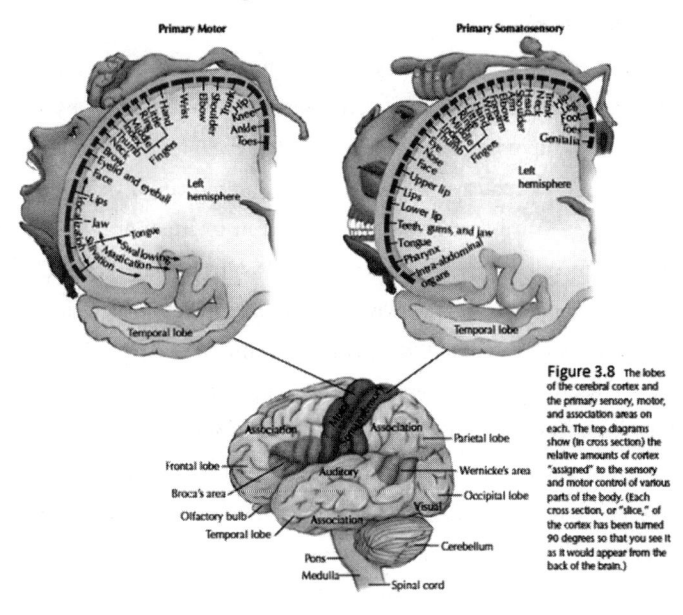

Figure 3.8 图片引自《心理学导论》（第11版 p.69 John O. Mitterer 著）

Motor and Somatosensory Cortex

The areas of cortex that move parts of the body (motor cortex) and receive sensory input from body parts (somatosensory cortex) occupy neighboring regions on each side of the central sulcus. These regions appear in both hemispheres; here we show only those on the left side, looking from the back of the brain toward the front. The cross–sections also show how areas controlling movement of neighboring parts of the body, like the foot and leg, occupy neighboring parts of motor cortex. Areas receiving input from neighboring body parts, like the lips and tongue, are near one another in the sensory cortex.

(Reprinted with permission of Macmillan Publishing Company from The Cerebral Cortex of Man by Wilder Pen field and Theodore Rasmussen. Copyright©. 1950 by Macmillan Publishing Company, renewed 1978 by Theodore Rasmussen.)

As you might expect, association areas form a large part of the cerebral cortex in human beings. This is one reason why damage to association areas can create severe deficits in all kinds of mental abilities. One of the most devastating, called aphasia, involves difficulty in producing or understanding speech.

Damage to association cortex in the frontal lobe near motor areas that control facial muscles can cause problems in the production of speech. This part of the cortex on the left side of the brain is called Broca's area (see Figure 3.7) It was named after Paul Broca, who in the 1860s described the speech difficulties that result from damage to the region. Damage to Broca's area causes the mental organization of speech to suffer. A person can still sing with ease but has great difficulty speaking, and what the person says is often grammatically incorrect. Each word comes slowly. One patient who was asked about a dental appointment said haltingly, "Yes–Monday–Dad and Dick...Wednesday 9 o'clock...10 o'clock...doctors...and...teeth" (Geschwind, 1979). The ideas dentists and teeth are right, but the fluency is gone.

Damage to a different association area can leave fluency intact but disrupt the ability to understand the meaning of words. Wernicke's area, described in the 1870s by Carl Wernicke, is also on the left side, in the temporal lobe, near the primary, receiving area in the cortex for hearing, as Figure 3.7 shows. Wernicke's area is involved in the interpretation of speech and, because it also receives input from the visual cortex, is also involved in interpreting written words. Damage to Wernicke's area produces complicated symptoms. A person with Wernicke's aphasia may have difficulty comprehending speech and may also produce speech that is fluent but difficult to comprehend. For example, a patient asked to describe a picture of two boys stealing cookies behind a woman's back said, "Mother is away here working her work to get her better, but when she's looking the two boys looking in the other part. She's working another time" (Geschwind, 1979).

Based on the symptoms of damage to brain areas, combined with anatomical evidence of connections among these areas, Wernicke and, later, Norman Geschwind proposed a model of how language is understood and produced. According to this model, language information reaches Wernicke's area from either the auditory cortex for spoken language or from the visual cortex for written language. In Wernicke's area, the words are interpreted and the structure of a verbal response is formed. The output from Wernicke's area gobs to Broca's area, where exist a detailed program for vocalization is formed. This program is relayed to adjacent areas of the motor cortex to produce speech. The neural structures involved in transforming the output into writing are not known.

The Divided Brain in a Unified Self

A striking idea emerged from observations of people with brain damage. Damage to limited areas of the left hemisphere causes some loss of the ability to use or comprehend language; damage to corresponding parts of the right hemisphere usually does not. Perhaps, then, the right and left halves of the brain serve different functions.

This is not an entirely new concept. It had long been understood, for example, that most pathways to sensory organs or muscles cross over as they enter or leave the brain. As a result, the left hemisphere receives information from and controls movements of the right side of the body, whereas the right hemisphere receives input from and controls the left side of the body. But these functions, although divided, are performed by both sides of the brain. By the nineteenth century, it was apparent that language centers, such as Broca's area and Wernicke's area, are almost exclusively on the left side of the brain. This suggested that one hemisphere is specialized for a function with which the other side seems not to be involved at all. During the 1960s, studies by Roger Sperry, Michael Gazzaniga, and their colleagues firmly established that there are indeed some differences between the hemispheres.

Split–brain studies

The people Sperry studied had such severe epilepsy that their seizures began in one hemisphere, then spread to engulf the whole brain. As a last resort, the two hemispheres in these people were isolated from each other by an operation that severed the **corpus callosum** massive bundle of more than a million fibers that connects the two hemispheres.

Using a special apparatus, the researchers presented visual images to only one side of these patients' split brains and found that severing the tie between the hemispheres had dramatically affected the way these people were able to think and deal with the world. For example, when the image of a spoon was presented to the left, or language oriented, side of patient NG's brain, she could say what the spoon was. But she could not describe the spoon in words when it was presented to the right side of her brain. Her right hemisphere knew what the object was, however. Using her left hand (controlled by the right hemisphere), NG could pick out the spoon from a group of other objects by its shape. When asked what she had just grasped, she replied, pencil. In other tests, the image of a nude woman was presented to NG's right hemisphere. The right hemisphere recognized the picture (NG blushed and giggled), but the patient could not describe it because the left (language) half of her brain did not see it (Sperry, 1968).

The language specializations of the left hemisphere are sometimes described as resulting in uniquely human capabilities that other animals do not possess. There are controversies about whether nonhuman animals have language abilities, but it is worth noting that monkeys' left hemispheres are specialized to recognize sounds made by other monkeys (Heffner & Heffner, 1984). Damage to the left temporal lobe results in a loss of the ability to distinguish different vocal noises, coos, made by other monkeys, but damage to the right temporal cortex has no effect on this ability. Therefore, even though primates may not be capable of language as such, it does appear they have an analog to Wernicke's area in humans.

Though the right hemisphere has no control over spoken language in most people, it does have some language ability. A split brain patient's right hemisphere can guide the left hand in spelling out words with Scrabble tiles (Gazzaniga & LeDoux, 1978). Communicating in this way, the right hemisphere has revealed that it has self-awareness and normal learning abilities. In fact, the right hemisphere is superior to the left on tasks dealing with spatial relations, especially drawing three-dimensional shapes. The right hemisphere is also much better than the left at recognizing human faces.

Lateralization of normal brains

Sperry concluded from his studies that each hemisphere in the split brain patient has its own "private sensations, perceptions, thought, and ideas all of which are cut off from the corresponding experiences in the opposite hemisphere...In many respects each disconnected hemisphere appears to have a separate mind of its own" (Sperry,1974). But when the hemispheres are not disconnected, are their functions different? Are certain functions, such as mathematical reasoning or language skills, **lateralized**, or performed more efficiently by one hemisphere than by the other?

To find out, researchers have presented images to just one hemisphere of people with normal brains and then measured lateralization by assessing how fast they could analyze information. If information is presented to one side of the brain and that side is specialized to analyze that type of information, a subject's responses will be faster than if the information must first be transferred to the other hemisphere for analysis. These studies have confirmed that the left hemisphere has better logical and language abilities than the right, whereas the right hemisphere has better spatial, artistic, and musical abilities (Springer & Deutsch,1985). PET scans of normal people receiving varying kinds of auditory stimulation also demonstrate these asymmetries of function.

The precise nature and degree of lateralization vary quite a bit among individuals. For example, among about a third of left-handed people, either the right hemisphere or both hemispheres control language functions (Springer & Deutsch, 1985). Only about 5 percent of right-handed people have language controlled by the right hemisphere. Surprisingly, left-handed people are also more likely to be brilliant mathematicians, be nearsighted, suffer allergies, stutter, and have reading difficulties.

Although the two hemisphere are somewhat specialized, the differences between them should not be exaggerated. People are not left-brained or right-brained in the same way that they are left-or right-handed. Normally the corpus callosum integrates the functions of the two hemispheres so that people are not aware of their "two brains." The hemispheres work so closely together, and each makes up so well for whatever lack of ability the other may have, that people are normally unaware that their brains are made up of two partially independent, somewhat specialized halves. In fact, even if the activity of one hemisphere is dominant, the effect is usually detectable only as differences in certain mental abilities or cognitive styles. For example, a person with a dominant right hemisphere may lean toward musical rather than foreign language studies. As we will see in later chapters, lateralization may also produce effects on the expression and suppression of emotion.

第四节 心理的化学过程
(THE CHEMISTRY OF PSYCHOLOGY)

So far, we have seen that the cells of the nervous system communicate by releasing neurotransmitters at their synapses. And we have outlined some of the basic structures of the nervous system and their functions. Now we need to pull these topics together, by examining which neurotransmitters occur in these structures and describing how these chemicals affect our behavior and mental processes.

Recall that different sets of neurons use different neurotransmitters. A group of neurons that communicates using the same neurotransmitter is called a neurotransmitter system. Usually the suffix–ergic is added to the name of a neurotransmitter to make it an adjective. Thus, for example, a group of neurons using the chemical dopamine as a neurotransmitter is called a dopaminergic system.

Neurotransmitters became interesting to biological psychologists when it became apparent that certain neurotransmitter systems might be related to particular behaviors and disorders. There is good evidence, for example, that one neurotransmitter system plays a role in some types of senility, whereas another system has been tied to some types of depression. Keep in mind, though, that a neurotransmitter can fit into more than one type of receptor in different parts of the brain or even in different parts of the same cell. As a result, a neurotransmitter can serve multiple functions, sometimes stimulating the firing of neurons in one area of the brain while at the same time inhibiting firing in another.

Five Neurotransmitters

At least fifty chemicals are known to act as neurotransmitters, and new ones are being discovered every year. Five of the most important and most intensely studied are acetylcholine, norepinephrine, serotonin, dopamine, and GABA.

Acetylcholine

The first compound to be established as a neurotransmitter was acetylcholine (pronounced "a-set-ill-coal-ene"). Neurons that communicate by using acetylcholine are called cholinergic. These neurons occur in both the peripheral and the central nervous systems. At the junctions of neurons and muscles, cholinergic neurons control the contraction of muscles. In the brain, cholinergic neurons are especially plentiful in the striatum (Part of the forebrain), where they occur in circuits that are important for movement. Axons of cholinergic neurons also make up major pathways in the limbic system and other areas of the cerebrum that are involved in memory (Bartus et al., 1982).

Indeed, cholinergic neurons may hold the key to Alzheimer's diseases severe brain disor-der which causes a progressive and devastating loss of memory and degeneration of personality. Some estimates suggest that as many as 5 percent of people over the age of sixty-five have Alzheimer disease (Coyle, Price & DeLong, 1983) .The problem seems to stem from a nearly complete loss of cholinergic neurons from a nucleus in the basal forebrain that sends fibers to the cerebral cortex (Whitehouse et al., 1983). Activating cholinergic neurons, usually with drugs that act as acetylcholine would, can facilitate memory processes somewhat. At present there is no effective way to reverse the effects of Alzheimer's disease, but research is currently active.

Norepinephrine

Like acetylcholine, **norepinephrine** occurs in both the central and the peripheral nervous systems. Collections of neurons that use norepinephrine or its close relative epinephrine are called adrenergic systems. The name makes sense because norepinephrine is also called noradrenaline, and epinephrine is also known as adrenaline. Approximately half of the norepinephrine in the brain is contained in cells located in the locus coeruleus ("blue spot") near the reticular formation in the hindbrain. There are only about 3, 000 cells in the locus coeruleus, but each sends out an axon that branches so extensively that it makes contact with as many as 100, 000 other cells (Moore & Bloom, 1979; Swanson, 1976).

Because adrenergic systems cover a lot of territory, it is logical that norepinephrine shapes several broad categories of behavior. Indeed, there is good evidence that norepinephrine is involved in the appearance of wake and sleep, in the process of learning, and in the regulation of mood, including depression and elation. For example, compared with others, depressed people have lower levels of norepinephrine or its metabolites (Bunney, Goodwin & Murphy, 1972; Crow et al., 1984), but researchers have not yet determined whether these low levels are a cause or an effect of depression.

Serotonin

The neurotransmitter **serotonin** is similar to norepinephrine in several ways: (1) most of the cells that use it as a neurotransmitter occur in a restricted region along the midline of the hindbrain;(2) serotonergic axons send branches throughout the forebrain, including the hypothalamus, the hippocampus, and the cerebral cortex; and (3) serotonin affects sleep and moods, Serotonin is also active in the neural circuits that descend from the brain to help block brain sensations.

Serotonin differs from norepinephrine, however, in that one of the substances from which it is made, tryptophan, can be used by the brain directly from the food a person eats. This is in one way in which dietary factors may affect mood or drowsiness. For example, compared with a high -protein meal, a meal high in carbohydrates produces increased levels of serotonin and, at least in women, drowsiness. In men, the reported mood change is "calmness" (Spring et al., 1982–1983).

Dopamine

The neurons that use **dopamine** as a neurotransmitter are more restricted than those that use norepinephrine or serotonin, and their axons do not branch as extensively. The functions of dopaminergic neurons ae also more restricted.

Some neurons that release dopamine are involved in movement; their degeneration is the cause of Parkinson's disease, which produces shakiness and extreme difficulty in initiating movements. Like Alzheimer's disease, Parkinson's is most common in elderly people. The neurons that degenerate have their ceil bodies in the substantia nigra of the midbrain; their axons travel in a very organized way to the striatum, by way of the nigrostriatal pathway. Other dopaminergic systems send axons from the midbrain to the forebrain, including the cerebral cortex. Malfunctioning of these dopaminergic neurons may be responsible for schizophrenia, a psychological disorder in which there are severe distortions in perception, movement, emotional expression and thought. People diagnosed as schizophrenic may see or hear imaginary things and may act or think very strangely.

GABA

The major inhibitory neurotransmitter is **GABA**, which stands for "gamma-amino butyric acid." GABA reduces the likelihood that the postsynaptic neuron will fire an action potential. It is used by neurons in widespread regions of the brain.

For example, when you fall asleep, neurons that use GABA deserve part of the credit. Dysfunctions in GABA systems may be related to the appearance of severe anxiety. In fact, GABA has been implicated in a variety of behavioral disorders, including Huntington's disease and epilepsy. Huntington's disease is an inherited disorder that results in the loss of many GABA activated neurons in the striatum. Normally these GABA systems inhibit dopamine systems. When they are lost in Huntington's disease, the dopamine systems may run wild, with effects that are in some ways the opposite of those of Parkinson's disease. Instead of facing an inability to begin movements, the victim is plagued by uncontrollable movement of the arms and legs, along with a progressive loss of cognitive abilities. Epilepsy is a brain disorder that produces intense repetitive electrical discharges, known as seizures, along with convulsive movements. Repeated or sustained seizures can result in permanent brain damage; fortunately, drug treatments can reduce their frequency or severity. Because epilepsy results from wildly spreading excitation through large populations of neurons, it is logical that a deficiency of GABA, the major inhibitory neurotransmitter, could be part of the problem.

Drugs, Neurotransmitters, and Behavior

Like naturally occurring neurotransmitters, psychoactive drugs are chemicals that may affect behavior, mental processes, and conscious experience. Included among these drugs are those, like cocaine, that are used mainly for pleasure or escape and those that are used to treat mental disorders. The study of psychoactive drugs and their effects is called psychopharmacology.

Most psychoactive drugs act by altering neurotransmission in at least one of four ways: (1) by altering the amount of neurotransmitter released by a neuron; (2)by mimicking the neurotransmitter at the receptor site; (3)by blocking receptors for certain neurotransmitters; or (4)by blocking reuptake of the neurotransmitter from the synapse. Because a single drug often produces more than one of these effects, it can be difficult to determine how the drug creates some observed result. We will consider each of these mechanisms.

Altering the amount of neurotransmitter released

The treatment for Parkinson's disease illustrates how a drug may act by altering the amount of neurotransmitters available to be released. Recall that Parkinson's disease involves the death of many dopamine cells in the nigrostriatal system, making movement very difficult. The search for a drug to combat the disease began with the assumption that, if the amount of dopamine in the remaining nigrostriatal neurons could be increased, those neurons might partially compensate for the lost cells. To devise a way of increasing the amount of dopamine available, researchers used the knowledge that dopamine is made in the brain from a compound called L—dopa, once L—dopa is in the brain, dopaminergic neurons take it up and convert it to dopamine.

Giving L—dopa to victims of Parkinson isease turned out to be an effective treatment, but for some unknown reason, the treatment is effective only for several years. Something about the dopaminergic system adjusts, so that L—dopa no longer relieves Parkinsonian symptoms. Because this adjustment is related to the length of treatment, physicians try to delay using L—dopa for as long as possible.

Other drugs cause more neurotransmitter to be released from the presynaptic endings. For example, the stimulant amphetamine releases such neurotransmitters as norepinephrine and dopamine, which normally activate large parts of the brain. This creates signals to the affected neurons that are similar to those that would occur if rapidly firing neurons were flooding the synapses with a neurotransmitter. Like L—dopa, amphetamine changes the neurotransmitter system if the drug is used regularly. With amphetamine, one result is the appearance of mental disturbances similar to one type of schizophrenia.

Mimicking neurotransmitters

If a molecule is very similar to a certain neurotransmitter, it may fool that transmitter's receptors and occupy them itself. Many drugs, called agonists, mimic neurotransmitters in this way, fitting snugly into the receptors and changing a cell's membrane potential just as the neurotransmitter would. For example, ephedrine is a drug that mimics norepinephrine and therefore has arousing properties. It is used clinically to treat narcolepsy, a disease in which a person falls asleep abruptly and unpredictably during the day (Goodman, Good—man & Gilman, 1980).The drugs mentioned earlier that may improve memory in Alzheimer's disease by acting like acetylcholine are also agonists.

Blocking receptors

Some drugs are similar enough to a neurotransmitter to occupy its receptor sites on nerve cells, but not similar enough to fit snugly and change those cell's membrane potential. These drugs are called **antagonists**. As long as they are attached to receptors, they compete with and block neurotransmitters from occupying and acting on the receptors.

One prominent application of antagonists is in the treatment of schizophrenia. No one has a "cure" for schizophrenia, but the drugs that partially relieve its symptoms have one feature in common: they are all antagonists that occupy dopamine receptors and prevent dopamine from producing its normal effects. Dopamine antagonists may relieve schizophrenic symptoms by blocking dopaminergic activity in neurons that send axons to the frontal lobes of the cerebral cortex. There, it is hypothesized, excess dopamine may disrupt thought, producing schizophrenic symptoms.

Unfortunately, the drugs that relieve these symptoms also prevent dopamine from reaching its receptors in other parts of the brain. As noted earlier, too little dopamine in the nigrostriatal tract produces inability to initiate certain movements and other symptoms resembling those of Parkinson's disease. Furthermore, as the brain adapts to prolonged use of dopamine blocking drugs, even more serious, of ten irreversible, movement disorders may appear. For example, tardive dyskinesia causes grotesque, uncontrollable, repetitive movements of the body and face.

Blocking reuptake

Many drugs interfere with the removal, or reuptake, of a neurotransmitter from synapses. The result is that the concentration of neurotransmitter remaining in a synapse increases, and the normal actions of the neurotransmitter are enhanced. Many drugs that are used to treat depression, for example, seem to work by blocking the reuptake of norepinephrine and serotonin, thus making more of these chemicals available and in turn improving mood. The mechanism by which these drugs relieve depression is still not entirely clear, however, because some drugs that block the removal of norepinephrine do not combat depression. Cocaine, for example, blocks the removal of norepinephrine, increases arousal, and lifts one's mood, but it does not relieve severe depression.

Other drugs block the deactivation of acetylcholine in synapses between neurons and at the junctions of neurons and muscles. The result is excessive contraction of all muscles, leading to death. Insecticides that are vital to modem agriculture, for example, act by blocking the removal of acetylcholine. Because nerve gas also works in this way, military agencies have been very interested in cholinergic neurochemistry.

第五节　内分泌系统
(ENDOCRINE SYSTEMS)

Neurons are not the only cells that can communicate with one another in ways that affect behavior and mental processes. Another class of cells that can do this is found in **endocrine systems**. The cells in these systems group together in special organs, called glands, which communicate, much as neurons do, by secreting chemicals. In this case, the chemicals are called **hormones**.

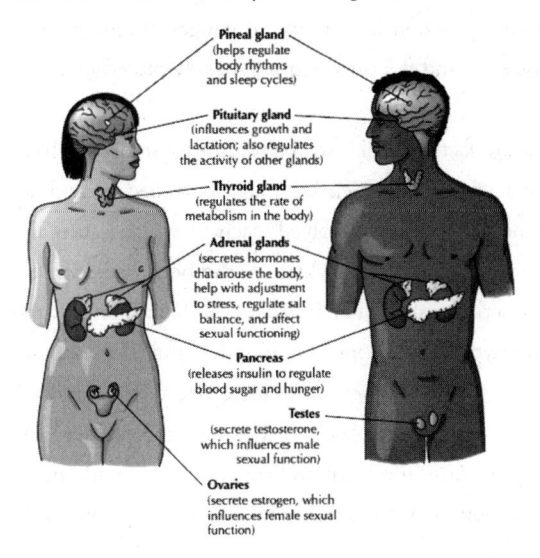

Obviously, hormones are similar to neurotransmitters. In fact, some chemicals, such as adrenaline, act both as hormones and as neurotransmitters. But, whereas neurons secrete neurotransmitters into synapses, glands put their, chemicals into the bloodstream, which carries them throughout the body. In this way, glands can stimulate remote cells to which they have no direct connection. Thus, neural communication is rather like the telephone, through which information is given out over wires to particular people.

Endocrine communication is more like a newspaper, which circulates information to a large number of people.

Figure3.9　图片引自《心理学导论》（第 11 版 p. 74 John O. Mitterer 著）

Some Major Glands of the Endocrine System

Each of the glands shown releases its hormones into the bloodstream. Even the hypothalamus, a part of the brain, regulates the adjacent pituitary gland by secreting hormones. Each hormone acts on many organs, including the brain, producing coordinated effects (such as the fight-or-flight syndrome) throughout the body.

Figure 3.9 shows the location and functions of some of the major endocrine organs. Hormones from these organs stimulate cells in both the peripheral and the central nervous systems. Usually they affect the growth and metabolism of various tissues and produce very general changes in behavior and mental processes. Some hormones affect general energy levels, arousal, and learning. Others regulate such basic behaviors as hunger and eating, thirst, aggression, and sexual behavior. The secretion of almost all hormones is affected by psychological processes, especially stress.

Just as neurotransmitters have their own receptors, there are target tissues, or target organs, whose cells have receptors that respond to particular hormones. The target organs for a hormone typically form a coordinated system. For example, when the sex hormones estrogen and progesterone begin to be secreted by a woman's ovaries, they travel through the blood-stream, activating her reproductive system. They cause the uterus to grow in preparation for nurturing an embryo; they enlarge the breasts to prepare them for their feeding function; and at the same time, they stimulate the brain and pituitary gland to cause a mature egg to be released for fertilization.

The action of adrenal hormones provides another example of a coordinated endocrine system. When the brain interprets a situation as threatening, it causes the adrenal glands to release adrenaline into the bloodstream. This produces a coordinated set of responses called the **fight-or-flight syndrome**, which prepares the animal or person for action in response to danger: the heart beats faster, the liver releases glucose into the bloodstream, and the organism is generally placed in a state of high arousal.

The fight-or-flight syndrome illustrates the fact that, like so many other systems we have described, endocrine systems are set up in feedback loops, which both are controlled by and act on the brain. Actually, a chain of several hormones is usually involved, each of which causes the secretion of another hormone. The chain begins with the brain, which, as the body's executive's active in both the nervous system and the endocrine system. For instance, the brain controls the pituitary gland by releasing hormones from the hypothalamus into the bloodstream. The pituitary secretes many different hormones, some of which stimulate other glands to secrete their hormones. These hormones then act on cells in the body, as well as feed back to the brain and pituitary. As with a thermostat and furnace, this feedback may cause the brain and pituitary to provide more stimulation or to reduce the stimulation. If the output of the final gland falls below some level, feedback causes the brain and pituitary to stimulate increased secretion. This system tends to keep the output of hormones within a certain range.

第六节 未来研究趋向
(FUTURE DIRECTIONS)

In trying to understand behavior and mental processes, some psychologists have paid little attention to biological factors, preferring to look at humans and animals as "black boxes" that receive stimuli from the outside world and generate responses. For them, the study of the biological and mental processes that go on inside the box is not of great concern. However, the desire to better understand these processes drives much current psychological research.

Today, knowledge of these biological systems is increasing at an explosive rate. Scientists far from understand the details of brain functions and how those functions translate into what people experience as the mind, but impressive progress is being made. People from a wide variety of scientific disciplines are applying their techniques to understanding the nervous system. Medical researchers, anatomists, biochemists, physiologists, and psychologists are all beginning to see themselves as neuroscientists.

Neuroscience is now in an era in which technical breakthroughs have allowed a tremendous amount of information to be gathered in a short time. Radioactive compounds have been used only in the last couple of decades; PET scans have been in use only for a few years. Other techniques, such as those of molecular biology, are even more recent. Advances in computer technology greatly aid all of these approaches to understanding the biological bases of behavior, because they allow scientists to gather more and more details of basic biological processes.

Specific biological factors in such disease processes as Alzheimer's disease and schizophrenia will be found and will be identified that will help determine who might be susceptible to certain kinds of disorders, such as alcoholism, making it possible to offer help long before the problem becomes extreme. Progress will be made in reversing some degenerative diseases, perhaps by aiding the body's own restorative powers. If scientists succeed in transplanting brain tissue, so that damaged tissue can be replaced and lost functions regained, they will face an obvious ethical and practical dilemma: Who gives up the brain tissue to be transplanted? One possibility is to use tissue from spontaneously or medically aborted fetuses, but this would not be acceptable to some people. Another alternative is a cross species transplant. Scientists have already successfully transplanted tissue from a mouse into a rat (Bjorklund et al., 1982).

In the case of Parkinson's disease, a person can be both donor and recipient of transplanted tissue. This is because cells of the adrenal gland, which have neuronlike properties, become neurons when placed in the brain. Since a person can live with just one adrenal gland, the other adrenal gland can be grafted into the caudate nucleus. This procedure has been done in humans with encouraging, even spectacular, results. Two Parkinson's patients who received this graft dramatically improved in their ability to walk and produce fine movements, such as handwriting (Madrazo et al., 1987).

It is also likely that a molecular basis for learning and memory will be found, and it will probably relate to a variety of changes in the nervous system. The ways that complex neural networks allow the brain to sense information and solve complicated problems will be unraveled, and perhaps the principles derived from such work will be applied to the creation of computers that can more efficiently solve problems too complex even for the human brain.

Future technologies will surely be added to those already used to study the brain and other biological structures. Currently, PET scans and electrical recordings are limited in how much information they can glean from the brain or how quickly they can trace changes in activity. New techniques, many using the latest supercomputers, will allow more rapid, more detailed, monitoring of brain activity. As these techniques are developed and shown to be safe, more research on how the brain works will be conducted with normal people instead of laboratory animals or medical patients.

The larger question of how the nervous system is responsible for the mind will be more difficult to answer. How do all the details fit together? More information than any individual can master is being generated about such questions. It will take some great minds, probably working with great computers, to synthesize this information into a vision of how the inside of the "black box" generates experience and behavior.

If you are interested in taking part in this collective adventure, either as a participant scientist or as an informed spectator, you can prepare yourself by learning more about both physical and psychological sciences. Relevant courses offered by most psychology departments include physiological psychology, sensation and perception, learning and memory, motivation and emotion, and abnormal psychology. Many departments now offer courses in drugs and behavior. Courses in other departments are also relevant; take as much chemistry, physiology, anatomy, and computer science as you can. Studying the relationships between body and mind is an inter-disciplinary adventure, so having a broad background will help you greatly in many different areas of life.

词汇（**Vocabulary**）

1. abacus   n. 算盘、顶板
2. acetylcholine   n. 乙酰胆碱
3. adrenaline   n. 肾上腺素
4. adrenergic   adj. 肾上腺素能的
5. agonist   n. 主动肌、主缩肌、兴奋剂、激动剂
6. antagonist   n. 对抗肌、对抗剂、对抗药、对抗者、对手
7. aphasia   n. 失语症、语言不能
8. axon   n. 轴突
9. callosum   n. 胼胝体
10. cerebellum   n. 小脑

11. cerebral hemisphere   n. 大脑两半球
12. cholinergic   adj. 释放乙酰胆碱的
13. convolution   n. 盘旋、缠绕
14. corpus callosum   n. 胼胝体
15. corpus striatum   n. 纹状体
16. CT scanning   n. CT检查
17. debilitate   v. 削弱……力量使人衰弱
18. decipher   v. 解释（密码等）
19. dendrites   n. 树突、树枝状
20. diagnosis   n. 诊断结论、调查分析判断结论、特征简介
21. diencephalon   n. 间脑
22. dopamine   n. 多巴胺
23. dopaminergic system   n. 多巴胺系统
24. eavesdrop   v. 窃听
25. electroencephalograms   n. 脑电图
26. ephedrine   n. 麻黄碱、麻黄素
27. epileptic seizure   n. 癫痫突然发作
28. euphoria   adj. 舒适、安乐、愉快、心情愉快、兴奋、欣快症、欣快异常
29. excitable surface membrane   n. 活性表面膜
30. fiber tract   n. 纤维素
31. fight-or-flight syndrome   n. 运动失调综合征
32. fissure   n. 裂隙
33. fronted lobe   n. 额叶
34. glial cell   n. 神经胶质细胞
35. glucose   n. 葡萄糖、淀粉糖
36. grotesque   adj. 古怪的、奇形怪状的、奇异风格的、怪物、怪人
37. gyri   n. 圆形或螺旋形
38. hippocampus   n. 海马
39. homeostasis   n. 体内平衡
40. homunculus   n. 小人（特指炼金术士在烧瓶中人工制造的小人）
41. hypothalamus   n. 下丘脑
42. isotope   n. 同位素
43. lateralization   n. 脑侧
44. L-dopa   n. 左旋多巴
45. limbic system   n. 边缘系统
46. mammillary body   n. 乳头体
47. medulla   n. 神经纤维外鞘髓部
48. mimic   v. 模拟，是……仿制品   adj. 模仿的、模仿者（人、动物）
49. mitochondrion   n. 线粒体

50. molecule   n. 分子
51. myelin   n. 髓磷质
    nuclear magnetic resonance imagingn 核磁共振成像
52. naloxone   n. 纳络酮，一种强力的麻醉性药物拮抗剂
53. neuron   n. 神经元
54. neurotransmitter   n. 神经递质
55. norepinephrine   n. 去甲肾上腺素，又作 noradrenaline
56. nucleus   n. 神经核（pi）. nuclei
57. occipital lobe   n. 枕叶
58. opiate   n. 鸦片剂
59. outer membrane   n. 外膜
60. parasympathetic branches   n. 副交感神经
61. parietal lobe   n. 顶叶
62. peripheral nervous system   n. 外周神经系统
63. placebo effect   n. 安慰剂作用（病人经治疗后情况好转，但不能认为系由于所应用的特效治疗所致）
64. polarizer   v. 赋予极性、使极化
65. positron emission   n. 正电子发射（指 β 衰变过程中核发射一个正电子和一个中微子）
66. postsynaptic   adj. 随联会之后的、后联会的
67. psychopharmacology   n. 神经药理学
68. receptor   n. 受体、感受器
69. refractory period   n. 不应期或不应相
70. reside   n. 泡、胞、囊
71. reuptake   v.（神经细胞对化学物质的）再吸收、再摄取
72. Schwann cell   n. 施旺氏细胞、神经的鞘细胞
73. self-propagating   n. 自繁殖
74. septum   n. 隔膜中隔、间隔、隔板
75. serotonin   n. 血清素主要存于血清和脑髓中
76. sodium   n. 钠
77. somatic nervous system   n. 躯体神经系统
78. somatosensory cortex   n. 躯体感觉皮层区
79. sphinx   n. ①斯芬克斯 ②神秘的人物
80. spinal cord   n. 脊髓
81. spinothalamic   adj. 脊髓丘脑的、与脊髓丘脑相连的
82. split-brain   n. 脑裂
83. substantia nigra   n. 黑质
84. sympathetic branches   n. 交感神经
85. synapse   n. 突触

86. stroke   n. 中风
87. tardive dyskinesia   n. 延迟性运动障碍
88. telencephalon   n. 端脑、终脑
89. temporal lobe   n. 颞叶
90. thalamus   n. 丘脑
91. thermostat   n. 恒温器
92. tomography   n. X线断层照相机

第四章 感觉
（SENSATION）

本章要点（Chapter Outline）
感觉系统（Sensory System)
听觉（Hearing)
视觉（Vision)
嗅觉（Olfaction)
味觉（Gustation)
躯体感觉（Somatic Sense)

在日常生活中，人们每时每刻都在与外界事物接触，而任何事物都具有许多属性，如颜色、形状、大小、软硬、气味等等。事物的这些个别属性通过感觉器官直接作用于人脑所引起的心理现象就是感觉。感觉是一种最简单的心理现象，它虽然简单，但它在人们的生活和工作中具有重要的意义。首先，通过感觉，人们能够认识并了解外界事物的属性，从周围环境中获得必要的信息，从而保证机体的正常生活。其次，通过感觉，人们还能认识自己机体的各种状态，因而就有可能实现自我调节。最后，感觉是一切较高级、较复杂的心理活动的基础。人的知觉、记忆、思维等复杂的认识活动，必须借助于感觉提供的原始资料。没有感觉，一切较复杂、较高级的心理现象都无从产生。本章主要讨论感知过程的初级阶段，对感官如何获得信息并将其转变为大脑所能接受的形式这一过程做了详尽描述。至今，虽然在该领域积累了大量的研究成果，但仍有许多未解之谜，像如何科学地解答大脑通过感官获得信息这一中心问题，将无疑会把人工智能领域的研究及计算机的创新革命带入一片崭新的天地。

George H. sees and hears things that other people do not. This is not because he has especially good vision and hearing, but because he suffers from schizophrenia, a severe form of mental disorder. George sees and hears things that are not really there, but the accusing voices he hears and the stern faces he sees on the walls are real to him. In fact, he has been in a mental hospital for nearly thirty years, in part because he cannot ignore his version of reality long enough to hold a job, let alone a normal conversation. George's case highlights the fact that, in order to get along with human society, one must hold a view of reality that is similar to that held by others.

But what is reality, and how do people recognize it? Philosophers have debated this deceptively simple question for centuries. The seventeenth-century British philosopher John Locke held that, whatever reality is, people can gain knowledge about the outside world only through the senses. This empirical, or data based, approach has become the basis for the scientific study of psychology. It presumes that contact with reality and knowledge of the world come to us as they come to Georgeonly through the senses.

A SENSE is a system that translates data from outside the nervous system into neural activity, giving the nervous system, especially the brain, information about the world. For example, vision is the system through which the eyes convert light into neural activity that tells the brain something about the source of the light (for example, that it is bright) or about objects from which it is reflected (for example, that a round, red object is out there). These messages from the senses are called sensations and comprise the raw information that affects many kinds of behavior and mental processes (see Linkages diagram, pp.120−121).

Traditionally, psychologists have distinguished between sensation the initial message from the senses and perception or the way the message is interpreted and given meaning in terms of previous experiences. Thus, you do not actually "sense" a cat lying on the sofa; you see shapes and colors visual sensations. But, because of your previous knowledge of the world, you interpret, or perceive, these sensations as a cat. However, recent research has made it more and more difficult to draw a clear line between sensation and perception. That research has shown that the process of interpreting sensations takes place at many levels, beginning in the sense organs themselves and continuing into the brain. Even previous experience can shape what people sense, causing you not to notice, for example, the familiar chiming of the living room clock, but leaving you very sensitive to the slightest sound when you walk down a dark alley at midnight.

In this chapter, we cover the earlier parts of the sensation−perception process, examining the ways in which the senses pick up information and convert it into forms the brain can use. In the next chapter, we will discuss the later segments of the sensation−perception process, along with psychophysics, the laws that govern how physical energy is converted into psychological experience. Together, these chapters will illustrate how human beings create, with the sense organs and the brain, their own worlds and their own realities.

第一节 感觉系统
(SENSORY SYSTEMS)

The senses gather information about the world through the various forms of energy they can detect, such as sound, light, heat, and physical pressure. For example, the eyes detect light energy, the ears detect the energy of sound, and the skin detects the energy of heat and pressure. These sensory systems are far from perfect, though. For one thing, they cannot detect such energy sources as X rays and microwaves. Further, there are limits to how much energy they can deal with at the same time. Humans depend primarily on vision, hearing, and the skin senses to gain information about the world; they depend less than other animals on smell and taste. There are also senses that provide information to the brain from the rest of the body. All of these senses must detect stimuli, encode them into neural activity, and transfer this coded information to the brain.

Steps in Sensation

There are six steps in sensation
1. Energy: contains information about the world.
2. Accessory structure: modifies energy.
3. Receptor: transduces energy into a neural response.
4. Sensory nerve: transfers the coded activity to the central nervous system.
5. Thalamus: processes and relays the neural response
6. Cortex: receives input and produces the sensation.

At each step, information is processed in some ways. In some sensory systems, the first step in sensation involves **accessory structures**, which modify the stimulus. The lens of the eye is an accessory structure that changes incoming light by focusing it; the outer part of the ear is an accessory structure that collects sound. The second step in sensation is **transduction**, the process of converting incoming energy into neural activity. Just as a radio receives energy and transduces it into sounds, the ears receive sound energy and transduce it into neural activity that people recognize as voices, music, and other auditory experiences. Transduction takes place at structures called **receptors**, cells that are specialized to detect certain forms of energy. Next, sensory nerves transfer the receptors activity to the brain. For all the senses but smell, the information is taken first to the thalamus, which relays it to cerebral cortex.

Each nerve cell that carries sensory information responds to only a small part of the incoming energy. This portion of the world that affects a given neuron is its receptive field. For example, in the visual system, one neuron might respond to light that is in a small area at the top of whatever you look at: this area is the receptive field for that neuron.

THE PROBLEM OF CODING

When receptors transduce energy, they must somehow code the physical properties of the stimulus into firing patterns that, when organized by the brain, allow one to make sense of the stimulus; to tell, for example, whether you are looking at a dog or a cat. Each psychological dimension of a sensation, such as the brightness or color of light, must have a corresponding physical dimension that is coded by sensory receptors.

As a way of thinking about the problem of coding, suppose that, for your birthday, you are given a Pet Brain, a new product inspired by the people who brought us Pet Rocks and Cabbage Patch dolls. Your Pet Brain is definitely alive (the guarantee says so), but it does not seem to respond when you talk to it. You show it an ice cream sundae; no response. You show it pictures of other highly attractive brains; no response. You are about to deposit your Pet Brain in the garbage disposal when you suddenly realize that you are not talking the same language. You should be buzzing the brain's sensory nerves with action potentials to send it messages and recording from its motor nerves to discern its responses.

After having brilliant insight and setting up a little electric shocker, you are faced with an even more awesome problem. How do you describe an ice cream sundae in terms of action potentials? This is the problem of coding. **Coding** is the translation of a stimulu's physical properties into a pattern of neural activity that specifically identifies those physical properties. Now you realize that, if you want the brain to see the sundae, you should probably stimulate its optic nerve (the nerve from the eye to the brain) rather than its auditory nerve (the nerve from the ear to the brain). This idea is based on the doctrine of **specific nerve energies**: stimulation of a particular sensory nerve provides codes for that one sense, no matter how the stimulation takes place. For example, if you close your eyes and apply gentle pressure to your eyeball, you will produce activity in the optic nerve. You will sense this activity as a light stimulus and see little spots of light. Similarly, electrical stimulation of the optic nerve is coded and sensed as light; electrical stimulation of the auditory nerve is coded and sensed as sound.

Having chosen the optic nerve to convey visual information, you must next code the specific attributes of the sundae stimulus: the soft white curved of the vanilla ice cream, the dark richness of the chocolate, the bright redness of the cherry on top. These dimensions must be coded in the language of neural activity. As described in the previous chapter, this language is made up of membrane potentials in dendrites and cell bodies and action potentials in axons.

Some attributes are coded fairly simply. For example, stimulus intensity is often coded by a neuron's rate of firing. A bright light will cause some neurons in the visual system to fire faster than will a dim light. The codes can be very complex, and information can be recoded at each of several relay points as it makes its way through the brain. Sensory psychologists are still working on deciphering the codes that the brain uses; your Pet Brain may have to wait a while to appreciate the beauty of an ice cream sundae.

REPRESENTING STIMULI IN THE BRAIN

As sensory systems transfer information to the brain, they also organize that information. This organized information is called a representation. If you have read Chapter 3, you are already familiar with some characteristics of sensory representations. In humans, representations in the cerebral cortex of vision, hearing and the skin senses share the following features;

1. A primary area of sensory cortex receives information through the thalamus from each of these senses.

2. The representation of the sensory world in the cortex is contralateral to the part of the world being sensed. Thus, for example, the left side of the primary visual cortex "sees" the right side of the world, and the right side of the somatosensory cortex "feels" the left side of the body. This happens because nerve fibers from each side of the body cross on their way to the thalamus. As noted in Chapter 3, the same thing happens in the motor cortex, so that the left side of the brain controls the right side of the body and vice versa.

3. The primary cortex contains a map or topographical representation, of each sense. This means that any two points that are next to each other in the stimulus will be represented next to each other in the brain. The proportions on the sensory map may be distorted, but the relationships

among the various points are maintained.

4. The density of nerve fibers at any given part of a sense organ determines the extent of its representation in the cortex. For example, your fingertips, which have many receptors for touch, have a larger area of cortex representing them than does the skin on your back.

5. Each region of primary sensory cortex is divided into columns of cells that have similar properties. For example, one column of cells in the visual cortex might respond most to diagonal lines; another column might respond most to edges.

6. For each of the senses, regions of cortex other than the primary areas do more complex processing of sensory information. Called association cortex, some of these areas contain representations of more than one sense: others provide additional representation areas for a given sense. Hearing, for example, is represented in several association areas.

In short, sensory systems convert some form of energy into neural activity. Often the energy is first modified by accessory structures; then a sensory receptor converts the energy to neural activity. The pattern of neural activity codes physical properties of the energy. The codes are modified as the information is transferred to the brain and processed further.

In the rest of this chapter, we describe individual sensory systems. We will consider (1) the form of energy that is detected by the sense; (2) the accessory structures and receptors that transduce the energy; (3) the coding and information processing that occurs at the receptor; and (4) the transfer of information from the receptor to the brain.

第二节 听觉
(HEARING)

When Neil Armstrong stepped onto the moon in 1969, he proclaimed, "That's one small step for a man, one giant leap for mankind." Many people on earth heard him because the words were transferred back to earth by radio. But if Armstrong had taken off his space helmet, I thrown it high over his head, and shouted "Whoo! I can moonwalk" not even an astronaut standing nearby could have heard him, Why? Because he would have been speaking into airless, empty space, sound is a repetitive fluctuation in the pressure of a medium like air, and it cannot exist in a place like the moon, which has almost no atmosphere.

Sounds

The fluctuations in pressure that constitute sound are produced by the vibrations of an object. Each time the object moves outward, its energy increases the pressure in the medium immediately around it. As the object moves back, the pressure drops. In speech, for example, the vibrating object is the vocal cords, and the medium is air. When you speak, your vocal cords vibrate, producing fluctuations in air pressure that spread as waves. A wave is a repetitive variation in pressure that spreads out in three dimensions. The wave can move great distances, but the air itself barely moves (if the air were moving, your vocal cords would create a breeze, not sound). Imagine a jampacked line of people waiting for a movie. If someone at the rear of the line violently shoves the next person, a wave of people jostling against people may spread all the way to the front of the line, but the person who shoved is still no closer to getting into the theater.

THE PHYSICAL CHARACTERISTICS OF SOUND

We can represent sound graphically as a waveform, as in Figure 4.1. The waveform represents in two dimensions and the wave moves through the air in three dimensions.

Three characteristics of the waveform are important in understanding sounds. First, the difference in the air pressure of the peak and of the trough is the **amplitude** of the sound. Second, the distance from one peak to the next is the wavelength. And third, **frequency** is the number of complete waves, or cycles, that pass by a given point in space every second. Frequency is described in hertz, abbreviated Hz (for Heinrich Hertz, a nineteenth-century physicist who studied energy waves). One cycle per second is hertz. Because the speed of sound is constant, frequency and wavelength are inversely related; that is, the longer the wavelength, the lower the frequency. Likewise, highfrequency sound is short wavelength sound.

The simplest waveform has just one frequency and can be represented by what is known in mathematics as a sine wave; the waveform in Figure 4.1 is an example. A sound that can be represented by a perfect sine wave is called a pure tone. In contrast, most sounds are mixtures of a large number of frequencies and amplitudes and correspond to complex waveforms.

PSYCHOLOGICAL DIMENSIONS OF SOUND

The frequency and amplitude of sound waves determine the sounds that you hear. These physical characteristics of the waves produce the psychological dimensions of sound known as pitch, loudness, and timbre.

Pitch—how high or low a tone is—is the psychological dimension determined by the frequency of sound waves. High-frequency waves are sensed as sounds of high pitch. The highest note on a piano has a frequency of about 4000 hertz; the lowest note has a frequency of about 50 hertz. Humans can hear sounds from about 20 hertz to about 20,000 hertz. Loudness is determined by the amplitude of the sound wave; waves with greater amplitude produce sensations of louder sounds. Loudness is described in units called decibels, abbreviated dB. By definition, O decibels is the minimal detectable sound for normal hearing. Timbre is the quality of sound that identifies it, so that, for example, a middle C played on the piano is clearly distinguishable from a middle C played on a trumpet. The timbre depends on the mixture of frequencies and amplitudes that make up the sound.

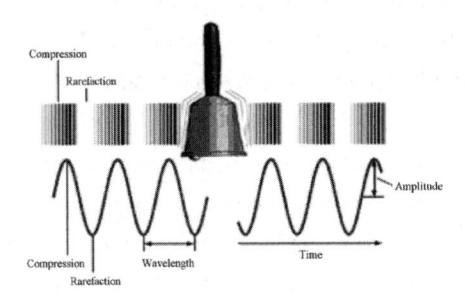

Figure 4.1

Waveforms, a Representation of Sound Waves

The molecules of air around a sound source are unevenly distributed. Regions of greater compressinon of air molecules alternate with regions of lesser compression because of the to-and -frovibrations of the object generating the sound. The variations in air molecule compression can be represented as a waveform of pressure across time, with greater pressure indicated by the peak in the curve. The point where the air is compressed the most is the peak of the graph. The lowest point, or trough, is where the air pressure is lowest.

fundamental frequency   (a)piano

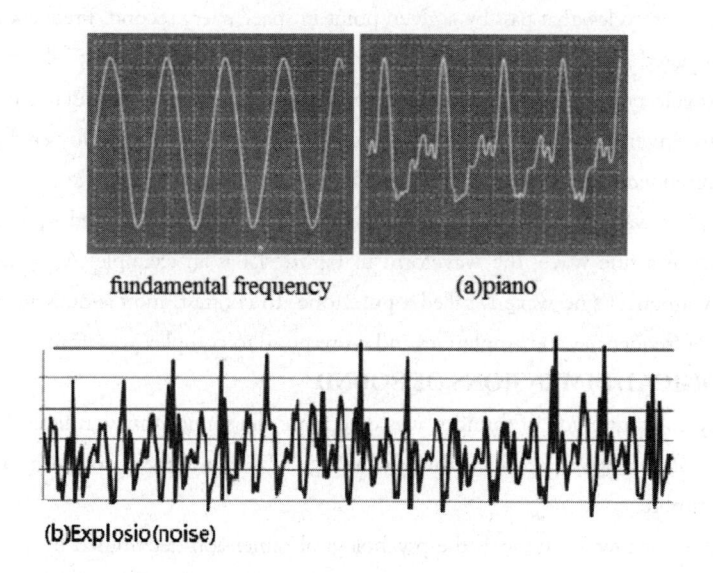

(b)Explosio(noise)

Figure 4.2
Timbre

Even when playing a single note, musical instruments produce complex waveforms, (a) The waveform produced by a piano playing one note, C below middle C. The fundamental frequency is 130 hertz, but multiples of this fundamental frequency also contribute to the sound. Because the components of the complex wave have a simple relationship to the fundamental frequency,the sound is musical, (b) The waveform produced by an explosion. Explosions are normally considered noise rather than music, because their waveforms are very irregular, rather than repeating (Part a from Speech and Hearing (revised ed), by Harvey Fletcher, D. Van Nostrand Company, lnc. 1952. Part b reprinted by permission of John Wiley and Sons, Inc .From E. G. Boring et al., Foundations of Psychology. Copyright (c) 1948.)

Figure 4.2 illustrates how one basic sine wave is apparent in a musical note from a piano, with other waves added onto the basic shape. The basic sine wave is called the fundamental frequency: the other waves give the tone its timbre. Because the added waves are multiples of the fundamental frequency of the note, the result does not sound out of tune. The regularities of the wave make it sound musical. In contrast, a noise does not have such regularities. Instead, it is a random sum of waveforms that are not related to one another in any regular way, as Figure 4.2 shows.

The Ear The ear converts sound into neural activity through its accessory structures and a fascinating series of transduction mechanisms. This transduction begins the process that allows us to experience the world of sound.

Auditory accessory structures Sound waves are collected in the outer ear, beginning with the **pinna**, the crumpled, oddly shaped part of the ear on the side of the head. The pinna funnels sound down through the ear canal. At the bottom of the ear canal, the sound waves reach the middle ear where they strike a tightly stretched membrane known as the eardrum, or **tympanic membrane**. The waves set up vibrations in the tympanic membrane that match the sound waves.

These vibrations are transferred through a chain of three tiny bones named for their shapes: the malleus ("**hammer**"), the **incus** ("**anvil**"), and the stapes ("**stirrup**"). Each passes on whatever vibration it receives to its nearest neighbor. At the end of this chain of bones is another membrane, the **oval window**. The bones focus the movements of the tympanic membrane onto the smaller oval window, thereby amplifying the changes in pressure produced by the original sound waves. Conduction deafness occurs if the junctions between these bones fuse, reducing or preventing accurate reproduction of vibrations. A hearing aid that amplifies the input to the eardrum or surgery to loosen the bones can sometimes combat conduction deafness.

Auditory transduction When the sound vibrations pass from the stapes through the oval window, they enter the inner ear, a world of fluid-filled spirals. They are now in the cochlea, the structure in which transduction actually occurs.

The cochlea is wrapped into a coiled spiral (cochlea is derived from the Greek word for "snail"). If you unwrapped it, you would see that a fluid-filled duct runs down its length. The **basilar membrane** forms the floor of this long duct. The sound waves pass through the fluid in the cochlea just as they traveled through the air. Whenever a wave passes through the fluid in the duct, it moves the basilar membrane, and this movement deforms **hair cells** that touch the membrane.

The hair cells are exquisitely sensitive to any change in their shape, and they make connections with fibers from the **auditory nerve**, which sends its axons into the brain. If either the auditory nerve or the hair cells are damaged, an irrevrsible impairment called nerve deafness may result. This condition cannot be improved by conventional hearing aids, though it can be alleviated to some extent in some patients by cochlear implants. These sophisticated electronic devices can translate sounds gathered by a tiny microphone into electronic signals that reach the brain by way of an electrode implanted in the cochlea.

The mechanical deformation of hair cells causes a change in the electrical activity of the auditory nerve. In the following sections, we will show how this activity codes information about the amplitude and frequency of sound waves, allowing people to sense the loudness and pitch of sounds.

The Coding of Intensity

The auditory system can respond to a wide range of sound intensities. On the low end, the faintest sound that can be heard moves the hair cells less than the diameter of a single hydrogen atom

(Hudspeth,1983). On the high end, sounds more than a trillion times more intense can also be heard; sounds this intense can be sensed even by the skin. Between these extremes, the auditory system codes intensity in a generally straightforward way: the more intense the sound, the more rapid the firing of a given neuron. Some cells may increase their firing rate as the intensity increases, up to a point: then they decrease their firing rate as the intensity increases further. And sometimes the firing rate of individual neurons in the auditory nerve depends on both the frequency and the intensity of the stimulus.

Frequency Coding

How do people tell difference between one note and another? Recall that the pitch of a sound depends on its frequency. Differences in frequency appear to be coded in two ways, which are described by place theory and the volley theory.

Place theory Georg von Békésy did some pioneering, but gruesome experiments to figure out how frequency is coded. He opened the skulls, of human cadavers, exposed the cochlea, and made a hole in the cochlear wall to observe the basilar membrane. He then presented his "volunteers" with sounds of different frequencies by mechanically vibrating a rubber membrane that was installed in place of the oval window. With sensitive optical instruments, von Békésy observed ripples of waves moving down the basilar membrane. He also noticed something very important. The outline of the waves, called the envelope, grows and reaches a peak; then it quickly tapers off to smaller and smaller fluctuations, much like an ocean wave that crests and then dissolves. Figure 4.3 illustrates this traveling wave. Its critical feature is that the distance along the basilar, membrane to the peak of the wave envelope depends on the frequency of the sound. High–frequency sounds produce a wave that peaks soon after it starts down the basilar membrane. Lower–frequency sounds produce a wave that peaks farther along the basilar membrane, farther from the stirrup.

What do these differences in peak ponits mean? According to place theory (also called the traveling wave theory), the peak of the wave represents the greatest response by hair cells. In other words, hair cells at a particular place on the basilar membrane respond most to a particular frequency of sound. Thus, if exposed to a very loud, damaging noise of a particular frequency, a person loses hair cells at one spot on the basilar membrane, as well as the ability to hear sounds of that frequency place theory is also supported by studies showing that each neuron in the auditory nerve is most sensitive to a specific frequency, which is called its characteristic **frequency.**

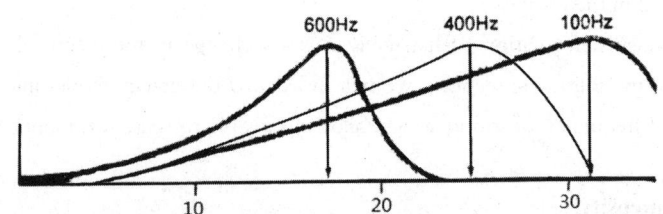

Figure 4.3
Movements of the Basilar Membrane That Support the Place Theory of Frequency coding
As vibrations of the cochlear fluid spread along the basilar membrane, the membrane is deflected

and then recovers. The point at which the bending of the basilar membrane reaches a maximum is different for each sound frequency. The arrows indicate the location of hair cells that receive the greatest stimulation for sounds of differing frequencies. (Adapted from Experiments in Hearing by G. von Békésy. Copyright 1960 . Reprinted with permission of Mc Graw–Hill Book Company. From G. L. Rasmussen and W. F. Windle, Neural Mechanisms of the Auditory and Vestibular Systems, 1960. Courtesy of Charles C Thomas, publisher, Speringfield, illionis)

Frequency matching: The volley theory Though place theory accounts for a great deal of experimental data on hearing, it cannot provide a complete explanation of how frequency is coded. In particular, it cannot account for the coding of very low frequencies, such as that of a deep bass note, because there are no auditory nerve fibers that have very low characteristic frequencies. But, since humans can hear frequencies as low as 20 hertz, they must be coded somehow. How?

Frequency matching seems to be the answer. **Frequency matching** means that the firing rate of a neuron matches the frequency of a sound wave. For example, one neuron might fires at every peak of a wave. Thus, a sound of 20 hertz could be coded by a neuron that fires twenty times per second.

Since no neuron can fire faster than one thousand times per second, clearly no neuron can match frequencies of, say, 10,000 hertz. However, the summed activity of a group of neurons can match sounds of moderate frequencies; each neuron in the group might fire at every other wave peak or at every fifth peak for example. Because a group of neurons fire in a sort of volley, the frequency-matching theory is sometimes called the volley theory of frequency coding.

In summary, the nervous system apparently uses more than one way to code the full range of audible frequencies. The lowest frequencies are coded by matching the frequency with the firing rate of auditory nerve fibers (frequency coding). Low to moderate frequencies are coded by both frequency matching and the place on the basilar membrane where the traveling wave peaks. And high frequencies are coded exclusively by the place where the traveling wave peaks.

Auditory Pathways and the Auditory Cortex

Before we can hear sounds, the information coded in the activity of auditory nerve fibers must be conveyed to the brain and processed further. The auditory nerve fibers must be conveyed to the brain and processed further. The auditory nerve, which makes one or two synapses before reaching the thalamus, brings the information to the brain. From the thalamus, the information is relayed to the auditory cortex. On their way to the thalamus, the fibers of the auditory nerve cross to the opposite side of the brain. As a result, the left side of the auditory cortex receives input from the right ear, and the right auditory cortex receives sounds reaching the left ear.

The first cells in the cortex to receive information about sounds are called **primary** auditory cortex. This area, in the temporal lobe, is connected to areas of the brain involved in language perception and production. Cells in the auditory cortex have preferred frequencies, just as neurons in the auditory nerve do. Neighboring cells in the cortex have similar preferred frequencies; thus the auditory cortex provides a map of sound frequencies . This arrangement is called a **tonotopic**

organization.

The cortex is not just a passive warehouse of information coded by the nervous system; it must further process the information if we are to hear. For example, although each neuron in the auditory nerve has a "favorite," or characteristic, frequency, each responds to some extent to a range of activity of frequencies. Therefore, the nervous system must examine the pattern of a number of neurons in order to determine the frequency of a given sound.

第三节 视觉
(VISION)

Fatal automobile accidents are much more likely to occur at night than in the daytime, even though people drive far fewer miles after dark. Fatigue and alcohol certainly contribute to this phenomenon. However, another important reason is that people tend to drive as fast and as confidently at night as they do in the daytime, in spite of the fact that their ability see deteriorates dangerously as illumination falls (Leibowitz & Owens, 1986). In other words, most people do not understand the limitations of the visual system. The visual system is one of the most remarkable senses, with its ability to transduce light energy into neural activity that, when processed in the brain, results in the precious experience of sight.

Light

What we call light is a form of energy known as electromagnetic radiation. Unlike sound, light does not need a medium to pass through; it has some of the properties of waves and some of the properties of particles. Light waves are like particles that pass through space, but they vibrate with a certain wavelength. Therefore, it is correct to refer to light as either light waves or light rays. Most electromagnetic radiation, including X rays, radio waves, television signals, and radar passes through space undetected by the human eye. **Visible Light** is electromagnetic radiation that has a wavelength from about 400 nanometers to about 700 nanometers, (A nanometer is one-billionth of a meter.)

Our sensations of light depend on two physical dimensions of light waves: intensity and wavelength. **Light intensity** refers to how much energy the light contains; it determines the brightness of light. What color we sense depends mainly on light wavelength. At a given inten-sity, different wave lengths produce sensations of different colors. For instance, 440-nanometer Light appears violet-blue, and 600-nanometer Light appears orangish-red.

Focusing Light: Accessory Structures of the Eye

Light energy is transduced into neural activity in the eye. But first, the accessory structures of the eye get more information from the light by focusing light rays into a sharp image. First, the light rays enter the eye by passing through the curved transparent protective layer called the **cornea**. Then the light passes through the **pupil**, the opening just behind the cornea. The **iris**, which gives the eyes their color, adjusts the amount of light allowed into the eye by constricting to reduce the size of the pupil or relaxing to enlarge it. Directly behind the pupil is the **Lens**. Like the cornea and like the lens in a camera, the lens of the eye is curved so that it bends light rays, focusing them on the surface at the back of the eye, called the **retina**.

How does the lens bend light rays from a point source so that they meet at a point on the retina? If the rays meet either in front of the retina or behind it, the image will be out of focus. The muscles that hold the lens adjust its shape so that either near or far objects can be focused on the retina. If you peer at something very close, for example, your muscles must tighten the lens, making it more curved, to obtain a focused image. This ability to change the shape of the lens to bend light rays so that objects are in focus is called **accommodation**. With age, the lens loses some of its flexibility, and accommodation becomes more difficult. This is why most older people need reading glasses.

Converting Light into Images: Visual Transduction

The retina, the structure where visual transduction takes place, is actually an intricate network of cells,. before transduction can occur, light rays must pass through several layers in this network to reach photoreceptor cells. The photoreceptors in the retina code light energy into neural activity. First we will consider the photoreceotrs and how they work; then we will describe how other cells in the retina operate.

Photoreceptors Photoreceptors can change light into neural activity because they are specialized nerve cells that have **photopigments**, or chemicals that respond to light. When light strikes a photopigment, the photopigment breaks apart, changing the membrane potential of the photoreceptor cell. As we noted in Chapter 3, this change in membrane potential provides a signal that can be transferred to the brain.

The retina has two basic types of photoreceotors: **rods** and **cones**. As their names indicate, these cells differ in shape, but there are other important differences as well. For one thing, the photopigment in rods includes a substance called rhodopsin, whereas the photopigment in cones includes one of three varieties of iodopsin. The fact that there are three different pigments in cones allows the cone system to distinguish colors. Rods and cones also respond somewhat differently to light. Rods are more sensitive to light than cones, but because they have only one pigment, the rods are unable to discriminate colors. Thus, rods allow us to see even when there is very little light, as on a moonlit night. But if you have trouble trying to match a pair of socks in a darkened bedroom, you now know the reason: because the light is dim, you are seeing with your rods, which cannot discriminate colors. At higher light intensities, the cones, with their ability to detect colors, become most active in vision.

The rods and cones also differ in their distribution in the eye. Cones are very concentrated in the center of the retina, a region called the **fovea**. This concentration of photoreceptors makes spatial discrimination, or **acuity**, greatest in the fovea. Indeed, the fovea is perecisely where the eye focuses the light coming from objects you look at. There are no rods in the fovea. With the increasing of distance from the fovea, however, the number of cones gradually decreases, and the proportion of rods gradually increases. Thus, if you are trying to detect a small amount of light, such as that from a faint star, it is better to look slightly away from where you expect to see it. This focuses the weak light on the very light sensitive rods outside the fovea. Because cones do not work well in low light, looking directly at the star will make it seem to disappear.

Dark adaptation After a photopigment has broken down in response to light, new photopigment molecules are put together. This takes a little time, however. When you first come from bright sunshine into a dark place like a theater, you cannot see because your photoreceptors, especially your rods, do not yet have enough photopigment. In the dark, your photoreceptors synthesize more photopigments, and your ability to see gradually increases. This increasing ability to see in the dark as time passes is called dark adaptation.

The different properties of rods and cones shape the course of dark adaptation. Cones adapt to the dark more quickly than rods; but even when they are completely dark-adapted, the cones are not nearly as sensitive to light. The rods take about 40 minutes to adapt completely to darkness. Thus, when you enter a dark theater, there is some immediate increase in sensitivity to light as your cones adapt; then sensitivity rises more slowly as your rods adapt. Overall, your sensitivity to light increase some ten thousandfold after an hour or so in a darkened room. This is too slow to avoid tripping over someone in a theater, but helps immensely if you are working for a long time in a darkroom.

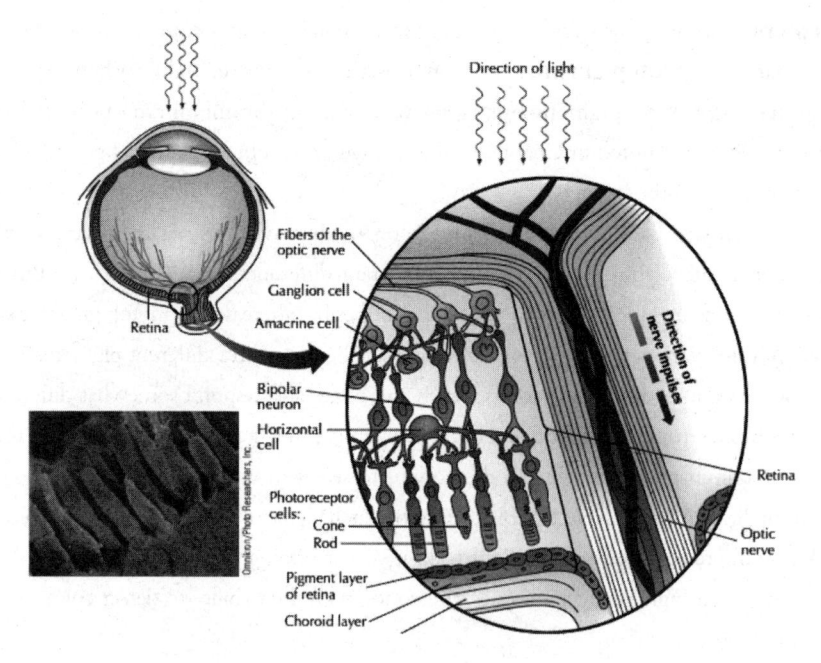

Figure 4.4

Organization of cells in the Retina

Light rays actually pass through several layers of cells before striking the photoreceptive rods and cones. Signals generated by the rods and cones then go back toward the surface of the retina, passing through the bipolar cells and on to the ganglion cells. Axons from the ganglion cells form the optic nerve that sends signals to the brain. Interconnections among the horizontal cells, the amacrine cells, the bipolar cells, and the ganglion cells allow the eye to begin analyzing visual information even before that information leaves the retina. In effect, the cells of the retina are outposts of the brain.

Interactions of cells in the retina The eye actually sharpens visual images, so that they are clearer than the light image that strikes the retina. To explain how the eye does this, we need to describe the interactions among the cells that make up the retina. Figure 4.4 illustrates some of the cells in various layers of the retina. The most direct connections from the photoreceptor cells to the brain go first to **bipolar cells** and then to ganglion cells; the axons of ganglion cells form the optic nerve that extends out of the eye and into the brain. However, the path is often far more complicated.

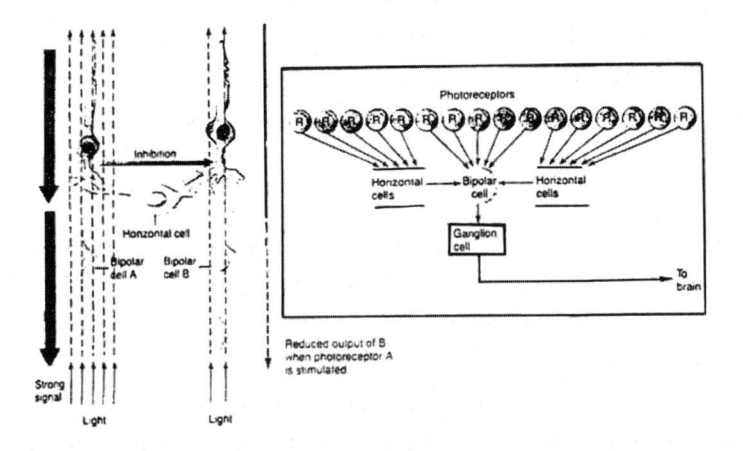

Figure 4.5
Convergence and Lateral Inhibition Among Retinal Cells
Right: Input from many photoreceptors converges onto bipolar cells in the retina. Many receptors feed directly into a given bipolar cellt and many receptors have indirect input to bipolar cells by influencing horizontal cells. As shown at left, the input from horizontal cells to bipolar cells is often inhibitory. The bipolar of photoreceptor A makes a connection to a horizonal cell that synapses on the bipolar cell of photoreceptor B. When A is stimulated, it excites the horizontal cell, which inhibits the bipoar cell of B. Thus, light shining on photoreceptor A actually inhibits the signal that photoreceptor B sends to the brain. Light striking photoreceptor A both sends a signal to the brain that there is light at point A and makes it appear as if there is less tight at point B than there really is.

Two complications are especially important. First, most bipolar cells receive, this arrangement is called convergence. Second, photoreceptor cells make connections of other types of cells in the retina, including horizontal cells and amacrine cells, which make lateral connections between bipolar cells. Through these connections, the response to light by a cell at one point on the retina can excite or inhibit the response of a neighboring cell. The bottom portion of Figure 4.5, for example, illustrates **lateral inhibition**; here the stimulation of one cell is producing a signal that makes it seem as if there is less light at another cell than there really is.

Together, these interactions enhance our sensation of contrast, and they influence the sensitivity and acuity of our vision. First consider a case of lateral inhibition. Most of the time, the light reaching one of two photoreceptors will be slightly greater than that reaching the other brie As Figure 4.5 illustrates, the photoreceptor receiving more light will suppress the eventual output to the brain from the photoreceptor receiving less light. Therefore, the output to the brain is a comparison of the light hitting two neighboring points. Whatever difference exists between the light reaching the two photoreceptors is exaggerated.

This exaggeration is important, because differences in amounts of incoming light are created by specific features of objects. For example, the visual image of the edge of an object contains a transition from a lighter region to a darker region. Lateral inhibition in the retina enhances this difference, creating contrast that sharpens the edge and makes it more noticeable. Convergence of input from photoreceptors to bipolar cells (as shown in Figure 4.5) also enhances contrast by allowing bipolar cells to compare the amount of light on larger regions of the retina. Thus, convergence and lateral connections combine to increase the eye's sensitivity to differences in the amount of light failing on different parts of the retina.

The degree of convergence also influences the sensitivity and acuity of cells. Convergence increases the sensitivity of each bipolar cell, because light striking any of the photoreceptors to which it is connected will stimulate it. It should come as no surprise, therefore, that there is a great deal of convergence in areas surrounding the fovea, where the light–sensitive rods predominate. However, convergence confuses bipolar cells, making it diffcult for them to tell which phcitoreceptor was actually hit by light. This reduces the accuracy, or acuity, of rod vision.

In the fovea, however, there is much less convergence. One cone tends to excite just one bipolar cell, making the area less light sensitive, but far more able to detect tiny details.

Ganglion cells and their recetptive fields Photoreceptors, bipolar cells, and horizontal cells communicate through the release of neurotransmitters. But, as we noted in Chapter 3, neuro–transmitters cause only small, graded changes in the next cell's membrane potential, which may not be strong enough to produce a sequence of action potentials that will reach the brain. **Ganglion cells** are the cells in the retina that generate these action potentials. As shown in Figure 4.4, they are stimulated by bipolar cells, and their axons extend out of the retina and travel to the brain.

What message do ganglion cells send to the brain? To find out, we could theoretically place an electrode in the axon of one of your ganglion cells, record the signal it sends to your brain when we present various visual stimuli, and thus determine what this one cell sees. "In other words, we could determine the ganglion cell's receptive field, which is that part of the retina and the corresponding part of the visual world to which that cell responds. What we would find is that most ganglion cells have what is called a center–surround receptive field. That is, most ganglion cells in effect compare the amount of light stimulating rods and cones in the center of their receptive fields with that stimulating the rods and cones in the surrounding area. Some center–surround ganglion cells are activated by darkness in the center of the field and by light in the regions surrounding the dark center. Their activity is inhibited by light in the center of the field and by dark spots in the surrounding area. Other center—surround ganglion cells work in just the opposite way. They are activiated by light in the center and darkness in the surrounding area.

The result of the center—surround receptive fields, is to optimize the detection of variations such as edges and small spots of light or dark. In fact, people see a sharper contrast between darker and lighter areas than actually exists. By enhancing people's sensation of edges and other important features, the retina is reporting to the brain an improved version of the visual world.

Color Vision

Perhaps the most salient feature of visual sensation is color. An advertising agent might tell you about the impact of color on buying preferences. A poet might tell you about the beauty of color, but we will tell you about how it works—which is itself a thing of elegance and beauty.

Wavelengths and color sensations We noted earlier that, at a given intensity, each wave length or light is sensed as a certain color. Sunlight is a mixture of all wavelengths of light. When this full spectrum of white light shines on grass, the grass absorbs most of the wave lengths and reflects a combination of wavelengths that appears green. When sunlight passes through a droplet of water, the different wavelengths of light are bent to different degrees, thus separating into a colorful rainbow.

The sepectrum of color found in the rainbow illustrates an important concept: the sensation produced by a mixture of different wavelengths of light is not the same as those produced by separate wavelengths. Further, there are three separate aspects of the sensation of color: hue, saturation, and brightness. These are psychological dimensions that correspond roughly to the physical properties of light. **Hue** is the essential color, determined by the dominant wave—length of the light. Black, white, and gray are not considered hues because no wavelength predominates in them. **Saturation** is related to the purity of a color. A color is more saturated and more pure if a single wavelength is relatively more intense than other wavelengths. If we add a broad variety of wavelengths to a pure hue, the color is said to be desaturated. For example, pastels are colors that have been desaturated by the addition of whiteness. **Brightness** corresponds to the overall intensity of all of the wavelengths making up light. However, as we will discuss in Chapter 5, on perception, our experience of the brightness of a particular color also depends on the brightness and hue of stimuli in other parts of the visual field.

These colors produced by either a single wavelength or a mixture Spectral Hues

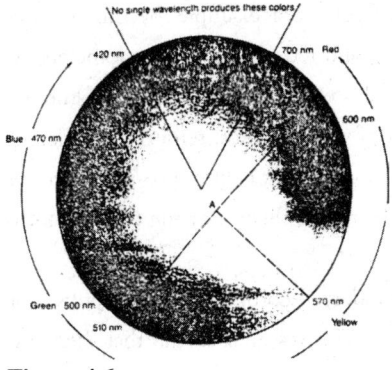

Figure 4.6

The color circle
Ordering the colors according to their psychological similarties results in a circle that reveals some interesting things about color vision. For example, although there are pure wavelengths that are sensed as red or green, there is no single wavelength that corresponds to purple. The color circle also allows one to predict the result of additive mixing of two colored lights. The resulting color will be on a line between the two starting colors, the exact location on the line depending on the relative proportions of the two colors. For example, mixing equal amounts of pure green and pure red will produce yellow, the color that lies at the midpoint to the line connecting red and green. This circle also reveals how purple can be generated: by mixing red and blue light.

The color circle shown in Figure 4.6 is made up of hues arranged according to their perceived similarities. If you mix light of two different wavelengths but equal intensity, you produce the color that is at the midpoint of a line drawn between the two original colors on the color circle. You are probably familiar with a different form of color mixing in which paints are combined. Like other physical objects, paints of different colors reflect certain wavelengths and absorb all others. As a result, mixing paints subtractive color mixing the two paints absorb, or subtract, more wavelengths of light than either one does alone. Because of this subtraction, mixing two paints usually produces, a darker color Thus, if you keep combining different colored paints, all of the wavelengths will eventually be subtracted, resulting in black (you usually get a disgusting mud color on the way to black). In contrast, mixing two lights of different wavelengths is additive color mixing, because the effects of the wavelengths from each light are added together, stimulating more cones. Mixing lights usually produces lighter color. Thus, if you keep adding different colored lights you eventually get white (the combined color of all wavelengths).

By mixing lights of just a few wavelengths, you can produce different color sensations. How many wavelengths are needed to create any color? The answer has helped lead scientists to an important theory of how we sense color.

The trichromatic theory of color vision   Early in the nineteenth century, Thomas Young and, later, Hermann von Helmholtz established through experimentation that any color could be matched by mixing pure lights of just three wavelengths of light. For example, by mixing blue light (about 440 nanometers), green (about 510 nanometers), and red (about 600 nanometers) in different ratios, you can produce any other color. Based on this evidence, Young and Helmholtz postulated that there are three types of visual elements, each of which is most sensitive to different wavelengths, and that information from these three elements combines to produce the sensation of color. This theory of color vision is called the Young–Helmholtz theory, or the **trichromatic theory.**

Support for the trichromatic theory has come from modern recordings of the responses of individual photoreceptors to light of a particular wavelength. This research reveals that there are three types of cones. Although each type responds to a broad range of wavelengths, each is most sensitive to particular wavelengths. short-wavelength cones are most sensitive to light of 440 nanometers (a shade of blue). Medium-wavelength cones are most sensitive to light of about 530 nanometers (a shade of green). Finally, long-wavelength cones respond best to light of about 560 nanometers (reddish yellow). Recently, scientists have found the basis for this differential sensitivity in the form of genes that direct different cones to produce pigments sensitive to blue, green, or yellow-red (Nathans et al. 1986; Nathans, Thomas & Hogness, 1986).

Note that no single cone, by itself, can signal the color of a light. The ratio of the activities of the three types of cones indicates what color will be sensed. Color vision is therefore coded by the pattern of activity of the different cones. For example, you will sense a light as yellow if it has a pure wavelength of 570 nanometers; this light stimulates both medium and longwave-length cones. But you will sense the same color when the same two cone types are stimulated by mixtures of other lights that stimulate the same pattern of activity in these two types of cones.

The opponent-process theory of color vision Some aspects of color vision cannot be explained by the trichromatic theory in its simplest form. For example, it cannot account for color afterimages. what was yellow in the original image will be in the afterimage, and green before will appear red.

This type of observation led Ewald Hering to offer an alternative to the trichromatic theory, called the **opponent-process theory**, It holds that the visual elements sensitive to color are grouped into three pairs and that the members of each pair oppose, or inhibit, each other. The three pairs are a red-green element, a blue-yellow element, and a black-white element. Each element signals one color or the other—red or green, for example—but never both. This explains why certain colors, such as greenish red or yellowish blue, never occur, even though it is quite possible to see bluish green or reddish yellow. Hering's opponent-process theory also explains color afterimages. It proposes that, when one part of an opponent pair is no longer stimulated, the other is automatically activated. Thus if the original image you looked at were green, the afterimage would be red.

The opponent-process theory is also consistent with characteristics of the color circle. Every color on the circle has a complementary color. Two colors are **complementary** if gray results when lights of the two colors are mixed together. On the color circle (Figure 4. 6), complementary colors are roughly opposite. Red and green are complementary, as are yellow and blue. Notice that complementary colors are opponent colors in Hering's theory. According to opponent-process theory, complementary colors stimulate the same visual element (for example, red-green) in opposite directions, canceling each other out. Thus, the theory helps explain why mixing complementary colors produces gray. The opponent-process theory also explains why colors such as purple appear on the color circle, but not in the spectrum of visible light. Purple is actually a product of stimulating the blue element and the red element in the visual system.

A synthesis The trichromatic and opponent-process theories seem quite different, but both are correct to some extent, and together, they can explain most of what we now know about color vision. Electrical recordings made from different types of cells in the retina paved the way for a synthesis of the two theories.

At the level of the photoreceptors, the trichromatic theory is right: as we said, there are three types of ones. However, we also noted that output from many photoreceptors feeds into each ganglion cell, and the output from the ganglion cell goes to the brain. Recall that the receptive fields of most ganglion cells are arranged in center–surround patterns .The center and the surround are color coded, as illustrated in Figure 4.7. The centere responds best to one color, and the surround responds best to a different color. This color coding arises because varying proportions of the three cone types feed into the center and surround of the ganglion cell.

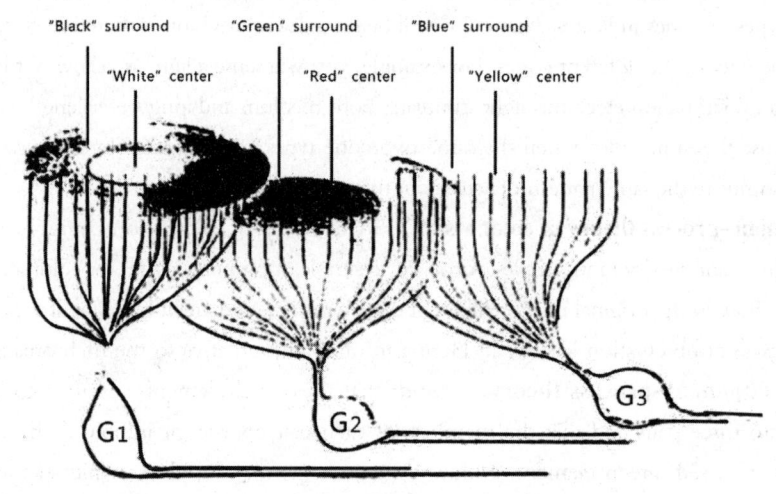

Figure 4.7
Color Coding and the Ganglion Cells
The center and surround of the ganglion cell receptive fields form the anatomical basis for opponent colors. Some ganglion cells, like G2, have a center whose photoreceptors respond best to red wavelengths and a surround that responds best to green wavelengths. Other ganglion cells pair blue and yellow. Some ganglion cells have receptive fields that are not particular about color; they receive input from all types of photoreceptors. The receptive fields of some ganglion cells overlap.

When either the center or the surround of ganglion cell is stimulated, the other is inhibited. In other words, the colors to which the center versus the surround of a given ganglion cell are most responsive are opponent colors. Recordings from many ganglion cells show that three very common pairs of exponent colors are those predicted by Hering's opponent–process theory: red–green, blue–yellow, and white–black. White–black cells receive input from all types of cones, so it does not matter what color stimulates them. Stimulating both the center and the surround cancels the effects of either light, producing gray. This is the basis for complementary colors. In dim light, cones are not responsive, but rods are, and all ganglion cells lose the color–coding aspect of their center–surround properties.

In summary, color vision is possible because three types of cones have different sensitivities to different wavelengths, as the trichromatic theory suggests. The sensation of different colors results from stimulating the three cone types in different ratios. Because there are three types of cones, any color can be produced by mixing three different wavelengths of light. But the story does not end there. The output from cones is fed into ganglion cells; the center and surround of the ganglion cells respond to differnt colors and inhibit each other. This activity provides the basis for the phenomena of complementary colors and afterimages. Therefore, the trichromatic theory embodies the properties of the photoreceptors, while Hering's opponent process theory embodies the properties of the other layers of the retina. Both theories are needed to account for the complexity of visual sensations of color.

Color blindness   What kind of color vision would a person have if he or she had cones containing only two of the three color-sensitive pigments mentioned earlier? Many people have this condition, and they are decribed as color blind. They are not actually blind to all color; they simply discriminate fewer colors than other people.

The most common form of color blindness involves red and green. To people with red-green color blindness, red and green look the same; they probably appear much like brown does to people with normal vision.

Visual pathways to the Brain

In addition to all the retinal visual processing that we have described, even more elaborate processing takes place within the brain. Information is brought there by axons from ganglion cells. These, axons, which are several inches long, leave the eye as a bundle of fibers called the **optic nerve**. The axons from all of the ganglion cells converge and exit the eyeball at one point. This exit point has no photoreceptors and is therefore insensitive to light, creating a **blind spot**.

After leaving the retina, about half the fibers of the optic nerve cross over to the opposite side of the brain at a structure called the **optic chiasm** (chiasm meand "cross"). Whether a fiber crosses over depends on the location of its receptive field. Fibers from the inside half of each eye, nearest to the nose, cross over; fibers from the outside half of each eye do not. This arrangement makes sense when you realize that the same half of each eye is looking at the same part of the visual field. Thus, the crossing at the optic chiasm brings all the visual information about the right half of the visual world to the left hemisphere of the brain and information from the left half to the right hemisphere of the brain.

The optic chiasm is part of the bottom surface of the brain; beyond the chiasm, the fibers ascend into the brain itself. The axons from most of the ganglion cells in the retina finally end and form synapses in the thalamus, in a specific region called the **lateral geniculate nucleus (LGN)**. Neurons in the LGN then relay the visual input to the **primary visual cortex**, which lies in the occipital lobe at the back of the brain. The most complex processing of visual information occurs in the visual cortex. There sensations finally become conscious. Two important characteristics of the visual cortex that influence these sensations are the receptive fields of the cortical cells and the organization of the cortex.

Feature detectors   Unlike the cells of the retina or the LGN, few cells in the cortex have center-surround receptive fields. They respond instead to certain featutes of objects in the visual field (Hubei & Wiesel, 1979). For example, a specific cell in the cortex might respond only to vertical edges. No matter where in the receptive field a vertical edge is presented, this cell in-creases its firing rate. Another class of cells might respond only to moving objects; a third might respond only to objects with corners. These cells in the cortex that respond to specific features of objects are called feature detectors. How do they work? Feature detectors might function by combining the input from a number of center–surround ganglion cells.

One theory of how the cortex puts together information from the ganglion cells to produce feature detectors is called the hierarchical feature–detection model. This model holds that any object seen is a compilation of features and that complex, feature detectors are built up out of more and more complex connections of simpler feature detectors (Hubel & Wiesel, 1979). For example, several center–surround cells might feed into one cell that is a line detector, and several line detectors might feed into one cell that responds to a particular spatial orientation, such as the vertical. With further connections, a more complex detector, such as a "box detector," might be built from the simpler line and corner detectors.

The problem with using this model to explain how people see patterns and objects is that they would need a high–order feature detector corresponding to each recognized object. An example of such a high–order feature detector would be a "grandmother cell," a cell that fires whenever you see your grandmother, from any angle, no matter what she is wearing. Although a hierarchical feature–detection model has a certain simplicity, the question of whether we actually have the immense number of specific feature detectors needed to sense each of the vast array of visual stimuli is still unanswered.

Spatial freguency Analysis
One alternative to the feature–detection model is the spatial frequency filter model. According to this model, the brain analyzes patterns; not by patterns, together information about lines, edges, and other features, but by analyzing gradual changes in brightness over broad areas. Compared with the feature–detection model, this view is much more difficult to appreciate intuitively, but it does not require a specific cell for every type of visual sensation.

The spatial frequency model points out, first, that any pattern, no matter how complex, can theoretically decomposed into component regions of light and dark, which can be represented by sine waves, just as any sound can be synthesized by combining sound waves of many different amplitudes and frequencies. Look at Figure 4.8a, which shows how a pattern of light and dark bars can be represented by a sine wave. The pattern of bars is called a sine–wave grating. Narrow areas of light and dark are represented by a highfrequency sine wave, and broader area of light and dark are represented by a lower–frequency sine wave.

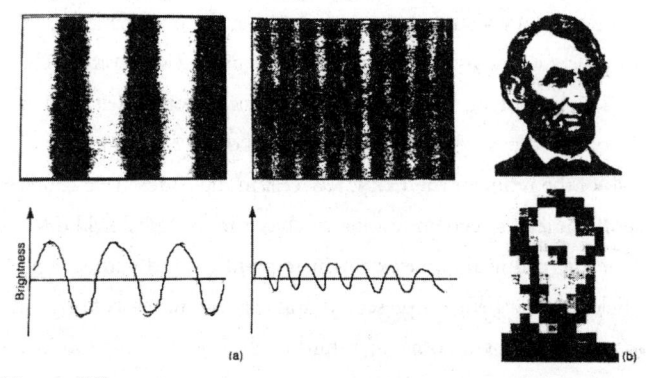

Figure 4.8

Spatial Frequency

The visual system has detectors for different spatial frequencies. (a) These gratings illustrate two different "pure" spatial frequencies, analogous to two pure tones. The one on the left is of low spatial frequency and high amplitude; the one on the right is of higher spatial frequency and low amplitude. By adding together appropriate sine waves representing pure spatial frequencies, it is possible to represent images that do not initially appear anything like sine waves, (b) An illustration of how the visual system can extract information based on a spatial frequency analysis of a visual pattern. The image on the bottom was generated by a computer, which took an average of the light–dark level within each block of the figure on the top. The blocks are therefore a low spatial frequency analysis of the figure, but the edges of the blocks are a high spatial frequency component that interferes with "seeing" the figure. To see just the low spatial frequency components, take off your glasses (if you wear them), and blur your vision by squinting. The figure on the bottom will now look as much like Lincoln as the one on the top, and much more so than the blocked figure viewed normally.

(*part a*: From *Fundamentals of Sensation and Perception* by M. W. Levine and J. M. Shefner, Addison–Wesley, 1981. Part b: Leon B. Harmon and Bela Julesz, science. 180: 1194–97 (1973). Copyright 1973 by the AAAs.)

If you combined many gratings like those in Figure 4.8a with different frequencies and orientations, you would end up with a complex pattern. The spatial frequency filter model suggests that the brain does the opposite. It holds that the brain analyzes the visual world by reducing it to patterns of alternating light and dark of differnt frequencies. It says that your brain in effect, can analyze waveforms using complex. Fourier analysis (pronounced for yay). Fourier analysis decomposes a complicated waveform into the simple sine waves that created it (see Figure 4.8b). Even if a pattern of light and dark did not start out as sine waves, it can be in the brain as a collection of many sine waves.

What evidence is there that your visual cortex might do this complicated kind of mathe‐ matics? If you shine a series of sine‐wave gratings (like those in Figure 4.8a) on the retina and record the activity of cells in the visual cortex, you find that each neuron responds best to a bar and space grating with a particular frequency. You can take a specific cell and find its preferred sine wave; the same cell will also have a preferred bar stimulus.

There is another clue that the visual system might work according to the spatial frequency filter model. If there were specific feature detectors for each object or shape in a particular cortical location, removing one part of the visual cortex should eliminate the ability to see a certain type of object. But removing part of the cortex does not have this effect. This suggests that a large part of the visual cortex might participate, through Fourier analysis, in sensing each object.

This description of spatial frequency analysis should demonstrate that there is a great deal to learn about the way the brain makes use of its sensory input. The mysteries are by no means solved, and there is evidence to support at least two drastically different theories of how people see things.

Organization of cortex   If you poked around in the visual cortex with an electrode, recording the activity of cells while presenting a variety of visual stimuli, you would discover that the retina's topographical map of the visual world is maintained all the way to the brain. That is, neighboring points in the retina are represented in neighboring cells in the cortex. The map is a distorted one, however. A larger area of cortex is devoted to the areas of the retina that have many photoreceptors. For example, the fovea, which is densely packed with photoreceptors, is represented in an especially large segment of cortex.

If you explored the surface of the cortex with an electrode, you would also find that there is more than one complete map of the retina. In fact, there are more than ten complete representations of the visual world on primates' visual cortex (Merzenich & Kaas, 1980). Other senses also have multiple representations; the large number for vision may reflect its special importance, but no one yet knows for sure.

Another thing you would notice about the visual cortex is that each point on the topographical map is made up of functional columns of cells that share a common property, such as responding to one type of visual stimulus. These columns are arranged perpendicular to the surface of the cortex. For example, if we locate a cell that responds to diagonal lines in a particular spot in the visual field, most of the cells in a column above and below it will also respond to diagonal lines. Other properties are represented by whole columns of cells, so that we could record the of a column in which all of the cells are most sensitive to a particular color.

第四节 化学性质的感觉：嗅觉和味觉
(THE CHEMICAL SENSES: SMELL AND TASTE)

There are animals without Vision, and there are animals without hearing, but there are no animals without some form of chemical sense; that is, without some sense that arises from the interaction of chemicals and receptors. Smell, or **olfaction**, detects chemicals that are airborne, or **volatile**. Taste, or gestation, is the sense that detects chemicals in solution that come into contact with receptors inside the mouth.

Olfaction

We sense odors in the upper part of the nose. Receptors there detect molecules that pass from the air into the moisture of the lining of the nose. Molecules can reach these receptors either through the nose or through an opening in the palate at the back of the mouth. Thus, the olfactory sense is a dual sense: unlike the other senses, it detects objects that are either internal (in the mouth) or external (Rozin, 1982).

In any event, olfaction is the only sense that does not send its messages to the thalamus. The axons from the nose pass a short distance, through a bony plate, directly into the brain, where they synapse in a structure called the olfactory bald. Connections from the olfactory buld spread diffusely through the brain, but they are especially plentiful in the amygdala, a part of the brain involved in emotional experience. This anatomical fact is consistent with the psychological fact that smells are emotionally powerful.

Not all smells affect everyone equally, since almost everyone is incapable of sensing certain odors. For example, about 33 percent of people are unable to smell cineole, the odor of camphor and about 3 percent cannot detect sweat. People in these categories may count themselves lucky, but for sewer workers unable to smell deadly hydrogen cyanide gas, such "odor blindness" can be dangerous.

Gustation

The chemical sense system in the mouth is gustation, or taste. The receptors for taste are in the taste buds, which are grouped together in structures called **papillae** on the tongue. There are about ten thousand taste buds in the normal person's mouth, most of them on the tongue. Others are located at the back of the throat.

Our taste system detects only a very few elementary sensations: sweet, sour, bitter, and salty. Each taste bud responds best to one or two of these categories, but it also responds weakly to other categories. The sensation of a particular substance results from the coded pattern of responses by many taste buds, none of which is completely specific for a given taste. However, different regions of the tongue are more sensitive to different tastes. For example, the back of the tongue is most sensitive to bitterness, and the front of the tongue is most sensitive to sweetness.

Taste Receptors and Sugar Substitutes

Scientists are still trying to determine the properties that allow chemicals to stimulate specific types of taste receptors. Among the facts they do know is that sweetness is signaled when a chemical fits into receptor sites at three points (Raloff, 1985). This knowledge has allowed chemists to design new chemicals that fit receptors just that way making a substance taste sweet. If the new chemical is also safe and has few calories, it is bound to be a popular and profitable artificial sweetener.

For a time, it was thought that saccharin was such a chemical. It is a very potent stimulator of sweetness receptors, but, because it appears to cause cancer, saccharin has now been largely replaced by aspartame (marketed as NutraSweet).

NutraSweet is described by its manufacturer (Searle) as safe and the most thoroughly tested compound ever marketed. Its use was approved by the Food and Drug Administration (FDA), Nevertheless, there is some controversy about whether aspartame causes problems in the central nervous system. Most of the concern has focused on the Phenylalanine in aspartame. Phenylalanine is a precursor, or preliminary form, of several neurotransmitters (sub-stances that allow commnication between neurons). and it competes for entry into the brain with other neurotransmitter precursors. The amount of a precursor in the brain can alter the amount of neurotransmitter in the brain, and this, in turn, can alter a person's behavior or mood. Some people have claimed that aspartame causes sleep problems, headaches, and can even increase appetite by affecting the neurotransmitter serotonin. But the FDA has judged that the changes are not significant enough to cause the problems that aspartame's critics attribute to it.

Another artificial sweetener on the horizon, called RTI−001, does not contain phenylate−

nine (Raloff, 1985). It has passed initial safety tests, but it must undergo years of testing before it is ready for the market.

There is another way to produce sweet sensations without sugar; use chemicals to modify the taste receptors so that they will send coded signals for sweetness to the brain. For example, miracle fruit, native to Africa, contains a substance that modifies sweetness receptors so that they respond to acids like vinegar, which normally taste sour (Bartoshuk et al., 1974). If you first eat miracle fruit, anything that normally tastes sour will instead taste sweet.

Smelly, Taste, and Flavor

There are some reasons to consider smell and taste as two components of just one sensori-perceptual system, **flavor** (Roein, 1982). Most of the properties that make food taste good are actually odors detected by the olfactory system, not activities of the taste system. And there is some evidence that the olfactory and gustatory pathways converge in some areas of the brain (van Buskirk & Erickson 1977). Still, no one knows yet how smell and taste come to seem like one sensation.

Flavor is also affected by the temperature of food. When the temperature is high, the chemicals in food become more volatile, releasing aromas that rise from the mouth into the nose and create better taste sensations. This is why many people find hot pizza delicious and cold pizza disgusting. Even the texture of food can alter its flavor. The texture and the heat of food are sensed through nerve endings in the mouth that are sensitive to temperature, pressure, touch, and pain-sensations that we examine in the next section.

第五节 躯体感觉和前庭系统
(SOMATIC SENSES AND THE VESTIBULAR SYSTEM)

Some senses are not located in a specific organ, such as the eye or the ear. These are the **somatic senses**, also called **somatosensory systems**, which are spread throughout the body. The somatic senses include the skin senses of touch, temperature, and pain, and kinesthesia, the sense that tells the brain where the parts of the body are. Even though it is not strictly a so-matosensory system, the vestibular system will also be considered in this section because its function-telling the brain about the position and movements of the head is closely related to kinesthesia.

Touch and Temperature

Touch is vitally important. Blind people survive and prosper, as do deaf prople and people without taste. But a person without touch would have difficulty surviving. Without a sense of touch, you could not even swallow food.

The stimulus and receptors for touch The energy detected and transduced into neural activity by the sense of touch is a mechanical deformation of tissue, generally the skin, frequently by stimulation of the hairs on the skin. Hairs do not sense anything directly (an observation you must have made, gratefully, when you got your first haircut), but when hairs are bent, they deform the skin beneath them.

Presumably, the receptors that respond to this deformation are in or somewhere near the skin. The skin covers nearly two square yards of surface, weighs more than twenty pounds, and includes many nerve endings that are candidates for the role of touch receptor. Some nerves that enter the skin from the spinal cord simply end; these are called free nerve endings. Many other nerves end in a variety of elaborate, specialized strutures. However, there is no relationship between the type of nerve ending and the type of sensory information carried by the nerve. Our best information at present suggests that there are no specialized receptors for touch. Instead, many types of nerve endings respond to mechanical stimuli, but the exact process through which they transduce mechanical energy is still unknown.

People do more than just passively respond to whatever happens to come in contact with bodies; jellyfish can do that much. For humans, touch can also be an active sense that is used to get specific information. Much as you can look as well as just see, you can also touch as r well as feel. When people are involved in active sensing, they usually use the part of the sensory apparatus that has the greatest resolution, or sensitivity. For vision, this part is the fovea; for touch, the fingertips have the greatest sensitivity and accuracy. Fingertip touch is the main way we explore the textures of surfaces. It can be extremely sensitive, as is evident not only in sensual caresses but also in the speed with which blind people can read Braille. The mouth, especially the lips, also has many touch receptors (one reason why kissing is so popular). You probably no longer depend on your lips to explore the world, but for infants and young children, who have not developed the ability to coordinate hand movements, the sense of touch in the mouth is an important way of learnig about the world.

Adaptation of touch receptors   Constant input from all the touch nerves would provide an abundance of unnecessary information. Once you get dressed, for example, you do not need to be constantly reminded that you are wearing clothes and in fact do not continue to feel your clothes against your skin. Changes in touch (for example, that your jeans have suddenly dropped to your kness). constitute the most important sensory information.

The touch sense emphasizes changes and filters out excess information through adaptation, the process through which responsiveness to a constant stimulus decreases over time. Typically, a touch nerve responds with a burst of firing when a stimulus is applied, then quickly returns to baseline firing rates, even though the stimulus may still be in contact with the skin. If the touch pressure increases, the nerve again responds with an increase in firing rate, but then it again slows down. A much smaller number of nerves adapts' more slowly, continuing to fire at an elevated rate as long as pressure is applied to the skin tion about three aspects of an object in contact with the skin: How heavy is it? Is it vibrating? and Where is it? The intensity of the sitmulus how heavy it is—is coded by both the firing rate of individual nerves and the number of nerves stimulated. A heavy object produces a higher rate of firing and stimulates more nerves than a light object. Vibrations are simply rapid fluctuations in pressure, and information about them is also coded by changes in the firing rate. Location is coded much as it is for vision: by the organization of the information.

In the sense of touch, this organization is called somatotopic (somato means body, and topos means place). Basically, the information is organized so that signals from neighboring points on the skin stay next to each other, even as they ascend from the skin through the spinal cord to the thalamus and on to the cortex. Consequently, just as there is a topographical map of the visual field in the brain, the area of cortex, called somatosensory cortex, that receives touch information resembles a map of the surface of the body. For example, the cells in the cortex that receive input from the wrist and the hand are close to each other, because the wrist and hand are close to each other on the surface of the skin. As with the other senses, these representations are contralateral; input from the left hand and wrist goes mainly to the right side of the brain.

Temperature   When you lie on a beach in the summer and dig your toes in the sand, you experience a pleasant stimulation, part of which comes from the sensation of the warmth of the sand. But are touch and temperature separate senses? To some extent they are. Electrical recordings made from sensory nerves on the skin show that some of them clearly respond to a change in temperature, but not to simple contact by a thermally neutral stimulus. There are warm fibers that increase their firing rates when the temperature changes in the range of about 95° to 115° F (35° to 47 °C). Temperatures above this range are painful and stimulate different fibers. Other fibers are "cold fibers" ; they respond to a broad range of cool temperatures.

Still, many of the fibers that respond to temperature also respond to touch. Even free nerve endings in the skin can convey touch, temperature, or pain. Different patterns of activty in a single nerve fiber can code different stimuli. For example, in one nerve a brief, smooth in crease in firing might signal touch, a sustained, regular increase in the same nerve might signal warmth; and variable, high-frequency activity could signal pain (Wall & Cronly-Dillon, 1960). But because no one knows how the different stimuli set up different patterns of firing, scientists have so far been unable to resolve whether each of the various skin senses has a separate existence or whether they are just aspects of the touch sense. Because the same nerves sometimes respond to both touch and temperature, you might expect that these sensations sometimes interact. This does, in fact, happen. For example, either warm or cold objects feel much heavier than thermally neutral objects—up to 250 percent heavier (Stevens 1982).

Pain

The skin senses can convey a great deal of pleasure, but a change in the intensity of the same kind of stimulation can create a distinctly different sensation: pain. Pain provides you with information about the impact of the world on your boby; it can tell you, You have just crushed your left thumb with a hammer. Pain also has a distinctly aversive emotional component. Researchers trying to understand pain have focused on the information carrying aspects of pain, its emotional components, and the various ways that the brain can adjust the amount of pain that reaches consciousness.

Pain as an information sense   If we consider just the information carrying aspect of pain, it is very similar to touch and temperature. The receptors for pain are free nerve endings, but no one knows how the free nerve endings that signal pain differ from other free nerve endings. Much is still unknown about just how pain is created, but it appears that painful stimuli damage tissue and cause the release of bradykinin, a chemical that fits into specialized receptors in pain nerves, causing them to fire.

Two types of nerve fibers carry pain signals from the skin to the spinal cord. A−delta fibers carry sharp pain, and C fibers carry several types of pain, including chronic, dull aches. These same C fibers also respond to nonpainful touch, but with a different pattern of firing. Both A−delta and C fibers carry the pain impulses into the spinal cord, where they form synapses with neurons that carry the pain signals to the thalamus and other of the brain.

Emotional aspects of pain   All senses can have emotional components, mots of which are learned responses. For example, the smell of baking cookies may make you feel happy because it has been associated with happy childhood times. The emotional response to pain is more direct Specific pathways carry an emotional component of the painful stimulus to areas of the medulla and reticular formation, activating aversion.

Nevertheless, the overall emotional response to pain depends greatly on cognitive factors. For example, experimenters have compared two groups' responses to a precise, painful stimulus. The two groups involved (1) people who were informed about the nature of the stimulus and when to expect it and (2) people who were not informed. Knowing about pain seemed to make it less aversive, even though the sensation was reported to be just as intense (Mayer & Price, 1982). Just how cognitive factors influence what people perceive and feel will be explored in the chapters on perception, emotion, and stress.

Modulation of pain: The gate theory   Pain is an extremely useful sense, because in the long run, it protects a person from harm. However, there are times when enough is enough. Fortunately, the nervous system has several mechanisms for controlling the experience of pain. One explanation of how the nervous system controls the amount of pain that reaches the brain is the gate theory (Melzack & Wall, 1965). It holds that there is a functional gate in the spinal cod that either lets pain impulses travel upward to the brain or blocks their progress. According to the theory, this gate can be closed by two mechanisms.

First, input from other skin senses can come into the spinal cord at the same time the pain gets there and can take over the pathways that the pain impulses would have used. Thus, nonpainful and painful sensations coming into the spinal cord in effect compete for pathways to the brain. This appears to be why rubbing the skin around a wound reduces the pain you feel, why electrical stimulation of the skin around a painful spot relieves the pain, and why scratching relieves itching (Itching is actually low−level activity in pain fibers). This mechanism may also partly explain the effectiveness of acupuncture, the Oriental method of relieving pain by twirling fine needles in the skin.

Second, the brain can close the gate by sending signals down the spinal cord. These messages from the brain block pain signals when they synapse in the spinal cord. The result is analgesia the absence of the sensation of pain in the presence of a normally painful stimulus. Suport for this aspect of the gate theory has come from the discovery that electrical stimulation of certain parts of the brain produces analgesia (Reynolds, 1969). For example, if part of a rat's. brainstem is electrically stimulated, the pain signal generated by heating the tip of the animal's tail never reaches the brain.

Natural analgesics How messages from the brain block pain signals is not entirely clear, but two classes of substances seem to play a role (1) the neurotransmitter serotonin, which is released by nerves descending from the brain, and (2) natural opiates called endorphins, enkephalins and dynorphins, these natural painkillers act at many levels of the pain pathway, including the spinal cord, where they block the synapses of the fibers that carry pain signals from the skin and other parts of the body. Natural opiates also relieve pain when the adrenal and pituitary glands secrete them into the bloodstream as hormones.

Most of the time, the endorphin system is not active as an analgesic. This makes sense; chronic analgesia would defeat the purpose of pain which is to cause you to escape or avoid damaging stimuli. Constant activity of the natural opiate system would not solve the problem of pain anyway, since, as with the opiate drugs on consciousness, tolerance and addiction can also develop with endorphins.

What conditions cause the body to ease its own pain? Again, we do not have all the answers, but we do know that certain physiological conditions can activate natural analgesic systems. For example, there is evidence that a hormonal endorphin, system operates during the late stages of pregnancy to reduce the mother's labor pains somewhat and create an apparent state of bliss in the fetus (Pert, 1979). Further, as we saw in Chapter 3, an endorphin system is activated when people believe they are receiving a painkiller, even when they get only a placebo. We also know that physical or psychological stress can activate natural analgesic systems. Different types of stress apparently bring different analgesic systems into action (Watkins & Mayer, 1982). For example, ridiculous as it may seem, shocking a rat's front feet activates a different system than shocking its hind feet. Stress-induced release of endorphins may account for instances in which severely injured soldiers and athletes continue to perform with no apparent pain.

If biological psychologists can determine how narural analgesic systems are brought into action, perhaps it will be possible to activate them in an alternating sequence, to relieve pain without producing tolerance and addiction (Watkins & Mayer, 1982). There is certainly a great need for this. Despite modern drugs, the pain of arthritis, migraine headaches, back pain, cancer, and other physical disorders imposes a heavy burden, causing suffering and disability to millions and costing more than $ 70 billion a year in medical costs, lost working days, and compensation (Bonica, 1984).

Proprioception

Most sensory systems receive information from the external world, such as the light reflected off green grass or the feeling of cool water washing over your feet. But as far as the brain is concerned, the rest of the body is "out there" too, and we know about where we are and what each part of our body is doing only because sensory systems provide this information to the brain. These sensory systems are called **proprioceptive** (received from one's own).

Kinesthesia The sense that tells you where the parts of your body are with respect to each other is kinesthesia. You probably do not think much about kinesthetic information, but you definitely use it. For example, even with your eyes closed, you can usually do a decent job of touching two fingers together in front of you. To do this, you must know where each finger is with respect to your body. You also depend on kinesthetic information to guide all your movements. Otherwise, it would be impossible to develop or improve any motor skill, from basic walking to complex athletic movements. These morement patterns become simple and fluid because, with practice, the brain uses kinesthetic information automatically.

Kinesthesia also plays an important role in a personas sense of self. Consider the case of Chritina, the disembodied woman Christina has a rare neurological disease that for unknown reasons, causes degeneration of the spinal nerves that provide kinesthetic information (Sacks, 1984). At first, Christina had difficulty holding onto objects; she would either grab them too tightly or let them slip out of her hands. Then she had trouble moving; she would rise from bed and flop onto the ground like a rag doll. Soon she began to feel she was losing her body; she was becoming disembodied, like a ghost. Once she became annoyed at her roommate for tapping her fingers on a table top. Then Christina saw that it was not her roommate, but Christina herself who was tapping. Her limbs were on their own, and her body was doing things she did not know about. The disease progressed until Christina had on sense of where her body was or what it was diong, even though all of her other senses were intact. If she leaked at her hand and concentrated very hard, she could guide its movements. But she had a permanent loss of her sense of self. Today she still feels separated from herself, a stranger in her own body.

Normally, kinesthetic information comes from both muscles and joints. Receptors in muscle fibers send information to the brain about the stretching of muscles, although their main role is to control muscle contraction (McCloskey, 1978). The primary source of kinesthetic information comes from joint receptors. These are nerve endings similar to those in the skin, but they are located where two bones meet, and they respond to deflections of the joint. When the position of the bones changes, joint receptors transduce this mechanical energy into neural activity, providing information about both the rate of change and the angle of the bones. This coded infomiation goes to the spinal cord and is sent from there to the thalamus along with sensory information from the skin. Eventually it goes to the somatosensory cortex and to the cerebellum. which is involved in the coordination of movements.

Vestibular sense Whereas kinesthesia tells the brain about where body parts are in: relation to one another, the vestibular sense tells about the position of the body in space and about its general movements. It is often thought of as the sense of balance. We usually become aware of the vestibular sense only when we overstimulate it and become dizzy.

Two vestibular sacs and three semicircular canals which are part of the inner ear are the organs for the vestibular sense (You can see the semicircular canals in Figure 4.4; the vestibular sacs connect these canals and the cochlea.) The vestibular sacs are filled with fluid and contain small crystals called otoliths (ear stones) that rest on hair endings. Because gravity pulls the otoliths toward the earth, they shift.when the head tilts, stimulating the hair endings and pro−viding information to the brain about the position of the head with respect to the earth. Astronauts beyond the pull of the earth's gravity do not receive this information, which contribute to space sickness.

Thsemicircular canals give information that is independent of the earth. They are fluid-filled, arc-shaped tubes that afe oriented in three different planes. Tiny hairs extend into the fluid in the canals. Whenever the head moves or changes its rate of movement, in any direction, the fluid in at least one of the (finals moves, bending the hairs. This bending stimulates neurons that travel with the auditory nerve, signaling to the brain the amount and direction of head movement.

The vestibular system has neural connections to the cerebellum, to the part of the autonomic nervous system that affects the digestive system, and to the muscles of the eyes. The connections to the cerebellum help coodinate bodily movements. The connections to the eye muscles create vestibular ocular reflexes. For example, when your head moves in one direction, your eyes reflexively move in the opposite direction. This allows your eyes to fixate on a point in space even when the head is moving around. You can demonstrate this reflex by having a friend spin you around on a bar stool for a while; when you stop, try to fix your gaze on one point in the room. You will be unable to do so, because the excitation of the vestibular system will cause your eyes to repeatedly move in the direction opposite to that in which you were spinning.

The vestibular-ocular reflexes allow remarkable feats of coordination. Consider, for example, a professional baseball player chasing a fly ball. Despite the fact that his boby and eyes are moving up and down as he runs, he can continue to fixate on the ball (which is also moving) well enough to judge its exact trajectory and intercept it.

第六节 未来研究趋向
(FUTURE DIRECTIONS)

In this chapter, you have seen how sensory systems allow people to make contact with the outside world as well as with what is going on within their own bodies. The study of these systems has been somewhat unusual. On one hand, it is tied up with very abstract issues, with questions at the core of philosophy, such as: What is reality? How can we know what it is? On the other hand, the study of sensory systems has led to some of the most concrete, down to earth research in psychology. This work focuses on learnig more about just how sensory systems detect energy, transduce it, and send it to the brain in a usable form. As we will describe in the next chapter, there has also been intense research on how people interpret sensations to build reality.

Psychologists have accumulated a tremendous body of knowledge in these areas, but much remains unknown or poorly understood, and the research goes on. For some senses, such as olfaction, we still need to learn more about transduction. For other senses, the major questions relate to how the brain processes the information it receives. When it comes to the transition from sensation to perception, to how the pathways and conections give rise to perception and subjective reality, we still know very little. For the major senses, the task is to learn what the relevant "features" are if the brain indeed codes features and to describe how connections in the cortex generate feature detectors. This task has practical applications: researchers in the field of artificial intelligence would like to build computers that can see and recognize objects, for both industrial and military purposes. But building a computer that can extract the relevant features of an image and recognize objects from any angle has turned out to be more difficult that many scientists thought (Waldrop, 1984). If we knew how the brain does it, perhaps we could construct computers that could do it.

There are still some peculiarities of color vision that scientists do not fully understand. One visual aftereffect is particularly bizarre because it lasts for a very long time. Variations of this aftereffect are often reported by people who use personal computers and word processors, including your authors. The scrolling green and black horizontal bars on many computer screens can set up aftereffects of pinkness when a white object is inspected (especially when surrounded by a black background), and the effects can last for weeks. In contrast to most afterimages, which result from retinal responses, these longer aftereffects are thought to reflect the way images are processed in the brain. We do not understand how.

These are just a few of the as-yet-unsolved mysteries of sensation. For more detailed information on sensory systems and how they work, consider taking courses on sensation and perception, biological psychology, vision, or speech and hearing.

词汇 (Vocabulary)

1. accessory structure   辅助结构
2. action potentials   动作电位
3. acuity   n. 视敏度
4. acupuncture   n. 针刺疗法、针灸
5. adaption   n. 适应
6. adrenal   n. 肾上腺
7. amacrine cell   无长突细胞
8. amplitude   n. 振幅
9. amygdala   n. 杏仁核
10. analgesia   n. 痛觉缺失
11. anatomical   a. 解剖学上的
12. aromas   n. 香味
13. arthritis   n. 关节炎
14. aspartame   n. 阿斯巴特（一种糖精）
15. association cortex   联合皮质
16. auditory   a. 听觉的
17. autistic   a. 孤独症的
18. autism   n. 孤独症
19. axon   n. 轴突
20. basilar membrane   n. 基底膜

21. bipolar cell   n. 双极细胞
22. bliss   n. 狂喜、极乐
23. bradykinin   n.（化）缓激肽
24. brightness   n. 明亮度
25. cadaver   n. 尸体
26. calorie   n. 卡路里（热量单位）
27. camphor   n. 樟脑
28. cerebellum   n. 小脑
29. cerebral cortex   大脑皮质
30. chronic   a. 长期的、慢性的
31. cineole   n. 桉树脑
32. cochlea   n. 耳蜗
33. cochlear implant   n. 耳蜗移植
34. color afterimages   n. 视觉后像
35. color blindness   n. 色盲
36. color vision   颜色视觉
37. complementary   a. 互补的
38. conduction deafness   n. 传导性耳聋
39. cones   n. 视锥细胞
40. contralateral   a. 双侧的
41. convergence   n. 汇聚形式，（生）趋同现象
42. cornea   n. 角膜
43. dark adaption   n. 暗适应
44. decibel   n. 分贝
45. decipher   n. 解释
46. degeneration   n. 退化、变质
47. dendrite   n. 树突
48. diagonal   a. 斜的
49. dynorphins   n. 强啡肽
50. electrode   n. 电极
51. electromagnetic radiation   n. 电磁辐射
52. empirical   a. 全凭观察实验的
53. endorphins   n. 内啡肽
54. enkephalins   n. 脑啡肽
55. envelope   n. 包膜
56. feature detector   n. 特征觉察器
57. fluctuation   n. 波动
58. fourier analysis   傅立叶式分析（傅立叶，19世纪法国空想社会主义者）
59. fovea   n. 中央凹

60. free nerve ending   n. 自由神经末梢
61. frequency matching   n. 频率对应
62. fundamental frequency   n. 基频
63. ganglion   n. 神经节
64. gustatoryn   a. 味觉
    gustation   n. 味觉
65. hair cell   n. 毛细胞
66. hierarchical feature-detection model   等级特征觉察模式
67. horizontal cell   n. 水平细胞
68. hue   n. 色调
69. incus   n. 砧骨
70. iodopsin   n. 视紫红质
71. iris   n. 虹膜
72. itching   n. 痒
73. kinesthesia   n. 运动觉、动觉
74. lateral   a. 侧面的
    lateral geniculate nucleus   n. 外侧胶状体
    lateral inhibition   n. 侧抑制
75. lens   n. 晶状体
76. malleus   n. 锤骨
77. medulla   a. 髓鞘的
78. membrane potential   n. 膜电位
79. migraine   n. 周期性偏头痛
80. modulation   n. 调节
81. motor nerves   n. 运动神经元
82. mallews   n. 锤骨
83. nanometer   n. 毫微米（十亿分之一米）
84. nerve deafness   n. 神经性耳聋
85. neurological   a. 神经病学方面的
86. neuron   n. 神经原、神经细胞
87. neurotransmitter   n. 神经冲动
88. occipital lobe   n. 枕骨叶
89. odor   n. 气味
90. olfaction   n. 嗅觉
91. opiate   n. 麻醉剂
92. opponent-process theory   对抗过程理论（四色说）
93. optic chiasm   n. 视交叉
94. optic nerve   n. 视神经
95. otolith   n. 耳石

96. oval window   n. 卵圆窗
97. palate   n. 腭
98. papilla   n. 乳头状的小突起 pi. papillae
99. perpendicular   a. 垂直的
100. phenylalanine   n. 苯
101. photopigment   n. 感光色素
102. photoreceptor   n. 光感受器
103. pigment   n. 色素
104. pinna   n. 耳廓
105. pitch   n. 音高
106. pituitary gland   n. 脑垂体
107. place theory   行波理论
108. primary visual cortex   初级视觉皮质
109. proprioception   n. 内部感觉
110. pupil   n. 瞳孔
111. pure tone   n. 纯音
112. receptor   n. 感受器、接受器
113. receptor field   n. 敏感区
114. reticular   a. 网状结构的
115. retina   n. 视网膜
116. rods   n. 视杆细胞
117. sac   n. 液囊
118. saccharin   n. 糖精
119. saturation   n. 饱和度
120. schizophrenia   n. 精神分裂症
121. semicircular canal   n. 半规管
122. sensation of contrast   感觉对比
123. serotonin   n. 5-羟色胺，血清紧张素
124. sine wave   n. 正弦曲线
125. skull   n. 颅骨
126. somatic senses   躯体感觉
127. spatial frequency filter model   空间频率过滤模式
128. specific nerve energy   n. 特定神经能
129. spectrum   n. 光谱
130. spinal cord   n. 脊髓
131. stapes   n. 镫骨
132. synapse   n. 突触
133. synthesis   n. 综合
134. taste bud   n. 味蕾

135. thalamus   n. 丘脑
136. the trichromatic theory   n. 三色说
137. the volley theory   n. 齐射说
138. threshold ix   n. 阈限
139. timbre   n. 音色
140. topographical representation   区域分化表
141. transducer   n. 传感器
    transduction   n. 传导
    transduction mechanism   转变机制，传导机制
142. tympanic membrane   n. 鼓膜
143. vestibular   a. 前庭的
    vestibular sense   平衡觉
    vestibular sac   前庭囊
144. vibration   n. 振动
145. visual pathway   视觉通路
146. volatile   a. 易散的、易挥发的
147. wavelength   n. 波长

第五章 知觉
（PERCEPTION）

本章要点（Chapter Outline）
从感觉到知觉（From Sensation to Perception)
知觉的特征（Some Features of Perception）
心理物理学（Psychophysics)
阈限（Thresholds)
知觉组织（Perceptual Organization)
知觉理论（Theory on Perception)

  通过前一章的学习，我们知道了什么是感觉。存在于眼睛、耳朵和其他感官中的感受器接受到光、声和其他刺激的能量，并将这些能量转化为神经冲动；神经冲动沿传入神经传到大脑和相应区域，并在此进行加工，从而形成感觉。然而，感觉只为我们提供了关于环境的原始信息，只反映客观事物的个别属性，我们不能从感觉得知客观事物的整体属性。飞机驾驶员在飞行中对周围环境作出准确判断正确操纵飞机，不是依靠感觉，而是依靠知觉。

  知觉是人脑对直接作用于感觉器官的客观事物的整体反映。人们运用已有的知识对来自环境的原始感觉加以综合和解释，形成有意义的经验——知觉。要理解知觉，首先要明白知觉除了以各种感觉为基础外，还要借助于人的过去的知识和经验。知觉不是简单地被动地吸收和解译原始的感觉，而是根据过去的知识经验，把当前客观刺激中缺少的东西在主观上进行补充，对所感觉到的东西赋予完整的意义，形成连贯一致的知觉世界。如果缺少相应的知识和经验，知觉就不能形成。例如：一个对环境的理解确实贫乏的人，他的视觉景象会不断地变化，呈现混淆的光色镶嵌体，他们听觉世界会是充满嗡嗡声、尖叫声的嘈杂世界。知觉同心理学的其他许多研究领域有关，记忆、表象、思维、情感、意志等都以知觉为基础。在许许多多活动中，知觉起十分重要的决定作用，大到飞行员驾驶飞机，小到一般人的日常阅读。

  通过本章的学习，我们将对知觉有清楚的认识。本章首先回答以下问题：大脑怎样把杂乱的感觉加工成有组织的、可以认出的知觉？在知觉加工过程中通过哪些方式解释原始的感觉信息？人们怎样认出熟悉的物体，怎样知道该物体的尺寸、形状和颜色？人们怎样知道物体在空间中所处的位置？其次，本章将列举一些错觉，甚至连最老练的知觉者在某种特定的情景中也会犯的令人迷惑的错误。

A pilot makes an approach to an airport must perceive very accurately how far away the runway is and the angle of approach in order to control the plane's speed and altitude for a touchdown at the end of the runway. For the pilots of four Boeing 727s in 1966, thin perception failed disastrously, causing plane crashes in Chicago, Salt Lake City, Cincinnati, und Tokyo. The four incidents had three factors in common. First, they all took place on clean nights, with the runway well in sight; the pilots did not have to rely on instruments. Second, they involved approaches over dark water toward runways lying on a background of upward–sloping city lights in the distance. Third, all of the planes crashed short of the runway.

Conrad Kraft, an engineering psychologist at Boeing Aircraft Corporation, gathered these findings. Kraft believed that the absence of altitude cues from the dark water below the aircraft in combination with an upward–sloping, lighted terrain, led the pilots to misperceive their alaltitude. He suggested that the pilots assumed that the airport and city lights lying on a flat rather than an upward–sloping surface, believed they were flying at a higher altitude than they actually were (higher than they should be), and therefore tried to "correct" their altitudes, bringing the planes down too low and crashing.

In fact, this was exactly what happened. But how did Kraft reach his correct diagnosis? The principles of sensation that we described in the previous chapterhow receptors in the eyes, ears, and other senses receive light, sound, and other types of energy and convert them into signals that are sent to the brain could not by themselves provide the answers. Sensations provide raw information about the environment but do not give much meaning to that information. It was Kraft's knowledge of the basic principles of perception that led him to a correct diagnosis.

Perception is the process through which raw sensations from the environment are interpreted, using knowledge and understanding of the world, so that they become meaningful experiences. Perception is related to many other areas of psychology (see Linkages diagram) and, as we will see, is critical to a wide range of actions, from flying an airplane safely to reading a book.

The first thing to understand about perception is that it is not a passive process of simply absorbing and decoding incoming sensations. If it were people's understanding of the environment would be poor indeed. The visual scene, for example, would be a constantly changing, confusing mosaic of lights and color. The auditory world would be a din of buzzing, humming and shrieking. Instead, human brains take the sensory stimuli that bombard everyone and actively create from them the coherent world that is perceived. People filled in missing information and drew on past experiences to give meaning to what they see, hear, or touch. For example, the raw sensations come from the stimuli in Figure 5.1 inform you only that there are four straight lines that contact one another ninety–degree angles. Yet you instantly see this pattern as a meaningful object: a square.

At last in this chapter we will describe many other examples about how perception creates people's experience of the world as an organized, recognizable place. We will discuss the various ways in which perceptual processes interpret incoming sensations. We will answer such questions as how do people know what is out there in the physical world? How do they recognize familiar

• 95 •

Figure 5.1
What Do You See?

objects and understand their size, shape, and color? How do people know where things are in space? We will illustrate some perceptual illusions, the facinating mistakes that even the most sophisticated perceiver can make under certain circumstances. We will consider the complex process of attention, because part of perception involves attending to some things and ignoring others. We will see that people make such choices about what to notice based partly on what they already know and hope will happen. Finally, we will look at some applications of research on perception.

第一节 从感觉到知觉：概述
(FROM SENSATION TO PERCEPTION: AN OVERVIEW)

Whereas the senses create a physical code from a stimulus, perception's job is to go beyond this code and draw on knowledge of the world to interpret what is but there. Suppose, for example, that your retinas transmit signals to your brain indicating that a stimulus below and just in front of you is brown in color and long, narrow, and wavy in shape. Is the stimulus a snake or a rope? The answer, in the form of an interpretation of the stimulus by your perceptual apparatus, will prompt you to ignore the object, run from it, or pick it up.

Some Features of Percption

This example helps illustrate six characteristics of perception that we will mention repeatedly. First,perception is generally knowledge based. If you do not know what snakes or ropes look like, especially if you do not know how to tell the difference between them, your chances of surviving in the woods are poor.

　　Second, perception is often inferential. People do not always complete sensory infomation at hand, but the perceptual system uses people's knowledge to make inferences about what not be able to hear, see, or feel. Thus, if you know what a snake looks like, you will perceive it as a snake even though the underbrush conceals the last few inches of the stimulus. You would not say. "Wow, if that thing had a tail, I'd swear it was a snake." Or consider the blind spot that we discussed in the chapter on sensation. The blind spot has no light receptors, but people do not perceive the resulting "hole" in the visual world, because their perceptual apparatus fill it in.

　　Third, perception is categorical; it allows people to place apparently different sensations in the category on some common features. Thus, you may not know exactly what kind of snake you are looking at, but it has enough "snakey" characteristics (long, round, scales, tapered tail, forked tongue, beady little eyes) for you to place the stimulus in the snake category. Similarly, people can instantly place certain sounds in a category called "human voice," even if they sound unlike any other voice they have ever heard.

Fourth, perception is relational. You perceive a stimulus pattern as a snake, not only because it has snakey features, but also because these features are related to one another in a coherent and consistent way. The tapered tail appears at the end of the body, not in the middle; there is a beady little eye on each side of the head, which is at the end opposite the tail. In the same way, your ability to perceive that someone is unusually tall requires that you see him or her in relation to more normally proportioned people.

Fifth, perception is adaptive, allowing people to focus on the most important information for handling a particular situation. For example, peripheral vision is very sensitive to moving stimuli. This is adaptive in that it allows people to react quickly to potential threatening motions across a wide range of space. Further, your perceptual apparatus firstly focuses first on whether the stimulus you suddenly encounter is a snake or a rope, not on whether it is a king snake or a python. The details will be filled in later, perhaps from a safer distance. On the other hand if you worked at the zoo and were told to feed the boa constrictor, species identification would be very adaptive indeed, especially if you wanted to keep your job. This aspect of perception helps us to quickly identify stimuli associated with food or other desirable goals, as well as those that are likely to be dangerous.

Finally, many perceptual processes operate automatically, you do not have to stop and consciously ask yourself, "Is that a rope or a snake?" The question is asked and answered much more quickly—so quickly, in fact that you are unaware of having done it.

Relating Sensation and Perception

As noted in the previous chapter, sensation and perception overlap somewhat. The sensory processes do not register everything in the outside world with equal emphasis; they highlight certain features. Thus, interpretation of a stimulus begins even before information about the stimulus reaches the brain. For example, the cells of the retina emphasize edges and changes, so that you see more contrast than the physical stimulus actually contains. When you look at the sky on a rainy day, the stimuli reaching your eyes actually include several different wavelengths of light; but your eyes themselves combine with data about those wave lengths and the eyes "tell" the brain that it is seeing one color: gray. Thus, perception appears to add additional information, based on prior knowledge. to what comes into the sensory systems. In this sense, perception may be a primitive version of the knowledge—based processes on thought and language. These processes allow people to learn concepts, make judgments, and reach decisions.

How perception actually does work and which of its six features are therefore most important are still matters of considerable debate. On one side of the question are researchers like Peter Lindsay and Donald Norman (1977). who emphasize the knowledge—based, inferential charactristics of perception. Called constructionists, they argue that the perceptual system must often construct an image of reality from fragments of sensory information, much as an archaeologist reconstructs an entire dinosaur from a few bits of bone. This, they suggest, how the mind can perceive the images in Figure 5.2 as a triangle and a face, even though much of the sensory information is incomplete.

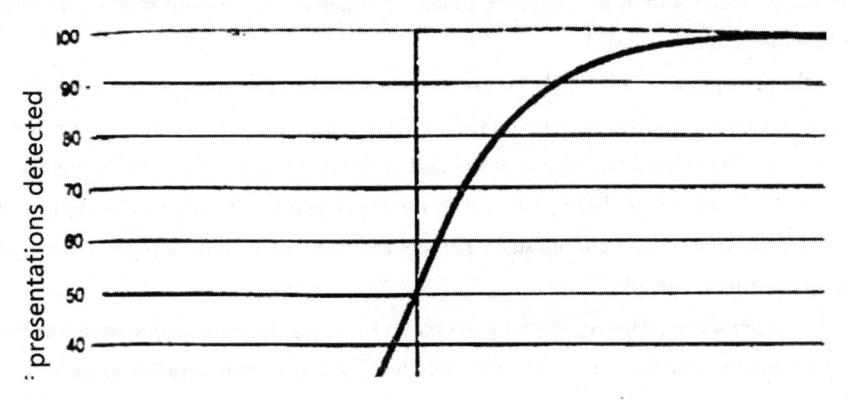

Figure 5.2
The Cmstractionist View of perception
These stimulus demonstrate the constructionist view of perception: when you look at them, you perceive is more than actually in the sensory information.

On the other side are those such as James Gibson, who stress the adaptive and automatic properties of perception. Gibson (1979) argued that most of the cues humans need in order to get along in the natural world are available from the stimulus themselves and are usually registered directly by the senses. Because of his emphasis on the rich sources of information available in the natural environment, Gibson's approach to perception is often called ecological. In his view, stimuli needs reconstruction, like those in Figure 5.2 occur only in the artificial world of the psychologist's laboratory. When people perceive deeply, for example, they do not first perceive stimuli as two-dimensional and then construct a three-dimensional version of the world. Instead, the stimuli that reach the eye tell people automatically about depth.

The debate about these opposing points of view remains unresolved, partly because, as so often happens in psychology, both have value. Constructtonist principles often hold for the process of recognizing object the "What is it?" aspect of perception. This recognition must often be performed in fleeting glances, when sensory evidence is incomplete. Yet the ecological view seems to describe accurately and precisely. The way people perceive their own movement through the word, as well as the specific properties of objects, such as their distance from the viewer and their color, shape, and orientation—the "What kind?" and "Where?" of perception.

第二节 心理物理学
（PSYCHOPHYSICS）

Human perccptual processes range from the very simple, such as listening for a faint sound in a quiet house, to the very complex, such as evaluating and appreciating an architect's design. The most basic perceptual processes—assessing whether a stimulus is present and, if present, how strong or intense it is might appear to belong in the chapter on sensation, but there is an important reason for covering them here. As you will see, even deciding whether a stimulus is present depends on what people know about the world, what they expect, and even what they want to perceive.

Absolute Thresholds: Is Something Out There?

The simplest perceptual categorization involves deciding whether a stimulus is present. This process begins with and depends on the sensory receptors and raw sensations. Indeed, the receptors, sensitivity to small amounts of energy can be a matter of life and death. If you are lost in the woods on a dark night, your safety may depend on detecting a faint glimmer of light or hearing the distant call of a search party.

Determining thresholds The minimum detectable amount of light, sound, pressure, or other physical energy is called the absolute threshold. This threshold can be amaxingly low. Normal human vision, for example, can detect the light equivalent to a single candle flame burning on a dark rnght thirty miles away! Table 5.1 presents values of the absolute thresholds for vision, hearing, taste, smell, and touch.

The information in Table 5.1 was derived from careful experiments by psychologists whose specialty is **psychophysics**, an area that focuses on the relationship between the physical energy of environmental stimuli and the conscious psychological experence those stimulus produce. Psychophysical research involves not only finding adsolute thresholds for the senses but also determining how sensitive people are to changes in the intensity or other qualities of those stimulus. These very basic questions get at the foundation of how people make contact with and become conscious of the world; it is not surprsing that the earliest psychologists concerned themselves primarily with psychophysical research.

To get an idea of how psychophysial research is done, consider a topical esperiment on the absolute threshold for vision. A subject is brought into a laboratory, and the lights are turned out. After the subject's eyes have adapted to the adrkness. many brief flashes of light presented one at a time at varying intensities, from less than that of candle burning thirty miles away to levels considerably higher. Each that, the subject is asked if the stimulus was seen. The pattern of yes or no responses to the varying light intensities usually forms a curve similar to that shown in Figure 5.3, As you can see, the absolute threshold is actually not absolute. Sometimes a stimulus of a particular intensity will be perceived, and at other times, it will not. Because of this variability, the exact amount of energy corresponding to any particular person's absolute threshold cannot actually be determined. To get around this problem, psychophysicists have redefined the **absolute threshold** as the minimum amount of energy that can be detected 50 percent of the time.

Table 5.1

Value of the Absolute Threshold

Examples of stimuli at the absolute threshold for five primary senses.

Sense	Absolute Threshold
VisionA	A candle flame seen at thirty miles on a dark, clear noght.
Hearing	The tick of a watch under quiet conditions at twenty feet.
Taste	One teaspoon of sugar in two gallons of warer.
Smell	One drop of perfume diffused into the entire volume of a six–room apartment.
Touch	The wing of a fly falling on your cheek from a distance of one centimeter.

SOURCE: Galanter, E. (1962). Contemporary psychophysics. In R. Brawn (Ed.) New Directions in psychology. NEW York: Holt, Rinehart & winston.

Sources of threshold variation Why should there be variability in an "absolute" threshold? Psychologists have long been aware of two reasons: internal noise and response bias.

Internal noise is the spontaneous, random firing of nerve cells. It occurs because the nervous system is never inactive. Thus, a person trying to detect a faint ray of light in an otherwise dark environment or trying to hear a soft sound in an otherwise quiet place does so against a background of the spontaneous firing of nerve cells of varying intensity. Sometimes this firing occurs in the brain's sensory areas or in receptor cells of the eye, ear or other sense organs. It is a little like "snow" on a television screen or static on the radio. If the level of internal noise happens to be high at a particular moment it may be mistaken for an external light or sound. If the level of internal noise is extremely low, the energy added by a faint light or sound may not create enough neural activity to make that stimulus noticeable (see Figure 5.4).

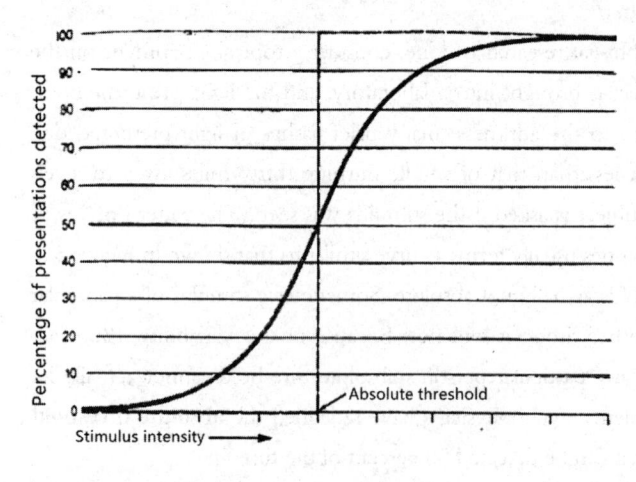

Figure 5.3
The Absolute Threshold
This graph shows the relationship between the percentage of times that a signal is detected and the intensity of that stimulus as measured in physical units. If the absolute threshold were indeed absolute, a signal of a particular intensity would always be detected, and any signal below that intensity would never be detected. In that case, the graph would show the relationship indicated by the dashed line, with no reports when the stimulus is below the threshold and 100 percent of the reports above it. Instead, the absolute threshold is defined by the horizontal line, which intersects the curve at the intensity at which the signal is detected with 50 percent accuracy.

The second source of variation in absolute threshold, **response bias**, is a person's willingness or reluctance to respond to a stimulus. It reflects motivation and expectancies. For example, people being paid for every correct detection of a faint light may tend to report seeing it even if it is not there. In contrast, people who are penalized for every incorrect detection may be cautious and fail to report detected signals unless they are very confident in them. Similarly, a person who expects a stimulus to occur will be more likely to detect it than one who does not.

Going Beyond the Threshold: Signal Detection Theory

Obviously, then, perception of a stimulus is not determined by the intensity or other characteris of the stimulus alone. Since neural noise and response bias can never be entirely eliminated, researchers in psychophysics have gone beyond trying to determine threshold and have turned to signal detection theory (Green & Swets, 1965) to understand how sources of variation affect perception.

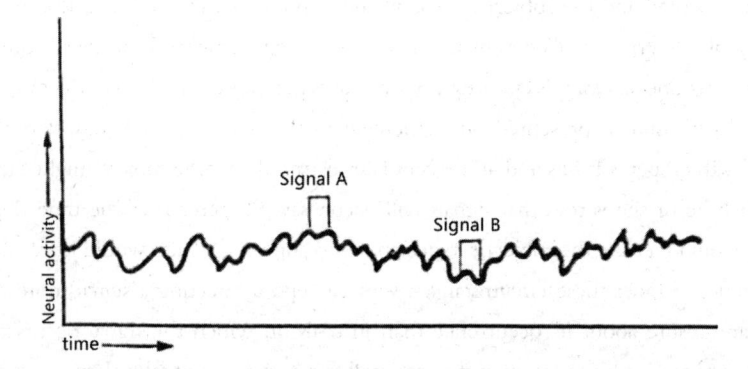

Figure 5.4
Neural Noise and Its Effects

This graph shows art example of the randomly changing neural noise in the part of the brain where detection of, say, sound takes place and the added energy caused by two signals, marked A and B. Because the random activty is already high when signal a occur, the signal and noise together generate enough total activity to stand out from the average activity level; therefore, signal will probably be detected. But signal B occurs when the noise happens to be low, and the total energy of the signal and noise is no greater than the average noise level alone. Thus, signal B will probably not be detected.

Signal detection theory is a formal mathematical model of what determines people's reports that a near-threshold stimulus has or has not occurred. It permits psychologists to identify the effects of response bias. It also allows them to compare different people's ability to detect sensory stimuli even when circumstances create different response biases and thus different patterns of absolute threshold. Instead, it assumes that perception of a stimulus depends on two factots: sensitivity and the response criterion. **Sensitivity** refers to the ability to detect a stimulus: it is influenced by neural noise and by the intensity or the stimulus, as well as by the capacity of the sensory system. The **response criterion** is the amount of energy necessary for a person to justify reporting that a signal has occurred. It is the internal rule a person uses to decide whether or not to report a stimulus, and it reflects the person's motivation and expectation.

To separate the effects of these two factors so that each can be measured, signal detection theory provides a special set of methods. The researcher presents stimuli on some trials but nothing on others. The no-stimulus trials are called catch trials, because they are designed to catch the subject's tendency to respond (perhaps because of sensory noise or Bias) when nothing is there. Instead of letting the response bias vary in unknown ways, which would interfere with measuring sensitivity, signal detection theorists alter the bias, either by offering money or by changing the person's expectations. Then they look at what happens to the person's responses. To alter a subject's expectancy that a stimulus will occur, for example, the researcher might change the percentage of trials on which it actually does occur.

Figure 5.5a shows the possible outcomes when the signal detection method is used. When a stimulus is presented and the subject detects it, the response is called a hit. If the subject fails to detect the signal, the error is called a miss. A false alarm occurs when no stimulus is presented, but the subject reports one anyway. Reporting no stimulus when none is given a correct rejection.

Suppose a stimulus is presented on 50 percent of the trials, and the subject responds as in Figure 5.5b, with 60 percent hits and 40 percent false alarms. The same subject might then be given trials on which he or she is told that signals will occur, say, 90 percent of the time (Figure 5.5c). This change would increase the subject's expectancy of a stimulus, which would lower the subject's response criterion. Under these circumstances, subjects report detecting a signal more often—even when they are unsure about its occurrence than in trials on which the signal occurs only rarely. Thus, The percentage of hits goes up, but so too will the percentage of false alarms.

Researchers estimate subject's sensitivity by examining the overall pattern of hits and false alarms that occurs as the experimenter manipulates the response criterion by changing the percentage of catch trials of altering the rewards offered. Figure 5.6 shows examples. The resulting curve is known as a **receiver operating characteristic (ROC) curve**, and its chape provides a measure of a subject's sensitivity. The more bowed the curve, the greater the sensitivity. Sensitivity in signal detection theory is measured in units called d' (d prime).

Consider the case in Figure 5.6a. The ROC curve shows that increasing the percentage of trials with a signal increased the subject's hit rate faster than the false-alarm rate. That means that the person discriminated between trials with the signal and trials without the signal; in other words, the subject was sensitive to the difference between the two kinds of trials. Thus we would conclude that this person is quite sensitive to the stimulus. Certainly he or she is more sensitive than the person whose data are plotted in Figure 5.6b, where increasing the percentage of trials on which the signal occurred increased the false-alarm rate about as fast as it increased the hit rate—perhaps indicating that the person was merely guessing. Here, d'= 0.

Sensitivity, and thus the shape of the ROC curve, depends not only on a person's capacity to detect stimuli but also on stimulus intensity. Thus, the shape of the carve will change if the stimulus changes, as Figure 5.7 illustrates. For a particular stimulus, however, differences in ROC curves indicate differences in people's ability to detect stimuli.

Figure 5.5
Signal Detection
(*a*) *The possible outcomes of signals trails and catch trails.* (*b*) *Outcome percentages when a stimulus is presented 50 percent of the time.* (*c*) *Outcome when a stimulus is presented 90 percent of the time.*

Stimulus presented?

		Yes	No
Subject's response	Yes	Hit	False alarm
	No	Miss	correct rejection

(a) possible outcomes

Stimulus presented?

		Yes	No
Subject's response	Yes	Hit 60%	False alarm
	No	Miss 40%	correct rejection 60%

(b) stimulus presented on 50% of trails

Stimulus presented?

		Yes	No
Subject's response	Yes	Hit 90%	False alarm 50%
	No	Miss 10%	correct rejection 50%

(c) stimulus presented on 90% of the trials

Some Applications of Signal Detection Theory

Signal detection theory is important not only because it allows psychologists to separate the contributions of sensitivity and response criteria to perceptual performance, but also because it can help them analyze why people sometimes fail to detect importnt signals.

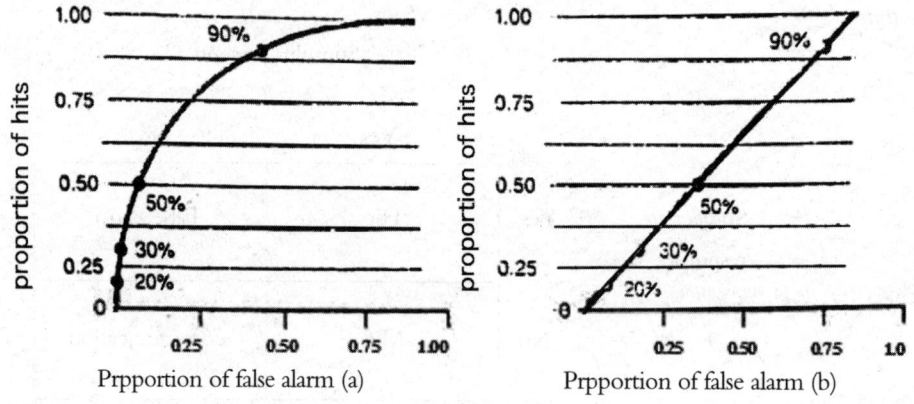

Figure 5.6
Receiver Operating Characteristics (ROC) Curves
Here we see the proportion of hits and false alarms that occur as the expectancy for a stimulus is changed by changing the percentage of trials on which a target stimulus is presented, (a) The bowed shape of the ROC curve indicates that the subject is quite sensitive to the signal. (b) The sensitivity (d') here is.

Consider an airport security guard looking for images of bombs or weapons on a video display showing X rays of passenger luggage. Why might the guard sometimes fail in this important task? The problem might be inadequate sensitivity. After hours on duty, the guard might nod off briefly just as a signal occurs (a miss) of, on suddenly jerking awake, misperceive a hair dryer as a gun (a false alarm). A second possibility relates to response criteria. Perhaps the guard's airport is particularly quiet, and no one has ever tried to conceal a weapon there; knowing this, the guard's expectancy level is low. Or perhaps the guard wants to avoid a false alarm that might unnecessarily upset the terminal crowd. In either case, the guard's, response criterion is high: another way of saying this is that the guard has a conservative response bias. The result is that mildly weaponlike images on the screen are not likely to provoke a warning from the guard.

Recognition of these possibilities has led spychoiogists to make a variety of recommendations to help those working at signal defection tasks maintain vigilance and an optimal criterion (Warm, 1984; Wickens, 1984a). Some of their recommendations are quite simple. For example, people driving long distances are advised to take breaks every so often in order to combat fatigue and boredom. On tasks offering monotonous stimulation, such as truck driving or inspecting parts as they move down an assembly line, detection accuracy may be maintained by having workers engage in mild physical exercise, listen to musics, or receive other varied sensory input. Psychologists also recommend setting the pace and complexity of a detection task so that it provides enough challenge to keep workers alert without overwhelming them, One Japanese bottling plant, for example, improved its inspectors' accuracy simply by slowing the rate at which bottles moved by. Finally, giving workers information about their performance in the form of feedback about hits and false alarms can lengthen the duration of detection accuracy. This can be done in many ways, including purposely presenting defective parts, phony target signals, or other critical stimuli from time to random time. This occasional feedback, plus knowledge that performance is being monitored, may help minimize signal detection errors.

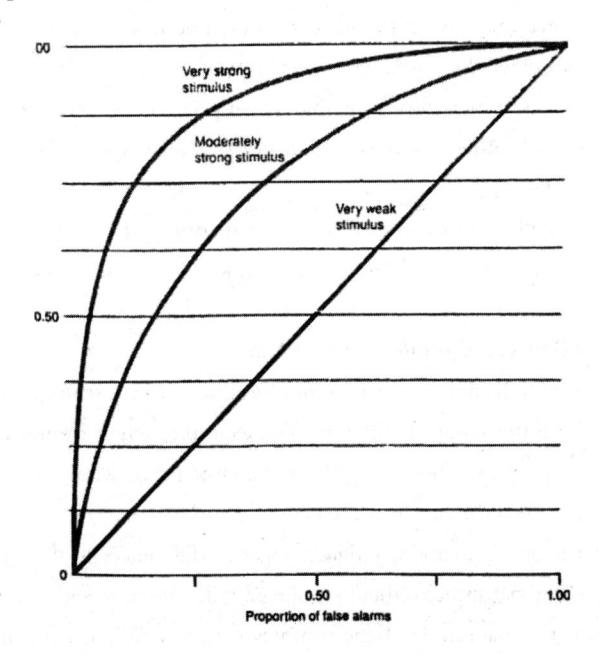

Figure 5.7
ROC Corves and stimulus Intensity
When a person detects a loud sound, hits increase much faster than false alarms as the per centage of stimulus trials increases, as the top curve shows. The curve for a quieter sound might show less sensitivity (middle curve), and for an extremely soft sound, it might look like the straight diagonal line. The d' value for the diagonal line is o and d' increases for the more bowed ROC curves. Note: A very loud sound would always show hits, and never show false alarms, and d' would be infinite.

Some psychologists have applied signal detection theory to situations involving the recognition of events in memory, in particular to eyewitness testimony. For example, when a crime witness tries to identify a suspect in a police lineup, the interests of justice demand that the detection process be as sensitive as possible, producing the fewest possible misses (failures to identify the suspect) and false alarms (erroneously identifying an innocent person). Typically, a lineup consists of people similar in appearance to the suspect, so that none will be automatically ruled out. But when this precaution is taken, several factors can distort a witness's response to a lineup, producing either misses or false alarms.

As in any other detection task, witnesses bring with them a response bias. Some witnesse's fear of seeing an innocent person tried or punished may create a very high response criterion, making them unlikely to identify an alleged crimianal. Other witnesses may want to see someone, anyone, convicted when a crime has been committed; their response criterion may be so low that they will very likely identify someone in any lineup as the criminal. These people have what is called a rishy bias.

On the basis of signal detection theory, psychologists have recommended that officers remind witnesses that the criminal they saw at the scene of the crime might not actually be in the lineup. This reminder tends to lower the witnesses expectation of seeing the criminal and, in turn, raises the response criterion. Researchers also argue that the suspect and others in the lineup should look equally dissimilar from each other to reduce the chance that the suspect will be chosen by guessing (Ellison & Bucknout, 1981).

These and other applications of signal detection theory alert people to problems related to perception in legal, medical, industrial, and other settings. They also suggest ways of combating those problems.

Judging Differences Between Stimuli: Weber's Law

Often people must not only detect the presence or absence of a stimulus but also determine whether two stimuli are the same or different. For example, when tuning up, musicians must determine if notes played by two instruments have the same pitch; when repainting part of a wall, you may need to determine if the new paint matches the old.

It turns out that people's ability to judge changes or differences in the amount of a stimulus depends on how much of that stimulus there is to begin with. More specifically, the ability to detect defferences declines as the magnitude of the stimulus increases. When comparing the weights of two envelopes, you will be able to detect a difference of as little as an ounce, but when comparing two boxes weighing around fifty pounds, you may not notice a difference unless it is a pound or more.

This relationship between the initial intensity of a stimulus and ability to detect a change in its magnitude is described by Weberns law, one of the oldest in psychology. Named after the nineteenth-century German physiologist Ernst Weber (pronounced "vayber"), Weber's Law describes the smallest detectable the smallest detectable ctifference in Stimulus energy, a quantity known as the **just-noticeable difference (JND)**. It states that the just-noticeable difference is a constant fraction of the intensity of the stimulus. The constant fraction, labeled K, is different for each sensory system and for different aspects of sensation within those systems. In algebraic terms, Weber's law is JND=K1, where I is the amount, or intensity, of the stimulus. For example, the value of K for weight is 0.02. If an object weighed 25 pound (I), the JND would be only half a pound (25 pounds × 0.02=0. 5 pounds). In other words, for 25 pounds of luggage, barbell, or other liftable object, a half-pound increase is necessary before one can detect a change.

The value of K represents the ability to detect differences. The smaller the value of K, the more sensitive a sense is to stimulus differences. For example, K for vision is 0.017, which indicates a high degree of sensitivity; only a small change in the intensity of light is needed to notice a difference in its brightness. Table 5.2 lists the value of K for a variety of sense modalities and reveals the variability in people's ability to judge differences in stimuli. Weber's law is found to be valid over a wide range of stimulus amplitudes, but it does not hold when stimuli are either very intense of very weak.

The fact that the judgment of differences follows Weber's law illustrates the adaptive nature of perception: the ability to discriminate differences generally matches the need to discriminate these differences in everyday life. For example, people rarely need to exercise fine discriminations between large quantities (such as the brightness of a flashbulb versus that of a spotlight), but such judgments are often required between small quantities, such as the subtle differences in the shading of an X ray that might indicate a tumor. The adaptive nature of perception is also illustrated by the senses' different sensitivities to change (see Table 5.2). Humans depend on vision far more than they do on the sense of taste; so it is sensible that K is smaller, and sensitivity greater, for vision than for taste.

Weber's law also applies to more complex stimuli. You might be concerned about a twenty-cent increase in a forty-cent bus fare; this 50 percent increase (20/40) is well above the JND for noticing changes in cost. But the same twenty-cent increase in your monthly rent would be less than a JND and thus unlikely to cause notice, let alone concern.

Table 5.2
Weber Constants (k) for Different Sense Modalities *The value of Weber's constant fraction differs from one sense to another. senses that are most important for survival tend to be the most sensitive*

pitch	.003
Brightness	.017
Weight	.020
Loudness	.100
Pressure on skin	.140
Saltiness of tastt	.200

Judging Stimulus Magnitude; Fechner's and Stevens's Laws

Weber's law describes the fact that the morethere is of some stimulus to begin with, the more the amount must change in order for any change to be noticed. In 1860 Gustav Fechner proposed that Weber's law could also be used to understand the psychological experience, or perception and stimulus magnitude. That is, it could help answer such questions as how much brighter a lightbulb must be to appear twice as bringht as a 100-watt bulb.

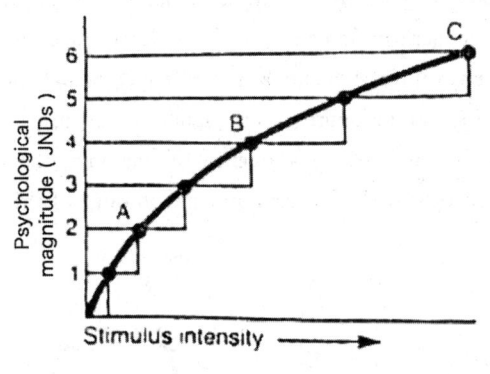

Figure 5.8
Fechner's Law Applied to Visual Stimulus
Larger and larger increases in physical energy (the horizontal axis) are required to produce

equal increases in psychological perception (JNDs, on the vertical axis). Thus, points A and B are perceived as equally differnt from each other, as are points B and C. Note that the increase in energy required to make a light appear two JNDs brighter is much greater when going from the fourth to the sixth JND (point B to C) than from the second to the fourth TND (point A to point D). Another way of saying this is that, as our perceptual experience increases arithmetically (from 1 to 2 to 3), the stimulus energy involved increases geometrically (from, say 1to 4 to 9 to 16,). The purple line shows what this function looks like.

Fechner reasoned that, since the JND is the smallest detectable change in the subjective magnitude of a stimulus, then the total subjective magnitude or intensity of any stimulus should be related to the number of JNDs by which that stimulus different from zero. That is, one should be able to measure subjective magnitude by adding JNDs. Furthermore, since JNDs become progressively larger that isn't require more stimulus energy as a stimulus grows more intense, larger and larger increases in physical energy will be necessary to obtain equal changes in subjective intensity when stimuli are of greater magnitude. In other words, constant increases in physical energy will produce progressively smaller increases in subjective magnitude. More prephysical **Fechner's Law** states that the perceived magnitude of a stimulus is the product of K for the particular sensory system involved and the logarithm of the stimulus intensity. Figure 5.8 depicts this relationship for a visual stimulus.

Although Fechner's law describes fairly well how people judge the loudness of sounds, the brightness of lights, and the intensity of many other sensations, it does not apply to some stimuli. For example, contrary to Fechner's law, each successive increase in the perceived intensity of electric shock takes less and less of an increase in physical energy.

S.S. Stevens found a way around this problem. By asking subjects to estimate the relative magnitude of stimuli of varying intensities, he found that their response followed a formula that became known as **Stevense's power Law** (stevens, 1957). It is somewhat more complex than Fechner's law, but it also works better. Figure 5.9 contains the formula and an example of how it generates accurate functions relating energy to subjective intensity for almost any kind of stimulus. To better understand the everyday importance of Fechner's or Stevens's Law, consider the problem of designing the volume control for a radio. How do you make the knob turn so that each angle of rotation of the dial will cause the same subjective increase in loudness to the listener? The answer is provided by the power law for sound. Starting from zero, each constant angle of rotation marked on the dial should produce an increasing amount of stimulus energy, and the amount of this increase is given by the power law.

Figure 5.9
Stevens's Power Law
Stevens's power law is S=klb, where S is the perceived magnitude of the stimulus, K is the constant, l is the physical intensity of the stimulus, and b is a power law generates equally accurate descriptions of the relationships between

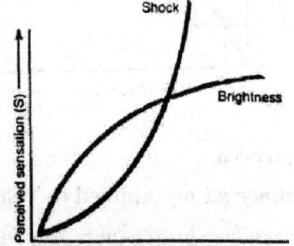

stimulus intensity and psychological perception for brightness (which follows Fechner's law) and for shock (which does not).

Important as it is, the detection of faint amounts of energy and of relative magnitudes of pure stimuli are only tiny components of the perceptual activities that most people perform every day. Perception also involves organizing all the sensations coming from the world. It is to this organizational aspect of perception that we now turn.

第三节 组织知觉世界
(ORGANIZING THE PERCEPTUAL WORLD)

Suppose for a moment that you are driving down a busy road while searching for Barney's Diner, an unfamiliar restaurant where you are to meet a friend. The roadside is crammed with signs of all shapes and colors, some moving, some rotating, and some standing still. If you are ever to recognise the one sign that says "Barney's Diner," you must impose some sort of organization on this overwhelming cafeteria of visual information.

Most people do this sort of thing all the time, but how? How do you know where one sign ends and another begins? How do you distinguish between signs and the background against which you perceive them? How do you realize that a sign remains the same size as you approach it, even though its image on your retina gets larger as the sign gets closer? In this section, we will describe some of the organizational processes that allow people to understand the jumble of lights and sounds in the world.

Principles of Perceptual Organization

You finally recognize the "Barney's Diner" sign because the sign's letters match the pattern or letters that you have stored in your memory. Before this march can take place, however, your perceptual system must first separate these letters from the larger background of lights, colors, letters, and other competing stimuli. Two basic principles of perceptual organization—figure-ground perception and grouping—**guide** this initial organization.

Figure and ground When you look at a complex visual scene or listen to a noisy environment, your perceptual apparatus automatically picks out certain objects or sounds to be figures (that is, the features to be emphasized) and relegates others to be ground (that is, background). For example, you drive up to an intersection, a stop sign becomes a figure, standing out clearly against the background of trees, houses, and cars. A **figure** is the part of the visual field that has meaning, stands in front of the rest, and always seems to include the contours or borders that separate it from the relatively meaningless background (Rubin, 1915).

The relationship between figure and ground is usually, but not always, clear cut. Consider Figure 5.10. What do you see? The fact that you can now look at Figure 5.10 and repeatedly reverse figure and ground to see faces, then a vase, then faces again clearly illustrates that perception involves an active interpretation of stimuli. Figure 5.10 also illustrates a second point: as we noted earlier, perception is categorical. That is, when people perceive sensory evidence, they usually assign it to one category or another, rarely to both or to something in between. You cannot, for instance, easily perceive Figure 5.10 as both a vase and two faces at the same time.

Figure 5.10

Figure–Ground Perception

what do you see? At firsts you may perceive two faces staring at each other. If so, the space between the two faces is the ground–the meaningless, contourless background behind the faces that form the figure. But look again. You may also perceive the figure as a vase or candle holder. Now the spaces an each side, which formerly had been meaningful figures, take on the meaningless properties of ground.

Grouping Why is it that certain parts of the perceptual world become figure and others become background, even when nothing in particular stands out in the physical pattern that falls on the retina? The answer is that certain inherent features of stimuli lead people to group them together, more or less automatically, into coherent objects or sounds.

Early in this century, a group of German psychologists described the principles behind this grouping of stimuli. They argued that people perceive sights and sounds as organized wholes. These wholes, they said, are different from and more than just the sum of the individual sensations, much water becomes something more than just an assortment of hydrogen and oxygen atoms. Because the German word meaning roughly "whole figure" is Gestalt, these researchers became known as Gestalt psychologists. They proposed six prinsiples or properties that lead the perceptual system to "glue" raw sensations together in particulsr ways, organizing stimuli into a world of shapes and patterns. These principles, which are illustrated in Figure 5.11.

(a) Proximity   (b) Similarity   (c) Continuity

(d) Closure   (e) Orientation   (f) Simplicity

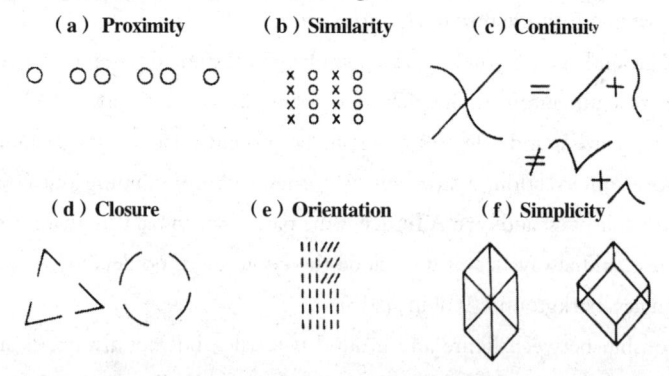

Figure 5.11

Gestalt principles of perceptual Grouping

You probably perceive a as being made up of two groups of two dots plus two single dots, rather than as three groups of two dots or some other arrangement. In b, you see two columns of X's and two columns of O's, rather than four rows of XOXO illustrating the principle of similarity, You see the symbol in c as being made out of two continues lines—one straight and one curved not one of the other discontinuous forms shown in. the figure. You immediately perseive the disconnected line segments of d as triangle and a circle. In e, the different orientation of the lines in one quadrant of the square makes that quadrant stand out from the others. In f, both figures are the same three—dimensional cube viewed from different angles but the one on the left is normally perceived as a two dimensional hexason with lines running through it; the other, as a three—dimensional cube.

1. proximity The closer objects are to one another, the more likely they are to perceived as belonging together, as in Figure 5.11a.

2. Similarity Similar element are perceived to be part of a group, as in Fgure 5.11b. People wearing the same school colors at a stadium will be perceived as belonging together even if they are not seated close together.

3. Continuity Sensations that appear to create a continuous form are perceived as belonging together, as in Figure 5.11c.

4. CLosure People tend to fill in missing contours to form a complete object, as in Figure 5.11d.

5. Orientation When basic features of stimuli have the same orientation (such as horizontal, vertical, or at an angle), people tend to group those stimuli together (Beck, 1966; Olson & Attneave, 1970). Thus, you group the vertical lines of a grove of standing trees together and see those trees separately from their fallen neighbors in the undergrowth. Figure 5.11e provides another example. The feature—detecting cells in the visual cortex, appear to be responsible for this aspect of perceptual grouping.

6.Simplicity People tend to group stimulus features in a way that provides the simplest interpretation of the world (Hochberg & McAlister, 1955), as in Figure 5.11f. Consider what it takes to describe each pattern. To describe the figure on the left in two dimensions to describe each pattern. To describe the figure on the left in two dimensions, you need only say that it is a hexagon with six radii of equal lengths. To describe it as a three—dimensional figure, you would have to say that it is a cube with sides of equal length, which is being viewed from a certain unusual angle. The simpler, more economical, two—dimensbnal perception will prevail. For the second figure, on the other hand, the two—dimensional interpretation is not nearly as simple to describe, because the shape is no longer a simple hexagon. You would have to describe it as "two overlapping squares with lines connecting their corresponching comers," The three—dimensional interpretation (a cube) is now simpler and more naturally perceived.

Having considered some of the ways people organize sensations into perceptions, consider some of the things these perceptions convey about the environment.

Perceptual Constancy

Suppose that, one sunny day, you are watching a friend walking toward you along a treelined sidewalk. The raw sensations generated by this movement are actually rather bizarre. For one thing, the size of the image on your retinas keeps getting larger as your friend gets closer. To demonstrate this effect to yourself, look at a distant person and hold your hand out at arm's length in front of your eyes. The image of your hand will completely block your view of the person, because the retinal image of the person is so small. Try the same thing when the person is three feet away. Your retinal image of the person will now be so much larger that your hand can longer cover all of it. But you perceive the person as being closer now, not bigger. Simillarly, as you friend walks along, passing from bright sunshine through the dark shadows of trees, the sensation reaching your eyes would suggest that your friend becomes darker in color, then darker again. But instead you perceive an indivdual whose coloring remains the same.

This example illustrates **percepotual constancy**, the perception of objects as constant in size, shape color, and other properties despite changes in their retinal image. Without this aspect of perception the world would be an Alicein−Wonderland kind of place in which objects continuously changed their properties.

Size constancy Why does the perceived site of objects stay more of less constant, no matter what changes occur in the size of their retinal image? Part of the reason is that perception is knowledge based, and experience tells us that most objects (aside from balloons) do not spontaneously change size. However, familiarity is not the only source of size constancy. Years ago, people in an experiment were asked to estimate the size of an unfamiliar object viewed at varying distances by adjusting a disk of light until the light disk seemed to be the same size as the object. If lack of familiarity with the objects had eliminated size constancy, the estimszed sizes should have been similar to the size of the retinal image, and closer objects would have been judged to be larger. In fact, the people came quite close to an accurate perception of the unfamiliar objects' true size (Holway & Boring, 1941).

What produced this accurate perception of size? As objects move doser or farther away, the brain perceives the change in distance and automatically adjusts the perception. The formula Describing this adjustment is

Perceived size = retinal image × perceived distance

In other words, the perceived size of an object is equal to the size of the retinal image multiplied by the perceive distance (Holway & Boring, 1941). Here again, we see that perception is relational: the retinal image is interpreted in relation to perceived distance. As an object moves closer, its retital image increases, but the perceived distance decreases at the same rate, and the Perceived size remains constant. If instead, a balloon is inflated in front of your eyes, the retinal image increaaes, but perceived distance remains constant, and the perceived size (correctly) increases.

As another example, hold the retinal image constant by fixing your eyes on a bar of light (a bright fluorescent light is a good choice) and stare at it for thirty seconds or ao, in order to form a good afterimage. This afterimage represents a retinal image of a constant size. Now shift your gaze from the light to a distant wall. The perceived size of the afterimage will now be larger because the retinal image is now being multiplied by a larger perceived distance.

The relationships in the perceptual system among retinal size, perceived size. And perceived desirable distance do always produce effects. People may perceive objects with smaller retinal images to be farther away than those with larger images, even when the distance is in fact the same. One experiment suggested that this error may be responsible for the higher accident rate among drivers of small car (Eberts MacMillan. 1985). A small car produces a smaller retinal image at a given distance than a larger one, possibly causing the driver of a following vehicle to overestimate the distance to the small car and therefore fail to brake in time to avoid a rear−end collision.

Although the perceptual system usually produces size constancy correctly and automaticalliy, it can sometimes fail. we will be clear when we consider depth perception a bit latter.

Shape constancy The perinciplcs of shape constancy are closely related to those of size constancy. To see shape constancy at work, remember what page you are on, clone this book, and tilt it toward and away from you several times. The book will continue to look rectangular, even though the shape of its retinal image changed dramatically as you moved it. The brain automatically integrates infomation about retinal images and distance as movement occurs. In this case, the distance information involved the difference in distance between the near and the far edges of the book.

Brightness Constancy No matter how the amount of linght striking an object change, its perceived brightness remains constant. You could demonstrate this constancy by watching a friend walk by a leafy tree on a sunny day or by placing a lump of coal in sunlight and a piece of white paper in some shade next to it. The coal still looks very dark and the paper still looks very bright, even though a light meter would reveal much more light energy reflected to the eyes from the sun −bathed coal than from the shaded paper.

Of course, one reason why the coal continues to look dark, no matter what the illumination, is that you know that coal is black, illustrating once again the knowledge based property of perception. Another reason is that the coal is still the darkest object relative to its back−ground in the sunlight, and the paper is the brinhgtest object relative to its background in the shade. The brighteness of an object is perceived in relation to its background.

Constancy and the nature of perception All of these perceptual constancies demonstrate the characteristics of perception that we described at the beginning of this chapter. Perception, we have noted, is both knowledge based and relative. For example, we have shown how the size of an object is perceived in relation to distance and its brightness in relation to its background. Sometimes the relational nature of perception can trick one into misperceivipg the world.

Nevertheless, perceptual constancies also demonstrate the adaptive nature of perception. Thanks to the constancies of perception, people perceive constant, stable objects. Imagine trying to deal with a world in which objects changed their form as constantly as their images changed on your retinas. Perceptual constancy also demonstrates the principle of simplicity at work. The world is far simpler if one can assume that objects are constant and that distances and lighting change, rather than assuming that the objects themselves change.

Depth Perception: Experiencing the Third Dimension

You have seen how one of the most important factors underlying size and shape constancy is perceived distance perception. Perception of distance, or **depth perception**, also allows people to experience the world in three dimensional depth, not as a two-dimensional movie. How can this be, when all visual information come through a set of two-dimensional retinas? There are two reasons. The first involving a wide variety of cues provided by the environment. The second is a set of properties of the visual system itself.

Stimulus Cues To some extent, people perceive depth through the same cues that an artist uses to create the impression of depth and distance on a two-dimensional canvas. These cues are actually specific characieristics of visual stimuli. Figure 5.12 illustrates several of them.

Figure 5.12 Suimalus cues for Depth Perception

Look first at the two men at the far left of the picture. They illustrate the principle of **relative size**: objects producing larger images on the retina are perceived as closer than those producing smaller ones.

Another cue comes from height in the visual fields more distant objects arc usually higher in the visual field than those nearby. The woman near the man at the front of Fingure 5.12 therefore appears to be farther away. (By the way, this is why size constancy was violated in Figure 5.12; the more distant ballplayer lower, not higher in the visual field).

The woman standing by the car in the middle of the picture illustrates another depth cue called **interposition**. Closer objects block one's view of things farther away.

The figure at the far right of the picture is seen as still farther away, in part because she is standing near a point in the road where its edges, like all parallel lines that recede into the distance, appear to converge toward a single point. This apparent convergence provides a cue called **linear perspective**. The closer together two converging lines are, the greater the perceived distance.

Finally, the road in the picture disappears into a hazy background. Since greater distances usually produce less clarity, **reduced clarity** is interpreted as a cue for greater distance. The effect of clarity on perceived distance explains why a mountain viewed on a hazy day appears to loom larger than the same mountain on a clear day. The haze acts as a cue for greater distane, but the size of the mountain's retinal image is unchanged. The same retinal image accompanied by a greater perceived distance produces a larger perceived size.

· 114 ·

Two additional stimulus cues for depth come from **gradients**, which are continuous changes across the visual field. A **textural gradient** is a graduated change in the texture, or "grain," of the visual field. Texture appears finer and less detailed as diastance increases; so as texture changes across the retinal image, people perceive a change in distance.

The second gradient cue is the **movement gradient**, which is the graduated difference in the apparent movement of objects. Faster relative movement across the visual field indicates less distance. The next time you are riding in an car in an open area, look out the side window at an object of intermediate distance (for example, a house). The telephone poles and other objects closest to you will apear to fly across your visual field at a rapid rate; in contrast, distant trees may seem motionless or even appear to move along with you. It is this difference in relative movement that provides cues to the difference in distance.

Cues based on properties of the visual system Because each eye is located at a slingtly different spot on the head, each receives a slightly different view of the world, as Figuure 5.13 illustrates. The difference between the two retinal images of an object is called **binocular disparity** and is responsible for creating the experience of a solid, three-dimensional object. For any particular object, this disparity decreases with increasing distance. Nevertheless, with both eyes open, the brain combines the two images, perocesses information about the amount of dispatity and the distance, and generates the impression of a single object having its correct depth, as well as height and width. Binocular disparity is one of the strongest cues of depth perception.

In the late nineteenth century, an understanding of binocular disparity was used to produce the stereoscope, a hand-held device that creates the appearance of depth by displaying to each eye a separate photograph of an object or scene, each taken from a slighiy different angle. The same principle is used today to create the impresston of three dimensions in Viewmaster slide viewers and in 3-D movies.

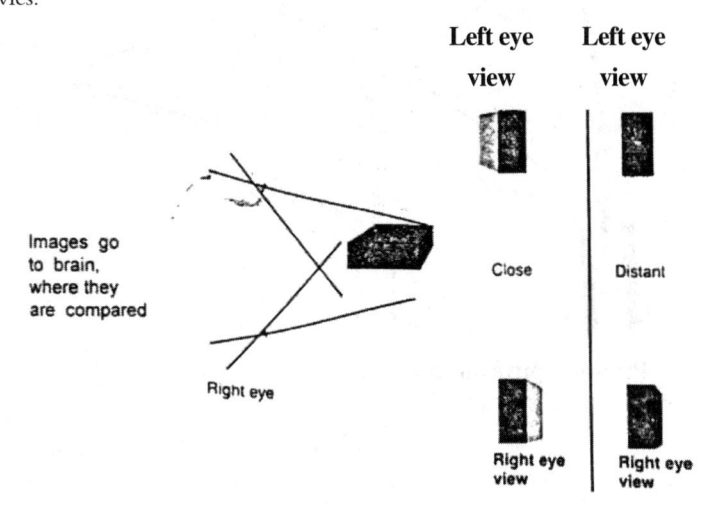

Figure 5.13
Binocular Disparity
Each eye has a slightly different view of the cube. The difference between views is greater when

the cube is close than when is far away. For a quick demonstration, how a pencil up vertically about six inches in front of you. Close one eye and take note where the pencil is relative to the objects, the backgrounld. Now open that eye and close the other one. Notice how the pencil seems to shift slightly and how it obscures slightly different parts of the background.

These are two views your eyes have on that pencil. If you now hold the pencil at arm's length or look at some other anrrow vertical object some distance away, there less difference in the angles at which the two eyes see the object, and the amount of disparity (or shift) decreases.

A second consequence of having two eyes located at slightly different places is that the eyes must converge, or rotate inward, in order to project the image of an object on each retina. This convergence provides another cue to depth. As Figure 5.14 shows, the closer the object is, the more "crosseyed" the viewer must become in order to achieve a focused image. The brain receives and processes informaton from the eye muscles about the amount of muscular activity;the greater the activity, the greaten the object is perceived to be .

What binocular disparity does for depth perception, the placement of the ears does for sound localization, that is, determining the directions from which sounds arise. The cues that are used to locate sounds depend on the fact that people have two ears, If a sound is continuous. the peak of sound waves coming toward the right side of the head will reach the right ear before they reach the left ear. Similarly, a sound coming from the right side of the head will be a little bit louder to the right eat than to the left ear, because the head blocks some of the sound from left ear. Thus. the nervous system uses both timing cues and intensity to locate sounds, This ablity to localize sounds requires sophistcated analysis of auditory input by the brain.

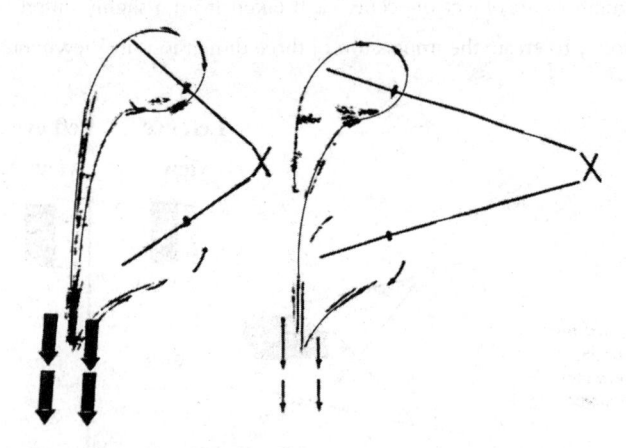

Proprioceptive information

Figure 5.14
Convergence
The arrows along the nerve fibers coming from the eyeballs represent the strength of proprioceptive information about muscle activity

The final depth cue based on the anatomy of the eye is related to facts we noted in the chapter on seasation. To bring an image into focus on the retina, the lens of the eyeball changes shape, or accommodates or accoplish this feat, muscles surrounding the lens must either tighten, to make the lens more curved for focusing on close objects, or relax, to flatten the for focusing on more distant objects. Information about the muscle's activity is relayed to the brain, and this accommodation cue helps creat the perception of distance.

Watching the World Go By: The Perception of Motion
As a tennis player brings her racket to return a shot, the most important thing is that she must perceive about the ball is not its size or shape or even its precise location and distance. The critical property is its motion: how fast it is going and where it Is heading.

The perception of motion usually occurs as visual patterns move across the surface of the retina. Like distance perception, it requires that one somehow translate this two-dimensional retinal image into a three-dimensional experience. People make this translation automaticully by using both visual cues and information about the movement of parts of the body.

Consistent with his ecological theory, Gibson (1966) argued that informaition indicating motion occurs in the visual stimulus itself. The movement gradient we discussed carlier provides a good example. Imagine you are riding in a car that is moving forward toward the horizon. When you are looking forward in the moving car. objects in your visual field appear to diverge from a single point, the point where the road disappears into the horizon. and move progressively faster as they move away from this vanishing point. This pattern is automaitically perceived as the forward movement of your own body toward and past unmoving objects.

Looming which is a rapid expansion in the size of an image so that it fills the available space on tlie retina, provides another cue to motion. As noted earlier, when an image looms, there is an automatic tendency to perceive it as an approaching stimulus, not an expanding object viewed at a constant distance.

Although the movement of light across the retina is normally associated with motion, it is not always sufficient to create the perception of motion, If movement of the retinol image were the only factor necessary for motion perception; then when you swing your head around, or even rotate your eyeballs from side to side, you should perceive everything in the visual field to be moving in the opposite direction. This is not the case, because as we discussed in the chapter on sensation, the brain also receives and processes information about the motion of the eye and head. If the brain determines that all of the movement of light on the retina is due to such bodily movement, the outside world is perceived as stable, not moving.

Sensations of head and eye movement can actually compensate for external motion, slowing down and smoothing out the perception of moving objects. For example, by moving your head and eyes, you perceive a speeding race car as a focused, smoothly moving object. But if you hold your head and eyes still the car goes by, you will perceive it as a much more rapidly moving blur.

Perceptual Illusions
The perceptual cues we have described coustantly and automatically convey precise information about the features of a multitude of objects and surfaces. As a result, you can walk down stairs, toss

a wad of paper into a distant trashcan, avoid collisions while driving, and accomplish a thousand other everyday acts with little hesitation and without a second thought. In fact, you are unlikely to become aware of perceptual cues at all unless you read about them or unless they create an inaccurate or distorted view of reality. In Chapter 6, on consicousness we will describe how distorted perceptions can come about through sleep, hypnosis, drugs and other circumstances; here we are concerned with those distoirtions of reality known as perceptual illusions.

Illusions of motion   One such illusion is stroboscopic motion, the perception of motion produced when snapshot images; each slightly different from the next, are presented one after the other. This is the principle behind the motion picture, which produces perceptions of motion from a series of still shots.

The "moving" neon lights seen on advertising signs are an application of another type of stroboscopic motion, an illusion called the phi phenomenon. If the timing is right, a series of lights flashing on and off sequentially at slightly different locations is perceived as just one light moving from one point to the next. movement is perceived even though nothing is actually moving.

The perception of movement in these cases is consistent with the principle of simplicity. It is simpler to assume that there is one object moving in space rather than several stationary objects, each of which turns on and off in sequence.

Illusory movement may also occur if you adopt the wrong frame of reference or the wrong hypothesis. Normally, when there is relative movement between figure and ground, the figure is more likely to be perceived as moving and the background as stable. If you therefore perceive a figure to be moving when it is not, the illusion is called induced motion. You may experience this effect when you sit in a stationary car in a parking lot, and the vehicle next to you begins to move slowly backward. You are likey to perceive your own car as drifting forward—even though cues from the vestibular senses tell you that you are not moving, and your kinesthetic senses say that your foot is planted firmly on the brake.

Why are these vestibuluar and kinesthetic cues temporarily ignored? The answer lies in a phenomenon known as **visual dominance**. When information received by the visual system conflicts with information coming from other sensory modalities, the sense of vision normally wins the battle and is perceived as accurate (Posner, Nissen & Klein, 1976).

Illusions of shape, size, and depth   Figure 5.15 presents five other perceptual illusions. The first three (a through c) involve distortions of shape; they support the Gestalt principle that the whole is different from the sum of its parts. Sections d and e show illusions of size and depth.

The Ebbinghaus illusion is shown in Figure S. 15d. Look at the circles in the center of each pattern. The one on the left probably looks smaller to you than the one on the right, though both are in fact the same size. This illusion illustrates again that perceptual judgments take place relative to some context. In the left—hand pattern, the context (or background) for the center, which consists of larger objects, creates the perception that the center circle is relatively small. The right—hand center circle appears in a context of smaller objects, making you perceive it as larger. Dieters should keep this in mind: a small meal looks more substantial if served on a small plate. Diet—food advertisers use this fact to make their products look more filling.

Other illusions involving size result from the way in which the perceptual system automatically "grabs onto" any cue to depth in order to provide a three-dimensional interpretation of a stimulus. The Ponzo illusion(Figure 5.15e) is a perfect example. line segment A looks loger.

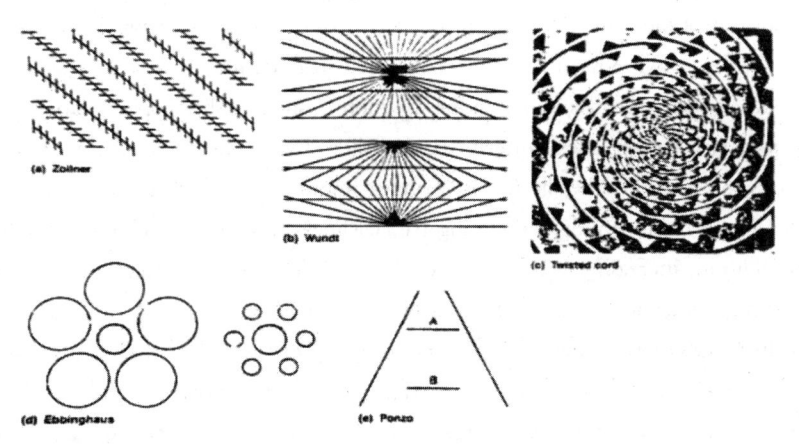

Figure 5.15
Five perceptual Illusion
(a) in the Zollner illusion, you can focus attention directly on a pair of parallel lines to establish that they are in fact parallel, but if you draw back to consider the entire figure, you get the clear impression that they are not parallel, (b) The lines in the Wundt illusion are actually parallel, and (c) the twisted cord is actually made up of concentric circles, (d) The Ebbinghaus illusion is a direct analogy to the misjudgment of brightness, (e) The Ponzo illusion uses converging lines to create the impression that the top horizontal line is at a greater distance than the bottom one. This greater perceived distance, multiplied by the top line's retinal size, gives it a larger perceived size (length) than the bottom line, even though the two are identical.

Than segment B, yet they are same length. You misperceive their lengths because the perceptual they are the same length. You misperceive their lengths because the perceptual system uses the converging lines as its primary depth cue (recall linear perspective. onpage180). Thus, you view the region where the lines are closer together as more distant. Then the priciple of relative size takes over; recall that when two objects have retinal images of the same size, the one perceived as farther away is seen as larger. As a result, the line seen as more distant here is also seen as longer.

Perceptions of size constancy and distance also serm to interact in the moon illusion, the perception that the moon is much larger when it is near the horizon than when it is high in the night sky, even though the size of the retinal image of the moon stays the same. Lloyd Kaufman and Irvin Rock (1962) have argued that when one looks at the moon on the horizon, the interventing space is filled with objects (houses, trees, or mountains) that convey a sense of greater distance than when one looks straight up and sees nothing but the moon. The greater perceived distance apparently makes the moon on the horizon look larger.

Probably the best-known and most studied perceptual illusion is the Müller-Lyer illusion, shown in Fingur 5.16a. Of the two arrow shafts in the figure, the one on the left seems shorter, despite the fact that the two are of equal length, Richard Gregory (1968, 1973) has argued that this illusion, like the Ponzo illusion, represents a misapplication of the depth cue of linear perspective. The convergence of the arrowheads on each side of the shaft on the left makes the shaft appear to be the closest part of the scene (like the outside corner of the house in Figure 5.16b), whereas the divergence of the arrowheads on the right makes that shaft seem to be toward the back. By the logic applied to the Ponzo and moon illusions, the more "distant" shaft appears to be larger.

The idea that depth cues underlie the Muller—Lyer illusion has been supported by investigations showing that the illusion is stronger among subjects who have more experience making depth and distance judgments using parallel lines and corners (Gregory1968; Segalletal, 1963). In addition, increasing the amount of three-dimensional information in the drawing increases the magnitude of the illusion (Liebowitz et al, 1969).

Attractive and simple as the depth perception theory of the Müller—Lyer illusion may seem, it cannot account for some phenomena. A striking example is shown in Figure 5.16c. In this figure, there are no converging lines to suggest distance, and the figure does not give a feeling of three-dimensionality; yet it does create a misjudgment of distance like that in the Müller—Lyer illusion. Why? One proposed explanation is that the perceived length of an obj ect is based on the "frame" of which it is a part. when the frame is perceived as larger, as it is in the right side of Figure 5.16c, so is the line segment included within it (Rock, 1978).

This example shows that explanations of some perceptual illusions remain incomplete. Perhaps the best conclusion to offer at this point is that illusions such as the Müller—Lyer are multiply determined. After all, since perception is based on many princirles, it seems reasonable that illusions could reflect the violation of more than one of them.

Distortions of perception may also be created, not by cues peovided by the environment, but by the same factors that create response bias in detecting stimuli: motivation, experience, bias, and expectancy. In one classic study, children were asked to estimate the size of poker chips by adjusting a disk of light to match a displayed chip. Chidren who had been told could use the poker chip to buy candy estimated the chip to be significantly larger than other children did, a result suggesting that objects that are more important may be perceived as larger (Lambert, Solomon & Watson,1949). You will see in the next section that the motivational and other individual-differnce factors highlighted in our discussion of signal dection theory can also affect the speed and accuracy with which people are able to recognise objects in world.

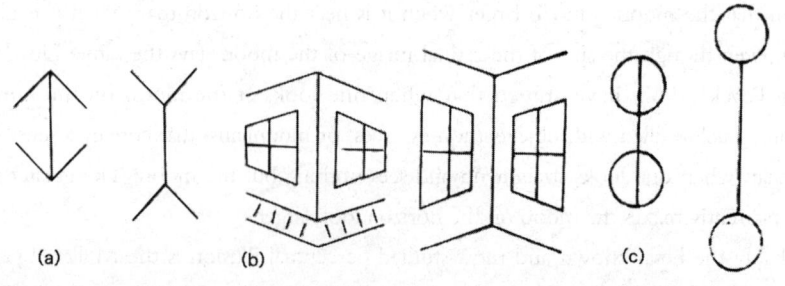

Figure 5.16

Variatiom on the Muller – Lyer Ilusion

(a) The Müller-Lyer illusion. (b)The Müller-Lyer illusion in a three-dimensional context, in which the vertical line is used to form the outside corner of a house and the inside corner of a room. The inside corner looks taller. (c) A demonstration of the illusion that does not involve perception of three dimensions.

第四节 识别知觉世界
(RECOGNIZING THE PERCEPTUAL WORLD)

In discussing how people organize the perceptual world by segregating it into figure and ground and then assessing the properties of objects, we have so far ignored one vital question: How do people recognise what the object is? If you are driving in search of Barney's Diner, exactly what happens when your eyes finally locate the pattern of light that spells out "Barney's Diner"? How do you recognize it as the place you are seeking?

Basicaily, the brain must analyze the incoming pattern of light and compare that patten to what is stored in memory. If it finds match, recognition takes place. Thus, recognition depends on the stimuli, sensations, and memory, But the factors create response bias in the detection of stimuli motivation and expetancy-also influence recognition if you desperately want to see the sign, perhaps because a long-lost lover waits at the diner, you will see it sooner than if you are going to meet some unexciting person. And you will recognize the sign more easily if it appears precisely at the corner where your map says you should expect it rather than a block earlier.

There are two types of processing that appear to be involved in recognition. Those aspects of recognition that begin at the "top" guided by higher-level cognitive processes and by psychological factors like expectations and motivation, are called **top-down processing** (Lindsay & Norman, 1977). Other aspecets of recognition depend first on the information about the stimulus that comes to the brain from the sensory receptors; this is called **bottom-up processing**. First, how does bottom-up processing work?

Feature Analysis

Some psychologists have suggested that recognition occurs through the firing of a particular set of neurons in the brain that become active only when they find their match in the perceptual world (Lindsay & Norman, 1977), much as only one fork in a row of tuning forks will vibrate when its matching pitch is played. We described this view, the hierarchical feature-detection model, in the chapter on sensation.

As we noted there, one problem with this model is that you would need a different feature detector for every one of the seemingly infinite number of specific sights, sounds, smells, and other stimuli that you recognize. (We also noted that the spatial frequency model may provide another description of how the brain analyzes patterns; this is not yet confirmed). Nevertheless, there are specific feature detectors in the visual cortex that respond to particular lines, edges, corners, angles, and other features of stimuli (Hubei & Wiesel, 1979). And there are cells that fire only in response to features corresponding to different pitches, loudnesses, and timbres of sounds.

This evidence that cells of the brain respond to specific features of stimuli supports the view that recognition occurs by means of **feature analysis**. According to this view, any stimulus can be described as a combination of features. The letter A, for example, can be described as existing of one horizontal and two angular lines, connected at an acute angle. The sensory system analyzes a stimulus into a set of such features. Then the brain compares this set against the lists of features of perhaps prototypes of objects in memory to find the best match. If there is a match, recognition occurs.

Feature analysis not only explains how people recognize stimuli that are exactly like familiar ones, but also perovides a plausible explanation for the fact that differnt stimuli can be given the same interpretaion. When you look at, say, a dachshund, Saint Bernard, of poodle, you recognize each animal as a dog, because each presents a pattern of features that corresponds to a stored catgory you know. But what happens when a combiation of features comes close to, but doesnot quite match, a stored perceptual category, as when you see a three—legged dog? here, the recognotion process places the stimulus in the closest category, while also noting the features that do not fit that category. thus, you say, "That's a dog with three legs" you do not say, "That's a milking stool ."

Figure 5.17
Limitations of Bottom–up processing
Because the same physical stimulus can be recognized in different ways from time to time, perceptual processing must depend in part on internal factors not just on the nature of the stimulus itself.

Feature analysis can nicely explain how a set of diverse stimuli (a dachshund and a Saint Bernard for example) can be assigned to one category as long as the stimuli share many of same features But feature analysis cannot easily explain how people handle ambiguous stimuli, assigning a stimulus sometimes to one category and sometimes to another. In Figure 5.10, for example, you could recognize the stimulus sometimes as a vase and sometimes as two faces. And in Figure 5.17, one stimulus pattern can be recognized as the number 13 or the letter B; another can be perceived as a lowercase b or as a baseball cap. Since these shifting recognition are based on the same stimulus patted the differences in perception cannot be attributed to feature analysis or some other bottom–up processing.

Top–down processing
The differences in your perception of patterns in Figure 5.18 must have something to do with the comet in which these stimuli are embedded. The ambiguous patterns are likely to be perceived in

relation to what is around them: they are perceived as a number when next to other numbers, as a letter when accompanied by other letters, as a hat when on top of a head. The context, creates an expectancy about what will be perceived. Along with motivation wants mad needs—expectancy is a major factor that influences perception through top-down processing.

Expectancy Look at Figure 5.18a. How old is the woman you see? Look again because like the vase-face example in Figure 5.10, this is an ambiguous figure. Some people immediately see attractive young woman wearing a feathered hat and turning her head away, Others see an old Hag with a large nose and a protruding chin (Boring, 1930).

Which one you recognize first can be influenced by what you expect to see. If you spent last summer working among high-fashion models, you might be more likely to see the young woman than if you had been working in a nursing home. The effect of expectancy was demon-stated in the laboratory by Robert Leper (1935) who showed people either Figure 5.18b, in which the young woman's strongly emphasized, or Figure 5.18c which makes the old woman stand. Then he showed Figure 5.18a, emphasizing the young woman continued to see her in the ambiguous figure, whereas the old woman was indentified first by those who seen the version emphasizing her.

Thus, past experience, like context, can create a certain expectancy, biasing perception toward one recognition or another under different circumstances. In other words, expectancy creates a **perceptual set**, a readiness or predisposition to perceive a stimulus in a certain way. This effect of expectancy applies to sounds as well as to sights. The raw sound "eye scream" takes on two very different meanings when heard in the context of "I scream whenever I am angry" as opposed to "I love ice cream."

The expectancy created by a familiar context can help people recognize objects. For example, in one experiment, people were shown a familiar scene, like a kitchen. Then they were given a very brief glimpse of an object that would be expected in that context (for example, a loaf of bread) or one that would be unexpected (for example, a mailbox). Although the two objects were roughly the same size and shape, the subjects more readily recognized the object that fit the context than the object that did not (Palmer, 1975). Similarly, in another experiment, people had a more difficult time recognizing objects when certain expected properties were violated (Biedermanet al. 1981). For example. in scenes like those in Figure 5.19, the fire hydrant was more easily perceived when it was on the ground than when it

Figure 5.18 An Ambiguous Figure (a)hich face do you see?(b)-(c) unambiguous portraits of the young and old woman, respectively.

• 123 •

was on the mailbox; the car was recognized more readily on the street than floating inside a house.

Motivation Suppose you are very hungry as you drive down the street of an unfamiliar city. You don't care if you find Barney's Diner or not; you'll eat anywhere. In this state of mind, you are likely to show many false alaims, slamming on the brakes and salivating at the sight of "Eaton's Furniture", "Burger's Body shop", Cherry Hill Estates, or any other sign that even hints at food.

Figure 5.19
Context and Recognition
These are examples of stimuli used by Biedeman et al. (1981). On the left, the fire hydrant is harder to perceive because it is in the wrong location and unsupported. On the right, the car is harder to see because of its inappropriate size and location. (From Human Factors, 1981.23,152–163. Copyright 1981, by the Human Factors society, Inc. and reproduced by permission).

Many motives besides hunger can alter perceptions. If you have ever watched an athletic contest, you probably remember a time when an obviously blind or demented referee incorrectly called a foul on the team you wanted to win. You knew the call was wrong because you clearly saw the other team player at fault. But suppose you had been cheering for the other team. the chances are good that you would have seen the same call as the right one. the effect of motivation on the categorization of ambiguous stimuli was also demonstrated in a classic laboratory study (Schafer & Murphy 1943). Figure 5.20 explains the experiment. The results indicated that people are biased toward recognizing stimuli that fall in a category that is associated with reward.

Top–down and Bottom–up Processes Together

Though we have discussed them separately, bottom–up and top–down processing work together in a constant interaction that creates the experience of a recognizable world. In fact, one kind of processing will "fill in" when the other becomes impaired. We described this phenomenon as closure when we discussed the perception of objects. In Figure 5.11d, for example, top–down processing took over to allow recognition of an object, even though the poor stimulus quality of an incomplete drawing made bottom up processing difficult.

For word recognition, too, top–down processing can compensate for an ambiguous stimulus that could not by itself promote good bottom–up processing. In fact, reading illustrates the interaction of bottom–up and top–down processing beautifully. Even when the quality of the

• 124 •

raw stimulus on the printed page becomes quite poor, top-down processes compensate to make continued reading possible.

They allow you to fill in where words are not well perceived and processed, thus giving a general idea of the meaning of the text. Even though the middle char-character in the words TAE and CAT may be of poor quality, the letters surrounding it provide a context that allows a top-down process to tell you it is an H in the first case and an A in the second. This sort of thing would not work if the world were not redundant, giving multiple clues about what is going on. If you lose or miss one stimulus in a pattern, others can fill in the gaps so that you can still recognize the total pattern. There is so much redundancy in written language, for example, that many of the words and letters you see are not needed. Fo-ex-mp-e y-u c-n-ad-hi-se-te-ce-it-ev-ry hi-dl-tt-rm-ss-ng.

For the spoken word, too, top-down processing can compensate for ambiguous stimuli, a fact that was nicely illustrated in a laboratory experiment in which subjects heard strings of five words, such as "wet brought who socks some," read in a background that was so noisy that an average of only 75 percent of the words could be recognized (Miller, Heise & Lichten, 1951), Under these conditions, "bottom-up" processing was difficult, because the quality of the raw stimuli was poor. But when the same words presented under the same noisy condition, they were reordered to make a meaningful sentence (for example, "who brought some wee socks"), a second group of subjects was able to recognize almost every word. In fact, in order to reduce their performance to tante of the first group, the noise level had to be doubled ! Why? When the word was no help in identifying the next. The meaningful sentence provided a more familiar context, allowing for some top-down processing in which hearing one word helpful the listener make a reasonable guess (based on knowledge and experience) about the others.

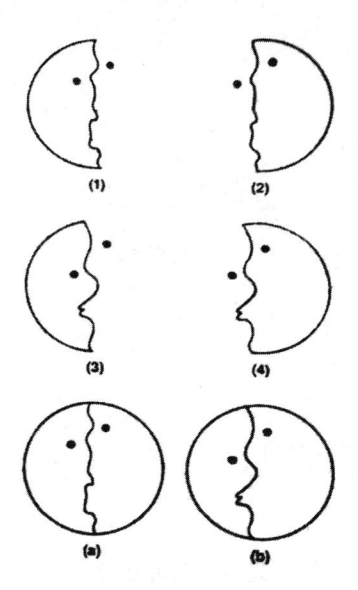

Research on the effect of top-down processing also shows how much truth there is in touch sayings as "beauty is in the eye of the beholder" Indeed, the reality that people perceive and often assume is just like only everyone else's is actually somewhat different for each person. This is not only important in understanding perceptual processes, but also, as we will discuss in Chapters 14 and 15 helpful understanding the basis of individual personalities and behavior disorders.

Figure 5.20
Motivation and Recognition
Schafer and Murphy (1943) trained people to associate names with profiles 1, 2, 3, and 4. The

people received money when two of the profiles were presented and lost money when the other two appeared. After trainings the propel were shown brief glimpses of ambiguous figures created by combining one rewarded and one punished profile (sections A and B) and were asked to name the face they perceived. The people reported seeing the rewarded face significantly more than half the time.

词汇 (Vocabulary)

1. absolute threshold   绝对阈限
2. accommodate   v. 调节
3. adaptive   adj. 适应的
4. automatically   adv. 无意识地
5. binocular disparity   双眼视差
6. blind spot   盲点
7. brightness constancy   明度恒常性
8. bottora-up processing   自下而上的加工
9. catch trial   捕捉试验
10. categorical   adj. 类别的、范畴的
11. closure   n. 闭合性组合
12. conservative response bias   保守性反应倾向
13. constructionist   n. 结构主义者
14. continuity   n. 连续组合
15. convergence   n. 辐复
16. cortex   n. 大脑皮质
17. decode   v. 解译
18. depth perception   深度知觉
19. Ebbinghaus illusion   艾宾浩斯错觉
20. ecological   adj. 生态学的
21. feature analysis   特征分析
22. Fechner's law   费希纳定律
23. figure and ground   对象和背景
24. gradient   梯度
25. grouping   n. 分组
26. hierarchical   adj. 等级制度的、分成等级的
27. hypnosis   n. 催眠状态
28. illusions of motion   运动错觉
29. illusions of shape, size and depth   形状、大小和深度错觉
30. induced motion   诱发性运动
31. inferential   adj. 可推理的、推论的
32. internal noise   内部干扰

33. interposition   n. 对象的重迭（遮挡）
34. just-noticeable difference (JND)   最小可觉差
35. knowledge based   以知识经验为基础的
36. linear perspective   线条透视
37. looming   n. 隐隐出现
38. match   n. 匹配物
39. Miller-Lyer illusion   缪勒—莱耶／错觉
40. moon illusion   月亮错觉
41. motivation   n. 动机
42. movement gradient   运动视觉梯度
43. neuious   n. 神经元
44. orientation   n. 定向组合
45. overlap   v. 部分重迭
46. perceptual apparatus   感觉器官
47. perceptual constancy   知觉恒常性
48. perceptual illusion   错觉
49. perceptual set   定势
50. phi phenomenon   n. 似动现象
51. Ponzo illusion   潘佐错觉
52. property   n. 特性、性质
53. proximity   n. 接近组合
54. psychophysics   n. 心理物理学
55. selective attention   选择性注意
56. sensory modality   感觉形式
57. sensation   n. 感觉
58. sensitivity   n. 敏感度
59. shape constancy   形状恒常性
60. signal detection theory   信号检测论
61. similarity   n. 相似组合
62. simplicity   n. 简单化组合
63. size constancy   大小恒常性
64. Steven's power law   史蒂文森神定律
65. stimulus cues   刺激线索
66. stroboscopic motion   频闪观测器运动
67. receiver operating characteristic curve (ROC curve)
    接收器操作特征曲线
68. reduced clarity   清晰度的减弱
69. relational   adj. 关联的
70. relative size   相对大小

71. response bias   反应倾向
72. response criterion   反应准则
73. retina (pl.) retinas/retinae   n. 视网膜
74. risky bias   冒险倾向
75. textual gradient   纹理梯度
76. timbre   n. 音质、音色
77. top-down processing   自上而下的加工
78. twisted cord   螺旋形曲线
79. visual dominance   视觉控制
80. Weber's law   韦伯定律
81. Wundt illusion   冯特错觉

第六章 注意与意识
(ATTENTION AND CONSCIOUSNESS)

本章要点（Chapter Outline）
什么是意识？（What is Consciousness?)
意识的状态（States of Consciousness)
注意与意识（Attention and Consciousness)
特殊的意识状态（Special Conscious State)

人类是动物界演化的最高产物，心理已发展到了意识水平，是心理发展的最高阶段。意识为人所特有的反映形式，是在人的劳动中和语言一道发生发展起来的。在人的一生中，意识也不是与生俱来的，新生婴儿在一段时间内只具有简单的心理，如感觉、知觉、情绪等，并没有意识，意识是通过后天活动中的学习才形成的。人具有了意识，就使活动有了目的性、方向性，使人能主动地适应世界和改造世界，使人具有了无限的创造力。意识的起源、本质、活动机制一直是人类科学之谜，吸引了历史上众多科学家为之呕心沥血，这种努力一直持续到现在。意识问题不仅在心理学理论中占中心地位，也与人类的生活息息相关。注意不是认识过程，而是心理过程的一种属性，是一种意识活动状态。这种属性是指人在认识事物过程中意识的指向和集中。一切认识过程如果没有注意的参加，就会变成视而不见、听而不闻，也就是所谓"心不在焉"。所以它是一切认识过程必不可少的条件和基础。

Consciousness is undeniably an important aspect of human behavior, yet very little is known about it. The fact that we have thoughts and feelings that we are aware (or conscious) of is perhaps one of the most distinctive qualities of human behavior. Thus the comprehensive study of behavior should attempt to understand what consciousness is and how it functions. The chief approach to the study of consciousness has been to study altered or abnormal states of consciousness in the hope that a complete analysis of altered states will shed light on the meaning of normal consciousness.

Any instance in which the overall functioning of one's mind takes on a pattern quite different from normal is called an altered state of consciousness (abbreviated SoC). In our normal, waking SoC there are many variations in function, aside from the particular thoughts that we are aware of at any moment. Some days our mental processes seem sharp, other days dull. Sometimes we sense the world in a very clear fashion, other times we feel isolated from it, as, for example, in the simple case of having a cold. Such quantitative variations are all within the normal or ordinary SoC. Yet when we wake up from a dream or if we have taken a powerful psychedelic drug, we feel that the overall functioning of our consciousness was in a qualitatively different pattern, not just as if we experienced a little more or less of some aspect of ordinary consciousness. Altered SoCs have attracted considerable interest and excitement because of the extraordinary psychological phenomena said to accompany them, such as profound insights, bizarre visions and perceptions, and incredible relaxation.

Knowledge about SoCs comes from a variety of sources, including commonsense assumptions based on personal experience, philosophical speculation, metaphysical and spiritual doctrines and observations, and (probably the smallest category) "hard" scientific data. The emphasis in this chapter will be on scientific knowledge, although this is often so fragmentary that knowledge from other domains is used to round out our discussion. The major kinds of altered states we will discuss are draining, out-of-body experiences, hypnosis, possession states, alcohol intoxication, marijuana intoxication, psychedelic experience, meditation, and biofeedback-induced states.

For each SoC discussed, we will look at a variety of psychological processes, including the subject's perceptions and awareness, emotions, cognitive processes, subconscious processes, memory functions, feelings of identity, perception of time, and moto functions. Often, however, some of these categories will be omitted, for our knowledge of most SoCs is far from complete. For convenience, we will diverge from our usual two-part chapter organization and mention applications and uses as each SoC is examined. Much of our knowledge about SoC is examined. Much of our knowledge about SoC comes directly from anecdotes involving applications, and at this point there is no clear or sensible way to separate what we know from what it means.

It is difficult to know exactly where, in a book that plans to progress from simple to complex principles, to locate a discussion of altered states. We have chosen to undertake the discussion at this point, even though some of the topics covered are directly connected with later analyses of personality, because our information about altered states primarily concerns relatively simple behaviors involving perceptual, motor, and learning processes. But, admittedly, our decision was largely arbitrary.

第一节 什么是意识
(WHAT IS CONSCIOUSNESS)

The definition of consciousness has tantalized philosophers for centuries and psychologists for a hundred years, yet no common answer is in sight (Ornstein, 1977). Natsoulas (1978, 1983) has identified seven meanings of the term. Loosely, consciousness may be said to be current awareness of external and internal stimuli, that is, of objects in the environment and of bodily sensations, memories, daydreams, and thoughts. But how should the attributes and aspects of consciousness be described?

In Western civilization, a spatial metaphor, or image, has typically been used to characterize the conscious mind (Jaynes, 1976, pp. 54-56). People speak of or consider their minds as containers or spaces in which ideas and memories are stored (Lakoff and Johnson, 1980; Roediger, 1980). They hold ideas in mind, or they have idea in the front or back or at the top of their minds. Ideas may also lie in the mind's dark corners or dim recesses. Some people are said to have broad or deep or open minds, while others' minds are described as narrow. shallow, or closed. Consciousness, accordingly, can be thought of as the processes that occur in this mental arena the spotlight of the mental space and events which people are currently aware of stand in the spotlight of consciousness.

William James, using a rather different metaphor, described consciousness as a "stream" of awareness. He wrote, "Our normal waking consciousness, rational consciousness as we call it, is but one special type of consciousness, whilst all about it, parted from it by the filmiest of screens, there lie potential forms of consciousness entirely different (1902).

A primary quality of normal, rational consciousness is that it is limited in capacity. People can be conscious of only so many things sensations of external objects or internal memories and thoughts at one time. One related issue, then is attention: how can people pay attention to some things and ignore others, even when the others may be more intrusive? But before we explore the answer and delve into unusual states of consciousness (sleep, dreams, hypnosis, meditation, and the effects of drugs), we must make some distinctions among states of consciousness.

Problems with studying consciousness. The study of consciousness has recently become a subject of renewed interest to psychologists. For some years past, the subject had received little scientific attention, primarily because the behavioristic viewpoint dominated psychological research for so long. Behaviorists, as we have seen, will accept only measures of overt performance as legitimate scientific data, and the primary data about SoCs come from subjects' introspective reports of their perceptions and experience. Behaviorists have continually warned against the use of self-reports in psychological studies because such reports are apt to be incomplete and biased. Still, self-reports are forms of behavior after all, and their potential scientific value cannot be entirely overlooked.

A more important problem in the scientific study of SoCs is the frequent report of many subjects that certain aspects of their experience are ineffable that is, cannot be put into words. There are three ways this kind of data can be handled. First, the psychologist can investigate what can be readily investigated and simply note but not otherwise treat reports of ineffable experiences. Second, he may attempt to develop more adequate language for communicating the experiences of altered SoCs. Or finally, he may attempt to induce the same SoC in himself, and then, although the experience itself may not be expressible in words, he may be able to communicate about it with other people who have had the same experience. From their combined discussions, a more adequate way of communicating to others might evolve. The latter approach is regarded with suspicion by many psychologists, although it is not necessarily incompatible with the basic tenets of science. The ambivalence about this approach was manifested during the peak of research on LSD in the early 1960s. Investigators who had not take the drug themselves were accused of being basically ignorant of the phenomena they were supposed to be studying, while those who had taken the drug were accused of having lost their objectivity!

The problem of obtaining unbiased data about SoCs is further compounded by the fact that the particular content of many SoCs is highly responsive to what the subject expects to happen. For example, research has shown that hypnotic behavior depends on the instructions given the subject about what will take place when he is hypnotized. People's expectations can determine the specific experiences they have without their realizing it. When LSD was first extensively investigated by psychiatrists who conceived of it as a way of creating model psychoses, many psychotic symptoms were manifested by those taking the drug. In retrospect, it is clear that psychotic symptoms can be experienced with LSD if the expectations given to the subject call these forth, but they are not an inevitable effect. Thus the observer is a focal part of the observation process in studies of SoCs, and the characteristics of the investigator—observer must be taken into account in interpreting the data. At present there is no certain way of doing this, and as a result, much of the data that have been obtained are contaminated by the (unknown) biases of the observers.

第二节　意识的状态
(STATES OF CONSCIOUSNESS)

Psychologists have found it useful to distinguish four mental states: conscious, preconscious, unconscious, and no conscious. External and internal events on which the mental spotlight is focused are said to be in consciousness. Not many memories and thoughts will be in consciousness at any one time, and they may be in either preconscious or unconscious states.

If memories can be called into consciousness fairly easily, they are described as being in a preconscious state. For example, as you read this you may not be thinking of the name of your psychology professor, or the names of your best friends, or your brothers and sisters. Yet if you are asked for them, they are available in memory, and immediately accessible to conscious experience (Tulving&pearlstone, 1966).

Unconscious ideas and memories are those that cannot be brought to mind easily. Sigmund Freud popularized the idea that many important memories and thoughts reside in an unconscious state. Through his study of neurotic patients, Freud came to believe that the major factor in emotional problems was childhood trauma. Memories of painful experiences were repressed, or converted into an unconscious mental state, from which they could not easily be made conscious.

The concept of the unconscious remains controversial in modem psychology. Psychologists often try to study phenomena of the unobservable inner world of the mind indirectly by observing overt behavior, just as astrophysicists strive to demystify black holes in space by noting their effects on light and neighboring bodies. Since unconscious mental processes, like black holes, cannot be observed directly, how can psychologists measure repressed memories? If repression simply embodies any memories that are not easily called into consciousness then repression undoubtedly occurs (Erdelyi &Goldberg, 1979). But if repression is taken to mean the unconscious suppression of a painful last, it becomes harder to study.

It is important to distinguish unconscious from no conscious mental processes. We categorize a process as no conscious when it cannot be hauled into consciousness, but as unconscious if it can be brought into consciousness, but only with great difficulty. Many processes go on in our bodies of which we are not aware. For example, we are not directly conscious of the workings of the rods and cones of our eyes described in Chapter 3, or of the chemicals in the blood coursing through our arteries and veins, or of the functioning of the kidneys, lungs, and heart, which the autonomic nervous system controls. We can become conscious of the effects of no conscious processes—heavy breathing, a pounding heart—but we cannot normally become conscious of the processes themselves.

Freud summarized these distinctions in a colorful metaphor in which he likens the different states of consciousness of ideas to their presence in different rooms of a house(1924, pp. 305–306). The crudest conception of these systems conscious, unconscious, and preconscious states is the one we shall find most convenient a spatial one. The unconscious system may therefore be compared to a large anteroom, in which the various mental excitations are crowding upon one another, like individual beings. Adjoining this is a second, smaller apartment, a sort of reception room, in which consciousness resides. But on the threshold between the two there stands a personage with the office of doorkeeper, who examines the various mental excitations, censors them, and denies them admittance to the reception room when he disapproves of them...Now this metaphor may be employed to widen our terminology. The excitations in the unconscious; in the antechamber, not visible to consciousness, which is of course in the other room, so to begin with they remain unconscious. When they have pressed forward to the threshold and been turned back by the doorkeeper they are "incapable of becoming conscious" ; we call them then repressed. But even those excitations which are allowed over the or threshold do not necessarily become conscious; they can only become so if they succeed in attracting the eye of consciousness. This second chamber therefore may be suitably called the preconscious system.

States of Consciousness and You

A recent Gallup poll showed that some 50 percent of college students had tried marijuana, many had used more powerful psychedelic drugs, and many are practicing various kinds of meditation. Thus the topic of SoCs is not only of intellectual interest but also of great personal interest to many students. The question of Should I try to alter my SoCs by such—and—such a method is a real one for many students, and it must be answered by the individual himself. But the decision should be made in the light of available knowledge, which, at best, is very slim. We will briefly discuss some of the known advantages of experiencing altered SoCs and some of the disadvantages.

The advantages claimed for such SoCs as meditative states and drug—induced states are of two kinds, namely, psychological pleasure and insights and spiritual insights. For example, the experienced marijuana user not only reports greatly enhanced pleasure in all that he does but also commonly feels that he has obtained important psychological insights that contribute to his personal growth. Similarly, systematic use of some meditative SoCs is claimed by some to aid spiritual growth, a process extending beyond physiological or normal psychological growth. In this context, spiritual growth is defined in terms of actualizing various human potentialities that supposedly put one in a more harmonious relationship with the universe or God.

On the other hand, the dangers of experiencing some SoCs are real. A person knowledge of the possible dangers must be weighed against the possible advantages, and, if the person goes ahead, he should realize that he is taking a calculated risk. We can consider four broad categories of dangers: physical, psychological, legal, and spiritual.

Physical dangers may come about through the exertion required in some meditative techniques or through the deleterious side effects of some drugs. Psychological dangers may result from a person coming into contact with repressed aspects of his personality that he cannot defend himself against in the altered SoCs, thus experiencing traumatic emotional difficulties. For some people who are already neurotic or prepsychotic, the experience of an altered SoC can act as a trigger to a psychotic episode. The legal dangers apply primarily to the use of drugs; most psychedelic drugs are illegal in the United States, and there are severe penalties for their possession. Regardless of whether one feels that laws are just, spending time in jail is not only unpleasant but generally results in adverse effects on ones psychological health.

In traditional spiritual disciplines the systematic and supervised use of altered SoCs is considered necessary for certain aspects of spiritual growth, but the same techniques and SoCs are often considered highly dangerous if indulged in without proper guidance. A particular spiritual danger, especially with drug–induced states, is that a person will generate and become attached to a counterfeit of a real spiritual experience, thus blocking his further progress.

We conclude with an apology for the sorry state of scientific knowledge about psychological processes under altered SoCs. This lack of knowledge is regrettable, for the topic is both fascinating and important. Unfortunately, in the past there has been considerable resistance by the general public and reluctance by trained psychologists to undertake research on altered states. But, although the area has been an unfashionable one, all signs point to a rapidly changing awareness of and growing interest in these phenomena among psychologists. The immediate future promises much more penetrating psychological analyses of altered SoCs than can be offered at this writing.

Certainly the general public is now greatly intrigued by the phenomena of altered SoCs. In fact, the public often does not exhibit intelligent skepticism about the topics we have discussed here. We do not believe that the validity of all these phenomena has been adequately demonstrated. we wish to conclude this chapter by pointing out that there is ample reason to be skeptical about how to interpret the reality and uniqueness of many of the topics in this chapter, particularly phenomena such as possession states, lucid dreaming, and Our knowledge in these areas is so minimal that there is reason to doubt whether the phenomena are qualitatively different from other more established and better understood behaviors. For example, is a possession state any different from what we typically refer to as mental illness? Even the validity of hypnosis as a separate state of consciousness is doubted by some investigators.

The topics covered in this chapter are about as controversial as any topics in psychology. We hope that you will not blindly accept everything you hear and read about such phenomena. But it is probably just as foolish to decide blindly that any phenomenon you do not understand is not a real one. It is only through careful, tedious, objective analysis that an understanding of consciousness will emerge. Until then, retain a healthy skepticism and an objective, inquisitive mind.

第三节 注意与意识
(ATTENTION AND CONSCIOUSNESS)

More things happen than a person can attend to at any one time; the frequently resulting state is called **information overload**. Thus, people need to concentrate on only part of the information available and to ignore other events. Attention may be defined as a focusing of perception that leads to a greater awareness of a limited number of stimuli. In terms of our earlier metaphor, stimuli to which people pay attention are in the spotlight of consciousness. How do people decide where to direct the spotlight of consciousness? As you stare at this page you could be paying attention to the voice of a radio disc jockey or to other noise in the background, or to a tingling in your feet, or to the rumbling of a hungry stomach. You could be daydreaming, having sexual fantasies, remembering what happened to you last night, or planning what you will do tomorrow. As you well know, paying attention to what you are reading is often difficult. Competition among many stimuli impedes concentration on one type of information to the exclusion of others.

Selective Attention

Paying attention to some things and ignoring others is described as selective attention. How does someone select one message from the environment and ignore others? Psychologists came interested in this question in the 1950s when they were asked to solve a problem involving the information overload with they were asked to solve a problem involving the information overload with which air traffic controllers were burdened. To coordinate departures and arrivals and prevent mid-air collisions, the controllers had to receive reports from a number of pilots and to tell each what to do, without help from today's electronic wizardry. Pilots voices and messages often sounded alike, so controllers erred on occasion, with regrettable results. The psychologists' assignment was to determine how a controller could attend to one important message amid competition from other messages.

To study the problem, the psychologists devised a test called **speech shadowing** (Cherry, 1953). The subject wore headphones through which two different messages entered, one sent to each ear. The listener was instructed to repeat back as well as possible all the words that reached one ear and to try to ignore the words that entered the other ear. Imagine that the message to the right ear was about astronomy and the one to the left ear about baseball. You can get some idea of what this experiment was like by placing yourself between two radios (or a radio and a television set) tuned to different channels on which there is continuous chatter. Try to repeat back everything you hear from one source and to ignore the other.

The result of your experiment should confirm what psychologists found in the 1950s. Even when the accepted message was delivered at 150 words per minute, much faster than normal speech, its recipient could repeat it back with few errors and remembered it fairly effectively. The rejected message was remembered poorly. One experimenter reported that people he tested could not recognize the rejected message above a chance level even when it was repeated 35 times (Moray, 1959). Information for a single sound may be retained for a second or two, but then it was lost(Glucksberg & G'wan, 1970) . Since the two messages usually are equally loud and otherwise physically similar, poor memory for the rejected message is purely psychological, reflecting lack of attention to the material. The psychologists working on the air controllers' problem helped to solve it by discovering the characteristics that make messages easily distinguishable. Almost any physical differences between messages, such as those of loudness or pitch, aid selective attention (Cherry. 1953).

A considerably less crucial but much more common example of information overload shows up at noisy parties. You may be listening to someone speaking softly while loud conversations go on about you, and music adds to the din. You follow one voice and ignore the others by selective attention, an experience sometimes called the cocktail party phenomenon. Both auditory cues and visual ones since you look at the face of your partner in the conversation arc employed .But what really happens in a scientific sense?

Models of Attention

Since the mid 1950s, psychologists have developed several different models to explain selective attention. We consider the most prominent examples here.

FILTER THEORY. The first important theory of how attention works was developed by Donald Broadbent(1957,1958); it is called **filter theory**. Broadbent proposed that just as engineers can map the flow or electricity through a wiring system, psychologists could chart the passage of information through the mind. He postulated the existence of two general systems, the sensory and the perceptual, with different properties. The sensory system retains information only briefly after it reaches the sense organs. It can hold more than one sort of information at the same time, so it is said to have parallel transmission. The perceptual system is roughly equivalent to conscious attention. It selects one of the signals in the sensory system and decides what to pay attention to, according to the individuals current needs. Broadbent(1958) held that processing in the perceptual system was serial, with a person paying attention to one thing, then another. He also assumed that if the perceptual system did not process information soon after it reached the sensory system, the information would be lost. Thus, he assumed that there was a filter between the sensory and perceptual systems that screened out data that was not selected by the perceptual system. Hence, the theory was named after its crucial active component.

The basic problem of selective attention is to discover how it is possible to attend to one message in the face of other competing messages that may be equally prominent perceptually. Broadbent's filter theory proposed that the competing messages are filtered out at the level of the senses, before the information is processed. Since the attended signal is selected early in processing for further attention, filter theory can be called an early selection theory of attention.

Filter theory has been used to help explain many everyday experiences. For instance, if you are listening intently to one conversation at a cocktail party, you are barely aware of the others which seem to be "filtered out" before their meaning is processed. But if your name is mentioned nearby, you often hear it and switch your attention. If you are filtering out the other conversations at a sensory level, before you have determined the meaning of the signal, how can you catch your name in a competing conversation? Broadbent suggested that people did so by occasionally switching the setting of the filter to other perceptual channels to sample the information there, as a shortwave radio fan might twist the dials to hear what Radio Moscow or Radio Beijing was proclaiming. On the other hand, contrary to Broadbent's filter theory, the words from another conversation might not be filtered out at a sensory level, but may be unconsciously perceived. Important signals, such as your name, would break through into consciousness after their unconscious registration. If signals from the environment are registered without benefit of conscious attention, then it may be that the effect of attention does not occur at a sensory level (as Broadbent theorized), but later in the sequence of perceptual processes. This possibility is realized in late selection theories of attention.

LATE SELECTION MODELS. Broadbent's filter theory was important because it was the first model of attention. Also important was the theory demonstration that mental processes could be conceived as a flow of information. However, the validity of the idea is contradicted by evidence that not all information in ignored messages is screened out at the level of the senses.

The mind seems to process some signals automatically without conscious awareness. In one experiment Neville Moray (1959) delivered different messages to the subjects two ears, and required the recipients to repeat one of the messages; however, he occasionally instructed his subjects, through the headphones, to switch their attention from one message to the other. If the subjects were repeating the baseball message entering the right ear, they might be told to attend to the message about astronomy in the left ear. When Moray embedded the instruction in the accepted message, the subjects usually switched without trouble, but when the instruction was put in the rejected message, they missed it every time.

This part of the experiment supports filter theory. If the rejected message were filtered out before it had been processed beyond the sensory level, the listener would not perceive the instruction and so could not act on it. However, when the instruction to switch ears was placed in the rejected message and was preceded by the subject's name(Mary, switch ears). Moray found that it was followed 30 percent of the time. Thus it must be concluded that ignored information is not shut out the level of the senses; some of it apparently seeps through, to be processed for meaning. A person's name is a particularly sensitive cue that seems to be perceived almost automatically.

Evidence thus mounts that ignored information is not filtered out at a sensory level, Instead, as with the example above, automatic processing occurs for some information of which people are unaware. This indicates the existence of unconscious perceptual processes, an example of which is discussed in "The Research process" (see below).

Most current theories of attention assume a **late selection**, that is, cheesing information after a sensory level (e.g, Norman, 1969; Schneider & Shiffrin, 1977). These theories maintain that although people are still not conscious of the different signals at that point, some kind of decision making opens the door to consciousness for the most important or expected signal. (See Figure 6.1 for a schematic outline of "late selection" model of attention, contrasted with filter theory.) Such unconscious perception is called **subliminal perception**, which describes perception of things below the threshold of awareness (Dixon, 1971; Erdelyi, 1974). Controversy has swirled about the concept for years, but there do seem to be several good demonstrations of it, such as the one recounted in "The Research Process." Subliminal perception is difficult to substantiate, however, and any effects of subliminal stimuli are probably short−lived.

A   FILTER (EARLY SELECTOIN)

Stimuli → → → → Sensory Registration (S) → Perceptual Analysis (P) → Selection of Response

B A LATE SELECTION THEORY

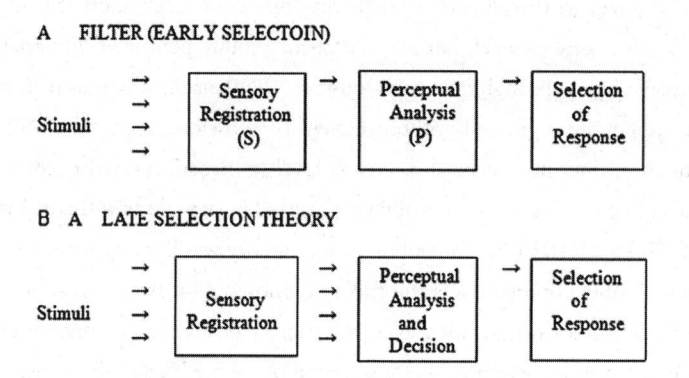

Stimuli → → → → Sensory Registration → → → → Perceptual Analysis and Decision → Selection of Response

Figure 6.1
Two Models of Selective Attention
According to filter theory (A), a person selectively attends to information by filtering at a sensory level. The signal that receives perceptual analyses guides a person s response. According to late selection theories(B), all stimuli receive some perceptual processing but only one is attended to and is used to make responses.

Automatic and Controlled Processing

Researchers interested in consciousness and attention have recently proposed a distinction between **automatic and controlled processing** (Posner and Snyder, 1975; Schneider and Shiffrin, 1977). The basic idea is that some mental (and physical) processes are under a person conscious control, while others occur automatically without one's awareness or intention. When you were learning to drive, steering the car, shifting gears, and using the accelerator and brake required much effort. You had to concentrate simply to stay on the road. This attention is an example of controlled processing. However, once a person has learned to drive, the same activities take little mental effort. The skilled driver can hold a conversation or listen to the radio while cruising the highway. The act of driving has become more automatic, so mental effort can be diverted to other tasks with no loss in driving efficiency. Of course, if some new event arises a child runs into the road it would be necessary once again to shift attention to driving and away from conversation. Many drivers say they sometimes suddenly snap to on the highway and realize that they have not been paying attention to what they were doing for minutes, as though they were driving on automatic pilot.

Another chore that seems to involve automatic processing is the **stroop task**, named for its discoverer (Stroop, 1935). In this experiment people identify colors as rapidly as they can. In one control condition people name patches of color, and in a second control condition words are written in different colors and people name the ink colors (not the words) as fast as possible. Ina third condition, the one of greatest interest, people again name the ink colors, but this time the words are the names of other colors. So, for example, a person may see the word red written in blue ink and their task would be to say "blue." (An example of the Stroop task is in Color plate 12). The finding from this experiment is that people name the ink colors much more slowly in the third condition, when the words name colors other than the ink colors. People are somewhat slower at naming the ink colors when they form unrelated words than at naming color patches, but this difference is quite small when compared to the case in which the words are color names (Dyer, 1973).

To try this experiment, you should time yourself as you name the ink color in each of the three panels of color Plate 12. Most people find naming colors in the third condition a relatively slow and frustrating experience.

The difficulty in performing the Stroop task is usually taken to indicate that people read words automatically. When a person sees the word blue and is supposed to respond with the name of the color of ink—black in this case the name of the word is automatically activated nonetheless. Even people who have been given extended practice at the Stroop task and have been told to try to suppress or ignore the printed word are still slower to name the colors in the third condition (Dyer, 1973). Apparently, reading is such an overlearned skill that people cannot avoid reading words presented to them. (Try looking at a word but disregarding its meaning). One theory of the Stroop effect is that there is a mental race between processes involved in naming the color and those in reading the word. Since people have much more practice in reading words than in naming colors, the reading response wins the race and slows color naming. The difficulty in performing the Stroop task is then attributed to automatic processes, ones that occur without a person's volition (or even contrary to it) and cannot be brought under conscious control. (However, Logan and Zbrodorr; 1979 have argued that some measure of conscious control can be brought to bear in the Stroop task).

Posner and Snyder (1975) have proposed a general theory to distinguish automatic from controlled processing. By this theory, a person processes an event automatically if processing (a) is rapid, (b) does not depend on a persons's trategy, and (c) does not take cognitive resources, or conscious attention. Controlled processing, on the other hand, (a) occurs more slowly, (b) depends on a persons's trategy, and (c) uses limited cognitive resources.

SUMMARY

1. Consciousness is the current awareness of internal and external stimuli. Its capacity is limited, so that there are only so many things of which individuals can be conscious at one time. Preconscious ideas can easily be called into consciousness, while unconscious thoughts cannot be easily retrieved. Nonconscious processes are those which, in principle, we cannot be aware of.

2. People often must deal with information overload, when more things happen to them

than they can attend to. The problem of selective attention is how to concentrate on one stimulus and ignore others. Broadbent's filter theory maintained that people filtered out ignored signals at the level of the senses. Experimental evidence has caused others to reject this view; they think that attention does not affect sensory processes, and that information is selected for attention only after it has been processed by the senses. These are called late selection theories.

3. There are two kinds of processing of information: automatic and controlled. One theory proposes that automatic processing occurs rapidly; it does not depend on a person's strategy, or method of approaching a task; and it does not require conscious attention, or cognitive resources. Controlled processing is the opposite: it is slower, depends on a person's strategy, and uses cognitive resources.

4. The brain's two hemispheres specialize in different activities in most people. The left hemisphere controls verbal tasks, such as speech production, while the right hemisphere commands imaginable and spatial abilities. The unity of consciousness is maintained by communication via the corpus callosum. In people whose corpus callosum has been surgically severed, tests show that in some circumstances the two hemispheres compete to direct behavior.

5. The origins of consciousness are not easily discovered. Jaynes has proposed that consciousness has existed in humans only for the last 2,000 to 3,000 years, Before consciousness was developed, according to Jaynes, the right hemisphere exerted control of behavior by sending the left hemisphere instructions as auditory hallucinations, or "voices of the gods." Jaynes's theory has generated a good deal of controversy.

6. An altered state of consciousness is experienced daily when people sleep and dream. Sleep is studied through analyzing patterns of brain waves. There are five distinct stages of sleep. The one that has attracted the most attention is Rapid Eye Movement, or REM, sleep. In this stage, the brain gives off electrical signals similar to those emitted when people are awake.

7. When people are deprived of sleep, they response in widely different ways, so no firm conclusions can be drawn currently about the effects of sleep deprivation, or the functions and purpose of sleep.

8. The function of dreams is also not clear. However, if people are kept from dreaming, they dream more than normal on later nights. This phenomenon is termed REM rebound.

9. Insomnia embraces a variety of sleep disorders. Almost everyone occasionally suffers from situational insomnia, brought on by stress. Arrhythmic insomnia may occur after jet travel or with a job with other than usual daylight hours. In sleep apnea, people stop breathing when asleep; in narcolepsy, they fall asleep uncontrollably no matter what they are doing.

10. The hypnotic trance may be a special state of consciousness in which people are quite responsive to others' suggestions. Often, hypnotized people can do things which they could not door would not try to do when they were not hypnotized. People cannot be hypnotized against their will, and they were not hypnotized. People cannot be hypnotized against their will, and they will not perform antisocial acts under hypnosis. People differ greatly in how susceptible they are to hypnotic suggestion.

11. Drugs are frequently used to alter consciousness. Stimulants are used to perk people up, but strong ones may lead to addiction. Depressants are used as relaxants, but they may affect coordination. When depressants such as sleeping pills and alcohol are combined, they may kill. Hallucinogens produce vivid hallucinations that some people believe reveal a hidden reality. Most strong drugs have negative effects on the physiology of the body and are addictive. Their use outside the field of medicine is usually illegal.

第四节 特殊的意识状态
(SPECIAL COUSCIOUS STATE)

Sleep and Functions of Sleep

Why do you sleep? "That's easy," you reply. "I sleep because I get tired." Well, yes, but you are not tired in the sense of muscle fatigue. You need almost as much sleep after a day of sitting around the house as after a day of intense physical or mental activity (Horne & Minard, 1985; Shapiro Bortz, Mitchell, Bartel, & Jooste, 1981). Furthermore you could rest your muscles just as well while awake as while asleep. (In fact, if your muscles ache after strenuous exercise, you probably find it difficult to sleep.) You feel tired at the end of the day because inhibitory processes in your brain force you to become less aroused and less alert. That is, we evolved mechanisms to force us to sleep.

Sleep serves many functions. During sleep, we rest our muscles, decrease metabolism, rebuild proteins in the brain (Kong et al., 2002), reorganize synapses, and strengthen memories (Sejnowski & Destexhe, 2000). People deprived of sleep have trouble concentrating and become more vulnerable to illness. Young adults deprived of a night's sleep show deficits on memory tasks (Yoo, Hu, Gujar, Jolesz, & Walker, 2007). Mice deprived of sleep for even 4 hours show impairments in their ability to alter synaptic activity (Kopp, Longordo, Nicholson, & Lü thi, 2006) Clearly, we need to sleep for many reasons.

Stages of Sleep

How does brain activity change when you fall asleep? Sleep activity can be measured with an electroencephalograph (eh-LEK-troen-SEF-uh-lo-graf), or EEG. The brain generates tiny electrical signals(brain waves) that can be amplified and recorded. When you are awake and alert, the EEG reveals a pattern of small fast waves called beta waves (Figure 6.2). Immediately before sleep, the pattern shifts to larger and slower waves called alpha waves. (Alpha waves also occur when you are relaxed and allow your thoughts to drift.) As the eyes close, breathing becomes slow and regular, the pulse rate slows, and body temperature drops. Soon after, four separate sleep stages occur.

Stage 1

As you enter light sleep (stage 1 sleep), your heart rate slows even more. Breathing becomes more irregular. The muscles of your body relax. This may trigger a reflex muscle twitch called a hypnic (HIP-nik: sleep) jerk. (This is quite normal, so have no fear about admitting to your friends that you fell asleep with a hypnic jerk.) In stage 1 sleep the EEG is made up mainly of small, irregular waves with some alpha waves. Persons awakened at this time may or may not say they were asleep.

Stage 2

As sleep deepens, body temperature drops further. Also, the EEG begins to include sleep spindles, which are short bursts of distinctive brain-wave activity (Gottselig, Bassetti, & Achermann, 2002). Spindles seem to mark the true boundary of sleep. Within 4 minutes after spindles appear, most people will say they were asleep.

Stage 3

In stage 3, a new brain wave, the delta wave, begins to appear. Delta waves are very large and slow. They signal a move to deeper sleep and a further loss of consciousness.

Stage 4

Most people reach deep sleep (the deepest level of normal sleep) in about 1 hour. Stage 4 brain waves are almost pure delta, and the sleeper is in a state of oblivion. If you make a loud noise during stage 4, the sleeper will wake up in a state of confusion and may not remember the noise. After spending some time in stage 4. the sleeper returns (through stages 3 and 2) to stage 1. Further shifts deeper and lighter sleep occur throughout the night.

Changes in brain-wave patterns associated with various stages of sleep. Actually, most wave types are present at all times, but they occur more or less frequently in various sleep stages.

Dreams

Ordinary Dreaming Ordinary dreaming refers to the experience almost all of us have had of waking up and recalling scenes and events that seemed to take place in a nonphysical world, a world we retrospectively consider to be purely imaginary. Although there have been many laboratory and home studies of dreams, most people in our culture have not learned to be good observers of their dreams. Thus much of what is known about dreams has come from piecing together the reports of poor observers.

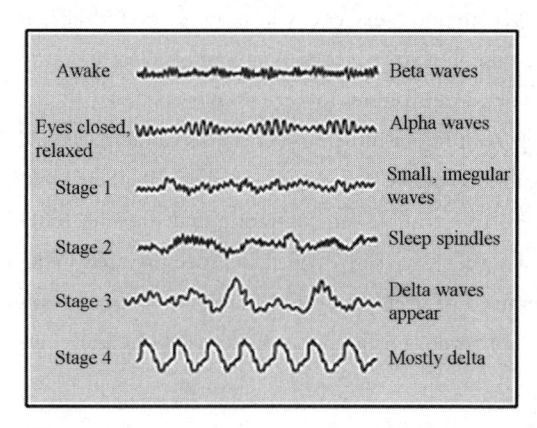

Figure 6.2
Brain waves, sleep, and dreaming

Functions of REM Sleep

An average person spends about one third of his or her life asleep and about one fifth of sleep in REM, totaling about 600 hours of REM per year. Presumably, REM serves a biological function. But what is it?

One hypothesis is that REM is important for memory storage, especially for weakening the inappropriate connections (Crick & Mitchison, 1983). REM and non-REM sleep may be important for consolidating different types of memories. Depriving people of sleep early in the night (mostly non-REM sleep) impairs verbal learning, such as memorizing a list of words, whereas depriving people of sleep during the second half of the night (more REM) impairs consolidation of learned motor skills (Gais, Plihal, Wagner, & Born, 2000; Plihal & Born, 1997).

Another hypothesis sounds odd because we tend to imagine a glamorous role for REM sleep: David Maurice (1998) proposed that REM just shakes the eyeballs back and forth enough to get sufficient oxygen to the corneas of the eyes. The corneas, unlike the rest of the body, get oxygen directly from the surrounding air. During sleep, because they are shielded from the air, they deteriorate slightly (Hoffmann & Curio, 2003). They do get some oxygen from the fluid behind them, but when the eyes are motionless, that fluid becomes stagnant. Moving the eyes increases the oxygen supply to the corneas. According to this view, REM is a way of arousing a sleeper just enough to shake the eyes back and forth, and the other manifestations of REM—including dreams are just by products.

Dream Theories

Psychodynamic Dream Theory

Sigmund Freud's landmark book, The Interpretation of Dreams (1900), first advanced the idea that many dreams are based on wish fulfillment (an expression of unconscious desires). Thus, a student who is angry with a teacher might dream of embarrassing the teacher in class, a lonely person may dream of romance, or a hungry child may dream of food.

Freud's psychodynamic theory of dreaming emphasizes internal conflicts and unconscious forces. Although many of his ideas are attractive, there is evidence against them. For example, volunteers in a study of starvation showed no particular increase in dreams about food and eating. In general, dreams show few signs of directly expressing hidden wishes (Fisher & Greenberg, 1996).

Freud's response to critics, no doubt, would have been that dreams rarely express needs so directly. One of Freud's key insights is that ideas in dreams are expressed as images or pictures, rather than in words. Freud believed that dreams express unconscious desires and conflicts as disguised dream symbols (images that have deeper symbolic meaning). For instance, death might be symbolized by a journey; children, by small animals; or sexual intercourse, by horseback riding or dancing. Similarly, a woman sexually attracted to her best friend's husband might dream of stealing her friend's wedding ring and placing it on her own hand, an indirect symbol of her true desires.

Do all dreams have hidden meanings? Probably not. Even Freud realized that some dreams are trivial "day residues" or carryovers From ordinary waking events. On the other hand, dreams do tend to reflect a person's current concerns, so Freud wasn't entirely wrong (Nikles et al., 1998).

The Activation–Synthesis Hypothesis

Psychiatrists Allan Hobson and Robert McCarley have a radically different view of dreaming. They believe that during REM sleep, brain cells that normally control eye movements, balance, and actions are activated. However, messages from the cells are blocked from reaching the body so no movement occurs. Nevertheless, the cells continue to tell higher brain areas of their activities. Struggling to interpret this information the brain searches through stored memories and manufactures a dream (Hobson, 2000).

How does that help explain dream content? Let's use the classic chase dream as an example. In such dreams we feel we are running but not going anywhere. This occurs because the brain is told the body is running, but it gets no feedback from the motionless legs. To make sense of this information, the brain creates a chase drama. A similar process probably explains dreams of floating or flying.

Hobson and McCarley call their view the activation-synthesis hypothesis. Hobson explains that several parts of the brain are "turned on" (activated) during REM sleep. This triggers sensations, motor commands, and memories. The cortex of the brain, which also becomes more active during REM sleep, synthesizes this activity into stories and visual images. However, frontal areas of the cortex, which control higher mental abilities, are mostly shut down during REM sleep. This explains why dreams are more primitive and more bizarre than daytime thoughts (Hobson, 2000). Viewed this way, dreams are merely a different type of thinking that occurs during sleep (McCarley, 1998).

Note that the activation-synthesis hypothesis doesn't rule out the idea that dreams have meaning. Because dreams are created from memories and past experiences, they can tell us quite a lot about a person's mental life, emotions, and concerns (Hobson,2000). However, many psychologists continue to believe that dreams have deeper meaning (Shafton, 1995; White & Taytroe, 2003). There seems to be little doubt that dreams can make a difference in our lives: Veteran sleep researcher William Dement once dreamed that he had lung cancer. In the dream a doctor told Dement he would die soon. At the time, Dement was smoking two packs of cigarettes a day. He says, "I will never forget the surprise, joy, and exquisite relief of waking up. I felt reborn." Dement quit smoking the following day. (For more information about dreaming, see this chapter's Psychology in Action.)

词汇 (Vocabulary)

1. absurdity   n. 荒谬的事物
2. anecdote   n. 轶事、趣闻
3. arbitrariness   n. 武断、专横
4. arena   n. 舞台
5. bizarre   n. 古怪的、奇异的
6. inspeltor   n. 检查员、审视者
7. chamber   n. 房间、内庭
8. compound   adj. 复合的、结合的
9. container   n. 容器
10. diverge   v. 分歧
11. domain   n. 领域、范围
12. episode   n. 插曲
13. focal   adj. 焦点上的
14. incongraity   n. 不和谐之事物
15. inguisive   adj. 好管闲事的
16. kidney   n. 肾
17. tedious   adj. 沉闷的、乏味的
18. vein   n. 静脉
19. volition   n. 意志、意志力

第七章 记忆
(MEMORY)

本章要点 (Chapter Outline)
记忆系统概述 (The Scope of the Memory System)
基本记忆过程 (Basic Memory Process)
感觉记忆 (Sensory Memory)
短时记忆 (Short-Term Memory)
长时记忆 (Long-Term Memory)
构建着的记忆 (Constructing Memory)
提高记忆 (Improving Your Memory)

记忆是过去经历过的事物在人脑中的反映。记忆储存着过去的知识经验，没有记忆心理活动无法实现；记忆发生局部障碍，正常的心理活动也会发生困难，日常生活秩序也会受到破坏。从信息加工角度看，记忆是一个信息加工过程。根据记忆中信息的输入、编码方式和储存信息时间的不同可把记忆分为三种类型：瞬时记忆（又称感觉记忆）、短时记忆、长时记忆。在信息加工过程中，记忆受着过去的经验的影响，表现出选择、意义化等特点；记忆的监控、管理调节成分——元记忆在起着重要的作用；有效的记忆方法有利于提高记忆效果；信息的加工处理离不开心理和行为的生理基础，特别是人脑，脑内的各部分以功能联合的方式保证记忆的正常进行。在对记忆的研究中，将来有可能更深入地研究人类的记忆有多少种，在减少前后抑制等的消极影响方面会有些突破。本章对上述内容较为详细地作了阐述。

There is a scene in the film On Golden Pond in which an elder Henry Forda strolls away from the cabin he has shared with his wife every summer for decades and, after having gone some distance, suddenly becomes disoriented. He can neither remember where the cabin is nor recall how to get to town. Panicked, he begins to run and eventually gets safely back home, but is badly shaken. Experience like this, which can plague older people highlight dramatically the importance of that indispensable mental capacity called memory. Memory allows people to learn and to survive. Without memory, you would not know how to shut off the alarm, take a shower, get dressed, or find your way home. You would be unable to communicate with other people, because you would not remember what words mean or even what you had just said. You would be unaware of your own likes and dislikes, and you would have no idea of who you were in any meaningful sense.

Yet memory is full of paradoxes. It is not unusual, for example, for people to remember the name of their firstgrade teacher, but not the name of someone they met just a minute ago. In other words, remarkable as it is, the human memory is far from perfect.Like perception,memory is selective; people retain some information and lose some. And what people recall can be shaped by a surprisingly or simplify what they report.

In this chapter, we describe what is known about both memory and forgetting. Some of the material here may be of immediate use to you in studying for exams and recalling what you have learned.

第一节 记忆系统概述
(THE SCOPE OF THE MEMORY SYSTEM)

Mathematician John Griffith has estimated that, by the time the average person dies, he or she will have stored five hundred times as much information as can be found in the Encyclopedia Britannica (Hunt,1982). In your own encyclopedia of memories you could include the meanings of thousands of words. You could fill a volume simply by describing your personal experiences. You could also fill a volume with such procedures as how to play checkers, wind a watch, tie a shoelace, and so on. And this list does not even begin to exhaust the inventory of an average person's memory(Taylor, 1981).

The impressive capacity of human memory reveals a complex mental system. Our exploration of this system begins with a look at the kinds of information it can handle. Then we describe the mental processes involved in memory and the stages through which information passes in order to become permanent memories.

Three Types of Memory

In which hand does the Statue of Liberty hold her torch? When was the last time you spent cash for something? What part of speech is used to modify a noun? The first question is likely to elicit a visual image; to answer the second, you must recall a particular event in your life; and the third requires general knowledge unlikely to be tied to a specific event. Some theorists argue that answering each of these questions requires a different type of memory (Brewer&pani, 1984). How many types of memory are there? No one is sure,but most research suggests that there are at least three basic types.Each is named for the kind of information it handles; episodic, semantic, and procedural (Tulving, 1985).

Any memory of a specific event that happened while you were present is an episodic memory—what you had for dinner yesterday or where you were last Friday night. More research has been devoted to episodic memory than to any other type. **Semantic memory** contains generalized knowledge or the world that does not involve memory of a specific event, or episodic. For example, most people can answer the questions like who were the first president of the United States? Are wrenches pets or tools? Most people know that wrenches are tools without remembering any specific episode in which they learned that fact. As a general rule, people convey episodic memories by saying, "I remember when..." whereas they convey semantic memories by saying "I know that..." (Tulving, 1972, 1982). **Procedural memory**, also called skill memory, involves how to do things. Knowing how to ride a bicycle, read a map, swim—these and thousands of other example are types of procedural memory. Often, stored procedures involve complicated sequences of movements that cannot be described adequately in words. A gymnast, for example, might find it impossible to describe the exact motions required for a particular routine; an automobile mechanic might not be able to say exactly how to set an engine's timing correctly.

Many activities require all three types of memory. Consider a game of tennis. Knowing the rules of the game or how many sets are needed to win a match involves semantic memory. Remembering the score or which side served last requires episodic memory. Knowing how to lob or volley involves procedural memory. Some theorists argue that no distinction among types of memory is necessary, because all three are represented and retrieved in the same way (Anderson, 1976). No matter how the controversy is resolved, however, the three types remain useful labels for the contents of memory.

Basic Memory Process

Most people have a favorite story about forgetfulness. For example, one of the authors sometimes drives to work and sometimes walks. On one occasion, he drove, forgot that he had driven, and walked home. When he failed to find his car in its normal spot the next morning, he called the police to report the car stolen. After about twenty-four hours, the police called to let him know that they had found the car parked next to the psychology building on campus and that it had been towed to a storage area. When he went to retrieve the car, it was embarrassing enough for the author to explain that he had made a mistake, but particularly so when he realized that he was once again stranded because he had forgotten to bring his car keys. What went wrong? There are several possibilities, because remembering the contents of episodic, semantic, or procedural memory requires the flawless operation of three fundamental processes encoding, storage, and retrieval outlined in **Figure7.1**. A breakdown of any one of these processes will produce some degree of forgetting (Melton, 1963).

First, information must be put into memory, a step that requires **encoding**. Just as incoming sensory information must be coded so that it can be communicated to the brain, information to be remembered must be put in a form that the momery system can accept and use. In the memory system, sensory information is put into various memory codes, or mental representation of physical stimuli. On thought, mental representation can take many forms. For example, people sometimes put information into **acoustic codes**, which represent information as sequences of sounds. **Visual codes** represent stimuli as pictures. **Semantic codes** represent an experience by its general meaning. Thus, if you see a billboard that reads "Huey's Going Out of Business Sale 50% Off Everything in Stock," you might encode the sound of the words as if they had been spoken (acoustic coding), the image of the letters as they were arranged on the sign (visual coding), or the fact that you saw an ad for Huey's (Semantic coding). The way stimuli are coded can influence what is remembered.

For example, semantic coding might not be able to remember the make,model, or no color (Bahrick&Bouvher, 1968).

The second basic memory process is **storage**, which simply means maintaining information in the system over time. Episodic semantic, or procedural memories can be stored for a very long time.When you find it possible to use a pogo stick or perform some other "rusty" skill or to recall facts and events from many years ago, you are depending on your memory storage capacity.

Figure7.1
Basic Memory Processes
Successfully remembering something requires three basic process. First, the item must be encoded, or put in a form that can be placed in, memory. Second, it must be stored, or maintained, in memory. Finally, it must be retrieved, or recovered, from memory. If any of these processes fails to operate properly, forgetting will occur.

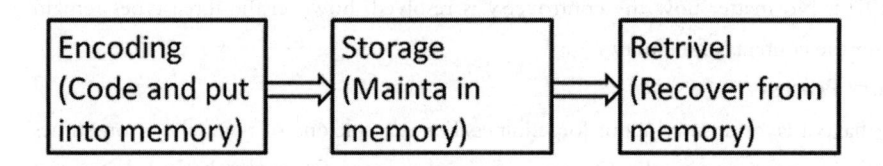

```
┌─────────────┐     ┌─────────────┐     ┌─────────────┐
│ Encoding    │     │ Storage     │     │ Retrivel    │
│ (Code and put│ ──▶ │ (Mainta in  │ ──▶ │ (Recover from│
│ into memory)│     │ memory)     │     │ memory)     │
└─────────────┘     └─────────────┘     └─────────────┘
```

Retrivel is the process of finding information stored in memory and bringing it into consciousness. Retriving stored information like your address or telephone number is usually so fast and effortless as to seem automatic. Only when you try to retrieve other kinds of information such as the answer to a quiz question that you know but cannot quite recall do you become ware of the searching process.

Encoding, storage, and retrieval are all vital links in the memory chain. The author's forgetfulness might thus be traced to information about his car's location being(a)never properly encoded, (b)encoded but never stored, or(c)stored but never retrieved.

Three Stages of Memory
As noted in the sensation and perception chapters, a great deal of information reaches people, but only a fraction of it is perceived. Similarly, people remember some incoming information far better and far longer than other information. For example,suppose your friends throw a surprise party for you. On entering the room, you might barely notice, and later fail to recall,the flash from a camera. And you might forget in a few seconds the name of a person you met at the party. But if you live to be a hundred, you will never forget where the party took place or how surprised and pleased you were. Why do some stimuli leave no more than a fleeting impression and others remain in memory forever? There are a number of factors to consider, the most influential theories of memory suggest that, in order for information to become firmly embedded in memory, it must pass through three stages of processing. Sensory memory, short—term memory and long—term memory (Atkinson&Shiffrin,1968; see **Figure7.2**).

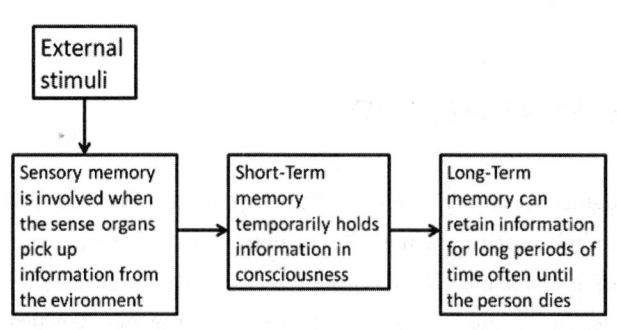

Figure7.2
The three Stages of Memory
Here is a very basic overview of the human memory system. In the first memory stage, the eyes, ears, or other sense organs pick up visual, auditory, and other information from the environment. The second stage involves the detection and brief holding in consciousness of distinct patterns of energy, such as recognizable images or understandable words. The third stage allows information to be retained for use hours, days, or even years later.

[External stimuli] → Sensory memory is involved when the sense organs pick up information from the evironment → Short-Term memory temporarily holds information in consciousness → Long-Term memory can retain information for long periods of time often until the person dies

In the first, sensory memory stage, sensory registers hold information from the senses sights or sounds, for example for a fraction of a second. Information in the sensory registers may be attended to, analyzed, and encoded as a meaningful patten; as we described in Chapter 5, this process is known as perception. If the information in sensory memory is perceived, it can enter the second, or short-term memory stage where, if nothing further is done, it will disappear in twenty seconds or so. If you further process the information in short-term memory. it may be encoded into long-term memory, where it may remain indefinitely.

Your reading this sentence is an example of ail three stages of memory. As you read, light energy reflected from the page is converted to neural activity and registered in sensory memory. If you pay attention to these stimuli, your perception of the patterns of light can be held in short-term memory. While you read, you are constantly recognizing words by matching your perceptions of them with the patterns and meanings you have stored in long-term memory. In addition, you are also holding the early parts of the sentence in short-term memory, so that they can be integrated and understood as you read the rest of the sentence. Thus, all three memory stages are necessary for you to understand a sentence.

In the following sections we describe the three stages of memory one by one along with the encodingy storage, and retrieval processes associated with each one—Some of the words and methods we use may seem to suggest that each stage of memory is a box that passively receives information from the preceding stage. But the memory system is not a chain of fancy recorders that passively collect what the world presents. Instead, memory (like perception) is an active process in which the three stages interact. As shown in the example of reading a sentence, en coding new information usually requires retrieving information already stored in memory and linking the new information to the old. Thus, what is already in long-term memory constantly influences how new experiences are encoded.

第二节 感觉记忆
(SENSORY MEMORY)

We have said that, in order to recognize incoming stimuli, the brain must analyze them and compare them to what is already stored in long-term memory. This process is nearly, but not quite, instantaneous. As a result, the impression that stimuli make on the senses must be maintained for a short time. "This is the job of the sensory registers, as Figure 7.2 shows. The **sensory registers** hold incoming information long enough for it to be processed further. This type of memory, called **sensory memory**, is very primitive and very, very brief, but it lasts long enough to connect one impression to the next, so that people experience a smooth flow of information.

Capacity of the Sensory Registers

Most of what we know about sensory memory comes from studies of the sensory register for visual information. For many years, researchers puzzled over how much information this register could hold and for how long. Several answers came out of experiments on how the eyes look at the world. When you look around, it seems as if your eyes are moving slowly but smoothly, like a movie camera scanning a scene. In fact, they are not. As noted in the perception chapter, your eyes fixate at one point for about one-fourth of a second and then rapidly jump to a new position. This rapid jumping from one fixation point to another is called saccadic eye movement.

How much information can a person glean from just one eye fixation? Several experiments addressed this question by showing people a display that included from one letter to twelve different letters arranged in rows. Each display was presented for such a short time (for example, one-tenth of a second) that the subjects did not have a chance to move their eyes while it was. visible; they saw it in only one fixation. Then, with the display removed, they were asked to report as many letters as possible (McDougall, 1904). People typically reported only about four or five items, even when the display included more than five. In other words, it appeared that there is a limit to how much information people can glean in a single fixation and that the limit is about four or five items. This limit is called the span of apprehension.

George Sperling (1960) was working on his doctoral dissertation when he noticed something very important about these experiments. The subjects often claimed that, although they could report only about four or five items, they had in fact seen the entire display. Why was this important? If the subjects were correct, then the span of apprehension indicated, not a limit on how much they could see, but a limit on how much they could remember and report see, but a limit on how much they could remember and report.

1. An array with a varying number of letters is displayed for 50 milliseconds.

2. Immediately after the display is turned off a tone is sounded that tells the subject which row to report.

3. The subject tries to report the letters in the appropriate (signaled) row.

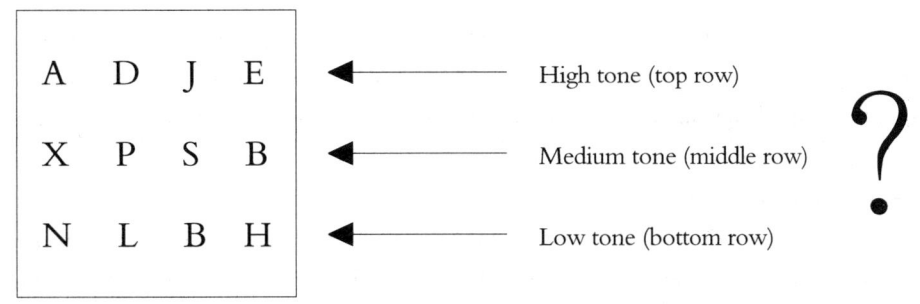

```
A  D  J  E   ◄─── High tone (top row)
X  P  S  B   ◄─── Medium tone (middle row)
N  L  B  H   ◄─── Low tone (bottom row)
```

?

Number of letters in the stimulus array

Figure 7.3
Studying Sensory Memory with the partial–Report Procedure
Subjects are presented with an array of from three to twelve letters for fifty milliseconds (or one-twentieth of a second) and are then asked to report some of what they saw. Because they do not know which row they are to recall until after the display has disappeared, they must keep all the letters in memory to successfully complete the task.
(*From Human Memory: The Processing of Information by G. R. Loftus and E. F. Loftus Copyright 1976 by Lawrence Erlbaum Assciates. Inc.*)

How could these two types of limitations be disentangled? Recall that the subjects were shown a display for a very brief time and then were asked to report all of the letters in the display; this is called the whole–report procedure. Sperling devised a partial report procedure, outlined in Figure 7.3.

person was shown a display of three rows of letters and, just after it was shut off, heard a tone. If the tone was high pitched, the subject was supposed to report only the top row of letters. If the tone was medium pitched, only the middle row was to be reported. And if the subjects heard a low–pitched tone, only the lowest row was to be reported. Notice that the subjects did not know which row was supposed to be reported until after the display had been shut off. As a result, they had to pay attention to the entire display and then retrieve the requested items from memory.

With this procedure, Sperling believed he could distinguish limitations on what people can see from limitations on what they can remember. To understand why, consider the trials in which subjects were shown twelve letters, as in Figure 7.3. How many letters must a person have available in memory in order to report all four letters in any row, regardless of which tone is sounded? Since subjects did not know which tone would sound until after the display was removed, perfect performance could occur only if the person had all twelve letters stored in memory.

By using the partial–report procedure in this way, Sperling estimated the number of items that were both seen and available in memory. Figure 7.4 shows the results. Clearly, many more items were available in people's memory than had been thought. Why, then, could subjects report only four or five letters? By increasing the time between the presentation of the letters and the tone, Sperling found that subjects' memory of the display faded continuously and decayed completely after about one second. Thus, by the time the subjects in the whole–report condition could report four or five items, the memory of the other items had decayed, or faded. In other words, what subjects had been claiming all along was correct: they were able to see more items than they could report. The span of apprehension reflected a limit, not on how much they could see, but on how long information could be held in the sensory register.

Properties of Sensory Memory

Experiments like Sperling's helped establish the fact that the sensory register retain mental representations of visual images only for a very brief time. The representations are called icons, and the sensory register for them is called **iconic memory**. Most icons last no more than one second, but there are conditions in which an icon can last a bit longer. The major determinant of how long an icon lasts is the strength of the visual stimulus (for example, its brightness). The stronger the visual stimulus, the more slowly the icon fades (Long & Beaton, 1982). As we noted in the chapter on perception, unusual persistence of an icon may play a role in the reading disorder known as dyslexia.

Thanks to iconic memory, people do not notice their saccadic eye movements, and the flow of information does not stop with every blink. The image from each fixation lasts long enough to give one the perception of a smooth flow of images when watching a movie (Loftus, 1983) or when one object passes in front of another (Mace & Turvey, 1983). Another interesting property of iconic memory is that it can lay one image on top of another, so that information is summed, as in Figure 7.5.

Figure 7.4

Results of a Sensory Memory Experiment

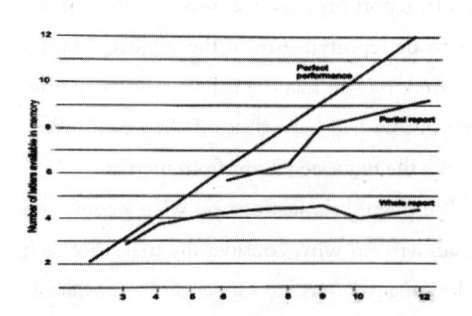

By using the partial–report procedure, Sperling found that subjects can retain nine or ten letters out of a twelve–letter display. However, because forgetting is extremely rapid, usually taking place within a second or two, performance is poor in the whole–report procedure. In the time it took people to report about four letters, they had already forgotten the rest.

(From G. Sperling,"The Information Available in Brief Visual Presentation."74, pp.129, Psychological Monographs Copyright 1960 by the American Psychological Association Adapted by permission of the author.)

Psychologists believe that each of the other senses has its own type of sensory register; among them, only echoic memory has received much study so far. Echoic memory is the sensory register for auditory sensations; an echo in this context is the mental representation of a sound in sensory memory. Experiments like Sperling's indicate that iconic and echoic memory have essentially the same properties, with one exception. Unlike an icon, an echo characteristically lasts up to several seconds, probably because of the physiology of the ear. For both the echo and the icon, research suggests that encoding is minimal. Both icons and echoes are very faithful reproductions of the physical stimulus, virtual copies of the information provided by the senses (sakitt & Long, 1979).

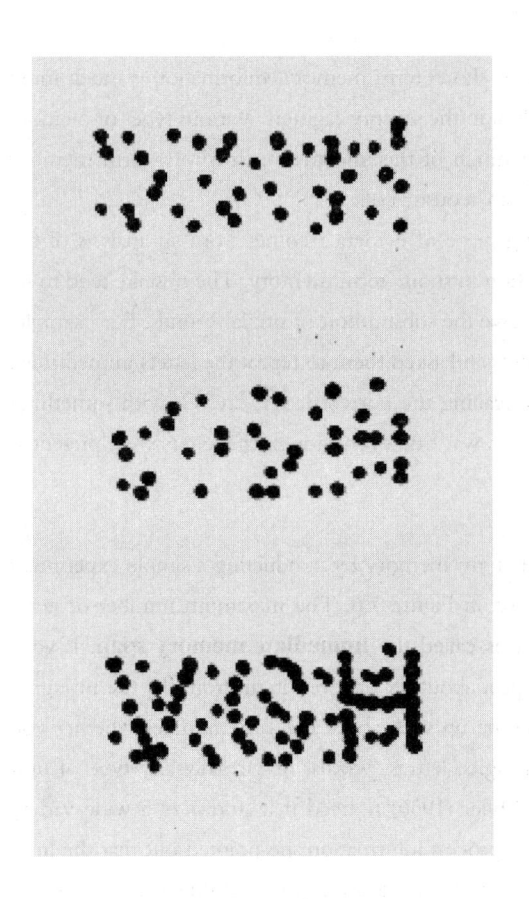

Figure 7.5
Summation of Information in Iconic Memory
Researchers showed subjects the top panel for six milliseconds, shut it off, and then presented the middle panel for six milliseconds. Subjects were able to identify the nonsense syllable (VOH) because the two iconic images or mental representations, became superimposed. The superimposed image is shown in the lower panel (From"Some Temporal Characteristics of Visual Pattern Perception"by Ericksen and Collins, Journal of Experimental Psychology 74, pp. 476–484. Copyright 1967 by the American Psychological Association Adapted by permission of the authors.)

Without further processing, icons, echoes, and other sensory memories simply fade away. The process controlling what information in sensory memory will be captured is called selective attention, which is described in the chapter on perception. Thus, perception itself processes and captures the elusive imressions sensory memory, transferring them to short-term memory.

• 153 •

第三节 短时记忆
(SHORT-TERM MEMORY)

Whereas sensory registers typically store information for only a second or so, the information in **short-term**, or **working**, **memory** can last from one second to more than a minute. When you look up a phone number and then dial the phone or check your TV Guide and then change the channel, you are using short-term memory. In fact, you might say that people live in short-term memory, because it provides much of their consciousness of the present. As its name implies, however, short-term memory can be fragile. For instance, you might forget the number you just looked up before you can dial it. In the following sections, we discuss how information in short-term memory is encoded, stored, and retrieved.

Encoding

If you attend to and perceive a stimulus, it enters short-term memory. Information is much more elaborately encoded in short-term memory.Then in the sensory registers. Various types of memory codes can be used, but research suggests that much of the information in short-term memory particularly verbal information is represented by an acoustic code.

How do we know this? One convincing piece of evidence comes from an analysis of the mistakes people make when encoding information in short-term memory. The mistake tend to be acoustically related, which means that they involve the substitution of similar sounds. For example, R. Conrad (1964) showed people strings of letters and asked them to repeat the letters immediately. The mistakes they made tended to involve replacing the correct letter, say, C, with something that sounded like it, for example, D, P,or T. This was true even though the letters were presented visually, without any sound.

Storage

You can easily determine the capacity of short-term memory by conducting a simple experiment designed by Darlene Howard (1983) and shown in Figure 7.6. The maximum number of items you can recall perfectly after one presentation is called the **immediate memory span**. If your memory span is like most pepple's, you can repeat about six or seven items from the test in Figure 7.6. The interesting thing is that you should come up with about the same number whether you estimate your immediate memory span with digits, letters, words, or virtually any type of unit (Hayes, 1952; Pollack, 1953). When George Miller (1956) noticed that studies of a wide variety of tasks showed the same limit on the ability to process information, he pointed out that the limit seems to be a "magic number" of 7 plus or minus 2. This is the capacity of short-term memory; it applies, not to a certain number of discrete elements, but to the number of meaningful groupings of information, called **chunks**.

The capacity of short-term memory is almost always between five and nine chunks. For example, read the following letters to a friend, pausing at each dash: FB-ITW-AC-IAI-BMB

—MW. The chances are very good that your friend will not be able to repeat this string of letters perfectly. Why? There are fifteen letters, which is more than most people's immediate memory span. But if you pause when you read the letters, so that they are grouped as FBI–TWA–CIA–IBM–BMW, the chances are very good that your friend will be able to repeat the string back easily (Bower, 1975). They are the same fifteen letters, but they will be processed, not as fifteen separate letters, but as five meaningful chunks of information.

9 2 5	G M N
8 6 4 2	S L R R
3 7 6 5 4	V O E P G
6 2 7 4 1 8	X W D X Q O
0 4 0 1 4 7 3	E P H H J A E
1 9 2 2 3 5 3 0	Z D O F W D S V
4 8 6 8 5 4 3 3 2	D T Y N R H E H Q
2 5 3 1 9 7 1 7 6 8	K H W D A G R O F Z
8 5 1 2 9 6 1 9 4 5 0	U D F F W H D Q D G E
9 1 8 5 4 6 9 4 2 9 3 7	Q M R H X Z D P R R E H

CAT BOAT RUG
RUN BEACH PLANT LIGHT
SUIT WATCH CUT STAIRS CAR
JUNK LONE GAME CALL WOOD HEART
FRAME PATCH CROSS DRUG DESK TREE LAW
CLOTHES CHOOSE GIFT DRIVE BOOK TREE HAIR THIS
DRESS CLERK FILM BASE SPEND SERVE BOOK LOW TIME
STONE ALL NAIL DOOR HOPE EARL FEEL BUY COPE GRAPE
AGE SOFT FALL STORE PUT TRUE SMALL FREE CHECK MAIL LEAF
LOG DAY TIME CHESS LAKE CUT BIRD SHEET YOUR SEE STREET WHEEL

Figure 7.6
Capacity of Short–Term Memory

These materials can be used to test your immediate, or short–term, memory span. Have a friend read the items in the top row at the rate of about one per second; then try to repeat them back in exactly the same order. If you are able to do this perfectly, have your friend read the next row. Each row contains one additional item. Continue until you make a mistake Most people are perfect at this task until they reach six or seven items. The maximum number of items you can repeat back perfectly is your immediate memory span.

(Adapted with permission of Macmillan Publishing Company from Cognitive Psychology:

Memory, Language, and Thought by Darlene V. Howard. Copyright 1983 by Darlene V. Harvard.)

Chunks of information can become very complex. For example, if someone read to you, "The boy in the red shirt kicked his mother in the shin," you could probably repeat the sentence very easily. Yet it contains twelve separate words and forty-three individual letters. How can you repeat the sentence so effortlessly? The answer is that people can build bigger and bigger chunks of information (Simon, 1974). In this case, you might represent "the boy in the red shirt" as one chunk of information rather than as six words or nineteen letters. Similarly, "kicked his motherl" and "in the shin" represent separate chunks of information.

Notice that chunking in this way also demonstrates the interaction of short-term and long-term memory. You cannot come up with a meaningful grouping of information if you do no more than passively take it in. Chunking requires that you relate the informaion being encoded in short-term memory to information already in long-term memory.

The Power of Chunking

Learnig to use bigger and bigger chunks of information can noticeably improve the amount of information held in short-term memory. For example, as noted in the chapter on development, children's memories improve in part because they gradually become able to hold as many as seven chunks in memory, but also because they become better able to group information into chunks.

A notable demonstration of the power of chunking comes from an experiment with a college student of average intelligence, with no unusual memory skills (Chase & Ericsson, 1979). At the beginning of the experiment, his immediate memory span was seven digits. The experimenters began by presenting a small number of digits and asking the student to repeat them in the same order. If he was correct, they increase the number of items on the list by one and repeated the procedure. Whenever the student made a mistake, the number of items was decreased by one and the procedure was repeated. He received a new random set of digits on each trial. This procedure was continued for one hour a day, approximately four days a week. After six months, the student's immediate memory span had increased to thirty-eight items (Ericsson, Chase & Faloon, 1980). After two years, it had increased to approximately two hundred items (Chase & Ericsson, 1981).

Other people's increased memory abilities are not restricted to strings of random numbers. Many cocktail waitresses, for example, can remember a much longer list of drinks than the average person (Bennett, 1983). One waiter taught himself to remember up to sixteen complete dinner orders without taking notes (Chase & Ericsson, 1981). All of these people owe their remarkable abilities to continued practice with some, useful method of grouping items—such as drinks or meals—into larger and larger chunks. For example, because the student in Chase and Ericsson's (1979) experiment was a runner, he encoded long sequences of digits as times in a race. If the first four digits were 3-2-7-8, he encoded them as the chunk 3:27.8 and thought of it as "3 minutes, 27.8 seconds, close to a world's record for the mile." In short, although the capacity of short-term memory is more or less constant, at seven plus or minus two chunks of meaningful information, the size of those chunks can vary. Learn to group more items into a meaningful chunk, and you can greatly increase your memory span.

Notice, however, that memory improvement takes many hours to practice and requires not only elaborate chunking, but also encoding and organizing new information in terms of knowledge already stored in long–term memory. In other words, though chunking alone can improve short–term memory, it is most effective when combined with strategies for relating short–term memory chunks to information in long–term memory. Learnig to move information rapidly back and forth between short–term and long–term memory is also particularly effective. One simple example is companie's use of meaningful, and thus memorable, chunks in such toll–free customer–assistance numbers as 1–800–REACH US or CALL GTE. And renowned chess masters, who have been known to play and win several games at once, even when blindfolded, have learned to chunk visual images of each gamers layout and use prior knowledge to encode new information quickly and efficiently into both short–term and long–term memory. We discuss some of these more elaborate memory improvement methods later in the chapter.

Duration

By rehearsing information, repeating it to yourself, you can maintain it in short–term memory for as long as you want. But people usually forget information in short–term memory quickly unless they continue to rehearse it. You have undoubtedly experienced this yourself. In order to hold a telephone number in short–term memory while you walk across the room to dial the phone, you must rehearse the number over and over. If a friend comes in and interrupts you, even for a few second, you may forget the number. But this limitation of short–term memeory is actually useful. Imagine what life would be like if you kept remembering every phone number you ever dialed or every conversation you ever heard.

How long does unrehearsed information stay in short–term memory? To answer this quesion, researchers needed a way to prevent rehearsal. In two famous experiments published almost simultaneously, John Brown (1958) in England and Lloyd and Margaret Peterson (1959) in the United States devised a method for doing so, which is called the **Brown–Peterson procedure**. A subject is presented with a group of three letters, such as GRB. Then the subject counts backward by threes from an arbitrarily selected number until a signal is given. Counting prevents the subject from rehearsing the letters. On the signal, the subject stops counting and tries to recall the letters. By varying the number of seconds the subject counts backward. The experimenter can determine how much forgetting takes place over a given amount of time.

As you can see in Figure 7.7, forgetting of information in short–term memory happens gradually but quite rapidly; after eighteen seconds, subjects can remember almost nothing (Peterson & Peterson, 1959). This is a striking demonstration of the importance of rehearsal for keeping information in short–term memory. Evidence from these and other experiments suggests that unrehearsed information can be maintained in short–term memory for no more than about twenty seconds. As noted earlier, although this can be a blessing, it can sometimes be dangerous. For example, on May 17, 1986, an air traffic controller at Chicago's O'Hare Field forgot that he had just instructed an aircraft to land on one runway and allowed another plane to take off on an intersecting runway. The two aircraft missed each other by only twenty feet.

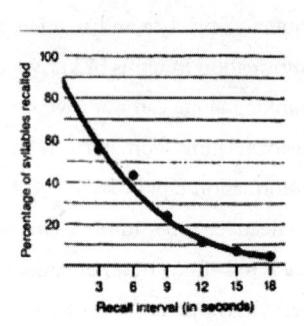

Figure 7.7

Forgetting in Short–Term Memory

The graph shows the percentage of nonsense syllables recalled after various intervals during which rehearsal was prevented. Note that there was virtually complete forgetting affer a delay of eighteen seconds (From"Short Term Retention of Individual Verbal Items"by Peterson and Peterson, Journal of Experimental Psychology, 58, pp. 193–198. Copyright 1959 by the American Psychological Association. Adapted by permission of the authors.)

Causes of forgetting Why do people forget information in short–term memory so rapidly? Researchers have found that either of two processes may be the cause (Reitman, 1971, 1974; Shiffrin, 1973). One process is decay. The mental represent as on a piece of steel are eaten away by rust and become less distinct over time. Forgetting also occurs because of interference from other information. For example, the appearance of new information in short–term memory can result in the displacement of information already there. Like a workbench, short–term memory can hold only a limited number of items; when additional items are added, the old ones tend to "fall off" (Klatzky, 1980).This is one reason why the phone number you just looked up is likely to drop out of short–term memory if you read another number before dialing. Rehearsal prevents displacement by reentering the same information into short–term memory.

Displacement is an example of **retroactive interference**, in which new information placed in memory interferes with the ability to recall information already in memory. There can also be **proactive interference**, in which previously learned information, now residing in long–term memory, interferes with the ablility to remember new information. Mistakenly saying the English word window instead of the German equivalent that you just learned is an example of proactive interference. It is easier to keep the two types of interference straight if you remember that proactive interference operates forward in time (the past interferes with the present), whereas retroactive interference operates backward in time (the present interferes with the past).

What is stored? You have seen that information is usually encoded into short–term memory acoustically (by how it sounds); that how much is remembered depends on how the information is grouped; and that, unless it is rehearsed, information is very quickly forgotten. There is yet another question to consider about the storage of information in short–term memory. How is the information represented mentally when it is stored?

To find out, Delos Wickens (1973) used a variation of the Brown–Peterson procedure and came up with a surprising answer. Each of four groups of subjects was given four recall trials Table 7.1 lists the types of items given to each group. One, called the "fruit group," was given the names of three kinds of fruit on each trial. The vegetable group was to remember the names of three vegetables on the first three trials, but on the fourth trial, they were given the names of three fruits.

• 158 •

As Table 7.1 shows, the type of words given on the fourth trial was also shifted for the flower and the profession groups.

Table 7.1

A Release from Proactive Inhibition Experiment

Control subjects were given the names of three fruits on each of four trials. Experimental groups were given lists of vegetables, flowers, or professions on the first three trials, then a list or fruits on the fourth trial.

Group	Trial 1	Trial 2	Trial 3	Trial 4
Fruit (control)	Fruits	Fruits	Fruits	Fruits
Vegetable	Vegetables	Vegetables	Vegetables	Fruits
Flower	Flower	Flower	Flower	Fruits
Profession	Profession	Profession	Profession	Fruits

The results are shown in Figure 7.8 The performance of the fruit group declined steadily across trials because of increasing proactive interference. The other groups showed a similar decline across the first three trials. However, their performance improved on the fourth trial, when the category of the words they tried to remember was shifted. This improvement, caused by changing the category of information to be remembered, is called a release from proactive interference. Notice that there were different amounts of release from proactive interferene, depending on the degree of similarity between word categories. When the words to be learned shifted from vegetables to fruits, the improvement was quite small. Improvement was intermediate for the shift from flowers to fruits and very large for the shift from professions to fruits. Why?

One possibility is that the words were represented in memory, not as single unites, but as collections of attributes or features, such as what the item looks like, what it tastes like, where one finds it, and so on. Because fruits and vegetables have many features in common, one category still interferes a great deal with the other, and the amount of release from proactive interference is quite small. However, fruits and professions have virtually nothing in common, so the shift in this case creates almost complete release from proactive interference (Wickens, 1972).In other words, old information interferes less with new information if the new information is very different from the old. Thus, your old phone number might interfere with your recall of a new phone number, but it would not interfere with your remembering the name of a new friend.

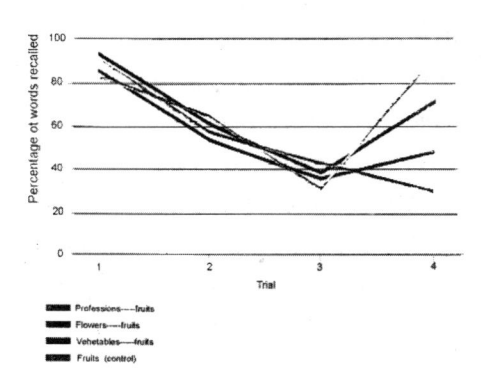

Figure 7.8 Release from Proactive Interference

Control subjects showed a steady decline in performance over four trials in which lists of fruits were recalled. This reflects a buildup of proactive interfernce from one list of fruit to the next. The other groups showed a release from proactive interference when—after three trials with lists of vegetables, flowers, or professions—they were to recall a list of fruits. The release effect on trial 4 was complete when the change in category was from professions to fruits, because professions share virtually no features with fruits Thus, subjects recalled the fruit list on trial 4 as well as they had recalled the professions on the first trial (From "Some Characteristics of Word Encoding" by Wickens. Memory and Cognition, 1, pp. 485–490. Copyright 1973 Psychonomic Society Publications.)

The idea that words are represented in short-term memory, not as single units, but as bundles of multiple features is very important, and we will return to it later in this chapter.

Retrieval

Imagine that you are holding certain information in short-term memory, for example, the digits 4–2–6. When asked for this information, you can give it, but the process is not as instantaneous as it may seem. Your ability to report what is in short-term memory depends on a process of search and retrieval.

How does retrieval work? Saul Sternberg (1966, 1969) looked at two theoretical possibilities, known as parallel Search and serial search. In a **parallel search**, all of the information in short-term memory is examined in parallel, or all at once. In a **serial search**, information is examined serially, or one piece at a time. To determine which type of search is used, Sternberg gave people several digits to remember and then gave them a probe number. The subjects' task was to determine whether the probe number had been part of the original set of digits. In order to answer, subjects had to compare the probe number with the numbers in memory. People can perform this task very rapidly, and they almost never make a mistake. But do they scan the digits in memory all at once or one by one?

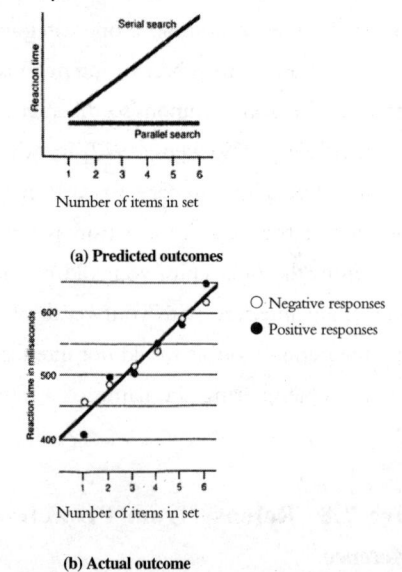

Figure 7.9

Short–Term Memory Scanning

How does the time needed to retrieve an item from short–term memory change as a function of the number of items? Predictions for a serial search model and a parallel search model are shown in (a). Typical empirical data are shown in (b); researchers have concluded from results like these that the search process in short–term memory is serial.

(From "High Speed Scanning in Human Memory" by S. Sternberg Science, VoL 153. #3736. pp. 652–654, August 5, 1966. Copyright 1966 by the American Association for the Advancement of Science.)

Sternberg reasoned that time and the size of the number set are keys to the puzzle. If items in memory are examined all at once (a parallel search), the number of digits presented in the original set should have no effect on the time which it takes to respond to the probe number. But if items in memory are examined one at a time (a serial search), the time needed to respond to the probe.

should increase as the length of the original list increases, Some of Sternberg's findings are shown in Figure 7.9. As you can see, they follow the pattern predicted by the serial search model: for each item added to the list, there is a corresponding increase in the time taken for the search. To be precise, it takes about 1/25 of a second to scan a single item in short–term memory.

Sternberg found another interesting result by comparing the time taken for yes and no responses. Obviously, a person would need to search all the items in the set in order to determine that the probe number was not in the set. But you would think that, in order to say yes, subjects would have to search only long enough to find the probe number; this should take less time. This is not what happens. People took the same amount of time to make a positive or a negative response. In other words, the search does not stop when a match to the probe number is found. Instead, the search continues through the entire set. In short, the evidence indicates that people retrieve information from short–term memory through an exhaustive serial search. Figure 7.10 summarizs much of what we have said about short–term, or working, memory.

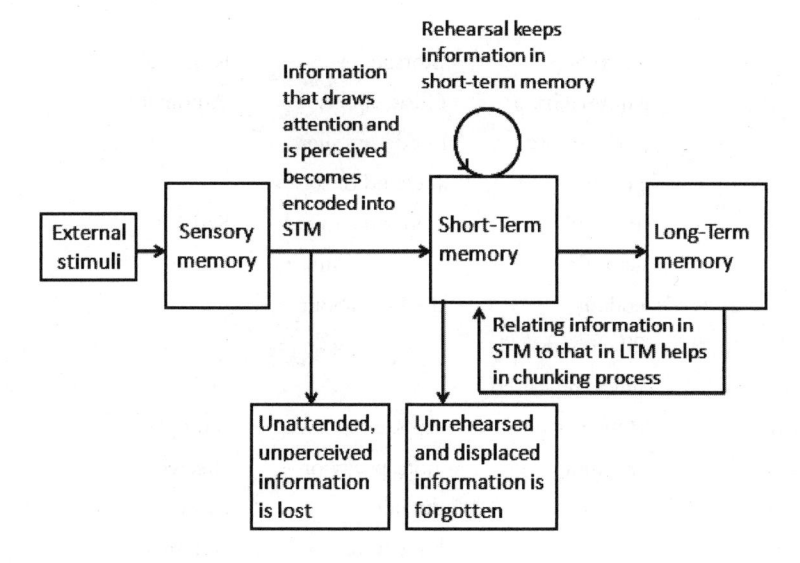

Figure 7.10

Another View of the Memory System

We have now seen that information that is attended to and perceived is encoded into short–term memory. If it is not rehearsed or is displaced by new information, this information will be lost. Chunking, aided by information already in long–term memory, can help hold more information in short–term memory.

第四节 长时记忆
（LONG-TERM MEMORY）

Table 7.2 contrasts the characteristics of short-term memory with those of sensory and long-term memory. Since long-term memory and short-term memory interact constantly, should they are considered as two storage systems or one?

Distinguishing Between Short – Term and Long – Term Memory

Psychologists studying memory have distinguished short-term from long-term memory because the two appear to be governed by different scientific laws and therefore seem to be quali-tatively different. For one thing, as Table 7.2 shows, there are good reasons for believing that both the encoding and storage processes in long-term memory differ from those of short-term memory. (We will describe these differences shortly). Evidence which information is transferred from short-term memory to another type of storage also supports the view that short-and long-term memory should be considered distinct. This evidence comes from experiments on recall and from research on the biology of memory.

Stage of Memory	Encoding	Storage	Retrieval
Sensory memory	Minimal;has a pure sensory guality	Great capaciy, but decays sffer a second or so	Automatic
Short-term Memory	Primarily acoustic coding	Capacity limited to 7±2 chunks; duration about 20 seconds unless rehearsed	Serial search
Long-term memory	Primarily semantic coding	Appears to have no capacity or duraion limitations	Strongly affected by how well the information is integrated is integrated with existing knowledge

Table 7.2

The Three Stages of Memory

Encoding, storage, and retrieval processes have somewhat different characteristics at each stage of memory.

(Serial–position curves) Look at the following list of words for thirty seconds, then look away and try to recall as many words as you can, in any order: bed, rest, quilt, dream, sheet, artichoke, mattress, pillow, night, snore, pajamas. Which words you recall depends in part on their position; that is, on where the words were in the list, as Figure 7.11 shows, Figure 7.11 is a serial–position curve, which is a plot of the chances of recalling the words in each position in a list. For the first two or three words in a list, recall is very good, a characteristic that is called the primacy effect. The probability of recall decreases for words in the middle of the list and then rises dramatically for the last few words. The ease of recalling words near the end of a list is called the recency effect.

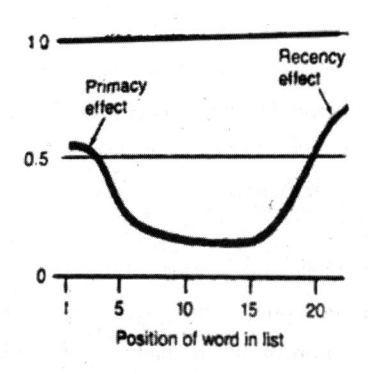

Figure 7.11
A Serial–Position Curve
The probability of recalling an item is plotted as a function of its serial position on a list of items. Generally, the first several items are likely to be recalled (the primacy effect); items in the middle of the list are much less likely to be recalled; and the last several items are recalled very well (the recency effect).

The primacy effect occurs because the words at the beginning of a list are rehearsed much more often than any of the other words on the list (Rundus, 1971). But why does the recency effect occur? If short–term and long–term memory are indeed distinct, then one possibility is that, when the test is given immediately after the list is read, the last four or five words in the list are still in short–term memory and thus are easily recalled. On the other hand, the beginning and the middle of the list must be retrieved from long–term memory.

To test this hypothesis, Murray Glanzer and Anita Cunitz (1966) gave a list of words to two groups of people. They asked one group to recall the list immediately after it was given. The second group was given a list, immediately performed a mental arithmetic task for thirty seconds, and then tried to recall as many words as possible. As Figure 7.12 shows, no recency effect occurred among those in the second group. Performing the arithmetic task before recalling the list displaced the last several words from short–term memory, making them no more likely to be recalled than those in the middle of the list. Since the performance of the two groups was otherwise very similar, the normal recency effect appears to be the result of keeping the last several words in short–term memory until the test is administerd.

Biological research Evidence that information is transferred from short–term memory to another, distinct system also comes from observations of how certain brain injuries and drugs affect memory. For example, damage to the hippocampus, which is part of the limbic system described in the chapter on biological psychology, often results in **anterograde amnesia**, or a loss of memory for any event occurring after the injury.

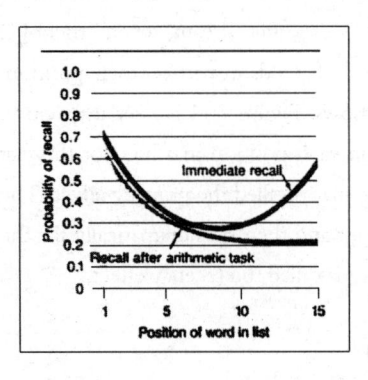

Figure 7.12

Separating Short–Term from Long–Term Memory

The serial–position curve shows both a primacy and a recency effect when subjects recall the list immediately after the last item is presented. It appears that the recency effect is based on retrieving the last several items from short–term memory, because when subjects perform an arithmetic task after hearing the last item, the recency effect disappears. The arithmetic task apparently displaces the words in short–term memory, leaving only those in long–term memory, leaving only those in long–term memory available for retrieval. (From"Two Storage Mechanisms in Free Recall, "by M. Glanzer and A. R. Cunitz In Journal of Verbal Learning and Verbal Behavior 1966.5, 351– 360 Copyright 1966 by Academic press, Inc, Reprinted by permission.)

A striking example is the case of a man with the initals HM (Milner, 1966). Part of his hippocampus had been removed in order to end severe epileptic seizures. Afterward, both his long–term memory and his short–term memory appeared normal, but he had a severe problem. He had had the operation when he was twenty–seven years old. Two years later, he still believed that he was twenty–seven. When his family moved into a new house, HM could not remember the new address or even how to get there. When he was told that his uncle had died, he grieved in a normal way. But soon afterward, he began to ask why his uncle had not visited him. Each time lie was told of his uncle's death, HM became just as upset as when he was first told. In short, the surgery had apparently destroyed the mechanism that reansfers information from short–term to long–term memory. HM could not learn anything new.

Another condition, **retrograde amnesia**, involves a loss of memory for events prior to some critical injury. Often, a person with this condition is unable to remember anything that took place in the months, or even years, before the injury. In most cases, the memories return gradually. The most distant events are recalled first, and the person gradually has better and better memory for events leadig up to the injury. But recovery is seldom complete, and the person may never remember the last few seconds before the injury. For example, a man received a severe blow to the head after being thrown from his motorcycle. After regaining consciousness, he claimed that he was eleven years old. Over the next three months, he gradually recalled more and more of his life. He remembered when he was twelve, thirteen, and so on—right up until the time he was riding his motorcycle the day of the accident. But he was never able to remember what happened just before the accident (Baddeley, 1982). Those final events must have been encoded into short–term memory, but apparently they were never successfully transferred into long-term memory.

Drugs, too, can disrupt the transfer of information from short-term to long-term memory. Smoking marijuana, for example, does not appear to affect the retrieval of information from short-term memory (Darley et al., 1973a). Nor does it affect retrieval from long-term memory (Darley et al., 1973b). But marijuana does inhibit the transfer of information from short-term to long-term memory.

The damage to memory in all these cases is consistent with the view that short-term and long-term memory are distinct systems; the problems are tied to an inability to transfer information from one system to the other. But psychologists do not yet know exactly how, physiologically, this transfer occurs. One view is that it involves tracing consolidation. In other words, some physiological trace that coding the experience must be gradually transformed, fixed, and consolidated if the memory is to endure.

It seems likely that the primary mechanism for trace consolidation is the movement of electrical impulses within clusters of neurons in the brain. For example, information in short-term memory is erased by any event that suppresses neural activity in the brain. Physical blows to the head, anesthetics, and various types of poisoning such as that from carbon monoxide all suppress neural activity, and all erase information from short-term memory. Similarly, information in short-term memory is erased by events that usually cause strong but random sets of electrical impulses, such as the electroshock treatments. The information being transferred from short-term to long-term memory seems to be vulnerable to destruction for only a minute or so (Chorover, 1965).

Encoding

Despite uncertainty about the physiological details of consolidation, psychologists have learned a good deal about how people encode information into long-term memory. Much information appears to be encoded automatically with little or no effort. This is particularly true for tasks that are well practiced. People learn and remember many things while driving, reading, or walking down the street, for example, even though they do not consciously attempt to memorize them—At other times, however, encoding is more effortful. As noted earlier, one of the primary mechanisms used to intentionally remember things is rehearsal. The importance of rehearsal was demonstrated by Hermann Ebbinghaus, a German psychologist who began the experimental study of long-term memory about a hundred years ago.

The early investigations of Ebbinghaus   Today, Ebbinghaus' methods seem rather quaint.

He used only himself as a subject. To time his experiments, he used a metronome, a mechanical device that makes a sound at constant intervals. His aim was to study memory in its "pure" form, uncontaminated by emotional reactions and other preexisting associations between what was already in memory and new material. To eliminate such associations, Ebbinghaus created the nonsense syllable, a meaningless set of two consonants and a vowel. iPOF, XEM, and QAL are examples. Ebbinghaus read aloud, to the beat of the metronome, a list of nonsense syllables. Then he tried to recall the syllables. He measured how difficult it was to learn a list by determining how many trials (repetitions through the list) were needed before he could repeat the entire list without making any errors. On just one trial, he could learn a seven–item list (the capacity of short–term memory). But as the number of items increased slightly, three to four times as many repetitions were required for perfect recall.

Rehearsal   Ebbinghaus learned his lists by rehearsing them, but his attempts to study memory uncontaminated by associations limited the type of rehearsal he could use. There appear to be two basic types of rehearsal: maintenance and elaborative. **Maintenance rehearsal** involves repeating an item over and over, as you might do to use a new phone number. This method can keep an item active in short–term memory, but it is very ineffective for encoding information into long–term memory. Far more effective is **elaborative rehearsal**, which involves thinking about how new material relates to information already stored in long–term memory.

Many of the most common failures of memory result from ineffective rehearsal strategies. For example, just repeating a new person's name to yourself When you are introduced is not a very effective strategy for memorizing it. Instead, if you have difficulty remembering new names, try thinking for a moment about how the new person and the new name are related to things you already know. Children's memories improve during their school years in part because they learn to rehearse, not just by repeating words, but by organizing items according to consistent concepts or meanings (Bach & Underwood, 1970) or by associating them through mental pictures or rhymes.

Rehearsal and Levels of Processing

Table 7.2 summarized considerable research evidence suggesting that sensory, short–term, and long–term memory can be distinguished not only by differences in their durations and capacities, but also by differences in their characteristic encoding processes. Some psychologists have suggested, however, that this research does not necessarily prove that there are three stages of memory. Fergus Craik and Robert Lockhart (1972), for example, have proposed an alternative view, which holds that differences in how well something is remembered reflects a single dimension: the degree or depth to which incoming information is mentally processed. From the perspective of this increasingly **influential level of processing model**, most incoming information immediately disappears from memory because it is not attended to or processed enough to create anything more than a briefimpression. According to this view, the icons, echoes, and other representations of information selected by attention and perception for further processing tend to be enccxied better and thus to stay in memory longer. How long depends on how elaborate the mental processing and encoding becomes—how much is thought about, organized, and related to existing knowledge.

Much of the research on rehearsal's role in memory has been conducted within the framework of level–of–processing theory. In one experimemt, college students were allowed to look for one minute at a picture of a living room. One group was told that several small X's had been embedded in the picture and that they were to try to locate them by scanning the picture vertically and horizontally. This is a relatively shallow level of processing, because the subjects could complete the task without ever thinking about the objects in the room. A second group was told that the X's had been placed at the edges of objects in the picture and that they should direct their attention to the contours of the objects. A third group was told to look at the picture and to think about what they would do with the various objects if they owned them. As a result, they had to relate the new information in the picture to other information stored in long-term memory. Following this relatively deep level of processing, these people recalled about thirty objects from the picture—roughly eight times as many as the other two groups (Bransford, Nitsch & Franks, 1977).

The most important conclusion to be drawn from research conducted within the level-of-processing framework is that memory is much more strongly determined by internal than by external factors. External factors, such as how the information is displayed and how long a person is exposed to it, are not nearly as important as how the person thinks about it in relation to existing knowledge. For example, noticing distinctive features—attributes of new information that are noticeably different from what you already know or expect—make that information more memorable (Graesser & Nakamura, 1982). The importance of distinctiveness was illustrated earlier when you probably recalled the unusual and non sleep-related word artichoke, even though, on the basis of its position in the middle of the sequence, you might normally have forgotten it. You might also have done particularly well at memorizing that list by thinking about most of the items as being related to something you already know about: sleep.

Semantic coding The successful encoding of information into long-term memory is the result of a relatively deep level of processing that tends to "imprint" the information. However, in doing this deep processing, people tend to ignore physical features and other details about the information and to concentrate on its underlying meaning. Thus, whereas short-term memory involves primarily an acoustic coding of information, long-term memory normally involves semantic coding. In other words, people encode general meanings or general ideas and not many of the specifics.

The dominance of semantic coding in long-term memory is highlighted by the errors that people make in recall. We have seen that the most common recall mistakes in short-term memory are acoustic; a person may incorrectly report something that sounds like the corrrect word. In contrast, mistakes in recall from long-term memory tend to involve substitutions that mean the same as the correct word. For example, a subject who has processed into long-term memory the list "watch, coffee, car, school" probably encoded four general ideas. Thus, errors in recall might appear as "watch, coffee, automobile, school."

The loss of detail that comes with semantic coding was demonstrated in a classic study by Jacqueline Sachs (1967), in which people first listened to tape-recprded passages. Then Sachs gave the subjects sentences and asked them whether each exact sentence had been in the taped passage. People did very well when they were tested immediately (using mainly short-term memory). But after only twenty-seven seconds, at which point the information had to be retrieved from long-term memory, they could not determine which of two sentences they had heard if both sentences expressed the same meaning. For example, they could not determine whether they had heard "He sent a letter about it Galileo, the great Italian scientist" or "A letter about it was sent to Galileo, the great Italian scientist. " In other words, they remembered the general meaning of what they had heard, but not the exact wording.

People are clearly capable of encoding images, as well as general meaning, into long-term memory. In one study, for example, people viewed 2,500 pictures. (It took sixteen hours just to present the stimuli!) Still, the subjects later correctly recognized more than 90 percent of the pictures tested (Standing, Conezio & Haber, 1970). One reason why pictures are remembered so well is that they have many distinctive features, which are likely to attract attention and to be perceived and encoded. Another reason is that such stimuli may be represented in terms of both a visual code and a semantic code—Such a dual coding theory suggests that information is better rememberd when it is represented in both codes than in only one (paivio, 1978).

Individuals with eidetic imagery(遗觉象), commonly called photographic memory, go far beyond recognizing recently seen pictures; they have automatic, long-term, detailed, and vivid images of virtually everything they have seen. About 5 percent of all school-age children have eidetic imagery, but almost no adults have it (Haber, 1979; Leask, Haber & Haber, 1969; Merritt, 1979). Why the ability to store detailed images disappears with age is not known.

Storage

Whereas the capacity of short-term memory is quite limited, there is reason to believe that long-term memory has an unlimited, or at least an undetermined, capacity (Tulvng, 1974). Evidence for this conclusion comes from studies on how and why people forget.

The course of forgetting The systematic study of forgetting was also begun by Ebbinghaus, To measure forgetting, he devised the method of savings, which involves computing the difference between the number of repetitions needed to learn a list of words and the number of repetitions needed to relearn it after some time has elapsed. This difference is called the savings. If it took Ebbinghaus ten trials to learn a list and ten more trials to relearn it, there would be no savings, and forgetting would have been complete. If it took him ten trials to learn the list and only five trials to relearn it, there would be a savings of 50 percent. As you can see in Fingure 7.13 Ebbinghaus found that some savings existed even thirty-one days after the original learning. In general, savings decline (and forgetting increase) as time passes. However, the most dramatic drop in what people retain in long-term memory occurs during the first nine hours, especially in the first hour. After this initial decline, the rate of forgetting slows down considerably.

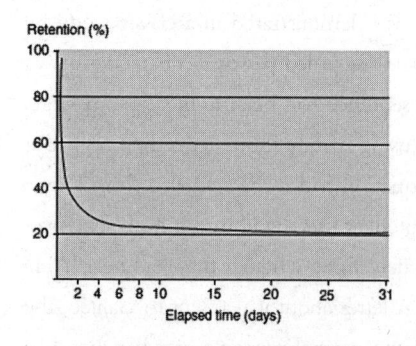

Figure 7.13

Ebbinghaus's Curve of Forgetting

Ebbinghaus found that most forgetting occurs during the first nine hours affer learning, especially during the first hour. After that, forgetting continues, but at a much slower rate (Ebbinghaus, 1885).

Ebbinghaus's use of nonsense syllables has been criticized by contemporary psychologists, who have substituted real words, sentences, and even stories. However, Ebbinghaus's curve of forgetting has been repeatedly confirmed. Although people remember sensible stories better than nonsense syllables, the shape of the forgetting curve is the same no matter what material is involved (Davis & Moore, 1935), There is virtually always a strong inital drop in memory, followed by a much more moderate decrease over time (Slamecka & McElree, 1983).

Savings can be very long-lasting. You may well forget something you have learned if you do not use the information, but it is very easy to relearn the material if the need arises. This is true of virtually everything—from meaningless passages in a foreign language, to motor skills like riding a bicycle, to academic subjects like physics.

Causes of forgetting   Whatever the benefits of long-term savings, you are more likely to be aware of the frustrations of forgetting. Drama critic and humorist Robert Benchley offered an extreme, if facetious, example. He claimed that when, several years after graduating, he tried to recall everything he had learned in college, he came up with just thirty-nine items. They included statements like "Charlemagne either diedor was born or did something with the Holy Roman Empire in 800" and "Marcus Aurelius had a son who turned out to be a bad' boy. " Is that all he learned in four years? Not at all. The typical college student will learn literally thousands of things, and many of them will be represented in memory until death. But people do forget. Why?

In our discussion of short-term memory, we noted the two main causes of forgetting: decay and interference. **Decay theory** suggests that, if people do not use information in long-term memory, it gradually fades until it is lost completely. In contrast, **interference theory** holds that forgetting information in long-term memory is due to the influence of other learning. As noted earlier, one way it can occur is through retroactive interference, in which learning new information interferes with the ability to rememeber old information. The person given something to learn and then tested on it after various delay intervals remembers less and less as the delays become longer. But is this due to decay or to interference? It is not easy to tell, because longer delays produce not only more decay but also more retroactive interference, because the subject is exposed to further information while waiting.

Karl Dallenbach thought that he could determine the cause of forgetting by creating a situation in which time passed but there was no accompanying interference. Evidence of forgetting in such a situation would suggest that decay, not interference, was operating. The subjects in one such experiment were, of all things, cockroaches (Minimi & Dallenbach, 1946), These creatures have a natural tendency to avoid light, but the researchers conditioned them to avoid a dark area of their cage by shocking them there. After learning to stay in the light, some of the roaches were returned to their normal laboratory environment. Members of another group were placed individually in small cotton-lined boxes, in which they could breathe but not move. The researchers reasoned that this group would not experience the interference associated with normal physical activity.

Later, the researchers calculated savings scores as each group of cockroaches again learned to avoid the dark area. Figure 7.14a shows the results. The performance of the two groups was very similar when reconditioning was done after only a half-hour's delay, but as the delay lengthened, the difference between the groups grew. Savings declined only slightly for the immobilized cockroaches but dropped dramatically for those that had been nonnally active. These results strongly support the notion that forgetting, at least in this situation was due to interference, not to decay.

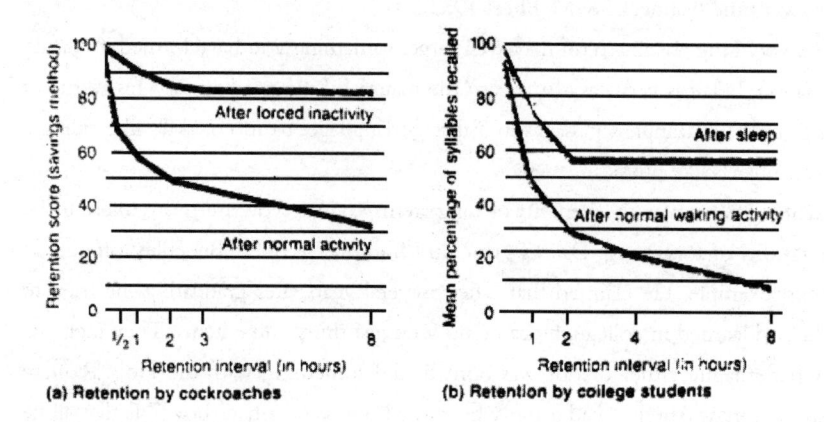

Figure 7.14
Retention of Memory over Time
Forgetting occurs much more rapidly over time if (a) cockroaches or (b) college students engage in normal activity after learning than if the interval before recall is spent quietly. These results suggest that interference is much more important in forgetting than the passage of time. (1946 by the Board of Trustees of the University of Illinois.)

So much for cockroaches. What about humans? In another of Dallenbach's experiments, college students learned a list of nonsense syllables and then either continued with their waking routine or were sheltered from interference by going to sleep. Again, while the delay (and thus the decay) was held constant for both groups, the greater interference associated with being awake produced much more forgetting, as Figure 7.14b shows (Jenkins & Dallenbach, 1924). Results like these suggest that interference is the key to forget. As we have seen the interference can be retroactive, in which new information interferes with recalling of older information, or proactive, in which old information interferes with learning new information. Table 7.3 outlines the types of experiments used to study the influence of each form of interference on long–term memory.

Retrieval

A great deal of research indicates that interference produces forgetting mainly by creating failures of retrieval. In one study, for example, people were presented with different numbers of word lists. Each list contained words from six semantic categories, such as types of buildings (hut, cottage, tent, hotel) and earth formations(cliff, river, hill, volcano). Some people learned a list and then recalled as many of the words as possible. Other groups learned the first list and then learned different numbers of other lists before trying to recall the first one. The results were dramatic. As the number of intervening lists increased, the number of words that people could recall from the original list declined consistently (Tulving & Psotka, 1971).

Proactive interference

Group	Time1	Time2	Time3	Result
experimental	Learn	Learn	Recall	The experimental group will suffer from proactive interference, and the control group will be able to recall more material form list B.
	listA	listB	listB	
control	nothing	learn		
	listB	listB		

Retroactive interference

Group	Time1	Time2	Time3	Result
experimental	Learn	Learn	Recall	The experimental group will suffer from proactive interference, and the control group will be able to recall more of the material form list A.
	listA	listB	listA	
control	Learn	Nothing	Recall	
	listB		listA	

Table 7.3
Procedures for Studying Interference
Proactive interference occurs when previously learned material interferes with the learning of new material. Retroactive interference occurs when learning new information inhibits the recall of previously learned information.

These results reflected strong retroactive interference. Then the researchers gave a second test, in which they provided people with a cue by telling them the category of the words (such as types of buildings) to be recalled. Then the number of interveing lists had almost no effect on the number of words recalled from the original list, as Figure 7.15 shows.
This result indicated that the words were still represented in long-term memory, but that peple were unable to retrieve them without appropriate cues. In other words, the original forgetting was due to a failure in retrieval. Findings like these have led some theorists to conclude that all forgetting from long-term memory is due to some form of retrieval failure (Eysenck, 1977; Raaijmakers & Shiffrin, 1981; Tulving 1974). Does this mean that everything in long-term memory remains there until death, even if we cannot always, or ever, recall it? Some theorists say yes, others say no, arguing that interference may also cause, information to be displaced from long-term memory. No one yet knows for sure. What we do know is that a great deal of information remains in the system for years or even decades.

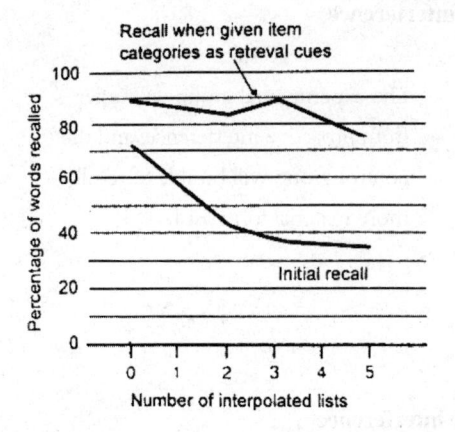

Figure 7.15
Retrieval from Long−Term Memory
Performance at recalling a list of items is strongly influenced by the number of other lists learned before recalling the initial list; this reflects the effect of retroactive interference. However, when retrieval cues are provided on a second recall test for the original list, the interfering effect of the intervening lists disappears. In other words, information that could not be retrieved under one set of conditions (without cues), could be recalled under different circumstances (with cues). (From"Retroactive Inhibition in Free Recall: Inaccessibility of Information Available in the Memory Store"by Tulving and Psotka. Journal of Experimental Psychology, 87, pp. 1−8, 1971. Copyright 1971 by the American Psychological Association Adapted by permission of the authors.)

Retrieval cues Stimuli like the category cues given in the Tulving & Psotka's (1971) experiment can help people retrieve information from long−term memory. These stimuli, called **retrieval cues**, allow people to recall things that were once forgotten and help them to recognize information stored in memory. In general, recognition tasks are easier than recall tasks because they contain more retrieval cues. For example, most students find it easier to recognize the correct alternative on a multiple−choice exam than to recall matenal "cold" on an essay test.

The cues are most effective at aiding retrieval depends on the degree to which they tap into information that was encoded at the time of original learning (Tulving, 1979; Tulving & Thomson 1973). This is known as the **encoding specificity principle**. Because long−term memories are often encoded semantically, cues that evoke the meaning of the stored information tend to work best. For example, imagining people learning a long list of sentences, one of which is either (1) "The man lifted the piano" or (2) "The man tuned the piano". Giving the cue "something heavy" during a recall rest will help subjects remember the first sentence, because they probably encoded something about the weight of a piano. "Something heavy" would probably not help in recalling the second sentence, however, because the subjects probably encoded something about the piano's sound rather than its weight. The cue "makes nice sounds" would be likely to help subjects recall the second sentence, but not the first (Barclay et al., 1974).

Context and state dependence In general, people remember more when their efforts at recall that take place in the same environment in which they learned, because they tend to encode features of the environment where the learning took place. These features later act as an effective cues. Members of a university diving club provided one demonstration of this principle. They learned lists of words while either on shore or submerged twenty feet underwater. Then they tried to recall as many of the words as possible, again whether on shore or underwater. Those who originally learned underwater scored much better when they were tested underwater than when they were tested on shore. Similarly, those who had learned the words on shore did better when tested on shore (Godden & Baddeley, 1975).

When memory can be helped or hindered by such similarities in context, it is called context−dependent. For example, one study found that students remember better when tested in the classroom in which they learned material than when tested in a very different classroom (Smith, Glenberg & Bork, 1978). This context dependency effect is not always strong (Saufley, Otaka & Bavaresco, 1985), but some students do find it helpful to study for a test in the classroom where the test will be given.

Like the external environment, your internal psychological environment can be encoded when you learn, and it, too, can act as a retrieval cue. When a person's internal state can aid or impede retrieval, memory is called state−dependent. For example, if people learn new material while under the influence of marijuana, they tend to recall it better if they are also tested under the influence of marijuana (Eich et al., 1975). Similar effects have been found with alcohol (Cowant 1976), with various other drugs (Eich, 1980), and with positive or negative mood states. College students remember more positive incidents from their diaries and more positive events from early childhood when they are in a positive mood at the time of recall. More negative events tend to be recalled when people are in a negative mood (Bower, 1981). State−dependent memory effects are particularly noticeable in people with bipolar disorder, a condition characterized by dramatic changes in mood, which was once known as manic−depression. These people recall information learned in the manic state much better when they are in another manic state than when they are depressed. And information learned in a depressed state is recalled best when the person is again in a depressed state (Hemy, Weingartner & Murphy, 1973).

The retrieval of incomplete knowledge   One final and important characteristic of long−term memory retrieval is examplified by the feeling−of−knowing experience (Hart, 1965, 1967; Nelson et al., 1982; Nelson & Narens, 1980). In a typical experiment, subjects are asked trivia questions. When subjects cannot answer a question, they are asked to estimate the probability that they could recognize the correct answer if they were given several options. People are surprisingly accurate at this task; the correlation between their predictions and their actual ability to recognize the items is as high as 70. Apparently people have incomplete knowledge of some answers—they know that they know the answer but simply cannot recall it.

In another example of incomplete knowledge, dictionary definitions of certain words were read to people (Brown & McNeill, 1966). If they could not recall a defined word, they were asked whether they could identify particular features of the word such as how many syllables it has, what letter it begins with, of what words it rhymes with. Again, people are proved to be quite good at this task.

How is it possible to have incomplete knowledge? Earlier we described research that suggests that information in short−term memory is represented as unique bundles of features. Similarly, it seems that individual words, as well as answers to trivia questions and other information, are represented in long-term memory as unique collections of features. Often people can retrieve some of the features (how many syllables a word has, what it rhymes with, and so on) but not enough features to identify the word.

Figure 7.16 summarizes much of the material we have covered on long-term memory and other aspects of the human memory system.

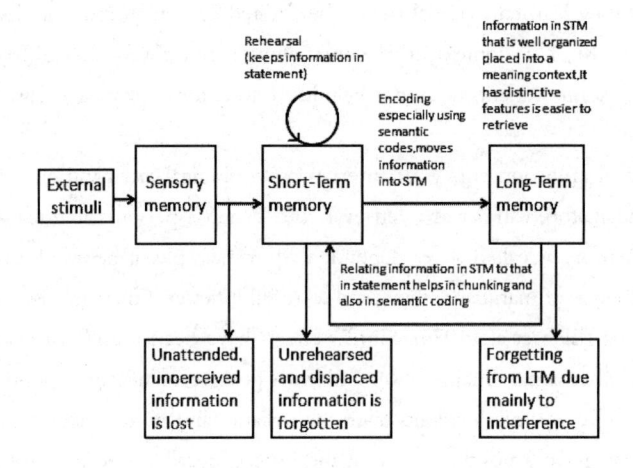

Figure 7.16
A Final Overview of the Memory System
You have now seen how sensory memory, short-term memory, and long-term memory relate to one another to create a complex, yet highly organized system for encoding, storing, an retrieving information.

第五节 构建着的记忆
(CONSTRUCTING MEMORY)

We have now described how information is encoded, stored, and retrieved through sensory, short-term, and long-term memory processes. As noted earlier, this remarkable memory system is not just an automatic record-and-playback machine. You saw, for example, that what gets encoded, stored, and retrieved can be affected by factors such as what information is already in the system. Among the other factors affecting memory are how people perceive and think about incoming information. In other words, to some extent, people can construct their memories.

Memory is costantly affected by the generalized knowledge about the world that each person has stored in long-term semantic memory. Much of this knowledge is represented in terms of schemas, or organized clusters of information about objects, events, or people. For example, simply hearing the words baseball game or sexually transmitted disease is likely to activate whole clusters of information in long-term memory. As noted in the next chapter, this generalized knowledge provides a basis for making infernce about incoming information during the encoding stage.

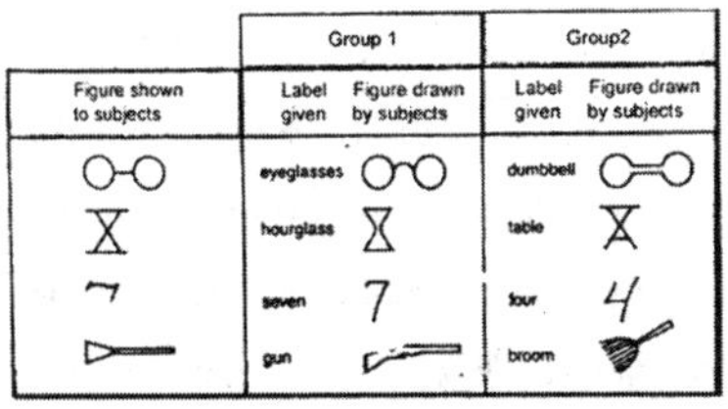

Figure 7.17 Reconstructive Memory

Carmichael, Hogant and Walter(1932) shaxved people figures like these along with various labels. In the first case, for example, the experimenter might comment, "This tends to resemble eyeglasses [or a dumbbell]." When the subjects were Later asked to reproduce the fig ures, their drawings were likely to resemble the items mentioned by the experimenter. In other words, the labels given to ambiguous items altered the subject's memory of them.

As shown in Figure 7.17, generalized knowledge also affects the way information is recalled. Another example is provided by an experiment in which researchers had undergraduates wait for several minutes in the small cluttered office of a graduate student (Brewer & Treyens, 1981). When later asked to recall everything that was in the office, most of the students mistakenly "remembered" that books were present, even though there were none. Apparently, the general knowledge that graduate students read many books influenced the sub ject's memory of what was in the room.

People must organize new information as they receive it. However, they use their existing knowledge to fill in gaps in that information. In this way, memories are constructed. To study this process, Rebecca Sulin and D. James Dooling (1974) asked their subjects to read a long passage about a dictator. In one case, the dictator was a fictitious character named Gerald Martin; in another, Adolph Hitler Later, subjects were asked if the passage contained the statement "He hated the Jews particlarly and so persecuted them. "This statement was not in the passage, but those who had been told that they were reading about Hitler "remembered" the statement more often than subjects who had read about Gerald Martin.

第六节 提高你的记忆
（IMPROVING YOUR MEMORY）

In psychology, as in medicine, physics, and other sciences, practical progress does not always require theoretical certainty. Even though some basic questions about what memory is and how it works resisty final answers, psychologists know a great deal about how memory changes over the years and how people can improve their memories. The two keys are metamemory and mnemonics (pronounced "knee monies").

Metamemory

How people try to remember something, and consequently how well they perform, is shaped to a great extent by what they know about memory. **Metamemory** is the name for knowledge about how your own memory works. It consists of three types of knowledge (Flavell, 1985; Flavell & Wellman, 1977).

First, metamemory involves understanding the abilities and weaknesses of your own memory. Preschool children are notoriously weak in this kind of understanding. They know that the way people look does not affect their memory, that noise interferes with remembering, and that it is harder to remember many items than a few. But in their self-confident naivete, they deny that they ever forget anyting and claim that they can remember quantities of information beyond their own (or anyone else's) capacity (Flavell, Friedrichs & Hoyt, 1970). Only in the school years do children learn the limits—and the strengths—of their memories. This knowledge obviously influences how a person goes about learning something. You might, for instance, be comfortable memorizing a list of directions; another person might write the directions down immediately.

Second, metamemory involves knowledge about different types of tasks. For example, children ieam to use different strategies for memorization when they know they will face a short-answer test, which requires recall, rather than a multiple-choice test, which for the most part requires only recognition (Horowitz & Horowitz, 1975).

Third, metamemory involves knowledge of what types of strategies are most effective in remembering new information. This is the aspect of metamemory that is most likely to change dramatically with age and experience (Fabricius & Wellman, 1983). Consider the use of the rehearsal strategy—repeating information until it is fixed in memory. Children as young as five may rehearse items when they are asked to remember something (Flavell, Beach & Chinsky,1966; Istomina, 1975; Keeney, Cannizzo & Flavell, 1967). But most five-year-olds do not use rehearsal to help them remember. They learn to rehearse in elementary school, and they refine their rehearsal strategies over the school years.

For example, suppose two groups of children, one consisting of five-year-olds and one of ten-year-olds, are asked to memorize lists of words. The two groups will probably do equally well if the word lists are short, but the older group will do much better than the younger on a long list. Why? Rote rehearsal, the younger children's iraian strategy, is very effective for recalling short lists. But when the older children are given a long list, they tend to combine rote rehearsal with more elaborate strategies, such as stringing the words into meaningful sentences or fitting them into different categories. Young children do not realize that rote rehearsal is no longer effective with a longer list, and they continue to use it. In this sense, their metamemory is not as good as that of older children; as a result, their performance is much poorer. This difference can be largely eliminated by teaching younger children to use a different strategy. We therefore know that the difference in performance is due, not to ability, but to the strategy used (Brown, 1975).

Investigations of metamemory hold great promise for furthering the understanding of various types of memory deficits. The difficulties of retarded children are one example. Investigations of metamemory have pointed out differences between retarded and normal children that are similar to those between younger and older normal chidren. For example, normal ten-year-olds use rote rehearsal to remember a short list of items, but elaborative rehearsal when given a long list.

Retarded ten-year-olds, however, like normal five-year-olds, tend to use rote rehearsal regardless of the length of the list. Again, the difference between groups can be eliminated or substantially reduced by teaching retarded children to use a more effective strategy (Butterfield, Wambold & Belmont, 1973; Campione & Brown, 1977; Resnick & Glaser, 1976). Teaching them to do so, however, is difficult, as we will describe when we discuss mental retardation in Chapter 10.

Mnemonics

Mnemonics are strategies for placing information in an organized context in order to remember it. For example, to remember the names of the Great Lakes, you can simply remember the mnemonic HOMES, and the lake names will follow easily: Huron Ontario Michigan, Erie, and Superior. Verbal organization is the basis for many other mnemonics. For example, you can link items by weaving them into a story, or you can create a sentence or a rhyme. To remember the spelling of arithmetic, some children learn "A rat in Tom's house might eat Tom's ice cream."

Classical mnemonics Two very simple but powerful methods that can be used to remember almost anything are the peg-word system and the method of loci. The first step in using the peg-word system is to learn a list of words to serve as memory pegs. One of the most popular of these lists is: one is a bun, two is a shoe, three is a tree, four is a door, five is a hive, six is a stick, seven is heaven, eight is a gate, nine is a line, and ten is a hen. Once you learn such a list, you can use it to help you remember anything. For each item to be remembered, create an image or association between it and the previously learned peg word. In general the more novel and vivid you make the images and the better they interrelate the objects involved, the more effective they will be.

One of the authors was introduced as a college student to another popular mnemonic. His roommate, who was known to brag a bit, said that he could remember any one htmdred words if he had enough time to think about them. A bet of $ 100 was made, the words were read, and the author lost. It was, as they say, a real learning experience. The author's friend had used a powerful and ancient mnemonic called the method of loci (pronounced "low sigh"), or the method of placed. The first step in this method is to think about a set of familiar geographic locations. For example, if you use your home, you might imagine walking along the sidewalk, up the steps, through the front door, around all four comers of the living room, and through each of the other rooms. Step two is to imagine each item to be remembered in one of these locations. Whenever you want to remember a list, you use the same locations, in the same order. As with the peg-word system, particularly vivid images seem to be particularly effective (Bower, 1970). For example, tomatoes smashed against the front door or bananas hanging from the bedroom ceiling might be helpful in recalling items from a grocery list.

These and other mnemonic systems share one characteristic: each requires that you have a well-learned body of knowledge (such as peg words or geographical locations) that can be used to provide a context for organizing incoming information. Thus, the success of these strategies provides yet another demonstration of the importance of relating new information to knowledge already stored in memory.

Remembering textbook material Most of the procedures discussed so far were devised for remembering arbitrary lists. When you want to remember more organized material, such as a chapter in a textbook, the same principles apply. In other words, you should create a context in which to organize the information.

More specific advice comes from a study that examined how successful and unsuccessful college students approach their reading (Whimbey, 1976). Unsuccessful students tend to read the material straight through; they do not slow down when they reach a difficult section; and they keep going even when they do not understand what is being said. In contrast, successful college students monitor their own performance, reread difficult sections and periodically stop to review what they have learned before going on. In short, effective learners engage in a very deep level of processing. They are active learners, thinking of each new fact in relation to other material. As a result, they not only learn to see similarities and differences among facts andideas, but also create a context in which many new facts can be organized effectively. You can create a context for new knowledge by, for instance, taking the role of an instructor and trying to explain to a friend the information you are learning. His or her questions will not only reveal any gaps in your memory for the material, but the lecture you create will establish an outline of framework into which you can place new information

Based on what is known about memory, we can suggest two specific guidelines for reading a textbook. First, make sure that you Understand what you are reading before moving on. Second, use the SQ3R method, which is one of the most successful strategies for remembering textbook material (Anderson, 1978; Frase 1975: Rickards 1976: Thomas & Robinson, 1972). SQ3R stands for the five activities that should be followed when you read a chapter: survey, question, read, recite, and review. These activities are designed to increase the depth to which you process the information you read.

1. Survey One of the best ways to begin a new chapter is by not reading it. Instead, take a few minutes to skim the chapter. Look at the section headings and any boldface or italicized terms. Obtain a general idea of what material will be discussed, how it is organized, and how its topics relate to one another and to what you already know. Some people find it useful to survey the entire chapter once and then survey each major section in a little more detail before reading it.

2. Question Before reading each section, stop and ask yourself what content will be covered and what information should be extracted from it.

3. Read Read the text, but think about the material as you read. Are the questions you raised earlier being answered? Do you see the connections between the topics?

4. Recite At the end of each section 9 stop and recite the major points. Resist the temptation to be passive by mumbling something like. "Oh, I remember that" . Put the ideas into your own words.

5. Review Finally, at the end of the chapter, review all the material. You should see connections not only within a section, but also among the sections. The objective is to see how the author has organized the material. Once you grasp the organization, the individual facts will be far easier to remember as well.

Is there anything to add to all of this? Yes. At the end, take a breake. Relax. Approach each chapter fresh. There is nothing to be gained from cramming. Following these procedures will not only allow you to learn and remember the material better, but also save you considerable time.

Lecture notes   Lectures are very common in colleges and universities, but they are far from an ideal method for conveying information. Important details in lectures are usually remembered no better than unimportant ones (Gool kasian, Terry & Park, 1979). In fact, jokes and parenthetical remarks in a lecture seem to be remembered far better than major topic statements (Kintsch & Bates, 1977).

Taking notes does help people remember what was said in a lecture (Peper & Meyer, 1978). Unfortuately, effective note taking is not an easily acquired skill. The major difficulty, is that the learner has no control over the pace of the lecture. But by using what you know about memory, you can devise some simple strategies for taking and using notes effectively. A first step is to realize that, in note taking, more is not necessarily better; it may be worse. Taking detailed notes of everything requires that you pay attention to everything that is said the unimportant as well as the important—and leaves little time for thinking about the material. In fact, the thinking involved in note taking is often more important than the writing, because it provides a framework for the facts. (This is why borrowing notes from other people is not nearly as effective as taking your own. It is very difficult to read notes if you do not have the general framewonk of the lecture already stored in memory). Note takers who concentrate on expressing the major ideas in relatively few words remember more than those who try to catch every detail (Howe, 1970). In short, the best way to take notes is to think about what is being said, draw connections with other material in the lecture, and then summarize the major points clearly and concisely.

Once you have a set of lecture notes, what should you do with them? Review the notes as soon as possible after the lecture so that you can fill in missing details and decipher your scribbles. Do not wait until a few days before an exam. As you saw earlier, most forgetting from long–term memory occurs within the first few hours after learning.

When the time comes for serious study, resist the urge to read your notes passively. Use them actively, as if they were a chapter in a textbook. Look for the "big picture". Write a detailed outline. Think about how various points are related to one another and how the topics themselves are interrelated. Once you have organized the material, the details will make more sense and will be much easier to remember. Go slowly and do it well. In the end, you will save yourself considerable time by being organized and efficient the first time you go through your notes.

第七节 未来研究趋向
(FUTURE DIRECTIONS)

Our understanding of memory has advanced considerably since Ebbinghaus began experimental investigations of the topic a hundred years ago. Many of the laws that govern sensory memory, short-term memory, and long-term memory have been discovered; and a great deal is known about how information is encoded, stored, and retrieved from each of these memory systems.

During the next decade, prominent topics of debate and research are likely to include the controversy about how many types of memory there are, the value of levels-of -processing theory, and questions about how memory works in everyday life. The study of how memory functions in eyewitness testimony during criminal trials is one specific example. Another is the examination of the role that sensory memory plays in the processing of complex information from the natural environment (Adelson, 1983; Coltheart, 1980, 1983; Finke, 1983; Finke & Freyd, 1985; Klatzky,1983).

Researchers are also investigating the causes and consequences of becoming an expert. For example, how do physicians learn radiological anatomy-the science of the relationships between anatomical structure and the patterns seen on X ray plates (Lesgold, 1984; Lesgold et al., 1981)? Whereas true experts store huge bodies of organized information in memory and can read X rays easily, students tend to make certain systematic and predictable errors. Why? In this and other areas of expertise, experts' mental representations of information in their field tends to change over the course of several years. Individual facts are integrated with one anoter, and the entire body of knowledge is organized more effectively. As a result, experts suffer less than nonexperts from both proactive and retroactive interfemce (Reder & Anderson, 1980; Smith, Adams & Schorr, 1978). Exactly how this improvement occurs something of a mystery. In the next chapter, we will look more closely at the thought processes of experts, as well as at efforts to "teach" computers to perform like experts.

Finally, there is enormous excitement about relating what is known about normal and abnormal memory. For example, if patients suffering from anterograde amnesia (the inability to remember anyrthing after some traumatic event, such as a head injury) play a complicated game, they later have no recollection of having played the game. But some of them play the game better the next time, improving their performance at the same rate as one would expect from a person with normal memory. One interpretation is that, although these patients have no episodic memory of ever having played the game, their semantic knowledge of the game has increased. Another possibility is that whatever caused the amnesia leaves the procedural memory system unaffected, even though it is divorced from any episodic memory. How the episodic experience is translated into semantic or procedural knowledge, and how they can become completely disassociated in memory, are unanswered questions.

There are, of course, many other unresolved issues. Courses on learning and memory provide an excellent starting place for learning more about the latest research, as well as for studying the basic principles of memory in more detail. Other relevant courses include cognitive psychology and experimental psychology.

词汇 (Vocabulary)

1. acoustic codes   听觉编码信息
2. acoustic coding   听觉编码
3. acoustically related   与听觉有关的
4. acetylcholine   n. 乙酰胆碱
5. amnesia   n. 记忆缺失、遗忘
6. amygdala   n. 小脑扁桃叶
7. anatomy   n. 解剖
8. anesthetics   n. 麻醉剂
9. anterograde amnesia   n. 顺行性遗忘（创伤或疾病后一段时间记忆力的丧失）
10. axon   n. 轴突
11. bipolar amnesia   n. 神经元两级的
12. blink   vi. 眨眼
13. brown-peterson procedure   n. 布朗—彼得逊法
14. carbon monoxide   n. 一氧化碳
15. cholinergic   adj. 释放出乙酰胆碱的
16. chunk   n. 厚厚的一块、组块
17. constructing memory   记忆建构
18. context-dependent   外部环境的影响
19. decay   n. 衰退
    decaytheory 衰退说
20. displacement   n. 移置
21. dual coding theory   双码理论
22. duration   n. 保持
23. dyslexia   n. 读字困难、阅读能力失常
24. echo   n. 反响
    echoic memory 反响记忆
25. elaborative rehearsal   详尽重复
26. eidetic imagery   遗觉像
27. engram   印迹（一种记忆的痕迹）
28. encoding specificity principle   编码特定性原则
29. epileptic seizure   n. 癫痫病的突然发作
30. episodic seizure   情景记忆
31. exhaustive serial search   彻底系列搜索
32. feeling-of-knowing experience   知情经验
33. fixate   vt. 注视
34. fragile   adj. 易破坏的
35. glean   vt. 搜集
36. hippocampus   n. 海马

37. icon(iconography)　n. 标志、标记
    icon memory 标记记忆
38. immediate memory span　瞬时记忆容量
39. inhibit　v. 抑制
40. instaneous　瞬时的、即时的
41. interference　干扰
    interference theory　干扰说
42. ion　离子
43. level-of-processing model　过程—水平模式
44. limbic system　边缘系统
45. long-term memory　长时记忆
46. maintenance rehearsal　保持重复
47. mammal　哺乳动物
48. mainc-depression　躁狂抑郁性精神病
49. meaningful groupings of information　信息组织
50. method of savings　节省法
51. meta memory　元记忆
52. metronome　节拍器
53. mnemonics　记忆法
54. neural activity　神经活动
55. neurotransmitter　n. 神经递质
56. nonsense syllable　无意义音节
57. nostril　鼻孔
58. olfactory　adj. 嗅觉的
59. parallel search　相似搜索
60. partial-report procedure　局部报告法
61. peg-word system　主题—词汇系统
62. primacy effect　首因效应
63. procedural memory　运动记忆
64. proactive interference　前摄抑制
65. recall task　回忆
66. recency effect　近因效应
67. rehearsing　复述、重复
68. release from proactive interference　前摄抑制的排除
69. retarded children　有障碍的孩子
70. retrieval　提取
71. retroactive interference　倒摄抑制
72. retrograde interference　逆行性遗忘（在休克和疾病发作不久前出现的遗忘）
73. rudimentary　adj. 初步的

74. saccadic eye movement n. 单挛运动（眼睛由一个注视点转到另一个注视点的迅速移动）

75. savings   n. 绝对节省值

76. selective attention   n. 选择性注意

77. semantic codes   语义编码信息

78. semantic memory   语义记忆

79. sensory registers   感觉登记

80. seral search   系列搜索

81. serial-position curves   系列位置曲线图

82. skill memory   技能记忆

83. span of apprehendsion   笼统观察事物的能量

84. subcortical   皮质下的

85. synapse   n. 突触

86. thalamus   n. 丘脑

87. trace consolidation   记忆痕迹通路

88. visual codes   视觉编码信息

89. whole-report procedure   整体报告法

第八章 思维与语言
（THINKING AND LANGUAGE）

本章要点（Chapter Outline）

人类信息加工系统
(The Human Information-Processing System)
认知过程（Cognitive Process）
思维（Thinking）
概念意象推理（Concepts Image Reasoning）
问题的解决（Problem Solving）
风险决策（Risky Decision Making）
语言的要素（The Elements of Language）
语言的发展阶段（Stages of Language Development）
语言的获得（How is Language Learned）

    思维是心理学中最复杂，也是最重要的问题之一。关于思维的研究，虽然开始得比较早，但至今仍有许多不明确的问题，思维是人类认知的核心，是在人的感知觉等初级心理过程的基础上发展起来的。

    言语则被称为是思维的外壳，它与思维是密不可分的。至今，言语的机制和言语的获得都是心理学中研究已久但久无定论的问题。

    本章在语言与知觉、语言与思维的关系问题上，为我们开拓了新的研究视角。此外，思维中关于概念掌握、解决问题、制定决策等课题日益要求我们在实验心理学、认知心理学、心理语言学及工程心理学各领域中不断深入研究。

Dr. Joyce Wallace, a New York City internist, was having trouble figuring out what was the matter with Laura McBride, a forty-year-old woman who reported pains in her stomach and abdomen, aching muscles, irritability occasional dizzy spells, and general tiredness (Rouech. 1986). The doctor's hypotheses was iron-deficiency anemia, a condition in which the level of oxygen-carrying hemoglobin in the blood is too low. There was some evidence to support that hypothesis. A physical examination revealed that Laura's spleen was somewhat enlarged, and blood tests showed low hemoglobin and high red blood cell production, suggesting that her body was attempting to compensate for the loss of hemoglobin. However, other tests revealed normal iron level. Perhaps she was losing blood through internal bleeding, but a stool test ruled that out. Had Laura been vomiting blood? She said no. Blood in the urine? No. How about abnormally heavy menstrual flow? Nothing unusual there. During the next week, Dr Wallace puzzled over the problem while additional tests showed a worsening hemoglobin situation and Laura reported more intense pain, now accompanied by cramps, shortness of breath, and severe loss of energy. Clearly, this woman's blood was becoming less and less capable of sustaining her, but if it was not actually being lost, what was happening to it? Finally, the doctor decided to look at a smear of Laura's blood on a microscope slide. What she saw? A condition called basophilic stippling—indicated that some kind of poison was destroying Laura s red blood cells. But what would poisoned her? Laura spent most of her time at home, repairing and restoring paintings, but it could not be anything there because none of her teenage daughters was affected at all. Or was something poisoning her? Dr Wallace asked herself, "What does Laura do that the girls do not?" Well, She works with paintings. Paint Lead! She might be suffering from lead poisoning! When the next blood test showed a lead level seven times higher than normal, Dr, Wallace knew she was right at last.

To solve this medical mystery and prescribe the appropriate treatment? Dr. Wallace relied on her ability to think, solve problems, and make judgments and decisions. She employed these higher mental processes to weigh the pros and cons of contrasting hypotheses and to reach decisions about what tests to order and how to interpret them. These same high-level mental processes also played a central role in other aspects of the case, as Dr. Wallace consulted with the patient and other physicians using that unique human capability known as language.

The work of a physician is an example of the thinking, judging, decision-making, problem-solving, and linguistic communication that occur in an unending stream in every human being all the time. These processes are involved in everything from a restaurant customer's choice between shrimp and roast beef to a national leader s decisions about actions that could lead to nuclear war. How good are human judgments and decisions? What factors can interfere with or influence them? How are thoughts transformed into language? Psychologists have been studying these questions for many years. In this chapter, we introduce some of their findings and highlight the importance of their research.

第一节 概要：从刺激到动作
（FROM STIMULUS TO ACTION:AN OVERVIEW）

If you think that Dr. Wallace had a difficult time diagnosing Laura's illness, consider the situation faced by the astronauts Apollo 13. As they approached the moon, on April 17,1970, they heard an explosion. An oxygen tank had ruptured. Faced with potential catastrophe, the crew had to take immediate action and answer some crucial questions. Was the damage so extensive that the mission should be aborted? Which systems still operated normally? How would the damage affect the crew's ability to return to earth? The crew needed to figure out how to survive with the depleted oxygen supply and how to navigate despite the damage. To solve these problems, they relied on extensive communication with ground control. As it turned out, the moon landing had to, be scrubbed, but ways were, found to conserve enough oxygen to sustain the crew until they could get back to earth.

The physician's task may appear far removed from the concerns of astronauts but the mental processes involved are surprisingly similar. In both situations, people have to perceive a complex pattern of incoming stimuli, much of it in the form of language; evaluate that pattern: and make decisions about it. Often these processes occur so quickly and appear so complicated that the task of analyzing them may seem like trying to nail jell–O to a tree. To describe and begin to understand what happens between the presentation of stimuli and the execution of responses, many psychologists in recent years have considered people mainly as information–processing systems.

The Human Information–Processing System

Any **information–processing system** receives information, represents information with symbols, and manipulates those representations. According to this model, information from a stimulus is passed through several stages before a response is shows these stages.

We have examined the first two stages in previous chapters. In the first stage, information about the stimulus reaches the brain by way of the sensory receptors. This stage does not require attention. In the second stage, the information must be perceived and recognized, a process involving the memory systems discussed in Chapter 7. Recall that, to recognize a stimulus, people match the perceived pattern to a pattern in long–term memory. In addition, various kinds of encoding are used to hold new information in memory; thus, information is further transformed at this stage. It demands relatively little attention. In the third stage, once the stimulus has been recognized, it is necessary to decide what to do with it. The information may simply be stored in memory. But if the decision is to take some actions, then a response must also be selected before the fourth stage–execution of the response can occur. This third stage demands more attention than perception. To begin exploring how information is processed during this third, decision making stage, consider a relatively simple example: a case in which a decision is made so quickly that you may not be conscious of thinking about it.

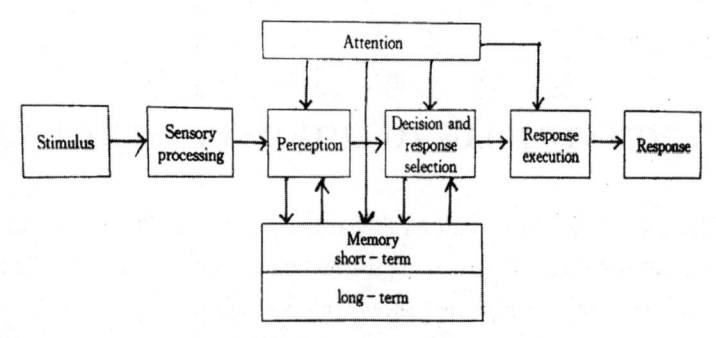

Figure 8.1

An Information–Processing Model

Information is transformed or changed by different operations or stages of information processing each requiring some minimum amount of time for execution. Certain of these stages requires heavy dependence on both short–term and long–term memory. And certain of the stages compete with short-term memory for attention, that limited supply of mental energy that is required for information processing to be carried out efficiently.

High-Speed Decision Making

Imagine that, as you are speeding down a road late at night, the green traffic light you are approaching suddenly turns yellow. In an instant you must decide whether to apply the brakes or floor the accelerator. Here is a situation in which a stimulus is presented, a decision must be made under extreme time pressure, and then the decision must be translated into action. Reaction times Psychologists have studied how people make decisions like this by examining reaction time, the elapsed time between the presentation of a physical stimulus and an overt response. Reaction time is.the total time needed for all the stages shown in Figure 8.1. In fact, the study of reaction time helped generate the information-processing approach. If cognition involves distinct stages, as the information-processing approach holds, then each stage must take some time. Therefore, one should be able to infer what stages or substages exist by examining changes in mental chronometry, the timing of mental events (Posner, 1978). The reaction time is not the time to execute the reaction, but the time required to stimulate the application of the organism to the apparent response.

Several factors influence reaction times. First, the reaction time to intense stimuli, such as bright lights or loud sounds, is shorter than to weaker stimuli. Second, the easier it is to discriminate between two or more stimuli, or the greater the difference between them, the shorter the reaction time will be. A third factor is the complexity of the decision; that is, the larger the number of possible actions that might be carried out in response to a set of stimuli, the longer the reaction time. Then reaction time is also influenced by stimulus-response compatibility. If the relationship between a set of possible stimuli and possible responses is a natural or compatible one, their reaction time will be fast. If it is not, then reaction time will be slow. Figure 8.2 illustrates compatible and incompatible relationships. Finally expectancy also affects reaction time. As we noted in the chapter on perception, expected stimuli are perceived more quickly than those that are surprising. Expectancy has the same effect on response time: people respond faster to stimuli that they anticipate and slower to those that surprise them.

In any reaction time task there is a speed-accuracy trade-off. If you try to respond quickly, errors increase, if you try for an error-free performance, reaction time increases (Pachella, 1974).

Figure 8.2

Stimulus-Response Compatibility

Suppose a cook is standing in front of the stove when a pot starts to boil over (a stimulus). The cook must rapidly adjust the appropriate dial to reduce the heat (the response). How fast the cook reacts may depend in part on the design of the stove. *In the stove shown in(a), the dials are placed next to the burners, and there is a clear and visually compatible association that determines which stimulus belongs to which response. In (b), however, this compatibility does not exist, and reaction time will be much slower.*

Important as reaction times are, however, they cannot directly measure what is going on between the presentation of a stimulus and the execution of a response.

But it cannot tell us how long it takes for response selection to begin, although there have been many ingenious efforts to make inferences about such things (Donders, 1969; Pachella, 1974). To analyze mental events and their timing more directly, psychologists have turned to other methods, such as the use of evoked brain potentials.

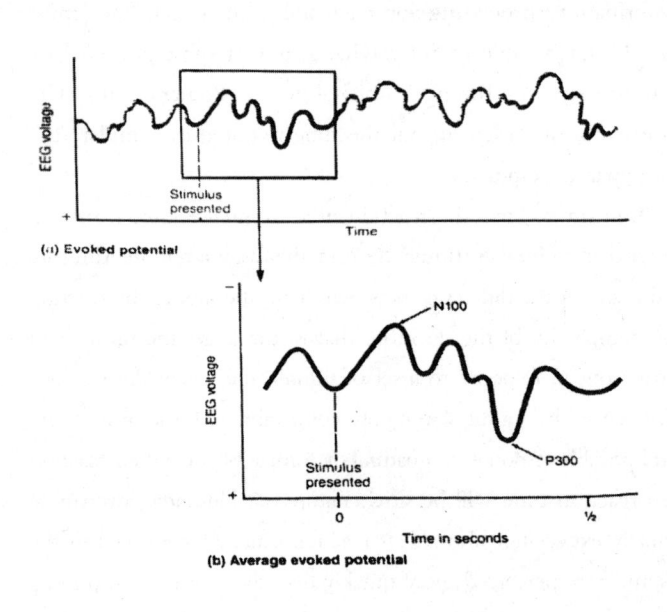

Figure 8.3
Evoked potentials
(a) *The EEG tracing produced when a subject s name is presented. The box indicates what is happening just after the name is presented. Although it is difficult for the untrained eye to see, there is a small temporary change in the voltage pattern. If several of these evoked potentials were averaged so that the random variations in the EEG tracings were eliminated, the result would appear as in (b), with a negative peak (N100) followed by a large positive peak (P300).*
(b)*Average evoked potential.*

Evoked brain potentials   Recall that the **evoked brain potential** is the small temporary change in voltage that occurs in response to discrete stimuli. By recording a series of responses to the same stimuli, researchers can determine the average evoked potential. Figure 8.3 shows an example. Each peak reflects the firing of large groups of neurons, within different regions of the brain, at different times during the information–processing sequence. Thus, the pattern of the peaks provides information that is more precise than overall reaction time.

The first negative peak, called N100, occurs around 100 milliseconds after the stimulus. It reflects initial sensory processing, and its voltage comes directly from the primary sensory cortex that processes the stimulus. Thus, N100s produced by auditory stimuli are different from those produced by visual stimuli. Stimuli that are in the focus of attention produce the larger N100s than those that are ignored (Hillyard, Picton & Regan. 1978).

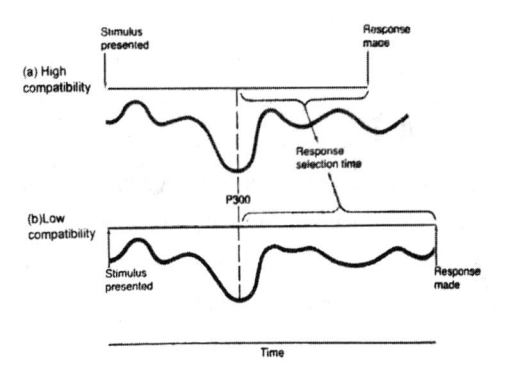

Figure 8.4

Effects of Stimulus–Response Compatibility

McCarthy and Donchin (1981)gave people two buttons and then presented the word right or left. Sometimes the subjects were told to give a compatible response, pressing to give a compatible response, pressing the right button in response to the word right and the left button in response to the word left. At other times, the assignment was incompatible to press the left button to the word right and vice versa. Here is a schematic picture of the results of McCarthy and Donchin's experiment. As you might expect, variation in compatibility had a strong effect, variation in compatibility had a strong effect on reaction time, but it did not affect the time of the P300. Therefore, the researchers concluded that stimulus response compatibility does not affect perceptual processing. When incompatibility lengthens reaction time, it does so by producing a delay in selecting the response.

Of particular interest is the positive peak called P300; as we described in the chapter on perception, it occurs roughly 300 to 500 milliseconds after a stimulus. It seems to signal the time at which perception of a stimulus is completed and the significance of that stimulus has been evaluated. Stimuli that are quite surprising, and therefore significant, produce large P300s compared to stimuli that are routine and expected (Donchin, 1981; Pritchard, 1981).

Once researchers had established the meaning of the P300, they could use it to study the timing of mental events. For example, Figure 8.4 describes an experiment on the effects of stimulus–response compatibility which shows that compatibility alters the speed of response selection but does not seem to alter the timing of perception.

Evoked potentials have also been used to determine the mental capabilities of patients who cannot communicate normally and to determine precisely what region of the brain has been damaged by a disease, accident, or poison.

Is Cognitive Processes same as language?

Decades ago, American behaviorist John Watson argued that thought is nothing more than covert speech. But if thought and speech are identical, why do people often have such a difficult time translating their thoughts into words? This intuitive case against Watson's view was bolstered in 1947 by a rather heroic experiment by Scott Smith (Smith et al., 1947) . If Watson's view were correct, Smith reasoned that paralyzing the speech muscles should disrupt thinking. Smith took a dose of curare a potentially lethal drug that temporarily paralyzes the peripheral nervous system, including the vocal apparatus. The paralysis was so complete that Smith needed respirators to help him breathe, but despite the drug's devastating effect on the speech system, Smith reported that he had lucid thoughts and could perform mental arithmetic and understand what was going on around him just as well as before taking the drug. This and other experiments have made a convincing case that thought is more than covert speech.

Another way of looking at thought is to consider it as part of the information-processing model. In this view, cognitive processes involve, a transformation and manipulation of information that has been encoded and stored in short-term and especially in long-term memory. Thinking thus can be defined as the manipulation of mental representations. Sometimes people perform these manipulations consciously, in order to reason, understand a situation, solve a problem, or make a decision. At other times, such as when people is daydreaming, the manipulations are less goal directed. In the next section, we look at what is meant by mental representations and how people manipulate them in thought.

<h2 style="text-align:center">第二节 思维
(THINKING)</h2>

In spite of its ephemeral nature, thinking does appear to be based largely on the ability to form, manipulate, and relate concepts. We therefore begin our discussion of thinking by considering concepts and concept formation. Later we consider how concepts are related to each other by propositions, how they are represented, and how these representations are used in thinking.

Concepts

The basic ingredients of mental activity, the building blocks of thought, are concepts—classes or categories of objects, events, or ideas with common properties. Concepts may be concrete and visualised, such as the concepts "round" or "red?" but they may also be abstract, such as the concepts "truth" and "justice." To have a concept is to recognize the set of properties or relationships that are shared by and define members of the category. For example, the concept bird includes such properties as having feathers, laying eggs, and being able to fly. Most birds have all of these properties, but even those, like penguins, that cannot fly are still birds, because they possess enough other bird properties (feathers, wings, and the like). But having just one bird property is not enough; snakes lay eggs and bats can fly, but neither are birds. It is usually the nation of properties that defines a concept. A concept is a general term for a class of things with common attributes.

Artificial and natural concepts For years, psychologists focused their researches on what are now called **artificial concepts**. These are concepts produced under the laboratory condition that can be clearly defined by a set of rules or properties, so that each member of the concept has all of the defining properties and no non-members does. For example, the concept square can be defined as "a shape with four equal sides and four right-angle corners." Any object that does not contain all of these features simply is not a square.

There are also examples of **natural concepts**, that have no fixed set of defining features but instead share a set of characteristic features. Members of a natural concept need not possess all of the characteristic features. One characteristic feature of the natural concept bird, for example, is the ability to fly; but an ostrich is a bird even though it cannot fly. The boundaries of a natural concept are fuzzy, and some members of the concept are better examples of the concept than others. The more characteristic features a particular example shares, the greater its degree of belongingness to the concept (Rosch, 1975). A robin, a chicken, an ostrich, and a penguin are all birds. But a robin is a better example than the other three, because a robin can fly and is closer to the size and proportion of what most people, through common and frequent experience, think of as a typical bird. A member of a natural concept that possesses all or most of its characteristic features is called a prototype or is said to be prototypical. Thus, the robin is a prototypical bird.

Mental Representations of Concepts

How are concepts represented in the mind? Our discussion of memory suggested one possibility. Recall that people encode into memory, especially long-term memory, not just individual pieces of information, such as words or pictures, and lists of the features or attributes of those items.

The more distinctive or unusual those features are, the easier the information is to remember. As people learn concepts, it may be the concepts' defining features that are mentally represented and encoded into long-term memory. This would help explain why artificial concepts, such as square, with their relatively few and usually distinctive features, tend to be easier to learn and remember than natural concepts, such as game, which are fuzzier, because they do not have a fixed set of defining features.

The notion that concepts are mentally represented as lists of features would also help explain research results like those of one particular reaction time experiment (Smith, Shoben & Rips, 1973). In the study, people were asked to say whether the sentences like "A robin is a bird" and "An ostrich is a bird" are true or false. Reaction times to correctly answer such questions were much faster when the sentence used prototypical examples of a concept ("A robin is a bird") than when the examples were not prototypical. Presumably this was because the prototypical example shared more easily identifiable features with the stored concept than did non-prototypical examples.

Concepts may also be mentally represented by visual images. Thinking of concepts such as beautiful, tranquil, or violent might instantly bring to mind mental pictures, or visual prototypes, of these concepts. Individual differences in how people tend to represent concepts and the kinds of concepts that tend to be represented as features or images are not well understood. Nor are we sure that there are not other still-undiscovered ways of mentally representing concepts.

Concepts are closely related to the idea of schemas, discussed in the chapter on memory. As we mentioned there, a schema is a mental representation of information about a class of events or things. Schemas preserve the average characteristics of several specific examples or cases, without retaining the specific details of any of them. In their ability to encapsulate the general characteristics of a large number of specific examples, schemas provide a very efficient way of representing and thinking about events and objects in the world.

Whether concepts are represented as features, as images, as schemas, or in other way, humans appear to combine them to form propositions and mental models.

Propositions   Concepts represent important building blocks of mental experience and essential components of the ability to think. Part of thinking involves relating various concepts to one another, and these relationships are usually represented by propositions. A proposition is the smallest unit of knowledge that can stand as a separate assertion. Usually taking the form of a sentence, propositions may be true or false. Propositions may represent the relationship between a concept and a property of that concept ("Birds have wings" or "Turtles cannot sing") or they may relate two or more concepts to each other (Dogs chase cats or Rob cheated on the test)?

Mental models   Recently, some psychologists have focused their attention on how concepts involving physical processes and mechanical or computational devices might be represented as mental models. **Mental models** are essentially large clusters of propositions that represent people's understanding of how things work and guide their interaction with those things (Gentner & Stevens, 1983; Johnson-Laird, 1983). For example, a mental model might describe a person's understanding of an electric wall switch (Brown, 1981), or a computer (Carey, 1982). Understanding people's mental models of, say, personal computers can be very important in teaching people to use them. If the teacher knows that the new student has an incorrect model (perhaps thinking of the machine's memory as impossible to erase), it is easier to understand and prevent the kinds of mistakes he or she is likely to make.

Propositions and mental models are abstract terms, which in conscious thought translate into the specific words and images people work with every day. For example, in solving a math problem about how long it would take three people to do a job, if you know how long it takes two people to do it, you might find yourself silently restating in words the concepts of the problem and their interrelationships. Here is a case of using words to represent concepts. In other cases, thinking involves the manipulation of images, as when you think about how an acquaintance would look in glasses.

We will save our discussion of thinking with words until the end of the chapter, when we look at language in some detail. Here, we look at the other modes of thought: images and cognitive maps.

Images and Cognitive Maps

Operations on images   To get a better visual image of an object, you might move closer to examine its details or use binoculars or a zoom lens. Do people do the same thing with mental images, and if so, how are mental images manipulated? In the last twenty years, some very clever investigations have addressed this question. For example, Steven Kosslyn (1976) asked people to form a mental image of an object such as a cat and then asked questions about it, such as "Does it have a head?" and "Does it have claws?" The smaller the detail in question, the longer people took to answer the question, as if they were indeed zooming in to the level of detail necessary to answer the question. The finer the detail required by the question, the greater the zoom and the longer the response time.

Roger Shepard and Jacqueline Metzer (1971) found evidence that people can imagine the rotation of objects in their minds. In their experiments, subjects viewed pairs of objects like those shown in Figure 8.6. Their task was to decide if the two objects were identical or mirror images of each other. Shepard and Metzler found that each added degree of difference in the orientation of the two objects added a constant amount of time to the decision. Thus, it looked as if the subjects imagined the rotation of one of the objects at a constant rate until it was lined up in the same orientation as the other.

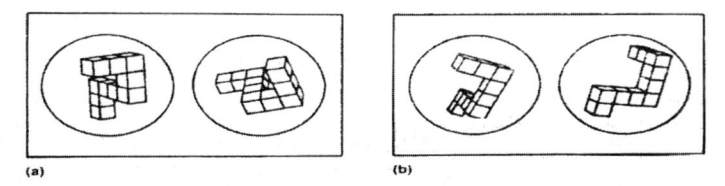

Figure 8.5
Imagining the Rotation of Objects
Subjects decide if the two objects in each pair are identical or not to do this, they must imagine the rotation of one of the objects so that it will be in the same orientation as the other. The objects in (a) are identical; those in (b) are different. The time needed to decide about each pair increases with the amount of rotation that subjects must imagine.

Though we cannot yet say exactly what goes on when people think by manipulating images, the information obtained so far suggests that, like other mental events, imagining involves its own systematic chronometry. Moreover the manipulations performed on images are very similar to those that would be performed on the objects themselves.

Maps and spatial cognition   Even people who do not usually use images in most of their thinking may employ them to navigate through a particular environment. Especially when that environment is new, people tend to imagine specific objects and landmarks as they try to go from one place to another. Finally, after gaining a lot of experience in the environment, people acquire an overall cognitive map of it.

Useful as they are, cognitive maps are not accurate copies of the environment; they include systematic distortions. One distortion results from rectangular bias, a tendency to impose a rectangular north–south–east–west grid on the environment. For those who love in flat mid-western cities, this represents no distortion at all, since these cities actually conform to that grid. But people's cognitive maps tend to distort the subtle twists and turns in many environments. For example, when asked to draw a map of Paris, most Parisians straighten out the bends of the Seine River in an effort to make it conform more closely to a north–south flow (Milgram & Jodelet, 1976). The rectangular bias also distorts the sense of relative locations. If you were asked where Reno, Nevada, is with respect to San Diego, California, you would probably answer, with little hesitation, northeast (Stevens & Coupe, 1978). After all, Nevada is east of California, and Reno is north of San Diego. But because California bends to the east, Reno is in fact northwest of San Diego.

In other words, people tend to simplify complex material in the world most of the time, this simplification is efficient and useful. But the costs humans must pay are certain systematic biases, such as false perceptions guided by top-down processes and expectancies, distortions of memory, and, as we have seen here, distortions of spatial cognition.

Reasoning

Whatever the units of thought are, the degree to which people achieve the goals of thinking depends on how they manipulate those units. If they manipulate them to reach a valid conclusion, then they are said to be rational. If someone tell you that negotiating with terrorists only leads to more terrorism, would you agree?

To determine your response, you would want to collect some evidence, but you would also need to exercise your powers of reasoning. Reasoning is the process by which you evaluate and generate arguments and reach conclusions. The procedures that yield a valid conclusion are known as logic.

At the core of the study of logic lie the rules for evaluating **syllogisms**, which are arguments made up of two propositions, called premises, and a conclusion based on those premises. For example, if all people on welfare are poor and, if all lazy bums are poor does it follow that all people on welfare are lazy bums? No. The rules of logic indicate that, whatever the empirical truth or falsity of each of the propositions, the conclusion drawn from this line of reasoning is not logically sound, or valid. Another example: All gun owner are people. All criminals are people. Therefore, all gun owners are criminals. These logically incorrect syllogisms illustrate a general principle of logic, namely, that if "All A's are B" and "All C's are B," it does not follow that "All A's are C." Scholars have also defined rules for determining the probability of events, and procedures for determining which of several possible decisions will yield the result most satisfying to the decision maker. Consider now how well these males for reaching rational conclusions and decisions actually describe how people think. Consider the following syllogism: (All psychologists are brilliant. The authors of this are psychologists. There fore, the authors of this text are brilliant.)

Do you agree? If you are the same as most people, you probably find yourself of two minds. On the one hand, the conclusion does follow logically from the preceding statements; the argument is valid. On the other hand, you probably are a little uncertain about our brilliance. Probably you reason that, although the logic of these statements is impeccable, the conclusion remains at odds with your general knowledge of the world, because the first statement is probably false. Obviously, reasoning depends on both knowledge of the world and an understanding of what is logical. If the premises are false, one should reject a conclusion flowing from them as invalids even if the logic of the argument is sound.

Psychologists have found, however, that people often accept a syllogistic argument as valid even when it is not, if the conclusion agrees with their attitudes. For example, consider the following syllogism: America is a free country. In a free country, all people have equal opportunity. Therefore, in America all people have equal opportunity.

William McGure(1960) found that people's belief in the validity of conclusions like this was based only in part on logical thinking. To a large extent, their reaction was influenced by the degree to which they believed that the conclusion was true, independent of the truth of the premises or the logic that followed from those premises. This tendency is sometimes demonstrated in the courtroom, when the defendant is a member of the clergy or a sweet, elderly woman, The jury may remain unpersuaded by the prosecution's logically sound arguments based on true premises, because the logical conclusion (that the sweet, old woman poisoned her sister) is at odds with the jury's beliefs about how the world operates. In other words, the conclusions that people reach are based on both logical and wishful thinking.

Heuristics and biases The idea that wishful thinking may sometimes overrule rational thinking could simply mean that people reason according to the laws of formal logic, probability, and rational choice, except when their thinking is marred by specific wishes or needs. But researchers begun to show that the laws of logic and probability do not always provide a good description of how people actually think. However intelligent, expert, or objective people are, they sometimes tend to violate these laws in their everyday thinking. Much thinking seems to be based instead on heuristics, which are mental shortcuts or rules of thumb (kahneman, slovic & Tversky, 1982; Tversky & Kahneman, 1974).

Suppose, for example, that you are about to leave home in the morning but cannot find your watch. You might search for the watch in every possible location, room by room. This approach involves using an **algorithm**, which is a systematic procedure that cannot fail to produce a solution. But to obtain the same outcome more quickly, you are likely to search first in the places where your past experience suggests the watch might be; this approach is a heuristic. Similarly, in deciding which political candidates to vote for, your rule of thumb might be to support all those in a particular party rather than researching the views of each individual. People use like these because they are easy and frequently work well. But heuristics can also bias cognitive processes and cause errors. For example, many of those who vote for everyone on a particular party s election ticket may later be chagrined to discover that they got the president they wanted, but they also got a local sheriff whose views they despise.

Other heuristics guide people's judgment about what events are probable or what hypotheses are likely to be true. Amos Tversky and Daniel Kahneman have described three heuristics that people seem to use intuitively to make many of these judgments (Kahneman, Slovic & Tversky, 1982).

The Anchoring heuristic. People use the **anchoring heuristic** when they estimate an event's probability by adjusting a preliminary estimate. In other words, people judge how likely it is that, they will be mugged in given city by using new information to alter whatever initial impression they might have had. This sounds like a reasonable strategy, but the preliminary starting value biases the final estimate. Once people have fixed a starting point, their adjust merits of the initial judgment tend to be inadequate. It is if they drop a mental anchor at one hypothesis or estimate and then cannot move very far from that original judgment. Thus, if a person assumes that the probability of being mugged in New York is 90 percent and then receives information about how improbable such events actually are, he or she may reduce the estimate to only 80 percent.

The representativeness heuristic. The representativeness heuristic involves judging the probability that a hypothesis is true or that an example belongs to a certain class of items by first focusing on the similarities between the example and a larger class of events or items, and then determining whether the particular example represents essential features of the larger class. For example, suppose you encounter a man who is tidy, small in stature, wears glasses, speaks quietly, and is somewhat shy. If asked whether this person is likely to be a librarian or a farmer, what would you say? Tversky and Kahneman (1974) found that most of their subjects chose librarian. But the chances are that this answer would be wrong. It is true that the description is more similar to or representative of the prototypical librarian than the prototypical farmer, but the fact that there are many more farmers in the world than librarians means that there are probably more farmers than librarians who match this particular physical description. Therefore, logic would dictate that a man matching this description is more likely to be a farmer than a librarian. When using the representativeness heuristic, people tend to ignore the overall probabilities, the baserate frequency, and focus instead on what is representative or typical of the available evidence. Base-rate logic would suggest that almost any set of male physical features is more likely to belong to a farmer than a librarian.

The availability heuristic. Even when people use base-rate probability information to help them judge group membership or assess the truthfulness of a hypothesis, they may employ a third heuristic that can bias their probability judgment. The availability heuristic involves judging the frequency or probability of an event or hypothesis by how easily the hypothesis or examples of the event can be brought to mind. Thus, people tend to choose the hypothesis or alternative that is most mentally "available" much as you might choose which sweater to wear on the basis of which is on top in the drawer, This shortcut tends to work well because, among other reasons, what we remember most easily are very frequent events or hypotheses, But the availability heuristic can lead to biased judgments, especially when mental availability heuristic can lead to based judgments, and when mental availability and actual frequency fail to correspond.

For example, television news reports showing the grisly aftermath of gang-land shootings and airline crashes may make these relatively rare events so memorable that people avoid certain cities or refuse to fly because they come to overestimate the frequency of crime or the probability of a crash (Slovis, 1984).

These heuristics represent only some of the strategies that people use intuitively and they create only some of the biases and limitations evident in our reasoning. We will see others in the following sections, as we take a closer look at two common goals of thinking: problem solving and decision making.

第三节 问题的解决
(PROBLEM SOLVING)

Four characteristics describe problem solving: (1) where you are (the problem) is not where you would like to be (the solution); (2) the path between the problem and its solution is not obvious; (3) often you must spend considerable effort to understand, or diagnose, the problem; and (4) to diagnose or eliminate the problem, you may need to form several hypotheses about which path is correct and then test those hypotheses. To diagnose the problem when a patient has an unfamiliar combination of symptoms, for example, a physician must relate the available information that is, the symptoms? To knowledge of the patient medical history and of a variety of possible disease, the physician might generate hypotheses about the patient's illness, review test results, try various treatments, and observe the effects on the patient. The many unnecessary teats performed in hospitals and the all too frequent cases of misdiagnosis testify to the fact that people's problem solving skills often leave much to be desired.

Problems in Problem Solving

Problem solving involves understanding the problem (diagnosis), devising a plan to solve the problem, executing the plan, and evaluating the results (Polya, 1957). Many problem solving difficulties occur at the start, with diagnosis. Proposing and testing hypotheses systematically is often an efficient, effective method of diagnosis, but it can lead to dead ends and frustrations that sometimes push people into trying to solve problems through blind trial and error. The frustration comes from five main sources.

Multiple hypotheses Often, people begin to solve a problem with only a vague notion of which hypothesis to test. For example, there may be a dozen reasons why a car will not start. Which hypotheses should be tested and in what order? People seem to have a difficult time entertaining more than two or three hypotheses at one time (Mehle, 1982). The limited capacity of short−term memory, may be part of the reason. As a result, the correct hypothesis is often neglected. Which hypothesis one chooses to consider may depend, not on which is most likely, but on the availability heuristic.

In other words, the particular hypothesis that is considered may be one that is remembered most readily, which may not be the best hypothesis at all. Several characteristics make particular hypotheses easier to remember, for example, their simplicity, their emotional content, and how recently they have been experienced (Tversky & Kahneman, 1974). Thus, the automechanic trouble shooting your car might diagnose the problem as being identical to one encountered the day before, simply because this hypothesis is most easily brought to mind.

Mental sets Sometimes people are so blinded by one hypothesis or strategy that they continue to apply it even when better alternatives should be obvious (a clear case of the anchoring heuristic at work). An example devised by Abraham Luchins (1942) is shown in Figure 8.7. The object of each problem in the figure is to use three jars with specified capacities to obtain a certain amount of liquid. For example, in the first problem you are to obtain 21 quarts by using three jars that have capacities of 8, 35, and 3 quarts, respectively. The solution is to fill jar B to its capacity, 35, and 3 quarts, respectively. The solution is to fill jar b to its capacity, 35 quarts, and then use its contents to fill jar A to its capacity of 8 quarts, leaving 27 quarts in jar B. Then pour liquid from jar B to fill jar C to its capacity twice, leaving 21 quarts in jar B [$27 - (2 \times 3) = 21$]. In other words, the solution

Figure 8.6
The Luchins Jar Problem
The problem is to obtain the volume of liquid shown in the first column by filling jars with the capacities shown in the next three columns. Each line represents a different problem. Such problems have been used to show that people often fall prey to mental sets that prevent them from using the most efficient solution.

Problem: Measure out the following quantities by using jars with the stated capacities:

		Jar A (quarts)	Jar B (quarts)	Jar C (quarts)
1	21 quarts	8	35	3
2	10 quarts	6	18	1
3	19 quarts	5	32	4
4	21 quarts	20	57	8
5	18 quarts	8	40	7
6	6 quarts	7	17	2
7	15 quarts	12	33	3

is to apply the equation B−A−2C. Now solve the remaining problems.

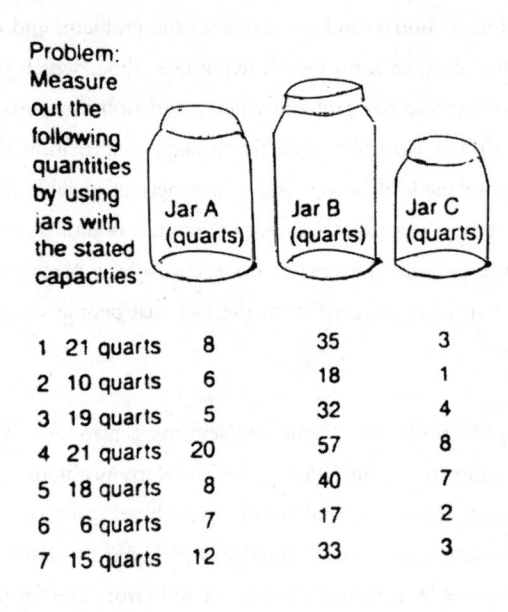

If you went through the problems in Figure 8.7 you found that a similar solution worked each tune. But what happened with problem 7? If you are like most people, you did not notice t it has a simpler solution (namely, A+C). Instead, you succumbed to a mental set, the tendency for old patterns of problem solving to persist (Sweller & Gee, 1978). In the Luchins jar problem, the mental set consists of a tendency to stick with a strategy or solution that worked m the past Figure 8.8 shows that a mental set may also restrict your perception of the problems itself. Figure 8.9 shows two ways of going beyond constraints to solve the nine−dot problem.

Figure 8.7
The Nine−Dot Problem
The task is to draw no more than four lines that run through all nine dots on the page without lifting your pencil from the paper. Many people find such puzzles difficult create artificial constraints on the range of solutions: drawing within the frame laid out by the dots and drawing through the middle of each dot.

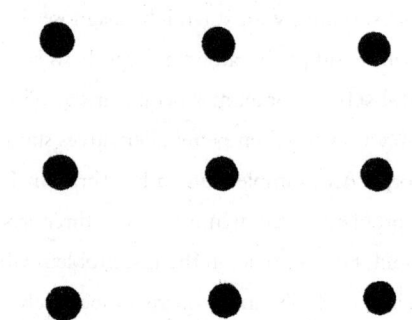

Yet another restriction on problem solving may come from experience with objects. Once people become accustomed to using an object for one type of function, they may be blinded to other ways of using it. Thus, experience may

• 198 •

produce functional fixedness, a tendency to avoid using familiar objects in creative, but useful ways. Figure 8.10 illustrates an experiment that provided an excellent example of functional fixedness (Maier, 1930).

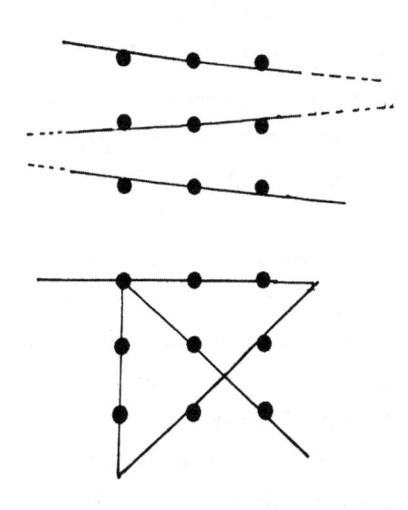

Figure 8.8
Two Creative Solutions to the Nine–Dot Problem

The confirmation bias Anyone who has suffered through a series of medical tests knows that diagnosis is not a one-shot decision. Instead, the physician choose an initial hypothesis on the basis of observed symptoms and then orders further problem is that humans have a strong bias to confirm rather than to refute the hypothesis they have chosen, even in the face of strong evidence against that hypothesis. People are quite willing to perceive and interpret data that support a hypothesis, but they tend to ignore factors the are inconsistent with it (Levine, 1966). Thus, the confirmation bias may be seen as a form of anchoring, in that it involves reluctance to abandon an initial hypothesis.

Figure 8.9
An Example of Functional Fixedness
People were asked to fasten together two strings hanging from the ceiling but out of reach of each other. Several tools were available in the room. The solution' was to take a heavy tool, such as a pair of pliers, attach it to one of the string, and swing it like a pendulum until that string could be reached while holding the other. The solution is not easily arrived at, however, because most people fixate on the usual function of the pliers as a hand tool rather than hypothesizing their role as a pendulum weight. Moreover, the people in the experiment were more likely to hit on the solution and use the pliers if the tools were scattered around the room, than if they were nearly

• 199 •

contained in a tool box. Apparently, when the pliers were in a tool box, their function as a tool was emphasized, and the mental set became nearly impossible to break.

(Rubenstein & Mason, 1979; Wickens, 1984). The control room operators could have formed either of two hypotheses about what might have been wrong inside the nuclear reactor. Either the water pressure in the reactor core was too high, creating the danger of an explosion, or it was too low, a condition that could lead to a meltdown. Several symptoms supported the correct hypothesis (the pressure was indeed low), but one defective meter indicated that the pressure was too high. Because the supervisors had used that meter to establish their original hypothesis of high pressure, they failed to appreciate other symptoms of the actual low pressure until after they had implemented the disastrous decision to shut down an emergency pump.

An experiment conducted by David Rosenhan (1973) provided a rather alarming example of the confirmation bias. Rosenhan and nine confederates presented themselves at ten different mental hospitals and complained of the same faked symptom: hearing a voice that said "dull, " "empty, " and "thud" . Otherwise, they reported only truthful facts about their very normal lives. Nevertheless, all were admitted, and most were diagnosed as schizophrenic, a severe condition described, on abnormal psychology. Once in the hospital, these patients behaved normally and reported no further symptoms, but even their normal actions were interpreted as symptoms of mental illness—evidence confirming the original, incorrect hypothesis that they were schizophrenic. For example, the "patients" took notes about their experiences in the hospital. In at least one case, the staff described this "writing behavior" as a symptom. Another "patient" accurately stated that he had a good family life, even though he sometimes had arguments with his wife and occasionally had to spank his children. This rather normal pattern was described in staff notes as follows, his attempts to control emotionality with his wife and children are punctuated by angry outbursts and, in the case of the children, spankings.

What is the source of confirmation bias? One possibility is that mental effort is required to abandon old hypotheses and construct new ones and that people tend to avoid complex mental operations (Rasmussen, 1981; Shugan, 1980). This cognitive laziness may discourage attention to alternative hypotheses. Furthermore, to admit that one is wrong may threaten self-esteem. This cognitive conceit (Fischoff, 1977) may lead people to search for and find confirming evidence and ignore contradictory evidence.

Ignoring negative evidence   Often, what does not happen can be as important as what does happen. For example, when troubleshooting a car, a symptom of headlight failure might lead you to hypothesize that the battery is low. Yet, if this were the case, other battery-powered equipment should also have failed. The fact that these symptoms are not present is important in disconfirming your original hypothesis. The absence of symptoms can provide important evidence for or against a hypothesis. Compared with symptoms that are present, however, people are less likely to notice and observe symptoms that do not occur (Hunt & Rouse, 1981). People have a difficult time using the absence of symptoms to help eliminate hypotheses from consideration.

Ignoring base-rate information

Hypothesis testing can also be impaired by the representativeness heuristic—the strategy of ignoring probability and focusing instead on what is most representative. For example, when a medical diagnosis is made, two variables should influence the choice of the hypothesis the evidence, or how closely the symptoms match those of the disease being considered, and the base rate, or how frequently the disease occurs. If a patient shows symptoms that match the textbook description of two diseases, call them fascitis and carlosis, but carlosis occurs 100 times more often, the physician's best choice is to diagnose carlosis. In fact, the base rate may make carlosis the best diagnosis even if the symptoms look a bit more like fascitis. However, when confronted with a situation like this, people tend to ignore base-rate information (Christensen-Szalanski & Bushyhead, 1981). It seems that the capacity of short-term memory is exceeded when new evidence and base-rate information must be combined. What is sacrificed is the more abstract less visible base rate.

Improving Problem-Solving Skills

How can you improve your ability to solve problems? Are there any easily taught techniques or methods that will give you the problem-solving skills of an expert? In the following sections, we try to answer these questions.

Avoiding the pitfalls   Perhaps the most obvious step that you can take to improve your problem solving is to avoid errors of syllogistic reasoning. Imagery can help. The pictures shown in Figure 8.11, called Venn diagrams, are an example. To solve a syllogism, you can draw the Venn representation of the two premises and see whether the conclusion is consistent with both. Less formally, you can imagine a scene that includes the elements in the syllogism (Johnson-Laird & Steedman, 1978).

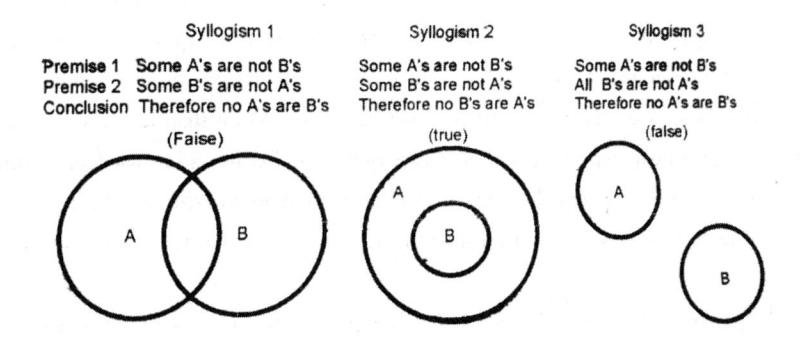

	Syllogism 1	Syllogism 2	Syllogism 3
Premise 1	Some A's are not B's	Some A's are not B's	Some A's are not B's
Premise 2	Some B's are not A's	Some B's are not A's	All B's are not A's
Conclusion	Therefore no A's are B's	Therefore no B's are A's	Therefore no A's are B's
	(False)	(true)	(false)

Figure 8.10

Venn Diagrams

These diagrams represent three different, but logically correct interpretations of the statement "Some A's are not B's". This statement is an equally valid description of "some Democrats are not New Yorkers," which is represented by (a); "Some federal employees are not senators", which is represented by (b); or "Some Albanians are not Chinese," which is represented by (c). Typically, however, people assume that only a diagram like (a) represents the

statement and therefore assume that the statement also implies "*some B's are not A's*" .
Other weaknesses in problem solving are more difficult to remedy psychologists have reasoned that it should be possible to train people not to fall prey in the biases that impair problem solving people, as Baruch Fischoff (1982) put it. Attempts to do this have produced some modest improvements in problem solving. For example, in a study, cautioning people against their tendency to anchor on a hypothesis reduced the magnitude of the confirmation bias and increased their openness to alternative evidence (Lopes, 1982).

Many anecdotal reports over the years have suggested that a technique called incubation may improve problem-solving ability. Incubation involves putting the problem aside for a while and turning to some other mental activity while the problem "incubates," perhaps at a subconscious level, as described in the chapter on consciousness. For example, French mathematician J. H. Poincare claimed that his insights into Fuchsian functions occurred suddenly as he was stepping onto a bus (Poincare, 1913). However, it appears that incubation aids problem solving only if the incubation period is preceded by a lengthy period of preparation (Silviera, 1971). Incubation may aid problem solving mainly by allowing mental sets and other biases to dissipate somewhat, engendering a fresh approach.

A heuristic known as decomposition may also help solve problems. Decomposition consists of breaking a problem into smaller elements by working backward from the final goal. Decomposition can be effective at breaking down even a large, seemingly unmanageable problem (such as writing a long term paper) into a series of smaller, more manageable subproblems (such as finding appropriate references, writing an outline, creating a first draft, and so on).

Imitating the expert   Scientists, engineers, physicians, maintenance technicians, auto mechanics, and labor negotiators, name just a few, are well-paid professionals, presumably because of their expertise in solving problems. What do these experts bring to a situation that a novice cannot? Experience and knowledge, for one thing. As a result, experts frequently proceed by looking for similarities and analogies between current and past problems. More than novices, they can relate new information and new experiences to past experiences and existing knowledge. This produces one of the most important general differences between the expert and the novice: the ability to use existing knowledge to organize new information into chunks, as we described in the chapter on memory.

Experts appear to have the ability to visualize problems more clearly and efficiently than novices, by using their past knowledge and experience to chunk a large number of problem elements into a smaller number of more meaningful units. One result is that experts seem to suffer less than non-experts from the interference problems described in the chapter on memory. Psychologists do not yet know why this is so. Another result is that experts may not need to decompose a problem into sub-problems. Once experts understand a problem, they can immediately bring to mind all of the steps from the problem to the goal, as if these were a single mental chunk.

Expertise also carries a danger: using logic to past experience can lead to the traps of functional fixedness and mental sets. As a Zen proverb says, "In the mind of the beginner there are many possibilities; in the mind of the expert, few". Top-down, knowledge-driven processes, bias people toward seeing what they expect or want to see. Thus, they can prevent people from seeing a problem in different ways. Indeed, there is a thin line between using past experience well and being trapped by it.

The benefits of experience may also be limited because feedback about a solution is delayed (Brehmer, 1981).Often, experts receive information about the correctness of a proposed solution only long after they have forgotten how they came to that answer. As a result, they cannot use the feedback to improve their problem-solving methods. Furthermore, the confirmation bias may prevent them from seeing that a proposed solution was incorrect (Fischoff & Siovic,1980).In short, experience alone does not ensure excellence at problem solving, and practice may not make perfect. A book by Christopher Cerf (1984) gives further reason for skepticism; it details fantastically erroneous predictions by experts.

Teaching the novice Despite the pitfalls and failures of expertise, it is fair to say that, for the most part, experts are better than novices in their area of expertise. This conclusion leads to an intriguing question. Are there shortcuts to achieving expertise? After carefully reviewing the literature, Richard Mayer (1983) concluded that claims of "instant" shortcuts to expertise must be viewed with some skepticism. The most important characteristic of any expert problem solver, he noted, is extensive knowledge in the problem area. For example, in a study, teaching students to use general strategies, such as diagrams, did improve their ability to solve mathematical problems, but only after the students had already mastered a good deal of mathematical knowledge (Schoenfeld 1979). Knowledge allows the expert to perceive the elements of a problem as a chunk, to understand the correlations between problem elements, and to draw on past analogies. In short, there seems to be no substitute for putting in the hard work needed to acquire knowledge. Once you possess this knowledge, however, you can learn shortcuts that will allow you to take maximum advantage of it.

Artificial Intelligence

The possibility of teaching expertise holds special interest for those who work in artificial intelligence, the field that studies how to program computers to imitate the products or human perception, understanding, and thought. To reach this goal, it is not necessary for the computer to imitate the processes of the brain, any more than airplanes must mimic a bird wing flapping. Nevertheless, just as aircraft have been improved by imitating some characteristics of birds in flight so, progress in artificial intelligence may depend on the careful study of human cognitive processes.

Researches in artificial intelligence have concentrated on imitating human perception, speech comprehension, and problem solving. A problem-solving computer needs to be supplied with two basic elements: (1) an extensive knowledge base about the area in which problems are to be solved; and (2) an inference engine, a set of procedures for using the facts in the knowledge base to solve problem. Computers, like people, can use two main types of procedures for problem solving; algorithms and heuristics. As noted earlier, algorithms are precise, step-by-step statements of logical and computational operations that guarantee a solution. Heuriatics, as we have seen, are mental rules of thumb or shortcuts that often work, but do not always.

Computers are good at following algorithms, because algorithms do not require much flexibility. Indeed, many problems, like solving differential equations or computing statistical tests, are best handled by algorithms, and therefore by computers. But algorithms are not terribly efficient. For example, an algorithm for a chess—playing computer might consider all possible moves, then all possible counter moves by the opponent, then all possible counter counter moves, and so on, until the "best" move is determined. After each move by opponent, the computer could determine which move would produce a sequence of moves that would result in victory the greatest number of times, and in loss the fewest possible times. The problem is that this algorithm is impossibly complex even for the fastest supercomputer; it would need to consider around 10120 possible sequences of moves, an astronomically large number that could occupy much of the worlds computer power for years (Solso, 1979). Many researchers working in artificial intelligence have concluded that the most effective procedures for problem solving are human—like heuristics. A heuristic for problem solving might specify the most logical place to start looking for a solution, or the rules under which different strategies or algorithms should be uses, or the most relevant kind of information about a problem. For chess playing, for example, a heuristic might immediately eliminate a number of potentially absurd moves, such as moving one s queen to a position where it will be taken.

Attempts to use computers for problem solving have had some success in the case of expert systems, one key to their success lies in the fact that they are used only in one specific area, for which a large knowledge base has been compiled. The difficulties encountered in developing these systems have highlighted critical ways in which human thought goes well beyond readily programmable heuristics and algorithms. Here are three of the most important problems.

1. Storing the knowledge base. Human experts have the knowledge that must be coded into the expert system, but often they cannot easily verbalize it in a way that can be coded by a programming language. Even when experts can articulate the facts, another problem remains: how the information is stored. Like a good library or like long—term memory, the knowledge base must be more than a warehouse of facts; it must have organization, cross—referencing, and careful tagging and labeling.

2. Building in common sense. Analysis of a problem sometimes brings you to conclusions that you know are wrong; they just do not make sense. Typically, you reject these conclusions and start again. But the most expert computer system will forge ahead single—mindedly.

3. Using wider knowledge. Expert systems typically store a great deal of knowledge about one specific area, but people often reach solutions by leaking at a problem from different perspectives and borrowing knowledge or analogies from other domains. It is often impossible to know what domains of knowledge will be useful until after the expert system has been used, and incorporating all potentially useful domains would make the computer program impossibly large.

Obviously, artificial intelligence has come a long way since the first algorithms were developed for arithmetic calculators in the sixteenth century. But it will be a very long time before anyone can create truly intelligent robots like C3PO of Star Wars or PIAL of 2001. There is an irony in the development of artificial intelligence. The more powerful computers and computer programs have become, the more psychologists have been forced to realize how much they do not yet know about human perception, understanding, and thought (Dreyfus & Dreyfus, 1979).

第四节 风险决策
(RISKY DECISION MAKING)

The ability to solve problems often overlaps with another critical skill: decision making. When you solve a problem, you must make decisions about what to consider. Even after you have correctly diagnosed a problem, you may be left with a difficult decision. For example, after a doctor determines that a patient's problem is cancer, someone must still make the crucial decision of whether to risk operating.

Simple decisions made when time is of the essence. In making these types of decisions, people generally err only when they try to respond too quickly. In contrast, many decisions, like those of jurors and physicians, take more time, are more complex, and are vulnerable to several types of errors. Sometimes a decision is difficult because each alternative has several characteristics. Often, the main problem is that the world itself is unpredicted and uncertain. Your decision to buy one car instead of another, for example, may be an error if the car turns out to be a lemon. But if there was no evidence that the car was faulty, you would chalk up the error to random factors in the world, not to a failure of your own decision making. You cannot see the future. Thus, decisions made in the face of the world's uncertainty are called risky.

Although many incorrect decisions result from the world's uncertainty, it is also true that people often make poor decisions because of limits, biases, and fallacies in information processing. In the following pages, we consider some techniques for making good decisions and some of the biases or limitations that influence decisions.

Rational Decision Making

Whenever you make a major decision, such as where to attend college or whether to accept a job offer, you consider several important characteristics or attributes, of the alternatives. In choosing a college, for example, the attributes might be tuition costs, closeness to home, social life, quality of the faculty, and so on. Unfortunately, people often fail to choose the alter-native that in the long run satisfies most of their important values.

One reason for such failure appears to be that, as in hypothesis testing, the limited capacity of short? Term memory prevents people from keeping in mind and considering all of the attributes in their relative order of importance (Edwards, 1977). Instead a decision may be guided by the availability heuristic, so that the choice is influenced only by the most available attribute, which is often the most salient characteristic. For example, you might choose the highest payed job without fully weighing the fact that it is also farthest from home and offers the least independence (Tverskey, 1977). To escape the frailties of short-term memory, you might use the technique shown in. Table 8.1, based on multi-attribute utility theory (Edwards, 1977). Whether you are trying to select an apartment or choose a site for an airport, this procedure can help you make a good choice (Edwards, 1977; Fischoff, Slovic & Lichtenstein, 1977. Wickens & Kramer, 1985).But the procedure assumes that the alternatives and attributes are all certain; it does not allow for the uncertainty about outcomes that complicates many decisions.

		(1) Alternatives			
(2) Attributes	Importance	(3) College 1	College 2	College 3	College 4
At$_1$ (cost)	3	4	1	3	2
At$_2$ (academics)	2	1	2	3	4
At$_3$ (social)	1	1	3	2	4
(4) Computing the products		3 × 4 + 2 × 1 + 1 × 1	3 × 1 + 2 × 2 + 1 × 3	3 × 3 + 2 × 3 + 1 × 2	3 × 2 + 2 × 4 + 1 × 4
(5) Summing the products		15	10	17	18

Table 8.1
Problem Solving Using Multiattribute Utility Theory

1. List all the alternatives (colleges) across the columns and all attributes that might possibly matter down the rows, in order of their importance.
2. Assign numerical weights to each attribute, giving 1 to the least important, 2 to the next, and so on.
3. Give each alternative a score for each attribute, with 1 again indicating the lowest score (such as most expensive, poorest academics).
4. Multiply the score in each cell by the importance weight for that row.
5. Add the products down each column.
6. Compare the columns. The column with the highest total is the winner and should be chosen.

	possible outcomes		
Possible actions	Repairs will succeed utility: +50 probability of outcome: 0.20 Expected utility: (+50)(0.20) = +10.00	Repairs will fail Utility: −200 probability of outcome: 0.80 Expected utility: (−200)(0.80) = −160.00	Expected utility: Of repairing the car: (+10.00) +(−160.00) = −150
Repair car			
Buy new car	New car will work Utility: −200 probability of outcome: 0.90 Expected utility: (−200)(0.90) = −180.00	New car will not work Utility: −500 probability of outcome: 0.10 Expected utiliy (−500)(0.10) = −50.00	Of buying a new car: (−180.00) +(−50.00) = −230

Figure 8.11
Application of Expected Utility Theory to Risky Decision Making

Following the steps described in the text, the action of repairing one s car is found to have a higher expected utility (is less negative) than the action of buying a new car. Hence the rational

• 206 •

decision maker should choose to repair the car.

Figure 8.12 shows how choices made under uncertainty can be analyzed. Suppose the choice is whether to buy a new car or fix the old one.

The steps for analyzing the situation and reaching a rational decision are:

1. List each possible action.
2. Define the possible outcomes of each action.
3. Assign a value to each outcome. Sometimes the value of the outcome might be simply its monetary cost, but often the value must instead be judged. Any subjective measure of value is called the **utility** of the alternative. For example, repairing the car would involve a significant cost in both time and money. If the repairs succeed, their cost might be more than compensated for by the utility of having a usable car, so a utility of + 50 is assigned. If the repairs fail, the continued anxiety, frustration, and cost of having to seek further repairs must be considered: hence the utility of this outcome is large and negative. The exact numbers assigned for the various outcomes are arbitrary; their relative size and direction are significant in making a decision.
4. Note the probability of each outcome. For example, you might estimate that, in view of your car's condition, there is only a 20 percent chance that repairs will be successful. (The probabilities in each row must add up to 1.00.)
5. Multiply the probability in each column of the table by the utility value in each cell. This product is the **expected utility** of each outcome.
6. Add the expected utilities for the possible outcomes of each action; this sum represents the expected utility for each action. The action with the highest total (the most positive or least negative) is the one that should be chosen. It is the rational choice, given this kind of systematic analysis of costs, benefits, and risks.

This procedure is so straightforward that it may seem surprising that people often make bad decisions. But a closer look at steps 3 and 4—the assignment of value and probability—will show that making decisions is far from simple.

Perceptions of Value

When people consider various alternatives, their preferences depend, not on simple differences between costs and benefits, but on how they judge the utility of outcomes and on whether each outcome is seen as risky or a sure thing. Numerous experiments have shown that people tend to have certain biases in making these evaluations (Tversky & Kahneman, 1981). Figure 8.13 shows the relationship between the objective value of an outcome and its judged utility. Equal changes in value do not give equal changes in utility, for several reasons (Edwards et al., 1965; Tversky & Khneman, 1981). First, the utility of a specific gain depends, not on the absolute in crease in value, but on what the starting point was. Suppose you can take some action to receive a coupon for a free dinner worth $ 10. Does this gain have the same utility as having an extra $ 10 added to a dividend check?

The amount is the same, but as Figure 8.13 shows, people behave as if the difference in utility between $0 and $10 (+U1 in the figure) is much greater than the difference between $100 and $110 (+U2). This calls to mind. Weder's law of psychology discussed in the chapter on perception. How much a difference in value means depends on how much you already have (Edwards, Lindman & phillips, 1965).

Second, gains and losses are perceived quite differently, as you can see by comparing −U1 and +U1 in Figure 8.13 each of which is the result of a ten−dollar difference in value. Gaining a certain value has less utility than avoiding a loss of the same value (Tversky & Kahneman, 1981). In other words, the pleasure of winning a certain amount is less than the pain of losing the same amount.

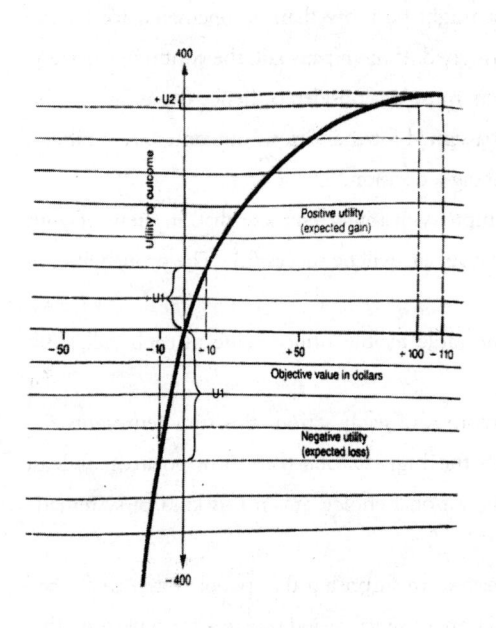

Figure 8.12
The Relationship Between Value and Utility
Notice that increases in value produce differing increases in utility, depending on the initial amount of value. For example, equal increases in value produce smaller increases in utility at higher initial values. Notice also that a $10 loss in value produces a much greater change in utility than does a $10 gain.

In addition, your preference among decision alternatives depends on whether the outcomes associated with them are risky or sure things, The reaction to risk depends on whether you are contemplating a loss or a gain. Suppose you are offered a choice between receiving one dollar for sure and gambling that dollar with a 50−50 chance of either winning two dollars or getting nothing. Which would you choose? The expected value of the outcome is the same for each option, but most people choose the smaller, but certain gain (Tversky & Kahneman, 1981). When people are faced a choice between two gains of the same expected value−one risky and one a sure thing−they generally choose the sure thing.

Now suppose you are forced to make the unpleasant choice between Using one dollar and accepting a gamble with a 50−50 chance of breaking even or losing two dollars. For either choice, the expected loss (outcome probability times outcome value) is one dollar. Most people accept the risky gamble. Thus, when offered the choice between risky loses and certain losses that have the same negative expected value, risk aversion vanishes, and people are more likely to select the risky rather than the sure alternative.

Because evaluation of an outcome is shaped by whether it is a gain or a loss, a risky or a sure thing, people can respond very differently to a decision, depending on how is framed (Tversky &

Kahneman, 1981). For example, a person might view the removal of a leg very negatively (as an expected loss) if it is contrasted with keeping the leg, but as an expected gain if the surgery prevents certain death.

Perceptions of probability

Differences between value and utility do not explain why people gamble. In reality, gambling involves choosing an expected loss instead of the sure thing of not gambling (If gambling yielded an expected gain for the gambler, Las Vegas and Atlantic City casinos would reap no profits). The explanation for gambling seems to come from a second element of risky decision making: people's perception of the probability that events will occur.

One way in which people's perception of probability differs from reality is called the **gambler's fallacy**. People believe that events in a random process will correct themselves. This belief is false. For example, if you flip a coin and it comes up heads ten times in a row, the chance that it will come up heads on the eleventh try is still 50 percent.

A second departure from reality results because people insistently overestimate the probability of very rare events and underestimate the probability of very frequent ones (Erlick, 1961; Tversky & Kahneman, 1981). In gambling or lotteries, the probability of a payoff is actually very rare (say, 1 percent). But if you perceive that your chances of winning are instead 5 percent, then the expected value of playing is artificially inflated and will be greater than the cost of entering. With this biased value, the decision to enter the gamble has a positive expected value.

There is one important exception to the tendency to underestimate frequent events, however.

When the event being estimated is the probability that one's own forecast or belief is correct, people tend to overestimate the probability, expressing overconfidence in their own predictions. Baruch Fisdhoff and Donald MacGregor (1982) used an ingenious approach to study this bias. They asked people whether they believed that a certain event would occur for example, that a certain sports team would win and how confident they were about this prediction. After the events, the accuracy of the forecasts was computed and compared with the confidence ratings assigned to the predictions. Sure enough, the confidence was consistently greater than the accuracy. That is, people tend to believe, more than they should, that they are going to be right.

This inflated confidence in prediction holds true even when people make predictions concerning the accuracy of their own memory. For example, Fischoff (1980) asked people questions based on general knowledge, such as: Which of the following causes is the most deaths in the United States: appendicitis, abortion, or childbirth? (The correct answer is appendicitis.) The people were also to indicate how confident they were that their answers were correct. Again, confidence was high, even though the answers were wrong more often than they were right.

Can debiasing eliminate this overconfidence? When Asher Koriat and his colleagues explicitly asked forecasters to list why their forecasts might be wrong, the forecasters offered forecasts that were less excessively optimistic (Koriat et al., 1980). They were able to reduce, but not eliminate, the tendency toward overconfidence. In short, be wary when people express confidence that a forecast is correct. They will be wrong more often than they think.

第五节 语言
(LANGUAGE)

So far, our discussion of thinking has assumed that people have a crucial skill: the ability to use language. This ability provides both a vehicle for the mind's communication with itself and the most important means of communicating with others. Other animals can communicate, but none appears to have the means to do so with the systematic rules, precision, and infinite range that human language allows. And only humans can pass communication through the ages, so that generation after generation can learn from and enjoy the heritage of its ancestors.

The Elements of Language

A **language has** two basic elements: symbols, such as words, and a set of rules, called **grammar**, for combining those symbols. These two components allow human language to be at once rule – bound and creative. With a vocabulary of no more than 50,000 to 100,000 words (the vocabulary of the typical college student), humans can create and understand an infinite number of sentence. All of the sentence ever articulate are created from just a few dozen categories of sounds.

The power of language comes from the way these rather unimpressive raw materials are organized according to rules. This organization occurs at several levels.

From sounds to sentences Organization occurs first at the level of sounds. **A phoneme** is the smallest unit of sound that affects the meaning of speech. Changing a phoneme changes the meaning of a word, much as changing a letter in a printed word changes its meaning. Tea has a meaning different from sea, and sight is different from sit.

Each spoken language consists of roughly thirty to fifty phonemes. English has twenty six letters, but it has about forty phonemes. The a in cat and the a in cake, for example, are different English phonemes. Many of the letter sounds are phonemes (including "ell", "aitch" and "em"), but so are the sounds "th" and "sh." Sounds that we consider different phonemes may be considered just one phoneme in another language, and sounds that are considered one phoneme in English are distinguished as different phonemes in other languages. For example, to English speakers the "p" in pin and the "p" in dip are one phoneme, but in the Thai language, they are two phonemes. In the Thai language, the "p" sound in pin combined with "-ay" gives a word meaning danger' the sound in combined with "-ay" creates a word meaning "to go".

Although changing a phoneme affects meaning, phonemes themselves are not meaningful. They are combined to form the second level of organization morphemes. A morpheme is the smallest unit of language that has meaning. Word stem like dog and run are morphemes, but so are prefixes like un-and suffixes like-ed, because they have meaning even though they can-not stand alone. Words are made up of one or more morphemes. Words, in turn, are combined to form phrases and sentences according to a set of rules called syntax. Compare the following sentences:

Fatal accidents deter careful drivers.

Snows sudden floods melting cause.

The first sentence makes perfect sense, but the second sentence violates English syntax. If the words were reordered, however, they would produce the perfectly acceptable sentence "Melting snows cause sudden floods" (Marks & Miller, 1964).

Even if you use English phonemes combined in proper ways to form morphemes strung together acceding to the laws of English syntax, you may not end up with an acceptable English sentence. Consider the sentence Rapid bouquets deter sudden neighbors. It somehow sounds right, but it is nonsense. Why? It has syntax, but it ignores the set of rules, called semantics, that govern the meaning of words and sentences.

Surface structure and deep structure   So far, we have discussed elements of language that are apparent in the sentences people produce. These elements were the focus of study for linguists and psycholinguists (psychologists who deal with language) for many decades. Then, in 1957, linguist Noam Chomsky started a revolution in the study of language. He argued that, if linguists studied only the language that people produced, they would never uncover the principles that account for all the sentences that people create. They could not explain, for example, how one articulated sentence, such as "This is my old friend" has more than one meaning (old can mean "aged" or "ling-standing"). And by looking only at sentences produced, linguists could not account for the very close relationships between the meanings of such apparently different sentences as Don't give up just because things look bad" and "The opera ain't over'til the fat **lady sings**."

To take these aspects of language into account, Chomsky proposed a more abstract level of analysis. Behind the word strings that people produce, called **surface structures**, there is, he said, a **deep structure**, an abstract representation of the relationships expressed in a sentence. For example, the surface structure "The shooting of the psychologist was terrible" may represent either of two deep structures: (1) that the psychologist had terrible aim, or (2) that it was terrible that someone shot the psychologist, Chomsky developed rules for transforming deep structures into surface structures and for relating sentences to each other.

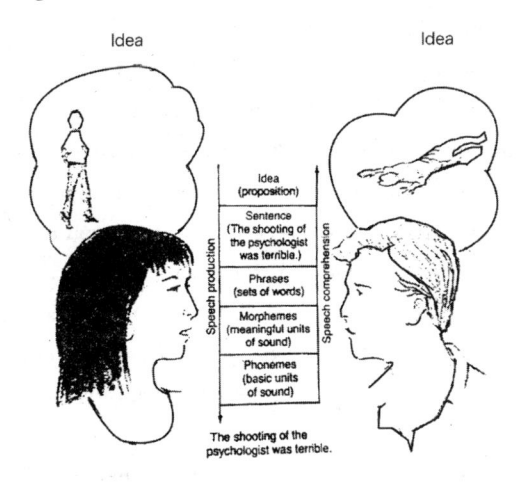

Figure 8.14

Producing and Comprehending Speech

The listener on the right has interpreted the speaker's message in a way that differs from the speaker's intended deep structure. Obviously, identical surface structures can correspond to distinctly different deep structures.

Since Chomsky proposed his first analysis of deep and surface structures, he and others have proposed many revisions of those ideas. The debates go well beyond what we can consider here. For our purposes, what is important about Chomsky's ideas is that they encouraged psychologists to analyze not just people's verbal behavior or the rules of grammar, but also the possible mental representations that verbal behavior reflects.

Communicating Through Language

When you speak, you have an idea or proposition to be conveyed, but sounds are transmitted. How is your idea translated into those sounds? If your communication is successful, your listener ends up, not simply with the sounds you transmitted, but with an idea or proposition that matches, or approximates, the one with which you began. How? Figure 8.14 illustrates an analysis of these processes. The speaker starts with an idea, which is translated, modified, and elaborated into a specific string of words, which are encoded into sounds by mechanisms of the throat and mouth. The listener must take this string of sounds and go through the reverse process in order to "decode" the message. If the encoding and decoding processes are error free, the ideas of speaker and listeners will match, and the communication will be successful. The specific words, however, may soon be forgotten. As we saw in the chapter memory, it is the underlying meaning, not the specific word string, that the listener is likely to encode and remember. Now consider how the decoding process occurs from the point of view of the listener.

Perceiving words When you listen to someone speak, what you perceive is a series of words. If sounds as if there is a (distinct pause between each word, while the phonemes within a word are heard as a continuous string. But this is not the case, **A speech spectrograph**, is a visual representation of the frequencies of speech as they unfold over time. The spectrograph shows that breaks occur, not between words, but within the words. You hear the breaks between, instead of within, words because of the top–down processing that we discussed in the chapter on perception. Because you know what the word should sound like, you recognize the sounds when they occur, and you perceive them as separate units, even if the physical stimuli are not separated. The top–down processing of speech also explains why speech in a language you do not understand sounds like a continuous stream and seems to be uttered at a much faster rate than speech in your own language. Because your brain does not know where each word in an unfamiliar language starts and stops, you do not hear the gaps between words; the gaps, after all, are not physically there. And because you do not perceive gaps between words, the sounds run together at what seems to be a faster than normal rate.

Understanding sentences Suppose you are asked to memorize two meaningless strings of words: "Hyaky deeb um flut recile pav togert disen" and "A–hyaky deeb reciled the dison togently um flutests pav." You might predict that it would be easier to learn the first string, which is shorter, because it should put a lighter burden on short-term memory. Surprisingly, William Epstein (1961) found that people learned the second string more easily. It is longer than the first, but it is also more sentence-like and more grammatical.

Apparently, the organization of the sounds into a sentence like structure, with the function words the and a and endings like-ed, allowed Epstein's subjects to chunk the sounds into more easily memorized units. Thus, the extra sounds added to the second sentence actually reduced the burden on short-term memory.

Experiments like Epstein's have demonstrated that syntax, the pattern of word order, plays a very important role in the comprehension of sentences. Instead of simply decoding speech word by word, researchers have found that people treat grammatical constituents, such as phrases, as separate units or chunks (Fodor. Bever & Garrett, 1974).

Although both syntax and word meanings are important to comprehension, they still do not tell the whole story. For example, knowing the meaning of words and proper word order does not explain why people understand that only one of the phrases, "Ruth eats fruit" and "fruit eats Ruth" is semantically correct. For this understanding, people also rely on knowledge of the world. Although both phrases are syntacically correct, you should have greater trouble reading the second string. Or if you read the strings in a hurry, your mind would probably automatically "recognize" the second sentence to another form, such as "the fruit was eaten by Ruth" (Fillenbaum, 1974). In other words, through top-down processing, people use their vast store of knowledge to find and impose meaning and organization, as well as grammatical structure, on words.

Understanding conversations Suppose we have been able to program a computer with all the rules and knowledge we have discussed so far with rules for decoding spoken phonemes and written letters into words, rules of syntax, a dictionary the meanings of words, and an encyclopedia of knowledge of the world. Now we ask our unfortunate computer to make sense of the following conversation:

    A: You going to the gym today to work out?
    B: Well, I aw flabby, but only if I can hook a ride with Jim. It's a long way.
    A: I'm afraid I heard his transmission's conked out, and it's at the shop.
    B: Oh[pause] then I guess it won't work out.

You probably had little trouble understanding this conversation, but the computer would be at a loss. The first problem is that the grammar is not complete. For example, the fact that the first sentence is a question would be indicated only by a rising tone of voice. Second, because both participants understand the general gist or the dialogue, certain ambiguous terms take on different meanings in different sentences (for example, it in lines 2, 3, and 4; work out in lines 1 and 4; and gym versus Jim in lines 1 and 2). Third, having the gist allows you to understand the meaning of words or phrases like hook, Tm afraid, and conked out, and to know that the transmission is actually part of Jim's car, not a part of Jim. These are things that the computer could not easily "understand."

In general, difficulties in programming a computer to understand conversations arise because the use of language is knowledge-driven and relies on the context in which words are spoken or written. This use of context creates one of the greatest challenges in the development of artificial intelligence for speech recognition. People use context to interpret and impose meaning on stimuli—including language. A statement like "How are you smart!" can be interpreted as "I think you're and idiot" depending on the context (perhaps the tone of voice). Thus, understanding language involves constructing meaning out of sounds, just as recalling stored memories sometimes involves constructing information based partly on the context in which that information is encoded or retrieved.

The context for understanding language may be created by the situation. Richard Mayer (1983) reported seeing a sign in a Laundromat in Santa Barbara, Califomia, that said, "Not responsible for clothes you may have stolen." The words themselves could easily mean "The owner is not responsible if you steal someone else's clothes." But, from the context created by the situation, it is obvious that the sign was meant to warn people not to leave their belongings unattended.

An individual's personal history also forms part of the context of a situation. Thus, people's educational and cultural backgrounds help shape their understanding.

Every Saturday night, four good friends get together. When Jerry, Mike, and Pat arrived, Karen was sitting in her living room writing some notes. She quickly gathered the cards and stood up to greet her friends at the door. They followed her into the living room but as usual they couldn't agree on exactly what to play. Jerry eventually took a stand and set things up. Finally, they began to play. Karen's recorder filled the room with soft and peasant music. Early in the evening. Mike noticed Pat's hand and many diamonds. As the might progressed the tempo of play increased. Finally, a lull in the activities occurred. Taking advantage of this, Jerry pondered the arrangement in front of him. Mike interrupted Jerry's reverie and said, "Let's hear the score." They listened carefully and commented on their performance. When the comments were all heard, exhausted but happy, Karen's friends went home (Anderson et al., 1977).

In a laboratory study, music majors tended to interpret this passage as describing a music practice session, whereas students in other fields typically read it as the description of a friendly card game (Anderson et al., 1977) .

Stages of Language Development

Once people have learned to speak, they use the many rules of language naturally and automatically to generate correct sentences and to reject incorrect ones, even though most people would have a difficult time stating the rules. For example, in an instant you know that the words "Bei mir bist du schoen" are not English and that the string of words. Quickly peaches sheep deserve is not an acceptable sentence. Children the world over learn language with impressive speed and regularity.

Developmental psychologists have painstakingly detailed the steps in this process. We discussed the earliest steps: the babblings of infants and the one-word speech of young children. By eighteen to twenty-four months of age, children usually have a vocabulary of some fifty-words. Then their language undergoes an explosion; it is not uncommon at this point for children to learn several new words a day and to begin to put words together.

At first, children's sentences consist of two-word pairs. These are more elaborate, less ambiguous, and somewhat less tied to gestures than children's one—word expressions. For example, to call attention to a dog, which was once done by pointing and saying, "Doggy," the child now says, "See doggy," Still, children's two—word utterances are telegraphic. Brief and to the point, they leave out any word that is not absolutely essential. If she wants her mother to give her a book, the twenty—month—old might first say, "Give book, then", "Mommy give," and, if that does not work, "Mommy book." The child also uses rising intonation to indicate a question ("Go out?"), and word stress to indicate location ("Play park")or asserted information ("Big car").

Three—word sentences come next in the development of language. They are still telegraphic, but more nearly complete: "Mommy give book." The child can speak in sentences that have the usual subject—verb—object form of adult sentences. Other words and word endings begging appearing, too (Brown, 1973; Dale, 1976). For most children, the suffixing comes first (I walking); then the prepositions in and on. The plural 5 comes next; then come some irregular past tenses ("It broke, " "I ate"). Later, children learn to use the suffixed for the past tense ("I walked"). But once they have mastered the rule for usinged—ed to express past events, they over apply the rule to irregular verbs that they previously used correctly, saying, for example, "It breaked" or "It broked" or "I eated."

Children also expand their vocabularies with adjectives. At first, they do not always get the antonyms straight. They know that tall and short both refer to height, more and less to quantity, wide and narrow to breadth; but they are likely to use both less and more to mean "more" or tall and short to mean "tall" (Donaldson & Balfour, 1968).

After acquiring some adjectives, children begin to use auxiliary verbs ("Adam is going") and to ask questions using wh words (where, whose, who, why, how, when, in roughly this order).They begin to put ideas together in sentences. They elaborate on nouns ("Here's the bail I was looking for") and link ideas together ("I want to draw if Jimmy does"). Until they are about five years old, however, children join events in the order in which they occur ("We went to the zoo and had ice cream") and understand sentences better if they follow this order (Clark, 1978; Kavanaugh & Jirkovsky, 1982), By age five, children have acquired most of the syntax of their native language.

How Is Language Learned?

Despite all that has been learned in recent years about the steps children follow in learning language, mystery still surrounds the question of just how they learn it. We know a great deal about what happens, but why and how it happens is still open to debate. Obviously, children pick up the specific content of language from the speech they hear around them. English children learn English, French children learn French. As parents and children share meals, playtime, and conversations, children learn that words refer to objects and actions and what the labels for them are. But how do they learn syntax?

Conditioning and imitation   Our discussion of conditioning in Chapter 7 suggest one possibility: perhaps children learn syntax because of the way their parents reinforce them. In fact, however, observations of parents and children suggest that reinforcement cannot fully explain the learning of syntax. Usually parents do not deliberately instruct their youngsters in the fine points of syntax. Most parents forego correcting the grammar of their young children or reprimanding them for syntactic mistakes. They are more concerned about what is said then about its form (Hirsch—pasek,

Treisman & Schneiderman, 1984). When the little boy with chocolate crumbs on his face says, not eat cookie, the mother is more likely to respond "Yes, you did eat it, rather than, asking the child to say, I did not eat the cookie." Parents may offer the child a correct version of the incorrect sentence, but they do not reprove the child.

Although adults do not give lessons on grammar, they, do greatly modify their speech when talking to their language—learning children. They shorten their sentences, and use con—Crete, basic nouns and active verbs—no pronouns, adjectives, conjunctions, or past tenses. They exaggerate, repeat, enunciate clearly, and stick to the here—and—now, in grammatically correct utterances. This kind of talk which parallels children's own has been called motherese although fathers, aunts, uncles, and older siblings also speak it. Parents seem to use motherese to help children understand what is being said. But does it help children acquire language? Apparently not. Children do not learn to speak correctly earlier if their mothers speak—down to their level (Chesnic et al., 1983; Nelson et al., 1983). In fact, within the range of language spoken by most mothers to their children, the more complex the mother's language, the earlier and more rapidly their children learn to speak in complex sentences (Clarke—Stewart & Hevey, 1981; Gleitman, Newport & Gleitman, 1984).

If the aim is to help a child learn syntax, expanding the child's utterances is more helpful than speaking motherese. Children learn syntax the most rapidly when adults offer simple revisions of their sentences, implicitly correcting their syntax, and continue with the topic they are discussing. For example,

Child: Mommy fix.

Mother: Okay, Mommy will fix the truck.

Child: It braked.

Mother: Yes, it broke.

Child: It broke.

Mother: Let s see if we can fix it.

This recasting obviously involves modeling correct speech forms, and modeling, or imitation, is an important source of learning. Especially if the child is given approval for imitating recast forms, adults recasting of language cannot help but shape language development.

But if children learned syntax by imitation, why would they overgeneralize rules for past tenses and plurals? Neither conditioning nor imitation seems entirely adequate to explain how children learn language. Children must still analyze for themselves the underlying patterns in the welter of language examples they hear around them.

Nature and nurture The ease with which children everywhere discover these patterns and learn language has encouraged some to argue that humans are "prewired" or biologically programmed to learn language. Chomsky (1957) has suggested that human beings possess an innate language acquisition device a LAD, for short, that processes speech and allows children to understand the regularities of speech and fundamental relationships among words. The LAD permits youngsters to gather ideas about the rules of language without even being aware of doing so. They then use these ideas to understand and construct their native language.

Evidence to support this hypothesis is hard to get, however. One suggestive finding is that there is some similarity in the syntax of all languages. Another is the fact that children born deaf and never exposed to language make up gestural systems that have several properties of natural spoken language, including placement of subjects before verbs and agent—action—object sequences, such as "June saw Bob" (Goldin—Meddow & Feldman, 1977).

Even if there is a LAD, it has a limited warranty. An unfortunate child was confined by her father to isolation and abuse in a small room until she was discovered and rescued at age 13 XA. (Curtiss, 1977). Like the Wild Boy of Aveyron, whom we described in Chapter 2, she had not heard any language, and she could not speak at all when she was discovered. After six years of therapy and language training, she still had not learned to use language forms like what, which, and that; possessive sentences; or auxiliary verbs. She could not combine ideas into a single sentence. Her speech was the equivalent of a two or three—year—old's. The Wild Boy was also unable to learn adult language. Such cases suggest that, to acquire complex features of language, it may be that a person must be exposed to speech before a certain age. That is, there appears to be a critical period for learning language similar to the critical periods for such developmental dimensions as binocular depth perception. This suggestion is supported by research showing that people who learn a second language after the age of thirteen or fourteen are unlikely ever to speak it without an accent (Lenneberg, 1967).

How Important Is Language?

The impressive power of language, and the complexities encountered when one tries to explain it, have helped generate many claims about its importance. Language, some say, is qualitatively different from all other forms of communication, is unique to humans, and sets humans apart from other creatures. Others suggest that language determines how people perceive the world or that, without language, there can be no thought.

Does language determine perception?   The language that people speak forms part of their knowledge of the world, and that knowledge, guides perceptions. This relationship raises the question of whether there is an even closer relationship between the two. Do differences among the languages of the world create differences in how people perceive the world? Benjamin Whorf thought that the answer was yes (Whorf, 1956). He noted, for example, that Eskimos have some twenty names for snow, whereas most Americans have only a few. Whorf proposed that this difference in language would lead to a greater ability to discriminate between varieties of snow—a perceptual ability—and when the discrimination abilities of Americans and Eskimos are compared, there are indeed significant differences. However, these results leave another question unanswered: Are the differences in perception the result of differences in language?

One of the most interesting tests of Whorf's ideas was conducted by Elenaor Rosch (1972). She compared the perception of colors by Americans with that by members of the Dani tribe of New Guinea. In the language of the Dani, there are only two color names, one for dark, "cold" colors and one for lighter, "warm" ones. In contrast, English speakers have names for a vast number of different hues. Of these, it is possible to identify eleven focal colors; these are prototypes, the particular wavelengths of light that are the best examples of the eleven major color categories (red, yellow, green, blue, black, grey, white, purple, orange, pink, and brown). Thus, fire-engine red is the focal color for red Rosch reasoned that, if Whorf's views were correct, then English speakers, who had verbal labels for focal colors, should recognize them better than nonlocal colors. For the Dani, the focal-nonlocal distinction should make no difference. Yet, in spite of the language differences between the groups, Rosch found that both the Dani and the Americans perceived focal colors more efficiently than nonfocal ones (Heider, 1972).

There are correlated differences in language and in perception between cultures. For example, Eskimos perceive and have verbal labels for subtle, but important differences among snow textures. Americans do not. But it appears doubtful that language causes the differences in perception, as Whorf claimed. It seems far more likely that, beneath the differences in both language and perception, there is a third variable: frequency of use and the society's need for certain objects. Eskimos, for example, live in a snowy world. Their lives depend on making fine discrimination about the snow between the snow bridge that is old and the one that will collapse, between the snow field that can be crossed easily and the one that must be avoided.

Hence, they learn to discriminate differences that are unimportant to people in warmer climates, and they attach names to those discriminated differences.

Is language ability necessary for thought? Much of human thought seems to be language-bound; people often use words to express ideas and silently spoken sentences to solve problems. We saw earlier that thought can be carried out without the muscular structures involved in language (Smith et al., 1947), but are the cognitive structures of language necessary to allow thought? Hans Furth (1964) looked for an answer to this question by studying the cognitive abilities of deaf children. Most deaf children are taught American sign language (A$L) quite early. But Furth studied children who were not taught any language, because their parents felt that learning ASL might retard their eventual acquisition of vocal speech and lip reading. Therefore, these children were language deficient. Were they also deficient in thinking ability? Furth carefully tested their ability to solve problems that did not involve language, and he found no cognitive deficits. At the very least, his experiment suggests that there can be thought without language.

Furth himself offered a stronger conclusion. Thought, he said, is unhampered by the loss of language. Many psychologists dispute this view, because language seems to provide an effective organizing tool for guiding people's thinking, as well as a rich vocabulary to help give meaning to concepts (Bruner, 1964).The precise relationship between thought and language may never be fully established, mainly because there is probably no single relationship involved. As we have seen, thinking sometimes requires language, but it can also be based on visual images. Further, the importance of language for thought varies from person to person.

第六节 未来研究趋向
(FUTURE DIRECTIONS)

As some of the simpler, more observable phenomena of cognition yield up their secrets, the challenge grows to understand the most complex mental phenomena, including thought, decision making, and problem solving. Techniques such as brain wave recording, verbal reports of thought processes, and computer simulations of thought have all been enlisted in this effort. For example, researchers are studying how well-established findings regarding reaction time can be used to build better computers, airplanes, automobiles, and other systems (This is the field of engineering psychology which was discussed in Chapter 1). Verbal narratives spoken by expert problem solvers, are used to help create computer programs that will solve new problems in the same way the experts do. Evoked potentials help us to understand precisely how the fastest decisions are carried out.

The issue of mental models is very much at the core of modem cognitive psychology. Among the questions still to be answered are: Do we need to talk about mental models at all in order to describe thought?

If so, are they verbal or spatial, neither or both, accurate or biased? How do they differ from experts to novices, or among people with differing mental abilities? How do we measure them? Designers of computers and other complex systems would like to know what the user's mental model of the system is, so that the system can be built in a way that is compatible with that model.

Numerous questions about problem solving and decision making are also on the agenda for coming years. How good or bad is human decision making (Einhorn & Hogarth, 1981)? To what extent do decision-making heuristics save work and produce good results? How often and to what extent do they get people into trouble? Does laboratory research on decision making by mock juries have applications in the real world? Can debiasing procedures be taught to improve decision making outside the laboratory? Several companies have marked products that are supposed to help people make decisions, but it is extremely difficult to evaluate the effectiveness of these aids. Their true value remains questionable (Wickens, 1984).

The study of artificial intelligence is one of the most rapidly expanding areas in science. It draws on concepts of psychology, engineering, computer science, and many other fields. One of the challenges in this multidisciplinary area is that of getting computers to think, reason, and communicate effectively. Most people remain skeptical that computers will ever be able to match human mental abilities (Dreyfus & Drejrfus, 1986). However, efforts to achieve this goal have already helped scientists learn more about the human mind and, as we have seen, have led to the design of computer-based expert systems that can help solve problems. Psychologists' involvement in future researches in this area will lead not only to more sophisticated computers, but also to a fuller understanding of complex mental processes in humans.

Indeed, cognitive psychology is rapidly becoming one of the most exciting areas in psychology. To learn more about the research explosion taking place in the areas of thought, decision making, problem solving, and language, you might take courses in experimental psychology, cognitive psychology (sometimes called higher processes or thinking), psycholinguistics, or engineering psychology (which is sometimes called human factors).

词汇 (Vocabulary)

1. algorithm   n. 算法式策略

2. anchoring heuristic　　n. 参照启发式策略
3. artificial concept　　n. 科学概念、人工概念
4. availability heuristic　　n. 提取性启发式策略
5. babbling　　n. 胡说，婴儿发出的咿哑声
6. base-rate frequency　　n. 基率频率
7. building in common sense　　共同理性的建构
8. chronometry　　n. 计时法
9. chunk　　n. 块
10. cognition　　n. 认知
11. compatibility　　n. 一致性、相容性
12. conceit　　n. 自大、自负
13. conditioning　　n. 条件作用、条件反射
14. confirmation bias　　n. 肯定倾向
15. conjunctive rule　　n. 合取规则
16. covert speech　　n. 内隐言语
17. cramp　　n. 痉挛
18. critical period　　n. 关键期
19. curare　　n. 箭毒
20. decode　　v. 解码、译码
21. decomposition　　n. 逆向分解法
22. deep structure　　n. 深层结构
23. disjunctive rule　　n. 析取规则
24. disrupt　　v. 分裂
25. dissipate　　v. 消除
26. distortion　　n. 变形
27. domain　　n. 知识范围
28. empirical　　经验的、全凭观察和实验的
29. enunciate　　v. 发音
30. ephemeral nature　　n. 瞬息性
31. err　　v.（正式用语）犯错
32. evoked brain potential　　n. 诱发电位
33. expectancy　　n. 期待
34. expected utility　　n. 预期效用
35. expert system　　专家系统
36. functional fixedness　　n. 功能固着
37. gist　　n. 要点、要质
38. hemoglobin　　n. 血红蛋白、血红素
39. heuristic　　n. 启发式（策略）
40. imitation　　n. 模拟

41. impeccable   a.（正式用语）不会错的
42. incubation   n. 酝酿期、孵化期
43. inference engine   n. 推断工具
44. intense stimuli   n. 强刺激
45. internist   n. 医学专家
46. language acquisition device（LAD）语言获得装置
47. manipulate   v. 操纵
48. mar   v. 损伤
49. menstrual   a. 月经的
50. mental chronometry   心理计时法
51. mental representation   n. 心理表象
52. mental set   心向、心理定势
53. mimic   v. & n 摹仿
54. morpheme   n. 词素
55. motherese   n. 母亲语
56. multiattribute utility theory   n. 多因素效用原理
57. multiple hypothese   n. 复合假设
58. natural concept   n. 日常概念
59. novice   n. 生手、初学者
60. nurture   n.（正式用语）儿童的教养、训练
61. overt   a. 公开的、公然的
62. peripheral nervous system   外周神经系统
63. phoneme   n. 音位、音素
64. pitfall   n. 圈套
65. premise   n. 前提
66. proposition   n. 命题、定理
67. prototype   n. 原型
68. psycholinguist   n. 心理语言学家
69. reaction time(RT)   反应时
70. rectangular bias   长方形倾向
71. representiveness heuristic   典型启发式策略
72. schizophrenic   n. 精神分裂症患者
73. semantics   n. 语义学
74. spatial cognition   n. 空间认知
75. speech spectrograph   言语摄谱仪
76. speed-accuracy trabeoff   速度—精确度交换
77. spleen   n. 脾脏
78. surface structure   n. 表层结构
79. syllogism   n. 三段论法

80. syntax   n. 句法
81. telegraphic speech   电文式言语
82. top-down process   自上而下的加工
83. vocal appratus   发声器官
84. voltage   n. 电压、伏特数

第九章 思维与教学
（THINKING AND TEACHING）

本章要点（Chapter Outline）

思维与理解的重要性
（The Importance of Thinking And Understanding)
概念的学习与教学（Learning And Teaching About Concept)
学习中问题的解决（Problem Solving in Learning)
思维的教学与学习（Teaching And Learning About Thinking)
迁移的教学（Teaching for Transfer)

  学习是以思维为核心的复杂活动，概念的学习是学生掌握知识的基础。概念掌握的基本形式有两种，即概念的形成和概念的同化，后者是学生获得概念的最基本形式，学生认知发展水平是影响其掌握概念的一个根本心理因素，已掌握的概念可以在不同的水平上加以应用。

  知识的掌握主要表现于解决问题，特别是创造性地解决问题。问题的解决可以使用一般和特殊两种策略，表现为一个过程，具有阶段性，解决问题的技能可以通过训练而得到提高。

  解决问题的核心是思维，发散思维尤为重要。学习迁移、学习方式、认知模型也是影响学习效果的重要因素。

第一节 思维与理解的重要性
（THE IMPORTANCE OF THINKING AND UNDERSTANDING）

Understanding is more than memorizing. It is more than retelling in your own words. Howard Gardner (1993b) defines understanding as:

> the capacity to take knowledge, skills, and concepts and apply them appropriately in new situations someone only parrots back what he or she has been taught, we do not know whether the individual understands. If that person applies the knowledge promiscuously, regardless of whether it is appropriate, then I would not say he or she understands either...But if that person know where to apply and where not to apply, and can do it to new situations, he or she understands.

Is thinking different from understanding? We could say that good thinking leads to understanding so thinking is the process that produces the outcome of understanding. What is good thinking? Some psychologists believe that thinking is the effective use of general strategies. Other psychologists associate thinking with problem solving and creativity. Still others talk about critical thinking skills such as evaluating evidence or making judgments.

A simple, practical definition is that good thinking is thinking that achieves its goal (Baron, 1985). Different goals require different kinds of thinking. In deciding which car to buy, critical thinking and the evaluation of advertisers' claims may be necessary. When faced with a flat tire and no jack, creative problem solving is required reach your goal (Perkins, Jay, & Tishman, 1993). In the following sections we will explore what is known about different aspects of thinking: problem solving, creativity, and critical thinking, and how teachers can support these paths to understanding. We begin with a discussion of the building blocks of thinking concepts.

第二节 概念的学习与教学
(LEARNING AND TEACHING ABOUT CONCEPT)

Most of what we know about the world involves concepts and relations among concepts (Schwartz & Reisberg, 1991). But what exactly is a concept? A concept is a category used to group similar events, ideas, objects, or people. When we talk about a particular concept like student, we refer to a category of people who are similar to one another—they all study a subject. The people may be old or young, in school or not; they may be studying baseball or Bach, but they can all be categorized as students. Concepts are abstractions. They do not exist in the real world. Only individual examples of concepts exist.

Concepts help us organize vast amounts of information into manageable units. For instance, there are about 7.5 million distinguishable differences in colors. By categorizing these colors into some dozen or some groups, we manage to deal with this diversity quite well (Bruner, 1973). Without the ability to form concepts, we would find life a confusing series of unrelated experiences. There would be no way of grouping things together, no symbols or shorthand for talking and thinking about similar objects and events. Nothing would be like anything else, and communication would be impossible (Reed, 1992).

Views of Concept Learning

Traditionally, psychologists have assumed that members of a category share a set of defining attributes, or distinctive features. Students all study; books all contain pages of printed, drawn or photographed materials that are bound together in some way. The defining attributes theory of concepts suggests that we recognize specific examples by noting key features.

Since about 1970, however, these long-popular views about the nature of concepts and category systems have been challenged (Benjafield, 1992). While some concepts, such as equilateral triangle, have clear-cut defining attributes, most concepts do not. Take the concept of party. What are the defining attributes? You might have difficulty listing these attributes, but you probably recognize a party when you see (or hear) one. What about the concept of birds. Your first thought might be that birds are animals that fly. But an ostrich is a bird. What about a penguin?

Prototypes and Exemplars. According to critics of the traditional view of concept learning, have in our minds a prototype of a party and a bird—an image that captures the essence of each concept. A prototype is the best representative of its category. For instance, the best representative of the "birds", category for many Americans might be a robin (Rosch, 1973). Other members of the category may be very similar to the prototype (sparrow) or similar in some ways but different in others (chicken, ostrich). At the boundaries of a category, it may be difficult to determine if a particular instance really belongs. For example, is a telephone a piece of "furniture"? Is an elevator a "vehicle"? Is an olive a "fruit"? Whether something fits into a category is a matter of degree. Thus, categories have fuzzy boundaries and graded membership (Schwartz & Reisberg, 1991). Some events, objects, or ideas are simply better examples of a concept than others.

Another explanation of concept learning suggests that we identify members of a category by referring to exemplars. Exemplars are our actual memories of specific birds, parties, furniture, and so on that category as our exemplar. For example, if you see a strange steel-and-stone bench in a public park, you may compare it to the chair in your living room to decide if the uncomfortable looking creation is still a chair or if it has crossed a fuzzy boundary into "sculpture".

Prototypes probably are built from experiences with many exemplars. This happens naturally because episodic memories of particular events tend to blur together over time, creating an average or typical chair prototype from all the chair exemplars you have experienced (Schwartz & Reisberg, 1991).

Concepts and Schemas. In addition to prototypes and exemplars, there is a third element involved when we recognize a concept our schematic knowledge related to the concept. How do we know that counterfeit money is not "real" money, even though it perfectly fits our "money" prototype and exemplars? We know because of its history. It was printed by the "wrong" people. So our understanding of the concept of money is connected with concepts of crime forgery, the federal treasury and many others.

Strategies for Teaching Concepts

Most of the current approaches to teaching concepts still rely heavily on the traditional analysis of defining attributes. Interest is growing, however, in the prototypes view of concept luring, partly because children first learn many concepts in the real world from best examples or prototypes, pointed out by adults (Tennyson, 1981). The teaching of concepts can combine both distinctive features and prototypes.

Lesson Components. Whatever strategy you use for teaching concepts, you will need to have tour components in any lesson: the name of the concept, a definition, relevant and irrelevant attributes, and examples and non-examples (Joyce & Weil, 1992). In addition, visual aids such as pictures, diagrams, or maps can improve learning of many concepts (Anderson & Smith, 1987).

The name of the concept is important for communicating, but it is somewhat arbitrary.

Simply learning a label does not mean the person understands the concept, although the label is necessary for the understanding.

A definition makes the nature of the concept clear. A good definition has two elements: a reference to any more general category that the new concept falls under, and a statement of the new concept's defining attributes (Klausmeier, 1976). For example, an equilateral triangle is defined as a plane, simple, closed figure (general category), with three equal sides and three equal angles (defining attributes) . This kind of definition helps place the concept in a schema of related knowledge.

The identification of relevant and irrelevant attributes is another aspect of teaching concepts. The ability to fly, as we've seen, is not a relevant attribute for classifying animals as birds. Even though many birds fly, some birds do not (ostrich, penguin), and some non-birds do (bats, flying squirrels). The ability to fly would have to be included in a discussion of the bird concept, but students should understand that flying does not define an animal as a bird.

Examples are essential in teaching concepts. More examples are needed in teaching complicated concepts and in working with younger or less-able students. Both examples and non-examples (sometimes called positive and negative instances) are necessary to make the boundaries of the category clear. So a discussion of why a bat (non-example) is not a bird will help students define the boundaries of the bird concept.

In teaching some concepts "a picture is worth a thousand words" or at least a few hundred. Seeing and handling specific examples, or pictures of examples, helps young children learn concepts. For students of all ages, the complex concepts in history, science, and mathematics can often be illustrated in diagrams or graphs. For example, Anderson and Smith (1983) found that when the students they taught just read about the concept, only 20 percent could understand the role of reflected light in our ability to see objects. But when the students worked with diagrams almost 80 percent understood the concept.

Lesson Structure.   Start your concept lesson with prototypes, or best examples, to help the students establish the category. For instance, if you were teaching the concept of liquid, you might start with examples such as water or juice. Then move to more difficult, less obvious examples such as cake batter, shampoo, or honey. These example show the wide range of possibilities the category includes and the variety of irrelevant attributes within a category. The formation helps students avoid focusing on an irrelevant as a defining feature. The cake batter example tells students that liquids can be thick opaque as well as thin and clear. The shampoo example indicates that liquids do not have to be edible. Including liquids that are thick and thin, clear and opaque, edible and inedible, will prevent undergeneralization, or the exclusion of some substances from their rightful place in the category liquid.

Nonexamples should be very close to the concept, but miss by one or just a few attributes. For instance, sand is not an example of liquid, even though it shares oneof the characteristics of liquids. You can pour it. Including nonexamples will prevent overgeneralization, or the inclusion of substances that are not liquids.

Once students have a good sense of a concept, they should use it. This might mean doing exercises, solving problems, writing, reading, explaining, or any other activity that requires them to apply their new understanding. This will connect the concept into the students web of related schematic knowledge. One new approach that you may see in some texts and workbooks is concept mapping (Novak & Musonda, 1991).

第三节　学习中问题的解决
(PROBLEM SOLVING IN LEARNING)

"Educational programs," Robert Gagne has written, "have the important ultimate purpose of teaching students to solve problems mathematical and physical problems, health problems, social problems, and problems of personal adjustment" (1977, p.177). A problem has an initial state the current situation, a goal the desired outcome, and a path for reaching the goal, problem solvers often have to set and reach subgoals as they move toward the final solution (Schunk, 1991a). **Problem solving** is usually defined as formulating new answers, going beyond the simple application of previously learned rules to create a solution Problem solving is what happens when routine or automatic responses do not fit the current situation. Some psychologists suggest that most human learning involves problem solving (Anderson 1993).

Problem Solving: General or Domain–Specific?

There is an interesting debate about problem solving. Some psychologists believe that effective problem solving strategies are specific to the problem area. That is, the problem solving strategies in mathematics are unique to math, the strategies in art are unique to art, and so on. Becoming an expert problem solver in an area requires that you master the strategies of the area. The other side of the debate claims that there are some general problem solving strategies that can be useful in many areas.

There is evidence for both sides of the argument. In fact, it appears that people move between general and specific approaches, depending on the situation and their level of expertise. Early on, when we know little about a problem area or domain, we may rely on general learning and problem solving strategies to make sense of the situation. As we gain more domain specific knowledge (particularly procedural knowledge about how to do things in the domain), we need the general strategies less and less. But if we encounter a problem outside our current knowledge, we may return to relying on general strategies to attack the problem.

Think of a general problem solving strategy as a beginning point, a broad outline. Such strategies usually have five stages. John Bransford and Barry Stein (1984) use the acronym IDEAL to identify the five steps:

I Identify the problem.

D Define and represent the problem.

E Explore possible strategies.

A Act on the strategies.

L Look back and evaluate the effects of your activities.

The first step, identifying that a problem exists, begins the process. This is not always straightforward. There is a story describing tenants who were angry about the slow elevators in their building. Consultants hired to "fix the problem" reported that the elevators were no worse than average and that improvements would be very expensive. Then one day, as the building supervisor watched people waiting impatiently for an elevator, he realized that the problem was not slow elevators but the fact that people were bored; they had nothing to do while they waited. When the boredom problem was identified, the simple solution of installing a mirror on each floor eliminated complaints.

Once a solvable problem is identified, what next? We will examine steps D, E, A, and L in some detail, because these are the heart of the process.

Defining and Representing the Problem

Defining and representing a problem often requires finding the relevant information and ignoring the irrelevant details. For example, consider the following problem adapted from Sternberg & Davidson (1982):

If you have black socks and white socks in your drawer, mixed in the ratio of four to five, how many socks will you have to take out to make sure of having a pair the same color?

What information is relevant to solving this problem? Did you realize that the information about the four-to-five ratio of black socks to white socks is irrelevant? As long as you have only two different colors of socks in the drawer, you will have to remove only three socks before two of them have to match.

In addition to identifying the relevant information in a problem, you must develop an accurate representation of the situation involved. This may require knowledge that is specific to the problem area. Let's assume we are dealing with story problems, problems that are stated orally or written out, like the socks problem above.

To represent these problems successfully, you must (1) understand the words and sentences, and (2) activate the right schema to understand the whole problem (Mayer, 1983a & b, 1992).

Understanding the Words. The first task in representing a story problem is linguistic comprehension, understanding the meaning of each sentence. Take, for example, the following sentence from an algebra story problem:

The riverboat's rate in still water is 12 miles per hour more than the rate of the river current.

This is a relational proposition. It describes the relationship between two rates, that of the riverboat and that of the current. Here is another sentence from a story problem:

The cost of the candy is $ 2.75 per pound.

This is an assignment proposition. It simply assigns a value to something, in cost of one unit of candy.

Research shows that relational propositions are harder to understand and remember than assignment propositions. In one study, when students had to recall relational and assignment propositions like those above, the error rate for recalling relational propositions was about three times higher than the error rate for assignment propositions (Mayer, 1982). If you misunderstand the meaning of individual statements in a problem, you will have a hard time representing the whole problem correctly.

The main stumbling block in representing many word problems is the students under-standing of part whole relations (Cummins, 1991). Students have trouble figuring out what is part of what, as evident in this dialogue between a teacher and a first grader:

Teacher: Pete has three apples; Ann also has some apples; Pete and Ann have nine apples altogether; how many apples does Ann have?

Student: Nine.

Teacher: Why?

Student: Because you just said so.

Teacher: Can you retell the story?

Student: Pete had three apples; Ann also had some apples; Ann had nine apples; Pete also has nine apples. (adapted from De Corte & Verschaffel 1985,p.19)

The students interprets "altogether" (the whole) as "each" (the parts).

Understanding the Whole problem.   The second task in representing a problem is to assemble all the sentences into an accurate understanding or translation of the total problem. Even if you understand every sentence, you may still misunderstand the problem as a whole. Consider this example:

Two train stations are 50 miles apart. At 2 p.m. one Saturday afternoon two trains start toward each other, one from each station. Just as the trains pull out of the stations, one bird springs into the air in front of the first train and flies ahead to the from of the second train. When the bird reaches the second train it turns back and flies toward the first train. The bird continues to do this until the trains meet. If both trains travel at the rate of 25 miles per hour and the bird flies at 100 miles per hour, how many miles will the bird have flown before the trains meet? (Posner, 1973)

Your interpretation of the problem is called a translation because you translate the problem into a schema that you understand. If you translate this as a tance problem ("I have to figure out how far the bird travels before it meets the oncoming train and turns around, then how far it travels before it has to turn again, and finally add up all the trips back and forth…"), then you have a very difficult problem on your hands. But there is a better way to structure the problem. You can represent it as a question of time and focus on the time the bird is in the air. If you know how long the bird is in the air, then you can easily determine the distance it will cover, since you know exactly how fast it flies. The solution could be stated like this:

Since the stations are 50 miles apart and the trains are moving toward each other at the same speed, the trains will meet in the middle, 25 miles from each station. Because they are traveling 25 mph, it will take the trains one hour to reach the meeting point. In the one hour it takes the trains to meet, the bird will cover 100 miles because it is flying at 100 miles per hour. Easy!

Research shows that students can be too quick to decide what a problem is asking. The subjects in one study made their decisions about how to categorize standard algebra problems after reading only the first few sentences of a problem (Hinsley, Hayes, & Simon, 1977). Once a problem is categorized "Aha, it's a distance problem!" a particular schema is activated. The schema directs attention to relevant information and sets up expectations for what the right answer should look like (Hayes, Waterman, & Robinson, 1977; Robinson & Hayes, 1978).

When students do not have the necessary schemas to represent problems, they often rely on surface features of the situation and represent the problem incorrectly like the student who wrote "15 + 24 = 39" as the answer to the question, "Joan has 15 bonus points and Louise has 24. How many more does Louise have?" This student saw two numbers and the word "more", so he applied the add to get more procedure. When students use the wrong schema, they overlook critical information, use irrelevant information, and may even misread or misremember critical information so that it fits the schema. Errors in representing the problem and difficulties in solving it are the results. But when students use the proper schema for representing a problem they are less likely to be confused by irrelevant information or tricky wording, like more in a problem that really requires subtraction (Resnick, 1981).

Translation and Schema Training. How can students improve translation and schema selection? To answer this question, we often have to move from general to area-specific problem-solving-strategic. In mathematics, for example, it appears that students benefit from seeing many different kinds of example problems worked out correctly for them. The common practice of showing students a few examples, then having students work many problems on their own, is less effective. Especially when problems are unfamiliar or difficult, worked-out examples are helpful (Gooper & Sweller, 1978). The most effective examples seem to be those that do not require students to integrate several sources of information, such as a diagram and a set of statements about the problem. This kind of attention splitting may put too much strain on the working memory. When students are learning, worked examples should deal with one source of information (Ward & Sweller, 1990). Ask students to compare examples. What is the same about each solution? What is different? Why? The same procedures may be effective in areas other than mathematics.

The Results of Problem Representation. There are two main outcomes of the problem representation stage of problem solving, as shown in Figure 9.1. If your representation of the problem suggests an immediate solution, your task is done. In the language of the cognitive scientist, you have activated the right schema and the solution is apparent because it is part of the schema. In one sense, you haven't really solved a new problem, you have simply recognized the new problem as a "disguised" version of an old problem that you already know how to solve. This has been called schema-driven problem solving, a kind of matching between the situation and your store of systems for dealing with different problems (Gick, 1986). In terms of Figure 9.1, you have taken the schema-activated route and have proceeded directly to a solution. But what if you have no existing way of solving the problem or if your activated schema fails? Time to search for a solution!

Figure 9.1
Diagram of the Problem–Solving Process
There are two paths to a solution. In the first, the correct schema for solving the problem is activated and the solution is apparent. But if no schema is available searching and testing may become the path to a solution. Source: M. L. Glck (1986). Problem–solving strategies. Educational Psychologist, 21,p.101. Adapted by permission of the publisher and author.

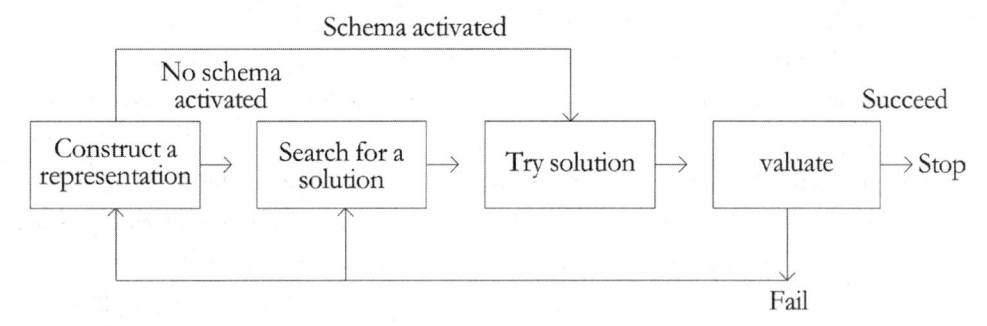

```
                    Schema activated
         No schema
         activated                                    Succeed
Construct a  → Search for a → Try solution → valuate → Stop
representation   solution
                                              ↓
                                             Fail
```

Exploring Possible Solution Strategies

If you do not have existing schemas that suggest an immediate solution, then you must take the search–based route indicated in Figure 9.1. Obviously, this path is not as efficient as activating the right schema, but sometimes it is the only way. In conducting your search for a solution, you have available two general kinds of procedures, algorithmic and heuristic.

Algorithms. An algorithm is a step–by–step prescription for achieving a goal. It usually is domain specific; that is, tied to a particular subject area. In solving a problem, if you choose an appropriate algorithm and implement it properly, a right answer is guaranteed. Unfortunately, students often apply algorithms haphazardly. They try first this, then that. They may even happen upon the right answer, but not understand how they found it.

In math classes you probably experienced some success applying algorithms. As long as you were careful in your computations, you were able to solve even such complicated problems as $17[43(90 + 15/78)]-[5/9(12356/2)]$. Later, if you were given geometry proofs to verify or equations to differentiate, you soon discovered that there were no algorithms guaranteeing a solution. At that point, if you did not learn some heuristics, you probably bailed out of math classes as soon as possible.

Heuristics. A heuristic is a general strategy that might lead to the right answer. Since many of life's problems are fuzzy, with ill–defined problem statements and no apparent algorithms, the discovery or development of effective heuristics is important. Let's examine a few.

In means–ends analysis, the problem is divided into a number of intermediate or subgoals and then a means of solving each is figured out. For example, writing a 20–page term paper can loom as an insurmountable problem for some students. They would be better off braking this task into several intermediate goals such as selecting a topic, locating sources of information, reading and organizing the information, making an outline, and so on. As they attack a particular intermediate goal, they may find that other goals arise. For example, locating information may require that they find someone to refresh their memory about using the library computer search system. Keep in mind that psychologists have yet to discover an effective heuristic for students who are just starting their term paper the night before it is due.

A second aspect of means–ends analysis is distance reduction, or pursuing a path that moves directly toward the final goal. People tend to look for the biggest difference between the current state of affairs and the goal and then search for strategy that reduce the difference. We resist taking detours or making moves that are indirect as we search for the quietest way to reach the goal. So when you realize that reaching the goal of completing a term paper may require a detour of relearning the library computer search system, you may resist at first because you are not moving directly and quickly toward the final goal (Anderson, 1993).

Some problems lend themselves to a working–backward strategy, in which you begin at the goal and move back to the unsolved initial problem. Working backward is sometimes an effective heuristic for solving geometry proofs. It can also be a good way to set intermediate deadlines ("Let's see, if I have to submit this chapter in three weeks, then it has to be in the mail by the 28th, so I should have a first draft by the 11th") :

Another useful heuristic is analogical thinking (Copi, 1961), which limits your search far solutions to situations that have something in common with the one you currently face. When submarines were first designed, for example, engineers had to figure out how battleships could determine the presence and location of vessels hidden in the depths of the sea. Studying how bats solve an analogous problem of navigating in the dark led to the invention of sonar.

Analogical reasoning can lead to faulty problem solving too. When they are first learning to use a word processor, some people use the analogy of the typewriter and fail to take advantage of the features of a computer. It seem that people need knowledge both in the problem domain and the analogy domain in order to use an analogy effectively (Gagne, Yekovich, & Yekovich, 1993).

Putting your problem–solving plan into words and giving reasons for selecting it can lead to successful problem solving (Cooper & Sweller, 1987). You may have discovered the effectiveness of this verbalization process accidentally, when a solution popped into your head as you were explaining a problem to someone else. Gagne and Smith (1962) found that when ninth and students were instructed to state a reason for each step they were taking, they were much more successful in solving the problem than students who did not state reasons.

Acting on the Strategies and Looking Back.
After representing the problem and selecting the approach, the next step is to execute the plan. If the plan primarily involves the use of algorithms, it is important to keep in mind that systematic "bug", or erroneous algorithms, may have developed in the procedures. Brown and Burton (1979) developed computer programs that located bugs created by students in solving subtraction problems. Their research indicated that children's algorithms contain many more bugs than teachers realize. One buggy algorithm they found, for example, was the consistent subtraction of the smaller from the larger number, regardless of which one was on top. Once teachers discover a bug, they can give specific tips for reworking problems. This corrective feedback is much more helpful than

merely advising the child to try again and be more careful.

After you choose a solution strategy and implement it, evaluate the results by checking for evidence that confirms or contradicts your solution. Many people tend to stop working before reaching the best solution and simply accept an answer that works in some cases.

In mathematical problems, evaluating the answer might mean applying a checking routine, such as adding to check the result of a subtraction problem or, in a long addition problem, adding the column from bottom to top instead of top to bottom. Another possibility is estimating the answer. For example, if the computation was 11×21, the answer should be around 200, since 10×20 is 200. A student who reaches an answer of 2311 or 23 or 562 should quickly realize these cannot be correct. Estimating an answer is particularly important when students rely on calculators, since they cannot go back and spot an error in the figures.

Factors That Hinder Problem Solving

Consider the following situation:

You enter a room. There are two ropes suspended from the ceiling. You are asked by the experimenter to tie the two ends of the ropes together and assured that the task is possible. On a nearby table are a few tools, including a hammer and pliers. You grab the end of one of the ropes and walk toward the other rope. You immediately realize that you cannot possibly reach the end of the other rope. You try to extend your reach using the pliers but still cannot grasp the other rope. What can you do? (Maier, 1933).

Functional Fixedness This problem can be solved by using an object in an unconventional way. If you tie the hammer or the pliers to the end of one rope and start swinging it like a pendulum, you will be able to catch it while you are standing across the room holding the other rope. You can use the weight of the tool to make the rope come to you instead of trying to stretch the rope. people often fail to solve this problem, because they seldom consider unconventional uses for materials that have a specific function. This difficulty is called functional fixedness (Duncker, 1945). Problem solving requires seeing things in new ways. In your everyday life, you may often exhibit functional fixedness. Suppose a screw on a dresser–drawer handle is loose. Will you spend 10 minutes searching for a screwdriver? Or will you think to use another object not necessarily designed for this function, like a knife or a dime?

Response set can be another block to effective problem solving. Consider the following:

In each of the four matchstick arrangements below, move only one stick to change the equation so that it represents a true equality such as V = V.

V = V I I   V I=X I   X II = V I I   V I = I I

You probably figured out how to solve the first example quite quickly. You simply move one matchstick from the right side over to the left to make V I = V I. Examples two and three can also be solved without too much difficulty by moving one stick to change the V to an X or vice versa. But the fourth example (taken from Raudsepp & Haugh, 1977) probably has you stumped. To solve this problem you must change your response set or switch schemas, because what has worked for the first three problems will not work this time. The answer here lies in changing from Roman numerals to Arabic numbers and using the concept of square root. By overcoming response set, you can move one matchstick from the right to the left to form the symbol for square root; the solution reads = I, which is simply the symbolic way of saying that the square root of 1 equals 1.

The importance of Flexibility Functional fixedness and response set point to the importance of flexibility in understanding problems. If you get started with an inaccurate or inefficient representation of the true problem, it will be difficult—or at least very time consuming—to reach a solution (Wessells, 1982). Sometimes it is helpful to "play" with the problem. Ask yourself: What do I know? What do, I need to now to answer this question? Can I look at this problem in other ways? Try to think conditionally, rather than rigidly and divergently rather than convergently Ask, "What could this be?" instead of "What is it?" (Benjafield, 1992).

If you open your mind to multiple possibilities, you may have what the Gestalt psychologists called an insight: Insight is the sudden reorganization or reconceptualization of a problem that clarifies the problem and suggests a feasible solution. The supervisor described earlier, who suddenly realized that the problem in his building was not slow elevators but impatient, bored tenants, had an insight that allowed him to reach the solution of installing mirrors by the elevators.

第四节 思维的教学与学习
(TEACHING AND LEARNING ABOUT THINKING)

Even if we are successful in teaching reading and the other basics, can we be sure that our students will be able to analyze and evaluate what they read? Will they be able to go beyond the information given to apply their knowledge make judgments, and generate new ideas? In other words, will they be able to think (Prawat, 1991)? Many educational psychologists believe that good thinking can and should be developed in school. But clearly, teaching thinking entails much more than the standard classroom practices pf completing worksheets, answering "thought" questions at the end of the chapter, and participating in teacher—led discussions. What else is needed?

One approach has been to focus on the development of thinking skills, either through stand-alone programs that teach skills directly, or through indirect methods that embed development of thinking in the regular curriculum.

Guideline: Encouraging Creativity

Accept and encourage divergent thinking.

Examples

1. During class discussion, ask: "Can Anyone suggest a different way of looking at this question?"
2. Reinforce attempts at unusual solutions to problems, even if the final product is not perfect.

Tolerate dissent.

Examples

1. Ask students to support dissenting opinions.
2. Make sure nonconforming students receive an equal share of classroom privileges and rewards.

Encourage students to trust their own judgment.

Examples

1. When students ask questions you think they can answer, rephrase or clarify the questions and direct them back to the students.

2. Give ungraded assignments from time to time.

Emphasize that everyone is capable of creativity in some form.

Examples

1. Avoid describing the feats of great artists or inventors as if they were superhuman accomplishments.

2. Recognize creative efforts in each student's work. Have a separate grade for originality on some assignments.

Be a stimulus for creative thinking.

Examples

1. Use a class brainstorming session whenever possible.

2. Model creative problem solving by suggesting unusual solutions for class problems.

3. Encourage students to delay judging a particular suggestion for solving a problem until all the possibilities have been considered.

Stand–Alone Programs for Developing Thinking

There are many different programs that teach thinking skills directly. A resource book for educators (Costa, 1985) lists over 15 different programs, including de Bono's CoRT system; Odyssey:A Curriculum for Thinking; Winocur's project Impact; Lipman's philosophy for Children; and Meeker's SOI. In these programs students learn skills such as comparing, ordering, classifying, and making inferences. The advantage of these stand alone thinking skills programs is that students do not need extensive subject matter knowledge to master the skills. Students who have had trouble with traditional curriculum may achieve success and perhaps an enhanced sense of self–esteem through these programs. The disadvantage is that general skills often are not used outside the program unless teachers make a concerted effort show students how to apply the skills in specific subjects; As you will see shortly when we discuss transfer, encouraging students to apply knowledge and skills to new situations is a challenge for all teachers (Prawat, 1991) .

Developing Thinking in Every Class

Another way to develop students' thinking encourage analysis, problem solving, and reasoning through the regular lessons of the curriculum. David Perkins and his colleagues (Perkins, Jay, & Tishman, 1993) propose that teachers do this by creating a culture of thinking in their classrooms. This means that there is a spirit of inquisitiveness and critical thinking, a respect for reasoning and creativity, and an expectation that students will learn and understand. In such a classroom, education is seen as enculturation, a broad and complex process of acquiring knowledge and understanding. We all learned language by being a member of a particular cultural group. We also learned rules of interaction, norms of appropriate behavior, and many other complicated rules and procedures through living in a culture that supports certain knowledge and values. Just as our home culture taught us lessons about the use of language, the culture of a classroom can teach lessons about thinking by giving us models of good thinking; providing direct instruction in thinking processes; and encouraging practice of those thinking processes through interactions with others.

Let's consider how this might happen in a classroom described by Perkins, Jay, and Tishman(1993).

Suppose an eighth-grade teacher wants his students to learn how to construct explanations that involve multiple causes. The class is studying the agriculture of eastern Asia, specifically the important rice crops. The teacher introduces a lesson by modeling good thinking about multiple causes:

Have you noticed that the roses in the park bloomed early this year? I'm asking myself why. What factors caused these early blooms? I recall it was a warm winter. That was probably an important factor. But certainly there are other factors involved probably some hidden ones and I know it is important to search for them. In fact, now that I have stopped to think, I remember that we had very heavy rains in March. This may be a factor too... (Perkins, Jay, & Tishman, 1993, p. 80)

After providing this model, the teacher points out other effects that have multiple causes such as winning a football game or staying healthy. Next, the teacher gives straightforward, direct instruction about how to analyze causes, such as considering how causal factors may work together or separately. He teaches the students to draw diagrams that depict multiple causes. Then he gives the students practice in analyzing multiple causes by asking them to diagram the causes involved in rice growth and how the causes work together or separately to produce rice. The teacher stimulates their thinking by suggesting that the students cast a wide net—consider many factors such as weather, soil, insects, and fanning practices.

When the students finish their diagrams, the teacher asks them to discuss their analysis with a partner. He guides the with questions such as "How did you identify causes?"

"Was it hard to figure out if causes worked together or alone?" "what questions can you invent about this multifactor causal analysis game?" "Can you envision other situations where you could use this kind of causal analysis?"

In this lesson, the four factors pf modeling, direct instruction, practice, and interaction help students become expert members of the thinking community.

The Language of Thinking How many words can you find in the above lesson that describe aspects of thinking? A quick look finds "search" , "asking why" . "hidden factors" , "analyze" "dentity"

"figure out" "envision" "effects" "contributing causes" and "invent" . My computer's thesaurus just found over 100 more words when I highlighted "thinking" . The language of thinking consists of natural language terms that refer to mental processes and mental products. Words like think—believe, guess,conjecture, hypothesis, evidence, suspect, doubt, and theorize from a vocabulary used to describe thinking (Perkins, Jay, & Tishman, 1993). The classroom should be filled with a clear, precise, and rich vocabulary of thinking. Rather than saying, "What do you think about Jamie's answer?" the teacher might ask questions that expand thinking such as, "What evidence can you give to refute or support Jamie's answer?" "What assumptions is Jamie making?" "what are some alternative explanation?" Students surrounded by a rich language of thinking, are more likely to think deeply about thinking.

Table 9.1 Examples of Critical Thinking Skills

Defining and Clarifying the Problem

1. Identify central issues or problems.
2. Compare similarities and differences.
3. Determine which information is relevant.
4. Formulate appropriate questions.

Judging Information Related to the Problem

5. Distinguish among fact, opinion, and reasoned judgment.
6. Check consistency.
7. Identify unstated assumptions.
8. Recognize stereotypes and cliches.
9. Recognize bias, emotional factors, propaganda, and semantic slanting.
10. Recognize different value systems and ideologies.

Solving Problems/Drawing Conclusions

11. Recognize the adequacy of data.
12. Predict probable consequnces.

Critical Thinking Critical thinking skills are useful in almost every life situation—even in evaluation the media ads that constantly bombard us. To evaluate the claim that 99 out of 100 dentist prefer a particular brand of toothpaste, you must consider such questions as: Which dentists were polled? How were they chosen? Was the toothpaste company involved in the polling process? If so, how could this bias the results of the poll? Or when you see a group of gorgeous people extolling the virtues of a particular brand of orange juice as they frolic in skimpy bathing suits, you must decide if sex appeal is a relevant factor in choosing a fruit drink.

Psychologists have not been able to agree on the skills that constitute critical thinking, but Table 9.1, taken from Kneedler (1985), provides a representative list of critical thinking skills. Source: P. Kneedler (1985). California assesses critical thinking, p.277. Alexandria, VA: Association for supervision and Curriculum Development and the author Copyright 1985 by ASCD ALL rights reserved.

No matter what approach you use to develop critical thinking, it is important to follow up with additional practice. One lesson is not enough, for example, if your class examined a particular historical document to determine if it reflected bias or propaganda, you should follow up by analyzing other written historical documents, contemporary advertisements, or news stories. Until thinking skills become overlearned and relatively automatic, they are not likely to be transferred to new situation. Instead, students will use these skills only to complete the lesson in social studies, not to evaluate the claims made by friends, politicians, toy manufacturers, or diet plans. What else is needed to apply good thinking?

Thinking as a "state of mind" . If people have a rich language for thinking and can be critical thinkers, they need one more quality to use their abilities—mindfulness. "mindfulness is a state of mind that results from drawing novel distinctions, examining information from new perspective, and being sensitive to context. It is an open, creative, probabilistic state of mind in which the individual might be led to finding differences among things thought to be similar and similarities among things thought to be different" (Langer, 1993, p.4) . The classroom culture should support the development of mindfulness by encouraging students to take intellectual risks, explore, inquire, seek challenges, and invest effort. Otherwise students will learn the language and skills of thinking, but seldom apply them outside the lessons of school. The challenge of transferring knowledge and understanding knowledge and understanding beyond the school house door has a long history of research in educational psychology.

第五节 迁移的教学
(TEACHING FOR TRANSFER)

Think back for a moment to a class in one of your high school subjects you did not go on to study in college. Imagine the teacher, the classroom, the textbook. If you can do all of this, you will be using your information processing strategies to search and retrieval very well. Now remember what you actually studied in class. If it was a science class, what were some of the formulas you learned? How about chemical reactions? Oxidation reduction? If you are like most of us, you may remember that you learned these things, but you will not be quite sure exactly what you learned. Were those hours wasted? These questions are about the transfer of learning.

Defining Transfer

Whenever something previously learned influences current learning, transfer had occurred. If students learn a mathematical principle in the first period and use it to solve a physics problem in the fifth period, then positive transfer has taken place. Even more rewarding for teachers is when a match principle learned in October is applied to a physics problem in March.

However, the effect of past learning on present learning is not always positive. Functional fixedness and response set are examples of negative transfer because they involve the attempt to apply familiar but inappropriate strategies to a new situation.

Specific transfer occurs when, a rule, fact, or skill learned in one situation is applied in another, very similar situation; for example, applying rules of punctuation to write a job application letter or using knowledge of the alphabet to find a word in the dictionary. General transfer involves applying to new problems the principles and attitudes learned in other, often dissimilar situations. Thus, general transfer might mean using problem-solving heuristics to solve issues in your personal life—for example, applying working backward to decide when to call for an appointment to have a dentist check a sore tooth in time to get any necessary treatment done before you leave for spring breaks.

A Contemporary View of Transfer, Gavriel Salomon and David Perkins (1989) describe two kinds of transfer, termed low-road and high-road transfer. Low-road transfer involves the spontaneous, automatic transfer of highly practiced skills, with little need for reflective thinking (p.118). For example, you probably have little trouble driving a friend's car, even though it is different from your car, because you have practiced the skill of arriving until it is automatic. You might have trouble, of course, if your friend's car has a standard transmission and you haven't driven a stick shift in years, because you lack recent practice with this kind of car. The key to low-road transfer is practicing a skill often, in a variety of situations, until your performance becomes automatic. So if you worked one summer for a temporary secretarial service and were sent to many different offices to work on all kinds of typewriters and word processors, by the end of the summer you probably would be able to handle most machines easily. Your practice with many machines would let you transfer your skill automatically to a new situation.

High-road transfer on the other hand, involves consciously applying abstract knowledge learned in one situation to a different situation. This can happen in one of two ways. You may learn a principle or a strategy, intending to use it in the future. For example, if you plan to apply what you learn in anatomy class this semester to work in a life-drawing course you will take next semester, you may search for principles about human proportions, muscle definition, and so on, This is called forward-reaching transfer, because you are looking forward to applying the knowledge gained. Background-reaching transfer occurs when you are faced with a problem and look back on what you have learned in other situations to help you in this new one. Analogical thinking is an example of this kind of transfer. You search for other, related situations that might provide clues to the current problem. The key to high road transfer is mindful abstraction, of the deliberate identification of a principle, main idea, strategy, or procedure that is not tied to one specific problem or situation but could apply to many. Such an abstraction becomes part of your meta-cognitive knowledge, available to guide future learning and problem solving. Table 9.2 summarizes the types of transfer.

Table 9.2 Kinds of Transfer

	Low-Road Transfer	High-Road Transfer
Definition	Automatic stransfer of highly practiced skill	Conscious application of abstract knowledge to a new situation
Key Conditions	Extensive practice Variety of settings and conditions Overlearning to automaticity	Mindful focus on abstracting a principle, main idea, procedure that can be used in many situations.
Examples	Driving many different cars Finding your gate in an airport	Applying PQ4R in reading texts Applying procedues from math in designing a page layout for the school newspaper

Teaching for Positive Transfer

Years of research and experience show that teachers cannot expect students to automatically transfer what they learn to new problems. We have seen repeatedly in this book that students will master new knowledge, problem-solving procedures, and learning strategies, but not use them prompted or guided. This is because learning is situated, that is, it is learned in particular situations. We learn solutions to particular problems, not general call purpose solutions that can fit any problem. Because knowledge is learned as a tool to solve particular problems, we may not realize that the knowledge is relevant when encounter a problem that seems different, at least on the surface. We tend to use knowledge only in situation where it is obviously appropriate (Driscoll, 1994; Singley & Anderson, 1989). How can you make sure your students will use what they learn, even when situations change?

What Is Worth Learning? First you must answer the question "What is worth learning?" The learning of basic skills like reading, writing, computing, and speaking will definitely transfer to other situations, because these skills are necessary for later work both in and out of school—writing job applications, reading novels, paying bills, locating and evaluating health care services, among others. All later learning depends on positive transfer of these basics to new situations.

Teachers must also be aware of what the future is likely to hold for their students, both as a group and as individuals. What will society require of them as adults? What will their careers require of them? As a child growing up in Texas in the 1950s and 1960s, I studied nothing about computers, even though my father was a computer systems analyst; yet now I spend hours at this word processor. Computer programming and word processing were not part of my high school curriculum, but learning to use a slide rule was taught Now calculators and computers have made this skill obsolete. Undoubtedly changes as extreme and unpredictable as these await the students you will teach. For this reason, the general transfer of principles, attitudes, critical thinking ability, and problem-solving strategies will be just as important to these students as the specific transfer of basic skills.

How Can Teachers Help? To have something to transfer, students must first learn and understand.

Students with be more likely to transfer information to new situations if they have been actively involved in the learning process, They must be encouraged to form abstractions that they will apply later. For example, Salomon and Perkins (1989) give this advice for teaching history:

[The] history teacher can introduce direct discussion of contemporary events. To provoke forward-reaching transfer, the teacher can select an episode in history and encourage students to seek contemporary analogs. To provoke Backward-reaching transfer, the teacher can choose a current phenomenon ... and urge students to reach into their historical repertoires for analogies and disanalogies. (p.136)

Newly mastered concepts, principles, and strategies must practiced in a wide variety of situations. positive transfer is encouraged when skills are practiced under authentic similar to those that will exist when the skills are needed later, Students can learn about multiplication by figuring how many ways they can makes $1.67 cents using only dimes and penies. They can learn historical research methods by researching their own family. Some of these applications should involve complex, unstructured problems, since many of the problems to be faced in later life, in school and out, will not come to students complete with instructions.

Greater transfer can also be ensured by overlearning, practicing a skill past the point of mastery. Many of the basic facts students learn in elementary school, such as the multiplication tables, are traditionally overlearned. Overlearning helps students retrieve the information quickly and automatically when it is needed.

词汇 (Vocabulary)

1. acronym   n. 首字母缩写词
2. algorithm   n. 分步法
3. analogical thinking   类比思维
4. concept mapping   概念图表
5. conjecture   vt. 推测
6. consultant   n. 商议者、顾问
7. convergently   ad. 集中地
8. counterfeit   a. 伪造的
9. defining attributes   定义属性
10. detour   n.& v. 弯路、绕道
11. dissent   n. 异议
12. divergently   ad. 发散地
13. edible   a. 可食用的
14. embed   vt. 嵌入
15. envision   vt. 想象
16. erroneous   a. 错误的
17. exemplar   n. 范例
18. frolic   vi. 嬉戏
19. functional fixedness   功能、固着
20. haphazardly   ad. 任意地
21. heuristic   a. 启发式的
22. insurmountable   a. 不可克服的
23. means—ends analysis   手段—目的分析
24. overgeneralization   n. 概括过宽（概念外延扩大）
25. oxidation   n. 氧化
26. parrot   vt. 简单重复
27. promiscuously   ad. 随意地
28. punctuation   n. 标点
29. repertoire   n. 全部节目
30. response set. 反应定势
31. skimpy   adj. 马虎的
32. subtraction   n. 减、减去
33. thesaurus   n. 词典、词库
34. tip   n. 提示
35. undergeneralization   n. 概念过窄（概念外延缩小）
36. working-background strategy   逆顺策略

第十章 情绪
（EMOTION）

本章要点（Chapter Outline）
情绪类型与诱因（Emotion Types and Incentives）
情绪的表现（Expression of Emotion）
情绪理论（Theories of Emotion）
情绪的性别差异
（Controversy: Are Man or Woman More Emotional）

人是活的有机体，同时又是社会的成员。在人的头脑里反映着个体与客体之间的各种客观关系。世界在人的头脑中的反映及人与社会的互动促使人们产生不同的个性与心理。情绪与情感是人的一种主观体验，包含了人对客观事物的喜怒哀乐。

情绪在人的生活中有重要的作用，无数作用于感官的刺激物，由于情感的产生而把其中某些刺激物分出来并把它们相互融合在一起，产生相应的印象并涂上某种情感色彩记忆并保存下来，而在日常生活中，人们通过面部、肢体语言及语气来表达情绪。

情绪和情感是怎样产生的，在个体的发展史中又是怎样分化的，这是心理学家们感兴趣的问题，围绕这些问题产生了詹姆斯—兰格理论、坎农理论及认知心理学的相互作用理论等众多理论。

第一节 情绪类型与诱因
（EMOTION TYPES AND INCENTIVES）

We are all emotional animals with the everyday feeling of love, hate, afraid, anxious, terrorized and so on. Furthermore, there are motivational consequences associated with these emotions such as a mindless fight out of anger. We can not bear the time without someone because of your love. And People are motivated to do all of things in order to escape or avoid unpleasant emotional factors(fear, anger, anxiety).We can clearly find out emotion and motivation are closely related topics. For our study, the concept of emotion has proved very complex and difficult to be confirmed scientifically, and, this is partly because so much of emotional experience is belong to private experience. Although there is still a long way to go, we can still say that the progress is being made.

Emotions and Incentives

A great deal of effort has been expended in an attempt to devise a classifications system for emotions. There are hundred of words in our language referring to different emotional experiences. Many of these overlap in meaning, however, or refer merely to slight differences in the intensity of the emotion. There are two primary dimensions of emotions:(1) the qualitative dimension of the pleasant unpleasant and (2) the quantitative dimension of intensity. Emotional states are basically pleasant or unpleasant, and they are vary in the intensity of the feeling of pleasantness or unpleasantness. Thus the difference between anger and rage is primarily one of intensity, as is the difference between happiness and ecstasy.

These two basic dimensions also determine the motivational consequences of emotional states. First, we can expect that unpleasant emotional states(and the things we have learned will produce them) will ace as negative incentives (we will be motivated to avoid or escape them). Likewise, pleasant states (and the things that will produce them)will be positive incentives (we well be motivated to achieve them).All because we learn about the world with a motivation to seek good feelings and to avoid unpleasant ones. Second, we can expect that the degree of motivation is depend upon the strength of the anticipate or experienced state. The stronger or more intense the emotion, the greater the motivation to approach or avoid. In other words, the emotional intensity will determine whether the incentive is positive or negative.

Anxiety and Anger

Psychologists have been particularly interested in the motivational consequences of two emotional states: anxiety and anger. Anxiety is of interest because it appears to play a central role in the motivation of abnormal behaviors as well as everyday behavior, so does anger because it is the standard emotion accompanying frustration, and anger probably underlies most acts of aggression, Together then, anxiety and anger represent two emotional states that may produce a great deal of undesirable behavior in people. Understanding these emotions may help us to control or eliminate much of our behavior.

Anxiety is like conditioned fear. The anxious person is anticipating that fearful or harmful things are about to happen. The state that occurs when you encounter an armed robber is fear, whereas the state in which you think you might encounter an armed robber is anxiety. Presumably anxiety is an unpleasant experience with negative incentive value, meaning that we will be motivated to escape anxiety when it develops and to avoid it if at all possible. Much of psychopathy behavior is thought to be motivated by the desire to escape anxiety. Behaviors that allow a person to escape anxiety will be reinforced and thus repeated, and eventually will become habits for dealing with anxiety. Similarly, objects, events and circumstances that we have learned will prevent or counteract anxiety become positive incentives, and we will direct our behavior toward achieving these goals.

The classic experiment demonstrating anxiety as a motivating force was done with rats by Neal Miller, using a shuttle box with two compartments, one black and one white. A rat was placed in the white compartment and electric shock was turned on, causing the rat to run into the black side of the box where he escaped from the shock. This routine was repeated for several trials until presumably the fear was conditioned to the white compartment. At that point, no further shocks were given. Despite the absence of shocks, the rat continued to show signs of fear when placed in the white side the rat was "anxious". The rat continued to run into the black side even though it was never shocked again. The white side took on negative incentive value and the black side probably took on positive incentive value. Next, a door was put in place between the compartments and a wheel was placed in the white compartment. This wheel, if turned by the rat, would open the door. The result was that the rats learned the wheel turning response to get out of the white compartment, even though shock was not administered. The rats were not escaping from real shock, but from the threat of shock. They were escaping from the white compartment because it had been associated with the shock. They were evidently motivated by the conditioned fear of anxiety produced by the white compartment. They may also have been motivated by the positive incentive of the black side of the box, because this side had repeatedly been associated with relief from the shock. And you might ask yourself about your own behavior at this point that how much of your behavior is motivated by the desire to escape or avoid an unpleasant consequence?

How about the feeling of "Anger and frustration"? Dollard et al.(1939)have suggested that all aggressive acts are cause by frustration, which is almost always accompanied by anger. This theory is known as the frustration aggression hypothesis. Inflicting harm on others is a major problem in our society and the world, and so it is important to understand the motivation for this aggression. There is very strong evidence that frustration is sufficient to produce aggression, although it is almost impossible to determine whether frustration is also a necessary factor that is, whether all aggression involves frustration. Consider just one study, in which a very hungry pigeon was trained to peck a key in a Skinner box in order to get grain. After the pigeon had learned this response, an "innocent bystander" pigeon was placed in the box with the trained pigeon and simultaneously the experimenter stopped giving grain for pecking (extinction). During this extinction period, the trained pigeon attacked the bystander by pecking at his head, throat and especially his eyes. There is little doubt that this was an attack reaction, apparently elicited by the frustration that was caused by the termination of the grain rewards.

The same kind of attack reactions were elicited in birds that had been reared in isolation, suggesting that there is a biological, innate component to this behavior, This conclusion accords with the suggestions of the ethnologists, who have argued that there is an aggressive instinct in human beings as well as in animals. However, although it may be true that there are aggressive instincts that result in predisposing us to fight when frustrated, it is clear that learning is also important, We learn aggressive tactic from seeing how others practice aggression, and limiting such observation may be one way of exerting some control on the development of aggression. This is why, for example, so many people are concerned about the violence on the mass media.

第二节 情绪的表现
(EXPRESSION OF EMOTION)

We can not experience another's emotion directly. But psychologists have found that emotion could be measured in four ways: by one's facial expressions, or his physiological responses, and even his description of the emotion and his daily behavior. There seems to be a genetic basis to facial expression of emotion and to physiological reactions that occur in emotion, In contrast, what individuals will say and do when they are emotional results primarily from learning. Our discussion will focus first on facial expression and physiological reaction, Later in the chapter we will discuss how one becomes particular emotion, frustration affected by learning.

Facial Expression

Cross-cultural studies indicate that facial expression of emotion is innate, at least for happiness, surprise, fear, anger, disgust, and sadness. Ekman and his colleagues (Ekman, Soren-son, & Friesen, 1969; Ekman,1972) presented photographs of different emotional expressions to members of varied cultures. The college educated subjects in Brazil, the United States, Argentina and Japan identified the same faces with the same emotional words, as did members of two preliterate cultures which had extensive contact with Western societies. All the cultures were exposed to similar mass media, however, so it could be argued that facial expressions had been learned.

To deal with this criticism, Ekman and Friesen did another study in 1971. People in a preliterate culture (the South Fore of New Guinea) who had had minimal contact with the West, who had seen no movies, and who neither spoke Mr. understood English, were shown a set of three faces and asked to select the face that matched the emotion of a story they were told. They interpreted faces as revealing the same emotions as did people from literate cultures. The only exception was that fear and surprise faces were not distinguished from one another, although they were distinguished from anger, sadness, happiness, or disgust.

Another reason to believe facial expression of emotion has an innate basis is that blind and deaf children express emotions in a manner highly similar to normal children (Eibl-Eibesfddt, 1973). Obviously, blind children could not have learned facial expressions by observing others, yet their smiles, for example, are like those of sighted children. A third source of support for an innate basis comes from the parallel ways in which people and animals show emotions. As long ago as 1872, Charles Darwin pointed out great similarities. Bared fangs in a dog or wolf, for example, seem like a sneer in a human and if you have a pet dog, you know how it can look happy or sad. Recent work has. substantiated remarkable similarity of facial expression in human and nonhuman primates (Chevalier-Skolniloff, 1973).

Physiological Reaction

The human body's physiological reactions in emotional situations also appear to be innate. Imagine yourself in any situation where you are concerned and unsure, perhaps just before having to address a group. You probably can name easily the bodily changes that you would experience: pounding heart, sweaty palms, dry mouth, tense stomach. The English language reflects this relationship between emotions and bodily reactions: "cold sweat, " "trembling with fear. " and "butterflies in the stomach. "

Of primary importance in the body's emotional reaction is the **autonomic nervous system**. As was mentioned before the autonomic nervous system consists of the sensory and motor nerves serving the heart and the glands and smooth muscles of the internal organs. The system has two branches: the **sympathetic nervous system** and the **parasympathetic nervous system**. The first tends to function more actively during strong emotion and the second to operate during relaxation and rest.

Figure 10.1 shows the major sympathetic and parasympathetic nerves and the organs controlled by each. Some organs, such as the sweat and adrenal glands, are associated only with the sympathetic nervous system, but most are controlled by both the sympathetic and parasympathetic nervous systems. In these cases, the bodily reactions produced by the two branches are opposites. The reactions associated with the sympathetic nervous system and emotional arousal consist of increased heart rate, increased blood pressure, pupil dilation, inhibition of salivation (causing dryness of the mouth), sweat secretion (suiting in clammy hands), constriction of blood vessels in the periphery of the body (producing cold hands and feet), and impeded digestion. The parasympathetic nervous system decreases heart rate and blood pressure, constricts pupils, and increases salivation and digestive processes. The parasympathetic and sympathetic nervous system work together. So you can simultaneously digest a meal, governed primarily by parasympathetic activity, while sweating if you are too hot, a reaction governed by the sympathetic nervous system.

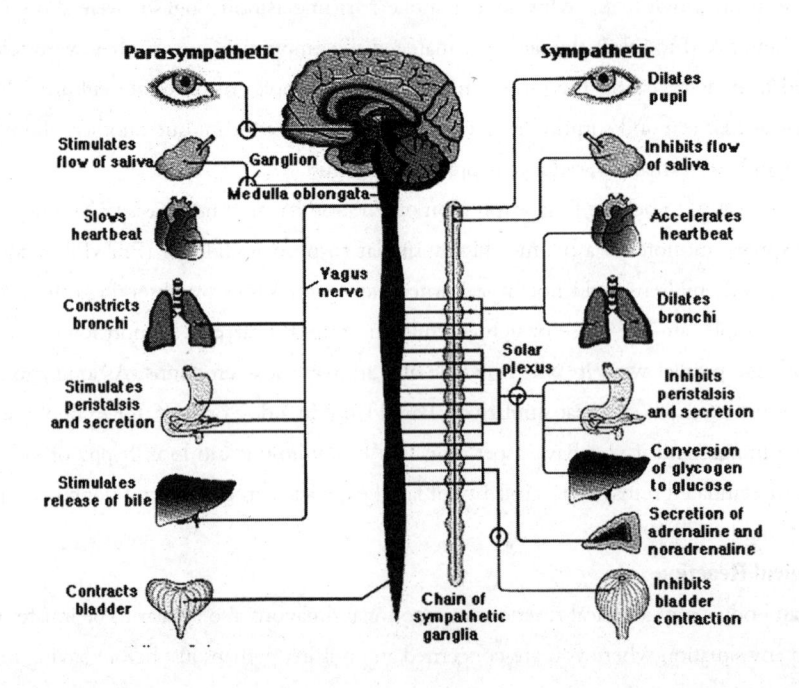

Figure 10.1 A Schematic View of the Autonomic Nervous System

There are two divisions: parasympathetic and sympathetic. Some organs are controlled only by one division; for example, the sweat glands and the adrenal glands are associated only with the sympathetic nervous system. Most organs are controlled by both the sympathetic and parasympathetic divisions. In these cases, the bodily reaction produced by the sympathetic nervous system. In emotional arousal the sympathetic nervous system is dominant (A ganglion is a collection of neural cell bodies).

The two branches differ significantly as well in the nature of the neurotransmitter substance that is active at the synapse. As discussed before communication between nerve cells occurs by means of chemical transmissions sent across the space separating these cells, the synapse. The major transmitter in the parasympathetic system is acetylcholine (ACh), and synaptic transmission using ACh is categorized as cholinergic transmission. In the sympathetic nervous system, the major synaptic transmitter is nor epinephrine. Synaptic transmission using nor epinephrine is designated as adrenergic. Nor epinephrine and the closely related epinephrine, once called adrenalin, are both released by the adrenal glands into the bloodstream. Once in action, they have effects on the body generally similar to those of arousal of the sympathetic nervous system. This is reflected in the phrase that "your adrenalin is flowing" to indicate excitement.

Emotion and Stress

The autonomic nervous system is of course strongly influenced by the brain. Some of the important brain areas involved in emotion have been identified, but the complete picture is not yet understood. One well-substantiated finding is that removal of the cerebral cortex the outermost layer of the brain where most higher functions seem to be organized will produce a highly excitable animal. Decorticate animals fly into a rage at the slightest provocation. Bard (1934) called this "sham rage" because it was short-lived, not clearly directed at the provocation, and seemly without conscious control. One interpretation of this finding is that the cerebral cortex normally inhibits emotion.

Emotions are also controlled by the hypothalamus. Stimulation of a particular portion of the hypothalamus elicits rage and provokes attack that can be well directed toward the provoking stimulus (Flynn, Vanegas, Foote, & Edwards, 1970; Panskepp, 1971). And, as we saw before, electrical stimulation of particular portions of the hypothalamus can produce strong pleasure reactions as well.

Because the sympathetic nervous system is active in emotion, one way to measure emotion is to measure physiological responses associated with the sympathetic nervous system. This is the idea behind the **polygraph**, or lie detector. Various parts of the machine record heart rate, blood pressure, palm conductance (which is affected by sweating on the palm), and breathing rate. The subject's response is measured when he or she is calm and answering neutral questions such as name and address. The critical questions which the investigator wants answered are interspersed. If the subject is lying, an emotional reaction to the lie will show up on the machine. But the machine doesn't measure lying, it measures physiological reactions associated with emotion, so anyone who can lie with no emotional reaction can fool the machine. And a person who is reacting Emotionally to certain questions, but is not lying, will be wrongly judged a liar.

In general, physiological reactions do not unequivocally measure emotion because the exact physiological reaction may differ from person to person (Grings & Dawson, 1978). One individual may show increased heart rate and little change in palm conductance, while in another individual palm conductance may change, but not heart rate (e. g., Lacey &. Lacey, 1958). Also, people vary in overall level of physiological reactivity in emotion, as discussed in Controversy. Facial expression is also not an infallible guide to emotion. People can smile without feeling happy and can feel happy without smiling. The best way to determine another person's emotion is to combine measures of facial expression and physiological response with what the person says and does.

第三节 情绪理论
(THEORIES OF EMOTION)

Theories of emotion try to explain what produces the experience of emotion. As we will see, one of the main issues dividing theories is the extent to which emotional experience is governed by reactions of the autonomic nervous system such as increased heart rate.

James–Lange Theory

Because of the evidence for an innate basis of emotional expression, and the apparent similarity of emotional expression in humans and other animals, emotion has traditionally been viewed as a primitive reaction of the body, with little control exercised by central cognitive processes. One view is that peripheral physiological reactions such as increased heart rate occur when an emotional stimulus is perceived, and subjective experience of these changes is the actual emotion. This is the **James–Lange theory of emotion**, proposed independently by the American psychologist William James (1885, 1968) and the Danish physiologist, Carl Lange (1885, 1967).

According to the James–Lange theory you do not cry because you are sad. You see something that makes you cry and the physiological fact that you are crying saddens you. You see a bear and you run and tremble, and your feeling of running and trembing constitutes fear. If you did not experience the physiological component of emotion, you could not feel emotional. If you saw a bear and your heart didn't pound and you didn't tremble you would not feel fear. Although this theory was proposed a long time ago, many current theorists also emphasize physiological reactions as critical determinants of emotional experience (see Grings & Dawson, 1978). Other scientists have disputed the James–Lange theory.

Cannon's Criticism of James–Lange Theory

In 1927 the physiologist Walter B. Cannon reviewed the experimental and clinical work relevant to the James–Lange theory and made a case against the theory. First, Cannon pointed out that separating the central nervous system from the peripheral nervous system so that peripheral physiological reactions cannot be felt does not eliminate emotional behavior. Cannon, Lewis, and Briton (1927) destroyed the sympathetic nervous system of a cat and obtained a normal rage reaction when the cat was put in the presence of a barking dog. Not all of the important nerve fiber pathways were destroyed in the experiments, as Fehr and Stern (1970) noted, so continued emotional behavior could have been due to the remaining connections. But the important question is not whether the cat acted angrily, but whether it felt angry. That is sue, of course, can be investigated only in humans. Patients who have suffered injuries to the spinal cord generally do report decreased emotional experience. The higher the lesion in the spinal cord, and thus the less the sensation received, the greater the decrease in emotional feeling reported. Yet, patients still report acting emotional. As one said:

Sometimes I act angry when I see some injustice. I yell and cuss and raise hell, because if you don't do it sometimes, I learned people will take advantage of you but it just doesn't have the heat to it that it used to. It's a mental kind of anger. (*Hohmann, 1966, p. 151*)

This evidence seems to show that the feeling of a physiological reaction may play some part in emotional feeling, but is not necessary for all emotional feeling.

Cannon's second criticism was that since the same peripheral physiological changes occur in diverse emotional and none motional states, how can researchers determine what emotion a subject feels? After all, running around the block will also increase your heart and breathing rates and make your palms sweat, but few would consider that an emotional experience. In one experiment, scientists positioned an attractive young woman to meet two groups of men, one group on a high, precariously swaying bridge, the other group on a low stable bridge. She intercepted the men coming off the bridges and asked their help in filling out a questionnaire. This was a pretext to give the men her phone number. A higher percentage of men who crossed the dangerous bridge called the women for a date, as though to say "my hands are sweaty, I'm breathing hard, she must be something" (Dutton & Aron, 1974) The experiment's results imply that a common physiological arousal state underlies different emotions. But some physiological differences have been measured between anger and fear (Ax, 1953), and there may indeed be different peripheral physiological changes in other emotional states as well. But no clear evidence now shows that physiological differences lie beneath all the varying emotions people experience.

The third point Cannon made was that peripheral physiological reactions are too slow to be the source of emotional feeling. It does appear that some emotional reaction occurs prior to physiological reaction. Have you ever been afraid, arid acted, and then started trembling?

Cannon's final major point was that artificial induction of the physiological changes which normally produce emotions fails to stir the emotion. Injections of epinephrine—adrenalin—cause physiological reactions similar to those of natural sympathetic nervous system arousal. When epinephrine was administered to 210 subjects, about 71 percent reported only physical symptoms such as tremor or palpitations (Maranon, 1924, cited in Schachter, 1964). The remaining 29 percent did note emotional reaction but described it "as if I feel as if I am afraid." Of course, injections of epinephrine do not produce the total range of peripheral physiological reactions which occur in normal emotional arousal, so these data are perhaps not that damaging to the James—Lange theory.

Cognitive–physiological Interaction in Emotion

More recent data suggest that situational and cognitive factors, which would be registered in the central nervous system and not the peripheral nervous system, are important in emotional reaction. It seems that the situation determines to a large extent what emotion an individual will experience when aroused by epinephrine. Stanley Schachter and Jerome Singer (1962) studied the effects of different situations on the emotion experienced when subjects were given epinephrine. One group of subjects received epinephrine and was correctly informed that "your hand will start to shake, your heart will start to pound, your face may get warm and flushed" A second group was told nothing about the face may get warm and flushed. A second group was told nothing about the drug's effects, and a third was misinformed and warned to expect itching, numbness, and headache.

The idea behind the experiment was that an emotional reaction requires two things: peripheral physiological arousal, and a situation which can explain the arousal in terms of an emotion. The specific emotion experienced will depend on what the situational cues suggest is appropriate, So groups which experience physiological arousal with a none motional explanation—those who were told the epinephrine would produce arousal—should not feel emotional. The other groups should feel emotional if there are situational cues that could explain the emotion. Schachter and Singer provided several explanations for the arousal to different groups to see if varying emotions would be produced.

Every subject waited in a room with another person who supposedly was also a participant in the experiment and had received the epinephrine. The other person actually had been hired by the experimenter to behave in particular ways' providing the subject with situational cues. In one condition the hired subject—or model—threw paper airplanes, shot wads of paper and was generally cheery. In the other condition, the model simulated anger, complained about the experiment, and displayed aggressiveness. The subjects were watched through one-way mirrors, and those uninformed and misinformed about the drug's effects acted angrier with the angry model than those who were informed. With the happy model, uninformed and misinformed subjects reported they were happier and tended to act happier than subjects who were informed. Thus Schachter and Singer concluded that two factors are involved in the experience of emotion—physiological arousal and an appropriate cognitive state. The arousal produced by the epinephrine was the same for "happy" and "angry" subjects, who inferred their emotion from the situation.

Recent work has demonstrated that the perception of bodily changes is sufficient to induce emotional feelings even if none actually occurs. Valins (1970) showed that male preference for pictures of female nudes was higher when the subject thought his heart rate had changed—he was told that it had—even though it remained constant. This work extends the Schachter and Singer findings. But other recent investigations suggest that situational factors do not totally determine interpretation of physiological reactions. They have shown that subjects experiencing unexplained physiological arousal tend to regard it as negative emotion regardless of the mood of the model (Maslach, 1979). Contrary to what Schachter and Singer (1962) found, more recently researchers have shown that if the model acts happy, subjects given epinephrine and misinformed about its effects do not different from subjects given a placebo in either reported emotion or in behavior (Marshall & Zimbardo, 1979). However, there is some controversy about what these results mean (see Marshall & Zimbardo, 1979; Maslach, 1979; and Schachter & Singer, 1979). Although they clearly show that unexplained physiological arousal is more likely to be interpreted as a negative rather than a positive emotion, it is not clear how to interpret these data. One view is that they show that physiological arousal determines the qualitative type of emotion experienced, at least for negative states, in conformity with the James—Lange theory. Alternatively, the results could mean that experience has taught most people that faily strong physiological arousal, such as that produced by epinephrine, is more likely to occur along with negative emotions, such as fear than with positive emotions This implies that not only does the current situation determine how an individual will interpret physiological arousal, but that previous experience with arousal and emotion affects how that individual interprets the arousal at the moment .

Although physiological expression and facial expression of emotion seem to have a genetic basis, what people do when they experience an emotion appears to be largely learned. Fear, for example, can evoke different responses: running, hiding, fighting. Which response will occur depends on the situation and how individuals have learned to confront it previously.

Do different emotions correspond to qualitatively different physiological states?

The James—Lange theory required a yes answer to this question, while the Cannon—Bard theory said no, there are just differences in degree of arousal. The evidence on several fronts went against the James—Lange theory. Cannon criticized the James—Lange theory because the evidence available at the time did not show different physiological patterns for different emotions. Cannon also thought that the physiological changes out in the body's periphery took place too slowly to be the primary source of emotion. Further in one study subjects were injected with adrenalin (epinephrine), which produces arousal in the autonomic nervous system, and yet these subjects did not report emotional experiences; the reason, according to Cannon, was that the central nervous system was not activated through the thalamus (there was no emotional stimulus). The overall picture is strongly against the James—Lange theory, although it is dying a slow death.

One reason the James—Lange theory still persists is that recent work has begun to demonstrate some differences in peripheral responses for different emotions. Most often cited is the work of A. F. Ax, who has demonstrated physiological differences between fear and anger. The adrenal glands secrete two different hormones, epinephrine and nor epinephrine. Ax found that during fear epinephrine seems to dominate, while during anger both epinephrine and nor epinephrine are ionpicated. Other studies have shown that animals that are preyed upon (and should thus be creatures of fear) secrete high amounts of epinephrine in contrast to the animals that do the preying. The preying animals (creatures of "anger" ?) show predominately nor epinephrine secretion. More recent work has centered on the biochemical substances that serve as neural transmitters in the central nervous system, which seem to be involved in different ways depending on the emotion. However, the evidence is not yet convincing, and so there is still a strong commitment to the notion that basically the emotional state is a general diffuse state of overall arousal or activation.

How important is cognitive appraisal of the situation

If the emotional state consists mainly of general arousal and there is not a different physiological state for the different emotions, how do we know whether we are happy or sad, pleased or angry? The answer probably comes from analyzing the total emotional experience into two basic parts:(1) the general arousal and (2) the cognitive appraisal or evaluation of the situation—such as "there is a dangerous animal loose in my room and it is about to attack me." In a simplified sense, the appraisal is designed to answer the question. "Why am I aroused to this degree?" There is a continual, interplay between the arousal and the appraisal, out of which emerges the emotional experience. The experience is thus a joint product of the arousal (including the degree of arousal) and the ongoing evaluation of the situation, which comes first is not of much concern in this theory, because arousal and appraisal are constantly changing and inter-acting with each other . Sometimes the arousal may precede the appraisal and sometimes it may come later.

The key new element in this interpretation is cognitive appraisal. The person is appraising the situation and at the same time is looking for something that the arousal can be attributed to (the bear is an obvious choice). This part of the theory comes from the attribution theory of Fritz Heider and has been investigated and elaborated by Stanley Schachte. Having something to attribute the arousal to and having a cognitive evaluation of that thing (such as it can harm me) are crucial. Without these components, there would be no emotional experience even if the arousal component has occurred. Thus, as mentioned earlier, subjects given injections of adrenalin which produces the arousal, do not become emotional because there is nothing to attribute the arousal to other than the injection, which is nothing to be happy, sad, angry, or ecstatic about. Presumably the subjects attribute the arousal to the injection (the doctor told them they would experience arousal) and then are not emotional. On the other hand, if the subjects were misled about the injection ("this is a vitamin shot") and were told that it would not produce arousal, then when they became aroused they would need an explanation, and would evaluate their predicament in seeking the explanation.

Schechter and Jerome Singer tricked subjects in just this way—the subjects received adrenalin but thought they were getting a vitamin shot. The subjects found their explanation for the experienced arousal (and thus their emotion) in the experienced arousal (and thus their emotion) in the situation. Half the subjects, after receiving the "vitamin" shot, were asked to wait in a room with someone else who was pretending to be very angry. These subjects reported that they became angry. The other half waited in a room with someone who was acting very happy, and these subjects said they were happy. They thus falsely attributed the arousal they were experiencing to the situation and experienced an emotional feeling that was consistent with their evaluation of the situation.

To emphasize the back-and-forth interplay between arousal and evaluation, we can point out that there is evidence that persons evaluate the degree of arousal as well as the situation that is apparently producing the arousal. And the evaluation of the degree of arousal will be fed back into the system and can affect the evaluation of the situation. In an ingenious experiment, Stuart Valins demonstrated this feedback feature. Male subjects were led to believe that they were listening to their own amplified heartbeat over a loudspeaker, when in fact what they heard was a prepared tape recording. Valins then showed these men pictures of nudes from Playboy; for half the nudes, the fake heart rate sounds were speed up when the picture appeared. This was designed to create the false impression in the subjects that they were especially aroused by these particicular nudes. Later the subjects were asked to rate the nudes on attractiveness, and, as predicted, they rated the nudes that had been associated with increased heart rate as more attractive than the other nudes. The reasoning is that the subjects, thinking they were aroused, searched for an explanation by more closely examining the nudes to find particularly attractive features in the photographs. Having found these features, the subjects would judge the photographs more attractive.

In fact, Valins has demonstrated that the subjects still rate these nudes as more attractive after they are told that the "heartbeats" were a fake. Fake or not, they caused the subjects to discover more attractive features. It has also been shown that the "heart-rate" effect does not take place if the nude photos are presented rapidly presumably because the subject does not have time to find the explanation for his arousal—he does not have time to find attractive features in the playmate.

The currently most popular account of emotional experience stems from a combination of general arousal theory (similar to the Cannon–Bard theory) and attribution theory. The experienced emotion is a complex function depending on the interplay among several factors (1) the arousal level the degree of arousal (or more accurately the degree to which the arousal level is changed some baseline) probably mediates the intensity dimension of emotion. (2) the cognitive evaluation of the situation producing the arousal change, which will at least partly deter mine the pleasantness—unpleasantness dimension; and (3) the evaluation of the arousal change, which may in turn affect the cognitive evaluation of the situation. A fourth factor is the specific physiological pattern of the arousal, which may partly determine the quality of the experience (is it fear or anger?). As yet, however, we know very little about what biochemical and physiological factors differentiate the various emotional states.

It is also possible that the degree of arousal change from the normal baseline may play a role in determining the pleasant–unpleasant dimension, in addition to determining the intensity dimension. If we assume that there is a homeostatic arousal system trying to keep arousal level in the moderate range, then we would guess that very large changes in arousal from this optimal level will, in general, be experienced as unpleasant. We might also expect that this homeostatic system will, in such cases, immediately attempt to counteract these large changes in arousal in an effort to return the arousal level to the moderate range.

The effect of opponent processes in emotions

Richard solomon and John Corbit have proposed just such an opponent–process model: Given a large change in arousal produced by either a pleasant or an unpleasant stimulus, the homeostatic system will immediately activate an opponent process to counteract the emotional reaction. The opponent process, in general, will have just the opposite effects of the initial process, meaning that the overall experience will be a combination of the opposing processes. If the initial experience is pleasant, it will be maximally pleasant process, which is by definition unpleasant, will soon be activated and begin to counteract the pleasant process. As the unpleasant opponent process gathers strength' the experience will become less and less pleasant. If the original stimulus situation that triggered the pleasant process were suddenly removed, we would experience only the opponent process in action, That is, we would experience an unpleasant emotion.

In contrast, suppose the initial state of arousal is unpleasant. Soon afterward, a pleasant opponent process will be activated to counteract the arousal such an experience will be maximally unpleasant only in the beginning because the opponent process will begin to temper or diminish the degree of unpleasantness. If at this moment the original unpleasant stimulus situation is suddenly removed, only the opponent process will be active and we will experience a pleasante—motion.

Solomon and Corbit use this theory to account for a variety of phenomena, among which they consider the following: Immediately after hatching, the newborn duckling gives every appearance of being quite satisfied with his new circumstances, though he may emit a few cries of distress. But then, according to imprinting studies, if the duckling is exposed to a white, moving object, he will stare at it intently. All movements and vocalizations tend to disappear. If the moving object is removed, there will be a burst of distress cries that may last for several minutes before subsiding. According to the typical ethological interpretation, the moving object has suddenly established a "following behavior" released by an adequate imprinting stimulus, a white moving object. In contrast, according to the Solomon Gorbit theory, the moving object is a stimulus that automatically releases in the duckling an affective state with pleasant emotional connotations. The stimulus—induced state is, however, opposed by an unpleasant process, of lesser intensity and designed to bring the organism back in the direction of emotional neutrality. When the triggering stimulus (the white object) is removed, only the unpleasant state remains, resulting in the distress reaction of the organism.

As another example, consider the studies by Epstein (1967) of the motivational bases and emotional accompaniments of parachuting. When the novice parachutist makes his first jump, he is terrified, judging by verbal reports, facial expressions, and changes in his autonomic nervous system. When the lands safely, he will appear stony faced or stunned for several minutes, only gradually recovering composure. The initial fear induced state of arousal is presumably opposed by a state of quiescence that persists for some period of time after the jump is complete.

A third example comes from the use of drugs, such as opium. Upon first use, an individual is likely to report an intensely pleasurable feeling known as the "rush." With the passage of time, as the drug effect wears off, the user will suffer aversive pain and frightening withdrawal symptoms. There may also be a feeling of craving for the drug. Presumably, this is the opponent process in action

Finally, consider the situation of a girl and boy falling in love. The initial state presumably experienced by both is characterized by pleasurable excitement, sexual highs, ecstasy, happiness, and, in general, good feelings. When the lovers are separated, the opponent process becomes evident. They feel lonely and depressed. Even when they anticipate reunion, loneliness may persist.

Reunion does, of course, reinstate the initial stimulus circumstances and thereby overwhelm the negative opponent process.

If we are repeatedly exposed to the identical emotional situation, the character of the emotional experience changes, Solomon and Corbit suggest that this happens because the opponent process gets stronger each time it is elicited. With enough repetition, the opponent process may become so strong that it overwhelms the initial stimulus-induced state and comes to dominate the emotional experience. Imagine your favorite food, the thing that gives you that most pleasant taste experience. Now imagine eating that food all the time, morning, noon, and night. Do you think the pleasure would disappear?

For the examples mentioned above, consider what happens when repetition takes place. For the ducklings, if the imprinting stimulus is presented and removed several times, the frequency and intensity of distress crying by a duckling will increase (the opponent process has been strengthened). For the parachutist, after many jumps he or she no longer reports terror and is instead eager to jump, although there may be a little anxiety or tension. The opponent process has been strengthened, and this turns the terror into the milder state of anxiety. After landing, the jumper is no longer subdued, but exuberant. Parachutists claim that they love to jump because of this exhilarating after-feeling (the strong opponent process). For the addict, after several weeks of opiate use, the "rush" begins to weaken, and it takes more of the drug to produce it. Moreover, the aftereffects become more intense and turn into an intensely unpleasant state of craving. Indeed, the opponent process has become so strong that the addict must take drugs all the time just to maintain his normal feelings. The drugs no longer produce the pleasant state, but just maintain the normal one, and the lack of drugs is what produces the abnormal state. Finally, consider the couple in love. After several weeks, months or years of repeated affectionate interaction, the qualitative and quantitative aspects of their love will change. Being together is a state of "contentment," normally, and comfort, not the same as the excitement, joy, and enthusiasm of the young lovers. Now, separation can have highly intense aversive effects, and in extreme cases grief and severe depression. It is as if the partners have become addicted to one another; being together is "normal," not exciting, and separation will result in withdrawal symptoms.

第四节 情绪的性别差异
(CONTROVERSY: ARE MAN OR WOMAN MORE EMOTIONAL)

One popularly accepted belief is that females are more "emotional" than males. But research suggests there are no differences in levels of emotional arousal between men and women. The sexes do differ, however, in how they express emotion.

As we have seen, facial expression is one measure of emotional arousal, In some studies (Buck, Savin, Miller & Caul, 1972) male and female subjects were shown color slides of seminude men and women, pleasant landscapes, a mother and child in a tender scene, repellent facial injuries tender scene, repellent facial injuries and strange photographic effects. Observes watched each subject's face over television and tried to judge which of the five kinds of slides the subject was seeing. When women were viewing, the observers proved to be correct much more often than when men were. So you might think females have greater emotional reactivity than males.

But emotional reaction can be measured physiologically as well. In a similar study that measured GSR (galvanic shin response), females had fewer responses than males (Buck et al., 1972). Craig and Lowrey (1969) found greater GSR changes for males than females who were watching someone receiving shock, but males rated themselves as experiencing less stress than females did. If appears that when overt responses such as facial expression and verbal report are measured, males show less emotional reactivity than females, but when physiological measures are taken, males exceed females.

One explanation is that expression of emotion is more socially acceptable for females than males. So males learn for inhibit their overt emotional reaction, causing increased physiological expression (Jones, 1950). In general it is true that low external expression of emotion is associated with high physiological reactivity (Lanzeffa & kleck, 1970). It is as though emotion must manifest itself somehow, so if overt expression is inhibited, physiological expression will increase.

Some observers have reasoned, therefore, that the blocking of expression of emotion can produce stress within the body, which may result in illness. It is indeed true that ulcers and heart disease are much more common among men than women. If this occurs because men inhibit expression of their emotions, then free expression of emotion would be desirable. However, free expression of emotion may also have detrimental effects, for it could create conditions where socially undesirable behavior such as aggression would be too frequent (Berkowitz, 1973).There are also other explanations of the differences between men and women in incidence of ulcers and heart disease. For one, female sex hormones appear to provide protection against these diseases. So it is not clear that either style of expressing emotion is more beneficial.

词汇 (Vocabulary)

1. addict   vt. 沉溺、嗜好
2. adrenalin   n. 肾上腺素
3. appraisal   n. 评估、评价
4. arousal   adj. 刺激的
5. aversive   adj. 厌恶的
6. cerebral   adj. 大脑的
7. connotation n. 含义、内涵
8. cortex   n. 表皮层
9. crave for   vt. 渴望、恳求
10. devastate   vt. 破坏
11. digestion   n. 消化、吸收
12. dilation   n. 扩大、膨胀

13. elicit   vt. 使……发出
14. enthusiasm   n. 热爱、渴慕
15. ethnologist   n. 人种家、人种学者
16. exhilarate   vt. 使……刺激、使……激动
17. extinction   n. 毁灭、绝种
18. ferocious   adj. 残忍的、凶暴的
19. fallible   adj. 易犯错误的
20. genetic   adj. 遗传学的、遗传因子的
21. impede   vt. 妨碍、阻碍
22. incentive   n. 刺激、诱因、动机
23. ingenious   adj. 有发明才能的、机敏的
24. lesion   n.（由受伤或疾病引起的）身体上的伤害
25. neurotransmitter   n. 神经传导
26. neutrality   n. 中性
27. normalcy   n. 标准、常态
28. nude   n. 裸体人像
29. novic   n. 初学者
30. opium   n. 鸦片
    opiate   鸦片剂
31. palpitation   n.（由于疾病、用力所致的）心脏急跳、心悸
32. parachute   vt. 空降、空投
33. periphery   n. 外用、表面
34. placebo   n. 安慰剂、宽心丸
35. precariously swaying   adj. 随意摆动的
36. predispose   vt. 使先倾向于、偏爱
37. prominent   adj. 突出的、显著的
38. provocation   n. 激怒、刺激
39. psychopathological   adj. 精神病心理学的
40. quiescence   n. 静止
41. salivation   n. 分泌唾液
42. stir   vt. 激起、惹起
43. tactic   n. 战术、兵法
44. termination   n. 结尾、结局
45. tremor   n. 颤动
46. videotape   n. 录影带

第十一章 动机
（MOTIVATION）

本章要点（Chapter Outline）
动机概念（The Concept of Motivation)
动机理论 (Theories of Motivation)
生理性动机 (Motives with a Biological Basis)
人类的性特征：最隐私的动机
（Human Sexuality:The Most Intimate Motive）
成就、权力、交往：人类特有的动机
(Achievement、Power、Affiliation: Some Uniquely Human Motives)

  人生活在世界上，每天都要做许多选择，那么人为什么做这样的选择而不做那样的选择呢？在背后的原因是什么呢？一个人的行为，大部分都是有目的、有意识的行动。这类行为的发生，有外部客观环境的促使作用，也有内部某些原因的驱动。仅就内部原因来说，最根本的动力源是人的需要。但由于种种复杂的原因，当人有了某种需要时，并不一定要产生满足需要的行动，只有这种需要达到了一定的强度，并且需要满足的目标被意识到可以实现时，人才有了真正开始行动的内驱力——动机。
  围绕人的动机产生了众多理论。在西方，综合诸多理论可以看出，生理需要、性行为、权力欲望被看作是人的基本动机。

第一节 什么是动机
(THE CONCEPT OF MOTIVATION)

  It is more difficult, if not impossible, to explain ones behavior solely in terms of external events or conditions. The concept of motivation helps us understand why people behave as they do. We can't observe this hidden, but by inferring it's existence we can often make sense out of actions which would otherwise seem confusing, puzzling, or bizarre. More formally, Psychologists define motivation as an inferred internal process that activates, guides, and maintains behavior (Geen. Beatty, and Arkin, 1984).
  In the remainder of this chapter we will examine several different aspects of human

motivation. First, we'll consider several contrasting perspectives on this process. Next, we'll examine two motives with an important biological basis: hunger and thirst. Third, we'll turn to a topic most people find fascinating: sexual motivation. And finally, we'll discuss several motives that seem to be uniquely human in scope: needs for achievement, power, and affiliation.

第二节 动机理论
(THEORIES OF MOTIVATION)

Why do people behave the way they do? Over the centuries providing different perspectives on motivation. We will focus here on three of these views: instinct theory, drive theory, and expectancy (cognitive) theory. Instinct theory, which is now rejected by most psychologists, suggests that many actions stem from innate urges or tendencies. In contrast, drive theory contends that many forms of behavior are "pushed" from within by basic needs. Since people often engage in actions that increase rather than reduce various drives, however, this theory, too, seems inadequate. A third perspective on motivation, expectancy theory, suggests that behavior is often elicited by the belief that engaging in certain actions will yield desirable outcomes.

Instinct Theory: A Biological Approach

In psychology, before the motivation is instinct. That is, before psychologists attempted to explain behavior in terms of motives, they sought to do so by means of instincts innate patterns of behavior which are universal in a species, independent of experience, and elicited by specific stimuli or conditions. For a time, this approach was quite popular. Thus, William James (1890), one of the founders of American psychology, included pugnacity, acquisitiveness, sympathy, and even curiosity on his list of basic human instincts. And Sigmund Freud, one of the most influential psychologists of all time, suggested that many complex forms of behavior aggression are heavily influenced by innate biological mechanisms.

To a large extent the origins of this instinct approach can be traced to Charles Darwin's theory of evolution. According to Darwin, human beings have evolved in the same manner, and in accordance with the same basic principles, as all other species on earth. Thus, the differences between us and other organisms are primarily ones of degree, not of kind. Since many other organisms possess instincts, he felt it was reasonable to suggest that human behavior, too, might be affected by built in tendencies.

Whether this is true or not remains somewhat controversial even today. Most psychologists doubt that innate patterns or tendencies play an important role in complex forms of human behavior, but some scientists (especially sociologists) contend that they do (Lumsden & Wilson, 1981). Quite aside from the outcome of this ongoing debate, though, it soon became apparent to most psychologists that instincts were not very useful from the point of view of understanding motivation. The basic problem was this: in most cases, the existence of an instinct was inferred from the behavior it was supposed to explain. For example, take the case of James's acquisitiveness. The existence of this instinct was inferred from the fact most people seek various possessions and usually become strongly attached to them. This instinct was then used to explain the occurrence of such behavior. In short, how do we know that people possess an acquisitive instinct? Because we can see them working hard to gain homes, cars, and so on. Why do they engage in such behavior? Because they possess an acquisitive instinct! As you can readily see, this is a useless type of circular reasoning. As realization of this fact grew, support for instinct theory waned, and it was soon replaced by a very different perspective in psychology drive theory.

Drive Theory: Motivation and Homeostasis

What do being hungry, thirsty, too cold, or too hot have in common? One answer is that they're all unpleasant and make us want to do something to eliminate such feelings. This basic fact provides the basis for a second major approach to motivation: drive theory. According to this view, biological needs arising within our bodies create unpleasant states of arousal the feelings we usually describe as "hunger", "thirst", "fatigue", and so on. In order to eliminate such feelings and restore the body's physiological balance (homeostasis), we engage in certain activities. Thus, according to drive theory motivation is basically a process in which various biological needs push or drive us to actions designed to satisfy these needs. Behaviors appropriate to help reduce drive are strengthen and tend to be repeated. Those that fail to produce such effects are weakened and will not be repeated when the drive is present once again.

In its original form drive theory focused primarily on biological needs and the aroused drives they produce. Soon, though, psychologists extended this model to other forms of behavior not so clearly linked to basic needs. For example, consider the famous frustration–aggression hypothesis (Dollard et al., 1939). According to this theory, frustration–aggression of our ongoing activities leads to the arousal of an aggressive drive which can be satisfied only by some kind of assault against the source of frustration. Here, as in many other extensions of drive theory, a powerful drive is supposedly aroused by external events rather than by internal biological needs.

Drive theory in psychology for several decades, there is widespread recognition of the fact that it have several serious drawbacks. The most important of these is this: contrary to what drive theory suggests, organisms (including human beings) often engage in actions that tend to increase rather than to reduce various drives. For example, have you ever delayed eating, even though you were hungry, in order to increase your enjoyment at the next meal (Zillmann et al., 1986)? If so, you already have first-hand evidence for the fact that we often seek to increase rather than to reduce various drives. Such effects are not restricted to human beings. For example, male rats learn to perform various responses that allow them to begin but not complete receptive sexual intercourse with females (Sheffield, Wulff, & Backer, 1951).

In the light of such evidence, most psychologists now believe that drive theory, by itself, does not provide a comprehensive framework for understanding human motivation. Thus, in recent years it has been largely replaced by the third view which greater emphasis on the cognitive aspects of motivation.

Expectancy Theory: A Cognitive Approach

Why are you reading this book? It is not, we'd guess, to reduce some biological drive! Rather, the chances are good that you are reading it because you expect that by doing so you will (1) learn something useful or interesting; and(2) get a higher grade on the next exam. In other words, your behavior is determined by your expectancies belief that your present actions will yield certain outcomes in the future. This basic point is the foundation for the third major theory of motivation we will consider, expectancy theory. This view suggests that motivation is not primarily a matter of being pushed from within by various urges; rather, it is more a question of being pulled from without by expectations of attaining desired outcomes or positive incentives. In short, while drive theory focuses mainly on the "stick" in the old carrot and-stick notion, expectancy theory focuses directly on the "carrot". So why do people engage in various behaviors such as reading this book, working too much, doing aerobics, or being videotaped at a dating service? Expectancy theory answers that they believe that doing so will yield outcomes they'd like to attain.

Expectancy theory has been applied to many different aspects of human motivation. Perhaps, though, it has found its most important use with respect to work motivation, such as the tendency to expend energy and effort on one's job (Mitchell & Larson, 1987). Research on this topic has consistently found that people will demonstrate a high level of work motivation only when (1) they believe that working hard will improve their performance, (2) good performance will yield various rewards (e. g., increases in pay, promotions), and (3) these rewards are ones they value.

In sum, expectancy theory suggests that our motivation to engage in a given activity will be high only when we expect that performing it will somehow pay off-yield outcomes or result we desire. In several respects, it is hard to imagine a more sensible statement about human motivation.

第三节 生理性动机：饥与渴
(HUNGER AND THIRST: MOTIVES WITH A BIOLOGICAL BASIS)

Why do we become hungry or thirsty? How do we know when we've had enough food or water to satisfy the needs from which these feelings arise? And why do some persons have so much difficulty regulating their intake of food, so that they gain or lose large amounts of weight? These are intriguing questions with important practical implications. Fortunately, research conducted by psychologists and others in the past few decades now allows us to offer partial answers. Since thirst has turned out to be the simpler (although far from simple), we'll begin with this motive and then turn to hunger.

Thirst: Regulating our Internal Fluid Balance

Both hunger and thirst involve the operation of regulatory mechanisms within our bodies. Both are affected by internal mechanisms that can (1) detect certain internal changes, (2) trigger corrective actions, and (3) bring these to a close when internal conditions return to optimal physiological values. If this sounds something like the operation of a thermostat in your home, you're on the right track. A thermostat detects departures from the temperature you've set, then turns on the furnace or air conditioning until the desired level is reached. But please note the internal mechanisms regulating hunger and thirst are far more complex than this, so the comparison is a useful one only if you keep this limitation firmly in mind.

During the course of daily life, our bodies lose a large amount of water through evaporation from the skin and lungs and the elimination of bodily wastes. In addition, we can also lose water in less routine ways (e. g., through bleeding or vomiting). How are such losses detected so that we feel the urge to drink? Two separate mechanisms seem to be involved.

First, some evidence suggests that certain cells in the heart, in the kidneys, and in veins detect changes in blood pressure produced by shifts in the volume of liquid outside the cells of the body (in the extracellular fluid compartment). When these baroreceptors are stimulated (primarily by a decrease in venous blood pressure), they trigger the secretion of ADH (antidiuretic hormone) by the pituitary glands. This hormone, in turn, causes the kidneys to reabsorb water which would otherwise be excreted as urine. In addition, other substances released by the kidneys in response to stimulation from the baroreceptors seem to stimulate receptors in the brain (especially in the hypothalamus), thus producing sensations of thirst.

Second, other neurons, located primarily in the hypothalamus, seem to respond to changes in the amount of water contained within cells of the body (in the intracellular fluid compartment). When the body's supplies of water are low, these osmoreceptors, along with many other cells, give up liquids to the blood and other bodily fluids. As they do, they shrink in size. This produces two effects: activity in the osmoreceptors stimulates the production of ADH, thus causing the kidneys to retain water, and it also generates sensations of thirst.

In sum, loss of water from our bodies is detected in two different ways. The sensations of thirst which result initiate drinking, and optimal physiological conditions are soon restored.

One final, interesting point: when we drink, sensations of thirst often cease long before the liquids we consume can reach either the extracellular or intracellular fluid compartments of our bodies. This suggests that receptors in the mouth and throat play a role in signaling satiety telling us when we've had enough(Carlson, 1986). Moreover, it appears that we can learn to anticipate our future needs with respect to liquid intake. For example, when rats are switched from a diet consisting mainly of carbohydrates to one rich in protein, which requires more water for digestion, they soon learn to drink more with their meals (Fitzsimmons & Le Magnen, 1969). Such findings suggest that, when coupled with the effects of learning, our internal mechanisms for regulating thirst can be effective indeed.

Hunger: Regulating Our Caloric Intake

Many persons find that the "battle of the bulge" a hard one to win. Despite their best efforts, their weight creeps up, and up, and up. Yet most individuals don't experience such difficulties. They simply eat what they want, when they want. In this section, we'll focus on how most organisms (including most human beings) are able to regulate their intake of food so precisely that they neither gain nor lose weight over long periods of time.

Are There Discrete Hunger and Satiety Centers in the Brain? At first glance, hunger and the regulation of eating seem quite simple: we eat when our stomachs are empty, and we stop when they are full. Unfortunately, early studies designed to test these straightforward notions showed that they are false. While individuals often do report experiencing hunger when their stomachs are active (Cannon & washburn, 1912), persons whose stomachs have been removed for medical reasons still report feeling hungry. This suggests that there is more to hunger than an empty stomach. Do brain mechanisms play a role? Intriguing hints that they might were provided by the medical histories of individuals who had suffered damage to the hypothalamus through surgery or accident. Such persons often experienced difficulty in regulating their weight, either gaining or losing large amounts.

These findings led some researchers to conduct systematic studies with animal subjects, studies in which portions of the hypothalamus were destroyed in order to observe the effects on eating. Initial results were dramatic. In fact, they seemed to point to the conclusion that the hypothalamus contained discrete "eating" and "satiety" centers.

The first of these, the supposed eating center, was located in the lateral hypothalamus. Destruction of this region greatly reduced subjects' interest in food. Indeed, animals who had undergone this operation often refused to eat or drink and would actually starve if not forced to take food. Further, they became quite finicky, refusing to eat any but the most palatable foods.

In contrast, destruction of a second region, the ventromedial hypothalamus, produced opposite effects. Animals who underwent this procedure became gluttons who consumed far more food than was true prior to the operation.

Such findings quickly gripped the attention of psychologists and even of the mass media. After all, if there were indeed discrete eating and satiety centers in the hypothalamus, perhaps effective solutions to the dieter's dilemma were just around the corner. Unfortunately, such hopes were soon dashed by other findings, which served to muddy this seemingly clear picture. First, animals who suffered destruction of the lateral hypothalamus gradually regained their appetites, at least in part. This contradicted the notion that this region serves as a discrete eating center. Second, animals who have undergone this operation show many other changes in behavior aside from a loss of appetite. For example, they fail to groom themselves, have trouble recovering their balance after a fall, and demonstrate little interest in almost any stimuli a phenomenon known as sensory neglect. In a similar manner, destruction of the ventromedial hypothalamus, too, produces a wide range of effects. Besides eliminating satiety, it appears to alter subjects' metabolism in basic ways, and these changes, not the elimination of a discrete satiety center, may account for their enormous appetites. In sum, the idea that the hypothalamus was a simple neurological key to understanding hunger and eating was soon discredited by additional research.

Detectors in the Liver and Elsewhere: A Less Dramatic but More Accurate Picture. If the hypothalamus does not contain eating and satiety centers, then what accounts for the ability most of us have to regulate caloric intake so precisely? (That it is precise is indicated by the following fact: if you eat just ten more calories than you need each day—less than the amount in a carrot—

you'll gain a pound every year.) The answer seems to involve several types of detectors located primarily in the liver, but existing elsewhere as well, which respond to different aspects of our diet (Stricker et al., 1977; Shimizu et al., 1983).

First, perhaps most important, such detectors respond to the amount of glucose in our blood, or perhaps they respond to the availability of our cells. When glucose levels are low (or when they are high but insulin levels are low, as diabetics) feelings of hunger result. When, in contrast, glucose levels are high and sufficient, insulin is also present, we experience satiety. Most of these glucose detectors are located in the liver, but some are present in the hypothalamus, too.

Second, some findings indicate that other detectors seem to respond to protein, more precisely, to amino acids. Thus, if we eat a meal high in protein (a thick, juicy steak, for example), we feel full even though the level of glucose in our blood may remain relatively low. Finally, still other detectors respond to lipids (fats). Again, even if glucose levels are low, when the amount of lipids circulating in our blood is high, we do not feel hungry.

Complex as all this may sound, it is still only part of the total picture. In addition, eating and hunger are also affected by what are sometimes termed head factors the sight, smell, and taste of food, as well as feedback produced by chewing and swallowing it. Such effects are illustrated by an interesting study conducted by Booth, Mather, and Fuller (1982). These researchers fed people three-course meals consisting of hot soup, small sandwiches, and a gelatin dessert. The number of calories in the soup could be varied by the addition of a tasteless but high-calorie starch. Subjects were not told about this difference, but spices were added so that the two versions were distinct in taste. On the first day subjects ate the same number of sandwiches after the high-calorie soup. Remember: subjects were not told that one version of the soup was higher in calories than the other. Rather, they were able to associate later feelings of being full or hungry with the taste of each soup, and adjust their eating appropriately. In this way, the taste of relatively high and low calorie foods can affect how much we eat, even if we know nothing about the foods' nutritional content.

As you can guess, feelings of hunger and satiety and their resulting impact upon eating are part of a complex internal system. Given such complexity, and the fact that several components of this regulatory system can be modified by learning, it is far from surprising that it sometimes gets out of whack. What happens when it does?

Obesity and Other Disorders in the Long-Term Regulation of Eating

There can be little doubt that in the late 1980s thin is "popular." Each year millions of persons spend billions of dollars in a continuing quest for slimness. In most cases, their desire to shed excess pounds stems primarily from concern with their appearance. But growing evidence suggests that there is strong medical justification for these efforts to counter obesity: being overweight has been linked to high blood pressure, diabetes, arthritis, and several other illness (Kolata, 1985). Why do so many people have difficulty regulating their eating and hence their weight? Unfortunately, many factors seem to play a role.

First, part of the problem seems to be learned. Many individuals acquire eating habits that are certain to generate excess pounds. They learn to prefer high-calorie meals (e. g., ones rich in protein and fats.) Further, they learn to associate the act of eating with many different contexts and situations. If you feel a strong urge to eat every time you sit down in front of the television or movie screen. Apparently, the desire to eat can be classically conditioned. Second, since eating often generates pleasant feelings, many persons learn to use this behavior as a means of coping with stress or unhappiness. Whenever they feel "down" or upset, they munch. Once again, such food intake is unrelated to bodily needs and can lead to unwanted pounds.

Genetic factors are important, too. As common sense suggests, individuals differently in basal metabolic rate. In other words, they vary in terms of the number of calories their bodies require at rest. Indeed, persons of the same age and weight performing the same daily activities can differ by a factor of two in this regard: one may require almost twice as many calories as the other. Persons with a high metabolic rate can eat much more than those with a low metabolic rate without gaining any weight. And now for the most discouraging part: when an individual diets, his or her metabolic rate tends to decrease. Moreover, the longer the diet continues, the greater this drop. Thus, as many dieters soon notice, the more weight they lose, the harder it lose still more because their bodies have adjusted to the apparent emergency (too few calories) by becoming more efficient!

Another inherited characteristic that may play a role in obesity is known as the **brown fat mechanism**. This system seems to provide a temporary means of storing extra calories. If they are not needed within a day after being consumed, they are released during periods of inactivity (e. g., during sleep) as heat. In contrast, white fat the type dieters fervently wish to shed stores excess calories in a more permanent manner.

That the brown fat mechanism can be very effective in maintaining fairly constant weight is shown by a study conducted by Rothwell and Stock (1979). Rats were fed a diet consisting of high calorie "junk foods." (Like people, rats seem to enjoy such foods and happily gobble them down.) On this diet subjects' caloric intake went up fully 80 percent. Yet their weight increased only 27 percent. What happened to the rest? One possibility, suggested by the fact that their oxygen consumption rose sharply, that it was simply released as heat by their brown fat mechanism. Since human beings, too, possess brown fat, it may play a similar role for us. Thus, those fortunate people you know who never seem to gain weight, no matter what they eat, may have a highly efficient brown fat mechanism. In contrast, those who seem to never lose weight, no matter what they eat, may lie at the opposite end of the scale in this respect. (We should hasten to note that this is largely informed speculation; such relationships have not yet been conclusively demonstrated among humans.)

Evidence for these effects has been reported by Herman and his colleagues (Herman et al., 1987). In this study, women who indicated that they were or were not currently dieting participate in a market survey involving flavors of gourmet ice cream. Before tasting the ice cream, one group was exposed to stress: they were told that after reporting their reactions, they would compose an advertising jingle for the ice cream and then sing it while being videotaped. The tape would then be shown to various marketing experts. In contrast, subjects in a second group were not exposed to such stress: they were told that after tasting the ice cream, they would merely be asked to list aspects of the product that should be stressed in future advertising. Both groups of participants were asked to refrain from eating for four hours prior to the study, so all were quite hungry.

Subjects were given containers of chocolate, vanilla, and strawberry ice cream and were told to taste as much as they wished. The containers were weighed before and after subjects received them, so the amount they ate could be carefully measured. It was predicted that among no dieters stress would reduce the amount of ice cream consumed, while among dieters the opposite would be true. These hypotheses have been supported. Given these results and the frequency with which most of us encounter stress during our daily lives, it is not at all surprising that many persons experience great difficulty maintaining a stable weight. The conditions around them seem to disrupt the self-control needed to restrict caloric intake.

Fifth, individuals who suffer from obesity seem to differ from other persons in one more respect that seems quite relevant to their problem: they tend to respond more strongly to external cues relating to food. In other words, they are more readily stimulated to eat by the sight or smell of food(Rodin & Slochower, 1976). Given the frequency with which such cues appear in many societies, it is hardly surprising that concern with obesity is a growing problem in many nations.

Finally, growing evidence points to the possibility that overeating, as well as several other ingestion related disorders (e. g., alcoholism), may involve excess production of, or sensitivity to, morphine, like substances produced by our own bodies, known as opioid peptides or endorphins. Several findings obtained in research with animals offer support for this hypothesis. First, small doses of morphine, which stimulate naturally occurring endorphin receptors in the brain, enhance the intake of several different substances (e. g., salt water, alcohol; Bertino et al., 1988). Second, the larger the dose of morphine administered, the larger such effects tend to be (Hubbell, Czirr, & Reid, 1987). Third, injections of drugs that counter the effects of morphine or endorphins (e. g., naxolone) reduce or even totally eliminate such results; rats receiving such drugs do not consume more of various substances (Hubbeli et al., 1988).

Together, these results suggest that endorphins prolong ingestion once it has begun, perhaps by enhancing the pleasant aspects of various tastes. Thus, some overweight persons (and perhaps some alcoholics, too) may experience personal difficulties because their internal mechanism for generating or responding to opioid peptides (endorphins) is somehow overactive. If this is indeed the case, then treatment for such problems based on the administration of opioid antagonists (drugs that counter the effects of endorphins) may prove effective. Research designed to test this possibility is currently under way.

Before concluding, we should note that there is another, and perhaps even more disturbing side to long-term weight regulation. In contrast to persons who are obese, some individuals tend to eat less than they need. In this condition, known as **anorexia nervosa**, individuals literally starve themselves until they lose dangerous amounts of weight. Surprisingly, anorexia nervosa does not seem to stem from the fact that they dislike food or find it unappealing. On the contrary, such persons are often preoccupied with it and enjoy preparing it. Their unwillingness to eat appears to derive from an unreasonable fear of becoming obese. This disorder occurs primarily among young women, who, of course, are the primary target of all those ads to be slim and be attractive, but it is sometimes found among older persons, too. Whether true anorexia nervosa ever occurs among males is as yet uncertain.

Because individuals suffering from anorexia nervosa sometimes show decreased activity in areas of the brain concerned with eating (e. g., the hypothalamus), some scientists believe it may stem from biological disorders (Leibowitz, 1983). At present there is not sufficient evidence to reach firm conclusions in this respect. One point, though, is clear: the psychological and physical damage caused by anorexia nervosa may be even greater than that associated with obesity.

Hunger and Thirst

Hunger and thirst are regulated by internal mechanisms that detect departures from optimal physiological conditions and initiate actions (eating and drinking) to correct such imbalances. The internal need for water is detected by baroreceptors which respond to reductions in blood pressure produced by loss of water from the extracellular fluid compartment, and by osmoreceptors which respond to the loss of water from cells themselves (the intracellular fluid compartment).

Hunger is regulated by many different factors, including cells in the liver and elsewhere which respond to changes in the levels of glucose, proteins, and fats in the blood. Hunger is also affected by head factors, such as the sight, smell, and taste of food. Many factors contribute to obesity. Among the most important of these are a learned preference for high-calorie meals, association of eating with various external cues, differences in basal metabolism, and contrasting reactions to stress. Some people suffer from anorexia nervosa and eat far less than they need to remain healthy.

第四节 性：最隐私的动机
(HUMAN SEXUALITY: THE MOST INTIMATE MOTIVE)

Are people in Western societies more preoccupied with food or sex? A stroll through the streets of any major city suggests that this is something of a toss-up. Signs and ads relating to both motives are present just about everywhere, although establishments concentrating on one or the other may be located in somewhat different districts. And, as we noted, most people report that thoughts and fantasies relating to sex are a frequent part of their daily lives (Lynn & Rhue, 1986). Since we're sure that you need no further convincing of the importance of sexual motivation, we'll turn at once to several of its key aspects.

Hormones and Sexual Behavior: Activation and Differentiation

As we noted before, puberty is marked by a tremendous increase in the activity of the sex glands or gonads—ovaries in women and testes in men. The hormones they produce (estrogen and testosterone, respectively) have many effects upon the body. The key question for purposes of this discussion, though, is this: do they influence sexual motivation? In most organisms other than human beings, the answer seems to be "yes." These hormones exert what are usually termed activation effects; in their absence, sexual behavior does not occur or occurs with a very low frequency (Geen et al., 1984). For example, removal of the ovaries (and the hormones they secrete) totally eliminates female sexual receptivity in many animals. Removal of the testes in males produces similar but somewhat less clear-cut results. Thus, for many species hormones play a key role in sexual motivation.

Human beings, though, are definitely the exception to this general pattern. Many women continue to engage in and enjoy sexual behavior after menopause, when the hormonal output of their ovaries drops sharply. Further, most do not report large changes in sexual desire over the course of their monthly cycle, despite major shifts in the concentration of various sexual hormones circulating in their blood. Thus, for humans hormones do not appear to related to sexual drive or behavior in a simple or straightforward manner. This is not to say that they play no role, however. Some women do report peaks of sexual arousal in the middle of their cycle and again prior to menstruation (Udry & Morris, 1968). Among men there is some evidence that testosterone levels are associated with differences in sexual arousal. For example, in one intriguing study Lange and his colleagues (1980) measured the speed with which men became sexually aroused (Experienced penile erections) while watching erotic videotapes. They found that men with high levels of testosterone in their blood became aroused more quickly than men with low levels. Of course, this in no ways implies that men in the former group have motivation or that they engage in sexual behavior more frequently or more vigorously than those in the latter group. These findings merely suggest that testosterone may be related to certain aspects of sexual motivation.

In addition to affecting adult sexual behavior, hormones produced by the gonads play another important role: they exert apparently irreversible effects upon the developing fetus. Recall that in humans the gonads begin to function by the seventh or eighth week of life; thus, the substances they produce are present early in life. Such organizational effects are quite varied in scope. First, these hormones affect the development of the genitals, so that males and females develop structures appropriate to their gender. Second, they seem to affect development of the brain in subtle but important ways. The differences produced, in turn, seem to predispose males toward male patterns of sexual behavior and females toward female patterns (Carlson, 1986).

Perhaps the impact of sex hormones on the development and future behavior of the fetus is most dramatically illustrated by the **androgen insensitivity syndrome** (Money & Schwartz,1978). In some individuals, a genetic defect prevents the cells of a genetic male from respond result to androgen (a hormone found in both sexes but which is more abundant in males). As a result, they are born with what appear to be female sexual organs. Since they lack a fully formed female reproductive tract, they cannot become pregnant, but if such individuals ate raised as girls, they develop in a seemingly normal manner. Indeed, most marry and report an average level of sexual motivation. If, instead, attempts are made to raise them as boys (their "true" genetic sex), serious problems can result. Administering testosterone to such persons when they reach puberty prevents the development of breasts, but it does not prevent them from remaining quite feminine in other ways (e. g., their voices stay high, they do not grow beards).

Opposite effects occur in a disorder known as the adrenogenital syndrome. Here, because of the presence of too much androgen, genetic females are born with what appear to be male reproductive organs. Many such persons undergo surgery shortly after birth to produce a more normal female appearance. When they reach puberty, they may also require injections of estrogen to counteract tendencies toward masculinization. (Their sex glands begin producing increased amounts of male hormone at this time.) Interestingly, although such individuals are raised as females, they show some behavioral characteristics of males. For example, they are often described as being tomboyish, and they often prefer wearing slacks to dresses. However, there is no indication that they are more likely to become homosexual than other persons (Money & Matthews, 1982). These findings call attention to an important point: although hormones affect the developing human fetus, social factors after birth are also extremely important. In sum, where human beings are concerned, hormones are only part of the total picture perhaps a relatively small part—with respect to sexual behavior.

Human Sexual Behavior: Some Basic Facts

Until the 1960s the only source of scientific information about human sexual behavior was that provided by surveys. The most famous of these were the carefully conducted Kinsey reports, published in the 1940s and 1950s. These surveys, which were based on interviews with more than ten thousand women and men, yielded many surprising facts. Although they were conducted decades ago, most men and nearly half of the women reported having engaged in premarital sex (Kinsey, Pomeroy, & Martin, 1948; Kinsey et al., 1953) Further, they indicated that many couples engaged in practices which were considered at the time to be objectionable by society (e. g., oral sex, a wide variety of sexual positions). If there is one basic theme in the Kinsey data, though, it is this: where sexual behavior is concerned that individual variation is enormous. Thus, while some people reported remaining celibate for many years, others reported having engaged in sexual relations with a large number of partners. And while some reported that orgasms were a rarity, a few indicated that they typically experienced them several times each day.

Of course, the type of data reported by Kinsey and other researchers is always open to question. First, there is the question of who agrees to participate. Are such persons younger, less inhibited, and better educated than the persons who refuse? Some evidence suggests that they are (Hyde, 1986). Second, do people report their experiences accurately, or do they describe the types and frequency of sexual behavior they think will put them in a favorable light? This is harder to assess but the latter certainly seems possible.

Starting in the 1960s, another source of information about human sexual behavior became available: direct and systematic observation of actual sexual activities. The first and still the most famous project of this kind was conducted by Masters and Johnson in the mid–1960s (Masters & Johnson, 1966). These researchers observed, filmed, and monitored the reactions of several hundred volunteers of both sexes as they engaged in sexual intercourse or self–stimulation. All together, more than ten thousand cycles of sexual arousal and satisfaction were studied. The results yielded important new insights into the nature of human sexuality. Perhaps the clearest finding was the fact that both males and females move through four distinct phases during sexual behavior.

First, in response to a wide range of sexual stimuli, they enter the excitement phase. During this phase many physiological changes occur, such as enlargement of the penis and clitoris, vaginal lubrication, and nipple erection.

If sexual stimulation persists, members of both sexes enter the plateau phase. The penis increases in circumference, and the outer third of the vagina becomes engorged with blood, reducing its diameter. Some persons experience a light rash on their chests or thighs, and muscle tension, respiration, heart rate, and blood pressure all rise to high levels.

After a variable period of direct stimulation, both males and females approach the orgasmic phase. This consists of several contractions of the muscles of the genitals, along with intense sensations of pleasure. Interestingly, the pattern of contractions, and even their timing, is virtually identical in both males and females.

The biggest difference between the two sexes occurs during the final resolution phase. Among males, orgasm is followed by a reduction in sexual tension and a drop in respiration, blood pressure, and heart rate. In addition, males enter a refractory period, during which they cannot be sexually aroused or experience another orgasm. Among females, two different patterns are possible. First, they, too, may experience reductions in tension and return to an unaroused state. Seconurning to this state.

The basic pattern we have just described seems to apply to all human beings, in all cultures. However, just about everything else seems to vary from one society to another. Different cultures accept widely different standards about such matters as (1) the age at which sexual behavior should begin, (2) the frequency with which it should occur, (3) physical characteristics considered attractive or "exy," (4) the particular positions and practices that are acceptable, (5) the proper time and setting for sexual relations, (6) which persons are appropriate partners, (7) how many marriage partners individuals should have at one time. So, we repeat, where human sexuality is concerned, variability is definitely the key term.

Human Sexual Behavior: What's Arousing and Why?
There can be little doubt that sexual motivation plays an important role in human behavior. Indeed. there is some indication that human beings engage in sexual activities much more frequently than the members of most other species, including primates. But what, precisely, stimulates such arousal? In some respects, human sexuality resembles that of other organisms. First, direct physical contact (e.g., kissing, touching, and other aspects of foreplay) produces such effects. Second, some researchers suggest that human beings, like other organisms, can be sexually stimulated by certain naturally occurring odors (Hassett, 1978). For example, in one study on this topic wives applied one of four perfumes at bedtime each night. One of these perfumes contained copulins, vaginal secretions that are presumably exciting to men. Results were mixed: some of the couples (about 20 percent) showed increased sexual activity on the nights when this perfume was worn; the others seemed unaffected. At present, then, we can't conclude with any certainty that naturally occurring scents play a role in sexual arousal. The existence of a huge and flourishing perfume industry, however, suggests that many people believe in the potential benefits of artificial aromas.

One potential source of sexual motivation, however, does seem to set human beings apart from other species: real or imagined erotic stimuli and images. In contrast to other organisms, human beings possess the capacity to generate their own sexual arousal on the basis of erotic fantasies or images. And they respond strongly to a wide range of erotic materials containing either visual images or verbal descriptions of sexual behavior.

With respect to self-generated imagery, recent findings indicate that many persons can produce intense sexual arousal, even orgasm, through internally generated sexual images (Money, 1985). Further, many report using sexual thoughts or images to enhance their pleasure during sexual intercourse or masturbation (Sue, 1979) or to speed up or delay the occurrence of orgasms (Davidson & Hoffman, 1986). In these and other ways our impressive cognitive abilities can play a major role in sexual motivation.

Turning to external erotic stimuli, it has been found that virtually every physiological reaction and behavior recorded by Masters and Johnson during actual sexual activity can occur in response to erotic passages, movies, tapes, or slides (Kelley and Byerne, 1983). Of course, all persons do not find all materials of this type equally exciting. Given stimuli they find attractive, though, it appears that most persons can be highly sexually aroused by such materials. Moreover, such arousal seems to affect overt sexual behavior. For example, Bryant (1985) asked a large sample of young men and women whether they had wanted to imitate the actions shown in the first X-rated movie or magazine they had seen, and whether they actually did imitate these actions with a willing partner. Most of the men and almost half of the women reported a desire to imitate these actions. And one-fourth of the men and about 15 percent of the women actually did imitate them.

If increases in sexual arousal and sexual behavior were the only effects produced by erotic materials, we could end our discussion of them here. Actually, though, they seem to exert a wide range of additional effects on persons who view them. Since some of these have important implications, we would be remiss if we did not at least mention them here.

One of the most unsettling of these effects is as follows: repeated exposure to X-rated materials seems to produce undesirable shifts in the viewers, attitudes about several aspects of sexual behavior. For one thing, such experience leads individuals to overestimate the frequency of several unusual and widely disapproved sexual practices (e. g., sadomasochism, human-animal sexual contact; Zillmann & Bryant, 1984). It may also cause some persons to view actions which are generally deemed inappropriate by society (e. g., an adult male seducing a twelve-year-old girl, extramarital affairs) as somewhat less objectionable (Bryant, 1985). We should hasten to add that such effects seem to occur only after exposure to a large number of X-rated films. Still, their existence suggests that viewing such materials can produce important changes in the way many people think about, and evaluate, sexual behavior.

In addition, it appears that exposure to explicit sexual materials, especially to films containing scenes of sexual violence (e. g., rape and other types of sexual assaults) can weaken the restraints of at least some males against aggression toward females (Malamuth, 1984). Moreover, such materials may also stimulate sexually aggressive fantasies in some viewers, and so perhaps increase their willingness to use force in sexual encounters (Malamuth, Check, & Briere, 1986). Clearly, such effects are disturbing, to say the least.

In sum, our ability to become aroused by external erotic stimuli or by our self-generated exotic fantasies seems to be something of a mixed blessing. It can enhance sexual arousal arid pleasure in some cases, but it may also lead to callous sexual attitudes and perhaps to unacceptable sexual practices as well. Whether the latter risks are justified, by the former benefits, of course, is largely a matter of personal values.

Sexual Orientation: An Unsolved Mystery

Estimates vary, but it appears that approximately 4 percent of all males and 2 or 3 percent of all females are exclusively homosexual who engage in sexual relations only with members of their own sex. In addition, many other persons (perhaps another2 or 3 percent of each sex) are bisexual who seek out and enjoy sexual contact with members of both sexes. What factors are responsible for these departures from the pattern, which is exclusively heterosexual? Decades of research on this issue have failed to yield any clear-cut answers (Geen et al.,1984). In fact, all of the most obvious possibilities appear to be false. Male homosexuals do not have lower levels of male sex hormones (androgens) than other persons. Moreover, exposing them to injections of such hormones (testosterone) does not reduce their homosexual tendencies if anything, these may be increased(Money, 1980). Similarly, study of the family background of homosexuals and heterosexuals has has failed to yield any reliable differences between them (Hammersmith, 1982). Homosexuals do not have different kinds of relationships with their parents or different sexual experiences during childhood.

Evidence concerning yet another possible explanation for differences in sexual preference one relating to prenatal hormones is still inconclusive. According to this view, homosexual preferences stem from the fact that during the prenatal period male sexual hormones exert too little effect on some male fetuses and too much impact on some female fetuses. The result: their brains are not suff iciently "masculinized" or "feminized," and they develop homosexual preferences as adults (Dorner, 1976). Definitive evidence for such differences does not exist, so this remains an intriguing but as yet unverified possibility:,

Finally, it has also been suggested that homosexual preferences may stem from experiences during puberty (Storms, 1981). According to this view, some individuals learn to associate their emerging sexual impulses with members of their own sex and so develop homosexual preferences. What might determine the nature of these associations? Perhaps the relative availability of members of each sex is the answer. For example, individuals attending schools that segregate the two sexes may be more likely to develop homosexual preferences than those attending schools containing both sexes. Is this view correct? At present no strong evidence for such effects exists. Moreover, many persons who are homosexual: report that they had homosexual fantasies and thoughts long before puberty. Thus, this theory is only food for thought and should not be viewed as proven.

In most mammals sexual motivation is strongly affected by sex hormones. These activate sexual behavior and affect the developing fetus in many ways. Hormones seem to play a smaller role in human sexual behavior, but they do affect development during the prenatal period. In addition, there is some indication that high testosterone levels males may be associated with more rapid sexual arousal.

Among human beings sexual motivation can be elicited by self-generated fantasies and by a wide range of external erotic stimuli. Exposure to such stimuli produces other effects in addition to such arousal (e. g., it may contribute to "callous" sexual attitudes).

In sum, the origins of homosexuality for that matter, of all sexual preferences—remain something of a mystery even today. Some person prefer partners of their own sex, but we don't yet know why this is so. What we do know, though, is this once established, such preferences are not readily changed. Hence, efforts by family, friends, and others to "reform" homosexuals (to change their sexual preferences) are usually unlikely to succeed.

第五节 成就、权力、交往：人类特有的动机
(ACHIEVEMENT、POWER、AFFILIATION: SOME UNIQUELY HUMAN MOTIVES)

Consider the following incidents:

An unhappy with the way in which a painting has turned out, destroys it rather than sell something that doesn't meet her standards.

An individual refuses to accept a transfer to a better job in his company because it will mean moving to another state and leaving many of his family and close friends behind.

A young woman gives up her high-paying law practice to run for public office, even though she has no real interest in the issues of the campaign.

How can such actions be explained? Many psychologists would answer: through reference to important human motives. The first example illustrates the **achievement motivation**—concern with meeting standards of excellence, "getting ahead", and accomplishing difficult tasks (McClelland, 1961). The second refers to **the affiliation motive** the desire to maintain close, friendly relations with others (Hill, 1987; McAdams, 1982). The third involves the **power motivation**—concern with being in change, having status and prestige, and bending others to our will (Winter, 1973). Such motives do not derive directly from basic biological factors, as do hunger, thirst, and, to some degree, sexuality; Yet they exert powerful effects upon behavior in many different contexts.

Achievement Motivation: The Quest for Excellence

Everyone gets hungry and thirsty, but as you probably known from your own experience, individual differ greatly in their desire for achievement. For some persons achievement difficult tasks and adhering to standards of excellence are important themes. For others just "getting by" is usually enough. How can differences in this motive be measured? How do they arise? And what are their effects? These are the issues upon which researchers have focused most.

Measuring Achievement Motivation.

The same basic method is used for measuring all three of the motives we will consider here (achievement, affiliation, and power). Originally, this consisted of showing individuals a series of ambiguous pictures, and asking them to make up stories about them. This is known as the **TAT**, or **Thematic Apperception Test**. The content of the stories was then evaluated, by means of carefully developed keys, to yield scores for achievement and other important motives (McClelland, 1975). More recently, however, Winter (1983) has developed a technique for scoring such motives directly from any type of verbal material, without the need for ambiguous pictures or stories about them.

The Origins of Achievement Motivation

Whatever measure is used, individuals are found to differ greatly in achievement motivation. How do such differences arise? Growing evidence suggests that they stem from certain differences in the child rearing practices used by parents. First, as you might expect, parents who place great emphasis on excellence and competition tend to produce children who are higher in achievement motivation than parents who do not emphasize such factors. Secondly parents who praise their children for success tend to produce youngsters who are higher in achievement motivation than ones who are indifferent to such outcomes (Teevan & McGhee, 1972). Third, parents who encourage their children to take credit for successes (who attribute such outcomes to the child's own effort or abilities) often produce youngsters higher in achievement than parents who do not adopt this practice (Dweck & Elliott, 1983). Finally, parents also serve as models of achievement motivation for their children. Those holding jobs requiring independent action and decision-making often have children who are higher in such motivation than ones holding jobs of a more routine nature (Turner, 1970).

The Effects of Achievement Motivation

Do individuals high and low in achievement motivation differ in other respects or in their life experiences? Existing evidence suggests that they do. First, as you might expect, individuals high in achievement motivation tend to get higher grades in school, earn more rapid promotions, and are more successful in running their own businesses than persons low in such motivation (Andrews, 1967; Raynor, 1970). Second, persons high in achievement motivation tend to prefer situations involving moderate levels or risk of difficulty; in contrast, those low in achievement motivation often prefer situations involving very low or very high levels of risk (Atkinson & Litwin, 1960). Why this difference? Because situations involving moderate risk or difficulty are ones with good chance of success, while also having sufficient challenge to make the effort worthwhile. Such situations are appealing to achievement-oriented people. In contrast, persons low in achievement motivation are more concerned about failure. Thus, they prefer situations in which either they are almost certain to succeed, or failure can be attributed to external causes (after all, the odds were so low, that almost no one succeeds).Finally, and perhaps most surprising, persons high in achievement motivation are not generally better managers than other persons. This seems to be true for the following reason: often, achievement-oriented people want to do everything themselves (so they can take full credit for success!). This is not an effective strategy in many work settings, where it is crucial to delegate tasks and responsibilities to others.

Sex Differences in Achievement Motivation: Do They Exist?

If you watch old films (ones made in the 1940s or 1950s), you may encounter the following situation: a teenage girl is brighter or more competent at some task than a teenage boy. However, she avoids making this fact known to him for fear that he will be threatened by this information and will, therefore, decrease her attractive.

In there any validity to this plot? In the past it appears there was. Traditional concepts of femininity seemed incompatible with high levels of competence, success, or achievement motivation. Taking note of this fact, Homer (1970, 1972) suggested that many women may actually fear success: they realize that striving for achievement can reduce their femininity in the eyes of others. And in fact, she found evidence for the widespread existence of such concerns (fear of success) among young women. More recent studies, though, have yielded a more encouraging pattern. At the present time clear differences between the sexes in this respect, or in overall achievement motivation, seem to be fading. Women still seem to have lower aspirations in some respects (e. g., they anticipate lower starting salaries than men in the same fields; Major & Konar, 1984), but the widespread fear of success reported by Homer seems to have all but disappeared (Terborg, 1977). Presumably, any remaining differences between the sexes with respect to achievement motivation will decrease further as traditional stereotypes of masculinity and femininity continue to shift.

Affiliation and Power Motivation: Two Sides of the Same Coin?

At first glance, the desire to be in charge (power motivation) and the desire to have close relationships with others (affiliation motivation) seem to be unrelated. After all, it's possible to imagine people high on both dimensions (people who want to "run the show", but who still like close ties with others), and people who are low on both (individuals who have little interest either in power or in friendly relations with others). In fact, however, research on these motivation suggests that in several areas of life, they do seem to be related or, at least, are perceived as being linked (Mason & Blankenship, 1987; Winter, 1987b).

First, consider the question of managerial success, an issue we mentioned earlier in connection with achievement motivation. What kind of individuals are most successful in this role? One possibility, suggested by McClelland and Boyatzis (1982), is that persons high in power motivation and low in affiliation motivation might be more effective than others in achieving success as managers. This makes good sense: after all, persons concerned with gaining power will focus on influence and status and may be more successful in "office politics." At the same time, their low concern with close interpersonal relations should permit them to avoid the kind of entangling ties that can prevent people from rising to the top (e. g., unwillingness to move from job to job or company to company).In fact, long-term studies suggest that individuals possessing this combination—known as the **leadership motivation pattern (LMP)**—who are high in power motivation but low in affiliation motivation—do rise to higher-level jobs than those not possessing it (McClelland & Boyatzis, 1982). Whether we'd want them for our boss, though, is quite another question.

Second, both motives seem to play a role in the occurrence of abuse in intimate relationships (Mason & Blankenship, 1987). Men high in power motivation report being more physically abusive toward their partners than men low in power motivation. And women high affiliation motivation and who are experiencing high levels of stress report being more psychologically abusive toward their partners than others.

Finally, both motives may play a role in the escalation of conflicts. The reason for this is as follows: each side may perceive their opponent as higher in power motivation and lower in affiliation motivation than they actually are. Such bias may then make it easier for both sides to take a "tough" stance and to refrain from making concessions.

FOCUS ON RESEARCH: The Cutting Edge
Does Having the "Right" Motives Make a Leader Great (or at Least Popular)?

Throughout history some leaders have been tremendously popular with their followers, while others have not. And some are now widely viewed as having been "great", while others are labeled as mediocre or worse. What accounts for these differences? Many possibilities exist, but one directly relevant to our discussion of motivation is as follows: perhaps popular or great leaders are ones whose motives match those of their society. In other words, perhaps the closer the "fit" between a leader's motives and those of his or her followers, the more popular the leader will be and therefore the more able to accomplish major goals. That this may actually be the case is suggested by the results of another ingenious study conducted by Winter (1987b).

In this investigation the inaugural addresses of ail thirty-four American presidents were subjected to careful analysis in order to obtain scores on three key motives: achievement, affiliation, and power. (See Table 11.1 for a sample of the findings.) In addition, the level of these motives prevailing in American society at the time of each president's election was also obtained. (This was derived from careful analysis of popular novels, children's readers, and hymns; McClelland, 1975). Obviously, there are many potential complications with respect to such data. For example, modem presidents don't usually write their own speeches. Thus, the content may reflect the motives of members of the president's staff as well as those of the president. Since presidents do choose their staffs and do approve their speeches, though, it can be argued that the themes present in them still reflect their own underlying motives. In any case, Winter (1987b) was certainly aware of such problems and attempted to collect these data as carefully and systematically as possible.

The motive scores for presidents and for society were then correlated with an index of each president's popularity (e. g., the percent of the popular vote he received) and with ratings of "greatness" provided by more than five hundred historians. Results were revealing. First, as predicted, the closer the match between a president's motives and those of society, the greater his popularity. Second, and more surprisingly, ratings of greatness correlated negatively with such congruence. The closer the match between each president's motives and those of society, the lower the rating he received from historians. In sum, it appeared that popularity is indeed a function of leader–society match, while greatness may stem from being different in this respect. (Included among the leaders most discrepant from society at the time were Washington, Lincoln, Truman, and kennedy.) These findings suggest that there may be some truth to the popular notion that in order to be great, leaders must truly lead and change their society in important ways.

Table 11.1

Careful analysis of their inaugural speeches suggests that American presidents have differed considerably in terms of their achievement, affiliation and power motivation. Scores are the number of images relating to each motive per 1,000 words in each president's inaugural speech. (Not all presidents are listed.)

president	Achievement	Scares on Each Motive Affiliation	power
George Washington	3.85	3.86	4.62
Thomas Jefferson	5.65	3.30	6.59
Andrew Jackson	4.48	2.69	5.38
Abraham Lincoln	3.34	2.23	6.97
Theodore Roosevelt	8.14	1.02	4.07
Franklin Roosevelt	6.37	2.12	8.50
Harry Truman	6.91	5.99	11.98
Dwight Eisenhower	4.50	4.50	6.14
John Kennedy	5.90	9.59	11.81
Lyndon Johnson	6.77	4.74	6.09
Richard Nixon	8.94	8.00	7.06
Jimmy Carter	10.60	4.89	8.16
Ronald Reagan	7.78	3.28	9.01

(*source*: Based on data in Winter, 1987b)

Intrinsic Motivation: How (Sometimes) to Turn Play into Work

Before concluding, we should call your attention to the following fact: there are many activities individuals perform simply because they find them enjoyable. Actions ranging from hobbies through gourmet dining arid lovemaking fit under this general heading. All may be described as stemming from intrinsic motivation: individuals perform them largely because of the pleasure they yield—not because of any hope of extern what happens if such persons are paid for sipping vintage wines or for pursuing their favorite hobby? Some research findings suggest that they may actually experience a drop in their intrinsic motivation. In short, they may be less motivated to engage in such activities than they were before. Why? One answer is as follows. Over rewarded persons may conclude that they chose to engage in these activities partly to obtain external rewards, to the extent they do, they may then perceive their own interest as lower than was previously the case. In short, such persons may shift from explaining their behavior in terms of intrinsic motivation ("I engage in this activity simply Because I enjoy it") to explanations in terms of external rewards ("I engage in this activity partly to obtain some external reward").

Many studies support this explanation. In such research, subjects provided with extrinsic rewards for engaging in some task they initially enjoyed later demonstrated less interest in the task than subjects not given such rewards (Deci, 1975; Lepper & Greene, 1978). These results seem to have important implications for parents, teachers, managers, and anyone else seeking to motivate others by means of rewards (the promise of toys or treats, raises, promotions, and bonuses). Presumably, if the target persons already enjoy various activities, offering them rewards for performing them may reduce. Such intrinsic motivation and may counter any benefits provided. Fortunately, recent research suggests this is not always the case. External rewards can be offered or administered without necessarily reducing intrinsic motivation. In particular, if they are offered as a sigh of competence or effectiveness, they may have positive rather than negative effects (Rosenfield, Folger & Adelman, 1980). Further, if such rewards are large and satisfying, they can maintain rather than reduce intrinsic motivation (Fiske & Taylor, 1984). These resets permit us to conclude on an optimistic note. While paying people for performing behaviors they enjoy can sometimes reduce their intrinsic motivation turn play into work—this is not always the case. When delivered with care, and in accordance with the principles outlined here, such rewards can enhance rather than reduce motivation and performance.

Achievement, power, and Affiliation

Individuals differ greatly in terms of three important motives: achievement, affiliation, and power. Persons high in achievement motivation often attain greater levels of success than persons low in such motivation. However, they prefer situations involving moderate risk or difficulty. Females seemed at one time to be lower in achievement motivation than males, perhaps out of fear that success would be incompatible with traditional views of femininity. Such differences appear to have decreased sharply m recent years. Persons high in power motivation but low in affiliation motivation are more successful as managers than others, but may be more likely to abuse their partners in intimate relationships. Newspapers often portray candidates they favor as lower in power motivation and higher in affiliation motivation than candidates they oppose.

When individuals are rewarded for performing actions they enjoy, their intrinsic motivation for engaging in these activities may be reduced. However, this does not occur if such rewards are provided for success or competence, or if they are large and satisfying to the persons who receive them.

词汇 (Vocabulary)

1. acquisitiveness   n. 获取、好求
2. activational effect   n. 激活效应

3. adrenogential syndrome 肾上腺性器综合征
4. androgen insensitivity syndrome 雄（性）激素不敏感综合征
5. aroma n. 芳香、香味
6. arbusal n. 唤起
7. arthritis n. 关节炎
8. baroreceptor n. 气压接受器、气压感受器
9. basal metabolic rate 基础代谢率
10. bisexual adj. 两性的
11. bizarre adj. 古怪的、怪异的
12. bleeding n. 流血、失血
13. callous adj. 冷淡的
14. caoric intake 热量摄取
15. carbohydrate n. 碳水化合物
16. carrot-and-stick 大棒与胡萝卜、软硬两手
17. celibate adj. 独身的
18. circumference n. 圆周
19. clitoris n. 阴蒂
20. concession n. 让步、妥协
21. copulate v. 性交
22. diabetes n. 糖尿病
23. engorge v. 使充血
24. erotic adj. 性欲的、色情的
25. escalation n. 增加、增强
26. estrogen n. 雌性激素
27. extracellular fluid compartment 胞外液区
28. femininity n. 妇女的气质
29. fetus n. 胎儿、胚胎
30. finicky adj. 对衣食苛求的
31. genitals n. 生殖器
32. gland n. 腺
33. glucose n. 葡萄糖
34. glutton n. 贪食者
35. gonad n. 性腺
36. heterosexual adj. 异性爱的
37. homeostasis n. 体内平衡
38. homosexual adj. 同性恋爱的
39. hormone n. 荷尔蒙
40. hypothalamus n. 下丘脑
41. inference n. 推断、推论

42. insulin   n. 本能
43. insulin   n. 胰岛素
44. introcelluliar fluid compartment   胞内液体
45. intrinsic motivation   n. 内在动机
46. kidney   n. 肾
47. lateral hypothalamus   侧生下丘脑
48. lipid   n. 类脂物
49. mammal   n. 哺乳动物
50. masculinity   n. 男性
51. masturbation   n. 手淫
52. menopause   n. 绝经期
53. menstruation   n. 月经
54. metabolism   n. 新陈代谢
55. monogamy   n. 一夫一妻制
56. morphine   n. 吗啡
57. nipple   n. 乳头
58. obesity   n. 过度肥胖
59. odor   n. 气味
60. optimal physiological values   最佳生理标准
61. orgasm   n. 高潮、情欲亢进
    orgasmic phase   高潮期
62. osmoreceptor   渗透感受器、渗透接受器
63. ovary   n. 卵巢
64. palatable   adj. 可口的、美味的
65. penis   n. 阴茎
66. pituitary gland   n. 脑垂体
67. plateau phase   平稳时期、停止时期、学习高原
68. positive incentive   n. 正刺激
69. predispose   v. 使倾向、偏向
70. prenatal   adj. 胎儿期的、出生前的
71. primate   n. 灵长类动物
72. protein   n. 蛋白质
73. puberty   n. 青春期
74. pugnacity   n. 好战、好斗
75. refractory period   不应期
76. regulatory mechanism   调节机制
77. resolution phase   消退期
78. respiration   n. 呼吸
79. sadomascochist   n. 施虐—受虐狂

80. satiety   n. 满足、饱足
81. secretion   n. 分泌液
82. seduce   n. 诱奸
83. stance   n. 看法、观点
84. starch   n. 淀粉
85. testosterone   n. 睾丸激素
86. Thematic Apperception Test(TAT) 主题统觉测验
87. thwart   v. 妨碍、阻挠
88. toss-up   n. 碰运气
89. trigger   v. 引发
90. vagina   n. 阴道
91. vein   n. 静脉
92. ventromedial hypothalemus   腹中下丘脑
93. vomiting   n. 呕吐
94. weird   adj. 怪诞的

第十二章 智力
（INTELLIGENCE）

本章要点（Chapter Outline）
什么是智力（What Is Intelligence）
智力理论（Theory of Intelligence）
智力的极端现象（The Extremes of Intelligence）

人类发展的重要因素之一是智力。每一个社会成员都担负着一定的社会责任和义务。工人生产、农民种田、学生学习、教师教学，所有的这些活动都必须通过特定的活动来完成，并且活动的效果反映着个体对社会所做出的贡献。因此，一个有责任心的社会成员，总希望能比较顺利地、成功地完成活动任务。可是，这一目标的实现并不以个人的强烈愿望而转移，也未必与个体的付出成正比，它要有一定的心理和行为方面的条件做保障。这种保障是多方面的，也是分层次的，其中所需要的最基本条件是能力保障。"智力是分析问题和解决问题的一种心理特性，也就是顺利完成智慧活动的能力"。因此了解和把握个体能力心理的规律，是认识和分析有效社会活动的重要理论基础。掌握个体能力形成的过程，则可以为社会培养有用的人才提供科学的理论依据。

第一节 智力的含义
（WHAT DOES INTELLENCE MEAN）

The idea that people vary in what we call intellence has been with us for a long time. Plato discussed similar variations over 2,000 years ago. most early theories about the basic nature of intelligence involved one or more of the following three themes: (1) the capacity of learn; (2) the total knowledge a person has acquired; and (3) the ability to adapt successfully to new situations and to the environment in general.

In this century, there has considerable controversy over the meaning of intelligence. In 1921,14 psychologists offered 14 different views about the nature of intelligence in a symposium on the subject, reported in the Journal of Educational Psychology (Neisser,1979).Sternberg and Detterman reported this process in 1986, asking 24 experts for their definitions of intelligence.

Again, opinion was divided. One point of disagreement in 1921(and still today) is whether intelligence is a signal ability or many separate abilities.

Intelligence: One Ability or Many? Some theorists believe intelligence is a basic ability that affects performance on all cognitively oriented tasks. An "intelligent" person will do well in computing mathematical problems, analyzing poetry, taking history essay examination, and solving riddles. Evidence for this position comes from correlation evaluations of intelligence tests. In study after study, moderate to high positive correlations are found among all the different tests that are designed to measure separate intellectual abilities (Lohman, 1989; McNemar, 1964).What could explain these results?

Charles Spearman (1927) suggested there is one factor or mental attribute, which he called g or general intelligence, that is used to perform any mental test, but that each test also requires some specific abilities in addition to g. For example, performance on a test of memory for numbers probably involves both g and some specific ability for immediate recall of what is heard. Spearman assumed that individuals vary in both general intelligence and specific abilities, and that together these factors determine performance on mental tasks.

Critics of Spearman's position insisted that there are several "primary mental abilities," not just one. Thurston(1938) listed verbal comprehension, memory, reasoning, ability to visualize abilities underlying intellectual tasks. But tests of these "separate" factors showed that ability in one area was correlated with ability in the others.

第二节 智力理论
(THEORIES ON INTELLIGENCE)

Multiple Intelligences. J. P. Guilford (1988) and Howard Gardner (1983) are the most prominent modem proponents of the concept of multiple cognitive abilities. Guilford suggests that there are three basic categories, or **faces of intellect:** mental operations, or the processes of thinking; contents or what we think about; and products, or the end results of our thinking (see Figtxe 12.1). In this model, mental operations are divided into six subcategories: cognition (recognizing old information and discovering new), convergent thinking (where there is only one answer or solution), divergent thinking (used when many answers may be appropri ate)? evaluation (decisions about how good, accurate, or suitable something is), memory recording (immediate memory), and memory retention (memory over several days). The contents on which people operate are divided into five subcategories: visual content, auditory content, word meanings, symbols, and behaviors. The different products that may result are units, classes, relations, systems, transformations, and implications.

According to this view, carrying out a cognitive task is essentially perform a mental operation on some specific content to achieve a product. For example, listing the next number in the sequence 3, 6, 12. 24,...requires a convergent operation (there is only one right answer) with symbolic content (numbers) to achieve a relationship product (each number is double the one before). Pointing an abstract conception of a still life requires a divergent thinking opera tion(many possible "answers") about visual content to create a transformational product (the actual objects are transformed into the artist's view). There are 180 combinations of operations, contents, and products—$6 \times 5 \times 6$.

Guilford's model of intelligence broadens our view of the nature of intelligence by adding such factors as social judgment (the evaluation of other' behavior) and creativity (divergent thinking). On the other hand, even though human mental abilities are complex. Guilford's model may be too complex to serve as a guide for predicting behavior in real situations or for planning instruction. In addition, when people are tested on these different abilities, the abilities prove to be related. The problem of explaining the positive correlations among all these supposed separate mental abilities remain unsolved.

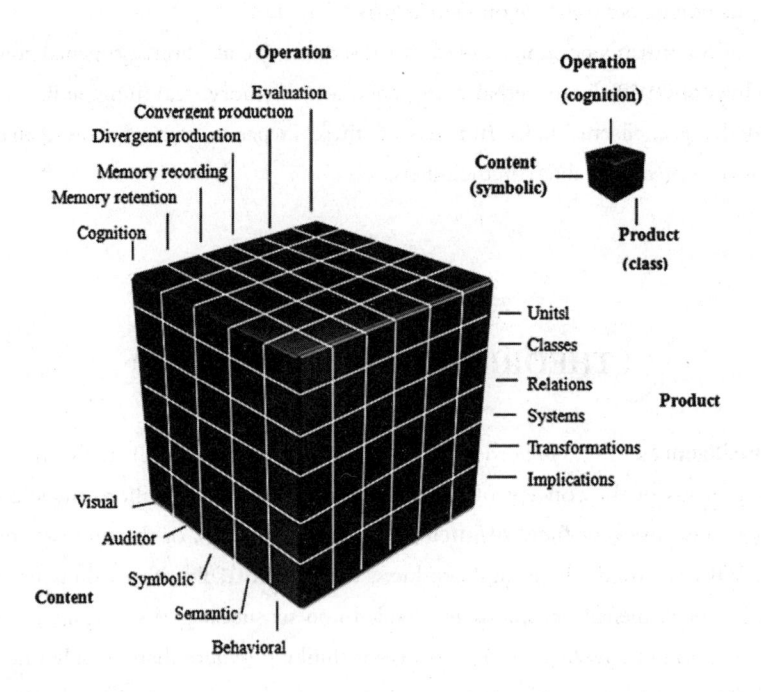

Figure 12.1 Guilford's Model of the Structure of Intellect

Each of Guilford's three dimensions of intellectual abilities—operation, content, and product—has many attributes. Through various combinations and these dimensions and these attributes produce 180 separate factors.

Howard Gardner (1983, 1993c) has proposed a theory of multiple intelligences. According to Gardner there are at least seven separate kinds of intelligences:linguistic(verbal),musi—

cal, spatial, logical−mathematical, bodily kinesthetic, understanding of others (interpersonal), and understanding of self (intrapersonal) (see Figure 12.2). Gardner has based his notion of separate abilities in part on evidence that brain damage (from a stroke, for example) often interferes with function in one area, such as language, but does not affect functioning in other areas. Gardner has also noted that individuals often excel in one of these seven areas but have no remarkable abilities in the other six. **Intelligence as a Process**. As you can see, the theories of Spearman, Thurston, Guilford, and Gardner tend to describe how individuals differ in the content of intelligence− the different abilities underlying intelligent behavior. Recent work in cognitive psychology has emphasized instead the thinking processes that may be common to all people. How do humans gather and use information to solve problems and behave intelligently? New views of intelligence are growing out of this work.

Robert Sternberg's (1985, 1990) triarchic theory of intelligence is an example of a cognitive process approach to understanding intelligence. As you might guess from the name, this theory has three parts.

The first describes the mental processes of the individual that lead to more or less intelligent behavior. These processes are defined in terms of components. A component is "an elementary information process that operates upon internal representations of objects or symbols" (Sternberg, 1985, p.97). Components are classified by the functions they serve and by how general they are. There are at least three different functions served. The first function−higher−order planning, strategy selection, and monitoring−is performed by met components. Examples of met components are identifying the problem, allocating attention, and monitoring how well a strategy is working. A second function served by components−executing the strategies selected is handled by performance components. One performance component allows us to perceive and store new information. The third function−gaining new knowledge is performed by knowledge−acquisition components, such as separating relevant from irrelevant information as you try to understand a new concept (Sternberg, 1985).

Some components are specific; that is, they are necessary for only one kind of task, such as solving analogies. Other components are very general and may be necessary in almost every cognitive task. For example, met components are always operating to select strategies and keep track of progress. This may help to explain the persistent correlations among all types of mental tests. People who are effective in selecting good problem−solving strategies, monitoring progress, and moving to a new approach when the first one more likely to be successful on all types of tests. Met components may be the modern−day version of Spearman's g.

Figure 12.2 Seven Intelligences
Howard Gardner's theory of multiple intelligences suggests that there are seven different categories of human abilities. An individual might have strengths or weaknesses in one or several areas. The figure gives explanations of each capacity and examples of occupations that draw upon that ability.

Intelligence	End States	Core Components
Logical–mathematical	Scientist Mathematician	Sensitivity to, and capacity to discern, logical or numerical patterns; ability to handle long chains of reasoning.
Linguistic	Poet Journalist	Sensitivity to the sounds, rhythms, and meanings of words; sensitivity to the different functions of language.
Musical	Composer Violinist	Abilities to produce and appreciate rhythm, pitch, and timbre; appreciation of the forms of musical expressiveness.
Spatial	Navigator Sculptor	Capacities to perceive the visual–spatial world accurately and to perform transformations on one's initial perceptions.
Bodily kinesthetic	Dancer Athlete	Abilities to control one's body movements and to handle objects skillfully.
Interpersonal	Therapist Salesman	Capacities to discern and respond appropriately to the moods, temperaments, motivations, and desires of other people.
Interpersonal	Person with detailed, accurate self–knowledge	Access to one's own feelings and the ability to discriminate among them and draw upon them to guide behavior; knowledge of one's own strengths, weaknesses, desires and intelligence.

Source: H. Gardner and T. Hatch (1989). *Multiple intelligences go to school. Educational Researcher, 18(8), p.6.* Copyright 1989 by the American Educational Research Association. *Reprinted by permission of the publisher and the authors.*

The second part of Sternberg's triarchic theory involves coping with new experiences. Intelligent behavior is marked by two characteristics: (1) insight, or the ability to deal effectively with novel situations, and (2) the ability to become efficient and automatic in thinking and problem solving. So intelligence involves creative thinking in solving new problems and **automaticity-quickly turning new solutions into routine processes that can be applied without much cognitive effort.**

Figure 12.3 Sternberg's triarchic theory of intelligence
Sternberg's triarchic theory suggests that intelligent behavior is the product of applying thinking strategies, handling new problems creatively and quickly, and adapting to contexts by selecting and reshaping our environment.

Contextual Intelligence	Experiential Intelligence	Componential intelligence
Ability to adapt to a changing environment and to shape one's world to optimize opportunities. Contextual intelligence deals with an individual's ability to prepare for problem solving in specific situations. For example, some students take their telephones off the hook or put a "do not disturb" sign on the door while studying, because they know they will be distracted by calls and visitors.	*Ability to formulate new ideas and combine unrelated facts A test of experi-ential intelligence assesses a person's ability to deal with novel tasks in an automatic manner. Examples include learning to remember all the words containing the letter t in a particular paragraph and diagnosing a problem with an automobile engine.*	*Ability to think abstractly, process information, and determine what needs to be done Tasks that can be used to measure the elements of componential intelligence are analogies, vocabulary, and syllogisms.*

The third part of Sternberg's theory highlights the importance of choosing an environment in which a person can succeed and adapt to that environment or reshaping it if necessary. Here, culture is a major factor in defining successful choice, adaptation, and shaping. What works in one cultural group will not work in another. For example, abilities that make a person successful in a rural farm community may be useless in the inner city or at a country club in the suburbs. People who are successful often seek situations in which their abilities will be valuable, then work hard to capitalize on those abilities and compensate for any weaknesses. Thus, intelligence in this third sense involves practical matters such as career choice or social skills. Figure 12.3 summarizes the elements of Sternberg's triarchic theory of intelligence and shows how they may relate mental abilities to one another and to the thinking processes underlying these abilities.

第三节 智力的极端现象
(THE EXTREMES OF INTELLIGENCE)

The atypical individual has always been of interest to psychologists. Intellectual atypicality has intrigued many psychologists and drawn them to study both the mentally retarded and the gifted.

Mental Retardation

The most distinctive feature of mental retardation is inadequate intellectual functioning. Long before formal tests were developed to assess intelligence, the mentally retarded were identified by a lack of age-appropriate skills in learning and caring for oneself. With the development of intelligence tests more emphasis was placed on IQ as an indicator of mental retardation. But it is not unusual to find two retarded individuals with the same low IQ, one of whom is married, employed, and involved in the community and the other requiring constant supervision in an institution. These differences in social competence led psychologists to include deficits in adaptive behavior in their definition of mental retardation. The currently accepted definition of **mental retardation** refers to an individual who has a low IQ, usually below 70 on a traditional test of intelligence, and who has difficulty adapting to everyday life. About 5 million Americans fit this definition of mental retardation (Zigler, 1987).

There are different classifications of mental retardation. About 80 percent of the mentally retarded fall into the mild category, with IQs of 50 to 70. About 12 percent are classified as moderately retarded, with IQs of 35 to 49; these individuals can attain a second-grade level of skills and may be able to support themselves as adults through some type of labor. About 7 percent of the mentally retarded are in the severe category, with IQs of 20 to 34; these individuals learn to talk and engage in very simple tasks, but they require extensive supervision. Only 1 percent of the mentally retarded fall into the profound classification with IQs below 20; they are in constant need of supervision.

What causes mental retardation? The causes are divided into two categories: organic and cultural-familial. Individuals with **organic retardation** are retarded because of a genetic disorder or brain damage; organic refers to the tissues or organs of the body, so there is some physical damage that has taken place in organic retardation. Down's syndrome, a form of mental recordation, occurs when an extra chromosome is present in the individual s generic make-up, for example. It is not known why the extra chromosome is present, but it may involve the health of the female ovum or the male sperm. Although those who suffer organic retardation are found across the spectrum of IQ distribution, most have IQs between 0 and 50.

Individuals with **cultural-familial retardation** make up the majority of the mentally retarded population; they have no evidence of organic damage or brain dysfunction and IQs range from 50 to 70. Psychologists seek to find the cause of this type of retardation in the impoverished environments these individuals probably have experienced (Broman, Bien, &Shaughnessy, in press). Even with organic retardation, though, it is wise to think about the contributions of genetic–environment interaction. Parents with low IQs not only may be more likely to transmit genes for low intelligence to their offspring but also tend to provide them with a less enriched environment.

Giftedness

Conventional wisdom has identified some individuals in all cultures and historical periods as gifted because they have talents not evident in the majority of the people. Despite this widespread recognition of the gifted, psychologists have difficulty reaching a consensus on the precise definition and measurement of giftedness. Some experts view the gifted as the top end of a continuum of intelligence (Humphreys, 1985; Zigler & Farber, 1985). Some of these advocates view this ability as a unitary characteristic that is perhaps hereditary. Others see the gifted as individuals who express specific talents that have been nurtured environmentally (Wallach, 1985). A comprehensive definition of **gifted** is an individual with well–above–average intelligence (an IQ of 120 or more) and/or a superior talent for something. Most school systems emphasize intellectual superiority and academic aptitude when selecting children for special instruction; however, they rarely consider competence in the visual and performing arts (art, drama, dance), psychomotor abilities (tennis, golf, basketball), or other special aptitudes.

A classic study of the gifted was begun by Lewis Terman (1925) more than sixty years ago. Terman studied approximately 1,500 children whose Stanford–Binet IQs averaged 150. His goal was to follow these children through their adult lives the study will not be complete until the year 2010.

The accomplishments of the 1,500 children in Terman's study are remarkable. Of the 800 males, 78 have obtained PhDs (they include two past presidents of the American Psychological Association), 48 have earned MDs, and 85 have been granted law degrees. Nearly all of these figures are ten to thirty times greater than found among 800 men of the same age chosen randomly from the overall population (Getzels & Dillon, 1973). These findings challenge the commonly held belief that the intellectually gifted are disturbed emotionally or maladjusted socially. This belief is based on striking instances of mental disturbances among the gifted. Sir Frances Galton suffered from an anxiety disorder and had two nervous breakdowns, for example. Sir Isaac Newton, Van Gogh, da Vinci, Socrates, and Poe all had emotional problems.

But these are the exceptions rather than the rules; no relation between giftedness and mental disturbance in general has been found. A number of recent studies support Terman's conclusion that, if anything, the gifted tend to be more mature and have fewer emotional problems than others (Janos & Robinson, 1985).

In another investigation, individuals with exceptional talents as adults were interviewed about what they believe contributed to their giftedness (Bloom, 1983). The 120 individuals had excelled in one of six fields–concert pianists dnd sculptors (arts), Olympic swimmers and tennis champions (psychomotor), and research mathematicians and research neurologists (cognitive).

They said the development of their exceptional accomplishments required special environmental support, excellent teaching, and motivational encouragement. Each experienced years of special attention under the tutelage and supervision of a remarkable series of teachers and coaches. They also received extensive support and encouragement from their parents. All of these stars devoted exceptional amounts of time to practice and training, easily outdistancing the amount of the time spent in all other activities combined.

Creativity

Most of us would like to be both gifted and creative. Why was Thomas Edison able to invent so many things? Was he simply more intelligent than most individuals? Did he spend long hours toiling away in private? Somewhat surprisingly, when Edison was a young boy his teacher told him that he was too dumb to learn anything! Other examples of famous individuals whose creative genius went unnoticed when they were young include Walt Disney, who was fired from a newspaper job because he did not have any good ideas; Enrico Caruso, whose music teacher told him that his voice was terrible; and Winston Churchill, who failed one year of secondary school. Among the reasons such individuals are underestimated as youngsters is the difficulty of defining and measuring creativity.

The prevailing belief of experts who study intelligence and creativity is that the two are not the same thing (Monroe, 1988; Wallach, 1985). One distinction is between c**onvergent thinking**, which produces one correct answer, and **divergent thinking**, which produces many different answers to the same question (Guilford 1967). For example, this intellectual problem—solving task has one correct answer and thus requires convergent thinking: "How many quarters will you get in return for sixty dimes?" But this question has many possible answers and requires divergent thinking: "What are some unique things that can be done with a paper clip?" A degree of creativity is needed to answer this question. Other examples of divergent thinking are generated by the following: Name words that belong to a particular class. For example, name as many objects as you can that weigh less than one pound. Even when you are not asked to, do you give divergent answers? For example, if you are asked what unique things can be done with a paper clip do you spontaneously generate different categories of use for the clip?

Creativity is the ability to think about something in a novel and unusual way and to come up with unique solutions to problems. When individuals in the arts and sciences who fit this description are asked what enables them to produce their creative works, they say that they generate large amounts of associative content when solving problems and that they have the freedom to entertain a wide range of possible solutions in a playful manner (Wallach & Kogan, 1965).

How strongly is creativity related to intelligence? A certain level of intelligence seems to be required to be creative in most fields, but many highly intelligent people (as measured by IQ tests) are not very creative.

In this chapter we have discussed many different aspects of intelligence. In the next section we turn our attention to development across the life cycle, beginning with the infant and childhood years.

词汇 (Vocabulary)

1. chromosome   n. 染色体
2. continuum   n. 连续之事物
3. convergent   a. 聚合的、聚集的
4. deficit   n. 不足之处
5. divergent   a. 发散的
6. excel in.   优于、胜过
7. multiple   a. 复合的
8. retardation   n. 障碍
9. rural   a. 乡村的
10. sculptor   n. 雕刻家
11. spatial   a. 空间的
12. symposium   n. 专题论文集
13. tutelage   n. 保护、监护、教导

第十三章 人格
（PERSONALITY）

本章要点（Chapter Outline）
人格（Personality)
心理动力论（The Psychodynamic Perspective)
特质论（The Trait Perspective)
行为主义观点（The Behavioral Perspective)
人本主义观点（The Humanistic Perspective)
人格特质的测量（Measuring Personality Trait)
探求人格动力：投射测验（Exploring Personality Dynamics: Projective Test）

第一节 人格概念
（CONCEPT OF PERSONALITY）

人格是一种多层次、多维度的复杂心理特征。因此各学者给人格所下的定义不尽相同，但有一点得到了大家的公认，这一点是：人格体现了个体的独特的行为模式、心理过程及个体与环境的交互作用。本章将描述个体的心理特征，并且阐述主要的四个派别的人格理论。第一个派别是以弗洛伊德为代表的心理动力论。心理动力论强调人格内部的心理动力。弗洛伊德认为人格形成的心理动力是生物驱力，特别是性驱力和攻击驱力，他提出了人格的三个结构、人格发展的五个阶段，以及八种自我防御机制。第二个派别是特质论。特质论认为人格是一些特质的集合。特质论中有两种理论，一种是类型理论，一种是特质理论，它们是特质论研究中的两个方面。类型理论主要研究人们之间共同的东西，特质论则强调人们之间的差异。第三个派别是行为主义观点。行为主义认为个性来源于外部事件，特别是强化。斯金纳的激进行为主义认为行为由行为的结果来决定，社会学习理论增加了许多认知因素，人和环境的交互作用论强调人和环境的相互作用。第四个派别是人本主义观点。以罗杰斯和马斯洛为代表的人本主义认为行为受个体独特的人生观所支配。人本主义强调人的内心世界、知觉、情感、自我实现的能力和所有内在潜能的充分实现。本章最后将介绍几种主要的人格测量方法。测量人格特质的人格调查表主要有明尼苏达多相个性量表和卡特尔16种人格因素量表。罗夏墨迹测验和主题统觉测验是探求人格动力的投射测验。

In the chapters you have been reading up until now, we have considered how specific human capacities work and how they develop. For example, we have discussed how the brain controls behavior and experience, and how human beings learn, remember, and reason. Furthermore, we have considered how capacities such as intelligence and the ability to interact with peers grow and change over time. In this chapter we will consider how the various human skills, capacities, needs, and motives come together in individuals human beings. This is the area of psychology known as personality.

Personality can be defined as the unique pattern of behavioral and mental processes that characterizes an individual and the individual's interactions with the environment. The subject of studying Personality, explores psychology is the study of individuals, with special emphasis on what makes a person unique. Henry Murray once stated that every person is in some like all other people, in other ways like some other people, and in still other ways like no other person (Murray & Kluckhohn, 1953). While personality psychology considers all these aspects, at present it gives more attention to how people differ.

In some cases personality psychologists study how groups or types of people differ; in other cases these psychologists study how the unique individual acts, feels, and thinks. Keeping in mind that our goal in this chapter is to understand what psychology can tell us about the psychological characteristics of the individual, let us consider how the different approaches to personality have evolved.

People have discussed the nature of personality for centuries. For example, the Greeks and Romans discussed a fourfold personality classification scheme based on the four cosmic elements—earth, air, fire, and water. Both Hippocrates and the Roman physician Galen suggested that the way these elements are represented in the personality creates four kinds of human temperament—melancholic, sanguine, choleric, and phlegmatic—corresponding to earth, air, fire, and water.

The modern psychological study of personality has been marked by the development of four major perspectives. The first and major milestone in the psychological study of personality was the work of Sigmund Freud. Freud mainly emphasized was on biological drives, especially sexual and aggressive drives, and the ways they were channeled by external forces. Freud's theories grew out of his work with psychologically disturbed individuals. From his observation of their difficulties, he formulated a theory of the structures of the personality, how they develop, and how they interact. His theory outlines the many ways that individuals satisfy their basic biological drives within an array of social and physical constraints.

Freudian theory and the theories of other psychologists basically sympathetic to Freud, called neo-Freudians, make up what is known as the psychodynamic perspective on personality. These theories all emphasize the dynamic forces within the personality that give rise to specific psychological characteristics.

The second major perspective on personality, the trait perspective, grew out of two criticisms of the Freudian approach. First, a disillusioned follower of Freud, Carl Jung, felt that not all people, or even most, were primarily motivated by sexual or destructive drives. He and others felt that humans had other needs and interests, and that people could be divided into personality types according to their different characteristics, A second group of critics felt that Freud's theories were not sufficiently supported by evidence. They felt that observations of psychologically disturbed people in a therapy setting were not sufficient data on which to build a theory. They also felt that more attention should be paid to measuring personality characteristics and describing people in terms of their individual traits, whether these traits be related to sex, aggression, or anything else. In short, the trait perspective attempts to consider a broad range of human characteristics and to devise ways of measuring the traits that individuals possess.

The third major perspective on personality is the behavioral, or social learning perspective. This perspective is strongly influenced by the work of B. F. Skinner and other learning theorists. It criticizes both the psychodynamic and trait perspectives. First, it objects to the psychodynamic concepts of intrapsychic structures and stages of development because they cannot be directly observed or operated. Furthermore, it rejects the emphasis of both the psychodynamic and trait perspectives on internal determinants of behavior. The psychodynamic perspective emphasizes inner drives; the trait perspective emphasizes internal traits. In contrast, the behavioral perspective emphasizes how external factors shape behavior and ultimately, through learning, a person's characteristics. Furthermore, because the behavioral perspective emphasizes people's responsiveness to external events and stimuli, it also emphasizes that people will behave differently in different situations and that personality characteristics vary from time to time and place to place.

The fourth, the humanistic perspective, like the trait and behavioral perspectives, grew out of dissatisfaction with other perspectives. Humanistic psychology especially rejects the psychodynamic and behavioral perspectives, primarily because they emphasize too much the determination of behavior, whether by internal drives or external stimuli, and do not consider sufficiently the extent to which people exercise free will and voluntarily direct their own lives.

第二节 心理动力论
(THE PSYCHODYNAMIC PERSPECTIVE)

The work of Sigmund Freud and his followers makes up the specific psychodynamic perspective known as the psychoanalytic theory of personality. We have already considered some of Freud's ideas in this book. Freud explored people's unconscious motives and conflicts using the techniques of dream interpretation and free association. His central idea was that personality characteristics, including the symptoms of psychological disorders, grow out of unconscious conflicts about sexual and of unconscious conflicts about sexual and aggressive drives. In addition, Freud emphasized that personality is largely determined during the first five years of life, when the person develops characteristic ways of dealing with internal drives and conflicts. In this section we will discuss in more detail Freud's ideas about the structure, development, and dynamics of personality (Freud, 1933, 1940).

The Structure of Personality

Freud's work with people suffering from various psychological disorders convinced him that the personality was composed of three different mental structures. He called these the id, the ego, and the superego. What a person thinks, feels, and does is a function of the actions or interactions of these three hypothetical structures. We will discuss them in order in which they develop in the personality.

The Id Freud held that at birth the child's personality consists solely of unconscious drives for pleasure. The name Freud gave the hypothetical mental structure in which these drives resided was the id. The id strives for immediate satisfaction of its drives for pleasure. According to Freud, this pleasure is obtained by the elimination of tension. When the id's tensions accumulate, satisfaction is achieved by a reduction in tension levels.

Freud specified two ways in which the id tries to achieve the reduction of tension. One mechanism is reflex action, or simply responding reflexively to stimuli in the environment. For example, a child's sucking on a nipple is reflex action. This reflex reduces tension and quiets an aroused and unhappy child. A second mechanism the id uses is primary−process thinking. This type of thinking involves creating a fantasy about the object or behavior that serves to reduce tension. For example, a child might imagine nursing. This fantasy partially reduces tension.

The Ego Primary−process thinking alone cannot ensure the survival of the child. Imagining feeding is pleasurable, but it does not satisfy nutritional requirements. For this reason, another mental structure develops. This mental structure is comprised of information that the child perceives, remembers, and of the cognitive processes that develop to process this information, such as thinking, reasoning, and planning. Freud called this mental structure the ego. The ego is largely conscious.

One important characteristic of the ego is that it develops in order to keep the id obtain real rather than imaginary satisfaction. It is able to do this because it uses **secondary−process thinking**, or realistic thinking, rather than simply fantasy, or primary−process thinking. Although it is more realistic than the id, the ego derives all its energy from the unconscious drives of the id and exists only to find effective ways of satisfying those drives. In short, the id is not suitably adapted to satisfy its own drives. The ego, on the other hand, is a reality−oriented mental structure that develops out of early experience to help the id obtain satisfaction.

The Superego The ego has to consider more than reality in obtaining satisfactions for the id. At about age five, the third major structure of the personality develops. This structure is called the superego. The superego contains moral principles and values, which have been acquired from the parents and society. It actually consists of two subparts. One part is the conscience, which contains moral prohibitions against certain behaviors, especially those expressing the sexual and aggressive drives of the id. The other part of the superego is the ego−ideal. This is the image of what one ideally can be and how one ought to behave. We can think of the conscience as containing dictates about what is immoral, or about what one should not do, and the ego−ideal as containing models about what is moral, or about what one should do.

The Key Role of the Ego If you have the feeling that the ego is caught in the middle, you are correct. It is this rational, reality-oriented portion of the personality that directs behavior. Unless it is overwhelmed by id tensions or superego dictates, the ego determines final decisions and actions. But in doing so it must provide some gratification for the id's drives and must also act within the moral constraints of the superego. Furthermore, it must choose behaviors that fit the constraints of reality. It is the executive of the personality but it must serve three masters: the id, the superego, and external reality. Later we will discuss some of the tools the ego uses in its dealings with the id, the superego, and reality.

Conscious, Preconscious, and Unconscious Regions Freud felt that the three structures of personality, the id, ego, and superego, functioned within overlapping portions of the conscious, preconscious, and unconscious regions of the mind (see Figure 13.1)

As noted before, the id is unconscious. Its drives operated only in unconscious form. The ego is largely conscious but has preconscious and unconscious portions as well. The preconscious portion of the mind contains thoughts, memories, and other kinds of information that are not conscious but that can easily be brought into consciousness. In addition, a portion of the ego is unconscious. This portion contains the ego-defense mechanisms, which we will discuss shortly. The superego contains conscious, preconscious, and unconscious areas. Its dictates can be felt in consciousness, or they can be preconscious, or they can operate unconsciously.

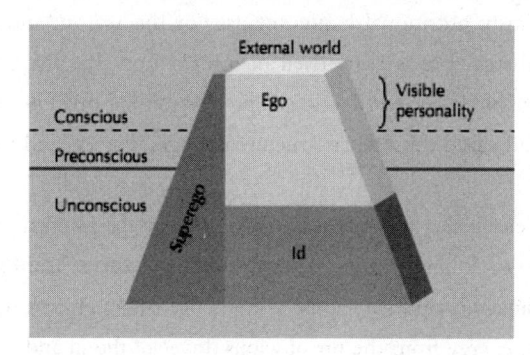

Figure 13.1
The relationship of the three structures of personality to levels of awareness.

The Development of Personality

We noted that the id strives to achieve pleasure by reducing tension. Freud believed that at different ages, human beings experience tension most intensely in different areas of the body, known as **erogenous zones**. He named the different psychological stages of development according to the zone that at a particular age is most sensitive to tension and most in need of tension-reducing stimulation.

The Oral Stage Freud proposed that during the first eighteen months of life, the most sensitive zone is the mouth. Thus the first stage is called the oral stage. The id strives to reduce tension in and around the mouth. This is achieved by sucking, even on a thumb or pacifier. The first thing that the child perceives and remembers is often related to when it is fed or how it might be able to obtain care and feeding from its parents.

The Anal Stage At about the age of eighteen months, the locus of gratification changes and the child enters the **anal stage**. The anal region becomes more sensitive, and the child derives satisfaction from stimulation in the anal region, either from the retention or elimination of feces. Also, parents begin to toilet train, their children at this age. Parents want to control when and where the child eliminates feces. Given the child's desires, this imposition of control comes at exactly the wrong time. A child's pleasure in retaining or eliminating feces at his or her choice of time and place and the parents' efforts to dictate new times and places can lead to conflict.

The phallic Stage   At about the age of three or four years, the genitals become the most sensitive area, and children derive pleasure from manipulating them. At this point, the child enters the **phallic stage**. Again, there is likely to be conflict with parental wishes. Parents typically try to curd behaviors such as masturbation or at least confine them to private settings.

Whether or not there is conflict about masturbation, the phallic stage is marked by the Oedipus or Electra complexes, a set of desires that produces conflict and discord within the family. The Oedipus complex is experienced by boys, and the Electra complex is experierued by girls. Freud proposed that all children experience a desire to have a sexual relationship with their parent of the opposite sex. Boys want to have a sexual relationship with their mothers, and girls with their fathers. These sexual wishes are one key aspect of the Oedipus and Electra complexes. The second key aspect of these complexes is a related wish to eliminate the parent of the same sex, who stands as a rival for the affections of the opposite-sex parent.

Like other desires emanating from the id, the Oedipus and Electra complexes are unconscious. The ego fears the consequences of expressing them and realizes that these drives cannot be satisfied directly. As a result, it holds the original sexual wish in the unconscious and seeks partial satisfaction for it. The ego obtains partial satisfaction by identifying with the parent of the same sex, the parent who has been the rival. Boys try to be as much like their fathers as they can, and girls try to be like their mothers. By being similar to the same-sex parent, children can vicariously enjoy the love that the opposite-sex parent expresses for the same-sex parent. For example, a little girl might be as much like her mother as possible and then enjoy the fact that she is very similar to the one the father loves. This process is known as identification.

In identifying with a parent, an important part of the personality is set in place. Many of our characteristic ways of behaving are determine by our identification with our mothers and fathers. One specific aspect of identifying with a parent is adopting, or introverting their values and morals. These incorporated values and morals form the third part of the personality, the superego, When the Oedipal conflict is resolved and the superego has been formed through incorporation of parental morality, the major structures of the personality are in place, and the phallic stage is over.

The Latency Period   Freud proposed that once the phallic stage is over at about five, there is a long, quiet period of psychological development in which no major unconscious drives press the ego for satisfaction. This is called the **latency** period, and it extends through late childhood to puberty. During this time children may learn a good deal about the world around them, other people, and their own skills and interests. However, there is little pressure from the id and little internal conflict.

The Genital Stage When the young person reaches puberty, or sexual maturation, he or she enters the final stage of development, the **genital stage**. In this stage, the person feels strong, adult, sexual desires for the first time. There may also be a reawakening of old Oedipal sexual and aggressive feelings. From this point on, the ego will have to work hard to balance the demands of the id for sexual gratification with the constraints of reality and the prohibitions and exhortations of the superego. The adult personality reflects how well the ego manages to do this.

The Concept of Fixation We have noted in discussing Freud's stages of development that the desires of the id change from age to age. However, Freud noted that sometimes individuals never lose their desire for a particular kind of gratification, such as oral stimulation. When this happens, the person is said to be fixated at the stage in which that kind of pleasure normally is sought.

What causes this fixation? According to Freud, when a child is either extremely frustrated in the pursuit of a pleasure or over gratified, he or she may become fixated. The person then becomes continuously concerned with obtaining the pleasure, and this concern becomes an enduring personality characteristic. For example, a person fixated at the oral stage will show continuous concern with getting some kind of oral gratification. Such a person might engage in behaviors that give direct oral stimulation, such as smoking or chewing oh pencils, or the person might symbolically pursue oral gratification. For example, he or she might want to acquire lots of money or knowledge, which may be compared to taking in nourishment through the mouth during the oral stage. A person fixated on the pleasures of expelling feces in the anal stage might be extremely sloppy, late, and disorganized as an adult. A person fixated on the pleasure of retaining feces might be excessively neat or orderly as an adult. Such a person might also be miserly, withholding money as he or she withheld feces as a child. Table 13.1 indicates the kinds of behaviors or characteristics that are associated with oral, anal, and phallic fixations. Thus the concept of fixation was Freud's way of explaining how important psychological characteristics and individual differences in personality development.

stage	characteristic
Oral	Optimistic
	Dependent
	Generous
	Demanding
	Sarcastic
Anal	Orderly
	Frugal
	Punctual
	Obstinate
	Rebellious
Phallic	Proud
	Self-assured
	Vain
	Timid
	Bashful

Table 13.1
(*Characteristics Associated with Fixations at Freudian Stages of Development*).

Based Fenichel (1945)

The Ego–Defense Mechanisms

As the "executive" of the personality, the ego strives to direct behavior in ways that satisfy the id, the superego, and the demands of reality. In attempting to achieve this goal, the ego develops several defense mechanisms. These defense mechanisms help keep the demands of the id and the dictates of the superego under control, and sometimes these mechanisms change perceptions of the external world so that reality appears less threatening. In doing so, the ego–defense mechanisms reduce feelings of anxiety and keep other feelings, such as guilt, conflict, and anger from overwhelming the ego. However, the ways of behaving and viewing the world that result from these mechanisms may not effective or realistic.

The defense mechanisms form a portion of the ego that operates unconsciously. People use them without being aware of doing so. In this way, the conscious part of ego is shielded from threatening perceptions, feelings, and impulses.

In discussing the defense mechanisms, we will divide most of them into three groups; (1) the behavior–channeling defense mechanisms; (2) the primary reality–distorting mechanisms; (3) and the secondary reality–distorting mechanisms. Other defenses will be noted as well.

Behavior–Channeling Defenses The three behavior–channeling defenses are identification, displacement and sublimation. These mechanisms direct behavior in ways that protect the person from conflict, anxiety, or harm. For the most part, they produce realistic behavior that the person feels is moral.

Identification is first used in resolving the Oedipal conflict. Later in life, people who are anxious about their behavior sometimes resolve their conflicts by identifying with another person who appears successful, realistic, and moral, trying to act as much like that person as possible. Freud regarded identification as a relatively healthy defense mechanism.

Displacement directs aggressive behavior away from someone or something that has aroused anger toward someone against whom it is both safe and morally acceptable to aggress. For example, a man who has been angered by his boss might fear being hostile toward him and might therefore honk his horn at a fellow commuter on the way home, shout at his wife, ridicule his soil, or kick his dog. In all of these instances, he is displacing aggression in a way that will not get him into trouble.

Sublimation entails expressing drives for pleasure or aggression in socially acceptable ways, In this way, the id obtains partial satisfaction while the superego's dictates are followed. For example, a person might sublimate his sexual drives into patenting highly respectable representations of nudes. Aggressive drives might be channeled into studying military history or playing contact sports. Freud felt that sublimation was extremely important for civilized existence and social achievement.

Primary Reality–Distorting Defenses One of the most basic ways protecting itself from feelings or perceptions that cause anxiety is simply not to feel or perceive them. The two defense mechanisms that protect the ego by keeping threatening feelings or perceptions out of awareness are repression and denial. They are called primary reality distorting mechanisms because they are the first line of defense. They protect the ego from even being aware of threats.

Repression entails blocking from awareness sexual feelings or impulses, aggressive thoughts or wishes, or feelings of guilt emanating from the superego. For example, a person who feds guilty for cheating on an exam may simply repress these feelings and not consciously experience them.

Denial is the defense mechanism used to keep threatening perceptions of the external world, rather than internal drives and feelings out of awareness. For example, a person living in California may singly refuse to admit that earthquakes threaten his life and home, or a smoker may deny that cigarettes are hazardous to her health.

Secondary Reality–Distorting Defenses Repression and denial simply push threatening feelings and perceptions out of awareness. However, other defense mechanisms often are called into play following denial or repression (White & Watt, 1981). The three secondary reality distorting mechanisms we will discuss are projection, reaction formation, and rationalization.

Projection involves perceiving personal characteristics in other people that you cannot admit in yourself. For example, a man might repress his own sexual feelings toward his brother's wife and then project those feelings onto her. Thus, the man will perceive that his brother's wife is sexually interested in him. Another common example is for people to project feelings of felt toward others onto those other people.

Reaction formation is consciously feeling or acting the strong opposite of one's true unconscious feelings because the true feelings are threatening. For example, a girl who hates her father may repress those feelings and consciously experience strong feelings of affection for him instead. These feelings are due to reaction formation.

Rationalization is a very common defense mechanism. It involves generating a socially acceptable explanation for behavior that may be caused by unacceptable drives. For example, a person may rationalize aggression by saying that another person deserved to be punished or harmed. A man may rationalize sexually harassing a woman by telling himself that she really wants to have sex with him, even if she does not admit it.

第三节 特质论
(THE TRAIT PERSPECTIVE)

In this section we will consider the trait perspective on personality. This perspective rejects the psychodynamic view that personality characteristics view that personality characteristics reflect unconscious drives, conflicts, fixations, and defenses. It assumes that personalities are defined by the various combinations of traits people possess. Traits are relatively stable characteristics of a person and can be measured. The trait perspective assumes that people's behavior in many different situations will reflect these personal traits, That is, behavior is generally caused by internal factors, traits, rather than external pressures and situations. Furthermore, this approach assumes that the appropriate way to study personality is to measure the amount of various traits which people possess, rather than inferring their unconscious needs and fears with projective tests. To illustrate this approach we will discuss three different personality-trait theories, beginning with an early theory that classified individuals into a limited number of psychological types. In addition we will discuss current controversies over trait-theory assumptions.

Type Theories

The trait perspective emphasizes individuality. It considers many different traits and the unique combinations that characterize individuals. Its predecessor, type theory, focused more on groups of people rather than on individuals. The basic assumption of type theorists is that individuals can be assigned to one of a small number of types or groups. All individuals within each type are assumed to be similar to each other on dimensions that define the type, and they are assumed to be quite different from individuals of another type. For example, a type theorist might hold that people can be divided into either active or passive types. Such a theorist would hold that active and passive people form two groups and that members of each group share many similarities.

One representative type theory was proposed by one of Sigmund Freud's most distinguished followers, the Swiss analyst Carl G. Jung. As a young physician, Jung admired Freud's work and began to research Freud's theory of dreams. In time, Jung became Freud's close colleague and was the heir apparent to the psychoanalytic school. However, after 1909, when Freud and Jung visited the United States together, both theoretical and personal differences separated them. From 1914 to 1939, when Freud died, they never communicated again. After their split, Jung went on to develop his own sophisticated theoretical system and published many books, including one called Psychological Types (1921).

In this book, Jung presented the idea that people could be grouped into one of two basic types, introverts and extraverts, on the basis of their attitude toward experience. Attitude was Jung's term for an individual's orientation toward experience. People who are introverted can be thought of as looking inward, while extraverts can be thought of as looking outward. The **introvert** is generally shyer and more withdrawn, cares less about other people, and is more oriented toward his or her own inner experiences. **Extraverts** are more interested in the people, objects, and events around them, and are more relaxed and cheerful around other people.

In addition, Jung discussed four functions, Jung's term for the ways the individual reacts to experience. Sensation and intuition are both methods, of taking in information about the world. Sensation and intuition are both methods of taking in information about world. Sensation refers to the perception of objects and persons using the five senses. Intuition is going beyond the five senses to seek the ultimate philosophical meaning of experience and its potential. Two other functions thinking and feeling, are used to make judgments about experience. Thinking refers to the use of reason in making judgments, while feeling refers to the use of emotions and values.

Generally, each individual will tend to rely primarily on one function, although Jung felt that the other functions could develop as the person matured. Combining the distinction between the introversion−extraversion attitude with the four functions produces, eight types in all, such as the introverted−feeling type. Interestingly Jung considered himself an introverted−intuitive type.

Jung's work was an ambitious attempt to understand personality in terms of the characteristics of different types of people. However, this perspective has changed considerably since Jung's early work. We will see how in the next section on trait theories.

Trait Theories

The primary assumption of any trait theory is that personality can be described in terms of how much of various traits individuals possess. Most modem trait theories owe a great deal to the pioneering work of Gordon All port (1961), All port contributed to the study of individuals and their traits from the 1930s through the 1960s, We will consider his contribution first. Then we discuss the theories of Hans Eysenck and Raymond Cat tell.

All port's Trait Theory All port thought of traits as internal structures that direct the behavior of an individual in consistent and characteristic ways. He distinguished several different kinds of traits. First, he distinguished common traits from unique traits, depending on whether they characterized many people or few. Second he distinguished cardinal, central, and secondary traits, depending on how pervasively they manifested themselves in an individual's personality. Common traits are characteristics such as friendliness or dominance, which are common to many people and on which individuals can be compared. For example, responsibility is a common trait. One can measure the extent to which different people show it. More important than common traits, All port felt, were what he called unique traits. These are unusual traits or trait combinations that characterize individuals and give them their unique personalities. They can include a particular style of humor or wit, a unique kind of ebullience and optimism, or a deep and crude cynicism and hostility that is hewn under pressure.

Both common and unique traits can be either cardinal, central, or secondary, depending on how pervasively they are manifested. The most pervasive of a person's characteristics are said to be cardinal traits. These traits direct behavior in consistent ways in many situations and thus make those situations "functionally equivalent" . That is, a cardinal trait leads a person to behave in similar ways in very different situations. For one individual, assertiveness may be a cardinal trait.

Such a person might be loud and active with a friend, authoritative with a sub-ordinate in a work situation, bold and outgoing with strangers, self-satisfied when praised. Thus, if assertiveness is a cardinal trait, it will show up in many different situations and will be an enduring characteristic of the person.

People may have only a few cardinal traits but several central and secondary traits. Central traits are similar to cardinal traits but are not as consistently manifested. Some common central traits are shyness, optimism, cheerfulness, and introversion There are unique central traits as well. Secondary traits are only seen in particular situations or at particular times. They are important characteristics of individuals, but they are not as pervasive as central or cardinal traits. Instead, they help give a more complete picture of the person.

Eysenck's Studies of Personality Traits Hans Eysenck is an English psychologist who has spent the last three decades studying the basic dimensions of personality. Using the techniques of factor analysis to analyze many measures of personality, behavior, and self-reported feelings and beliefs, Eysenck concluded that there are two basic dimension of personality (Eysenck, 1953). The first is the key dimension identified many years before by Jung, introversion versus extraversion, but Eysenck defines these traits slightly differently. Introversion according to Eysenck is comprised of reserve, lack of sociability, caution, and emotional control. Extraversion is comprised of sociability, activity, daring, and expressiveness. There may be few, if any, perfect introverts or extroverts, but there is an introversion-extraversion dimension. People may be near one of the extremes or at any point between them.

Eysenck's second dimension is stability versus instability, sometimes called neuroticism. The stable individual is well-adjusted, calm, relaxed and easygoing. The unstable or neurotic person is moody anxious, restless, and temperamental. Different individuals can be characterized on the basis of how much introversion-extraversion and how much stability they show in their personalities. All of your friends and classmates can be located on these dimensions.

Cattell's Basic Personality Traits   The psychologist Raymond B. Cattell has been an active investigator of personality traits for three decades (Cattell, 1950, 1966, 1973). He has argued that it is very important to find ways of measuring personality traits. He has been concerned with identifying the traits that people share and the traits that make them distinct. He has gathered many measures of traits through behavioral observation, records of people's life histories, questionnaires, and objective tests. He has then used factor analysis to assess these traits. In his work, Cattell found that two different kinds of traits, surface traits and source traits, underlie individual differences in personality.

Surface traits are reflected in consistent patterns of behavior, such as curiosity, altruism, and realism. The deeper source traits give rise to surface traits. These are characteristics such as dominance or submissiveness, or ego-strength, the capacity to withstand pressure. In various combinations and interactions, these source traits cause people to display surface traits. For example, ah individual with dominance and ego-strength as source traits might show surface traits such as persistence and leadership in decision-making situations. An individual with these source traits might have the surface a good military commander.

On the basis of his extensive research, Cattell concluded that sixteen basic source traits underlie individual differences in behavior. Cattell has developed a questionnaire that measures how people stand on these traits. We will discuss this questionnaire and the traits it measures in the next section.

Evaluation of the Trait Perspective

The findings of Eysenck and Cattell are consistent with Jung's introversion–extraversion distinction and other research that has attempted to define the basic trait dimensions of personality. For example, Norman (1963) has found the following to be basic traits: extraversion, agreeableness, conscientiousness, emotional stability, and cultural interest.

Despite these consistent findings, social–learning theorists, who we will discuss in the next section, have recently criticized the trait perspective. They feel behavior is caused more by external factors or the characteristics of specific situations, than by internal factors, or personality traits. All port argued that traits render situations functionally equivalent, and that people will consistently manifest their traits in different situations. The critics, as we shall see, argue that this has not been empirically demonstrated. For example, the critics argue that labeling an individual "aggressive" or "responsible" does not really predict how he or she will act in a specific situation. Will an aggressive woman blow her horn in traffic jams, be rude to waitresses, or be insensitive to her employees? The critics of the trait approach suggest that the answer is probably "not always" . They feel that human beings are too unpredictable for the simple listing of their traits to have much meaning.

In this section we will consider four different kinds of research that address the question of whether people's behavior is consistently related to personality traits. This research considers whether people behave consistently over time, whether they behave consistently across situations, whether some people are more consistent than others, and whether people are consistent if both traits and situations are considered together.

Consistency Across Time   The most impressive evidence in support of trait theory comes from studies of how people behave over a long time period. These kinds of studies are called longitudinal studies. An important study of 100 subjects who were tested and retested over twenty-five years found high levels of consistency on some important traits. Men showed consistent levels of dependability, emotional control, and aesthetic interest. Woman showed the same degrees of submissiveness, gregariousness, and nonconformity over time (Block, 1971). Thus, according to these studies, people are consistent. However, such studies do not show that we are all consistent all the time in all ways.

Inconsistency Across Situations   One of the leading critics of the trait approach has been Stanford University psychologist Walter Mischel (1968; 1980). Mischel reviewed research on peopled behavior in different situations and found that there is a rather low degree of consistency. For example, the person who is honest in one situation, for example, school, may not be honest at home. Similarly, people can show varying amounts of dependency, self–control, and aggressiveness in different situations. Mischel also reports that the correlation between a person's standing on personality tests and his or her behavior in specific situations is relatively low. That is, even if a person has a high score on a trait like extraversion, you cannot be sure that he or she will wave to a neighbor.

Mischel's work suggests that an individual's high or low standing on various traits is not always a good predictor of behavior. Many other factors determine how people act. One of these factors is individual differences in consistency.

Individual Differences in Consistency   When you think of specific people, for example, your mother, your best friend, or your favorite professor, you do not think of how they stand on all the important traits that researchers have investigated. Rather, you tend to think of them in terms of several conspicuous traits and trait combinations that really make them special. Perhaps it's your father's smile, his unending patience, and his ability to become even more calm and caring in stressful situations. You would expect him to be consistently patient in many different situations, but perhaps not consistently happy of outgoing. In other words, we expect certain people to be consistent in certain ways but not others. Bam and Allen (1974) have conducted research showing just this kind of consistency—different people are consistent, and inconsistent, in different ways.

Bam and Allen asked subjects whether they considered themselves consistent on various traits. For example, some subjects, said that they were consistently friendly but not consistently conscientious. Others said the opposite. Some people felt consistent on both traits, some on neither. Bam and Allen found that those who described themselves as consistently friendly were indeed consistent in various situations. Reports from these subjects' parents and peers correlated highly with ratings obtained from direct observation of subjects' behavior. For people who did not rate themselves as consistently friendly, the correlation between reports by others and direct observation was much lower, about the level found by Mischel.

What does the research into consistency tell us? People are probably consistent in some ways but not in others. The ways in which they are consistent, and perhaps inconsistent, give people their individuality. Although traits can be shown consistently across time and situation, knowing a person's traits does not allow us to predict behavior in every situation. In order to fully understand how people behave we need to consider both the person and the situation.

Considering Both Person and Situation   Work by Magnusson and Endler (1977, 1980) suggests that three key factors must be taken into account in order to fully predict behavior. First, we must consider the traits of the person. Is the individual often hostile and aggressive, generally kind, or perhaps anxious? Second, we need to consider the situation as perceived by the person. Does the person perceive a situation to be threatening or merely competitive? Finally, we need to ask how the person generally manifests particular traits in particular situations. That is, what is the person's characteristic mode of response to a given situation? For example, Endler and Hunt (1969) and Endler and Rosenstein (1962) have identified fourteen different manifestations of anxiety in various situations. These reactions include perspiration, immobilization, nausea, and dry mouth. Their research shows that people's behavior in a particular situation can be predicted accurately if we know their traits, how they perceive the situation, and how they characteristically manifest their traits in such situations. In short, both the person and the situation need to be considered, as well as how varied the expressions of a trait can be.

第四节 行为主义观点
(THE BEHAVIORAL PERSPECTIVE)

The fundamental assumption of the behavioral perspective on personality is that the characteristics of individuals result from external events, especially reinforcement. As a result of external forces, people learn specific patterns of behavior in specific situations and generalized them to similar situations. Also, the behavioral perspective does not assume that people will be consistent. They may learn quite different patterns of behavior in different situations. Furthermore, though patterns of behavior learned early in life may persist, personality is not necessarily stable, People can have new experiences and learn new patterns of behavior that will change their personality. The behavioral view of personality as constellations of learned behaviors maintained by reinforcement was a reaction to the Freudian approach of postulating unobservable, unverifiable psychic structures and dynamics. It also contrasts sharply with both the psychodynamic and trait perspectives in its contention that changeable, external factory rather than stable, internal factors shape personality and behavior.

B.F. Skinner's Radical Behaviorism

One of the most forceful proponents of the behavioral approach is B. F. Skinner (1953,1969). Skinner believes that we can make a great deal of progress in understanding people by focusing exclusively on their behavior and the external forces that have shaped it throughout their lives.

Skinner's key concept is that behavior is determined by its consequences. Skinner's movement, the experimental analysis of behavior, uses the concepts of reinforcement, generalization, and extinction to explain in detail how behavior is shaped by consequences. The most important factor in shaping behavior, according to Skinner, is reinforcement. For example, a young boy who is reinforced for sharing rather than taking toys for himself will learn to share toys. Next, the boy may generalize his tendency to share toys and thereby share and cooperate in many other situations. Furthermore, even if his sharing behavior does not receive immediate reinforcement in every situation 9 it may still persist because it is on a schedule of partial reinforcement.

Skinner suggests that most behavior that we observe in people is maintained because it is reinforced in some way. The reinforces in a person's life situations may not be readily apparent, but the behavioral viewpoint suggests that if one looks carefully enough, one is likely to find them. Specifically, Skinner suggests that we must conduct a functional analysis of an individual's behavior. This means analyzing both situations and behaviors to identify the situations and behaviors to identify the stimuli that function as discriminative stimuli and reinforces.

One of the great advantages of the behavioral perspective, and especially of the functional analysis of behavior, is that it can be readily applied to change behavior. Once it has been discovered that a person's behavior is maintained by certain reinforces, these reinforces can be withdrawn, leading to extinction, or used to reinforce alternative forms of behavior. Such processes are known as behavior modification.

Social Learning Theory

Many psychologist have found Skinner's basic emphasis on behavior and reinforcement welcome but have found the exclusive focus on behavior too extreme. Among these people are the social learning theorists who have added to their behavioral account of personality many cognitive factors (Bandura, 1977). As we shall see, variables such as a person's expectancies and values are important in the social learning perspective on personality.

Perhaps the most important departure of the social learning theorists from strict behaviorism has been to argue that people can learn by means other than direct reinforcement. To account for this, they have devised the important notion of observational learning,. This idea holds that people often learn not only by having their own behavior reinforced but also by observing other people perform behaviors and receive reinforcement. These other people are called models. For example, from observing models we can learn how to serve a tennis ball, insult strangers, or draw tulips. Sometimes we can learn how to perform a behavior by simply watching another person perform it once. In other instances we must observe many times and practice the behavior on our own extensively, as may be the case in learning how to nurture others or be assertive.

Observational learning is one way we might learn behaviors without reinforcement, but reinforcement remains very important in determining whether a person will actually perform a behavior. A person may have learned how to influence a group but may not engage in this behavior until some kind of reinforcement is available. This is often enough to induce the person to begin performing the behavior. However, the person will also perform the behavior because of vicarious reinforcement (Bandura, Ross, & Ross, 1963). Vicarious reinforcement takes place when we observe another person being reinforced for an action. It often leads us to expect that we also will be reinforced for performing the same action. For example, if we see that one of our neighbors earns money for recycling bottles, we may engage in these behaviors too, assuming of course that through observation we have learned how to perform them.

In introducing concepts such as observational learning and vicarious reinforcement, social learning theorists have demonstrated that cognitive processes are important in a full account of learning. For example, we have to consider attention, memory, and expectancy to understand how people learn and to predict how they will act. In addition, social learning theorist Walter Mischel (1973) proposes that the following five "person variables" are important in understanding how people interact with their environment.

1. Competencies. Each person has different capacities and abilities. These may be mental abilities, such as intelligence, creativity, or memory; physical capacities, such as running speed or the ability to pitch a baseball; or artistic ability, such as singing, painting, or dancing. People's competencies affect what they can do and often what they attempt to do.

2. Encoding strategies and personal constructs. These terms refer to the ways people take in or

encode information about objects and events in the environment, and to the concepts or constructs individuals, use to perceive and categorize other people. None of us pays attention to everything or perceives everyone else entirely accurately. However, our perceptions, accurate or not, strongly influence our behavior.

3. Expectancies. We have already noted that expectancies are key variables in determining action. Because of our experience and behavior and what we see, hear, and read about others, we have expectancies about the consequences of our actions. Most important, of course, are expectations about whether certain actions will lead to reinforcement. If one expects that they will, one is more likely to perform them.

4. Values. What people value, or what they find reinforcing is critical in determining their behavior. Behaviors that produce the most valued outcomes for us are the behaviors we will pursue.

5. Self-regulatory systems and plans. Self-regulatory systems include self-imposed goals and aspirations, which affect behavior. They also include the standards by which we assess our behaviors. Many people regulate their own behavior by rewarding or not rewarding themselves for certain actions. Some students decide that they will treat themselves to a movie or a chocolate ice-cream soda after they finish each term paper: If they stick to these plans, they have good incentive to get their work done. Giving themselves reward for doing the work is likely to establish a behavior pattern that matches personal standards and leads to many valued outcomes in the long run.

Reciprocal Interaction: The Person and the Environment

Social learning theorists see people as highly active, especially as processors of information. This idea is best expressed in the social learning concept of reciprocal interaction (Bandura, 1977), which holds that the person and the environment affect each other. Clearly the environment affects us. We cannot ignore it. But at the same time our behavior changes the environment. For example, our friendliness produces similar reactions in others. A far different environment would be produced if we were cynical or arrogant. This implies of course that, if we wish, we can choose how we would like to affect that environment. We can try to affect it in ways that will make certain behaviors of ours more adaptive of reinforcing. For example, we can attempt to interest others in art, perhaps by showing them a few interesting paintings. If we are successful, we will have friends who like to discuss art with us, thereby creating reinforcers for our interest in art. In short, we respond to the environment but the environment responds to us as well.

Before leaving social learning theory, it is important to note converging developments in the behavioral and trait perspectives on personality. Whether or not the proponents of various approaches explicitly acknowledge it, agreement on the best ways to understand persons seems to be emerging. As you will recall, the behavioral perspective at first considered only observable variable and external determinants of behavior, such as reinforces. Then, this position was extended into the approach, which began to consider important "person variables" . In contrast, the trait perspective began by considering only the internal dispositions of a person but then integrated some consideration of situational variables. Thus, at present both social learning and trait proponents agree that internal and external variables must be considered in fully understanding human action. Social learning theorists still emphasize concepts of reinforcement and situational control, while trait theorists emphasize what is inside the person. But there is much more agreement now than in the past. There may be even greater shared understanding in the future.

第五节 人本主义观点
(THE HUAMANISTIC PERSPECTIVE)

The humanistic perspective highlights the ideas that, people's behavior controlled by their unique perceptions of the world around them and that people have the potential for growth. We will illustrate this perspective by discussing the work of Carl Rogers and Abraham Maslow, two leading figures in the humanistic movement. We will see that their emphasis is on the person's own internal world, his or her perceptions and feelings, and on the individual's capacity for self-actualization, or the full realization of all inner potentials.

How did humanistic psychology develop? It grew largely in reaction to the perceived imbalances of the Freudian and strict behavioral perspectives on understanding the person: Psychologists such as Rogers and Maslow believed that there is more to human behavior than the simple repetition of patterns determined by unconscious dynamics during childhood, as emphasized by Freudians, and that there is more to psychology than simply predicting and controlling behavior, as emphasized and controlling behavior, as emphasized by behaviors. They felt that there needed to be more emphasis on what a person is like as an adult, how people perceive the world around them, how they feel, how they understand and how they grow and develop their full capacities. In addition, humanistic psychologists feel that more needs to be said about the positive side of human nature. They feel that within every human being is the capacity for good and that there is a richness and depth to personality slighted by Freudians and behaviorists. Various psychological factors, especially pressures to conform and the need to gain approval, may suppress this rich potential. This made it even more important for humanistic psychologists to create a "third force". that is, a force that supplements the Freudian and behavioral perspectives, to explore human potential and to learn how this potential can be more effectively realized.

Self-actualization, or the development of all that one is capable of being or becoming, is a central concept in humanistic psychology. We will see in the theories of both Carl Rogers and Abraham Maslow that while self-actualization is a key goal, it can be difficult to obtain.

Carl Rogers

One of Carl Rogers' central concepts is that of the organism, or the individual person (Rogers, 1951, 1959). Rogers contends that the organism strives toward maintaining, enhancing, land actualizing itself. In doing so it is drawn toward, and evaluates positively, all those experiences, feelings, and behaviors that further this goal. In contrast, the organism avoids and values negatively experiences that constrict, reduce, or block development. In short, the organism has a strong, inner tendency toward enhancing and actualizing inner potential.

The enhancement and actualization of the organism does not happen easily or without interference. In growing up, the child may learn a set of values from his or her parents that restrict the tendency toward self-actualization. Parents do not allow their children to perform all the behaviors that feel good and seem enhancing to them. Behaviors such as hitting a sibling when angry, dressing exactly as one pleases, or singing loudly during a church sermon will not be approved by parents. Children have strong needs for approval and affection, or as Rogers puts it, positive regard, and they quickly see that receiving positive regard may be conditional on behaving according to parental standards. Thus, behaving in ways that promote self-actualization can conflict with the need for positive regard, cramping the child's self-actualization.

A further development is that children construct a self-image or self-concept consistent with the values they learn from their parents. They see themselves as being people who generally meet parental standards. When their behavior and feelings are consistent with parental standards, their self-concept is enhanced and they feel worthy. When they behave in unapproved ways they feel unworthy. Thus, the fact that approval is conditional on certain kinds of behavior creates conditions of worth. Feelings of being worthy, and of being a good person, exist only when behavior is consistent with conditions of worth.

What are the consequences of conditional positive regard, conditions of worth, and the self-concept? The organism may strive for experiences that are inconsistent with the self-concept. The self concept in turn may not recognize or accept these strivings. In this way the self-concept can frustrate or block the organism's tendency toward self-actualization. It will deny feelings or urges that are contrary to the learned rules of the self-concept. In this way there can fee a great deal of conflict between the two central aspects of the person, the organism and the self-concept.

How much opposition between these two aspects of the personality typically exists? It is difficult to answer this question because there are great differences between individual. In the well-adjusted or fully functioning person, ail the organism's experiences are admitted and recognized. They are seen as consistent with the overall self-concept. However, when there is substantial inconsistency between the self-concept and the organism, serious psychological problems can result. People may be out of touch with their internal worlds. They can be unable to admit what is inconsistent with their self-concept. Under these circumstances, anxiety and other disturbing symptoms may develop and therapy may be required. Rogers is perhaps best known for the widely used therapy that he developed from his theories. Its central concept is unconditional positive regard, which unlike conditional positive regard, fosters self-actualization therapy more.

Abraham Maslow

Abraham Maslow is another humanistic psychologist whose ideas have been very influential. He is best known for two contributions, his theory of the hierarchy of human motives, and his re-search on the characteristics of self-actualizers (Maslow, 1968, 1970).

The Hierarchical Theory of Motivation Maslow proposed a hierarchical theory of motivation in which "lower" needs had to be satisfied before "higher" ones could be addressed. There are five kinds of needs: physiological needs, safety needs, belongingness and love needs, esteem needs, and, finally, the need for self-actualization. We shall consider each of these needs in turn.

Physiological needs are basic needs such as hunger and thirst. People must satisfy these basic life needs before other needs can be satisfied. If they are not met, people will direct all their resources at trying to meet them. The next set of needs that are addressed, after physiological needs are satisfied, are safety needs. These include needs for physical safety and needs for psychological safety or security. Maslow thought that Children experience this need more than adults, but adults who experienced little safety as children may be highly concerned with safety when they grow up. They feel less safe than others in the same situations and direct much of their energy to building safety and security. This prevents them from trying to satisfy higher needs.

People who have satisfied their physiological and safety needs can attempt to meet belongingness and love needs. These form the third step in the hierarchy. These needs include the need to be accepted by and included in groups, and the need for affection from parents, peers, and other loved ones. People who feel loved, and who feel their needs to be included are gratified, can move to the next step in the hierarchy. People who do not feel that these needs have been met will focus their energies on being accepted and being loved. These people may conform excessively or act in other ways to gain acceptance and approval.

Esteem needs are next in Maslow's hierarchy. Essentially, these needs relate to a desire to have a positive self-concept. They include the need to be competent, to achieve, to be effective, and to be free, autonomous, and independent. In addition, esteem needs include the desire to have one's achievements and competencies recognized and appreciated by others. This recognition gives one the added capacity to be effective in interactions with other people. As with other needs, people who lack positive self-esteem will be excessively concerned with gaining recognition.

The final step on the motivational hierarchy is the need for self-actualization. This is the need to develop all of one's potentials and capacities and to be all that one can be. It includes the need to appreciate the intrinsic worth of our surroundings and to experience the world deeply. It also includes the need to grow in harmony with the world around us.

The need for self-actualization is an entirely different kind of need from the lower needs in the hierarch. Maslow refers to the lower needs as deficiency motives. They are all stimulated by a lack or a deficit. The person experiencing them strives to get whatever it is he or she feels is missing. On the other hand, self-actualization is called a being motive or a growth motive. With this need, no specific deficit needs to be filled. The person simply wants to be and to grow as fully as possible. The need for self-actualization is never satisfied, as the other needs can be, because more growth and experiencing of the world are always possible. The need for self-actualization pulls people toward positive states rather than away from negative ones.

The Characteristics of Self-Actualizes According to Maslow very few people satisfy all their lower needs and reach the state where they experience no deficits, but only the need to grow, develop, experience, and appreciate. One of the most important studies in the humanistic tradition is Maslow's investigation of individuals whom he believes were self-actualized (Maslow, 1968).

Maslow began by selecting historical and contemporary figures who were, in his estimation self-actualized. These were healthy people whom Maslow felt had fully used their potentials. They included the American social worker Jane Addams (1860–1935), the physicist Albert Einstein (1879 –1955), the German composer Ludwig van Beethoven (1770–1827), the psychologist William James (1842–1910), the American presidents Thomas Jefferson (1743–1826) and Abraham Lincoln (1809–1865), First Lady Eleanor Roosevelt (1884–1962) and American writer Henry David Thoreau (1917–1862). In general, Maslow found that these people had needs for safety, belongingness, love respect, and self-esteem and thus were primarily motivated to achieve self-actualization. He felt that they were concerned with fulfilling all their potentials and talents, and that, compared to others, they had achieved a greater knowledge and acceptance of inner human nature. More specifically, Maslow found these healthy, self actualized people to have the following characteristics when compared to others:

1. A superior perception of the real world around them;
2. A greater acceptance of themselves, other people, and their Environment;
3. Greater spontaneity in their feelings and actions;
4. Greater focus on problems and tasks around them rather than on themselves;
5. More detachment from mundane matters and a desire for privacy;
6. More autonomy and more resistance to social pressures to conform;
7. Fresh appreciation of all that is around them, and rich emotional reactions;
8. Increased identification with all of humankind;
9. Strong and intimate interpersonal relationships with a few other people;
10. More democratic, egalitarian, and non-prejudiced attitudes;
11. Superior creativity;
12. A more deeply developed sense of values.

While many psychologists have found Maslow's work of great interest, others have criticized it. Many feel that his selection of self-actualized people is somewhat arbitrary. They are all individuals who achieved great things and who fulfilled some potentials, but many of them had severe personal problems as well. Eleanor Roosevelt, for example, had Very distressing relationships with her husband and children, and William James and Abraham Lincoln both had many periods of deep depression. Not all of them had all, or even most, of the characteristics of self-actualizers. Moreover, many of these characteristics are very difficult to define objectively and to assess. This is true of many of the concepts in humanistic psychology, such as the self-actualization concept itself. Thus, while the humanistic perspective has played a very important role in encouraging psychology to consider the whole person and the way he or she experiences the world and strives to grow, it lacks some of the empirical, objective research of the trait and social-learning perspective. In short, the ideals of humanistic psychology are notable, but its conclusions cannot be accepted uncritically.

第六节 人格特质的测量
(MEASUTING PERSONALITY TRAIT)

In this section we will consider several tests, or personality inventories that psychologists have devised to measure the extent to which individuals possess particular traits. Personality inventories differ from projective tests in two ways. First, they use unambiguous stimuli in the form of many true-false questions about personal characteristics or behavior. In contrast, the projective tests use stimuli that are purposely ambiguous and open to interpretation. Second, personality inventories are constructed and the results scored on the basis of research findings about the characteristics of individuals who give certain responses. Psychologists using projective tests, on the other hand, depend less on established findings and more on professional experience and in sight. For both of these reasons, the personality inventories are called objective tests.

The first personality inventors were devised many years ago, shortly after tests of intelligence began to flourish. During World War I, a test known as the Woodworth personal Data sheet was used to determine which soldiers were most likely to be disabled by stress in combat. Recruits were asked whether or not they had symptoms such as bad dreams or fainting spells. Persons with high scores were singled out for further evaluation. In the years since the end of that war many other tests have been developed. We shall consider three of them here: the MMPI and the 16 PF.

The MMPI

Probably the most famous and widely used inventory of personality traits is the Minnesota Multiphase personality Inventory, or MMPI. The MMPI was designed in the 1940s to help diagnose patients with psychological disorders. Since then it has been widely used with both normal and abnormal individuals to assess their personalities. We shall outline the steps involved in constructing the various scales of the MMPI and then discuss how it is used.

The Clinical Scales The first step in constructing the MMPI was to choose several groups, each made up of people diagnosed as having a specific psychological disorder, such as depression, hysteria, and schizophrenia, as well as a group of people with no previous history of psychological disorders, called the "Minnesota normal". Second, sets of true-false questions, or items (see Table 13.5) were submitted to the normal and each of the diagnostic groups. Third, items that were answered differently by the normal and any one of the diagnostic groups were identified and selected for inclusion on the test. In selecting items, no interpretation was made of the individual's answer. All that was significant was that the item distinguished the two groups. For example. if the item, "I like poetry" was answered differently by depressed individuals and normal, it would be included in the test. Items that were not answered differently were discarded. Fourth, new questions were tested and old ones were retested to find which ones reliably differentiated the normal from the diagnostic group. Finally, on the basis of this testing and retesting, items were organized into eight clinical scales, each one being composed of sets of items answered differently by the normal and a particular diagnostic group. There are also a masculinity–femininity (Mf) scale, which is composed of items answered differently by men and women, and a social introversion scale, which is answered differently by introverts and extraverts.

The Validity Scales   When personality inventories are constructed, the issues of reliability and validity need to be addressed just as in the construction of intelligence test. That is, there needs to be evidence that (1) people's responses are consistent at different times (reliability), and (2) that scores what they are intended to measure (validity). In addition, personality inventories present a special validity problem. Sometimes individuals responding to such a test will try to present a certain, image of themselves by lying or distorting their answers. Three scales, called validity scales, were thus added to the MMPI to measure these tendencies. They are the lie(L), frequency (F), and correction (K) scales.

Table 13.2 Some Representative Items from the MMPI

I am afraid of losing my mind
My way of doing things is apt to be misunderstood by others
I like to know some important people because it makes me feel important
I have had periods of days, weeks, or months when I could not take care of things because I could not get going
My mother often made me obey even when I thought it was unreasonable

The lie scale includes statements about standards of socially desirable behaviors that almost no one measures up to. An example would be "I sometimes feel angry". If people answer "false" to this statement they are probably lying. If a person endorses more than a few items on this scale, psychologists assume that the person is trying top har4 to present a favorable self–image. This suggests that other responses on the test may be distorted and that the results as a whole may not be valid for this individual.

The frequency scale consists of statements about negative or highly unusual behaviors. If persons admit to such behaviors of feelings, it probably indicates that they were careless or confused in answering the questions, or that they are "faking bad", perhaps to attract attention and help.

The collection scale is similar to the lie scale in that it considers how much people deny common but negative behaviors or claim praiseworthy but unlikely actions. However, the statements on the correction scale are less extreme. It measures not lying so much as the extent to people try to present themselves favorably and the extent to which they have adaptive psychological defenses. Moderate scores on the K scale are consistent with being psychologically healthy.

Using the MMPI   It is probably apparent to you by now how the MMPI is used. A person would score high on a scale, for example, depression, if answers to many of the scale–2 items matched those of the depressed diagnostic group. Thus a psychologist could compare a person's scores with those of individuals with specific psychological disorders symptoms and predict whether the person has those disorders.

While the MMPI was developed to determine the like hood that people were suffering from certain psychological disorders, it has been widely used with normal people as well. Normal people as well as disturbed people show typical; profiles or patterns. Profiles for both these groups can be very informative.

The 16 PF

The MMPI was constructed by the empirical method of selecting items that discriminate different groups of people. A somewhat different approach was taken to develop a test called the 16 PF. As part of his research into personality, Raymond Cattell (1972) identified sixteen basic personality traits, In addition, he developed the Sixteen Personality Factor Questionnaire, or 16 PF to measure the degree to which people have these traits. The questionnaire consists of more than 100 items to which people respond "yes" or "no". The scale has been shown to be a valid measure of people's standings on the sixteen traits. Cattell has done a great deal of research using the 16 PF, showing for example that airline pilots are more tough-minded, practical, self-assured and controlled than artists or writers. In contrast, artists and writers showed sensitivity, imagination and intelligence. The 16 PF is often used by high-school and college counselors to help students make personal and vocational decisions.

第七节 探求人格动力：投射测验
(EXPLORING PERSONALITY DYNAMICS:PROJECTIVE TEST)

According to Freudian and other psychodynamic theories, understanding peopled personalities may require indirect methods to get information about unconscious motives and conflicts, which subjects cannot report directly. Several interesting and provocative methods of gaining this kind of access are known as projective tests. In this section we will outline the general assumptions underlying the use of projective tests and discuss some of the specific techniques that are widely used.

The Assumptions of Projective Testing

The word projective holds the key to understanding these tests. In general it is assumed that people will project their needs, feelings, and conflicts onto ambiguous stimuli. Thus, many psychologists believe that if people are asked to respond to ambiguous stimuli such as inkblots or drawings, to give their associations to words, or to draw objects without specific instructions, their responses will reveal these unconscious needs, feelings, and conflicts. For example, if a person is asked to say the first word that comes into her mind she hears the word "mother", the answer will give a clue about her unconscious concerns. Thus, the response "rage" could be an indication of hostility between the subject and her mother. Two of the best-known projective tests are the Rorschach Inkblot Test and the Thematic Apperception Test (TAT).

Rorschach Inkblot Test In 1911 a Swiss psychiatrist named Hermann Rorschach published the first in a series of studies compiled later in a book called Psycho diagnostics (1942). These studies reported Rorschach's investigation of psychiatric patients' responses to ambiguous inkblots. Rorschach assumed that patients' perceptions of these ambiguous figures would reveal a great deal about their personalities and their manner of thinking. Unfortunately, Rorschach died at a young age, long before his work was complete. However, other psychiatrists and psychologists who were interested in projective testing continued his work.

Rorschach Inkblot Test consists of ten symmetrical inkblots, which are presented to subjects on cardboard cards. Figure 13.3 is similar to card 4. As you might imagine, different individuals see many different kinds of objects in this and other cards. Some cards generate certain common responses called "popular", Popular responses include witches, clowns, monkeys, cannibals, bats, Indians, baby faces, and climbing animals, In a Rorschach test, that people's responses reflect their particular needs, feelings, and conflicts. For example, a psychologist would take note if a person saw blood and destruction in many different cards.

The interpretation of responses is based on various scoring systems and the examiner's experience, that is, his of her careful comparison of one person's responses with those of many other people (Beck, Beck, Levitt, & Molish, 1961; Klopfer, Ainsworth, Klopfer, & Holt, 1954). Among the variables that are considered are the number of responses, how much human form is seen, and the ways colors (which appear in some cards) are perceived.

Many psychologists are satisfied that an experienced practitioner can make valid inferences use this test. However, because there is no agreed way to interpret any particular set of responses, the Rorschach test has been widely criticized. Some psychologists feel it constitutes lit–tie more than reading "tea leaves". Empirical studies have not shown that the Rorschach test has high, reliability or validity. Subjects often give different responses when tested at different times, indicating low retest reliability, and different psychologists make different inferences about an individuals personality based on the same responses (Buros, 1965).

Figure 13.2 *A sample card from Rorschach's test*

The Thematic Apperception Test

Another projective test that seems somewhat less mysterious than Rorschach's ink blot test is one that was developed by Christiana Morgan and Henry Murray (1935). This test is called the Thematic Apperception Test or TAT. The test is composed of nineteen pictures of people with ambiguous expressions in ambiguous situations and one blank card. The term apperception refers to the contention that people being tested do more than perceive what is there. They apperceive Which means that they bring their own interpretations into play in understanding the pictures. It is assumed that what people apperceive in the TAT cards will reflect central themes, that is motives, concerns, interests, and fears in their personalities.

Subjects are asked to look at a typical TAT card and other cards and to make up stories about what is going on in each picture. They are told each story should have a separate beginning, middle, and end, and that there should be a clear conclusion to the story.

One key assumption about the test is that the subject will identify with one of the figures in each picture, and will make this person the central figure or "hero". Then, many of the subject's own feelings will be projected onto this person. For example, if several heroes in a subject's stories have difficulties with their fathers or are extremely worried about sexual relations, an examiner might suppose that these matters are important problems for the subject.

The TAT is open to the same kinds of criticisms as the Rorschach. There are no objectively established criteria for interpreting overall personality structure from the TAT, and its reliability and validity have not been consistently demonstrated. Still, many experienced psychologists do feel that they get a great deal of information from TAT stories.

词汇（Vocabulary）

1. atlas   n. 图表集
2. converge   v. 汇聚、使集中
3. cramp   vt. 束缚
4. cynicism   n. 玩世不恭
5. deficiency   n. 缺乏、不足
6. ebullience   n.（感情）奔放
7. egalitarian   adj. 主张人人平等的
8. elimination   n. 消除
9. emanate   vi. 发源
10. erogenous zone   （与儿童的发展阶段有关的）性感带
11. fixation   n. 固结
12. genital   n. ［复］生殖器
13. gratification   n. 满足
14. immobilization   n. 固定、不动
15. intrinsic   adj. 内在的
16. interject   vt. 摄取、心力内投（与project相对）
17. longitudinal study   纵向研究
18. masculinity-femininity scale   男子气—女子气量表
19. masturbation   n. 手淫
20. nausea   n. 恶心
21. perspiration   n. 排汗
22. pervasive   adj. 遍布的、普遍的

23. practitioner   n. 开业者、实践者
24. preconscious   adj.& n. 前意识（的）
25. predecessor   n. 前辈、先驱
26. primary-process thinking   初级思维过程
27. profile   n. 外形、轮廓
28. provocative   adj. 引起争议的
29. puberty   n. 青春期
30. reciprocal interaction   交互作用
31. sublimation   n. 升华
32. thematic apperception test   主题统觉测验
33. the phallic stage   生殖器阶段
34. tuberculosis   n. 肺结核
35. unconscious   adj. 无意识的
36. vicarious reinforcement   替代强化

第十四章 人类行为
（HUMAN BEHAVIOR）

本章要点（Chapter Outline）

行为 (Behavior)
组织行为 (Organizational Behavior)
行为科学（The Behavioral Science）
人类行为的系统观（Human Behavior: a Systems View）
天性与教养的争论（The Nature-Nurture Controversy）
行为与环境（Behavior and Environment）
行为与态度（Behavior and Attitudes）
行为与认知过程（Behavior and Cognitive Processes）
行为与动机（Behavior and Motivation）

  行为是现代心理学研究的一个课题。作为心理学研究领域的行为通常指个体行为和组织行为。关于组织行为的研究是跨学科的研究，它关注发生在有组织的情景中的行为，它为高效率地完成集体目标提供指导。研究行为的行为科学是指不但能帮助我们理解组织行为，而且运用科学或准科学方法而产生知识的那些学科，主要包括文化人类学、社会学、社会心理学、经济心理学、政治心理学等。在组织行为的研究中必须明确的一个最基本的观点是：人类的行为过程是一个极度复杂、开放的输入—输出转换系统。

  导致人的行为的因素有哪些，这个问题引起天性与教养的争论。对这个问题的回答有三种答案，第一种是天性即遗传，第二种是教养即环境，第三种是天性与教养的结合。来自环境的经验被人们所知觉、加工、储存，从而产生行为。对人的行为产生重要影响的环境因素主要有文化、社会阶级及工作价值观等。文化对行为的影响最广泛、最深刻，不同的文化导致不同的行为模式。文化内化、文化适应、文化同化、文化迁就等术语都是专门用来描述文化对行为的影响的。社会阶级决定行为的类型是自我指导型还是遵从型。态度是产生某种行为的预先倾向，态度包括认知的、情感的、行为的三个方面。关于态度与行为之间的关系有两种不同的观点，一种观点认为二者之间没有因果关系；另一种观点认为二者之间有因果关系，并列举了与高成就者的行为对应的一系列态度特征。认知过程即思维过程是行为科学中极端重要的主题。知觉、学习、问题解决这些最重要的认知过程与我们的日常行为息息相关，是外界刺激与人类行为的直接联系者。动机是激发人类行为的内部力量，它影响行为的方向和效果。

第一节 行为
(BEHAVIOR)

"心理学"一词的英文是 Psychology，是希腊文 Psyche 与 logos 演变而成，前一词意为灵魂（Soul），后一词意为讲述（discourse），合起来意为心理学是阐释心灵的学问。到19世纪末，科学心理学萌芽，心理学一度被界定为是研究心理活动或意识的科学。20世纪初，美国心理学家华生（John B. Watson, 1878—1958）反对将意识作为心理学的研究对象，1913年创立了行为主义（behaviorism），认为心理学是研究行为的科学，当时出版的心理学教科书一般都将 Psychology 界定为 The science of behavior 或 The science of the behavior of man and animals。这一观点在西方心理学界持续了四十多年，随着行为主义学说局限性的日益显现，到20世纪70年代，几乎没有心理学家会认为自己是严格的行为主义者了。心理学的定义也改变为：心理学是对行为与心理过程的科学研究，即 The scientific study of behavior and mental processes 或 The scientific study of behavior and experience。我们现在将心理学定义为："心理学是系统研究心理活动及其规律，以及以心理作为内在条件的行为的科学。"很明显，心理（包括意识）和行为都是现代心理学研究的主题。

行为（behavior）一词有广狭两种意义，狭义指人表现于外并且能被直接观察记录或测量的活动。广义的行为，除了上述可直观观察的外显活动外，还包括以外显活动为线索，进而间接推知的内在心理活动或心理过程，即内隐行为。实际上，人的外显行为与内隐行为是不可分割的统一体，内隐行为即心理。苏联心理学中虽不用行为一词，但使用活动（activity）这一术语，认为人的心理是在他的活动中表现、形成和发展起来的。只有观察和研究人的活动，才能判断他的心理过程和心理特性。在这个意义上应当说人的心理和活动是统一的。因此心理学也研究人的各种活动（游戏的、学习的、劳动的和创造的活动）、活动的各个不同方面（熟练和作为任何活动的必要条件的注意等）。在现代心理学中，行为一词已远不是行为主义心理学中的含义了。

在这一章我们主要介绍关于行为的一些研究。

第二节 组织行为
(ORGANIZATIONAL BEHAVIOR)

Organizational behavior, as a field of study, concerns all aspects of human action in organizational or group context. It includes the effects of organizations on human beings and of human beings on organizations. From a pragmatic viewpoint, the concern is to determine how behavior affects the accomplishment of organizational goals.

The definition of organizational behavior includes more than the purely psychological aspects of individual action. A few of these additional implications are:

1. Organizational behavior includes the anthropological, sociological and economic, as well as the psychological, elements of behavior.

2. Organizational behavior explicitly recognizes factors such as structure and authority which are operative in organizations.

3. Organizational behavior introduces the utilitarian view of the common good.In other words, it conveys a normative connotation of the coordination of individual actions toward desirable goals.

These observations tell us several important things about organizational behavior. First, it is interdisciplinary and draws freely from the knowledge generated from a variety of sources. At the same time it maintains its own identity by concentrating on behavior that takes place in an organizational setting. Finally, it provides prescriptive guidelines for accomplishing collective goals effectively and efficiently. Whereas psychology, sociology, and anthropology seek only to understand and describe the actions of individuals and groups, organizational behavior is an applied field of study. It concern is to utilize knowledge of behavior in accomplishing desired results.

What we have proposed here is a complex field of study. If we are to analyze the subject effectively as we have defined it, we must understand the behavior of individuals, groups, organizations, and the environments within which they exist. Obviously, no one can be an expert in all these areas. If, however, we cannot become experts, we must at least become acquainted with a variety of disciplines.

第三节 行为科学
(THE BEHAVIORAL SCIENCES)

We learn about human behavior in a number of ways. Some things we know through our own personal experiences. We also learn about behavior by viewing it historically and through the more speculative insights provided by philosophy and theology.

In spite of the fact history, philosophy, and theology help us to understand human behavior, they are not considered part of the behavioral sciences. The term behavioral sciences is reserved for those disciplines that generate knowledge through the application of scientific or quasi-scientific methods. The primary emphasis of this text is on systematic findings and research, although at times there are inserted insights provided by studies that are more humanistic nature. Following is brief review of the fields on which we rely most in developing our understanding of organizational behavior. Cultural anthropology. Anthropology is the study of human culture. More specifically, cultural anthropology studies the history and evolution of human culture.

Research of this nature has implications for organizational behavior and management because it is useful in explaining the evolution of the value systems upon which individual and organizational goals are based. These factors can he instrumental in describing past and present trends in organizational goal formation. Moreover, this type of anthropological research provides assistance in implementing programs of planned organizational change.

Psychology.   Psychology is concerned with a number of aspects of individual behavior. A few of the more important areas include the cognitive or thinking processes of learning, perception, and problem solving, as well as personality formation, attitude development, and motivation theory.

The practical implications of pure psychological research are countless. A few of the more important include applied learning theory in the area of training and development, motivation research, and decision making as a practical application of human problem solving.

Sociology.   Sociology has been defined as the scientific study of human interaction and the way people relate to one another. Sociological research focuses on groups, and reaches into a number of areas ranging from the emergence of social institutions such as religion, education, and business, to the design of complex organizations.

Because we are concerned with human behavior in organizations, we naturally will concentrate on sociological research that has examined group interaction. We also will give attention to theory of organizational design.

Social psychology.   As name implies, social psychology is closely related to the fields of psychology and sociology. If we conceive of psychology as the study of individuals, and sociology as the analysis of institutions and organizations, we can think of social psychology as the study of interpersonal relations in small groups.

Organizational behavior draws heavily on social psychology because of the insights social psychology has generated in areas such as group dynamics, research methods, and more specific concepts such as conformity and group cohesiveness.

Other disciplines.   A number of other disciplines contribute significantly to our understanding of human behaviors in organizations. Economics, for example, provides an analytical framework for understanding human choice when constrained by limited resources. One area of increasing importance is economic psychology, which analyzes human choice and the effects of attitudes and motives on economic behavior.

Certain areas of political sciences also are relevant because of their concern for the scientific study of political behavior. Researchers have obtained impressive results in the areas of political psychology and voter behavior.

第四节　人类行为的系统观
(HUMAN BEHAVIOR: A SYSTEMS VIEW)

The process of human behavior is an extremely complex issue. It is also the most fundamental topic that must be examined in the area of organizational behavior.

Yet simple effective way to view human behavior is with an input–transformation–output system. The essential nature of this view is illustrated in the following diagram. The input–output formulation is important and valuable because it is consistent with the open–systems view of behavior. This open–systems concept does not view the individual as an isolated being; rather, it places him or be within an environmental matrix and allows us to easily see the relationship between the individual and the total environment.

```
                    ┌──────────────────┐
                    │  Transformationg │
        inputs ────▶│      process     │────▶ outputs
                    └──────────────────┘
```

Inputs, Transformations, and Outputs

In the general model proposed above, we see the individual as a being who takes certain inputs from the environmental matrix, performs certain processes on them, and behaves in a manner that results in outputs back into the environment.

On the surface, this explanation presents an unrealistically mechanistic image of human action. Therefore, it would be useful to reformulate the input – output model in behavioral terms. This is done in Figure 14.1 shall.

Figure 14.1
The process of Human Behavior

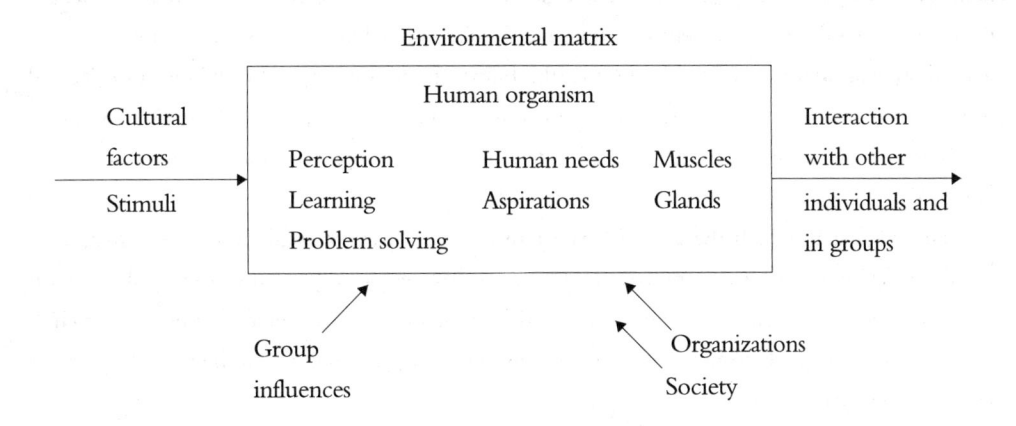

```
                          Environmental matrix
                   ┌──────────────────────────────────────┐
                   │          Human organism              │
  Cultural         │                                      │          Interaction
  factors          │  Perception    Human needs   Muscles │          with other
              ────▶│  Learning      Aspirations   Glands  │────▶     individuals and
  Stimuli          │  Problem solving                     │          in groups
                   └──────────────────────────────────────┘
                            ▲                  ▲
                           /                    \
                      Group                      Organizations
                      influences                 Society
```

The diagram illustrates that behavior begins with a stimulus or stimuli originating in the environmental matrix. The stimuli enter the human organism through the sense preceptors or the perceptual process. Perception is considered one of the human cognitive, or thinking, processes. Cognitive processes also include learning, judgment, reason, and so on. These thinking processes are instrumental in making external, such as attitudes, group norms, cultural factors, and similar phenomena, meaningful to and influential on the individual.

One's exposure to his or her environment, as well as certain inborn characteristics, the

• 323 •

emergence of important intrinsic factors such as needs, motives, aspirations, and so on. On the basis of complex interactions among cognitive processes, intrinsic factors, and effectors, actions result that cause people to interact with other individuals and in groups.

Thus, it is evident that human actions are determined by a complex set of environmental (experience-based) and hereditary factors. The relative importance of experience and heredity as determinants or behavior has consequently been a frequently discussed topic in the behavioral science literature. It would, therefore, be wise to examine the issue, at least briefly.

第五节 天性与教养的争论
(THE NATURE-NURTURE CONTROVERSY)

It is generally accepted by behavioral scientists that human action is caused, motivated, and goal-directed. Thus, behavior is neither without cause nor is it random. The question is, What causes human action and defines the goals toward which it is directed?

Kurt Lewin, a famous psychologist, provides a simple yet extremely useful functional explanation that can be expressed as follows:

B=f(P.E)

This expression states that behavior(B) is a function of the person or unique organism (P) and experience (E). As one might expect, not all researchers are content to say simply that behavior is both biologically and environmentally determined. Instead, various groups have sought to identify the importance of the two influential factors, and this has resulted in an interesting controversy.

The biological being. We all know that the human body is composed of billions of cells, and that each cell contains a nucleus, which in turn contains twenty-three pairs of chromosomes. These chromosomes are composed of genes, which determine the hereditary characteristics of the unique individual.

The manner in which the genetic characteristics of the parents combine in the formation of an offspring results in a variety of physical traits that, many people argue, can be quite influential on behavior. These traits can even be predicted with varying degrees of accuracy. Some traits, such as the color, are complex but predictable. Other traits, such as the general development of the nervous system, are less predictable.

In spite of the impressive results of genetic research, many, perhaps most, psychologists assign less importance to heredity than to experience in the formation of personality. shall examine this argument briefly at his point and say more about it later.

The experiential dimension. Human beings are exposed to numerous environmental influences from the moment of birth. Some people, for example, are born into deprived families and thus have limited educational opportunities, varying cultural value systems, and so on. Some people, on the other hand, have the best of everything from the beginning and thus develop in another way.

Many psychologists are quite insistent that family influences, group interactions, and similar factors are much more influential on behavior than heredity is. In fact, one researcher states clearly that "psychological development is fully dependent on stimulation from the environment."

A synthesis. The story is told that Abraham Maslow, early in his career, had the opportunity to work with the great psychologist E. L. Thorndike at Columbia University. One of Maslow's first assignments as Thorndike's assistant was to work out the percentage of human behavior resulting from heredity and the percentage resulting from experiential factors. Because he knew that behavior is caused by an interaction of both factors and was unable to work on anything that bored him, Maslow thought the project was "silly" and wrote Thorndike a note saying that he could not do the research because it was not worth doing.

Other people have experienced the same reaction although few have been so bold in expressing their views. However, Theodosius Dobzhansky argues specifically that all important traits are the result of the interaction of heredity and experience, so that any attempt to deal with them independently is untenable.

From the perspective of the behavioral sciences, perhaps the really important point is that, given the present state of knowledge, little can be done to alter biological properties. More success can be obtained in examining and understanding the environmental matrix.

第六节 行为与环境
(BEHAVIOR AND ENVIRONMENT)

When we suggest that experience, and the environmental forces contributing to this experience. influence behavior, we are admitting the importance of learning in the development of human behavior. A discussion of learning, however, necessitates an analysis of several other cognitive processes, such as perception and problem solving. At this point, we shall simply acknowledge that the human organism receives stimuli from various environmental forces as illustrated in Figure 14.1.These forces are perceived, processed, and stored, so that unique situations can evoke them, and past experience can be used for appropriate response relative to the individual's goals. At this point we shall look at some of he influential factors.

Culture

Culture is the broadest category of forces that influence behavior and, to some extent, includes all the other factors the environmental matrix. This is true because, as one writer notes, culture encompasses the "complex whole which includes knowledge, belief, art, morals, law, custom, and any other capabilities and habits acquired by man as a member of society". In line with this definition. Berelson and Steiner itemize the following four characteristics of culture.

    1. Culture is learned behavior. One acquires culture through his or her exposure to it over time.

    2. Culture is shared with others. In a given society, all, or most, members behave in a similar manner and share similar values.

3. Culture influences the manner in which biological needs are satisfied. All people require shelter. However, in a primitive society the shelter may be a cave, whereas modern men and women live in high-rise apartments.

4. Culture is consistent. All parts of the culture fit together in certain important ways.

Anthropologists use a rather specialized vocabulary to discuss various aspects of culture. For example, enculturation is the process by which a person is molded by a particular culture. When a person leaves the home or parent culture and changes to adapt to a new culture, the process is known as acculturation. When a person is integrated into a particular culture, assimilation takes place. If people do not completely integrate themselves into the culture, they may accommodate the culture on important matters so as to avoid conflict.

Numerous studies have been completed in an effort to specifically determine what factors within the broader culture are influential and how the influences actually emerge. At this point we shall briefly review a few of the more definitive influences.

Some evidence. Because it is often easier to see variations in cultures displaying gross differences, it is probably not surprising that much of the research on cultural influences has been done by examining behavioral patterns in divergent societies. Barry Richman has raised a number of interesting questions concerning the significance of cultural variables and their influence on organizational behavior. The really important aspect of this research is the way in which Richman identifies the variables that are likely to become operative. Two of the more important are sociological constraints (attitudes toward authority, the perceived value of achievement, and so on) and educational constraints (literacy levels, attitudes toward education, amount of formal education, and so on). Although Richman suggests that over time cultures may converge, differences certainly exist in the short run. Thus, cultural factors are sure to continue in their role as important determinants of managerial behavior and organizational goal accomplishment..

More specifically, some researchers have looked at the manner in which culture can influence such fundamental processes as the ways in which people perceive reality. For example, research suggests that natives of Western societies are more familiar with three-dimensional structures that have straight lines and right angles than are natives of other cultures.

Some useful insights have also been offered relating a culture's view of authority and family structure. In Germany, where the father is the dominant figure in the family, management practices tend to be more authoritarian. In England, the more cooperative attitudes of inter-organizational relations are associated with the mother's primary position in the family. Finally, in America, where the family is more child oriented, the responsibility of organizations for "servicing" individual needs has been emphasized.

All this illustrates one important point. Cultural factors can and often do result in differing behavioral patterns. The reason is easily explained in anthropological terms. The culture is instrumental in forming concepts of what should and should not be done in given situations and thus determines, to a great extent, the values possessed by a group of people. More, however, must be said of specific ways in which these values influence behavior in organizations.

Social Class And Work Values

Socialization may be viewed accurately as the process through which a culture bestows its values on an individual or group. This begins at birth and continues until death. The family is probably the first source of socialization, and the values the family conveys to its members are related to a variety of factors.

Social class has long been recognized as an important determinant of work values. Research studies have clearly illustrated the ways in which social class can influence one's orientation toward work. Based on the result of empirical data. Leonard Pearlin and Melvin Kohn argue that individuals exposed to a high social class position develop greater self-direction, while those from lower social positions tend more to conform to established traditions and norms. The dynamics of the process are explained by the fact that self-direction is consistent with an occupational system based on the assumption that one can accomplish what one desires to achieve. Conformity is based on an occupational system founded on the dangers of stepping out of line. Thus, it seems that a person's social environment may significantly influence how one relates to the authority structure of organizations.

Parent societies may also influence the degree of alienation one experiences from the institutional framework to which that person is subjected. One study illustrates how conflicts can develop between a person's orientation toward social institutions and the requirements of a given job situation. In this particular formulation, a distinction is drawn between a universalistic and particularistic orientation. The former refers to a view, such as that held by many people in the United States, that advocates an institutionalized view toward the good of society. The latter refers to a friend-directed view with less devotion to the common good. The results of the study illustrate how particularistic outlooks displayed by Mexicans resulted in alienation of these people when they were exposed to the work environment of a bank that was built on universalistic values. People from a more common middle-class American background, on the other hand, were not alienated in a universalistic setting that was consistent with their social value system.

第七节 行为与态度
(BEHAVIOR AND ATTITUDES)

Attitudes are defined as predispositions to react in some manner to an individual or a situation. The term is frequently equated with opinions, although an opinion can be more specifically defined as an expression of an evaluation or judgment with regard to a situation one confronts.

Conceptually, attitudes develop as illustrated in Figure 14.2. It is easy to see from the diagram that attitudes evolve from one's past experience and from the forces evoked from die individual's present environmental matrix. Of course, these two factors are not completely independent, in that the environmental matrix surrounding past experiences may be quite similar to the matrix operative in the present. Attitudes then become important aspects of past experience. However, the fundamental questions concerning us in relation to organizational behavior are. How do attitudes influence human action? and how can we measure these important forces?

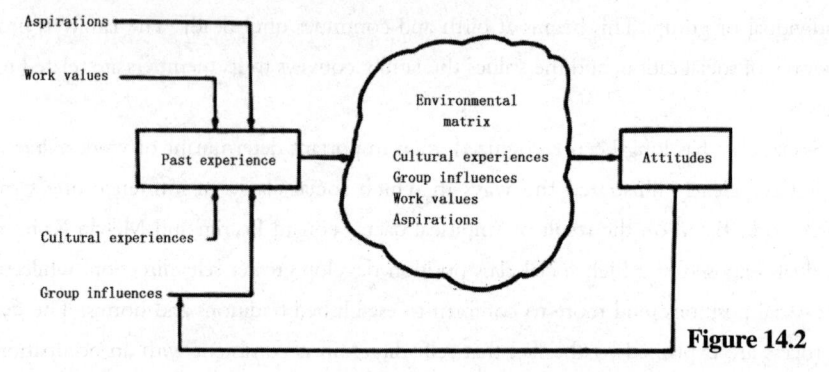

Figure 14.2

Discussions concerning attitudes generally revolve around three attitude components. The first is the cognitive, the perceptual process through which attitude objects (persons, places, things, and so on) are made known 10 individuals. In this chapter our emphasis has been on the second, or effective component, which relates to the reasons behind a person's feelings of good and bad. likes and dislikes and so on. Now we shall look briefly at the third, or behavioral component which is a person's action tendency toward an attitude object.

Several early studies in the behavioral sciences raised serious questions about the existence of any causal relationship between attitudes and behavior. Lapiere, for example, illustrated how innkeepers' apparent attitudes toward Oriental people vary substantially from their actions. In his study, the researcher was consistently refused reservations when he wrote letters stating that Orientals would be in the visiting party. However, when he actually appeared with Orientals and asked for accommodations, he was not refused.

Another study by Minard revealed interesting differences among reactions toward blacks on and off the job. According to Minard, of the coal miners studied, about 20 percent were free from prejudice on and off the job: this group interacted with blacks in the mine and in the community. Another 20 percent were prejudiced in both situations. The remaining 60 percent displayed an obvious inconsistency in behavior. In the mine, the miners acted as if they were free from prejudice. After work, however, their behavior changed, and while they were in the community their behavior appeared motivated by distinct race consciousness.

Frame 14.1

Attitudes Aad Action

Attitudes enable the release of human potential, which includes Talent, Education and Motivation. This is what Howard Westphall, of the J. W. Newman Corporation believes. Attitudes, in this case, are defined as how individuals feel about themselves and the world around them. Consistent with this, the Newman. Corporation has developed fourteen attitude patterns that are observed in high-performing people. The patterns of thinking are:

Self-esteem The high performer's self-image perceives one's self as valuable, important, and capable of achievement.

Responsibility The high performer accepts responsibility for the outcomes of actions. When one is successful, one is proud. When one is unsuccessful, accountability is acknowledged and mistakes are corrected.

Optimism Achievers expect1 things to be better because they are convinced that they influence the course of events.

Goal orientation A sense of goal direction is important to high performers. The goal is constantly directing behavior.

Imaginativeness High performers are not bound by the past. Their imagination is full of all things they will cause to happen.

Awareness Since achievers are goal oriented, they are more perceptive to useful signs and collect more information about what is happening.

Creativeness High performers are always searching for new and better ways of doing things.

Communicativeness Emphasis placed on getting the message through to others.

Growth orientation The emphasis is always on pushing ahead rather than standing still and meeting the world of change head-on.

Positive response to pressure The achiever functions best in a time of crisis. The reality of pressure is accepted as a challenge.

Trust The achiever believes others want to achieve and is willing to provide opportunities for responsible action.

Joyfulness The high performer experiences a genuine enjoyment in what he or she actually does.

Risk taking Achievers appreciate the reality of uncertainty and expect nothing better. The objective is excellence, not perfection.

Newness High performers make decisions and engage in actions in the present because they want to and enjoy doing so.

Adapted from "Attitudes The Secret of Super performers" Industry Week, 21 January 1974 pp. 36–38.

On the basis of these studies one is inclined to conclude that there is no consistent and certainly no causal relationship between attitudes and action. Other research, however, shows something quite different. Sherif and Hovland illustrated how people who joined certain types of organizations (such as advocates of prohibition) displayed significantly different attitudes from members of other organizations. Thus, the act of joining specific organizations appears quite consistent with attitudes. In another study, it was found that attitudes about participation in student political activities were closely correlated to whether or not the participants actually voted in a student election shortly before the survey was taken. Thus, again we have the dilemma of conflicting findings and must search for a synthesis.

第八节 行为与认知过程
(BEHAVIOR AND COGNITIVE PROCESSES)

Cognitive processes are thinking processes. As such, they are extremely important topics in the behavioral sciences. Some of the most significant cognitive processes are reasoning, evaluation, and judgment. All of these are important in the day-to-day behavior of individuals. For example, research illustrates that, although they rarely admit doing so, decision makers in organizations use judgment to complement facts in arriving at ultimate choices.

Figure 14.3 The Behavioral Process

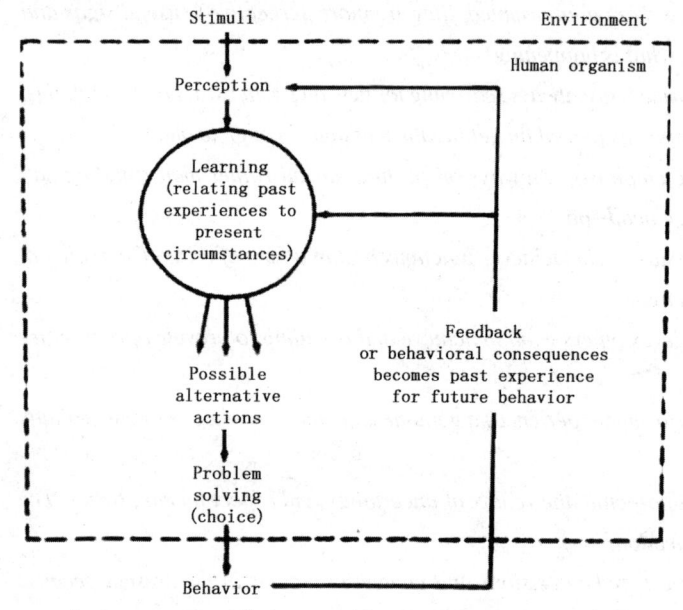

As important as all the cognitive processes are, we shall restrict our analysis to three of the most important. These are perception, learning, and problem solving, they are frequently referred to as the core **cognitive processes**. In reality, they form a direct linkage between the receipt of an external stimulus (or stimuli) and the resulting human behavior. This linkage is illustrated in Figure 14.3. In this diagram we see that the behavioral process becomes operative with the perception or reception of stimuli from che environmental matrix. The perceived stimuli are then assigned meaning through the learning process, at which point the individual's past experience is combined with the present circumstance and a series of possible responses are generated. One or more alternatives are then selected, and behavior results. This behavior may be an overt observable action or something less observable, such as the formation of an attitude. The consequences of the actions are then stored, influencing future perception and learning. Thus, we see that perception, learning, and problem solving are all core determinants and facilitators of behavior. Perception provides the link between the individual and the environment. Learning assists in providing meaning to unique and redundant stimuli. Problem solving is instrumental in determining the evoked responses.

第九节 行为与动机
(BEHAVIOR AND MOTIVATION)

To understand motivation, one first must comprehend the process of human behavior. It is for this reason that we discussed attitudes, needs, and cognitive processes before introducing this topic. Some behavioral scientists emphasize the importance of intrinsic forces in developing theories of motivation, while others place primary importance on cognitive factors. All, however, recognize the importance of both factors in formulating concepts of human action.

In very general terms, we can say that motivation is concerned with how behavior is activated, maintained, directed, and stopped. From a managerial perspective, part of a person or group to influence the direction and rate of behavior toward the accomplishment of organizational goals.

Analytically, we can illustrate the motivational process with the use of Figure 14.3. Here we see that the process begins with the motivational stimuli initiated by a manager, or by any other person wishing to activate behavior. The stimuli are then perceived by an individual. Perception, as we have seen is influenced by a variety of factors such as attitudes, personality, past experiences, and future expectations. Once the stimuli are perceived, they are interpreted according to the unique needs of the individual, and an information search is initiated. A series of possible courses of action is generated and evaluated, and a choice is ultimately made through the process of problem solving. The response is then evaluated by the individual, according to the intended result.

This process should illustrate the personal nature of motivation. At every point, the individual's uniqueness is important. Some people, because of their past experiences and aspirations, want money. Others desire fame, security, Or countless other outcomes. Frame 14.1 provides an unusual insight into the thinking of at least one production worker.

词汇 (Vocabulary)

1. accommodate   v. 文化迁就、容纳
2. acculturation   n. 文化适应
3. accuracy   n. 准确、精确
4. acknowledge   vt. 承认
5. advocate   vt. 辩护、拥护、提倡   n. 提倡者
6. alienation   n. (情感) 疏远
7. alternative   adj. 二者选其一的   n. 二者选一
8. anthropology   n. 人类学
9. aspiration   n. 志气、抱负、渴望
10. assimilation   n. 文化同化
11. authority   n. 权利、职权、权威

12. be content to 满足于
13. bestow...to... 把……给予……
14. biologically adv. 生物学地
15. capability 能力、才能
16. chromosome n. 染色体
17. cohesiveness n. 内聚力、紧紧地结合在一起
18. conformity n. 遵从性
19. conflict v. 冲突 n. 冲突
20. confound vt. 混淆
21. connotation n. 涵意、内涵
22. controversy adj. 争论、论战
23. consistent 一致的、连贯的
24. coordination n. 协作、配合、共济、同等
25. cultural anthropology 文化人类学
26. define vt. 解释、定义、限定
27. deprived adj. 贫穷的、被剥夺的
28. dilemma n. 进退两难
29. dimension n. 维度、方面
30. dominant figure 支配人物、起决定作用的人物
31. dynamics n. 力学、动力学、动力、动态
32. economic n. 经济心理学
33. effector n. 效应器
34. emergence n. 出现、浮现
35. encompass vt. 围绕、包含、包括、完成
36. enculturation n. 文化内化
37. environmental matrix 环境背景
38. essential nature 本质
39. esteem vt. & n. 尊重
40. evoke vt. 引起、唤起
41. evolve vt. 使发展、渐进
42. expert n. 专家、能手 adj. 熟练的、有经验的、内行的
43. feedback n. 反馈
44. formula n. 公式、程式、准则
45. function n. 函数、功能、机能、职责 vi. 运行、起作用
46. gene n. 基因
47. generate vt. 使产生、使发生
48. habit n. 习惯、习性、体质、举止
49. heredity n. 遗传、传统
50. human being n. 人、人类

51. the human race n. 人类
52. identify vt. 鉴别、认为……一致
53. image n. 示意图、像、心像
54. implication n. 含义、暗指、牵连、言外之意
55. inborn adj. 天生的、先天的
56. in line with 跟……一致、符合
57. innkeepers n. 小旅馆老板
58. insight n. 洞察、领悟、见识
59. instrument n. 仪器、器械、手段
60. intrinsic adj. 内在的、固有的、本质的
61. isolate vt. 隔离、孤立、分离
62. judgement n. 判断、审判、评价
63. matrix n. 矩阵、模型、来源
64. nervous system n. 神经系统
65. offspring n. 儿女、子孙、后代、结果、产物、幼苗
66. open-system view 开放系统观
67. operative adj. 操作的、有效的、起作用的
68. oriental adj. 东方人的
69. originate vi. 发源、发生 vt. 创始、发明、创作
70. philosophy n. 哲学、哲理、人生观、原理
71. physical trait 身体特点
72. political psychology 政治心理学
73. pragmatic adj. 实用主义的、重实效的
74. predictable adj. 可预言的
75. predisposition n. 预先倾向
76. quasi 类似、准、半
77. random adj. 任意的、随机的
78. redundant adj. 丰富的、过剩的
79. religion 宗教、信仰、有关良心的事
80. social psychology 社会心理学
81. sociological constraint 社会压力
82. speculative 思辨的、纯理论的、投机的
83. stimulus 刺激、刺激物、促进因素
84. tendency 倾向
85. theology 神学
86. to some extent 在某种程度上
87. utilitarian 功利的、功利主义的、功利主义者
88. variables 变量
89. voter behavior 选举人行为

第十五章 心理的发展
（PSYCHOLOGY DEVELOPMENT）

本章要点（Chapter Outline）
发展的概念 (Concepts in Human Development)
发展的规律性 (Principles of Development)
发展的理论 (Theories of Development)
认知的发展 (Cognitive Development)
社会性及情感的发展 (Social and Emotional Development)

"发展"一词是指个体身心整体的连续变化过程，不仅是数量的变化，更重要的是质的变化；不仅指向前推进的过程，也指衰退消亡的变化。本章主要涉及儿童心理的发展，即从不成熟到成熟的这一成长阶段。主要介绍一些西方的观点，包括儿童心理发展的基本规律，儿童心理发展的制约因素、认知及个性、社会性的发展。

第一节 人类发展的概念
（CONCEPTS IN HUMAN DEVELOPMENT）

Developmental psychology looks at changes that occur between conception and death. It endeavors to describe the nature of human characteristics at different ages, to identify predicable differences among different ages and sexes, and to explain the processes that account for developmental changes and differences. At a simple level, for example, developmental psychology describes what it is like to be a seven-year-old, how seven-year-old might be different from fourteen-year-olds, how seven-year-old got to be the way they are, and how and why they will continue to change. The information is obviously crucial to teachers, who must always be concerned with student's readiness, interests, and capabilities. Unfortunately, however, the information that developmental psychology has for us is not always simple and straightforward; it often must be qualified, and it is subject to a great many exceptions.

One of the factors particularly important to the developmental psychologist is the place and time in which individuals are born and raised. My son and I are clearly a case in point. we are as I have said, of different worlds; as developmental psychologists would say, we are of different cohorts.

A cohort can be described as a group of individuals who were all born within the same range of time. Thus, he 1940 cohort includes all individuals born during the year 1940. Thus, a cohort is initially of a fixed size and composition; it includes a specific number of individuals of both sexes and perhaps of a variety of ethnic and social backgrounds; and it cannot, after the time period that defines it has elapsed, grow in size. Instead, with the passage of time its size decreases as members die. and there are some predictable patterns of changes since male tend to die sooner than females throughout the world. Although there are 105 males born for every 100 females. The number of each still alive by early adulthood are approximately equal. And by the age of 65, only 69 males are still alive for every 100 females. These predictable changes, clearly have implications for understanding the lives of men and women.

From developmental psychology's point of view, the most important thing about a cohort is not that it includes only individuals who were born at the same time, but rather that these individuals have had a similar sequence of historical influences in their lives, particularly if their geography, social class, and other circumstances are also similar. and in interpreting the conclusion of developmental psychology, we have to keep in mind that a great many of these conclusions are based on research conducted with a small number of cohorts—often, only one—and that they might not be valid for other cohorts.

This chapter gives a brief overviews of some of what is known or suspected about human development. In order to clarify the issues involved in this discussion, four terms need to be defined: growth, maturation, learning, and development.

Growth refers primarily to physical changes such as increases in height and weight. These changes are quantitative rather than qualitative. That is, they are changes in quantity or amount rather than being transformations that result in different qualities.

Maturation, a somewhat less precise term than growth, is used to describe changes that are relatively independent of the environment. These changes are assumed to be closely related to the influences of heredity. In most areas of development, however, there is a very close interaction between heredity and environment. For example, Learning to walk depends on the development of certain muscle groups and on increasing control their movements(maturational developments)as well as on the opportunity to practice the various skills involved(environments; learning). An important illustration of maturation is the changes in early adolescence that lead to sexual maturity(puberty)—changes collectively labeled pubescence. Although their onset seem to be affected by environmental condition(menarche, the onset of menstruation, occurred progressively earlier between 1850 and 2970, apparently because of nutritional factors; see Frisch and Revelle,1970), the changes of pubescence are largely genetically programmed.

Learning is defined in terms of actual or potential changes in behavior as a result of experience. Thus, all relatively permanent changes in behavior that are not the result of maturation or of external factors whose effects are unrelated to environment(such as the temporary effects of drugs or fatigues)are example of learning.

Developments can be defined as the total process whereby individuals adapt to the environment. this total process involves growth, maturation, and learning.

第二节 发展的规律性
(PRINCIPLES OF DEVELOPMENT)

This section briefly summarizes important knowledge in developmental psychology. The summary takes the form of ten principles of development, each of which can be viewed as a concluding or explanatory statement. These principles are not an exhaustive summary of all of developmental psychology; rather, they have been selected largely in terms of their relevance to the teaching-learning process.

Nature and Nurture

Development is influenced by both heredity(nature) and environment(nurture). Both the meaning and the truth of this principle are obvious. What is not so obvious is the extent to which each factor contributes to development. We know, for example, that nature(heredity) is responsible for many of our physical characteristics, such as hair and eye color, facial features, and, to some extent, height and weight. But even here, the influences of heredity are not entirely simple and straightforward. While some characteristics(for instance, hair and eye color) do appear to be entirely under the control of our genes(Waddington, 1975), other characteristics(for instance, height and weight clearly) are also influenced by environmental factors.

The situation is far less clear in terms of personality and cognitive characteristics than in terms of physical characteristics. Thus, it has been extremely difficult to determine whether and how important qualities such as intelligence and creativity are influenced by heredity and the extent to which they can be modified by the environment. In attempting to clarify this crucial question, a large number of studies have focused on identical twins because, as Gould notes, they are "the only really adequate natural experiment for separating genetic from environmental effects in humans..." (1981, p.234). This is because identical(monozygotic) twins are genetically identical, a condition that is not true for any other pair of humans, including fraternal(dizygotic) twins. Thus, if intelligence, for example, is genetically determined, identical twins should have almost identical intelligence test scores(almost but not exactly identical, since we cannot measure intelligence very accurately). By the same token, the more people differ genetically, the less similar their intelligence scores should be. But if, on the other hand, intelligence is largely a function of the environment, ordinary siblings as well as fraternal twins should resemble each other about as closely as identical twins and far more closely than identical twins who are brought up in separate homes.

Many of the important studies of twins show that the correlation of test scores(a measure of relationship that ranges from 1 to +1) is lowest for those who are least alike genetically(unrelated persons) and becomes progressively higher as degree of genetic similarity increase. Intelligence is clearly influenced by heredity.

However, the correlations also increase with degree of environmental similarity. Thus, identical twins reared together are more alike in terms of measured intelligence than are those reared apart. Similarly, fraternal twins, who are no more alike genetically than are other siblings, nevertheless manifest higher correlations an observation most often explained by the fact that their environments are probably more nearly alike than are those of most siblings. Fraternal twins, after all, are of exactly the same ages and typically are subject to the same experiences at about the same time.

The conclusion, as we stated at the beginning of this section, developments is influenced by both heredity and environment. The two interact in complex and not clearly understood ways to determine what you and I become. What is most important about this principle, from education's point of view, is that many of our characteristics can be influenced by the environment. And while there is relatively little that we can do about heredity at this point, much of the environment still remains in our hands.

Different Growth Rates

Development takes place at different rates for different parts of the organism. This is not intended to mean that the left foot grows rapidly for a short while, then the right foot, and then one arm although from personal experience I know that some people do grow like that, and sometimes their development gets arrested at embarrassing stages. It does mean, however, that various parts of the body, as well as some aspects of personality and cognitive and perceptual ability, grow at different rates and reach their maximum development at different times.

The development of cognitive ability and personality traits ha been shown to be governed by this principle. Bloom(1964) found that for each personality trait, there is a characteristic growth curve. By the age of two and a half, half of a child's future height will have been reached. Half of a male's aggressiveness toward others is thought to be established by age three; and much of our intellectual potential has already been developed by age six, a fact that may be partly related to how and when the brain grows.

Investigations of brain development reveal several interesting and important facts. First, most of the neurons(nerve cells) that make up the human brain are formed during the prenatal period, although some additional neurons may form in the first few months after birth(Rosen–zweig and Leiman, 1982). At birth, the infant's brain weighs approximately one quarter of what it will weigh at its maximum, which is reached at about age 25. Most of the increase in brain weight between birth and adulthood seems to be caused by the growth of axons and dendrites(the elongated portions of the nerve cell, which permit neural transmission) and by myelination (the growth of a protective covering around the axon).

Second, brain growth too seems to be subject to varying rates. The brain does not grow at uniform rate between conception and birth, nor between birth and adulthood. Instead, it appears to grow in spurts. These growth spurts are reflected by increases in cranial(head) circumference. Examinations of head measurements have led Lewin(1975) to believe that there is a rather dramatic spurt in brain growth during the later stages of fetal development. Some rather alarming evidence suggests that this period of rapid brain development is a critical period during which the effects of malnutrition can be especially severe—as can also be true during the first few months of infancy, during which there is a continuation of the growth spurt(Parmelle and Sigman,1983). It is not surprising that in the majority of the world's undeveloped nations, where malnutrition is most prevalent, scientists have noted smaller than average head circumference among children(Winick,1976),

Epstein's(1978) examination of head circumference data leads him to the conclusion that significant and distinct spurts in brain growth take place during tour periods between birth and adulthood: two to three months; two to three years; six to eight years; and fourteen to sixteen years for males and ten to twelve years for females. He notes as well that these spurts occur during periods that correspond closely with periods of major cognitive change according to Piaget's theory and suggests the possibility that physical changes in the brain accompanying these growth spurts make cognitive development possible. Evidence to substantiate this supposition or to corroborate the consistency and significance of changes in cranial circumference is still scarce.

Another observation related to the principle of different growth rates is lateralization a term which refers to the fact that the two lateral halves(hemispheres) of the brain are some what specialized. For example, in the majority of individuals(95 percent of right-handed people and 70 percent of left-handed) the left hemisphere controls speech and other language functions, as well as reason and logic. And in the majority of people the right hemisphere is more concerned with the spatial and temporal—for example, are and music—as well as with the emotions. Thus, individuals who are logical are sometimes described as left-brain oriented; those who are more intuitive and artistic might be referred to as right-brained.

A number of researchers and theorists point out that our current educational practices emphasize left brain functions, as is reflected in our preoccupation with verbal learning, mathematics and science, and logic(see, for example, Sonnier, 1985). Arguing that our schools neglect right-brain functions, they present a number of compelling arguments for changing our educational fare and philosophy so as to educate both halves of our students' brains. The phrase holistic education has been coined to represent this point of view. Unfortunately, investigating the dual function of the brain has proven difficult, and much of what passes for information in this area may be more speculation than fact.

To summarize the second principle briefly: Development is not a uniform process for all features of an organism. To understand it, investigators are compelled to look at different aspects of development and at their interaction.

The description of growth curves for development has led Bloom(1964) to postulate a law that. if valid, is of major importance for education. It is given here as principle 3.

Timing of Environmental Influences

Variations in environment have greatest quantitative effect on a characteristic at its period of most rapid change, and least effect on the characteristic at its period of least rapid change (Bloom, 1964, p.vii). This principle is most clearly illustrated in the area of physical growth. It is evident, for example, that changes in environment are not likely to affect the height of subjects over age twenty.

On the other hand, dietary changes for children under age one could conceivably have a more significant effect on future height.

This principle also holds in the area of intellectual development. As mentioned earlier, brain growth seems highly vulnerable to malnutrition during a growth spurt, especially during prenatal and early postnatal development. In addition, several studies tend to confirm the principle. For example, a now famous study reported by 1951 examined the intelligence test scores of American blacks living in Philadelphia. Of two groups of blacks who had been born in the South. one had moved to Philadelphia prior to grade one. and the second had moved at grade four. The first group showed much greater increases in intelligence test scores than the second. In addition, the greatest changes occurred daring the first few years. A third group of blacks, born and raised in Philadelphia, scored higher than the other two groups at all grades. The implications for teaching are obvious. Stimulating educational particularly if they provide children with success and not with failure, may exert a lasting influence on intellectual development.

Sequential Development

Development follows an orderly sequence. In fetal development the heart appears and begins to function before the limbs reach their final form; the lips and gums form prior to the nasal pas-sages; the regresses before the permanent tooth buds are formed; and so on.

In motor development, children can lift their chins from a prone position before they can raise their chests; they can sit before standing; they can stand before creeping; and they can creep before walking (Shirley, 1933).

In intellectual development, the same principle can be seen to apply, although the sequences are less obvious and the stages less distinct. Piaget s theory is based on the assumption that hu-man development is characterized by distinct sequential stages. Piaget's analysis of the evolution of play behavior in children offers one example of sequential development in a nonvoter, non-physical area. The illustration selected deals specifically with the evolution of game rules in the child' an evolution that Piaget describes as comprising two aspects, both of which exhibit the orderly sequence of principle 4. On the one hand, there is the child's actual behavior in game sit-uations; on the other hand, there are verbalized notion of rules. These do not necessarily agree.

The following descriptions are based on observations of children playing the game of marbles.

Stage I (1 to 3 years): During Stage I. children behave as though there are no rules. Their marble games are those of free play.

Stage II (3 to 5 years): At around the age of three children begin to imitate aspects of the rule regulated behavior of adults. They think they are following rules, but in reality they are making their own. My son, when he, delighted in throwing toy cars across the room and then shrieking

"Sixteen points" . When his sister did likewise he occasionally allowed her to earn sixteen points, but more often than not he insisted that the car either went too far or not far enough. The rules changed continuously but aspects of the behavior were rule bound in a loose sense (for example, the notion of points is derived from adult games).

Stage III (5 to 11 or 12 years): In the third stage, children play in a genuinely social manner.

Rules are mutually and rigidly adhered to by all players. They are never changed.

Stage IV (from 11 or 12 years): The fourth stages is marked by a more complete understanding of the purpose and origin of rules. They are occasionally modified in the course of playing games.

Interestingly, while these four stages describe the way children play games, they do not describe the child's verbalized notions of rules. These follow a different sequence:

Stage I (1 to 3 years): The verbal notions of rules at this stage correspond to behavior. Children know no rules and play according to note.

Stage II (3 to 5 years): At Stage II. children play cording to rules, but change them continually. They make them up as they go along. If asked about rules, however, they go along. If asked about rules, however, they describe them as being external and unchangeable, and readily admit that new rules would be quite unfair.

Stage III (5 to 11 or 12 years): Whereas children at this stage follow rules rigidly without ever changing them, they believe that rules come from other children, and that they are, in fact, changeable.

Stage IV (from 11 or 12 years): Both in behavior and in thought, children at this stage completely understand and can modify rules.

These observations are typical of the method. Piaget employed in gathering data for the development of his theory. Two points crucial to an understanding of that theory are summarized in the next two principles.

Continuous Development

Development is continuous rather than discrete. In other words, stages of development are not separate but follow one from the other with no clear out break in the sequence. This means that the ages assigned to various steps in a developmental sequence are simply approximations.

This principle also recognizes the fact that, as a continuous process, development is relatively smooth and orderly. There are occasional spurts in various areas, but in the main the children's competence increases gradually enough that changes often go unnoticed by parents and teachers. Nevertheless, knowledge of children's capabilities and interests at different ages can be of considerable value for teachers in suggesting appropriate activities, instructional methods, and so on.

Individual Differences

There is a great deal of variability among individuals. This is related to the high plasticity of the human being, to different genetic characteristics, and to the effects of different environments on children. It remains true, nevertheless, that valid generalizations about children as a group can be made. But and this is extremely important—these generalizations apply to children as a group and not to any specific individual child. There is no normal, average child; the "average child" is a myth invented by grandmothers and investigated by psychologists.

Breaks in Continuity

Any breaks in the continuity of development will generally be due to environmental factors. Major disturbances in a developmental sequence can usually be accounted for in terms of experiential factors. On the one hand, there is the possible enriching effect of optimal environment on development the other, there are the possible deleterious effects of impoverished environment. Spit (1945, 1946) studied the effect of maternal deprivation on children in institutions. He found that, in general, institutionalized babies had an extremely high mortality rate, despite good medical attention, and that they were considerably retarded in motor and intellectual development. While the Spitz studies have been severely criticized (Pinneau, 1955), there is much corroborative evidence to suggest that impoverished environments have very harmful effects on children, and to some extent these effects are irreversible (Bowlby, 1952; Dennis, 1960). The Dennis study, for example, describes children brought up in very barren environments in an or–phanage in Tehran (Institution I)and compares them with children raised in a second institution (III), which provided the children with better care, more attention, and more stimulation. At the age of four, only about 15 percent of the children in Institution. I could walk. Surprisingly, most of those who could not walk did not creep or crawl but "scooted" instead that is, they propelled themselves sitting down, pushing with their hands and pulling with one foot. It appears that the sequence of motor development can be altered through environmental changes.

Much more significant for education are studies reporting attempts to remedy the effects of early deprivation. Without doubt, the most ambitious of all these attempts is Project Head Start in the United States, a massive program aimed at the preschool child from a low–income family. It is not yet clear from the numerous reports that have been published whether the Head Start program (and Project Follow Through) are effective in closing the educational gap. Many of the programs for slum children initially had to be too concerned with the child's physical needs to spend much time on cognitive activities. Evaluations did not always show positive changes–perhaps because tests measured the wrong things; perhaps because the programs themselves were mot always good (Bronfenbrenner, 1974,1977; Clarke and Clrke, 1976). Results of other research using more specific, and perhaps more sensitive, measures have been far more optimistic. There is little doubt that preschool programs can have markedly beneficial effects on children's cognitive, emotional, and social development (Belsky and Steinberg, 179; Bronfenbrenner, 1979).

Correlation and Compensation

Correlation, not compensation, is the rule in development. There is a popular notion that contradicts this principle. It is widely believed that individuals who are intellectually gifted are, of course, not nearly so well endowed in other areas. The "egghead" is believed to be a blundering social idiot; he is certainly unattractive and frail; his vision is weak; he is completely useless at any kind of task requiring even the smallest degree of dexterity; his breath smells; and his teeth are crooked. The athlete, a handsome and virile brute, is remarkably stupid; he spells his name with difficulty; he cannot write a check without a lawyer to correct it; he reads comic books and laughs uproariously at very unfunny events.

These stereotypes do not represent reality. In fact, the person who excels in one area is more likely to excel in others. This is supported by data from studies by Terman et al. (1925). The corollary is that people who are below average in one area tend to be below average in other areas as well and this too is true. While there are obvious exceptions to this principle, it nevertheless serves as a useful guide in understanding the overall development of children.

Stages of Development

Development proceeds in stages. This principle is often stated in developmental literature. In reality it is nothing more than a statement of a popular belief. In fact, it is probably as reasonable to assume that development does not proceed in stages, but rather progresses in a slow, continuous fashion (principle 5). But it is useful to describe development in stages. Stages give us convenient places to hang our facts. They simplify our understanding, help our organization, and facilitate recall. They have been used extensively by theorists such as Freud, Erikson, and Piaget. The interesting point is that the stages used by these theorists are not parallel. They are all expressions of different features of child development. Therefore, while it might appear reasonable to say that development proceeds in stages, it must also be made clear that the stages are invented by theorists to clarify and order their observations.

A third classification of developmental stages is provided by Erikson. It describes what he labels psychosocial crises. Each stage is labeled in terms of a conflict that tests the child. Resolution of this conflict is assumed to result in the development of a specific sense of competence essential for adapting to and coping with social reality.

Rate of Development

Development usually proceeds at the rate at which it started. A child who learns lo walk and talk at a very early age is more likely to be highly intelligent as an adult than is a child who begins developing more slowly. Data to support this contention are relatively difficult to find since early measures of intelligence are notably unreliable; however, Bloom(1964) has surveyed a large number of studies that, taken as a whole, suggest that human characteristics are remarkably stable. In other words, there is relatively little change after the initial period of rapid development that characterizes most physical and intellectual qualities.

Importance of Developmental Principles

The preceding developmental principles constitute an overview and summary of some of the most clearly valid and educationally relevant statements that can be made about developmental processes. While they do not suggest highly specific instructional implications, they can never theless provide teachers with general concepts that might be useful for understanding students better.

There is, of course, far more to human development than can be summarized in ten principles.

第三节　发展的理论

（THEORIES OF DEVELOPMENT）

To interpret their systematic observations and the information obtained from experiments, developmental psychologists have proposed theories that provide a framework for explaining how children develop. Theories are used to organize information on behavior and developmental change gathered from studies and to guide research. Theories present a cohesive view of our knowledge about child development and also identify areas that require additional study.

We introduce some of the theories used to account for the qualitative changes observed as children grow. All developmental theorists must take some stance on how genetic and environmental mental influences combine to guide development. Therefore, we start our discussion by examining the historical viewpoints that have influenced modem theorists in determining the roles of heredity and environment in development. We then identify those areas in which modem researchers are in agreement and the areas subject to ongoing debate. Following that, we turn to the role of theory in explaining development and describe how different theories interpret be—havioral changes.

Historical Viewpoints on Heredity and Environment
Darwin's theory of evolution and his hypothesis that natural selection favors transmission of traits that promote survival of a species have had a strong influence on the way many modern theories of development account or the biological basis for behavior. They have also influenced theoretical accounts of the significance of environment, for Darwin viewed environment, too, as critical for development: It provides the context for individual development and also determines which genetic traits are favored for transmission across generations. But even before Darwin's path breaking work, there was speculation on the roles of heredity and environment in shaping the development of an individual. These ideas did not focus on the evolution of species but on the basic nurture of humans and on how to account for the goodness or badness of individual children. They, too, have had a major impact on modem theories of development.

Historically, there have been two lines of thinking about human development, two ways of viewing the process of change from infancy to adulthood. One stems from an outlook expressed by the seventeenth century English philosopher John Locke. Locke saw the human infant as a tabula rasa, a totally blank slate to be written on by experiences that lie ahead. Children, in Locke's view, are neither good nor bad by nature; they become that way by virtue of their environments. If parents raise their children properly, according to Locke, the children will develop into responsible members of society. Today, traces of Locke's ideas can be seen in social learning theory. Social learning theorists stress the importance of rewards, punishments, and other learning experiences in shaping how children act.

Shortly after Locke died, a French philosopher whose ideas helped establish a different viewpoint was born. This Frenchman, Jean Jacques Rousseau, saw children as individuals from the moment of birth. Rousseau also believed that human development unfolds naturally in very positive ways, as long as society allows into do so. Parents, Rousseau argued, need not shape their children forcibly; they merely have to let maturation take its natural course. In this century, Rousseau's idea of a natural unfolding of development has appealed to those who focus on inherited potentials in children and to those who stress normative developmental patterns. Arnold Gesell. who conducted research at Yale during the 1920s and 1930s on children's physical and motor development, is probably the best known of the modem maturational theorists.

Today, few develop mentalists point solely to environment or maturation when trying to explain children's behavior. Most take an interactions view: They see a role for both inborn factors and environment working together. To an interactions, asking which factor (environment or maturation) is responsible for development is the wrong question to ask. It is like asking which factor (moisture or low temperature) is responsible for snow. Clearly, both are necessary. Those who stress the inborn factors still study the way in which environment affects inherited differences (e. g., Scarr and Grajek, 1982) . Those who emphasize environmental forces still acknowledge that human biology helps create some of the major developmental issues humans face (e.g., Erikson, 1963). As Robert Plomin (1983) has put it, the issue has become not "how" do heredity and environment influence development but "how much" do heredity and environment influence development.

The Common Core of Contemporary Positions

All modern developmental theories share the Darwinian assumption of a common human heredity and common developmental program. No theorist doubts the role of genetic factors in shaping various aspects of human capacity and the basic developmental timetable. In addition, ail recognize that characteristics of individuals are influenced by genetic factors. These include physical characteristics such as hair color and height and apparently also mental characteristics such as intelligence and some forms of depression. In animals, it is also easy to demonstrate genetic influences on behaviors uch as activity level, and such variations probably exist for human as well.

At the same time, develop mentalists recognize an important role for environment. Environmental factors influence not only psychological development but basic biological processes as well. Monkeys experiencing loss of a parent undergo biochemical changes in the brain that have been linked to depression (McKinney, 1977). When anorexic adolescent girls starve themselves, menstruation ceases. Thus, developmentalists generally share the view that both genes and environment powerfully influence behavior and that biology and experience continually interact.

Another widely shared viewpoint that human beings from the start are active organisms. This has two meanings. First, from birth human infants are active participants in their own experiences (Osofsky, 1979; Stone, Smith, and Murphy, 1973). Virtually no researcher currently sees the newborn as a blank slate waiting to be written upon. Infants are born with many capacities for both stimulating and responding to other people. This view of inborn factors interacting with environment is one you will meet repeatedly as you read about specific theories used in the study of children. Second, individual children are viewed as being active in creating their own environment, including the parenting they receive. Thus, inconsistent parenting may promote difficult behavior in the 2–year–old, but difficult behavior in the 2–year–old may at the same time promote inconsistent parenting. This is referred to as reciprocal determinism (Bandura, 1985) or bidirectional influence (Bell, 1968).

Continuing Theoretical Diversity

Despite a common core of agreement, develop mentalists continue to express a wide range of viewpoints concerning how heredity and environment work together. Researchers differ in the relative role they grant to one influence or the other and in their viewpoints on the nature of the interaction. For example, ail may believe that a 2-year-old given to frequent tantrums would be difficult to parent, yet they differ widely in their views of the origins of the 2-year-old s behavior. Some researchers may point to previous parenting. Likewise, one develop mentalist may argue that infants are largely responsible for creating their own early environments through the impact of their characteristics on parents (Scan and McCartney, 1983), another may argue that the quality of care experienced transforms the inborn characteristics of the infant and that only after the first months of life does the child play a major role in creating his or her own environment (Sroufe and Flesson, 1986). Both positions consider genetics and environment f but the relative emphasis is quite different.

Such disparities are not easily settled at the present time. For example, although differences in 2-year-olds are associated with parenting differences, interpretation of this situation is open: The differences among 2-year-olds may have been created largely through experience, and the parenting differences may have been influenced by the child in the first place. At present little evidence suggests that the characteristics of normal young babies influence the quality of parenting (Blehar, Lieberman, and Ainsworth, 1977; Egeland and Farber, 1984; Jacobvitz and Sroufe, 1987), but perhaps some will be forthcoming.

A major reason for the continuing diversity of opinion concerning the roles of heredity and environment is the difficulty of measuring both environment and important human qualities. Demonstrating the presence of genetic influences has been easy. Identical twins, even when reared apart, tend to be more similar on a number of characteristics, including intelligence, than no identical twins (Rowe and Plomin, 1978). Similarly, children who are adopted as infants often show the influence of their biological heritage. But until we can better define and measure environments, it is not possibly to say whether genetics or environment has a greater or lesser influence, precisely how much influence each factor has, or most important, how genetics and environment interact. Do some children develop better in one kind of environment, others in another? At the same time many human qualities are themselves quite difficult to measure. A child's amount of movement in a room is relatively easy to measure, distractibility and "impulse control" much harder. Harder still to measure are more abstract qualities such as creativity, confidence, and self-esteem. The influence of heredity on intelligence test performance is important), but the influence of heredity on more abstract qualities is hard to assess. Thus, there remains plenty of room for disagreement and controversy.

Still, agreement exists on the most basic proposition: Human development is powerfully influenced by both heredity and environment. Those who emphasize genetic or biological factors, such as individual differences in temperament or level of maturation, still see a role for environment in modifying these or in allowing behavior to be expressed. And those who stress the role of experience and quality of care look at these factors in, he context of human biology.

We now turn to the way theories are used to explain development Psychologists are interested in describing human development. But more fundamentally they also want to explain the changes they observe. In doing so, they propose theories. A theory is an organized set of assumptions about how things operate. It is an attempt to account for current observations and to predict future ones. Observations or isolated facts by themselves do not have much meaning. They take on meaning by being interpreted on the basis of some theory.

For example, a 3-year-old's selection of a Mick and a 6-year-old's choice of a tie as birthday presents for their fathers. The Swiss developmental psychologist Jean Piaget would have egocentric with age; 6-year-old are fundamentally less egocentric than 3-year-old, who in turn are vastly less egocentric than 1-year-old.

The same observation can take on different meanings when viewed through different theories. For instance, part of Sigmund Freud's psychoanalytic theory holds that beginning at around age 4 children strive to be like, or identify with, the parent of the same sex. This identification is an indirect way for children to feel they have power in the world. Viewed through Freudian theory, a 6-year-old boy who picks a tie for his father and a similar tie for himself is doing so partly because of identification with his father. Other theories would bring different interpretations to bear on the boy's actions. For example, some would stress that he has learned cultural stereotypes about gender-appropriate behavior. This is why he selects a tie for his father, not an apron, as he might for his mother.

In addition to providing framework for interpreting facts and findings, theories also serve to guide scientific research. Researchers could explore an infinite number of questions about human development. Theories help them decide which questions are important to ask and, to some extent, how to ask them. For example, if you held the theory that much of individual behavior is determined by heredity, you might give high priority to contrasting people with similar and dissimilar genetic makeup's (twins versus unrelated individuals, for instance). On the other hand if you thought that experience is a major determinant of behavior, you would conduct studies contracting people with different histories. A researcher with an interactions perspective might well try to examine both genetic and environmental variation in the same study.

Theories are evaluated in several ways. First, they must be sensible, plausible, and consistent. They must not contain propositions that are incompatible with each other or make assumptions known to be fallacious. But more than this, they must organize, integrate, and make coherent the body of research findings on child behavior and development, and they must provide a useful guide to further research. It must be possible to derive statements from the theory that are open to disconfirmation; that is theories must be specific and testable. However, the validity or usefulness of a theory in the behavioral sciences usually cannot be decided by one or two critical facts; rather, an ongoing check of findings and a convergence of results are necessary.

No single theory of child development prevails in the field. The reason is that "facts" often can be interpreted in different ways. For example, 1-year-old differ in the time they spend crying and fussing. This fact is consistent with (predictable from) a wide number of theories of child development, including those that emphasize inborn differences and those that emphasize learning or other environmental influences. A multiplicity of theories exists because different theorists have sought to explain different aspects of development and, in general, have focused on different questions. Piaget's theory and Freud's theory are very different in pan because Piaget was trying to explain the child's changing understanding of the world and Freud was trying to explain the origins of emotional disturbance.

第四节 认知发展
(COGNITIVE DEVELOPMENT)

Infancy

The infant's visual system matures gradually over the first two years. In early infancy, the abilities to focus. and to discriminate details all arc worse than adults'. Infants can see early only objects that arc large, close to them, and high in contrast and a parent's face during feeding, for instance, precisely fits this description. Infants also prefer to look at things with high contrast, contours, a moderate degree of complexity and movement.

Researchers have used several different techniques to determine that the perception of distance develops in infants when they are between 5 and 7 months old.

Newborns can hear the difference between loud and soft, high and low tones. But their hearing is not as acute as adult s throughout their first year of life. Infants prefer human speech to other sounds. They especially like baby talk, which typically has a high pitch, exaggerated tone, slow and repetitious wording, and drawn-out vowel sounds.

Newborns coordinate what they hear with what they sec. They can also taste and smell at birch.

Newborns pay attention to their environments and notice the onset of sights and sounds. An they mature, they can pay attention for longer periods. They actively explore with their senses and select things to focus on. They detect the invariance of objects in the environment and perceive what they can do with these things.

Investigations of how early and in what ways infants learn show that classical conditioning Generally is unsuccessful with infants under 2 or 3 months old. Operate conditioning with very young infants involves only reflexes; after 3 months of age or so, a broader range of behavior is affected by reinforcement.

By using various methods—paired comparison, habituation, retention of learned responses, and observing spontaneous behavior researchers have learned what and for how long infants remember. At first, apparently, memory consists of primitive sensory, wired-in recognition, without thought. Al about 3 months, memory becomes more cognitive, as infants begin to control what they look at, listen to, and pay attention to. By 8 to 10 months, infants form mental categories, which allow them to summarize information, thus reducing their memory load.

According to Jean Piaget, the early mental activity of infants, called sensor motor intelligence, is limited to what can be sensed and acted on. Out of their sensor motor experience with objects, infants develop action schemes. They organize—combine and integrate—their schemes and adapt them as their experience increases. Infants assimilate new objects and experiences into their existing schemes; they accommodate, or modify, schemes when they encounter new objects and experiences that do not fit their schemes.

According to Piaget, infants progress through an unvarying sequence of developmental stages, each of which incorporates the knowledge gained in the previous stage. During the sensor motor period, Piaget claimed, infants progress from a stage of practicing and repeating reflexes, to acquiring adaptations, to making interesting sights last. During this stage, they engage in magical–phenomenistic thinking. They also begin to develop object permanence, the knowledge that even when objects are out of sight they continue to exist. Later stages bring fuller under-standing of object permanence, cause and effect, the physical properties of objects and of the self as a separate being.

Other developmental psychologists have found problems in Piaget's theory of sensor motor development and his suggestion that infants do not begin to form mental representations of objects until the middle of their second year. They have found evidence that infants form mental representations of objects in the first year and suggest that Piaget's hidden object task is difficult for infants not because they don't realize that objects are permanent but because they are not good as searching for objects or remembering where they are hidden.

Infants act out their mental representations of actions through successively more advanced stages of imitation. They go from pseudo imitations—imitations of acts they can perform already—to true imitations of unfamiliar actions to deferred imitations, imitations that occur sometime after the infant has seen the original act. Infants seem to be tuned in to imitating other's mouth movements particularly early.

The sense of self develops in stages, too. Infants at first are interested in their mirror images but do not realize that they are seeing their own image. Later, they distinguish between their own and others' reflected images. Still later they understand that they have unique features that can be named and labeled with words.

Play is the work of infancy, the repetition of actions for sheer enjoyment. A major developmental change in play occurs when pretend play begins at the age of about 1 year.

Not all infants develop cognitively at the same rate, Psychologists test individuals' cognitive levels with infant intelligence tests. These tests are useful for assessing whether infants are pro grassing normally, but they generally do not predict individuals' later IQ scores. One reason is that intelligence tests in infancy center on perceptual and sensor motor abilities, whereas later intelligence tests center on verbal and abstract abilities. Infants' recognition of new and familiar stimuli is more predictive of later IQ scores than these infant IQ tests.

Language develops in infancy, too, out of basic capacities like speech perception and categorization, understanding of the meaning of words, the articulation aspects of babbling, and conducive learning environment. At first, because of their limited vocabularies infants may overextend words (using "dog" for cats, dogs, and rabbits) or under extend them (using "dog" just to Spot).

Unresponsive and intimidating care in infancy retards cognitive development. Although parents cannot create intelligence in their children, they can foster its development. Special programs to train and support parents to become more stimulating have been successful.

Early Childhood

Children use symbols that are verbal—a word, a made-up name—and physical—a drawing, a doll, a stick used as a gun. Piaget called personal symbols; he called shared symbols signs. Toddler's pretend play is the first evidence of their symbolic thinking. During the preschool period, pretend play changes from symbolic play with objects, to play in which children act out roles, to dramatic play with roles announced ahead of time.

In their drawing, children everywhere begin as scribbles, but after this stage, the pattern of their drawing is shaped by cultural convention.

Children between 4 and 6 years old think intuitively and therefore sometimes confuse the real with the imagined, the animate with the inanimate, and their own perspective with others'.

Young children cannot perform logical operations such as addition, subtraction, or multiplication, and so their thought, according to Piaget, is "preoperational". Their ability to classify objects is limited to basic, functional categories. They sometimes reason transductively from one particular to another rather than from the general to the particular although they are capable of simple deductive reasoning. Slowly, they acquire concepts of number and age.

Preschool children are neither as systematic nor as selective in paying attention as older children are, perhaps because they are less efficient at encoding information, because they do not understand what others think it is important for them to pay attention to, or because they cannot consciously direct their attention so that they focus only on relevant aspects of tasks. Memory improves with age, as children get better at encoding information. Children begin speaking in one word and then two word telegraphic utterances. Over regularization is a common kind of mistake children make as they are learning to speak in sentences and shows that they have learned the rules for making past tenses and plurals. Language is the result of both innate abilities and environmental input.

Although adults do not give children deliberate language lessons they speak to them in mothers, a special and simplified language adapted to young children's limited language abilities, and they expand their simple utterances into more complex sentences.

The number and kind of toys they play with, television shows they watch, and the stimulation they receive from their parents and peers all affect the cognitive development of children.

Program to improve the learning environments of young children, whether focused on the children or their parents or both, can improve children's performance on intelligence tests. Young children's cognitive development is also affected by their attendance at nursery school and day-care programs with an educational component.

Middle childhood

During middle childhood, children begin to grasp the logical relations among things' the orderly rules and constant properties that govern how things happen. Their logical reasoning is concrete —because they can reason only about concrete thing and operational because they can operate mentally on the things in an organized, integrated, and systematic way.

With these new abilities children come to understand the conservation of matter: that even though objects outward appearances may change, their length, quantity, mass, area, weight, and volume do not necessarily change. Children learn to arrange objects in a series and to make transitive inferences. They learn the direct relations between speed and distance and time and then the indirect relation between speed and time.

According to Piaget, children between 5 and 10 years old have an external morality, in which rules are seen as inviolable instructions from figures of authority. They do not understand that people may agree to discuss and remake rules. In Kohlberg's stages of moral reasoning, children are first concerned with getting rewards and avoiding punishment. Next they are concerned with making fair deals and trades. At the level of conventional moral reasoning, children think that moral behavior means following social rules and conventions.

School-age children remember more than younger children in part because they can use deliberate strategies for remembering, such as imagery, rehearsal, and organizing information into systematic categories, and in part because their broader knowledge of the world gives them organizing frameworks. Short-term memory capacity also increases somewhat with age. School-age children understand their own memory processes better than younger children do, but it is not clear that this understanding helps them to remember.

Learning to read requires several skills: attacking and mastering a visual code for spoken sounds; attending to and figuring out the written words on a page; and understanding what words and letters actually are. Poor readers are not as skillful as good readers at encoding words into short term memory.

Individual children develop at different rates and to different levels, and this is reflected in their performance on IQ tests are affected by the cultural content of the test itself and the testing situation as well as by their cognitive competence.

Mental retardation ranges from mild to profound. Profound clinical retardation is caused by chromosomal, genetic, and prenatal conditions and by severe malnutrition in infancy and childhood. Sociocultural retardation, which is usually mild, is caused by educational, economic, and social deprivation.

Children differ in their cognitive styles of perceiving and responding to the environment, some being reflective and others impulsive, some field dependent and others field independent.

Girls consistently average higher scores than boys on tests of verbal abilities, and boys, higher scores on tests of spatial abilities. Biological, social, and psychological factors contribute to these observed differences in intellectual abilities.

The openness of classes and classrooms, teachers' expectations of students, and academic performance, and the amount of time children actually spend on schoolwork all affect how well and how much children learn. Computers have the potential for being powerful teachers and motivators. They are especially valuable in teaching children how to write compositions and how to think logically and systematically as they write computer programs.

第五节 社会性及情感的发展
(SOCIAL AND EMOTIONAL DEVELOPMENT)

Infancy

In the first hour after birth, when an infant is alert and gazing and the mother's receptivity is heightened by high hormone levels, the mother begins to form emotional ties to the infant. Mothers who miss this sensitive period for bonding have many opportunities later on to grow emotionally attached to their infants.

Infants communicate with those around them with their appealing babyness, gazes, vocalizations, smiles, laughter, and cries. They communicate by facial expressions and bodily gestures. Mothers interpret babies' expressions and gestures as communication, even when the baby is not intentionally sending messages. Eventually, the infant does learn to communicate and becomes a truly interactive partner in these social exchanges. Mothers and infants take turns and play "duets" in feeding, vocalizing, and playing games.

In their interactions with adults, infants begin to learn their culture s rules about when and where they may display emotions. They learn to smile often and to control expressions of distress. Infants also respond to other people's expressions of emotions and use them to guide their own behavior.

The newborn is physiologically primed to pay attention to the kinds of stimulation provided by parents' faces-the contrasts between skin and hair, the moving eyes and red mouth. In turn, parents project their own feelings and rhythms onto the infant and act as though those actions were social. So begins the interactive "system" of parents and child.

Some mothers and infants mesh well, others not so well. Mothers may be over stimulating, anxious, insecure, depressed, even mentally ill. Some babies are temperamentally unresponsive, difficult, irritable, and rejecting of mothers' attempts at social communication.

Temperament is generally stable over time, although the coures of any infant's development depends to some extent on the fit of his or her temperament with parents' expectations and behavior.

The most important social and emotional development of an infant's first year is the formation of a lasting, loving tie with the person he or she interacts with the most. This attachment develops in the second six months of life. By observing infants and mothers in the "strange situation" psychologists have found that infants are either securely or insecurely attached to their mothers. Insecure infants avoid contact with their mothers or act ambivalently toward them.

Mothers who are loving, responsive, and sensitive are likely to offer the infant appropriate levels of stimulation and to foster secure attachments in their infants. Mothers who are tense and angry are likely to foster avoidance in their infants.

Secure attachments are likely to flourish when a baby has one regular caretaker who gives loving and sensitive attention and who keeps long separations to a minimum.

Securely attached infants typically become children who are more socially and emotionally competent than those who are insecurely attached.

Mothers do most of the physical care of infants. Fathers are more likely to play and rough-house. There are, of course, marked individual differences in how fathers behave with their infants.

In families, the behavior of each member is felt by all the others. The arrival of a new baby is a momentous event within any family and causes substantial change in family relationships.

Infants form relationships outside their families, with caregivers in day care, but they do not substitute for their attachments to their parents.

Early childhood

As they get older, children become more autonomous, get less upset at brief separations from their parents and seek less physical contact with them. Yet young children remain strongly emotionally attached to their parents. Patterns of attachment—secure, avoidant, and ambivalent—usually remain stable over time.

In the preschool period, parents begin to exert more control and discipline over their children. Parents with an authoritarian style of discipline are firm, punitive, unsympathetic, and do not value independence in their children. Their children tend to be suspicious, withdrawn, unfriendly, and unhappy. Permissive parents do not lay down rules or assert their authority over their children. Their children tend to be immature, dependent, and unhappy. Authoritative parents reason with their children, set few but firm limits, and keep conflict to a minimum. Their children are most likely to be friendly, competent, socially responsible, and happy.

Parents' interpretations of their children's behavior and children's characteristic affect the parents' disciplinary style and effectiveness. Mothers of easy children, and difficult children ignore, protest and talk back more to their mothers than other children.

Families with handicapped or difficult children may get caught up in seemingly endless vicious cycles of hostile, defeating action and reactions.

Many families, especially in America, experience the stress of divorce. Whether children have long-term problems as a result of divorce depends in large part on whether their parents part amicably or fight openly and on the relationships they maintain with the children.

Mothers' work also is a source of stress—and strength—to their children's development.

Daughters are more likely than sons to benefit from their mother's working.

In families with more than one child, siblings interact from infancy onwards. They imitate each other, compete for toys and their parents attention and affection, and have many positive interchanges. Older siblings may act like parents to their younger sibling by providing them with security and even speaking motherese to them. Sibling interactions are both reciprocal and complementary.

Over the preschool period, children have more chance to play with other children. As 2-and 3-year-old, their play is mainly parallel and ritualistic-repetitive, rhythmic exchanges or turns. Older preschoolers are more likely to engage in language play and pretend play, to play interactively and cooperatively.

Preschoolers children act in both prosocial and antisocial ways. They help, hit, hurt, disrupt, and fight with other children. Determinants of young children's aggressive behavior are many and complex. They include frustration; selective reinforcement; imitation of aggressive parents, teachers, other children, and television characters; certain hormones land physical unattractiveness.

Preschoolers make friends with children of the same sex, age, energy and activity levels as they, and with their friends they talk, agree and comply, offer sympathy and help, and inquire about one another's feelings.

As young children's social understanding improves, they better understand other people's emotions, modulate their own emotional expressions, communicate more effectively, and have smoother conversations.

The young child's self-concept is based on fleeting, sometimes inaccurate, perceptions. Young children usually define themselves in terms of physical actions, not psychological traits.

By the time they are 3 years old, boys and girls begin to act in different ways. Girls play house, pay attention to people's feelings and relationships; boys have grandiose power fantasies and games. Girls are more likely to be nurturant; boys are more likely to be aggressive. These differences stem, in part, from parents, teachers, and other children also acquire knowledge about sex constancy and gender roles and develop their gender identity.

Television is one way that young children get information about gender roles. They also learn from watching television what kinds of behavior are acceptable. If they watch violent programs, they are more likely to be aggressive. If they watch prosocial programs, they are more likely to be helpful and cooperative.

Middle Childhood

In middle childhood, the world is made up of family, school, and peers. School-age children feel deeply about their families. They need and want rules and restrictions, but the more controlling relationship between involved parents and younger, immature children gradually changes into a less controlling relationship in which both parents and child are responsible for the child's behavior.

Children of mothers who work outside the home are likely to become independent and self-reliant earlier and to value women and their abilities more. Daughters of working mothers tend to be more independent and outgoing and to do better in school than daughters of housewives. But in some middle-class families, sons of working mothers may do less well in school, score lower on intelligence tests, feel that their mothers are uninvolved, and therefore feel depressed and inadequate. School-age children form friendship cliques, with leaders and followers, in which they do such things together as watch television, go to the movies, play games, go to the beach, and talk. Girls have an intensive style of interacting with each other; they play with one other girl, express intense feelings about her, and share experiences and fantasies with her. Boys have an extensive style of interacting with each other. They play noisily in a group and usually focus on a game like baseball or soccer. In the age-segregated elementary school, boys and girls rarely mix.

Popular children are confident, outgoing, active, friendly, and cooperative. They are rarely aggressive, get along with anyone, and know what to say and when to say it. Children who are socially inept, aggressive, disruptive, and act inappropriately are often rejected.

Cooperation, helping, and showing concern for others increase during early childhood but decline toward the end of middle childhood. Competitiveness, individualism, and generosity increase over the school years.

Almost all schoolchildren sometimes cheat or fib. They also sometimes hurt each other. Children learn aggression from parents who are aggressive, rejecting, and unloving and who punish the children for aggression but do not reward them for sharing or cooperating. Children's peers reinforce, elicit, model, and absorb aggression. When children watch a lot of violent television shows, think that these shows are real, identify with aggressive television characters, are reinforced for their own aggressive behavior, and are objects of aggression, they are likely to act aggressively.

Children in open classes generally feel more positive about school and about themselves than children in traditional classes.

What children do after school largely depends on the neighborhoods they live in—whether there are parks, stores, community centers, busy streets, fenced yards, sidewalks, streetlights, and other physical features. With their friends, children roam around their neighborhoods on foot, bike, and skateboard, play sports, join clubs and Scout troops, and take lessons.

As they get older, children get better at understanding other people's feelings, moods, intentions, and motives. As their social understanding increases, their social competence increases, too.

The way that children see themselves changes in middle childhood as they begin to recognize that they have unique qualities. Children's self-esteem derives in part from others' opinions of them and in part from their mastery of developmental tasks, their performance in school, and their ability to deal with social situations.

Some temperamental traits—activity level, intensity, adaptability, and rhythm city—seem somewhat stable from infancy to early childhood. Across childhood and beyond, the most stable qualities are aggressiveness and sociability.

词汇 (Vocabulary)

1. ambivalently   adv. 情绪矛盾地
2. amicably   adv. 友好地
3. anal   n. 肛门期
4. animate   adj. 有生命的
5. anorexic   adj. 厌食的
6. articulation   n. (清楚的) 发音

7. autonomy vs. shame and doubt　　自主对羞怯和疑虑
8. axon　n. 轴突
9. babbling　n. 婴孩咿呀语
10. bidirectional influence　双向影响
11. bud　n. 萌芽、芽
12. chin　n. 下巴
13. chromosomal　adj. 染色体的
14. clique　n. 朋党
15. cohesive　adj. 有内聚力的
16. cohort　n. 股（动植物分类系统上所用的单位）、断层
17. compensation　n. 补偿
18. conception　n. 怀孕
19. conducive　adj. 有助于的
20. contour　n. 轮廓
21. convention　n. 风俗、习俗
22. convergence　n. 汇聚、整合
23. corollary　n. 必然的结果
24. corroborate　v. 确证、证实
　　corroborative adj. 确证的
25. cranial　adj. 头部的
26. deleterious　adj.（对身心）有害的
27. dendrite　n. 树突
28. dexterity　n. 灵巧、敏捷
29. distractibility　n. 分心、注意转移
30. dizygotic　adj. 异卵的
31. duet　n. 二重奏
32. egocentrism　n. 自我中心主义
33. explicit　adj. 明白表示的
34. fetal　adj. 胎儿的
35. fib　v. 撒小谎
36. foster parent-child　养父母—子女
37. fraternal　adj. 兄弟的
38. generosity　n. 宽宏大量
39. genital　n. 性器期
40. gum　n. 齿龈
41. heredity　n. 遗传
42. holistic education　整体性教育
43. identification　n. 认同、身份证明
44. identity vs. identity diffusion　同一性对角色混乱

45. impoverished   adj. 贫困的
46. industry vs. inferiority   勤奋对自卑
47. inept   adj. 不适当的
48. initiative vs. guilt   自主性对内疚
49. institution   n. 社会福利机构（孤儿院）
50. integrity vs. despair   自我完整对失望
51. interactionist view   互动观点
52. intimacy and solidarity vs. isolation   亲密团结对孤立
53. inviolable   ad. 不可违背的、不容亵渎的
54. irreversible   adj. 不可取消的
55. latency   n. 潜伏期
56. lateralization   n. 侧面化
57. limb   n. 肢臂
58. malnutrition   n. 营养不良
59. manifest   adj. 明显的
60. maturation   n. 成熟
61. menarche   n. 月经初期
62. menstruation   n. 月经
63. mesh   v. 使紧密配合
64. modulate   v. 调节
65. monozygotic   adj. 同卵的
66. mortality   n. 死亡率
67. multiplication   n. 乘法
68. myelination   n. 髓鞘化
69. nasal   adj. 鼻的
70. neuron   n. 神经元
71. nurture   n.（儿童的）教育、抚育
72. one-egg twins   同卵双生子
73. onset   n. 发生
74. optional environment   最佳环境
75. oral   n. 唇期
76. orphanage   n. 孤儿院
77. phallic   n. 生殖器期
78. plasticity   n. 适应性
79. plausible   adj. 似真实的、似合理的
80. postulate   v. 假定
81. prenatal period   胎儿期
82. pseudo imitation   n. 假模仿
83. puberty   n. 青春期

84. pubescence   n. 青春期
85. rear   v. 养育
86. reciprocal determinism   交互决定论
87. regress   v. 倒退
88. rhythmicity   n. 规律性
89. ritualistic   adj. 遵守程序的
90. scheme   n. 图式
91. sensorimotor   n. 感觉运动
92. sibling   n. 兄弟或姐妹、同胞
93. slate   n. 石板
94. speculation   n. 推测、思考
95. spurt   n. 奋进、猛发
96. substantiate   v. 证实
97. subtraction   n. 减法
98. tabula rasa   n. 白板、婴儿空白的心灵状态
99. tantrum   n. 发脾气
100. temperament   n. 气质
101. temporal   adj. 时间的
102. two-egg twins   异卵双生子
103. vicious cycle   恶性循环
104. virile   adj. 刚健的
105. vulnerable   adj. 易伤的、易受破坏的

第十六章 学习
（LEARNING）

本章要点（Chapter Outline）
行为主义学习观（Behavior Views of Learning)
认知理论学习观（Cognitive Views of Learning)
人本主义学习观（Humanistic Views of Learning)

学习是日常生活中常用的词，是人们普遍关心的问题，科学心理学在使用这一术语时有其特定的含义。最主要的学习定义有两种，一是行为主义心理学对学习的定义：学习是由经验引起的行为的相对持久的变化；二是认知心理学对学习的定义：学习是人的倾向或能力的变化，但这种变化要能保持一定时期且不能单纯归因于生长过程。可见学习有广义和狭义之分，从广义到狭义又可依次分为四个层次：第一层指人和动物在生活过程中获得个体的行为经验的过程；第二层指人类的学习；第三层指学生的学习；第四层指知识和技能的获得与形成，以及智力和非智力因素的发展与培养。

本章对行为主义、认知心理学及人本主义三个学派的学习观、基本特点等内容做了一一介绍，并进行了一些对比研究。

第一节 行为主义学习观
（BEHAVIORAL VIEWS OF LEARNING）

Definition

When we hear the word "learning" most of us think of studying and school. But learning is not limit to school and is not always intention. In the broadest sense, learning occurs when experience causes a relatively permanent change in an individuals knowledge or behaviors. The change may be deliberate or unintentional, for better or for worse. To qualify as learning, this change must be bring about by experience—by the interaction of a person with his or her environment. Changes due simply to maturate, such as growing taller or turning gray, do not qualify as learning. Temporary changes due to illness, fatigue, or hunger are also excluded from a general definition of learning, A person who has gone without food for two days does not learn to hungry, and a person who is ill does not learn to run more slowly. Of course, learning plays a part in how we respond or illness. Our definition specifies that the changes resulting from learning are in the individual's knowledge or behavior.

Classical Conditioning

The principle of contiguity that whenever two sensations occur together over and over again, they will become associated. Later, when only one of these sensations (a stimulus) occurs, the other will be remembered too (a response). Classical conditional focuses on the learning of involuntary emotional or physiological responses such as fear, increased heart beat, salivation, or involuntary sometimes called respondents because they are automatic responses to stimuli. Through the process of classical conditioning, humans and animals can be train to react involuntarily to a stimulus that previously had no effect—or a very different effect—on them. The stimulus comes to elicit, or bring forth, the response automatically.

Classical conditioning was discovered by Ivan Pavlov, a Russian physiologist, in the 1920s. In his laboratory, Pavlov was plagued by a series of setbacks. He was trying to answer questions about the digestive system of dogs, including how long it took a dog to secrete digestive juices after it had been fed. But the intervals of time kept changing. At first, the dogs salivated in the expected manner while they were being fed. Then the dogs began to salivate as soon as they saw the food. Finally, they salivated as soon as they saw the scientist enter the room. The white coats of the experimenters, the sound of their footsteps, all elicited salivation. Pavlov decided to make a detour from his original experiments and examine these unexpected interference in his work.

In one of his first experiment. Pavlov began by sounding a tuning fork and recording a dog response. As expected, there was no salivation. At this point, the sound of the tuning fork, was a **neutral stimulus** because it brought forth no salivation. Then Pavlov fed the dog. The response was salivation. The food was an **unconditioned stimulus** because no prior training or "conditioning" was needed to establish the natural connection between food and salivation. The salvation was an **unconditioned response**, because it occurred automatically no conditioning required.

Using these three elements the food, the salivation, and the tuning fork Pavlov demonstrated that a dog could be conditioned to salivate after hearing the tuning fork. He did this by contiguous pairing of the sound with food. At the beginning of the experiment, he sounded the fork and then quickly fed the dog. After Pavlov repeated this several times, the dog began to salivate after hearing the sound but before receiving the food. Now the sound had become a conditioned stimulus that could bring forth salivation by itself. The response of salivating after the tone was now a conditioned response.

Pavlov's work also identified three other processes in classical conditioning: generalization, discrimination, and extinction. After the dogs learned to salivate in response to hearing one particular sound, they would also salivate after hearing other similar tones, those that were slightly higher or lower. This process is called **generalization** because the conditioned response of salivating generalized or occurred in the presence of similar stimuli. Pavlov could also teach his dogs **discrimination** to respond to one tone but not to others that are similar by making sure that food always followed only one tone, not any others. **Extinction** occurs when a conditioned stimulus (a particular tone) is presented repeatedly but is not followed by the unconditioned stimulus (food).The conditioned response (salivating) gradually fades away and finally is "extinguished" it disappears altogether.

Operate conditioning

So far we have concentrated on the automatic conditioning of involuntary responses such as salivation and fear. These involuntary actions are often called **respondents**. Clearly, not all human learning is so automatic and unintentional. Most behaviors are not elicited by stimuli, they were emitted or voluntarily enacted. People actively "operate" on their environment to produce different kinds of consequences. These deliberate actions are called **operate**. The learning process involved in operate behavior is called **operate conditioning** because we learn to behave in certain ways as we operate on the environment. The person generally thought to be responsible for developing operate conditioning is B.F. Skinner (1953). Skinner began with the belief that the principles of classical conditioning account for only a small portion of learned behaviors. Many human behaviors are operate, not respondent. Classical conditioning describes only how existing behaviors might be pair with new stimuli; it does not explain how new operate behaviors are acquired.

Behavior, like response or action, is simply a word for what person does in a particular situation. Conceptually, we may think of a behavior as sandwiched between two sets of environmental influences: those that precede it (**its antecedents**) and those that follow it (**its consequences**) (Skinner, 1950). This relationship can be shown very simple as antecedent–behavior–consequence, or A–B–C. As behavior is ongoing, a given consequence becomes an antecedent for the next ABC sequence. Research in operate conditioning shows that operate behavior can be alter by changes in the antecedents, the consequences, or both. Early work focused on consequence.

To study the effects of consequences on behaviors under carefully controlled conditions, Skinner designed a special cage like apparatus. The subjects of Skinner's studies were usually rats or pigeons placed in the cages, which soon came to be called **Skinner boxes**. A typical Skinner box is a small enclosure containing only a food tray and a lever or bar (for rats) or a disk (for pigeons).The lever or disk is connected to a food hopper. Modifications of this basic box include lights close to the lever or disk and electrified floors used to give mild shocks to the animals. In one experiment, a hungry pigeon is placed in the box and proceed to explore it. Since pigeons tend to peck, the animal will eventually get around to pecking the disk. At that point a small food pellet will drop into the food tray. The hungry bird eats the pellet, moves around the box and soon pecks the disk again. There is more food, and before long the pigeon is pecking and eating continuously. The next time the pigeon is placed in the box, it will go directly to the disk and begin to pecking.

According to the behavioral view, consequences determine to a great extent whether a person will repeat the behavior that led to the consequences. The type and timing of consequences can strengthen or weaken behaviors. In order to understand consequences, reinforcement is the first problem to be discussed.

There are two types of reinforcement. The first, called **positive reinforcement**, occurs when a (usually pleasant) stimulus is presented following a particular behavior. Examples include the money or praise that students may receive when they bring home. As on report cards or the cheers and laughter of fellow students following the class clown's latest remark. Notice that positive reinforcement can occur even when the behavior being reinforced (silly remark) is not "ositive" from the teacher's point of view.

Whereas positive reinforcement involves the presentation of a desired stimulus, the second kind of reinforcement, called **negative reinforcement**, involves the removal of (or escape from) an aversion (unpleasant) stimulus. A stimulus is aversion if you would work to escape or avoid it. If a particular action causes an aversion stimulus to go away or allows you to escape or avoid something unpleasant, you are likely to repeat the action when you are faced with a similar situation. Consider the students who are repeatedly sent to the principal's office. Their rules breaking are probably being reinforced in some way because they continue to do it. The misbehavior may be getting them out of bad situations such as a test or a class that causes anxiety. If so, the misbehavior is being maintained through negative reinforcement.

Negative reinforcement is often confused with punishment. The process of reinforcement (positive or negative) always involves strengthening behavior. **Punishment**, on the other hand, involves decreasing or suppressing behavior. A behavior followed by a punisher is less likely to be repeated in similar situations in the future. Again it is the effect that defines a consequence as punishment, and different people have different perception of what is punishment. One student may find suspension from school punishing, while another student wouldn't mind at all.

Like reinforcement, punishment may take one of two forms. The first type has been called Type I punishment, but this name isn't very informative, so I use the term presentation punishment. It occurs when the appearance of a stimulus following the behavior suppresses or decreases the behavior. When teachers assign demerits, extra work, running laps, and so on, they are using presentation punishment. The other type of punishment (Type D punishment) I call removal punishment because it involves removing a stimulus. When teachers or parents take away privileges after a young person has behaved inappropriately, they are applying removal punishment. With both types, the effect is to decrease the behavior that led to the punishment.

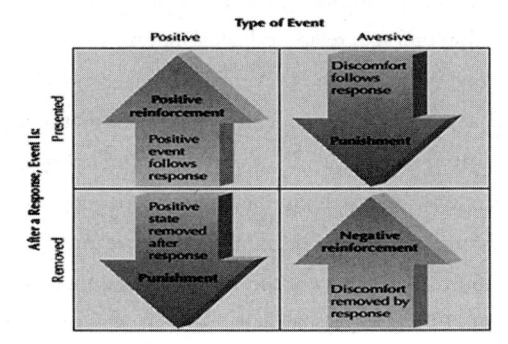

Figure 16.1

Types of reinforcement and punishment. The impact of an event depends on whether it is presented or removed after a response is made. Each square defines one possibility: Arrows pointing upward indicate that responding is increased; downward pointing arrows indicate that responding is decreased. (Adapted from Kazdin, 1975.)

• 361 •

When people are learning a new behavior, they will learn it faster if they are reinforced for every correct response. This is a **continuou reinforcement schedule**. Then, when the new behavior has been mastered, they will maintain it best if they are reinforced intermittently rather than every time. An **intermittent reinforcement schedule** helps students to maintain skills without expecting constant reinforcement.

There are two basic types of intermittent reinforcement schedules. One called an interval schedule is based on the amount of time that passes between reinforces. The other a ratio schedule is based on the number of responses learners give between reinforces. Interval and ratio schedules may be either fixed (predictable) or variable (unpredictable).

Speed of performance depends on control. If reinforcement is based on the number of response you give, then you have more control over the reinforcement: the faster you accumulate the correct number of responses, the faster the reinforcement will come. Therefore, people work faster on ratio than on interval schedules. In operate conditioning, a person or an animal will not persist in a certain behavior if the usual reinforce is withheld. The behavior will eventually be extinguished (stop). For example, if you go for a week without selling even one magazine door-to-door, you may give up.

Social Learning Theory

In recent years most behavioral psychologists have found that operate conditioning offer too limited an explanation of learning. Many have expanded their view of learning to include the study of cognitive processes that cannot be directly observed, such as expectations, thoughts, and beliefs. A prime example of this expanded view is Albf learning, while accurate, are incomplete. They give only part of the explanation of learning and overlook important aspects of the situation, particularly the important social influences on learning.

Bandura distinguishes between the acquisition of knowledge (learning) and the observable performance based on that knowledge (behavior). In other words, Bandura suggests that we all may know more than we show. Students may have learned how to simplify fractions but may perform badly on a test because they are anxious or ill or have misread the problem. While learning may has occurred, it may not be demonstrated until the situation is right. In social cognitive theory, therefore, both internal and external factors are important. Environmental events, personal factors (such as thinking and motivation), and behavior are seen as interacting, each influencing the others in the process of learning. Bandura calls this interaction of forces reciprocal determinism.

One factor overlooked by traditional behavioral theories is the powerful effect that modeling and imitation can have on learning. People and animals can learn merely by observing another person or animal learn, and this fact challenges the behaviorist idea that cognitive factors are unnecessary in an explain of learning. If people can learn by watching, they must be focusing their attention, constructing images, remembering, analyzing and making decision that affect learning.

Learning by Observing Others. For observational learning to occur, several things must take place. First, the learner must pay attention to the model and remember what was do. (A beginning auto mechanic might be interested enough to watch an entire tune-up, but unable to remember all the steps.) Next, the learner must be able to reproduce the model behavior. (Sometimes this is a matter of practice, but it may be that the learner will never be able to perform the behavior. We may admire the feats of world-class gymnasts, but many people could never reproduce them, no matter how much they practiced.) If a model is successful at a task or rewarded for a response, the learner is more likely to imitate the behavior. In general, models who are attractive, trustworthy, capable, admired, powerful, or high in status also tend to be imitated (Bandura & Walters, 1963; Brewer & Wann, 1998). Finally, once a new response is tried, normal reinforcement determines whether it will be repeated thereafter. (Notice the similarity to latent learning, described earlier.)

Elements of Observational Learning. Bandura (1986) notes that there are four important elements to be considered in observational learning. They are paying attention, retaining information or impressions, producing behaviors, and being motivation to repeat the behaviors.

In order to learn through observation, we have to pay attention. We typically pay attention to people who are attractive, popular, competent, or admired (Sulzer-Azaroff & Mayer, 1986). For younger children this could mean parents, older brothers or sisters, or teachers. For older students it may mean popular peers, rock stars, or TV idols.

In teaching, you will have to ensure students' attention to the critical features of the lesson by making clear presentations and highlighting important points.

In order to imitate the behavior of a model, you have to remember it. This involves mentally representing the model's actions in some way, probably as verbal steps (Hwa-Rang, the eighth form in Tae Kwan Do karate, is a palm-heel block, then a middle riding stance punch, then...), or as visual images, or both. Retention can be improved by mental rehearsal (imagining imitating the behavior) or by actual practice. In the retention phase of observational learning, practice helps us remember the elements of the desired behavior, such as the sequence of steps.

Once we "know" how a behavior should look and remember the elements or steps, we still may not perform it smoothly. Sometimes we need a great deal of practices, feedback, and coaching about subtle points before we can reproduce the behavior of the model. In the production phase, practice makes the behaviors smoother and more expert. A sense of self-efficacy, the belief that we are capable of performing the behavior is important at this phase and influences our motivation to perform.

As mentioned earlier, social cognitive theory distinguishes between acquisition and performance. We may acquire a new skill or behavior through observation, but we may not perform that behavior until there is some motivation or incentive to do so.

Reinforcement can play several roles in observational learning. If we anticipate being reinforced for imitating the actions of a model, we may be more motivated to pay attention, remember, and reproduce the behaviors. In addition, reinforcement is important in maintaining learning. A person who tries a new behavior is unlikely to persist without reinforcement (Barton, 1981; Ollendick, Dailey, & Shapiro, 1983). For example, if an unpopular student adopted the dress of the group but was greeted with teasing and ridicule, it is unlikely that the imitation would continue.

Bandura identifies three forms of reinforcement that can encourage observational learning.

First, of course, the observer may reproduce the behaviors of the model and receive direct reinforcement, as when a gymnast successfully executes a front flip/round off combination and the coach/model says, "Excellent!" But the reinforcement need not be direct it may be vicarious reinforcement as well. As mentioned earlier, the observer may simply see others reinforced for a particular behavior and then increase his or her production of that behavior. Most TV ads hope for this kind of effect. People in commercials become deliriously happy when they drive a particular car or drink a specific juice, and the viewer is supposed to do the same; the viewer's behavior is reinforced vicariously by the actor's obvious pleasure. The final form of reinforcement is self-reinforcement, or controlling your own reinforces. This sort of reinforcement is important for both students and teachers. We want our students to improve not because it leads to external rewards but because the students value and enjoy their growing competence. And as a teacher, sometimes self-reinforcement is all that keep you going.

Observational Learning in Teaching. There are five possible outcomes of observational learning: teaching new behaviors and attitudes, encouraging existing behaviors, changing inhibitions, directing attention, and arousing emotions. Let's look at each of these as they occur in classrooms.

Teaching New Behaviors. Modeling has a powerful effect on behavior. In a classic experiment, children watched an adult attack a large blow-up "Bo-Bom the Clown" doll. Some children saw an adult sit on the doll, punch it, hit it with a hammer, and kick it around the room. Others saw a movie of these actions. A third group saw a cartoon version of the aggression. Later, the children were frustrated by having some attractive toys taken away from them. Then, they were allowed to play with the Bo-Bo doll. Most imitated the adult's attack (Figure 8.25). Some even added new aggressive acts of their own! Interestingly, the cartoon was only slightly less effective in encouraging aggression than the live adult model and the filmed model (Bandura et al., 1963).

Figure 16.2 A nursery school child Imitates the aggressive behavior of an adult model he has just seen in a movie

Modeling, when applied deliberately, can be an effective and efficient means of teaching new behaviors (Bandura, 1986; Schunk, 1987). Studies indicates that modeling can be most effective when the teacher makes use of all the elements of observational learning described in the previous section, especially reinforcement and practice.

Models who are the same age as the students may be particularly effective. For example, Schunk and Hanson(1985) compared two methods for teaching subtraction to second graders who had difficulties learning this skill. One group of students observed other second graders learning the procedures, then participated in an instructional program on subtraction. Another group of students watched a teacher's demonstration, then participated in the same instructional program. Of the two groups, the students who observed peer model learning not only scored higher on tests of subtraction after instruction, but also gained more confidence in their own ability to learn. For students who doubt their own abilities, a good model is a low-achieving student who keeps trying and finally masters the material (Schunk, 1987).

Encouraging Already-Learned Behaviors. All of as have had the experience of looking for cues from other people when we find ourselves in unfamiliar situations. Observing the behavior of others tells us which of our already-learned behaviors to use: the proper fork for eating the salad, when to leave a gathering, what kind of language is appropriate, and so on. Adopting the dress and grooming styles of TV idols is another example of this kind of effect.

Strengthening or Weakening Inhibitions. If class members witness one student breaking a class rule and getting away with it, they may learn that undesirable consequences do not always follow rule-breaking. The class may be less inhibited in the future about breaking this rule. If the rule-breaker is a well-liked, high-status class leader, the effect of the modeling may be even more pronounced. One psychologist has called this phenomenon is the ripple effect (Kounin, 1970). The ripple effect can work for the teacher's benefit, When the teacher deals effectively with a rule-breaker especially a class leader, the idea of breaking this rule may be inhibited for the other students viewing the interaction. This does not mean that teachers must reprimand each student who breaks a rule, but once a teacher has called for a particular action, following through is an important part of capitalizing on the ripple effect.

Directing Attention. By observing others, we not only learn about actions, we also notice the objects involved in the actions. For example, in a preschool class, when one child plays enthusiastically with a toy that has been ignored for days, many other children may want to have the toy, even if they play with it in different ways or simply carry it around. This happens, in part, because the children's attention has been drawn to that particular toy.

Arousing Emotion. Finally, through observational learning people may develop emotional reactions to situations that themselves have never experienced, such as flying or driving. A child who watches a friend fall from a swing and break an arm may become fearful of swings. Students may be anxious when they are assigned to a certain teacher because they've heard frightening stories about how mean that teacher is. Note that hearing and reading about a situation are also forms of observation.

Criticism of Behavior Methods

Properly used, the strategies in this chapter can be effective tools to help students learn academically and grow in self-sufficiency. Effective tools, however, do not automatically produce excellent work. The indiscriminate use of even the best tools can lead to difficult. Critics of behavioral methods point to two basic problems that may arise.

Some psychologists fear that rewarding students for all learning will cause the students to lose interest in learning for its own sake (Deci1975; Deci&Ryan,1985; Kohn,1993;

Lepper&Greene,1978). Studies have suggested that using reward programs with students who are already interested in the subject matter may, in fact, cause students to be less interested in the subject.

Just as you must take into account the effects of a reward system on the individual, you must also consider the impact on other students. Using a reward program or giving one student increased attention may have a detrimental effect on the other students in the classroom. Is it possible that other students will learn to be "bad" in order to be included in the reward program? Most of the evidence on this question suggest that reward programs do not have and adverse effects on students who are not participating in the program if the teacher believes in the program and explains the reasons for using it to the nonparticipating students(Christy, 1975). If the conduct of some students does seem to deteriorate when their peers are involved in special programs, many of the same procedures discussed in this chapter should help them return to previous levels of appropriate behavior (Chance, 1992,1993).

第二节 认知理论学习观
(COGNITIVE VIEWS OF LEARNING)

Elements of the cognitive perspective

The cognitive perspective is both the oldest and the youngest member of the psychological community. It is old because discussions of the nature of knowledge, the value of reason, and the contents of the mind date back at least to the ancient Greek philosophers (Hemshaw, 1987). Then, from the late 1800s, cognitive studies fell from favor and behaviorism thrived. But research during World War II on the development of complex human skills, the computer revolution, and breakthroughs in understanding language development all stimulated a resurgence in cognitive research. Evidence accumulated indicating that people do more than simply respond to reinforcement and punishment. For example, we plan our responses, use systems to help us remember, and organize the material we are learning in our own unique ways (Miller, Galanter, &Pribram, 1960; Shuell, 1986). With the growing realization that learning is an active mental process, educational psychologists became interested in how people think, learn concepts, and solve problems (e.g., Ausubel, 1963; Bruner, Goodnow, & Austin, 1956).

Interest in concept learning and problem solving soon gave way, however, to interest in how knowledge is represented in the mind and particularly how it is remembered. Remembering and forgetting became major topic for investigation in cognitive psychology, and the information processing model of memory dominated research.

Today, there are other models of memory besides information processing. In addition, many cognitive theorists have a renewed interest in learning, thinking, and problem solving. The cognitive view of learning can best be described as a generally agreed-upon philosophical orientation. This means that cognitive theorists share basic notions about learning and memory.

Cognitive theorists believe, for example, that learning is the result of our attempts to make sense of the world. To do this, we use all the mental tools at our disposal. The ways we think about situations, along with our knowledge, expectations, feelings, and interactions with others, influence how and what we learn.

Comparing cognitive and behavioral views

The cognitive and behavioral views differ in their assumptions about what is learned. In the cognitive view, knowledge is learned and change in knowledge make changes in behavior possible. In the behavioral view, the new behaviors themselves are learned (Shuell, 1986). Both behavioral and cognitive theorists believe reinforcement is important in learning but for different reasons. The strict behaviorist maintain that reinforcement strengthens responses; cognitive theorists see reinforcement as a source of feed back about what is likely to happen if behaviors are repeated.

The cognitive view sees people as active learners who initiate experiences, seek out information to solve problems, and reorganize what they already know to achieve new insights. Instead of being passively influenced by environmental events, people actively choose, practice, pay attention, ignore, and make many other decisions as they pursue goals. Older cognitive views emphasized the acquisition of knowledge, but newer approaches stress its construction (Mayer, 1992).

Differences between behavioral and cognitive views are also apparent in the methods each group has used to study learning. Much of the work on behavioral learning principles has been with animals in controlled laboratory settings. The goal is to identify a few general laws of learning that apply to all higher organisms (including humans, regardless of age, intelligence, or other individual differences),

Cognitive psychologists, on the other hand, study a wide range of learning situations. Because of their focus on individual and developmental differences in cognition, they have not sought general laws of learning. This is one of the reasons that there is no single cognitive model of theory learning representative of the entire field.

The importance of knowledge in learning

Knowledge is the outcome of learning. When we learn a name, the history of cognitive psychology, the rules of tennis, or when to ask a friend for a favor, we know something new. Knowledge is more than the end product of previous learning; it also glides new learning The cognitive approach suggests that one of the most important element in the learning process is what the individual brings to the learning situation. What we already know to a great extent what we will learn, remember, and forget(Peeck, van den Bosch & 1982; Resnick.1981; Shuell, 1986).

A study by Recht and Leslie (1988) shows the importance knowledge in understanding and remembering new information. These psychologists identified junior high school students who were either very good or very poor readers. They tested the students on their knowledge of baseball and found that knowledge of baseball was not related to reading ability .So the researchers were able to identify four groups of students good readers high baseball knowledge, good readers/low baseball knowledge, poor readers/high baseball knowledge, and poor readers/low baseball knowledge. Then all the subjects read a passage describing a baseball game and were tested in a number of ways to see if they understood and remembered what they had read.

The results demonstrated the power of knowledge. Poor readers who knew baseball remembered more than good readers with little baseball knowledge and almost as much as good readers who knew baseball. Poor readers who knew little about baseball remembered the least of what they have read. So a good basis of knowledge can be more important than good learning strategies in understanding and remembering.

As a framework for examining learning and memory, we will use a well researched model, information processing.

Met cognition, Self–Regulation, and Individual Differences

One question that intrigues many cognitive psychologists are why some people learning and remember more than others. For those who hold an information processing view, part of the answer lies in the executive control processes, **Executive control process** guide the flow of through the information processing system.

We have already discussed a number of control processes, including selective attention, maintenance rehearsal, elaborative rehearsal, organization, and elaboration, These executive control processes are sometimes called met cognitive skills, **Metacognition** literally means knowledge about cognition. Donald Meichenbaum and his colleagues describe met cognition as people's "awareness of their own cognitive machinery and how the machinery works" (Meichenhaum, Burland, Gruson, & Cameron, 1985, p.5). Because people differ to their met cognitive knowledge and skills, they differ in how well and how quickly they learn.

Some of the differences in met cognitive abilities are due to development. As children grow older they are more able to exercise executive control and use strategies. For example, they are more able to determine if they have understood instructions (Markman, 1977, 1979) or if they have studied enough to remember a set of items (Flaveil, Friednchs, & Hoyt, 1970). Older children automatically use more efficient techniques than younger children for memorizing information(Flavell, 1985;Pressley, 1982). Met cognitive abilities begin to develop around ages 5 to 7 and improve throughout school. Most children go through a transitional period when they can apply a particular strategy if reminded, but will not apply it on their own (Gamer,1990).

Not all differences in met cognitive abilities have to do with age or maturation. There is great variability even among students of the same developmental level. Some individual differences in met cognitive abilities are probably caused by biological differences or by variations in learning experiences. Students can vary greatly in their ability to attend selectively to information in their environment. In fact, many students diagnosed as learning disabled actually have attention disorders (Hallahan & Kauffman, 1994), particularly with long tasks (Pelham, 1981). Attention is also influenced by the individual and cultural differences, such as learning abilities and preferences, cognitive styles, and cultural background. Students who are field dependent, for example, have difficulty perceiving elements in a pattern and tend to focus on the whole.

Met cognition involves at least two separate components: declarative and procedural knowledge of the skills, strategies, and resources needed to perform a task—knowing what to do and how to do it; and conditional knowledge to ensure the completion of the task—knowing when to do it. The use of these regulatory or met cognitive abilities is known as cognitive monitoring (Fla veil,1985). Let's examine some of the individual differences in met cognitive abilities that affect short-term memory and long-term memory.

Individual differences and working memory

As you might expect, there are both developmental and individual differences in short-term memory. Research indicates that young children have very limited working memories, but their memory span improves with age. It is not clear whether these differences are due to changes in memory capacity or improvements in strategy use. Case(1985a & b) suggests that the total amount of space available for processing information is the same at each age, but young children must use quite a bit of this space to remember how to execute basic operations, like reaching for a toy, finding the right word for an object, or counting. Using a new operation takes up quite a bit of the child s working memory. Once an operation is mastered, however, there is more working memory available for short-term storage of new information. Biology may play a role too. As the brain and neurological system of the child mature, processing may become more efficient so that more working-memory space is available.

As children growing older, they develop more effective strategies for remembering information. Most children spontaneously discover rehearsal around age 5 or 6. Siegler(1991) describes a 9-year-old boy who witnessed a robbery, then mentally repeated the license number of the getaway car until he could give the number to the police. Younger children can be taught to rehearse, and will use the strategy effectively as long as they are reminded. But they will not apply the strategy spontaneously. Children are 10 to 11-years old before they have adult like working memories.

According to Case (1985 a & b), young children often use reasonable, but incorrect strategies for solving problems because their limited memories. They try to simplify the task by ignoring important information or skipping steps to reach a correct solution. This puts less strain on memory. For example, when comparing quantities, young children may consider only the height of the water in a glass, not the diameter of the glass, because this approach demand less of their memory. According to case, this explains young children's inability to solve the classic Piagetian conservation problem.

There are several developmental differences in how students use organization, elaboration, and knowledge to process information in working memory. Around age 6, most children discover the value of using organizational strategies and by 9 or 10 they use these strategies spontaneously. So, given the following words to learn: couch, orange, rat, lamp, pear sheep, banana, rug, pineapples, horse, table, dog an older child or an adult might organize the words into three short lists of furniture, fruit, and animals. Younger children can be taught to use organization to improve memory, but they probably won't apply the strategy unless they are reminded. Children also become more able to use elaboration as they mature, but this strategy is developed late in childhood. Creating images or stories to remember ideas more likely for older elementary-school students and adolescents (Siegler,1991).

Besides development differences, there are other individual variations in short-term memory. Some people seem to have more differences in working memory may be associated with gift in math and verbal areas. For example, subjects in one research study were asked to remember lists of numbers, the locations of marks on a page, letters, and words (Dark & Benbow, 1991). Subjects who excelled in mathematics remembered numbers and locations significantly better than subjects talented in verbal area. The verbally talented subjects, on the other hand, had better memories for words. Based on these results, Dark and Ben bow believe that basic differences in information processing abilities play a role in the development of mathematical and verbal talent.

Because working memory is limited, students, particular younger and less able students, often try to simplify new information by ignoring some elements. This can lead to error. Case (1985b) suggests the following procedures for dealing with young children or with any students whose working-memory capacity is limited. First, observe the students who are failing at a particular task and deterring if they are trying to oversimplify the task. Second, find some ways to point out what they are ignoring and why their oversimplified approach won't work. Then demonstrate a better strategy. Finally, let the students practice the new approach. Throughout this process, try to minimize the amount of information the students have to remember by reducing the number of items involved, using familiar terms, emphasizing what is really important, keeping the steps small, and giving lots of practice so that each steep becomes as automatic as possible.

Individual differences and long-term memory

The major individual difference that affects long-term memory is knowledge. When students have domain-specific declarative and procedural knowledge, they are better at learning and remembering material in that domain. Think what it is like for you to read a very technical textbook in an area you know little about. Every line is difficult. You have to stop and look up towards or turn back to read about concepts you don't understand. It is hard to remember what you are reading because you are trying to understand and remember at the same time. But with a good basis of knowledge, learning and remembering become easier; the more you know, the easier it is to know more. This is true in part because having knowledge improves strategy use. Now that we have examined the information processing explanation of how knowledge is in memory, how memory might work, and the ways that individual students differ, let's turn to the really important question: What does this tell us about how teachers can help students learning and remembering better? How can teachers support the development of knowledge?

Constructivism: Challenging Symbolic Processing Models

The information processing presented in this chapter share several features, even if they differ in their views of memory. All of these approaches see the human mind as a physical symbol-processing system that converts sensory input into symbol structures (e.g. propositions, images, schemas) then processes those symbol structures so knowledge can be held in memory and research has focused on knowledge representation and memory, and recently on the learning of school subjects such as reading, writing, science, and mathematics.

Information processing theorists believe that we actively construct knowledge based on what we already know and the new information we encountered, so these approaches are constructivist, at least in a narrow sense. But, as you will soon see, many researchers and educators believe that these symbolic processing approaches do not take the idea of knowledge construction far enough (Derry,1992).

Even though symbolic processing models dominated cognitive research for many years, other views of learning were developing as well. Today, there is a strong challenge to cognitive views of learning—the **constructivist perspective**. This perspective is grounded in the research of Piaget, Vygotasky, the Gestalt psychologists, Bartlett, and Brunar as well as the educational philosophy of John Dewey, to mention just a few intellectual roots. As with information processing views, there is too no one constructivist theory of learning. For example, there are constructivist approaches in science and mathematics education, in education psychology and anthropology, and in computer-based education. Some constructivist views emphasize the shared, social constrction of knowedge; others see social forces as less important (Cognition,1991; Spiro Feltovich, Jacobsin & Coulson, 1991; Tobin, 1994; von Glaserfeld. 1990; Wittrock,1992).

One of the beginnings of constructivist approaches can be traced to studies of perception conducted early in this century in Germany (and later in the United States) by psychologists called Gestalt theorists. **Gestalt**, which means something like pattern or configuration in German, refers to people's tendency to organize sensory information into patterns or relationships. Instead of perceiving bits and pieces of unrelated Information, the human brain transforms objective reality into mental events organized as meaningful wholes (Schunk, 1991, p.129).F.C.Bartlett (1932) was another early constructivist theorist, His studies of the constructive nature of remembering (described earlier) highlighted the fact that remembering is more than recalling. As we remember, we often create meaning based on what we know and expect.

Knowledge: Accuracy Versus Usefulness

A fundamental difference between symbolic processing and constructivist perspectives is that symbolic theorists assume the world is knowable; there is an objective reality "out there" , and an individual can form a relatively complete understanding of it. This understanding may be more or less accurately. Our knowledge constructions may be filled with misconceptions about how the world operates. For example, young children sometimes construct a subtraction procedure that says,

"subtract the smaller number from the large number, no matter which number in a problem is on top."

Many of the more radical cognitive constructivist perspectives, on the other hand, do not assume that the world is knowable. They suggest that all knowledge is constructed and based upon not only prior knowledge, but also the culture and social context. They point out that what is true in one time and place—such as the "fact" before Columbus's time that the earth was flat—becomes false in another time and place. Constructivists are not concerned with accurate, "true"representation of the world, but only with useful construction.

Radical constructivists hold that we live in a relativistic world that can only be understood from individually unique perspectives, which are constructed through experimental activity in the social/physical world. No individual's viewpoint thus constructed should be viewed as inherently distorted or less correctly than another's although it is certainly true that one individual perspective can be more useful than another. (Derry, 1992, p.415).

Particular ideas may be useful within a specific **community of practice**, such as fifteenth century navigation, but useless outside that community. What counts as new knowledge is determined in part by how well the new idea fits with current accepted practice. Over time, the current practice may be questioned and even overthrown, but until such major shifts occur, current practice will shape what is considered useful.

A second difference between information processing and many of the current constructivist perspectives is that information processing theorists tend to focus on the individual information processor as he or she tries to make sense of the world. Thus cognitive psychologists study individual and developmental differences, but may ignore the social situation in which learning occurs. In contrast, social constructivist approaches affirm Vygotsky's notion that learning is inherently social and embedded in a particular cultural setting. Learning in the real world is not like studying in school. It is more like an apprenticeship where novices, with the support of an expert guide and model, take on more and more responsibility until they are able to function independently. For the social constructivist, this explains learning in factories, around the dinner table, in high school halls, in street gangs, in the business office and on the playground. Because learning takes place in a social situation, the norms of the group and the identity of the individual in the must be considered (Derry, 1992).

第三节 人本主义学习观
（HUMANISTIC VIEWS OF LEAMSING）

BASIC ASSUMPTIONS

If you were to ask ten randomly selected educational psychologists to describe the S-R and cognitive-perceptual views by listing basic assumptions, referring to key experiments, and noting teaching techniques derived from each position, their response would probably stress many of the same points. If you asked them to do the same for the humanistic view, however, their responses probably would differ to such an extent that you might wonder whether they were talking about the same thing. The disparity would be likely because the phrases humanistic psychology and humanistic education are used in a variety of ways and even those who identify themselves as humanistic psychology and educators stress different ideas. One reason for this diversity of opinion is that humanists and psychology and education come from varied back round's and do not share a common interest in do those who endorse the views of Skinner (learning) or Bruner (cognitive and discovery). Even though the humanistic view is not well defined, it does involves a cluster of assumptions and techniques that are sufficient different from the two views already to merit mention in a text on how to apply psychology to teaching.

The humanistic view is not based on experimental data, such as reports of the behavior of rats in a Skinner box or apes in problem situations; instead, it is based on observations, impressions, and speculations. To structure this discussion assumptions, the experiences and observation of the "elder statesmen" of humanistic psychology—Abraham H. Maslow, Carl R. Rogers, and Arthur Combs will be summarized.

Maslow: Let children grow

Maslow earned his Ph.D in a psychology department that supported the behaviorist associations position. After he graduated, however, he came into contact with Gestalt psychologists, prepared for a career as a psychoanalyst, and became interested in anthropology. As a result of these various influences, he came to the conclusion that American psychologists who endorsed the behaviorist position bud become so preoccupied with overt behavior and objectivity that they were ignoring some of the most important aspects of human existence. This conclusion was reinforced when his first child was born. Maslow observed later: "All the behaviorist psychology that I'd learn didn't prepare me for having a child. A baby was so miraculously and so wonderful all the work with rats...just did not help at all" (quoted in wilson, 1972, p.146), (B. F. Skinner by contrast, found that his with rats did help him bring up his children. He designed an ingenious combination crib-playpen for his daughter. Superficially, the Air Crib, as it is called, resembles a Skinner box. But it is not intended to shape a child's behavior. Instead, it serves as a controlled environment in which an infant can sleep, explore, and play in safety and comfort.)

Maslow became convinced that a strict Freudian view of behavior, which led to the conclusion that human beings beings desperately strive to maintain control of themselves, also had limitations, primarily because much of it was based on the behavior of neurotic individuals. When he observed the behavior of especially well-adjusted persons or self-actualizers, as an alternative to the behaviorist and psychoanalytic interpretation of behavior, Maslow proposed third force psychology. This view is good for them. Parents and teachers are therefore urged to trust children and to let and help them grow instead of interfering too much and trying to shape their behavior.

Rogers: learner-centered education

Caxl R, Rogers had experience quite similar to those of Maslow, and he came to similar conclusions. Rogers began his career at a psychotherapist who used psychoanalytic techniques. Eventually he came to a conclusion identical to that of Maslow: The psychoanalytic view sometimes made troubled human beings appear to be helpless individuals who needed the more or less constant help of psychotherapists to cope with their problems. Over a period of years Rogers developed a new approach to psychotherapy . He called it client centered (or nondirective) therapy to stress that the client, rather than the therapist, should be the central figure. (Or, as the term nondirective indicates, the therapist was not to tell the patient what was wrong and what should be done about it.) This view of therapy is h departure from psychoanalysis, where the analyst is the central figure who makes interpretations and offers prescriptions. It is also based on rejection of the strict behaviorist view of determinism, since It is assumed that the client will learn how to control his or her own behavior (and not merely be shaped by experiences).

As he practiced client-centered therapy, Rogers came to the conclusion that he was most successful when he established certain condition (1967, pp.53-54). He did not attempt to put up a false front of any kind, He established a warm, positive, accept attitude toward his clients, and he was able to empathize with clients and sense their thoughts and feelings. Rogers concluded that these conditions set the stage for successful experiences with therapy because clients became more self-accepting and aware of themselves. Once individuals acquired these qualities, they were inclined and equipped to solve personal problems without seeking the aid of a therapist.

In addition to functioning as a therapist, Rogers also served as a professor. As he analyzed his experience as an instructor he came to the conclusion that the principles of client-centered therapy could be applied just as successful to teaching. He proposed that education become learner-centered and that teachers try to establish the same conditions as client-centered therapists. Refers sums up the qualities of a teacher who wants to use a learner-centered approach in this ways:

One of the requisites for teacher who would facilitate this type of learning is a profound trust in the human organism...If we trust the capacity of the human individual for developing his own potentiality, then we can permit him the opportunity to choose his own way in his learning.

Another element of the teacher's functioning which stands out is his sincerity, his realness, his absence of facade. He can be a real person in his relationship with his students. He can be angry. He can also be sensitive and sympathetic...Thus he is a person to his students.

Another attitude which stands out is a prizing of the student, a prizing of his feeling and opinions.

Still another element in the teacher's attitude is his ability to understand the student's reactions from the inside, an emphatic awareness of the way the process of education and learning seems to the student. (1967, pp.59-60)

Rogers argues that the results of learner-centered teaching are similar to those of client-centered therapy: Students become capable of educating themselves without the aid of teachers.

Combs: The teacher as facilitator

Arthur Combs became an enthusiastic advocate of the humanistic view after having experiences similar to those of Maslow or Rogers. He also became disenchanted with behaviorism and psychoanalysis and sought an alternative. While Maslow based his conception of third force psychology on the study of motivation on and Rogers based his view on his experiences as a psychotherapist, Combs uses the cognitive view as a starting point for his speculations. He begins with the assumption that "all behavior of a person is the direct result of his field of perceptions at the moment of his behaving" (1965, p.12). (This is the same point emphasized by Kurt Lewin's concept of the life space.) From this assumption it follows that a teacher should try to understand any learning situation by speculating about how things seem from the students' point of view, this assumption also leads to the conclusion that to help students learning, it is necessary to induce them to modify their beliefs and perceptions so that they will see things differently and behave differently.

Some aspects of Combs's analysis of learning are similar to those of Bruner and other cognitive psychologists, but Combs places less stress on cognitive aspects of learning and more emphasis on personal perceptions of the learner.

Combs believes that how a person perceives herself or himself is of paramount importance and a basic purpose of teaching is to help each student develop a positive self-concept. Maslow and Combs both assert that human being are self-motivated, but Maslow explains in terms of a hierarchy of needs, while Combs proposes that all behavior is due to a single basic need for adequacy. If it is assumed that students are eager to become as adequate as possible in any situation, the role of the teacher is seen in a much different light than when it is assumed (as in S-R theory), that behaviors are shaped by reinforcing experiences. Combs observes, "The task of the teacher is not one of prescribing, making, molding, forcing, coercing, coaxing, or cajoling; it is one of ministering to a process already in being. The role required of the teach is that of facilitator, encourager, helper, assister, colleague, and friend of his students" (1965,p.16). Combs elaborates on these points by listing six characteristics of good teachers: (1) They are well informed about their subjects. (2) They are sensitive to the feelings of students and colleagues.(3) They believe that students can learn. (4) They have a positive self-concept. (5) They believe in helping all students do their best. (6) They use many different methods of instruction (1965, pp.20-23).

Cognitive and humanistic views: Similarities and differences

In many respect, the assumptions of the humanistic view are similar to those upon which the discovery approach to learning is based. Cognitive psychologists and humanistic educators share the view that extreme interpretations of the behaviorist-environmentalist associations position may lead to unfortunate school practices. Humanists agree with Bruner that observing only overt behavior is restrictive and that occurs when stimuli are responses may often be limited and may lacked personal meaning. Humanists differ from cognitive psychologists, however, in stressing the significance of emotions, feelings, personal fulfillment, and relationships with others. An example of this difference is provided by the reaction of Richard M. Jones to Bruner's approach to teaching Man: A Course of Study. In Fantasy and 1 sterile and that class activities with the MACQS materials should be arranged to stimulate pupils "emotional and imaginal response" (1968, p.9), He describes his own experiences in presenting MACOS and says that the most meaningful learning took place in a situation of "controlled emotion" (p.25).

A similar point is made by George Dennison, who asserts in The Lives of Children that Bruner is too concerned with control, social engineering, manipulation (1969, p.253). Dennison suggests that the discovery approach is most effective when it is arranged so that students can interact with the teacher and each other in situation in which they are free to reveal themselves. He presents his critique and describes ways to improve on the Bruner approach (as well as education in general) in Chapter 12 of his book.

Merging the cognitive, affective, and psychomotor domains

An argument often made by humanistic psychologists is that the tendency for behavioral scientists to subdivide topics and engage in specialized research has led to the assumption that human behavior must be compartmentalized. Many texts in psychology classify types of behavior into three major domains: cognitive (thinking), affective (emotions, attitudes, and values), and psychomotor (physical skills). It is essential to resort to such subdividing schemes when discussing complex topics, but humanistic psychologists and educators maintain that it is a mistake to try to subdivide behavior in classrooms. They recommend that teachers arrange for learning experiences so that students think and feel and perhaps also engage in physical activities at the same, instead of taking separate courses in subject matter, attitude formation, and physical education.

Still another point made by humanists is that students should be encouraged to explore their feelings and to engage in many form of self-expression. The term humanist reflects the idea that we should not lose sight of the fact that we are, after all, human. Maslow and Combs acknowledge that the behaviorist stress on objectivity and precise observation led to impressive advances in knowledge of human behavior, but they point out that it has also caused S-R theorists to sometimes equate humans with simple animals, machines, or computers. Machines and computers do not fall in love, experience, anger or jealousy, or become ecstatic about especially experiences. Animals may have such feelings, but they are incapable of analyzing them or of perfecting ways of expressing or communicating them with depth, subtlety, and permanence. The humanistic psychologist or educator believes that the unique qualities of human beings should be developed to the fullest possible degree.

A final point made by several psychologists who identify themselves as humanists is that students should be helped to become aware of and clarify their values. In the opening chapter of Values Clarification, Sidney B. Simon, Leland H. Howe, and Howard Kirshenbaum call attention to the fact that young people today are faced by many decisions and must choose from among many alternatives. The authors maintain that "everything we do, every decision we make and course of action we take, is based on our consciously or unconsciously held beliefs, attitudes and values"(1972, p.13). In Personalizing Education: Values Clarification and Beyond, Leiand W.Howe and Mary Martha Howe assert that "If our values are clear, consistent, and soundly chosen, we tend to live our lives in meaningful and satisfying ways" (1975, p.17). In addition to endorsing the basic assumptions proposed by Maslow, Rogers, and Combs, then humanistic psychologists and educators support the view that students should not only acquire knowledge and perfect intellectual and motor skills, they should examine their emotions, explore their feelings, learn how to communicate with others, engage in many forms of self-expression, and clarify their attitudes and values.

In the preceding portions on the S-R view and the cognitive-discovery view, the section following the outline of assumptions consisted of a description of experiments that serve as a foundation for and demonstration of the principles of each theory. It is impossible to insert such a section in this chapter because the humanistic view is not based on experimental evidence. There was, however, what might be thought of as a fifty-year "experiment" in humanistic education, and a brief account of this will be offered as a substitute for a description of systematic research.

An experiment in humanistic education

In 1921 A S. Neill, who had experienced difficulties and frustrations served as a teacher in English public schools, established his own school. He called it Summer hill, and after the school had been in operation for forty years, a compilation of his earlier writings was published in 1960 under the tide Summerhill. It became an immediate best seller and was frequently described as the most important book ever written on education. In the first chapter of Summer hill Neill states his basic philosophy, which is essentially the same as that of Maslow, Rogers, and Combs: "My view is that a child is innately wise and realistic. If left to himself without adult suggestion of any kind, he will develop as far as tie is capable of developing" (1960, p.4). Neill on this point in the third chapter, titled "SumiDerhill Education vs. Standard Education." In criticizing standard education, he argues, "Every time we show Tommy how his engine works we are stealing from that child the joy of life—the joy of over-coming an obstacle. Worse! We make that child come to believe that he is inferior, and must depend on help" (p.25).

In other parts of Summerhill, it becomes clear that Neill himself did not endorse this view in actual practice. There were teachers at Summerhill, and they offered lessons. Pupils were not compelled to attend the lessons, but if a child skipped several classes and then asked the teacher to take time to explain what had been missed, those who had attended regularly had the right to forbid him or her from coming to future sessions. Afternoons were free for both teachers and pupils to do as they wished. Most students spent their time on working on art or crafts projects, or writing and producing plays.

Every Saturday night a general meeting was held. Any person who had a grievance against any other individual could bring it up at these meetings, and all members of the school—faculty and students alike—were allowed to vote in determining if the complaint was just. If a majority agreed that a particular action infringed on: the rights of others, the offending party to promise not to repeat the action, and might also be required to pay a fine or give up a privilege. General school policies were also determined at these meetings. On one occasion, for example, Neill argued that children below the age of sixteen should not be allowed to smoke because tobacco is "a drug, poisonous, not a real appetite in children, but mostly an attempt to be grown up" (p.45).When the vote was taken, Neill's proposal was defeated by a large majority.

Neill proved that school based on the modified assumption that "children are innately wise and realistic" was workable. A significant point to keep in mind, though, is that Summerhill was a full-time boarding school and parents who sent their children to Neill asked him to serve not only as teacher but also as substitute parent. Accordingly, it hardly any of the polices in. Force at Summerhill can be used in public schools. Few parents of public school children are likely to support the view that children of all ages should select their own curricula, for example, nor are they likely to agree that students should be permitted to outvote teachers and administrators in determining school regulations. Thus, even though Neill successfully carried out a fifty-year experiment in humanistic education, the techniques he developed can be used in pure from only in small, private boarding schools. For information about techniques of humanistic education that might be used in American public school, it is necessary to turn to books, by other advocates of this view.

Criticisms of humanistic education

One of the most fundamental criticisms of the humanistic view Is that it is not based on empirical data or on a consistent set of principles. Programmed instruction and behavior modification are based on a substantial amount of experimental evidences. The cognitive–discovery view is derived from concepts of Gestalt psychology and field theory. As a consequence, it is possible to apply both the S–R and the cognitive view in the classroom by reasoning logically from a clearly stated theoretical position. Programmed approaches should feature a series of steps designed to lead the learner to specific goal; discovery session should be structured to encourage awareness of new relationships. Humanistic psychology, by contrast, is derived from an assortment of vaguely stated assumptions and observations. Proponents argue that teachers should trust children and let them grow without interference. But what, exactly, does that mean? How does one go about putting that philosophy into practice, and what happens if children are self–educated? One way to seek an answer to these questions is to evaluate Neill's Summerhill, since his school was the most consistent embodiment of the humanistic point of view.

How successful was Summerhill?

Neill maintained that "a child is innately wise and realistic. If left to himself without adult suggestion of any kind, he will develop as far as he is capable of developing" (1960, p.4). If taken literally, Neill's basic philosophy would mean that children should be expected to ignore all that adults of any kind have learned and try to discover everything for themselves. This is obviously an impossible task, which Neill himself recognized. He paid lip service to the joys of completely self–directed learning but hired teachers to provide lessons. Attendance at classes was voluntary, but peer pressure might has caused it to become at least partly compulsory. Furthermore, in describing some of the private lessons he provided Neill reveals that many Summerhill pupils sought and welcomed help from teachers.

Neill defended self–directed learning by arguing that his students learned as much as public school students and that they were much more likely to go into creative work after they left Summerbill. Neill's personal impressions were not supported by more objective observation made by others. A team of inspectors from the British Ministry of Education visited the school and wrote a report reprinted in Summerhill. They concluded, "On the whole the results of (the self–directed learning) system are unimpressive. It is true that the children work with a will and an interest that is most refreshing, but their achievements are rather meager" (p.80). The inspectors added that they felt the system would have worked better if the teachers had been more inclined to supervise, integrate, and guide the pupils.

Other evidence on the impact of Summerhillindioed was provided when a young American named Emmanuel Bernstein interviewed fifty graduates of the school. He reported (1968) that the occupations of the fifty were typical of the general population and did not include a disproportion ate number of creative individuals. When he asked the former Summerhillians for their general opinion of the school, ten of the fifty had nothing but praise. They left that their experiences at the school "had given them confidence, maturity, and had enabled them to find a fulfilling way of life" (p.38).On the other hand, seven of the fifty left Summerhill had been harmful them. Most of these felt that their experience at the school had "led them to find more difficult in life than they might have otherwise experience" (p.40). An interesting point emerged from the interviews was that those who had stayed at Summerhill for the fewest number of years tended to feel that they had benefited the most; those who had attended the longest "appeared most likely to have difficult and tenacious adjustment problems" (p.40). Perhaps the most significant point of all was the finding that "the majority of Summerhillians had only one major complaint against the school; the lack of academic opportunity and inspiration, couple with a dearth of inspired teachers" (p.41). Few of file graduates who had children of their own sent them to Summerhill. Some who did not have children at the time they were interviewed indicated that they might send their offspring to the school but only for a few years before the age of ten or so.

It appears then that when teachers are enjoined to trust children and let them grow, it is appropriate to add, "But don't expect them to make all the decisions themselves and give them help when they need it." Maslow himself recognized this when he made a distinction between bad choosers and good choosers. He suggested that only children who have their needs well satisfied and who enjoy close to optimal adjustment can be expected to make wise choices. Most children do not possess these desirable qualities and, if they are not guided by adults, will often make choices that are destructive.

"Humanistic teachers" do not have a monopoly on positive qualities

A criticism that is related to the idealistic, unrealistic, and vague nature of humanistic education probably deserves to be called a holier-than-thou attitude. Those who write on humanistic education sometimes describe themselves and those who endorse their views in ways that imply that all other types of educators are inhuman. Humanistic teachers are characterized as real persons who trust children. They prize students, believe in them, and sensitive to their needs. They want to help pupils do their best, and they do not prescribe, coax, or cajole but serve as facilitators and helpers. By implication, educators who do not endorse the views of Maslow, Rogers, and Combs are phony, distrustful, negative, dictatorial, insensitive pedagogues who don't care whether students learning and who fail to facilitate learning. The latter description may apply to a few no humanistic teachers, but a teacher who uses techniques of programmed instruction or the discovery approach can be just as real, trusting, and sensitive as a teacher who favors values clarification sessions or self-expressive activities. In terms of the results of learning experiences, it is probably reasonable to say that a teacher who gives a well-organized lecture on how to compute percentages for instance is being more of a facilitator and helper than one who leans against a windowsill and watches students engage in interpretations of melting ice cubes.

In addition to assuming a holier than-thou stance, some humanists also offer what might be classified as elaborate rationalizations for what they do. Suppose two teachers in an elementary school occasionally devote thirty minutes to interpretive dance. One, who has read several books on humanistic education, explains, "This is confluent education in which effective and cognitive elements flow together. It is intended to permit students to engage in a constructive dialogue with their fantasy lives, explore emotional responses to the world, break down interpersonal estrangement in order to facilitate communication and participation, and allow each unique individual to live fully and intensely here and now." The other teacher, who has not read any books on humanistic education, says, "The kids like to do this every now and then because it's fun and gives them a chance to move around and let off steam. Also, it saves me the trouble of preparing a lesson."

Humanistic educators claim too much

Humanistic educators make themselves vulnerable to criticism because they claim so much for the techniques they espouse. They aspire not to teach subject matter, but to create students who will be happy, well-adjusted self-actualizes with a firm sense of identity and a clear set of values. In Personalizing Education, Howe and Howe assert that "if our values are clearly, consistent, and soundly chosen, we tend to live our lives in meaningful and satisfying ways" . The Howe's use the phrase "soundly chosen," but they join other values clarification advocates in stressing that "Values Clarification is not an attempt to teach students 'right' and 'wrong' values. Rather, it is an approach designed to help student prize and act upon their own freely chosen values. Thus, V.C is concerned with the process by which students arrive at their values, rather than the content of these values" . There is no reason to assume, however, that students will automatically make sound choices when they engage in values clarification sessions. It is quite possible that when students are encouraged to develop clear and consistent values, they will choose those that focus on material possessions, power, self-indulgence, and the like. Considering the nature of high-pressure advertising in America and the kinds of individuals who achieve notoriety in our society, it would be surprising if such values were not favored by many young people. Simply because a person's values are made more consistent as a consequence of values clarification sessions, therefore, does not guarantee that the individual will live in a "meaningful and satisfying way" . It is just as likely that the opposite could be the case.

Furthermore, if Piaget's description of cognitive development is taken into account, there is reason to doubt that very many pupils will actually develop a consistent value system as a result of engaging in values clarification exercises. Many values clarification strategies are designed to be used with elementary school children who are at the concrete operations stage of cognitive development and unable to grasp abstract concepts or generalize. To cite just one example, when they are asked to indicate if they prefer ice cream, Jell-o, or pie for dessert (a question featured in a values clarification strategy intended to give children practice in choosing between alternatives), young children will probably react in a quite literal way. They will think about their favorite dessert but not about the principle of choosing between alternatives. There is no reason to believe that when they are faced with a choice involving values they will see any connection between picking a dessert and making a moral or ethical decision.

The same tendency to respond in literal ways is likely to be characteristic of many secondary school students as well, since the transition to formal thought is a gradual process. But even high school students who are capable of dealing with abstractions and hypothetical situation many don't develop a realistic or workable set of values, because novice formal thinkers tend to overlook realities. Secondary school students are also eager to impress others. If a high school girl volunteers to be interviewed by the class, for instance, she may supply glib and idealistic answers and be so preoccupied with making a good impression on classmates that there will be no carry-over to behavior outside of class. Simply because students can about positive values m discussing hypothetical situations, they will not necessarily act that way when the chips are down. Because of factors such as these, it is unrealistic to expect that use of values clarification strategies will equip students with a value system that will lead to a "meaningful and satisfying life."

Those who call themselves humanistic teachers may describe their philosophy of teaching in glowing (but vague) terms and make lavish claims about what they are doing to foster the development of better human beings. In actual practice, they are likely to make occasional use of games or strategies such as those described in books on values clarification. Many of these strategies are provocative and likely to arouse a positive response, but there is no substantive evidence that they have the intended effect. Typically, humanistic educators offer "proof" of the effectiveness of the techniques they recommend by providing diaries and impressions written by individuals who have had positive experiences with the methods described. Testimonials from selected students or teachers, however, do not prove anything. They are particularly unimpressive when one considers the claim that humanistic education leads students to live more meaningful and satisfying lives. Furthermore, in an era of accountability and low test scores, most parents, administrators, and school boards are not likely to be favorable impressed if teachers say that the primary goal of their instruction is to help students "explore or express themselves" or engage in "meaningful interpersonal relationships". You are reminded that in her criticism of Bruner's MACOS materials, Onalee McGraw delivered the opinion that "teaching children" to understand themselves' and be aware of themselves' is bunch of garbage. She went on to say, "By what authority are these people getting involved in the psychological development of, the child? And what right have teachers to probe into the delicate reaches of the child s mind and unleash the child's emotions?" (Shaar, 1975, p.5). Not all parents are as extreme or as out-spoken as McGraw, but many of them endorse, at least partially, the view that teachers should concentrate on helping children learn skills and subject matter and not try to set themselves up as psychotherapists in the classroom.

Suggestion for teacher: Appling the humanistic view in the classroom

1. Try to remain aware of the extent to which you direct and control learning—Whenever possible, permit and encourage students to make choices and to manage their own learning.

2. Establish a warm, positive, acceptant atmosphere. Do your best to communicate the feeling that you believe every student in the class can learn and that you want them to learn.

3. When it seems appropriate, function as a facilitator, encourage, helper, and assister. Before attempting to function as a colleague or friend, think about possible complications.

4. If you feel comfortable doing it, occasionally show that you are a "real person" by telling students how you feel. When you express anger, however comment on the situation, not on the personality traits of your students.

5. If you do not have strong positive feelings about yourself and how you function as a teacher, consider participating in individual or group counseling sessions, and also work at improve your skills as an instructor.

6. Do your best to help your students develop positive feelings about themselves. Empathize with them, and show you are sensitive to their feelings.

7. If appropriate, schedule occasional periods during which students are encouraged to examine their emotions.

8. If appropriate, schedule occasional periods during which students are encouraged to become more sensitive to the feelings of others.

9. If appropriate, schedule occasional periods when students are encouraged to express themselves through movement, physical contact, and creative dramatics.

10. If appropriate, ask students to participate in role playing, psychodrama, or simulation games.

11. Make systematic use of values clarification strategies.

a. Call attention to the process of values development.

b. Select and use strategies that seven steps in the process of values acquisition and call attention to ways an exercise illustrates one or more aspects of the sequence.

c. Use long-term strategies in class, and urge students to continue to use them on their own.

d. Look for ways to introduce values clarification strategies into lesson plans.

12. Use the Taxonomy of Educational Objectives: Affective Domain to identify specific goals of humanistic education.

13. Do you best to provide learning experience that will lead to the development of the habits and attitudes you want to foster.

14. Make use of object lessons. When illustrative incidents occur in the course of events, take advantage of them.

15. Set a good example.

16. Be aware of your students' level of moral development, and encourage understanding of subtle aspects of morality by presenting "moral dilemmas".

词汇 (Vocabulary)

1. ambivalently　　adv. 情绪矛盾地
2. adequacy　　n. 充分、适当
3. acquire　　vt. 获得、学到
4. aspire　　vi. 渴望
5. aversive　　a. 令人厌恶的
6. cognitive monitority　　认知监控
7. compartmentalize　　vt. 划分
8. competence　　n. 能力、胜任
9. complication　　n. 复杂的情况
10. consequencement　　n. 结果、后果

11. constructivism   n. 建构主义
12. contiguity   n. 接近、临近
13. delicate   a. 微妙的、难以处理的
14. demerit   n. 缺失、过失
15. demonstrate   vt. 证明、说明、证实
16. deteriorate   vt. 恶化、变化
17. determinism   n. 决定主义
18. detrimental   a. 不利的、有害的
19. discrimination   n. 分辨、区别
20. disenchant   vt. 使不抱幻想
21. disparity   n. 不同、不一致
22. distinguish   v. 区分、辨别
23. ecstatic   a 欣喜若狂的
24. efficacy   n. 功效、效验
25. elicit   vt. 诱发、引起
26. embodiment   n. 具体化、体现
27. emit   vt. 发出（刺激）、发表（意见）
28. emotional   a. 情绪（上）的、感情（上）的、易动感情的
29. empathic   a. 感情移入的
30. endorse   vt. 赞同
31. espouse   vt. 拥护、支持、采纳
32. extinction   n. 消失、灭绝
33. generalization   n. 泛化、概括、一般化
34. gestalt   n. 格式塔
35. glib   a. 流利的、喜辩的
36. grievance   n. 不满
37. holy   adj. 神圣的、至善的
38. innately   adv. 天生地
39. intensely   adj. 热情的
40. interact   vi. 相互作用、相互影响
41. intermittent   a. 间歇的、断断续续的
42. interpretive   a. 解释的、阐明的
43. involuntary   a. 不随意的、无意识的、偶然的
44. Ivan Pavlov   n. 巴甫洛夫
45. meager   a. 贫乏的、不足的
46. mention   vt. 提出、说起
47. merge   vt. 合并、结合
48. metacognitive skill   认知技能
49. minister   vi. 给予帮助照顾
50. model   n. 榜样、典型、原型
51. monopoly   n. 专利、独占
52. neutral   a. 中立的、中性的
53. notoriety   n 臭名昭著
54. novice   n. 新手、初学者
55. object lessons   实物教育课、直观教育课

56. operate   a. 操作性的
57. optimal   a. 最适宜的、最令人满意的
58. overt   a. 公开的、明显的
59. physiological   a. 生理学的、生理的
60. presentation   n. 表象
61. presentation punishment   n. 表象性惩罚
62. probe   n. 彻底调查
63. programmed instruction   程序化教学
64. proponent   n. 建议者、支持者
65. propocative   a. 引起争论的
66. reciprocal   a. 相互的、交互的
67. removal punishment   剥夺性惩罚
68. reinforcement   n. 强化
69. resurgence   n. 苏醒、复活
70. respondent   n. 反应、应答行为
71. retain   vt. 保持
72. retention   n. 保留、保持
73. ridicule   n. 嘲笑
74. salivate   vt. 流涎
75. seizure   n. 发作
76. spent   a. 用过的、精疲力尽的
77. stance   n. 姿态
78. sterile   a. 枯燥无味的、无效果的
79. substitute   n. 替代物、代用品
80. subtraction   n. 减法
81. suspension   n. 暂时停学、暂时中止、悬吊
82. Taxonomy of Education objectives   教育目标分类学
83. tease   vt. 取笑
84. tenacious   a. 固执的
85. testimonial   n.（资格、能力）证明书
86. unconditioned response   非条件反应
87. unconditioned stimulus   非条件刺激
88. unimpressive   a. 给人印象不深的、平淡的
89. unleash   vt. 释放
90. vicarious reinforcement   代替强化
91. vunerable   a. 易受责难的、易受伤的

第十七章 心理测量
（PSYCHOLOGICAL MEASUREMENT）

本章要点（Chapter Outline）
测量与评价（Measurement and Evaluation)
测量量表（Scales of Measurement)
测量与目标 (Measurement and Goal)
良好测量工具应具备的特征
(Characteristics of a Good Measuring Instrument)
标准化测验（Standardized Tests)
教师编制测验（Teacher-Made Tests)
参照标准测验（Criterion-Referenced Testing)

心理测量泛指依据某种特定规则，把所观察的心理现象及属性予以量化描述的过程，它是进行心理评价的基础。

心理测量工具的正确、可靠性是保证测量乃至评价准确的基础。因此，一个良好的测量工具应具备必要的特征，如较高的信度与效度等。心理测量的种类很多，可从不同的角度——测量的内容、测量的表现方式、测量的时间要求、施测人数、测验材料、解释测验结果的方式等进行分类。不同种类的测量工具在其编制、施测、记分、测量结果的解释等方面都有所差异，因而在实际研究中选择恰当的测量工具至关重要。

第一节 测量与评价
（MEASUREMENT AND EVALUATION）

The statement Alphonse Blodet has a nose that is five and a half inches long illustrates measurement. The statement Marie Robinet has a stupendous nose is an example of evaluation. Measurement involves the application of an instrument (a ruler in this case) to assess a specific quantity; evaluation is the formation of a judgment concerning certain qualities. In general, then, measuring is more precise and more objective; evaluating is less precise, more subjective.

Both measurement and evaluation are important parts of the instructional process. Instruction can be described as a sequence of procedures conducted before teaching, during teaching, and after teaching (see Table 17.1). In the before-teaching phase, measurement and evaluation may be involved in placing students, selecting instructional procedures, and determining student readiness. Plans for final assessment and evaluation should also be made at this stage. In the after-teaching phase, measurement and evaluation are employed not only to determine the extent to which instructional goals have been met, but also to assess the effectiveness of instructional strategies and to reevaluate student placement and strategies and to reevaluate student placement and readiness. Measurement is being employed when actual tests are used; it is essentially a quantitative process. Evaluation is being employed when teachers make decisions concerning the adequacy of instructional procedures, the readiness of students, and the extent to which curriculum goals are being met; it is a more qualitative process.

Evaluation don't need be based on measurement. Indeed, many teacher assessments of student behavior are not based on measurement. The countless value judgments made by teachers about the abilities of students, their motivation, their persistence, their pleasantness, and so on are often examples of evaluation without measurement. One of the major premise of this chapter is that evaluation should be based on measurement and, consequently, that the measuring instruments should be not only the best possible, but also used intelligently. It is possible to use them with something less than great wisdom. In order to simplify and clarify the content of this chapter, the term measurement will be predominant throughout. It should be kept in mind, however, evaluation often follows measurement.

Table 17.1 A model of the instructional process

Before Teaching

1. Establish goals

2. Determine student readiness

3. Select instructional strategies; collect required materials

4. Plan for assessment and evaluation

Teaching

Implement instructional strategies

After Teaching

1. Assess effectiveness of teaching strategies

2. Determine extent to which goals have been met

3. Reevaluate student readiness

第二节　测量量表
（SCALES OF MEASUREMENT）

There are a number of different ways of measuring things—a number of different scales of measurement that are appropriate for measuring different things (see Table 17.2). The crudest and least informative scale of measurement is a **nominal scale**. As its label implies, this level of measurement simply names. The numbers on the backs of football players or descriptive categories such as blue and red or house and barn are examples of nominal measurement. They tell us nothing about amount, but only indicate the categories to which things belong.

At a more advanced level, **ordinal scales** permit us to rank, or order, individuals on the basis of the characteristics we measure. For example, tasting different beverages might allow us to rank them in terms of sweetness. The ranking (or ordinal scale) tells us nothing about absolute amount of sugar, but does give us some information about relative amounts.

Table 17.2 Four scales of measurement

Scale	Characteristics and functions	Example
Nominal	Names: places things in categories	Labeling reading groups "giraffe", "zebras", and "Goats"
Ordinal	Ranks: tells us about relative amount (more than/less than)	Being in first grade, second grade, third grade, and so on
Interval	Measures in equal intervals: arbitrary Zero: permits precise measurement of Change, but not comparison of absolute amounts	Most psychological and educational measurement. We simply assume that score intervals are equal
Ratio	True zero and equal intervals: permits Comparison of absolute amounts	Weight: height

The third measurement scale, the **interval scale**, allows us to measure quantity in intervals that vary in fixed, predictable ways. We measure temperature using interval scales. We can say that a change from 0 to 10 degrees is equivalent to a change from 10 to 20 degrees or to a change from 20 to 30 degrees. But what the interval scale does not permit us to do is to say that 20 degrees is twice as hot (or half as cold) as 10 degrees or that 30 degrees is three times as hot as 10 degrees. In order to compare amounts in this way, we need to measure characteristics that conform to a **ratio scale**. A ratio scale has a true rather than an arbitrary zero. The zero in a temperature scale, for example, is completely arbitrary. It could have been set at any temperature and is, in fact, set different points in the Fahrenheit and the Celsius scales. Weight and age, on the other hand, have exct, no arbitrary zeros. And 40 pounds is twice as heavy as 20 punds.

Most of measurements in psychology and education make use of interval scales, although most of what we measure doesn't really fit this scale. That is, we assume that the difference between 60 and 70 percent on our standardized tests is roughly equivalent to the difference between 40 and 50 percent. The emphasis should be on the word roughly. In most instances, we have little evidence to support this assumption of equivalency.

While most measurement in education employs an interval scale, virtually none of it is direct. That is, no instruments have been devised yet that measuring knowledge directly, as a ruler measures distance or a scale measures weight. Measurement in education is like the estimation of temperature. The latter is inferred from the observation that a column of mercury or alcohol rises or descends in a hollow glass tube; the former is inferred from changes in behavior. Knowledge as a cognitive phenomenon is not measurable; but the assumption can be made that some of its effects on behavior are.

第三节 测量与目标
(MEASUREMENT AND GOALS)

The relationship between measurement in schools and educational goals is obvious. Less obvious is that specifying goals is essential to good measurement. It is difficult to imagine how teachers can assess the effectiveness of instructional procedures unless they know precisely what those procedures were intended to do. It is equally obvious that they will not know what procedures to employ unless they have already made a decision about the outcomes desired. A simple representation of the act of teaching comprises only three processes: specifying goals; implementing procedures to attain these goals; and evaluating the effectiveness of these procedures relative to the attainment of goals.

Goals

Goals are outcomes that are desired. School-related goals include not only the specific instructional goals of teachers but also the wider objectives of curricula, programs, principals, and communities. However, because questions relating to the wider objectives of education have been in the domains of philosophy, politics, and economics, rater than psychology, and because evaluation seldom goes beyond the goals of the classroom teacher, in this text we will discuss only the specific instructional goals of the teachers. Three approaches to specifying instructional objectives are mentioned here.

General Objectives. It is sometimes useful to begin the preparation of a unit or of an entire course by specifying in general terms what the final desired outcome of the instruction is. Such a statement may be of value in assessing the general effectiveness of the entire course or of a portion there. It is not likely to be of any real value, however, in determining the adequacy of specific instructional procedures or of particular lessons. For example, the general objectives of unit in the natural sciences may include a statement such as this:

The students should be familiar with the flora and fauna of the Rocky Mountains and adjoining foothills in North America.

While this statement of general objectives might serve as a guide for teachers, indicating to them that they need to prepare lessons about the flora and fauna of that area, it is not specific enough to serve as a blueprint for the construction of measuring instruments.

Specific Objectives. On the other hand, a specific instructional objective such as the following suggests means for evaluating the effectiveness of instructional procedures:

After the unit, the student should be able to recognize a lynx, a grizzly bear a cougar an elk a mountain sheep, and a moose when presented with these animals.

Any enterprising teacher can easily obtain bears, cougars, moose, lynx, elk, and sheep and use these both for instruction and for assessing the attainment of goals. A less enterprising teacher might settle for photographs or other visual aids. A useful exercise in the preparation of any lesson is to list specific objectives at the very outset. Not only useful for evaluative purposes, but they also often serve to clarify the teacher's thinking.

Bloom Taxonomy. Bloom et al. (1956) and Krathwohl, Bloom, and Masia (1964) have provided an exhaustive and useful list of educational objectives in the cognitive and affective domains. The usefulness of these lists of educational objectives (referred to as taxonomies) is that they can serve as guides in determining the goals for a lesson or course. The taxonomy of objectives for the cognitive domain, for example, describing a class of objectives, a list of educational objectives that correspond to this class, and test questions that illustrate it (see Table 17.3). The six hierarchical classes of objectives in that domain are, from the lowest to the highest level: **knowledge, comprehension, application, analysis, synthesis,** and **evaluation**. Each of these is broken down into subdivisions. You are referred to the handbook of objectives (Bloom et al., 1956) for a detailed consideration of a taxonomy of educational objectives (and to the box "Remembering and Thinking" for a preview of that detail) .

Table 17.3 Bloom's cognitive domain, defined and illustrated

Class of objectives	Example
1. Knowledge (items of factual information)	Who wrote A Midsummer Night s Dream? What was the author trying to say? Given what you know about the authenticity of the first quarto and about weather conditions in England in the summer of 1594, when do you think the play was written? Find the most basic metaphors in Act I, and explain their meaning. Identify the four themes in A Midsummer Night's Dream, and discuss how they contribute to the central action Do you agree with the statement that A Midsummer Night's Dream is Shakespeare's first undisputed masterpiece?
2. Comprehension (understanding; obtaining meaning from communication)	
3. Application (using information, principles and the like to solve problem)	
4. Analysis (arriving at an understanding by looking at individual parts)	
5. Synthesis (arriving at an understand−ing by looking at larger structure; by combining individual elements)	
6. Evaluation (arriving at value judgments)	

Blueprints for Teacher–Made Tests

We should emphasize at the outset that a test whether it is a teacher–made test or a standardized test is not like other common measuring instruments such as rulers, scales, and ther mometers. Rulers measure whatever they measure directly; our psychological and educational instruments measure indirectly. In effect, a student's test performance consists of a sample of behaviors (selected from a large number of potential behaviors) that, we assume, represents some knowledge, ability, or attitude, and on the basis of which we make inferences. It is important to realize that the inferences we make about knowledge, ability, or other student characteristics are never based on direct measurement; they are simply inferences—educated bits of speculation based on nothing more than a sample of behavior. Hence, the question of precisely which behaviors to sample is very important.

A **test blueprint** is, in effect, a table of specifications. It specifies the topics to be tested, the nature of the questions of the topics to be used, how many questions will relate to be sampled. Test sorts of cognitive processes to be sampled. Test blueprints don't need be developed only by the teacher but can also involve the collaboration of students. Constructing the blueprint can do a great deal to clarify instructional goals, both for the teacher and students. It can also contribute in important ways to the teacher's selection of instructional strategies as well as to the students' monitoring of their own learning processes.

Detailed test blueprints that take into consideration differences among possible learning outcomes can be based on systems such as Bloom's taxonomy. A typical test blueprint based on portions of this taxonomy takes the form of a table that lists all relevant topics down the side and all relevant domains across the top, and that specifies the number of items for each topic relating to each domain (see Table 17.4). Popham (1981) suggests, for example, that items be divided simply in terms of whether they involve recall or go beyond recall.

Table 17.4 A simple test blueprint – based on Bloom's taxonomy, cognitive domain – for Chapter 4 of this text

Cognition	Number of items by domain					
	Knowledge	Comprehension	Application	Analysis	Synthesis	Evaluation
Cognition	4	3	3	2	3	1
Bruner's theory	3	4	3	2	2	1
Ausubel's theory	3	3	2	2	2	1
Instruction	4	3	3	2	2	3
Total	14	13	11	8	9	6

There are a number of other ways to devise test blueprints, some of which are easier and more useful in certain subjects. In physical education classes, for example, where Bloom's taxonomy and other similar classifications are not highly relevant, teachers might simply make a listing of the skills that students are expected to acquire. This list of skills, together with an indication of the criteria that will be employed as evidence of skill mastery, serves as a test blueprint. Unfortunately, using this kind of test blueprint in physical education classes is rare. Most often, teachers rely on informal, intuitive evaluation. And although there is clearly a need for such evaluation, it is seldom as impartial as more formal evaluation. Nor does it serve nearly as well as a guide to instruction.

第四节　良好测量工具应具备的特征
（CHARACTERISTICS OF A GOOD MEASURING INSTRUMENT）

Validity

It might appear somewhat platitudinous to say that a good test must measure what it is intended to measure. It is true, however, that many tests probably do not measure exactly what they are intended to measure, or they measure many other things as well and are therefore difficult to depend on. Obviously, **validity** is the most important characteristic of a measuring instrument since, if it does not measure what it purports to, then the scores derived from it are of no value whatsoever.

There are four different ways of measuring or estimating validity—four indexes of validity (see Table 17.5). The first, **face validity**, is the extent to which the test appears to measure what it is supposed to measure. This is probably the easiest type of validity to determine; if a test looks valid, then it at least has face validity. This type of validity is particularly important for teacher-made tests, where students should know just by looking at a test that they are, in fact, being tested on the appropriate things. In other words' a mathematics test that has face validity will consist of items that look like mathematics items; similar items would not find their way into an English easefulness, of course, the teacher had, for some reasons, undertaken to deceive the students in order to measure their spontaneous knowledge of mathematics. This possibility might seem a little remote, but there are other circumstances under which test makers very carefully avoid any semblance of face validity. Tests designed to measure some personality characteristics such as honesty or openness, for example, are likely to be highly invalid if they appear to measure what they are actually intended to measure. Since we know that dishonest people might very well lie to us, we are not likely to obtain an accurate measure of their honesty if we let them know that that is what we are not likely to obtain an accurate measure of their honesty if we let them know that that is what we are interested in. Better to deceive them, lie to them, to determine what liars and scoundrels they really are.

Content validity, a second important index of the extent to which a test measures what it purports to, is assessed by analyzing the content of test items in relation to the objectives of the course, unit, or lesson. Content validity is perhaps the most crucial kind of validity when dealing with the measurement of school achievement. A test with high content validity includes items that sample all important course objectives (both content and process objectives) in pro-portion to their importance. That is, if some of the objectives of an instructional sequence are the development of cognitive processes, then a relevant test will have content validity to the extent that it samples these processes. And if 40 percent of the course content (and, consequently, of the course objectives) deals with knowledge (rather than with comprehension, analysis, and so on), then 40 percent of the text items should reflect knowledge. Determining the content, validity of a test is largely a matter of careful logical analysis. One of the great advantages of preparing a test blueprint of the kind described earlier is not only that it can guide instruction, but also that it should ensure content validity.

Table 17.5 Types of test validity: Determining that a test measures what it purports to measure

Face	The test looks like it measures what it says it measures
Construct	The test taps hypothetical variables that underlie the property being tested
Content	The test samples behaviors that represent the topics as well as the processes implicit in course objectives
Criterion−Related: Predictive	Test scores are valuable predictors of performance in related areas at a later time
Concurrent	Test scores are closely related to similar measures obtained by other means, at about the same time

It is important to note that tests and test items do not possess validity as a sort of intrinsic quality. That is, a test is not generally valid or generally invalid; rather, it is valid for certain purposes and with certain individuals and invalid for others. For example, if the following item is intended to measure comprehension, then it does not have content validity:

How many different kinds of validity are discussed in this chapter?
  a) 1
  b) 2
  c) 3
  d) 4
  e) 10

If, on the other hand, the item were intended to measure knowledge of specifics, then it would have content validity. And an item such as the following might have content validity with respect to measuring comprehension.

A third type, **construct validity**, is conceptually more difficult than face or content validity. It is somewhat less relevant for teacher−constructed tests but is highly relevant for many other psychological measures (personality and intelligence tests, for example). In essence, a construct is a hypothetical variable an unobservable characteristic or quality, very often derived from theory. For example, a theory might specify that individuals who are highly intelligent should be reflective rather than impulsive. One way of determining the construct validity of a test designed to measure intelligence would then be to look at how well it correlates with measures of reflection and impulsivity.

One of the principal uses of tests is to predict future performance. Thus, we assume that all students who do well on our year–end fifth-grade achievement tests will do reasonably well in sixth grade. And we also predict that those who perform very poorly on these tests would not do well in sixth grade, and we might use this prediction as justification for having them fail fifth grade. The extent to which our predictions are accurate reflects the fourth type of validity: **criterion–related validity**, One component of criterion–related validity, just described, is labeled **predictive validity** and is easily measured by looking at the relationship between performance on a test and later performance. Thus, a college entrance examination designed to identify those students whose chances of college success are high versus those who are not likely to succeed has predictive validity to the extent that its predictions are borne out. **Concurrent validity**, a second aspect of criterion–related validity, is the relationship between a test and other measures of the same behaviors. For example, the most accurated way of measuring intelligence is to administer a time-consuming and expensive individual test; a second way is to administer a quick, inexpensive group test; a third, far less consistent approach is to have teachers informally assess intelligence on the basis of what they know of their students' achievement and effort. Teacher assessments are said to have concurrent validity to the extent that they correlate with the more formal measures. In the same way, the group test is said to have concurrent validity if it agrees well with measures obtained in other ways.

A second requirement of a good measuring instrument is that it be reliable. This means that the test should measure consistently whatever it measures. An intelligence test that yields a score of 170 for a student one week and a score of 80 the next week is probably somewhat unreliable (unless something has happened to the student between the tests.) An instrument that is highly unreliable cannot be valid. In other words, if a test measures what it purports to and that attribute does not fluctuate erratically, then the test will yield similar scores on different occasions. Hence, one way of assessing reliability is to correlate results obtained by giving the test twice or by giving two different forms of the same test. This is called **repeated–measures** or **parallel forms reliability**, Another way, called **split–half reliability**, is to divide the test into halves and correlate the scores obtained on each half. If all items are intended to measure the same thing, the scores on the halves should be similar.

A number of different factors are involved in determining the apparent reliability of a test. One is the stability of what is being measured. Clearly, if a characteristic fluctuates dramatically over time, then measurements of that characteristic will also fluctuate. However, most of the things we measure in psychology and education are not expected to fluctuate unpredictably. That is, although we expect change in many characteristics, we can often predict the nature of the change. Students are expected to read better, understand more clearly, solve more problems, and generally improve cognitively through school. Tests that are valid and reliable should reflect these changes.

A second factor that affects test reliability has to do with the test rather than with the trait being measured and sometimes called **equivalence reliability** and sometimes called equivalence reliability (Wiersma and Jurs, 1985). Simply defined, equivalence reliability refers to the extent to which different forms of a test (either parallel forms or split halves) yield consistent results.

A third important factor, particularly with respect to teacher-constructed, multiple-choice or true-false tests, is chance. As an example, consider a test consisting of twenty true-false items. The chance of getting any single item correct, if the student knows next to absolutely Lady Luch is looking pointedly in the other direction, the average score of a large class of hypothetical know nothing should be around 50 percent. And some of the luckier individuals in this class may have astoundingly high scores. But a subsequent administration of this or of parallel examination might lead to startlingly different results, almost surely giving evidence of low reliability.

One way of increasing test reliability is obvious: Make tests longer. This does not mean that all short objective tests need to be avoided. In the long run, the effects of chance tend to even out: one hundred very short tests, taken all together, make up one very long, sometimes very reliable test. The most important admonition is simply that the teacher should not place undue confidence in the results of only a handful of short tests, in which the effects of chance cannot easily be controlled.

While a test cannot be valid without also being reliable, it can be highly reliable without being valid. Consider the following intelligence test.

第五节 标准化测验
(STANDARDIZED TESTS)

A test is a collection of tasks (items or questions) assumed to be a representative sample of the behaviors that tester wishes to assess. Given that human beings vary in countless ways, there are countless types of tests and countless examples of each type. A few examples of some psychological tests are referred as standardized tests, because they provide standards (also called norms) by which to judge the performance of individual students. Thus, intelligence tests are typically standardized in such a way that average performance is reflected in a score close to 100. In addition, the norms for intelligence tests tell us what distribution of scores we might expect for a large group.

A large collection of tests that are particularly important for classroom teachers are standardized achievement tests. These professionally developed tests are available for virtually every school subject and designed to provide teachers, school administrators, and parents with information.

Once you have determined that an achievement test is suitable and that grade-equivalent scores are therefore meaningful, it is then important to know precisely what their meaning is. A grade-equivalent reading score of 5 obtained by a fourth-grade student does not mean that the student should be in fifth grade. In fact, the raw test score (raw means the actual, untransformed score on the test) that corresponds to this grade-equivalent score is simply the average score of a large number of fifth-grade students. A few fifth-grade students will have scored much higher or much lower. Similarly, many of the fourth-grade students in the norming group will have raw scores as high as some of the fifth-grade pupils. Hence, an achievement test does not separate cleanly among different grade levels—it does not give us an absolutely accurate index of what grade level a student should be. Furthermore, achievement tests given at different times of the year can produce markedly different results. Bernard (1966) reports, for example, that those administered immediately after summer vacation often average a full half-grade lower than scores obtained the preceding June.

Although most achievement tests designed for use in schools provide grade-equivalent scores, many also provide one or more of other types of norms, including age equivalents (and others, such as Z-scores, T-scores, percentiles, and stanines, explained in the box "Norms and the Normal Distribution") **Age-equivalent scores**, as the label implies, are norms expressed in terms of ages rather than grades. Such norms make provisions for converting raw scores to age equivalents which can be interpreted as meaning that a student is functioning at a level comparable to the average for a specific age group. Age-equivalent scores are more common for intelligence tests and other measures of ability or aptitude than they are for achievement tests. It is largely because more meaningful to say that a person is intellectually at the level of a four-year-old or a nine-year-old than to say that someone reads at a four-year-old or a nine-year-old level. When interpreting age-equivalent scores, observe the same cautions as when interpreting grad equivalent scores. The most important caution is that these scores represent averages; hence there will be a wide range of scores within most groups. In addition, because standardized tests are far from completely valid or completely reliable, we should be careful not to rely on them too heavily.

Types of Standardized Tests

Several kinds of standardized tests are used in schools. If you have seen cumulative folders, with testing records for individual students over several years, you know the many ways students are tested in this country. There are three broad categories of standardized tests: achievement, diagnostic, and aptitude (including interest). As a teacher, you will probably encounter achievement and aptitude tests most frequently.

Achievement Tests

The most common standardized tests given to students are achievement tests. These are meant to measure how much a student has learned in specific content areas such as reading comprehension, language usage, computation, science, social studies, mathematics, and logical reasoning.

Achievement tests can be designed to be administered to a group or individually. Group tests can be used for screening to identify children who might need further testing or as a basis for grouping students according to achievement levels. Individual achievement tests are generally given to determine a child's academic level more precisely or to help diagnose learning problems.

Norm-referenced achievement tests that are commonly given to groups include the California Achievement tests, the Metropolitan Achievement Test, the Stanford Achievement Test, the Comprehensive Test of Basic Skills, the SRA Achievement Series, and the Iowa Test of Basic Skills. Individually administered norm-referenced tests include Part II of the Woodcock-Johnson Psycho-Educational Battery: Tests of Achievements; the Wide-Range Achievement Test; the Peabody Individual Achievement Test; and the Kaufman Assessment Battery for Children. These tests vary in their reliability and validity.

Using Information from a Norm-Referenced Achievement Test. What kind of specific information do achievement tests results offer teachers? Test publishers usually provide individual profiles for each student, showing scores on each sub test. Figure 17.1 is an example of an Achievement Test. Note that the Individual Test Record reports the scores in many different ways. At the top of the form, after the identifying information about Susie's teacher, school, district, grade, and so on, is a list of the various tests—Vocabulary, Comprehension, Mechanics, and so on. Each test several different ways of reporting the score:

GE: Susie's grade-equivalent score.

AAGE: Anticipated achievement grade-equivalent score, which is the average grade-equivalent score on this test for students around the country who are at Susie's grade level.

DIFF: An indication of whether the difference between Susie's actual and anticipated grade-equivalent scores is statistically significant (means her actual grade-equivalent score is scientifically higher than the average; means her score is significantly lower than the average).

SS: Susie's standard score.

LP: Susie's local percentile score; this tells us where Susie stands in relation to other students at her grade level in her district.

NP: Susie's national percentile score, telling us where Susie stands in relation to students at her grade level across the country.

RANGE: The range of national percentile scores in which Susie's true score is likely to fall. You may remember from our discussion of true scores that this range, or confidence interval is determined by adding and subtracting the standard error of the test from Susie's actual score. There is a 95 percent chance that Susie's true score is within this range.

Beside the score is a graph showing Susie's national percentile and stanine score, with the standard error bands indicated around the scores. Bands that show any overlap are probably not significantly different. But when there is no overlap between bands for two test scores, we can be reasonably certain that Susie's achievement levels in these two areas are actually different.

Interpreting Achievement Test Scores. Let's look at Susie's scores more carefully. In language mechanics she has a grade-equivalent score of 12.9, which is equal to a standard score of 763. This is at the 92nd percentile for Susie's district and at the 83rd percentile nationally. Her true national percentile score is probably in the range from 73 to 93 (that is, plus and minus 1 standard error of measurement from the actual score of 83). By looking at the graph, we can see that Susie's language mechanics score is equal to a stanine of 7. We can also see that her score bands on vocabulary and comprehension overlap a bit, so her achievement in these areas is probably similar, even though there seems to be a difference when you look at the NP scores alone. Comparing language mechanics and expression, on the other hand, we see that the bands do not overlap. Susie probably is stronger in mechanics than in expression.

You may also have noticed that the difference between Susie's actual and anticipated grade equivalent scores in language mechanics is significant. She scored significantly higher than the average student in her grade on this part of the test. But as discussed earlier, it is best not to interpret grade-equivalent scores literally. Susie is much better than the average 8th grader in language mechanics (in fact, she is as good as or better than 92 percent of students at her grade level locally), but it's very unlikely that she could handle 12th-grade English classes.

The profile tells us a number of things. First, we can see that Susie is apparently strongest in language mechanics and math concepts and applications and weakest in language expression and science. She is significantly below the average for her grade level only in science. By comparing the two columns under LP (local percentiles) and NP (national percentiles), we can see that the eighth graders in Susie's district are achieving below the national level on every test except math computations. This is evident because Susie's performance places her generally in the 70th to 90th percentile range for her district but only in the 50th to 70th percentile range nationally. For example, Susie's performance in vocabulary is well above average for her district (86th percentile) but only average (48th percentile) for eighth graders nationally.

The scores we have just described are all norm-referenced. However, standardized tests like the one Susie took can also be interpreted in a criterion-referenced way. The bottom portion of Susie's Individual Test Record in Figure 17.1 breaks down the larger categories of the top section and shows criterion-referenced scores that indicate mastery, partial knowledge, or no mastery for specific skills like use of synonyms and antonyms, character analysis in reading comprehension, and abilities in geometry and physics. Teachers could use these results to get a relatively good idea of Susie s strengths and weaknesses with these specific skills and thus to determine her progress toward objectives in a given subject.

Diagnostic Tests

If teachers want to identify more general learning problems, they may need to refer to results from the various diagnostic tests that have been developed. Most diagnostic tests are given to students individually by a highly trained professional. The goal is usually to identify the specific problems of a student. Achievement tests, both standardized and teacher made, identify weaknesses in dministered diagnostic tests identify weaknesses in learning processes. There are diagnostic tests to assess the ability to hear differences among sounds, remember spoken words or sentences, recall a sequence of symbols, separate figures from their background, express relationships, coordinate eye and hand movements, describe objects orally, blend sounds to form words, recognize details in a picture, coordinate movements, and many other abilities needed to receive, process, and express information.

Elementary-school teachers are more likely than secondary teachers to receive information from diagnostic tests. There are few such tests for older students. If you become a high school teacher, your students are more likely to be given aptitude tests.

Aptitude Tests

Both achievement and aptitude tests measure developed abilities. Achievement tests may measure abilities developed over a short period of time, such as during a week-long unit on map reading, or over a longer period of time, such as a semester, Aptitude tests are meant to measure abilities developed over many years and to predict how well a student will do in learning unfamiliar material in the future. The greatest difference between the two types of tests is that they are used for different purposes—achievement tests to measure final performance (and perhaps give grades), and aptitude tests to predict how well people will do in particular programs like college or professional school.(Anastasi, 1988).

Scholastic Aptitude.   The purpose of a scholastic aptitude test, like the SAT or ACT, is to predict how well a student is likely to do in college. Colleges use such scores to help decide on acceptances and rejections. The SAT may have seemed like an achievement test to you, measuring what you had already learned in high school. Although the test is designed to avoid drawing too heavily on specific high school curricula, the questions are very similar to achievement test questions.

Standardized aptitude tests such as the SAT (and the SCAT and PSAT for younger students) seem to be fairly reliable on predicting future achievement. Since standardized tests are less open to teacher bias, they may be even fairer predictors of future achievement than high school grades are. Indeed, some psychologists believe grade inflation in high schools has made tests like the SAT even more important. Others believe that the SATs are not good predictors of success in college for women or members of cultural or ethnic minority groups. The controversy continues.

IQ and Scholastic Aptitude   The IQ test as we know it could well be called a test of scholastic aptitude. IQ scores are distributed based on the results of the major individual tests. Now that you understand the concept of the major individual tests. Now that you understand the concept of standard deviation, you will be able to appreciate several statistical characteristics of the tests. For example, the IQ score is really a standard score with a mean ot 100 and a standard deviation of 15 (for the Wechsler Scales; the Cognitive Abilities section of the Woodcock-Johnson Psycho-Educational Battery; and the Global Scale of the Kaufman Assessment Battery for children) or 16 (for the Stanford-Binet and the McCarthy Scales for Children). Thus, about 68 percent of the general population would score between 1 and 1 standard deviations from the mean, or between about 85 and 115. Only about 2.5 percent of the general population would have a score higher than 2 standard deviations above the mean—that is, above 130 on the Wechsler Scales.

The difference of a few points between two students' IQ scores should not be viewed as important. Scores between 90 and 109 are within the average range. In fact, scores between 80 and 119 are considered to range from low average to high average. To see the problems that may arise, consider the following conversation:

Parent: We came to speak with you today because we are shocked at our son's IQ score. We can't believe he has only a 99 IQ when his sister scored much higher on the same test. We know they are about the same. In fact, Sam has better marks than Lauren did in the fifth grade.

Teacher: What was Lauren's score?

Parent: Well, she did much better. She scored a 103!

Clearly, brother and sister have both scored within the average range. The standard error of measurement on the WISC–R (Weschler Intelligence Scale for Children) varies slightly from one age to the next, but the average standard erf or is 3.19. So the bands around Sams and Laruens IQ scores—about 96 to 102 and 100 to 106—are overlapping. Either children could have scored 100, 101, or 102. The scores are so close that on a second testing Sam might score slightly higher than Lauren.

Vocational Aptitude and Interest. In schools, the guidance counselor is generally the person most concerned with students' career decisions. It is the responsibility of people in the guidance office to know what aptitude test scores really mean and how to help each student make an appropriate decision. Vocational aptitude tests and vocational interest tests may provide useful information for educational planning. But as with any tests, interpretion must be cautious.

If you teach, in a junior high or high school, your school may administer vocational aptitude tests to the students. One test designed to measure aptitudes relevant to career decisions is the Differential Aptitude Test (DAT), Students in grades 8 through 12 may take the test. Questions cover seven areas: (1) verbal reasoning, (2) numerical ability, (3) abstract reasoning, (4) clerical speed and accuracy, (5) mechanical reasoning, (6) space relations, and (7) spelling and language. The test results on the DAT are converted into percentiles, and a percentile band is reported for each sub test. After the tests have been scored, the guidance counselors in a school should be able to help students relate their DAT profile scores to career planning decisions.

The Uses of Testing in American Society

Today many important decisions about students, teachers, and schools are based on the results of standardized tests. Test scores may affect high school graduation, admission to special programs, placement in special education classes, teacher certification, and school funding. Because the decisions affected by test scores are so critical, many educators call this process high–stakes testing. Some groups are working to increase the role of testing—by establishing a national examination, for example, while others are working to cut back the use of standardized tests in schools (O'Neil, 1991).

In the next few pages we will consider two basic questions: What role should testing play in making decisions about people? Do some students have an unfair advantage in taking tests?

Tests are not simply procedures used in research. Many decisions about individuals are made every day based on the results of tests. Should Liz be issued a driver's license? How many and which students from the eighth grade would benefit from an accelerated program in science? Who belongs in a special class for the mentally retarded? who will be admitted to college or professional school? In answering these questions, it is important to distinguish between the quality of the test itself and how the test is used. Even the best instruments can be and have been misused. In earlier years, for example, many students were inappropriately classified as mentally retarded on the basis of valid and reliable individual intelligence tests. The problem was not with the tests but instead of the fact that the test score was the only information used to classify students, much more information must be considered before a student can be identified as retarded.

Behind all the statistics and terminology are issues related to values and ethics. Who will be tested? What are the consequences of choosing one test over another for a particular purpose with a given group? What is the effect on students of being tested? How will the test scores of minority-group students be interpreted? What do really mean by intelligence, competence, and scholastic aptitude; and do our views agree with those implied by the tests we use to measure these constructs? How will test results be integrated with other information about the individual to make judgments? Answering these questions requires choices based on values as well as accurate information about what tests can and cannot tell us. Let's look at three uses of testing: testing readiness, testing minimum competency, and testing teachers.

Readiness Testing. In 1988 Georgial became the first state to require that children pass a test before moving from kindergarten to first grade (Fiske, 1988; Linn, 1986). The test quickly became a symbol of the misuse of tests. Public outcry led to modifications of the policy and spurred many educators to reform the readiness testing process. In fact, the uproar over this group-administered, machine-scored, norm-refemced test for kindergarten children "probably did more to advance readiness assessment reform in this country than all other causes combined" (Engel, 1991, p.41).

Critics of readiness tests (Engel, 1991; Meisels, 1989; Shepard & Smith, 1989) believe:

1. Group-administered paper and pencil tests inappropriate for preschool children and thus should not be the basis for decisions about school entry.

2. Using readiness tests narrows the preschool curriculum, making it more academic and less developmentally appropriate.

3. The evidence shows that delaying entry into first grade or retaining students in kindergarten is not effective. Students who are retained do no better than similar student's who are not held back.

In spite of these criticisms, today almost every state uses testing at the state or district level to determine if a child is "ready" for first grade or to place a child in a special developmental kindergarten (Kirst, 1991a). Several states as well as a few test publishers are trying to develop appropriate ways to determine readiness. Engel (1991) suggests that such procedures would be ongoing assessments about many different aspects of readiness cognitive, social emotional, physical, and so on. These assessments would be indirect; that is, they would be completed by adults rather than requiring the children to answer questions directly on paper. The observations should provide useful information for teaching and should be conducted in a comfortable natural setting, often as part of the preschool program itself.

Minimum Competency Testing. A Nation at Risk (National Commission on Excellence in Education, 1983) reported that about 23 million American adults were functionally illiterate. About 13 percent of the teenagers in the United States (and up to 40 percent of minority youth) were also functionally illiterate. And in many studies comparing U. S. students with students from other industrialized nations, the American students have placed low in academic achievement (Educational Testing Service, 1992).

In response to this problem, many people believe that **minimum competency testing** should be used to determine high school graduation. Some people even suggest that a national examination would be helpful. "Escalating concern over low achievement, coupled with a growing belief that each pupil needs to be able to aim for a national standard of performance, has some policymakers, business leaders, and educators favoring a national exam (or set of exams) for all students" (O' Neil, 1991). Seventy-seven percent of the people surveyed in the 1991 Gcillup Poll of the public's attitude toward the public schools said they favored requiring the public schools in their community to use standardized national tests to measure the academic achievement of students (Elam, Rose, & Gallup, 1991). This idea is still under discussion and the debate rages.

Will requiring minimum competency tests or a national exam improve the situation? As usual, experts disagree. Barbara Lemer (1981) believes the close monitoring and clear standards required by minimum competency testing would encourage teachers and students to spend more time teaching and learning the basics. Since academic engaged time is one of the few factors that seems clearly associated with learning, this increased attention should improve achievement. Besides, "no other approach is demonstrably superior to it" (Lerner, 1981, p.1062)

However, many psychologists and teachers believe such tests are undesirable. The psychologists and teachers believe such tests are undesirable. Their argument is that teachers would have less and less freedom on deciding what and how to teach. The tests would control the curriculum. In working to get everyone to the minimum level, teachers would have to ignore the faster students. A few slower students might monopolize the teacher's attention. New ways of organizing classes would be necessary to prevent holding everyone back (Kirst, 1991a & b). And finally, tests might discriminate against minority students.

The last factor had a great impact when Florida instituted a functional literacy test for high school graduation. Although the citizens of the state were in favor of the testing, a federal judge ordered the process stopped on the grounds that the tests perpetuated the effects of past discrimination against minority students. Evidence presented during the trial Debra p. v. Turlington indicated that 20 percent of African-American seniors and only 2 percent of white seniors were denied diplomas on the basis of the tests. Many of the African-American students had spent some of their early school careers in segregated schools. The judge felt that denying them diplomas punished these students for having gone to inferior schools and thus violated their right to equal protection under the law (Haney, 1981).

Testing Teachers. Almost 90 percent of the people surveyed in the 1985 Gallup poll believed that teachers should have to pass a basic competency test before being hired. When teachers answered the same question a year earlier, 63 percent agreed that testing was a good idea (Gallup, 1984). By 1985, 30 States, mostly in the southern and western sections of the United States, reported that they had some kind of teacher-assessment programs, and a dozen more states indicated that serious discussions were under way.

Edward Haertel (1991) notes that, like other standardized tests, "the teacher competency tests now in common use have been streneuously and justifiably criticized for their content, their format, and their impacts, as well as the virtual absence of criterion—related validity evidence supporting their use" (p.3). In other words, high test scores do not predict good teaching.

New models of teacher assessments are in the planning and development stages. For example, the revision of the National Teacher Examination (NTE) is nearing completion as I am writing this page and may be available by the time you read these words. The revised NTE is a battery of tests given in three stages. Stage I tests basic skills early in the prospective teacher's education program. Stage II, given at the end of the undergraduate program, tests subject matter knowledge and knowledge of teaching. Stage III is a performance based on assessment conducted mostly through classroom observations.

Like the alternatives to standardized tests we will examine shortly, the NTE and other new teacher tests will make greater use of authentic performances and products. Teacher candidates might complete a lesson planning exercise and then be interviewed about what they planned and why. They might be asked to submit a portfolio containing an overview of a unit, details of two consecutive lessons, copies of student handouts, lists of the resources selected for background, a videotape of teaching samples showing large and small — group lessons, and other examples of the teacher's actual work.

These procedures are not yet refined, but many look promising. Of course, every innovation has its shortcomings. Can these porfolios and performances be evaluated objectively? Will we see an explosion of businesses that specialize in helping teachers build a beautiful portfolio? Will the wealthier teachers and teacher candidates have the beat portfolios and videos (Kirst, 1991b)?

Advantages in Taking Tests Fair and Unfair

In this section we will consider three basic issues: Are standardized tests biased against minority students? Can students gain an advantage on admissions tests through coaching? Can they be taught test—taking skills?

Bias in Testing. The average performance of students of lower socioeconomic status on most standardized measures of mental abilities, although the discrepancies are decreasing for some minority groups (Burton & Jones, 1982). Are tests such as the individual measures of intelligence or college admissions tests biased against minorities? This is a complex question.

Research on test bias shows that most standardized tests predict school achievement equally well for all groups of students. Items that might appear on the surface to be biased against minorities are not necessarily more difficult for minorities to answer correctly (Sattler, 1988). Even though standardized aptitude and achievement tests are not biased against minorities in predicting school performance however, many people believe there are factors related to the specific content and procedures of such tests that put minority students at a disadvantage. Here are a few factors they suggest:

1. The language of the test and the tester is often different from the languages of the students.

2. The questions asked tend to center on experiences and facts more familiar to the dominant culture than to minority—group students.

3. Answers that support middle—class values often are rewarded with more points.

4. On individually administered intelligence tests, being very verbal and talking a lot is rewarded, which favors students who feel comfortable in the situation.

5. Minority-group children may not be oriented toward individual achievement and may not appreciate the value of doing well.

Concern about cultural bias in testing has led some psychologists to try to develop culture-fair or culture-free tests. These efforts have not been very successful. On many of the so-called culture-fair tests, the performance of students from lower socioeconomic backgrounds and minority groups has been the same as or worse than their performance on the standard Wechsler and Binet Intelligence scales (Sattler, 1988).

Coaching and Test-Taking Skills. Courses to prepare students for college entrance exams are becoming more popular. As you probably know from experience, both commercial and public school coaching programs are available. It is difficult to evaluate the effects of these courses. In general, research has indicated that short high school training programs yield average gains of 10 points in SAT verbal scores and 15 points in SAT math scores, whereas longer commercial programs show gains of anywhere from 50 to as much as 200 points for some people (Owen, 1985). Kulik, Kulik, and Bangert (1984) analyzed the results of 40 different studies on aptitude and achievement tests training and found that there were more substantial gains when students practiced on a parallel form of a test for brief periods. The design of the coaching program, therefore, may be the critical factor.

Two other types of training can make a difference in test scores. One is simple familiarity with the procedures of standardized tests. Students who have a lot of experience with standardized tests do better than those who do not. Some of this advantage may be due to greater self-confidence, less tendency to panic, familiarity with different kinds of questions (for example, analogies like house: garage: rear), and practice with the various answer sheets (Anastasi, 1988). Even brief orientations about how to take tests can help students who lack familiarity and confidence.

A second type of training that appears to be very promising is instruction in general cognitive skills such as solving problems, carefully analyzing questions, considering all alternatives,

noticing details and deciding which are relevant, avoiding impulsive answers, and checking work. These are the kinds of met cognitive and study skills. Training in these skills is likely to generalize to many tasks (Anastasi, 1988).

New Approaches to Standardized Testing

Standardized tests continue to be controversial. In response to dissatisfaction with traditional forms of assessment, new approaches have emerged to deal with some of the most common testing problems. But each of these approaches has its own problems. We will examine proposed procedures for measuring learning potential, for making assessment more "authentic," and for improving the SAT.

a. Assessing Learning Potential

One criticism of traditional forms of intelligence testing is that such tests are merely samples of performance at one particular point in time. These tests critics say, fail to capture the child's potential for future learning. Reuben Feuerstein's Learning potential Assessment Device at tempts to look at the process of learning rather than its product (Feuerstein, 1979). The child is presented with various reasoning and memory tasks. When necessary, the examiner teaches the child how to solve the problems and then assess how well the child has benefited from in-striation, This approach reflects Vygotsky's ideas about the zone of proximal development—the range of functioning where a child cannot solve problems independently but can benefit from guidance. Results of the test have been difficult to interpret. Nevertheless, it offers a thought-provoking and radically different approach to intelligence testing.

b. Authentic Assessment

One of the major criticisms of standardized tests is that they test low-level skills that have no equivalent in the real world. Students are asked to solve problems or answer questions they will never encounter again; and they are expected to do so alone, without relying on any tools or resources, while working under extreme time limits. Critics say that real life just don't like this. Important problems take time to solve, and often require using resources, consulting other people, and integrating basic skills with creativity and high-level thinking. (Kirst, 1991a; Wolf, Bixby, Glenn, & Gardner, 1991).

How can standardized tests assess complex, important, real-life outcomes? This has been called the problem of authentic assessment, Some states are developing procedures to conduct authentic assessments. For example, Kentucky recently passed the Educational Reform Act of 1990. The act identifies six objectives for students, including such goals as applying knowledge from mathematics, the sciences, the arts, the humanities, and the social sciences to problems the students will encounter throughout their lives as they become self-sufficient individuals and responsible members of families, work groups, and communities.

According to Jack Foster (1991), the secretary of the Education and Humanities Cabinet for the governor of Kentucky. The task now is to create prototypes of complex tasks that students can perform to demonstrate all these objectives in an interactive context. The tasks must have multiple objectives and require higher levels of thinking than is demanded by most paper-and-pencil tests (p.35). the state assessments will be tied to ongoing school and class assessments that guide instruction. The process will: be criterion-referenced rather than norm-referenced, because students' performances will be compared to expected "benchmark" levels of attainment at grades 3, 5, 8, and 12.

Many of the suggestions for improving standardized tests will require stanaharized tests of the future may be more like the writing sample you may have submitted for college entrance and less like the multiple-choice college entrance tests you also had to take. Newer tests will feature more constructed-response formats. This means that students will create responses (essays, problem solutions, graphs, diagrams, etc.) rather than simply selecting the (one and only) correct answer. This will allow tests to measure higher-level and divergent thinking.

c.Changes in the SAT

Even the SAT is changing. The new SAT will have tests of verbal reasoning, mathematical reasoning, and subject matter. The verbal test will emphasize reading. The reading passages will be more engaging and more similar to the material that high school students have read in their classes. Each passage will be longer, and students will have to answer more questions about the passage. The verbal test will still have sentence completion and analogy questions, but the antonyms questions will be dropped. On the mathematical portion, students will generate their own answers (constructed response format) for 20 percent of the questions. Hand held calculators will be allowed but not required. There will be a writing test that is two-thirds multiple-choice questions and one-third essay. The new SAT is projected to be ready by spring 1994, and a new PSAT should be out by fall 1993, so students who take the PSAT in fall 1993 will encounter the same format when they take their SATs later (Smith, 1991).

With a move to more authentic assessment, standardized tests and classroom tests can better coordinated.

第六节 教师自编测验
(TEACHER-MADE TESTS)

A large majority of the tests employed in the classroom)m are made by classroom teachers, and some of these are highly representative of course objectives, are at an appropriate level of difficulty, and are used in reasonable and wise ways. Other tests are less gifted.

Teacher-made tests can be employed for a variety of purposes, only one of which is the assigning of grades. Other than this, a test can be employed to determine whether students are ready to begin a unit of instruction, to indicate to the teacher how effective instructional procedures are, to identify learning difficulties, to determine what students know and what they don't know, to predict their probability of success on future learning tasks, and to motivate students to learn.

Teacher-made tests are almost always of the paper-and-pencil variety. Only occasionally can a sample of nonverbal behavior be employed on a test. For example, in physical education, in art, in drama, and in some workshop courses, students are sometimes asked either to produce something or to perform. In most other courses they will be given an objective or an essay test or both. An essay test requires a written response of some length for each question.

Objective tests, however, normally require very little writing and the scoring procedure is highly uniform (hence objective). The four major types of objective test items are completion, matching, true false, and multiple choice. Examples or each are given below:

1. Completion

Test blueprints are often based on _____ taxonomy. Predictive and concurrent validity are two types of _____ validity.

2. Matching

—— Z-scores 1. mean = 50; standard deviation =10

—— T-scores 2. mean = 0; standard deviation = 1

_____ stanine 3. mean = 5; standard deviation = 2

3. True—False

_____ a. A good achievement test should almost always result in a grade—equivalent score of betvoeen 4 and 5 for an average fourth—grade class.

_____ b. Content validity can usually be determined by making a carefull logical analysis of the relationship of test items to course objectives.

4 .Multiple choice

The extent to which a test appears to measure what it is intended to measure defines:

a. content validity

b. face validity

c. construct validity

d. test reliability

e. criterion—related validity

Essay Versus Objective Tests

Objective tests of the kind just described and the more subjective essay tests can be used to measure almost any significant aspect of student behavior. However, some course objectives are more easily assessed with one type of test than the other. Several of the major differences between essay and objective tests are given below. These can serve as guide in deciding which to use in a given situation. Very often a mixture of both can be employed to advantage.

1. It is far easier to tap higher level processes (analysis, synthesis, and evaluation) with an easy examination, although it is possible to do the same thing with objective items. Essay exam—nations can be constructed to allow students to organize knowledge, to make inferences from it, to illustrate it, to apply it, and to extrapolate from it.

2. The content of essay examinations is often more limited than the content of the more objective tests. Since essay exams usually consist of fewer items, the range of abilities or of information sampled is necessarily reduced. The objective—question format, in contrast, permits coverage of more content per unit of testing time. While a student's range of knowledge is often apparent in an range of knowledge is often apparent in an essay test, the absence of that knowledge may not be so readily apparent.

3. Essay examinations allow for more divergence. It is not unreasonable to expect that students who do not like to be restricted in their answers will prefer essays over more objective tests.

4. Constructing an essay test is considerably easier and less time consuming than making up an objective examination. In fact, an entire test with an essay format can often be written in the same length of time it would take to write no more than two or three good multiple choice items.

5. Scoring essay examinations requires considerably more time than scoring objective tests. This is especially true where tests can be scored electronically (as objective tests are in most larger universities and in an increasing number of schools). The total time involved in making and scaring a test is less for essay examinations if classes are small (twenty students or fewer, perhaps) but is considerably less for objective tests as the number of students increases (see Figure 17.1)

Figure 17.1

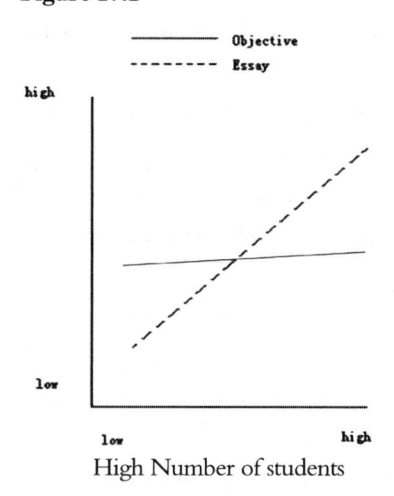

```
         ——— Objective
         ----- Essay
high



low
      low              high
      High Number of students
```

A representation of the relation-ship between size of class and test construction and scoring time.

6. The reliability of essay examinations is very much lower than that of objective tests, primarily because of the subjectivity involved in their scoring. Numerous studies attest to this fact. In one (Educational Testing Service, 1961), three hundred essays were rated by fifty-three judges on a nine-point scale. Slightly over one-third of the papers received all possible grades. That is, each of these papers received the highest possible grade from at least one judge and the lowest possible grade from at least one other. In addition, each received other possible grade from at least one judge. Another 37 percent of the papers each received eight of the nine different grades; 23 percent received seven of the nine.

Other studies have found that a relatively poor paper that is read after an even poorer one will tend to be given a higher grade than if it is read after a very good paper; that some graders consistently give moderate marks whereas others give very high and very low marks, although the average grades given by each might be very similar; that knowledge of who wrote the paper tends to affect scores, sometimes beneficially and sometimes to the student's detriment; and that if the first few answers on an essay examination are particularly good, overall marks tend to higher than if the first answer is poor.

There are a number of methods for increasing the score reliability of essay examinations, not the least of which is simply being aware of possible sources of unreliability. Some of the suggestions given below may be of value in this regard.

Suggestions for Constructing Tests

The advantages of a particular type of test can often be increased if its items are constructed carefully. By the same token, the disadvantages can also be made more severe through faulty item construction. Essay examinations, for example, are said to be better for measuring higher processes. Consider the following item:

List the kinds of validity discussed in this chapter.

If the tester's intention is to sample analysis, synthesis, or evaluation, this item has no advantage over many objective items. However, an item such as the following might have an advantage:

Discuss similarities and differences among three of the different types of validity discussed in this chapter.

Several specific suggestions follow for the construction of essay tests and of multiple-choice tests, the most preferred among objective-item forms.

Essay Tests. The following suggestions are based in part on Gronlund (1968):

1. Essay questions should be geared toward sampling processes not easily assessed by objective items (for example, analysis, synthesis, or evaluation).

2. As for ail tests, essay questions should relate directly to the desired outcomes of canning procedure. This should be clearly understood by the students as well.

3. The questions should be specific if they are to be easily storable. If the intention is to give marks for illustrations, the item should specify that an illustration is required.

4. A judicious sampling of desired behavior should comprise the substance of the items.

5. If the examiner's intention is to sample high-level processes, sufficient time should be allowed for students to complete the questions.

6. The weighting of various questions, as well as the time that should be allotted to each, should be indicated for the student.

7. The questions should be worded so that the teacher's expectations are clear both to the student and to the teacher.

Suggestions for making the scoring more objective are also available. One of these is to outline model answers before scoring the test (that is, write out an answer that would receive full points). Another is to score all answers for one item before going on to the next. The purpose of this is to increase uniformity of scoring. A third suggestion is simply that the scorer should intend to be objective. For example, if poor grammar in a languge arts test results in the loss of five points on one paper, grammar that is half as bad on another paper should result in the loss of two and a half points.

Multiple–Choice Items. A multiple-choice item consists of a statement or series of statements (called the stem) and of three to five alternatives, only one of which is the correct or best solution. The other alternatives are referred to as distracters. Each of the distracters is a response that will appear plausible if students do not know the answer. If they know the correct answer, distracters should, of course, appear less plausible.

Multiple-choice examinations have a number of distinct advantages over such objective formats as true-false, matching, and completion, not the least of which is that they are less susceptible to the effects of guessing. In addition, they can more easily be adapted to measure higher processes such as analysis, comprehension, and application, as well as simple recall.

Below are a number of suggestions for writing multiple-choice items. Most of them are common sense (which makes them no less valid).

1. Both stems and alternatives should be clearly worded, unambiguous, grammatically correct, specific, and at the appropriate level of comprehension. In addition, stems should be clearly meaningful by themselves.

2. Double negatives are highly confusing and should be avoided. Single negatives are not recommended either.

3. The items should sample a representative portion of subject content, but they should not be taken verbatim from the textbook. This is defensible only where the intention is clearly to test memorization.

4. All distracters should be equally plausible so that answering correctly is not simply a matter of eliminating highly implausible distracters. Consider the following example of a poor item:

10+12+18 =

a. 2,146

b. 7,568,482

c. 40

d. 10

5. Unintentional cues should be avoided. Ending the stem with a or an often provides a cue, for example.

6. Qualifying words such as never, always, none, impossible and absolutely should be avoided in distracters (though not necessarily in stems).

They are almost always associated with incorrect alternatives. Words such as sometimes frequently, and are most often associated with correct alternatives. In stems both kinds of qualifiers tend to be ambiguous.

Reporting Test Results

Having constructed, administered, and scored a test, the teacher is faced with the responsibility of making the wisest possible use of the information derived from it. Obviously, some of these uses are separate from the actual reporting of test results to students or parents; they are concerned instead of instructional decisions that the teacher must make. Are the students ready to go to the next unit? Should they be allowed to study in the library again? Should educational television be employed? Should a review be undertaken? Should the teacher look for another job?

Even if the test is primarily intended to let the teacher make decisions concerning questions such as those given above, results should also be reported to the students. The feedback that students receive about their learning can be of tremendous value in guiding future efforts. It can also be highly reinforcing in this achievement oriented society.

While raw scores can be reported directly to the student, they are of little or no value unless they are related to some scales about which value judgments can be made. A score of 40 on a test where the maximum possible score is 40 is different from a score of 40 on a test where the ceiling is 80. The traditional way of giving meaning to these scores is to convert them either to a percentage or to a letter grade that has clearly defined, though arbitrary, significance. Advanced students should probably be given more information than simply a percentage or a letter grade. To begin with, it is useful to know precise areas of weakness as well as strengths. In addition, even a percentage score is relatively useless the student has some knowledge about the scores obtained by other students. A simple way of giving a class this knowledge is to report the mean (average) as well as the range of scores (low and high scores).

The mean is called a measure of **central tendency**, since it indicates, in an approximate way, where the center of a distribution of scores is. There are two other common measures of central tendency: the **median** and the **mode**. The median is the exact midpoint of a distribution. It is the fiftieth percentile—the point above and below which 50 percent of all scores lie. The mode is simply the most frequently occurring score; as such, it is not particularly valuable for educational and psychological testing. It is of considerable interest to shoe and clothing manufacturers, however, since they are not interested in manufacturing average or median sizes, but those that occur most frequently.

As we saw when discussing standard scores, a measure of central tendency is not nearly as valuable by itself as it is when combined with a measure of variability. And the most useful measure of variability for normally distributed observations is the standard deviation. If students are sufficiently sophisticated, the standard deviation might be reported as an important dimension of test scores.

第七节 参照标准测验
(CRITERION-REFERENCED TESTING)

There is a small kingdom hidden in the steamy jungles of South America. One of its borders is the Amazon, which describes a serpentine half-circle around most of the perimeter of this kingdom. Its other border consists of an impenetrable row of harsh mountains. The inhabitants of the kingdom are therefore trapped by the river on one side (they dare not try to cross it) and by the mountains on the other (although they can climb the mountains to their very tops, the other side presents an unbroken row of vertical cliffs attaining dizzying heights of no less than 8,000 feet at any location). In this kingdom there are numerous, very ferocious man-eating beasts. Fortunately, all are nocturnal. I say fortunately because although the human inhabitants of the kingdom live on the mountainsides well beyond where their enemies can climb, they must descend the mountain every day to find food.

In this kingdom a test is given to all able bodied men, women, and children each day of their lives. It is a simple test. Before nightfall, each must succeed in climbing the mountain to a point beyond the reach of the predators. Failure to do so is obvious to all, for the individual who fails simply does not answer roll call that evening. Success is equally obvious. The situation, however, is not parallel to the ordinary testing practices of most schools. Passing the test does not require that an individual be the first to reach safety; it doesn't even require that he be among the first 90 percent to do so. Indeed, he will have been just as successful if he is the very last to reach the fire. He will be just as alive as the first (and perhaps he will be less hungry).

Consider the situation in schools where testing is of the traditional, **norm-referenced** variety. Assume that all students are expected to attain a certain level of performance in a variety of subjects, a level of performance that we will denote by the symbol X. In the course of the school year, teachers prepare a number of tests and determine, probably relatively accurately, that certain individuals usually do better than others on these tests. These students are, in effect, comparable to the people in the aforementioned kingdom who typically reach safety first. They are the students that the teachers can rightly assume have reached, or even gone beyond, X. But in assessing student performance and reporting grades, teachers don't often ask themselves which students have reached

X and which haven't. Instead, they compare each child to the average performance of all children and on that basis make judgments about the relative performance of students. Thus, in a very advanced class, students who have in fact reached X, but who fall well below average performance, are assigned mediocre marks. In a less advanced class, these same students might be assigned much higher grades.

Norm-referenced tests are therefore tests where the students performance is judged and reported in terms of some standard or norm that is derived from tropical student performance on the test. In other words, the results of such a test are based on comparisons among students (Haertel, 1985).

A second alternative is exemplified in the South American kingdom: Students are not compared one to the others, but performance is judged only in relation to a criterion. In that example, the reach of predators; success is survival and failure is death.

Criterion-referenced testing can also be employed in schools, and is, in fact, used extensively in mastery learning and other forms of individualized instruction. If teachers are able to specify what is involved in achieving X in terms of precise behavioral objectives, then they can judge whether a student has reached the criterion without having to compare the student to any other. Obviously, it is sometimes difficult and certainly very time consuming to define X with directly measurable objectives. On the other hand, it is quite possible to define aspects of X in those terms, in which case criterion-referenced tests can be employed. The teacher can decide, for example, that all fifth-grade students should be able to read a selected passage within five minutes and subsequently answer three questions about the content of the passage. This amounts quite simply to establishing a criterion. Students can then be tested to determine whether they have reached the criterion.

The principal difference between criterion-referenced tests and norm-referenced tests lies not in the nature of the tests themselves but in the use that the teacher makes of them. In criterion-referenced testing, the student's performance is compared to a criterion; in norm-referenced testing, an individual's performance is compared to that of other students. Individual differences are far less important in criterion-referenced testing. Indeed, the objective is to have all students succeed.

Literature on educational testing has sometimes been preoccupied with a minor controversy surrounding the relative merits of these two approaches to testing (for example, Popham, 1978; Shepard, 1979). Advocates of criterion-referenced testing point to the inherent justice of their approach. No student need consistently fail for performing less well than others after a fixed period of time. When students reach the criterion, they will have succeeded. Indeed, at that point, they will be as successful on that particular task as all others. And those students who have more to learn at the onset of instruction will not fail simply because they start at a different place and consequent the beasts, they will have succeeded. Criterion-referenced testing argues strongly for the individualization of instruction and of evaluation; it encourages students to work toward the goals of the system rather than against other students; and it forces teachers to make those goals explicit.

But criterion-referenced testing has certain limitations, as critics have been quick to point out. While it is relatively simple to specify that after taking typing lessons for six weeks a student should know after sitting in a social studies class for six weeks. A criterion-referenced test is clearly appropriate in the first instance, but much less so in the second.

A second limitation is that some students can perform better than the criterion. Some educators fear that exclusive reliance on criterion-referenced testing may thwart student incentive.

An advantage of norm-referenced testing is that it provides both students and those who would counsel them with very valuable information concerning their likelihood of success in academic situations where they will, in fact, be required to compete with others.

What should you do while the controversy rages around you? Very simply, both There are situations where norm-referenced tests are not only unavoidable, but also very useful. There are also many situations where students will respond very favorably to the establishment of definite criteria for success and where both their learning and your teaching will benefit as a result. Here, as elsewhere, there is no either-or question; your decisions should be based on the fundamental purposes of your instructional procedures in specific situations.

词汇 (Vocabulary)

1. achievement test   成就测验
2. admonition   n. 劝告、警告
3. aforementioned   adj. 前面提到的
4. Age-equivalent scores   年龄当量分数
5. allot   v. 分配、配给
6. aptitude test   能力倾向测验
7. authentic assessment   真实评估
8. beverage   n. 饮料
9. Celsius   n. 摄压温度计
10. central tendency   集中趋势
11. clerical   a. 抄写的
12. collaboration   n. 合作
13. compilation   n. 汇编
14. concurrent validity   同时效度
15. consecutive   a. 连续的
16. construct validity   构想效度
17. content validity   内容效度
18. criteria   n. 标准
19. criterion-related validity   标准关联效度
20. culture-fair test   文化公平测验
21. culture-free test   排除文化、影响测验
22. detriment   n. 损害、伤害
23. diagnostic test   诊断测验

24. Differential Aptitude Test (DAT)　不同能力倾向测验
25. discrepancy　n. 差异
26. distractor　n. 干扰项、迷惑题
27. enterprising　a. 有事业心的
28. equivalence reliability　等值信度
29. erratically ad　v. 不稳定地、不规律地
30. escalate　v. 增强
31. extrapolate　v. 推断
32. face validity　表面效度
33. fahrenheit　n. 华氏温度计
34. fauna　n. 动物群
35. flora　n. 植物群
36. fluctuate　v. 起伏不定
37. functional literacy test　功能性文化测验
38. grade-equivalent scores　年级等值分数
39. haphazard　a. 无计划的
40. hierarchical class　层次等级
41. impartial　a. 公正的
42. impenetrable　a. 不能穿过的
43. incentive　n. 动机
44. inherent　a. 固有的、内在的
45. intelligently　adv. 理智地
46. interval scale　n. 顺序量表
47. intrinsic　a. 固有的、内在的
48. judicious　a. 明智的
49. jurisdiction　n. 权限、管辖范围
50. justification　n. 正当理由
51. Learning Potential Assessment Device　学习潜能评估策略
52. manual　n. 手册
53. mean　n. 平均数
54. median　n. 中数
55. mediocre　a. 中等的
56. metacognitive　a. 元认知的
57. minimum competency testing　最低能力测验
58. mode　n. 众数
59. monopolize　v. 垄断
60. nominal scale　称名量表
61. nocturnal　a. 在夜间活动的
62. norm　n. 常模

63. norm-referenced test　　参照常模测验
64. ordinal scale　　顺序量表
65. orthogonal　　a. 垂直的
66. overlap　　n. 部分重迭
67. parallel-forms reliability　　复份信度
68. pendulum　　n. 舆论的钟摆
69. percentile　　n. 百分位
70. perpetuate　　v. 使永久存在
71. platitudinous　　a. 陈腐的
72. plausible　　a. 似有道理的
73. portfolio　　n. 文件夹
74. predator　　n. 食肉动物
75. predictive validity　　预测效度
76. premise　　n. 前提
77. profile　　n. 轮廓
78. proliferate　　v. 增多、扩散
79. prototype　　n. 原型
80. proximal development　　接近发展
81. ratio scale　　比率量表
82. readiness test　　准备测验
84. Scholastic Aptitude Test（SAT）　　学习能力倾向测验、学术性向测验
85. semblance　　n. 外观
86. serpentine　　adj. 蜿蜒的
87. split-half reliability　　分半信度
88. standard deviation　　标准差
89. stanine　　n. 九级评分制
90. stupendous　　a. 巨大的
91. susceptible　　a. 敏感的
92. synthesis　　n. 综合
93. terminology　　n. 专门术语
94. thereof　　adv. 其
95. thwart　　v. 挫败
96. undue　　a. 不适当的
97. validity　　n. 效度
98. verbatim　　adv.（照原文或原本）逐字地
99. vocational aptitude test　　职业能力倾向测验
100. vocational interest test　　职业兴趣测验

第十八章 心理变态与治疗
（MENTAL ABNORMAL AND THERAPY）

本章要点（Chapter Outline）
心理变态的界定 (The Definition of Abnormal)
变态行为的分类 (Classifying Abnormal Behavior)
心理障碍的治疗 (Therapy for Psychological Disorder)

　　心理治疗是根据心理学原理，以不使用药物为原则，对心理异常者所给予的帮助。变态心理学的研究，旨在探讨行为异常的类别与成因，从而建立系统理论，作为心理诊断与治疗的依据。用于解释心理变态的基本理论，有精神分析论、行为论及生理科学观等。学习和讨论各种心理异常者的行为特征与心理原因、症状，针对异常者的"病象"、"病情"与"病因"给予诊断和治疗，以达到身心健康的目的。健康的心理，旨在助人调适生活、预防疾病，更好地适应现代社会发展的节奏，建立有益于其个人与社会的生活目标，并使之在教育、职业及人际关系等各方面发展上，能充分展现其性向，从而臻于最佳的生活适应。

第一节　心理变态的界定
（THE DEFINITION OF ABNORMALITY: WHAT IS ABNORMAL BEHAVIOR）

　　There is a considerable debate among psychologists about how to define the subject matter of abnormal psychology. No single definition exists, but most approaches use one or more of the following criteria: statistical, cultural, and personal.

　　In terms of the statistical criterion, abnormality is defined as any substantial deviation from the average of typical behaviors of the group to which the individual belongs.

　　The cultural criterion views abnormality as a deviation from an ideal standard or norm. To be considered normal, behavior must be socially acceptable. This perspective emphasizes the value judgments involved in the concept of abnormality. What one person considers abnormal another may view as perfectly sensible. Indeed the "abnormal" at pass time could become the "normal" after some later years.

A third criterion, personal distress, considers abnormality in terms of the individual's subjective feelings. For example, several studies have demonstrated that thousands of young people have problems controlling their own weight, and consequently view themselves as unattractive.

These problems are not abnormal statistically, for they are frequent. They are abnormal, however, in an ideal sense, causing unhappiness to the sufferers.

None of these criteria statistical, cultural, or personal is completely satisfactory for diagnosing abnormality. In most instances all three are considered. A fourth criterion the legal definition of abnormality declares a person insane largely on the basis of his or her ability to judge between right and wrong or to exert control over behavior. This approach is even less useful for diagnostic purposes. Insanity is a legal term that is not employed by psychologists in discussing abnormality.

Abnormal and deviant behavior causes a great deal of unhappiness and distress to millions of people. It is impossible to say exactly how many people to millions of people. It is impossible to say exactly how many people are "abnormal", although some estimate that virtually 100 percent of the population will suffer some psychological problem, such as anxiety of depression, at some time, with 25 percent encountering serious psychological difficulties. The U.S. Surgeon General's report of 1979 predicted that one out of every eight individuals would actually require mental health care and now, It may be more fateful. In terms of individual suffering and the loss of human potential, the costs of these problems are enormous. The financial burdens of mental illness alone are put in the tens of billions of dollars annually; if the price of crime and other deviances is added, the figures quintuple.

CONCEPTIONS OF ABNORMALITY AND DEVIANCE

Words such as "abnormal" and "deviant" are emotionally powerful. So some Psychologists prefer terms like "behavior disorder" "emotional disturbance" "mental illness" and "psychological problem" . In this chapter we will discuss them one by one. But before we discuss, we shall first consider the historical development of the different approaches to abnormality. These include: (1) the superstitious, (2) the medical, (3) the psychoanalytic, and (4) the behavioral.

The Superstitious Approach

Some of the earliest explanations of abnormal behavior attributed it to supernatural powers. During The middle ages, for example, all natural phenomena were perceived as manifestations of God or Satan. Thus a person who acted abnormally was thought to have been possessed by a god or devil. For eviction of a satanic spirit, treatment might consist of torture, even execution.

The Medical Approach

Attitudes began to change in the late 1700s and early 1800s. With the Enlightenment came renewed interest in human rationality and thus the power of experiment and observation. Slowly, explanations for behavior based on reason replaced religious ones. The idea developed that people in asylums were not evil but ill. In Paris, the physician Philippe Pinel (1745–1826) promoted this view and removed the inmates' shackles and insured that they had sufficient food, fresh air, and exercise.

This medical perspective gained much support when it was found that some bizarre behaviors were due to brain damage and an identifiable physical cause. Classic among these was the discovery that syphilis, a sexually communicated microorganism, produced aberrant behavior through deterioration of the brain ten to twenty years after initial infection.

The medical model is, today, perhaps the single most influential perspective on abnormal behavior. Scientists now know that a number of diseases other than syphilis, as well as the intake of certain substances, can cause mental disturbances. Excessive use of alcohol or other drugs damages the brain. Ingestion of lead or mercury has been linked to delusions, hallucinations, and a lack of emotional control in industrial workers and in people who have consumed fish taken from industrially polluted waters. Finally, the medical model focuses research attention on the genetic inheritance of illness. Heredity has been implicated in a number of mental disorders, particularly schizophrenia.

The Psychoanalytic Approach

Not all physicians accepted the medical model's biological version of the origin of abnormal behavior. Sigmund Freud elaborated his view that psychological problems could be traced to childhood conflicts. These conflicts, if not resolved, could lead to a fixation at the stage of development where they occurred. Thus, for the adult distressed, the problems are assumed to be due to unconscious, unresolved conflicts from childhood. Impulses which have not been completely discharged and instead have been dealt with inadequately by defense mechanisms become transformed into the symptoms of the neuroses and psychoses. According to Freud:

Neurosis is the result of a conflict between the ego and its id, whereas psychosis is the analogous outcome of a similar disturbance in the relation between the ego and external (1959, p.250)

Fundamental of the psychoanalytic view, therefore, is the idea of an inner core of emotional or mental disturbances, i.e., disease, from which stimulate the observed symptoms.

Freud's ideas have profoundly affected how psychologists think about adjustment and the healthy personality. From the psychoanalytic perspective, well adapted individuals possess insight into their unconscious motives and a strong ego, and they do not waste psychic energy in distorting either wishes or reality itself (Meissner, 1980).

The Behavioral Approach

In contrast to the medical and psychoanalytic models, which view abnormal behavior as a surface manifestation of underlying problems, the behavioral approach regards the behavior itself as the problem. Its major aspect is its claim that abnormality and deviance are explained just like other behaviors through. According to this perspective, one person may have learned from the environment to be a hard-working business executive and another to be an easygoing teacher; still another may have learned to become alcoholic or schizophrenic.

One of the differences between the behavioral and medical perspectives lies in the labels the practitioners apply to abnormality and deviance. Behaviorally oriented psychologists prefer to use such terms as "behavior problem" . This is partly to avoid stigmatizing the whole individual as "mentally ill" or "emotionally disturbed" (see "Controversy" below).

第二节 变态行为的分类
(CLASSIFYING ABNORMAL BEHAVIOR)

Researchers interested in the classification of abnormality suggest that before diagnosticians can attempt to say whether or not a particular behavior problem is a mental illness or not, let alone isolate its origins, they must first describe it adequately. Classification has often been part of a developing science. The periodic table in chemistry, for example, has been revised as new elements have been discovered. Much of our understanding of evolutionary theory would not be possible without reliable classification of various species of animals and plants. Psychologists studying abnormal behavior are still in the early stages of developing a classificatory system.

A good clinical classification scheme for behavior has three particular values (Goldstein, Baker, & Jamison, 1980):

1. To predict the future course of a pattern of abnormal behavior, to make a prognosis.
2. To develop different treatment plans for distinct disorders.
3. To study the causes, or etiologies, of specific disorders.

Investigation, however, has not demonstrated the tripartite diagnostic systems to be very useful. Many researchers have scrutinized the reliability of diagnostic judgments that is, the extent to which experts agree about how to categorize a person or, indeed, whether the person should be categorized at all. These studies indicate that although the level of reliability has tended to be better than chance for the major categories, it has been disturbingly low for decisions that have so great an impact on peopled lives. The reliabilities have been low partly because the system has lacked clear criteria (Spitzer & Williams, 1980). For example, the system failed to specify when an emotionally cold, socially withdrawn person with oddities of thought should be judged as suffering from neurosis, personality disorder, or psychosis. Recently, a new classificatory scheme has been developed in an attempt to improve reliability.

DSM–III

In 1980, the American Psychiatric Association published the third edition of its Diagnostic and Statistical Manual (DSM–III). The volume, which names and classifies mental disorders, is used by virtually all clinical psychologists and psychiatrists. In the new edition, fifteen separate classifications of disorders are proposed (see Table 18.2). The American psychiatric Association worked closely with the World Health Organization to make the DSM–III similar to the International Classification of Diseases. In this way clinicians and research investigators around the world might have a common language.

DSM–III consists of five axes, or dimensions. The patient is rated on each. The first dimension consists of the fifteen disorders listed in Table 18.1. The second embodies twelve personality disorders that may be occurring in addition to the mental disorders of Axis I. Thus a person may suffer from both a mental disorder and a personality disorder (see Table 18. 2). The three remaining axes indicate any physical illness of potential relevance (Axis III); the presence of any current stress (Axis IV); and an assessment of the patient's highest level of adaptive functioning during the previous year (Axis V). In these ways, the authors of DSM−III hope to provide a fuller classification of a patient, using reliable and relatively well defined criteria. Although most psychologists and psychiatrists recognize DSM−III to be an improvement over previous classificatory schemes, it is still too soon to make a final judgment.

Table 18.1

The Major Categores of Mental Disorders According to DSM−III

Category of Mental Disorder	Example
1. Infant, Childhood, or Adolescent Disorders	Mental Retardation
2. Organic Mental Disorders	Senility
3. Substance Use Disorders	Alcoholism
4. Schizophrenic Disorders	Shizophrenia
5. Paranoid Disorders	Paranoia
6. Psychotic Disorders not Elsewhere Classified	Brief Reactive Psychosis
7. Affective Disorders	Depression
8. Anxiety Disorders	Phobias
9. Somatoform Disorders	Conversion Disorder
10. Dissociative Disorders	Multiple personality
11. Psychosexual Disorders	Sexual Masochism
12. Factitious Disorders	Factitious Illness
13. Disorders of Impulse Control	Pathological Gambling
14. Adjustment Disorder	Inability to Work
15. Psychological Factors Affecting Physical Condition	Migraine Headache

Source: From DSM−III Copyright The American Psychiatric Association, 1980. Reprinted by permission.

Critics of DSM−III have been concerned that this classificatory system increases the danger of labeling and stigmatizing as "abnormal", people who have relatively mild difficulties. Certainly any classificatory system can be misused if psychologists allow a diagnostic label to carry too much weight. They run the risk of overlooking the unique features of each case and expecting the person to conform to the classification. Another danger is forgetting that naming or classifying is only a first and tentative step in scientific understanding.

In presenting descriptions of the various disorders in this chapter, we will adopt a compromise position between the old−fashioned but familiar tripartite classification, and the new, modem one of DSM−III. Accordingly, we will divide abnormal behavior into the three broad classifications of neuroses, character disorders, and psychoses, and within each of these traditional domains we will describe the disorders according to the DSM–III terminology.

Table 18.2
The Major Types of Personality Disorder According to DSM–III

Category of Personality Disorder	Brief Description
1. Paranoid Personality Disorder	Unwarrantedly suspicious
2. Schizoid Personality Disorder	Emotionally cold
3. Schizotypal Personality Disorder	Having oddities of thought
4. Histrionic Personality Disorder	Overly dramatic
5. Narcissistic Personality Disorder	Grandiose sense of self–importance
6. Antisocial Personality Disorder	Continuously antisocial
7. Borderline Personality Disorder	Impulsively unpredictable
8. Avoidant Personality Disorder	Hypersensitive to rejection
9. Dependent Personality Disorder	Passively dependent on others
10. Compulsive Personality Disorder	Preoccupied with trivial details
11. Passive–aggressive Personality Disorder	Indirectly resisting demands
12. Atypical, mixed, or other Personality Disorder	Immature

Source: From DSM–III. Copyright The American Psychiatric Association. 1980. Reprinted by permission.

DSM–V was created in 1980, and this standard is not fixed. With the passage of time and the development of society, the previous standard has been difficult to suit the current requirements. So, in 2013, The American Psychiatric Association published the latest one–DSM–V. This version is better than the previous, more refined, and more in line with the current situation. DSM–V reintroduced "addiction" word, and added gambling disorder, substance use disorders, attenuated psychosis risk syndrome and some other new projects. But the new version still exists many problems, the part of the personality still stays in chaos. And the American standard may not be suitable other countries, DSM–V need more time to improve itself.

The Neuroses

The neuroses include a wide range of maladaptive behaviors that have anxiety as their most general characteristic. Neurotic disorders are primarily a less serious form of abnormal conduct, seldom requiring hospitalization. DSM–III refers to several separate disorders that we will in clude under the general heading of the neuroses. These include anxiety disorders, somatoform disorders, and dissociative disorders.

The anxiety disorders are characterized by high levels of apprehension in the presence of certain objects or situations and by the development of behavior patterns to avoid these stimuli. The most prevalent types of anxiety disorders are phobias, generalized anxiety disorders, and obsessive compulsive disorders.

Somatoform disorders involve physical symptoms suggesting physical disorder, but for which there are no apparent organic causes. The most common form of these disorders is conversion disorder.

Dissociative disorders involve a splitting off (dissociation) of a part of the individual's personality, so that memory or identity is disturbed. In amnesia, there is a loss of memory. In a fugue, a person takes on a new identity. In multiple personality, the person shows two or more distinct integrated personalities, each of which dominates at a particular time.

The Character Disorders

Like the category of neuroses, the term character disorder is somewhat old-fashioned and encompasses a number of behavior problems. In previous categorization systems, the character disorders have included delinquency and habitual criminality, drug abuse, sexual deviance, and difficulties of impulse control. The new DSM-III lists most of these as major mental disorders. In this section we will cover some of the more important of these disorders from the DSM-III perspective. We will also discuss crime and delinquency.

Substance use disorders involve excessive use of drugs. Alcohol is the most widely used drug. It is estimated that today, in the United States, more than 10 million people are alcoholics, or problem drinkers.

According to DSM-III, there are three basic sexual disorders. Gender-identity disturbance involves confusion between anatomic and psychological sexuality. Paraphilias (sexual deviations) involve focusing on particular sexual practices, such as fetishism or exhibitionism, as the sole means of sexual release. Psychosexual dysfunctions, such as impotence, involve difficulties in the initiation or completion of the sexual cycle. There is a clear trend away from labeling the individual who engages in homosexual behavior as emotionally disturbed.

The impulse disorders involve an intense drive to perform an act that is harmful to the individual or others. The more common manifestations include pathological gambling, kleptomania (compulsion to steal), and pyromania (compulsion to set fires).

Crime and delinquency are reaching epidemic proportions in American society. Some 10 percent of adult offenders are classified as psychopathic or sociopathic. These individuals demonstrate a lack of empathy, love, guilt, and shame. The psychopath's relationships with others tend to be exploitative and manipulative.

The Psychoses

The meaning of psychoses is a general term for severe disturbances of behavior and thought. The afflicted Individual's personality becomes so disorganized that hospitalization is often required. The psychoses refer to the type of disorder that makes us want to label the sufferer crazy, insane, or mad. Unlike neurotics, the psychotics have, in some ways, actually lost touch with reality. DSM-III refers to several separate disorders that we will describe under the general heading of the psychoses. These include organic, schizophrenic, paranoid, and affective disorders.

Organic disorders are directly related to brain damage. Blows to the head, toxic agents, and aging are the most usual causes. The main category of Organic Disorder in DSM-III is delirium and dementia, referring to a global disorientation of consciousness and memory loss.

Schizophrenic disorders are the most serious type of abnormal behavior and the most likely to require hospitalization. Schizophrenics experience thought disorder, delusions, and hallucinations. DSM-III lists four types of schizophrenic reactions: disorganized, paranoid, catatonic, and undifferentiated. Most scientists agree that some combination of genetic and environ-mental factors works to produce schizophrenia, Strong evidence for a genetic factor is provided by studies of children of schizophrenic mothers adopted shortly after birth and from studies of identical and fraternal twins.

Affective disorders involve disturbances of mood or emotion. People suffering from these disturbances are unrealistically depressed, inappropriately joyful, or both. Leaning theorists focus on reduced positive reinforcement and learned helplessness to explain depression.

Hope for the future

We have seen that mental disorders are common and encompass an enormous range of conditions. They cause a great deal of personal distress and impairment of social functioning. Many different explanations have been proposed for these varied problems, and many scientists are seeking the causes. Research has sometimes clarified a particular type of abnormal functioning, but more often it has simply given us clues that may lead to clarification. There is still conflict even about the definition of abnormal behavior. Under the circumstances, we must not expect to find one set of principles that accounts for all conditions that clinical psychologists deal with. One set may underlie schizophrenia, others depression, still others drug addiction, and so on. It is to be hoped that in the future, psychologists will understand the processes better, involved in the development of personality and will be able to reduce the incidence of mental disturbance. It is also to be hoped that the methods of treating these disturbances will improve to the point where the disturbances can be more readily cured. We turn to the methods of treatment in the following sections.

第三节 心理障碍的治疗
(THERAPY FOR PSYCHOLOGICAL DISORDER)

To judge from the history of attempts to treat psychological disorders, it would seem that our species has found its own problems mystifying. In the 2200 years since Eratosthenes correctly estimated the earth's circumference, we humans have charted the heavens, explored the solar system, reconstructed the basic history of life on earth, cracked the genetic code and eliminated or found cures for all sorts of diseases. Meanwhile, we have treated psychological disorders with a bewildering variety of harsh and gentle methods: by cutting holes in the head, and by giving warm baths and massages; by restraining, bleeding, or "beating the devil" out of people, and by placing them in sunny, serene environments; by administering drugs and electric shocks, and by chatting

—talking about childhood experiences, current feelings, or maladaptive thoughts and behaviors. We can now state with certainty the chemical composition of Jupiter's atmosphere, but when it comes to understanding and treating what is closer to home—the psychological disorders described we still are only beginning to make real progress.

A catalog of all therapies that have been tried at one time or another would have two main sections: the psychological therapies (therapies that involve an interaction between a trained professional and a client with a problem) and the biomedical therapies (therapies that alter the brain's structure or functioning). Although surefire "remedies" for most psychological disorders do not exist, as we will see, current psychological and biomedical therapies can be sometimes effective.

THE PSYCHOLOGICAL THERAPIES

The most common psychological form of therapy is psychotherapy, "a planned, emotionally charged confiding interaction between a trained, socially sanctioned healer and a sufferer" (Frank, 1982). From among the some 200 types of psychotherapy (Pines, 1982), we will consider several of the most influential. Although all the therapies we will consider are distinguishable in their pure forms, in practice, half of all psychotherapists describe themselves as eclectic, as using a blend of therapies (Smith, 1982). Depending on the client and the problem, an eclectic therapist will use or mix a variety of techniques.

Later, we will ask how successful each technique is and what common threads run through them all. But first, let us consider the basic aims and techniques of each therapy on its own terms. The major therapies are built upon familiar foundations the psychoanalytic, humanistic, and social–cognitive perspectives on personality.

Aims

Psychoanalysis assumes that psychological problems are fueled by unconscious impulses and conflicts, many of which develop and are repressed in childhood. Psychoanalysis aims to bring these repressed feelings into conscious awareness where they can be dealt with. By gradually gaining conscious insight into the origins of the disorder, the person in analysis works through the buried feelings. This releases the energy that was previously devoted to neurotic conflicts, allowing it to redirect toward healthier, and more anxiety—free living.

Methods

When Freud discarded hypnosis as an effective therapeutic technique, he turned to free association. Imagine yourself as a patient using the free association technique: The analyst invites you to relax in a comfortable position, perhaps by lying on a couch. He or she will probably sit out of your line of vision, helping you to focus your attention on your internal thoughts and feelings. Beginning perhaps with a childhood memory, a dream, or a recent experience, you state aloud whatever comes to your mind from moment to moment. It sounds easy, but soon you become aware of how often you edit your thoughts as you speak, by omitting material that seems trivial, irrelevant, or shameful. Even in the relatively safe presence of the analyst, you may pause momentarily before uttering an embarrassing thought or you may change the subject to something less threatening, and sometimes your mind may seem to go blank or you may find yourself unable to remember important details.

To the psychoanalyst, these blocks in the flow of one's free associations are resistances. They hint that anxiety lurks and that sensitive material is being blocked from consciousness. The analyst will want to explore these sensitive areas, first by making you aware of your resistances, and later by helping you to interpret their underlying meaning. The analyst's **interpretations** suggestions of hidden feelings and conflicts are considered an important avenue to insight. Through them you may become aware of what you are avoiding, and you may discover what your resistances mean and how they fit with other pieces of your psychological puzzle.

In addition to resistances, Freud believed that another clue to repressed impulses is the latent content of our dreams. Thus, after inviting you to report a dream, the analyst may try to interpret its hidden meaning, thereby adding yet another piece to your developing picture of yourself.

Psychoanalysis The goal of psychoanalysts is to help people gain insight into the unconscious origins of their disorders and to work through the accompanying feelings. To do so, they draw upon techniques such as free association and the interpretation of resistances, dreams, and the transference to the therapist of long repressed feelings. Like psychoanalytic theory, psychoanalysis is criticized for its after the fact interpretations and for being time consuming and costly. Although traditional psychoanalysis is not practiced widely, its influence can be seen in therapists who explore childhood experiences, who assume that defense mechanisms suppress emotion laden information, and who seek to help their clients achieve insight into the roots of their problems.

Humanistic Therapies Unlike psychoanalysts, humanistic therapists tend to focus on clients' current, conscious feelings and on their taking responsibility for their own growth. Carl Rogers, in his person centered therapy, uses active listening to express genuineness, acceptance, and empathy. With Gestalt therapy Fritz Perls sought to break down peopled defenses and to make them accept responsibility for their feelings. Many therapeutic techniques can also be applied in group therapy, as in the application of humanistic principles within encounter groups.

Behavior Therapies Behavior therapists worry less about promoting self—awareness and more about directly modifying problem behaviors. Thus they may counter—condition behaviors through systematic desensitization or aversive conditioning. Or they may apply operant conditioning principles with behavior modification techniques such as token economies. The newer cognitive—behavior therapies such as Ellis's rational—emotive therapy, Beck's cognitive therapy for depression, and Meichenbaum's self—instructional training, all aim to change self—defeating thinking by training people to look at themselves in new, more positive ways.

Evaluating Psychotherapies Because the positive testimonials of clients and therapists cannot prove that therapy is actually effective; psychologists have conducted hundreds of studies of the outcomes of psychotherapy. These studies indicate that (1) people who remain untreated often improve (a phenomenon called spontaneous remission); (2) those who receive psychotherapy tend to improve somewhat more, regardless of what kind of therapy they receive for how long; (3) mature, articulate people with specific behavior problems often receive the greatest benefits from therapy; but (4) placebo treatments of the sympathy and friendly counsel of paraprofessionals also tend to produce more improvement than occurs with untreated people.

THE BIOMEDICAL THERAPIES

Psychotherapy is one major way of dealing with psychological disorders. The other is to alter the brain's functioning by disconnecting its circuits through psychosurgery, by overloading its circuits with electroconvulsive shock, or by altering its electrochemical transmissions with drugs.

Psychosurgery

Because its effects are irreversible, **psychosurgery** surgery that removes or destroys brain tissue in an effort to change behavior—is the most drastic biomedical intervention. In the 1930s, Portuguese physician Egas Moniz developed an operation that came to be called a lobotomy. Moniz found that when he surgically cut the nerves that connect the frontal lobes with the emotion-controlling centers of the inner brain, uncontrollably emotional and violent patients were calmed. During the 1940s and 1950s literally tens of thousands of severely disturbed people were "lobotomized" and Moniz was honored with a Noble Prize.

Although the intention was simply to disconnect emotion from thought, the effect was often more drastic; it produced a permanently lethargic, immature personality. When during the 1950s calming drugs became readily available, psychosurgery was largely abandoned. Today, psychosurgery is used only in extreme cases. For example, if a patient suffers uncontrollable seizures, surgeons can deactivate the specific nerve clusters that cause the convulsions (Valenstein, 1980). Even such apparently beneficial operations are irreversible, however, and so are used only as a last resort.

Electroconvulsive Therapy

A less drastic manipulation of the brain occurs with the still widely practiced use of **electroconvulsive therapy (ECT)**. When first introduced in 1938, the wide-awake patient would be strapped to a table and jolted with roughly 100 volts of electricity to the brain, producing bone-rattling convulsions and momentary unconsciousness. Today, the procedure is much less terrifying and is used only with severely depressed patients (having been found to be ineffective in treating other disorders such as schizophrenia). The patient is first given a general anesthetic and a muscle relaxant. Then the shock is administered to the soundly sleeping patient for a fraction of a second causing a minute or so of convulsions. Within 30 minutes the patient awakens and remembers nothing of the treatment.

Drug Therapies

By far the most widely used biomedical treatments are the drug therapies. Introduced in the 1950s, they have reduced the need for psychosurgery and in many cases have reduced the need for hospitalization. New discoveries in psychopharmacology (the study of the effect of drugs on mind and behavior) have revolutionized the treatment of severely disordered people, enabling thousands to be liberated from confinement in mental hospitals.

TREATING THE SOCIAL ROOTS OF PSYCHOLOGICAL DISORDERS

Both the psychotherapies and the biomedical therapies locate psychological disorders within individuals and thus seek to remedy them by changing individuals. Thus we infer that people who act cruelly must be cruel people and that people who act "crazy" must be "sick". We attach labels to such people, thereby distinguishing them from the rest of us "normal" people. It follows, then, that we try to treat "abnormal" people by giving them insight into their problems, by changing their thinking, or by controlling them with drugs.

However, there is another way to view many psychological disorders as an understandable response to a disturbed and stressful society. According to this view, it is not just the individual who needs treatment, but also the social context in which the individual acts. The idea is that many of these problems do not suddenly spring up in an individual but develop from the person's history of stressful experiences in a particular environment.

词汇 (Vocabulary)

1. aberrant   a. 异常的、畸变的
2. asylum   n. 避难所
3. criteria   n. 参考标准、准则
4. deterioration n. 变坏的状况、日渐削弱
5. diagnose   v. 诊断
6. elaborate   v. 通过推理阐发使其完善
7. etiology   n. 病因、病源
8. hallucination n. 幻觉
9. manifestation n. 显现
10. neurosis   n. 神经官能症
11. scrutinize   r. 审查、检查
12. shackle   v. 剥夺自由
13. syphilis   n. 梅毒
14. symptom   n. 症状

第十九章 社会心理学
（SOCIAL PSYCHOLOGY）

本章要点（Chapter Outline）
态度与态度改变（Attitudes and Attitude Change）
归因与印象形成（Attribution and Impression Formation）
偏见与刻板印象（Prejudice and Stereotypes）
社会吸引（Social Attraction）
从众与服从（Conformity and Compliance）
攻击与利他（Aggression and Altruism）

社会心理学是对人的社会心理和行为规律进行系统研究的科学。社会心理学包括个体社会心理和社会行为、社会交往心理和社会行为、群体心理及应用社会心理学四个方面。每一个社会心理现象的产生都离不开特定的文化环境、特定的人群，以及与此一致的相应的社会交往方式和内容。社会态度的形成与改变过程中，认知因素、社会因素等对态度的变化形成都起着重要的作用。归因是对自己或他人行为的解释和预测，凯利的归因理论指出归因存在吝惜律和协变律。在归因中由于利益关系等易作出归因偏差和归因错误，印象和刻板印象是社会认知中的心理现象。这类社会认知现象的形成受权威者个性、传统的态度、认知因素等影响。社会交往中的心理现象、从众和服从也将在这一章讨论。此外对社会利他和攻击也从社会心理方面介绍了产生这些行为的机制，并给予相应的理论解释。

第一节 概述
（INTRODUCTION）

Social psychology is the scientific study of how people think about, influence, and relate to one another. Sociology and psychology are social psychology's parent disciplines. Social psychology tends to be more individualistic in its content and more experimental in its method than other areas of sociology. Compared to personality psychology, social psychology focuses less attention on differences among individuals and more attention on how people, in general, view and affect one another. There are many additional perspectives on human nature, each of which asks its own set of questions. Successful explanation of human functioning by one perspective does not invalidate explanation by other perspectives.

Most social psychological research is either correlation or experimental. Correlation studies, sometimes conducted with systematic survey methods, ascertain the relationship between variables, such as between amount of education and amount of income. Knowing two things are naturally related is valuable information, but it usually does not indicate what is causing what. When possible, social psychologists therefore prefer to conduct experiments in which cause and effect can be pinned down more precisely. By constructing a miniature reality that is under their control, experimenters can vary one thing and then another and discover how these things, separately or in combination, affect people. When participants are randomly assigned to an experimental condition, which receives the experimental treatment, or a control condition, which does not, then any resulting difference between the two conditions can be attributed to the experimental treatment. Ethical problems often encountered in conducting experiments have necessitated the development of ethical standards for research.

Social psychologists organize their ideas and findings into theories. A good theory will distill a bewildering array of facts into a much shorter list of predictive principles. These predictions can be used to confirm or modify the theory, to generate new exploration, and to suggest practical application.

Social psychology's findings may sometimes seem obvious. However, experiments indicate that outcomes are generally far more "obvious" after the fact are known than they are beforehand. This hindsight bias tends to make people overconfident about the validity of their intuition.

Social psychologists' values penetrate their work in obvious ways, like their choice of research topics. Less easily recognized are subtle ways in which values permeate social psychology. There is a growing awareness of the subjectivity of scientific interpretation, of values hidden in the concepts and labels of social psychology, and of the gulf between scientific description of what is and ethical prescription of what ought to be. This penetration of values into science is not unique to social psychology, nor is it anything to be embarrassed about. That human thinking is seldom dispassionate is precisely why we need systematic observation and experimentation if we are to check our cherished conjectures against reality.

第二节 态度和态度改变
(ATTITUDES AND ATTITUDES CHANGE)

Attitudes

Attitudes can be defined as positive or negative evaluation of people, objects, ideas, or events(Bem,1970). For example, a person's opposition to government regulation or support for solarenergy development are attitudes. Likewise, liking the New York Yankees or disliking disco music are attitudes.

Attitudes must be distinguished from beliefs. Beliefs are perceptions of factual matters, of what is true or false. For example, our ideas about how many teeth alligators have, what causes inflation, and whether artichokes grow on trees are beliefs. Beliefs do not have an evaluative, that is, a liking or disliking, component. Although attitudes and beliefs are different, what we say about one applies to the other. Here, we will concentrate on attitudes, but you should remember that our discussion also applies to beliefs. In the rest of this section we will look at how attitudes are formed and changed.

Attitude Formation

Psychologists have identified three major influences on the formation of attitudes: social influences, or the influence of other people; cognitive influences, or the influence of our reasoning; and behavioral influences, or the influence of our own behavior. These influences jointly mold our earliest attitudes, and they can change attitudes throughout our lives.

Social Influences on Attitudes

Attitudes strongly affect how we perceive and respond to other people. It is somewhat ironic, then, to recognize how strongly other people influence our attitudes. Our early attitudes are influenced by our parents. Later on, attitudes are influenced by peers. Both parents and peers influence attitudes through three processes: providing information, reinforcement, and identification.

Many of our earliest likes and dislikes are influenced by our parents(Oskamp, 1977). Some of the attitudes that we form on the basis of parental influence will change, but many will remain the same. For example, one of the best predictors of which political party a person will belong to is the party his or her parents belong to. Two-thirds to three-quarters of the adults in the United States vote for the same party as did their fathers. People's fathers' party preference is a better predictor of their own party preference than is social class or occupation, two other strong predictors(Hyman, 1959).

The first way parents influence our attitudes is by providing information about people, objects, policies, ideas and events in the world. Parents tell children what is good and what is bad. Young children, having no information to the contrary, believe what their parents say. For example, if children are told that they can learn a lot from playing with children of other religions, they will probably develop positive attitudes toward these children. In short, parents provide us with unchallenged information about whether certain things are good for us or bad. On this information we base many attitudes.

A second means by which parents influence attitudes is by administering rewards and punishments (Mc Ginnies, 1970). Very often, parents praise children for expressing some attitudes and disapprove when they express others. Such approval or disapproval has been shown to have a strong impact on people's attitudes.

A third social influence on attitudes is the process of identification(Kelman, 1961). In the course of growing up, we often try to emulate other people we admire. Part of this process of identification is adopting the others' attitudes. Freud suggested that the first people we identify with are our parents, especially our parent of the same sex during the resolution of the Oedipus complex.

Erik Erikson emphasizes that throughout childhood and adolescence we identify with many other people, such as relatives, celebrities, or older peers, in the process of forming an identify. Through these identifications we adopt many attitudes.

Parents are not the only people with whom children come in contact, and they are not the only people who influence our attitudes. By the time school starts, at age five or six, children are spending more and more time with peers. Peers influence attitudes in the same way parents do. They provide each other with information; they reinforce each other for expressing certain opinions; and they identify with each other. A study of peer influence at different ages suggests that it increases through the elementary school years, reaches its peak in junior high school (ages 12 and 13), and then begins to decrease. Subjects made judgments about the length of lines after being told how three other subjects of the same age judged them.

Cognitive Influences on Attitudes

Another very important source of attitudes is our own reasoning and logic. Very often we go beyond what we have been told by other people and figure things out for ourselves. Many studies of attitude change have shown that one attitude can be logically derived from others. Let us take as an example a study showing that, if one attitude changes, other logically connected attitudes change as well.

In this study, conducted by social psychologist William McGuire (1960), high-school students completed a questionnaire indicating whether they believed forty-eight different statements were true. Many of these statements were logically related, although related statements were dispersed throughout the questionnaire. For example, three related statements were: "Any form of recreation that constitutes a serious health menace will be outlawed by the City Health Authority". The increasing water pollution in this area will make swimming a serious health hazard. "Swimming at the local beaches will be outlawed by the City Health Authority". As you can see, the third statement is logically derived from the first two.

About a week after completing the questionnaire, some subjects who did not believe the first statement read essays that tried to persuade them that it was true. The other two statements were not mentioned in the essay. A questionnaire given immediately after the subjects read the essay showed that they were influenced by it and had come to believe in the first statement. In addition, the questionnaire showed that those who came to believe the first statement and already believed the second statement, that swimming was becoming a health hazard subsequently came to believe the third statement, that swimming would be outlawed, which was derived from the first two. A third questionnaire given a week later showed that the subjects still believed this conclusion. Thus we see that if people's beliefs are changed, other logically related beliefs will change as well.

Behavioral Influences on Attitudes

A third influence on people's attitudes is their own behavior. This may seem strange, since you may feel that attitudes influence behavior rather than vice versa. How can behavior influence attitudes? Leon Festinger's (1957) theory of cognitive dissonance helps explain how this happens.

The theory of cognitive dissonance relates to the research by McGuire discussed above. Both propose that people make their thoughts consistent. The theory of cognitive dissonance states that whenever two thoughts or cognitions are inconsistent, an unpleasant tension called cognitive dissonance will be produced. Festinger borrowed the term dissonance from music, where it means jarring, grating, or inharmonious. Because two inharmonious thoughts produce dissonance, people are motivated to reduce it. They can do this by changing one or the other of the inconsistent cognitions.

Dissonance also results if a person's cognition about a behavior is inconsistent with a cognition about an attitude. An experiment by Jonathan Freedman (1965) shows how this kind of process leads to attitude formation in young children. The hypothesis of this experiment was that children who were prevented from playing with an attractive toy would experience dissonance. The two cognitions, "That is a great toy" (attitude) and "I'm not playing with it" (behavior) would be inconsistent. Furthermore, Freedman predicted that unless subjects had a good reason for avoiding the toy, they would reduce dissonance by changing their attitude and coming to dislike the toy.

Young children were brought into a laboratory where an experimenter asked them a series of questions about their toy preferences. In the room was a Tonka tractor, a Dick Tracy toy rifle, a cheap, plastic submarine, a child's baseball glove, and an extremely expensive, battery-controlled robot. After a period of time the experimenter said that he had to leave the room for several minutes, but that while he was gone the child could play with some of the toys that were there. The only restriction, the experimenter stated, was that the child was not to play with the robot, which happened to be the most attractive toy!

The experimenter created two conditions by stating this restriction in one of two ways. In the mild-threat condition, he said, "It is wrong to play with the robot." In the strong-threat condition he added, "If you play with the robot. I will be very angry and will have to do something about it." In both conditions, almost none of the children played with the robot.

According to the theory of cognitive dissonance, the children should come to dislike the robot, a negative attitude consistent with their behavior. But which group's attitude would be more negative, the group that heard the mild threat or the one that heard the strong threat? You might expect that children who heard the very strong negative threat would have the most negative association to the toy. But dissonance theory predicts the opposite. Those who heard the strong threat had good reason, or sufficient external justification, for not playing with the toy. There would be serious consequences if they played with it. However, the mild-threat children did not have a good reason, or sufficient justification, for their behavior. These children would need to provide their own justification by deciding that they really did not like the toy. In this way, dissonance would be reduced.

The results shown in Table 19.1 supported cognitive-dissonance theory. About three months later, the children were brought back to the laboratory and told they could play with any toy they wanted. Fewer children in the mild-threat condition than those in the strong-threat condition played with the robot. They had formed a more negative attitude, an attitude consistent with their behavior of not playing with the robot in the face of only a mild threat.

Table 19.1 Results of the Freedman(1965) Toy Study

Condition	Percentage of subjects playing with attractive toy in second session
Strong threat	67%
Mild threat	29%
Control	66%

Adapted from Freedman,1965

Research on dissonance theory has provided many demonstrations that people will form attitudes that are consistent with and thereby justify their behavior (Wicklund & Brehm, 1976). Thus when parents make sure that their children do not hit their siblings or that they do their homework, the children should form attitudes consistent with these behaviors, especially if the tangible rewards for the behavior are small. The less the external justification, the more the children will adopt an attitude that is consistent with their actions. Focus: "Explanations for Dissonance Studies" discusses two other explanations for this process.

Persuasion and Attitude Change

In the course of growing up, people form many attitudes. These attitudes are useful in forming perceptions and making judgments about the world, and they help in guiding social interaction. However, the attitudes people form hardly ever escape pressures to change. In this section we will consider the factors that determine whether attempts to alter attitudes are successful.

Social psychologists are interested in attitude change because it may ultimately be the key to solving a number of longstanding social problems. For example, racial discrimination is deeply rooted in racist attitudes, and for discrimination to end, these attitudes need to be changed. We will first consider the role of the communicator's characteristics in influencing attitude change. Next we will consider the nature of the communicator's message. Finally, we will consider how attitude change is affected by the situation in which people receive a persuasive appeal.

Communicator Characteristics

Social psychologists have explored three characteristics that contribute to a communicator's effectiveness: credibility, attractiveness, and similarity. Communicators with high credibility, a reputation for expertise and honesty, produce more attitude change than communicators with low credibility (Zimbardo, Ebbesen & Maslach, 1977). For example, one study showed that an article describing a cure for the common cold was believed more if subjects thought it was printed in the New England Journal of Medicine rather than in Life magazine (Hovland & Weiss, 1951).

Attractive sources are often more effective than unattractive ones, possibly because we like to please attractive people by doing what they want, including adopting specific attitudes. In one study, a woman changed subjects' attitudes about education more when she was dressed attractively than when she appeared unkempt and homely (Mills & Aronson, 1965).

Another factor is the communicator's similarity to the listener. If someone else seems to be facing the same problems and situations in life that we are, we tend to feel they share our interests and we believe them. This was shown in a study of paint salesmen in a hardware store. The salesmen were more successful in influencing the brand of paint their customers bought when the salesmen's own painting experience was described as similar to the customers' instead of much more extensive (Brock, 1965). In general, then, communicators who are credible, attractive, and similar to their audiences are more persuasive than those who lack these qualities. However, the characteristics of the communicator are only one determinant of persuasion.

Message Characteristics

Obviously it does not matter who is trying to be persuasive if what they are saying is not convincing. But what makes a message persuasive? First, the message must appear unbiased. Second, the message must motivate its listeners to change their minds or take action.

Research on the influence of one versus two-sided communications demonstrates the importance of making a message seem unbiased. A one-sided communication discusses arguments for only one position. A two-sided communication mentions or describes arguments on the other side of the issue too.

In a classic experiment on which was more persuasive, American soldiers in the Pacific during world War II were told that the war with Japan would be long and then heard arguments about how long the war would last. Some communications were one-sided, presenting only reasons why the war would be long. Other communications were two-sided, and gave reasons why the war might be long and why it might be won quickly. The results showed that soldiers with more than a high-school education were more persuaded by the two-sided communication. The one-sided communication seemed biased, since these soldiers knew there were arguments on the other side of the issue. On the other hand, soldiers with less than a high-school education were more persuaded by a one-sided communication. To them, the two-sided communication seemed confusing (Hovland, Lumsdaine, & Sheffield, 1949).

Other experiments generally are consistent with these findings (Petty & Cacioppo, 1981). If an audience knows arguments opposing the position being advanced, a two-sided communication acknowledging the issues is more effective. However, if an audience does not know about arguments opposing the position being advanced, a two-sided communication which explains them produces doubt and confusion. Thus a communication written to be unbiased may run into another problem, lack of clarity.

Some messages contain threats or fear to try to change attitudes and related behavior, they state that unless you act or think in a certain manner, harmful consequences will follow. Fear is used in messages because it can motivate action. The first study on fear was conducted by Janis and Feshbach (1953) who predicted that high fear would increase attitude change by catching the audience's attention and motivating change. This experiment tried to make high-school students brush their teeth more often by detailing the consequences of tooth decay. One group of students, the low-fear group, was given a calm talk about the dangers of decay. A second group, the high-fear group, saw gory slides and was told that infections from tooth decay could spread and cause serious illness, including blindness. Quite surprisingly, the results showed that subjects in the low-fear group showed the most change in attitude.

Other experiments however, have shown contrary results, which support Janis and Feshbach's original hypothesis that high-fear is more persuasive. For example, in one study, subjects in a high-fear condition saw frightening films about the dangers of smoking. The films showed diseased lungs and actual surgery on lungs. Subjects in a low-fear condition saw milder, more clinical films with charts and graphs. Smokers were more persuaded about the dangers of smoking in the high-fear condition. (Leventhal, Watts & Pagano, 1967)

Most studies show that high fear is more persuasive than low fear, but there are exceptions such as the Janis and Feshbach findings. Psychologists are now studying the possibility that moderate fear is most persuasive because of its motivating qualities. Intense fear may lead listeners to attack the communicator or ignore the message. Other research shows that fear works best when subjects are given explicit recommendations on how to escape from danger (Harris & Jellison, 1971; Leventhal, 1970).

The Situation

How much we are affected by persuasive messages depends in part on the situations in which we receive them. Sometimes when people are reading or listening to a persuasive message they are distracted by other thoughts, sounds, or activities. Distraction can have a considerable impact on the effect of a persuasive message. A number of studies indicated that if people are distracted while they are listening to a message they will show more attitude change because the distraction interferes with silent counter arguing (Osterhouse & Brock, 1970).

In one study college students listened to a speaker arguing against fraternities. In one condition they simultaneously watched a film of the speech. In a second condition they watched an amusing but irrelevant film, an Academy Award-winning short called The Day of the Painter. Subjects in the second condition were more influenced by the speech (Festinger & Maccoby, 1964).

Distraction is just one of many situational factors that can increase persuasion. Another factor that makes people more susceptible to persuasive messages in simply pleasant surroundings. This phenomenon was shown in a study where students read essays while they ate peanuts and drank soda. Other subjects did not have these enjoyable refreshments. The subjects who ate while they read showed more attitude change than the other subjects (Janis, Kaye, & Kirschner, 1965). One possible explanation is that subjects who ate and drank while reading associated a pleasant stimulus (food) with the message and thus came to like the message better on the basis of classical conditioning.

The Persistence of Attitudes

Generally, research indicates that people will maintain the attitudes they have at any particular time, whether they are new or old, unless there are pressures to change. Thus a person who has his or her attitude changed is likely to maintain that new attitude unless some force, such as peer pressure, induces a change (McGuire, 1969). In this section we shall consider two studies pertaining to the persistence of changed attitudes. One shows that they can be stable over many years. The other suggests this might be true because adopting a new attitude can lead people to forget their old ones.

The Stability of Attitudes

An impressive demonstration of the persistence of changed attitudes comes from Newcomb's studies of Bennington students (Newcomb, Kocning, Flacks. & Warwick, 1967). After the 1960 and 1964 presidential elections, Newcomb surveyed women who had been students at Bennington in the 1930s and had become liberals. He wanted to see whether they were who went to colleges other than Bennington.

In the 1960 election, sixty percent of the Bennington graduates favored the Democrat, Kennedy, while only thirty percent of women who were similar in terms of social class, education, region, religion, and so forth, supported Kennedy, In the 1964 election, about sixty-five percent of these comparison women supported the Democrat, Johnson while ninety percent of the Bennington graduates did. Thus the Bennington graduates became more liberal than their peers in the 1930s and were still more liberal in the 1960s.

Newcomb et al.(1967) suggest this happened because the Bennington women tended to marry liberal husbands (or they converted their husbands), and their husbands supported their liberal attitudes. Women who had revered to their earlier conservative beliefs had married men who did not support liberal attitudes. Thus the Bennington studies show that new attitudes will persist unless there is pressure to change.

Forgetting Old Attitudes

Another important factor in the maintenance of new attitudes is the distortion of memory. When people change their minds, they could experience cognitive dissonance if they recognized they have been inconsistent over time. One way to reduce the dissonance is simply to distort the memory of your old attitude and to believe that the attitude you hold now is the one you have always held. An interesting demonstration of this point occurred in a study of attitude change among high-school students.

A week before the actual experiment, the students were given a survey dealing with several political issues. Then, groups composed of either all probusing or all antibusing students were called in for discussions of that issue. In the discussion, one of their peers, who was actually a confederate of the experimenter, tried to change the students' minds. The confederate spoke first, using clever two-sided statements and countering typical arguments from the other side of the issue. A questionnaire handed out after the discussion showed that the confederate had been remarkably successful in changing his friends' attitudes. The students were then asked to recall as accurately as they could how they had answered the questionnaire that they had completed before the experiment. Their memory was very accurate except on the busing issue (see Table 19.2). Nearly every subject remembered his or her initial busing attitude as having been identical to what it was after the discussion (Goethals & Reckman, 1973). Neisser (1982) reports similar findings. Thus people may hold to their new attitudes because they forget they ever felt differently.

Table 19.2 Error in Recall Scores.

All subjects were asked to duplicate their earlier responses on a thirty-one-point scale; the higher the score, the higher the error. These results indicate that subjects whose attitudes about busing had been changed as a result of group discussion recalled those earlier attitudes very inaccurately. However, the same subjects recalled their attitudes on other issues quite accurately, Futhermore, control subjects, who had not participated in a persuasive group discussion t recalled their busing attitudes and other attitudes highly accurately.

Condition	Bussing issue	Other issues
Experimental subjects(mean)	13.06	3.96
Control subjects (mean)	3.25	2.75

Adapted from Goethals & Reckman, 1973

第三节 归因与印象形成
(ATTRIBUTION AND IMPRESSION FORMATION)

Attitudes are a very important element in the way we perceive and evaluate objects, events, and other people. They help us organize a complex world. Another very important part of social perception is the processes by which we perceive people and form impressions of them. The most important process in perceiving people is the process of attribution, or explaining the causes of people's behavior. In this section, we will discuss the ways people make specific attributions about others and how they resolve discrepancies when they have conflicting information.

Attribution is the process of figuring out or explaining why people behave as they do. When we use attribution, each of us becomes an amateur detective trying to decide the cause of a behavior. At the heart of this process is deciding whether a person's behavior is caused by something in the person (an internal attribution) or by something in the situation or environment (external attribution). For example, we might overhear a neighbor yelling at the boy who delivers the newspaper. Is the neighbor yelling because he is a hostile grouch(internal attribution)? Or is he yelling because the paper has landed on the roof for the fifth day in a row (external attribution)? We will consider first the basic principles that people follow in making internal or external attributions. Then we will consider how attributions can be biased. Finally, we will discuss research on the ways people form impressions when they have conflicting information.

Kelley's Principles of Attribution

The distinction between internal and external causes of behavior was first discussed by Fritz Heider (1944,1958). Heider's work influenced all subsequent theory and research on attribution. A more recent theorist, Harold Kelley (1973), has specified how people actually decide whether a behavior is attributable to internal or external causes. In this section we will discuss Kelley's two key attribution principles, the discounting and covariation principles.

The Discounting Principle

The discounting principle holds that the internal causes of a behavior should be discounted if there are plausible external causes for the behavior. For example, we discount the internal causes of a celebrity's endorsement of brand of corn flakes if we know he is being handsomely paid for making the commercial. The money is a very plausible cause for his behavior, so we do not infer he has a positive attitude toward this brand of breakfast cereal.

One classic example of discounting was an experiment by Jones. Davis, and Gergen (1961). In this experiment, college students were told that they were to judge the personality characteristics of a sailor who was applying for a position in a Navy program. The subjects were to make these judgments after hearing the sailor's job interview.

Half the subjects were told that the sailor was applying for a job in an astronauts program. They were also told that this position required self-reliance and introversion, since astronauts sometimes spend long periods of time alone in space. The other half of the subjects were told that the sailor was applying for a submarine program. This position was described as extraversion, an ability to get along with others in close quarters over extended periods of time. Then, half the subjects in each of these two groups heard the sailor describe himself as introverted on a tape recording. The remainder beard him describe himself as extraverted. Thus four different experimental conditions were created (see Table 19.3).

Table 19.3 The Role of Discounting in Subjects Perceptions of Sailor's Personality.

When the sailor's self-description matched the position requirements the experimenters predicted that subjects would discount the self-description. The subjects ratings indicate that this occurred.

Position applied for	Sailor's self-description	Experimenters' prediction of Subjects' perception	Subjects' perception of sailor
Astronaut (requires introversion)	Introverted	Somewhat introverted (discounting)	24.1 (somewhat introverted)
Astronaut (requires introversion)	Extroverted	Highly extroverted (no discounting)	31.8 (highly extroverted)
Submariner (requires extroversion)	Introverted	Highly introverted (no discounting)	18.05 (highly introverted)
Submariner (requires extroversion)	Extroverted	Somewhat extroverted (discounting)	24.58 (somewhat extroverted)

The higher the score, the more the sailor was perceived as extraverted as opposed to introverted. Based on Jones, Davis, & Gergen, 1961.

According to the discounting principle, subjects should have had little confidence that the sailor actually had the traits needed for the job. They might reason that he described himself that way only to fit the job specifications. This plausible external explanation for his behavior should have led subjects to discount the possible internal cause, which is that the sailor really had the traits. On the other hand, the applicant for the astronaut program who described himself as extraverted and the applicant for the submarine program who describe himself as introverted had nothing to gain. Thus, subjects should not have discounted the internal cause, that the sailors really were as they describe themselves. The results of the experiment confirmed this discounting logic.

The Covariation Principle

The co variation principle explains how observers use logical processes when attributing a person's behavior to either internal or external causes.

Suppose for example that we want to know whether Joan enjoys a certain movie because of her good sense of humor or because the movie is very funny. In applying the co variation principle, we have to do a little detective work and find out about three characteristics of Joan's reaction: its distinctiveness, its consistency, and its level of consensus.

Distinctiveness refers to how unusual or unique Joan's response is. Does she often laugh or just at this movie? If her response to the movie is distinctive for Joan, we might consider the hypothesis that the movie caused the response. However, before accepting this hypothesis we would need to know about consistency.

Consistency refers to whether or not Joan's response is the same whenever she sees the film. If she were to see it again, would she still think it was funny? If her response is consistent, we might feel more strongly that the movie is funny (an external cause). If she yawns the second time we might attribute her initial reaction to a temporary mood (an internal cause). But we still need more information. We need to know how other people respond to the movie.

Consensus refers to how many other people laugh at the film. If many others laugh, Joan's response has high consensus. If no one else laughs, it has low consensus. If there is high consensus, we would think that the film is the cause of Joan's laughter. If there is low consensus, Joan's laughter would be attributed to something about her, perhaps her sense of humor or perhaps a temporary mood.

Figure 19.1

Kelley's Co variation principle	High	High	High consensus	External distinctiveness attribution	consistency
		Joan laughs just at this movie +	Joan usually laughs at + this movie	Many other people laugh at this movie =	This movie is funny
		Low distinctiveness	High consistency	Low consensus	Internal attribution
		Joan laughs often +	Joan usually laughs at + this movie	Few people laugh at = this movie	Joan is easy to amuse

How does the information from these three criteria, distinctiveness, consistency, and consensus, come together to make an attribution? In general, a response is attributed to an external cause, in this case the film Joan saw, if the response is distinctive, consistent. and has high consensus. On the other hand, if the response is consistent but not distinctive, and has low consensus, it is attributed to some trait of the person. If the response is inconsistent. It is generally attributed to a special circumstance or temporary mood (set Figure 19.2)

In a study showing the importance of kelley's criteria, subjects were given information such as the following: "Sue is afraid of the dog. She is not afraid of almost any other dag. In the past Sue has always been afraid of the dog. Almost everyone is afraid of the dog." According to Kelley's criteria, should subjects attributes Sue's fear to an internal cause(that she is a fearful person)or to an external cause(that the dog is frightening)? First, Sus's response is distinctive. Her reaction to this dog is unique. Second, her response is consistent. She is always afraid of the dog. Third, her response has high consensus. Others are afraid of the dog too. Subjects should thus make an external attribution to this distinctive, consistent, and consensual response. The results of the experiment show that they do(Mc Arthur,1972).

Biases and Errors in Attribution

Research shows that people do follow both the discounting and co variation principles. But this does not mean that people always follow them in the course of social interaction. Correctly applying attribution principles, especially the covariation principle, takes time, energy, and intellectual effort. However, people are not always rational, deliberative, and scientific. In all too many cases, they shortcut the principles that would lead to accurate social perceptions and jump to incorrect conclusions. These errors can lead to harmful mistreatment of individuals and groups. Thus, social psychologists are particularly interested in identifying errors and biases. In this section we will discuss two important, and related, biases in attribution: the fundamental attribution error and the actor−observer bias. Both biases suggest we often fail to take full account of all the factors affecting other people's behavior.

The Fundamental Attribution Error

The fundamental attribution error is the tendency for perceivers to underestimate the role of external causes of behavior and to overestimate the role of internal or dispositional causes (Ross, 1977). That is, it is a failure to use the discounting principle. For example, we might conclude that a young boy is unintelligent (internal cause) when his poor performance in school is really due to his unsettled home life (external cause). Or we might assume that a salesman is very helpful (internal cause) when his kindness is caused by his efforts to close a deal (external cause). In short, we err in the direction of paying too little attention to external causes of behavior.

A strong demonstration of this tendency was found in a study by Napolitan and Goethals (1979). College students individually discussed their views of a case study with a young woman who was either very friendly and supportive or very cold and critical. Some of the students were told that the woman was practicing various styles of interacting with others and some were told that she was being herself. Later, when students were asked what they thought the woman's personality was really like, they inferred she was the way she acted, either friendly or unfriendly, regardless of whether they had been told her behavior was forced or spontaneous. Only if they interacted with her twice and saw her act friendly one time and unfriendly the other did they begin to consider situational forces that might have caused her behavior. Then they formed impressions that more accurately considered why she might be acting friendly or unfriendly. Too often though, we jump to conclusions about what people are like when a full consideration of the situation would make us much more cautious about making inferences. Heider (1958) suggested we do this because of our need to feel that we understand other people and that we can predict them.

This and other studies of the fundamental attribution error suggest that when we judge the behavior of other people, it is easy to make internal attributions. In the next section, however, we will see that we do not make this error in explaining our own behavior.

The Actor–Observer Bias

Jones and Nisbett (1971) have proposed that attributions are influenced by an actor–observer bias. A person is likely to attribute his or her own behavior to external pressures or situations. An observer of the same behavior will, however, show a pervasive tendency to attribute another person's, or an actor's, behavior to internal dispositions and personality traits (see Figure 19.3).

Figure 19.2 *The actor–observer bias in attribution. (Based on Jones & Nibett, 1971)*

Behavior
Actor A walks down the street whistling

Actor's attribution	Observer's attribution
I'm whistling because it's such a beautiful day (External attribution)	A's whistling because A is a relaxed cheerful person (Internal attribution)

Many studies have demonstrated the actor–observer bias (Harvey & Weary. 1981). In one study. male college students were asked to take both roles. As actors they were asked to explain why they chose to major in a particular subject or why they were dating a particular girl. For the most part, their reasons had to do with external causes—the inherent interest of the subject matter or the attractiveness of their date. One subject wrote, "Chemistry is a very fascinating field." Thus, the subjects saw their behavior as natural responses to objects and people in the environment. However, when these same subjects were asked to play the role of observer and explain why a friend made the same choices, they tended to explain their friend's behavior in terms of internal needs, interests, and traits. One subject commented. "He needs someone he can relax with." (Nisbett, Caputo, Legant,& Marecek, 1973).

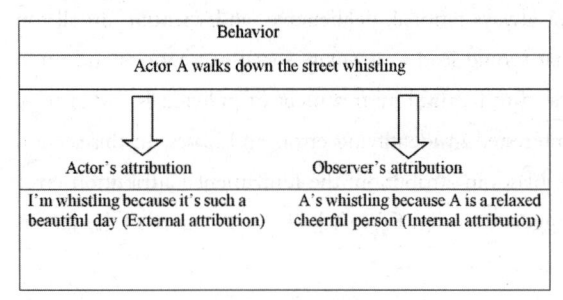

Three factors contribute to the actor–observer bias. First, as actor we are oriented to behaving adaptively in our environment. We are aware of its force and constrains and the need to be flexible and adaptive. Because of this orientation, we tend to see our behavior as being caused by these forces. As observers, other people are part of our environment and we want to understand them. Thus, we tend to attribute traits to others. Second, as actors we know our behavior is different in different situations. As observers, we assume others are likely to behavior similarly in different situations so we infer traits that will account for these presumably consistent choices. Third, people resist labeling themselves. We all hate to be pigeonholed. Therefore, we do not explain our behavior in terms of labels. But we have no objection to pigeonholing other people. We like to view ourselves as flexible and adaptive, and others as understandable and predictable (Jones and Nisbett,1971).

Who is correct, the actor or the observer? Most evidence seems to suggest that the actor is correct. It is not as easy to attribute stable traits to people as we might think. People are adaptive, complex, changing, and inconsistent. They are as hard to pigeonhole as we are.

Resolving Discrepancies: Primacy and Recency Effects

We have seen that people use the processes of attribution to make judgments about the causes of other people's behavior. What happens, however, when people later behave in ways that are inconsistent with our first impression? Consider, for example, what happens when a friend whom we thought was extremely intelligence starts getting Cs and Ds? What overall impression do we form of his or her intelligence? When people hold strongly to their first impressions, we refer to a primacy effect. When they weigh recent information more heavily in their final judgment and decide, for example, that their friend who just started getting poor grades is really unintelligent, they are showing a recency effect.

Which effect is more common, primacy or recency? In one study, subjects were asked to read one of two paragraphs about a boy named Jim (Luchisn,1957). Some subjects read the following:

Jim left the house to get some stationery. He walked out into the unfilled street with two of his friends. basking in the sun as he walked. Jim entered the stationary store, which was full of people. Jim talked with an acquaintance while waited for the clerk to catch his eye. On his way out, he stopped to chat with a school friend who was just coming into the store. Leaving the store, he walked toward school. On his way out he met the girl to whom he had been introduced the night before. They talked for a short while, and then Jim left for school. After school, Jim left the classroom alone. Leaving the school, he started on his long walk home. The street was brilliantly filled with sunshine. Jim walked down the street on the shady side. Coming down the street toward him, he saw the pretty girl whom he met on the previous Jim crossed the street and entered a candy store. The store was crowded with students, and he noticed a few familiar faces. Jim waited quietly until the counterman caught his eye and then gave his order. Taking his drinking he sat down at a side table. when he had finished his drink he went home. (pp.34–35)

In the part of this paragraph, Jim seems extraverted and friendly. But starting with sentence "After school..." Jim sounds much more introverted. One group of subjects read the paragraph as it was presented to you and came to the conclusion that Jim was very friendly. However, another group of subjects read the two parts of the paragraph in reverse order, starting with "After school..." and finishing with the part you read first. These subjects were more impressed with the early "introverted" information. Thus, subjects in both groups formed final impressions that were consistent with their first impressions and gave less weight to later information.

For the most part, people seem to interpret later, inconsistent information about the behavior of others as reflecting temporary moods or situational pressures. We noted when we discussed the fundamental attribution error that people do not generally pay much attention to the external forces that cause the behavior of other people. However, they are willing to attribute to external causes behavior that does not fit their preconceptions.

第四节 偏见与刻板印象
(PREJUDICE AND STEREOTYPES)

In the last two sections we have discussed attitudes and attributions, two critical aspects of social perception. Both attitudes and attributions affect how we assess and evaluate other people and how we behave toward them. Sometimes our attitudes and attributions lead to positive assessments and actions. Sometimes they lead to negative ones. Nowhere is the negative side clearer than in the case of prejudice and stereotypes.

Prejudice is a negative attitude toward or evaluation of a person due solely to his or her membership in a group. A stereotype is a set of beliefs about the characteristics of people in a particular group that is generalized to almost all group members. Also important is concept of discrimination, defined as the expression of prejudice in behavior. In this section we will consider three key psychological factors that lead to prejudice and stereotypes. These include authoritarianism, cultural attitudes, and cognitive factors.

The Authoritarian Personality

One of the most comprehensive studies of prejudice ever conducted was reported in the book, The Authoritarian Personality (Adorno, frenkel-Brunswick, Levinson & Sanford, 1950). The authors of this book were initially concerned with anti-Semitism, or prejudice against Jews. They had seen the slaughter of Jews that had taken place in Europe under Nazi fascism, and they wandered whether Americans had the same potential for fascism as Germans. They wanted to find what larger pattern of attitudes and personality characteristics was associated with prejudice and fascist tendencies. The authors of the book were very strongly influenced by Fredian personality theory. Thus, they believed that prejudice would be an expression of unconscious needs, conflicts, and defense mechanisms.

The subjects for the study were adults from many different social classes and occupations who lived near Berkeley, California, where the study was conducted. All subjects completed several long questionnaires about their attitudes and beliefs. A smaller number were interviewed and tested extensively in order to assess their personalities.

During the course of the study, a measure of prejudice called the E-scale was developed. E-stands for ethnocentrism, a glorification of one's own ethnic group and a hostility toward other groups. It was found that E-scale scores correlated with a measure of personality structure, the F-scale (see Table 19.4). People scoring high on the F-scale were said to have "authoritarian personalities" and a potential for fascism (thus the name F-scale).

Table 19.4 *Sample Items from Adorno's E and F scales*

Items from the Ethnocentrism (E) scale

1. One trouble with Jewish business people is that they stick together and prevent other people from having a fair chance in competition.

2. Negroes have their rights, but it is best to keep them in their own districts and schools and to prevent too much contact with whites.

3. The worst danger to real Americanism during the last fifty years has come from foreign ideas and agitators.

4. America may not be perfect, but the American Way has brought us about as close as human beings can get to a perfect society.

Items from the Fascism (F) scale

Obedience and respect for authority are the most important virtues children should learn.

When a person has a problem or worry, it is best not to think about it but to keep busy with more cheerful things.

People can be divided into two distinct classes: the weak and the strong.

What the youth needs most is strict discipline, rugged determination, and the will to work and fight for family and country.

An insult to our honor should always be punished.

Adapted from Adorno, et al. 1950

Adorno, et al. developed a theory to explain how the characteristics of authoritarian individuals develop and lead people to become prejudiced. These researchers found authoritarians had a strong interest in power and authority. They had a tendency to be very submissive and obedient toward those with more authority and very harsh and demanding toward those with less authority. They also had very conventional values, with little independent examination of moral questions. They tended to be intolerance of weakness and refused to admit weakness in themselves. They also were unable to accept sexuality and aggressiveness in themselves. Rather they projected these traits onto members of minority groups. Finally, they were thought to have the potential to accept fascist political appeals.

According to Adorno, et al. unconscious ego-defense mechanisms play a large role in the development of these characteristics. The parents of authoritarians are anxious about their own worth and status and use harsh disciplinary methods to enforce obedience and respect at home. They do not allow their children to expression feelings of weakness or anger toward the harsh discipline. As a result the children repress both their own feelings of weakness or inadequacy and the aggression they feel toward their parents. The weaknesses and inadequacy are projected onto members of certain ethnic groups, while the aggression felt toward the parents is displaced onto these groups. Finally, authoritarian individuals rationalize their hostility by thinking that these ethnic groups deserve harsh treatment in light of their inadequacies. Of curse, the perceived inadequacies of these groups have actually been projected onto them. The theory of the development of the prejudiced, authoritarian personality has been very controversial. Critics argue that authoritarians learn their prejudiced attitudes and other traits directly from their parents. The critics believe, further, that largely unconscious defense mechanisms developed in childhood are not the primary cause of prejudice (Brown 1965). Still, the F—scale and the concepts of authoritarianism are still generating research. Displacement of aggression tied to authoritarianism seems to account for some of the most extreme forms of prejudice.

Learning Culture Attitudes

After The Authoritarian Personality was published, some psychologists believed that the riddle of prejudices had been solved. People were prejudiced because they were authoritarian. Other psychologists, however, believed that not all prejudiced people were authoritarian and that not all authoritarians were prejudiced. They reasoned that with or without a personality type that provides the potential for prejudiced attitudes, some people will adopt such attitudes, just as they adopt other attitudes, on the basis of identification and the information and reinforcement provided by parents and peers.

One psychologist with this viewpoint, Thomas Pettigrew, published an important study on the role of both culturally learned attitudes and authoritarianism in prejudice. Pettigrew (1959) measured levels of prejudice and authoritarianism among whites in the northern and southern United States and in South Africa. Pettigrew found much higher levels of prejudice against black people in south Africa and the southern United States than he did in the northern United States. Yet, F—scale scores among people in these three regions were no different. Thus, the higher levels of prejudice did not reflect more authoritarianism. Rather, the prejudice seemed to stem from a history that led to negative culture beliefs about black people. These culture beliefs were, in turn, taught to children by their parents. Pettigrew found that Northerners most attached to their culture beliefs were the least prejudiced, while Southerners most attached to their culture were the most prejudiced. Thus, the extent to which people adopted their culture beliefs determined how prejudiced they were. This was true as well in South Africa, where the people who most accepted the culture beliefs were most prejudiced. In short, authoritarianism may account for extreme and aggressive forms of prejudice, but more often prejudice can be explained by people adopting the attitudes and stereotypes of the culture around them.

Cognitive Factor in Stereotyping

More recent work on stereotypes has emphasized that prejudice may be largely based on the way we process information (Hamilton,1979).This approach considers how cognitive factors alone may contribute to stereotypes.

As an example, let us consider how the memory for salient stimuli contributes to stereotyping. Salient stimuli are those that are especially noticeable, such as rare or unusual stimuli. For example, if blacks are in a minority they are more noticeable. Furthermore, let us assume that socially undesirable behaviors are more unusual and noticeable than socially desirable behaviors. This means that a black person performing a socially undesirable behaviors will be an especially salient stimulus. Whites may perform socially undesirable behaviors in exactly the same proportion as blacks, but blacks doing so will be more memorable. Thus, one might recall that blacks perform socially undesirable behavior more frequently than they actually do.

An experiment by Hamilton and Gifford (1976) showed exactly this kind of error in memory.

Subjects read approximately forty statements describing individuals from two groups. A and B. who performed behaviors that were either socially desirable or socially undesirable. One example was "John, a member of group A, visited a sick friend in the hospital." Individuals belonging to Group A were always described more frequently. Group B was the minority.

There were two conditions in the experiment. In both conditions, Group A and Group B performed an equal proportion of desirable or undesirable behaviors. In condition one, one third of the behaviors for both groups were socially desirable. In condition two, one third of the behaviors for both groups were undesirable. Table 19.5 shows the number of behaviors performed by both groups in the two conditions.

After subjects read all statements, they were asked to recall whether a member of Group A or Group B performed each behavior. As predicated, subjects tended to remember that the minority group, Group B, performed the more unusual behavior more frequently than was the case. Thus when the desirable behavior was less common (Variation 1), Group B was given more credit for performing it than was deserved. When the undesirable behavior was less common (Variation 2). Group B was also recalled as having performed it more frequently than was the case. Thus, if black people are in the minority, one might recall that they perform undesirable behavior more than they actually do. In this way, our memory for salient stimuli can contribute to stereotypes and prejudice.

Table 19.5 Comparison of Statements Describing and Later Attributed to Groups in Hamition &Gifford's Study of Stereotyping.

Groups and types behaviors	Number of statements describing each type of behavior	Number of statements attributed to each group
Variation I		
Group A		
Desirable behaviors	8	5.87
Undesirable behaviors	16	15.71
Group B (minority)		
Desirable behaviors	4	6.13
Undesirable behaviors	8	8 29
Variation II		
Group A		
Desirable behaviors	18	17.52
Undesirable behaviors	8	5.79
Group B (minority) Dvtirable		
Desirable	9	9.48
Undesirable	4	6.21

Adapted from Hamilton & Gifford.1976

第五节 社会吸引
(SOCILA ATTRACTION)

We will discuss social attraction, an area of social psychology that considers both social perception and social interaction. This area is sometimes called "liking and loving." We will first consider some of the factors that determine whether people become attracted and whether their attraction lasts. Then we will consider some special aspects of romantic love.

It is important to distinguish liking and love as we begin. Liking usually involves respect or high regard for another person. In addition, it often involves seeing the other as similar to oneself. Love usually involves liking plus three other factors: great attachment to and dependency on the other person; caring for or the desire to help the other person; and the desire for an exclusive, intimate relationship (Rubin,1973). Most of what we say in the first part of this section on the determinants of attraction applies to both liking and love, to relationships between same-sex and opposite-sex individuals, and to both intimate and non-intimate relationships.

The Determinants of Attraction

Several factors determine whether people become attracted. In studying these factors, psychologists have tried to take some of the mystery and myth out of the topic of liking and loving. The factors we will consider are proximity and familiarity, physical attractiveness, reciprocal liking, attitude similarity, and complementary needs.

Proximity and Familiarity

We can only come to like or love those whom we have a chance to meet and to get to know. Of course, the people we encounter and interact with most often are those who live or work close to us. Not surprisingly then, many studies have shown that nearness or proximity is a key factor in liking others. For example, a study of married couples in student housing showed that people chose friends on the basis of proximity. The closer one couple lived to another, the more they tended to like each other. Their best friends were usually the couple in the next apartment, and it was unusual for people to be very friendly with others who were more than four apartment units away. It was easy to predict who another couple's friends were by knowing where they lived (Festinger, Schachter & Back,1950).

How can we explain the power of proximity? One important factor, it may surprise you to learn, is sheer familiarity (Zajonc, 1968). The common wisdom that "familiarity breeds contempt" is more accurately translated to "familiarity breeds content" (Rubin, 1973). We like both people and objects more after we have been exposed to them for a long period of time. The exception is if we truly detest someone or something, in which case repeated exposure can lead to even more dislike (Grush, 1976). Still, repeated exposure does lead to increased liking if we originally felt neutral or slightly positive toward the person or object(Swap, 1977). In short, people who are near and become familiar stand a strong chance of becoming good friends.

Physical Attractiveness

Another important factor in the early stages of a relationship is appearance or physical attractiveness. People may not judge books by their covers, but they clearly do so with other human beings. In one study of the importance of physical attractiveness, students were randomly matched for a dancing date that they believed was part of a study of computer dating and attraction. At the beginning of the study, each subject's physical attractiveness was rated by other student judges. In addition, each subject completed several personality questionnaires measuring a range of traits, interests, and abilities. After the dance, subjects were asked how much they had like their date. There was a clear tendency for simple physical appearance to determine how much the students liked their dates. None of the personality traits that was measured played a significant role in liking during this single encounter situation. Only attractiveness mattered.

Many studies have shown that we seem to value physical attractiveness in other people. Is physical attractiveness important in ways other than that we are initially most attracted to beautiful people? As it turns out, physical attractiveness continues to be important in dating and even in marriage choice. People who are seriously dating or engaged are often much more similar in their level of attractiveness than would be predicted by chance (Murstein, 1972). That is, handsome men and beautiful women tend to pair off, as do average—looking men and average—looking women.

Perhaps this phenomenon can be understood in terms of a "matching process". Although most everyone will want to date those who are very attractive, they may think that they will probably be rejected by those who are significantly more attractive. Thus they limit their choices accordingly. Another possibility is that all of us attempt to attract the best—looking partners we can but only succeed with those who are similar. The evidence suggests that caution and realism probably limit some of our attempts at love (Shanteau & Nagy, 1979).

Reciprocal Liking

One of the most valued rewards people can offer each other is their affection. If people like us, they will probably help and care for us. Not surprisingly, research has shown that liking is reciprocal. We like those who like us in return. Because other people's liking for us is important, however, it can operate in subtle ways to influence just how much we like other people in return.

One subtlety with intriguing implications for long—term compatibility is when someone likes us rather than just how much they like us. In an important study on this question, Aronson and Linder (1965) proposed that we like people more if they first dislike us and then come to like us than if they have liked us all along. They also predicted that we have the least affection for people who like us at first but then later do not like us. In a test of these predictions, college women overheard a series of seven evaluations of them by an attractive girl who was either 1) consistently positive, 2) consistently negative, 3) at first positive and then negative, or 4) at first negative and then positive. The predictions were confirmed. As Table 19. 6 shows, subjects most liked the girl when she went from negative to positive evaluations, and least liked her when she went from positive to negative evaluations.

Table 19.6 Subjects' Liking for Confederate in Different Conditions.

Confederate's attitude toward subjects	Subjects' liking of confederate rated on a −10 to +10 scale
Negative to positive	7.67
Positive to positive	6.42
Negative to negative	2.52
Positive to negative	0.87

Adapted from Aronson & Linder, 1965

There are several possible explanations for these findings. One is that people who change their evaluations are perceived as being discerning. Perhaps they have more credibility, and so their liking (or disliking) means more. Another possible explanation for liking the negative−to−positive evaluator so much is that the early critical remarks create a need for affection or liking. Later positive evaluations fulfill this need and thus are much more satisfying than the evaluations of constantly positive person.

Do these findings imply that husbands or wives who have been consistently positive toward their spouses in the past cannot satisfy their spouses to a greater degree in the future? Perhaps a stranger who has been neutral, or even critical, arouses more liking when he or she is positive than does the reliable spouse. These concerns have led to the formulation of Aronson's law of marital infidelity (Aronson, 1980), which says that strangers are liked for their compliments more than are spouses, while critical remarks hurt more from the spouse than from the stranger. These ideas are intriguing, but Aronson goes on to say that this law probably does not apply in good marriages where communication is honest and open.

Attitude Similarity   One very important factor in determining how compatible and happy two partners in a relationship will be is their degree of attitude similarity. People with similar attitudes like each other in the short run and get along well over the long run. Laboratory studies of interpersonal attraction have shown that when students were told the attitudes of hypothetical strangers, there was a strong and direct relationship between attitude similarity and the students' reports of liking the stranger. It seems that we like people who share our attitudes about many issues more than those who share our attitudes on only a few issues (Byrne, 1971).

Theodore Newcomb (1961) conducted some important studies at the University of Michigan to investigate whether similarity is important in real, long−term relationships. He randomly assigned rooms to students who had agreed to live in an experimental dormitory for a year. At the end of one semester, Newcomb found that attitude similarity was a very strong predictor of how much the students reported that they liked each other.

Figure 19.3 *Balance theory predicts that two people, A and B, will like each other (as indicated by the plus sign) if their opinions about some object, person, idea, or event are the same. This situation is illustrated in the first two triangles where A and B both like X (Triangle 1) or dislike X (Triangle 2). Balance theory also predicts that A and B will dislike each other if they have different evaluations of X (Triangle 3). If A and B like each j other but disagree about X, the resulting imbalance can be resolved either by A or B changing his or her opinion about X or by A and B coming to dislike each other. (Based on Heider. 1946; Newcomb, 1953)*

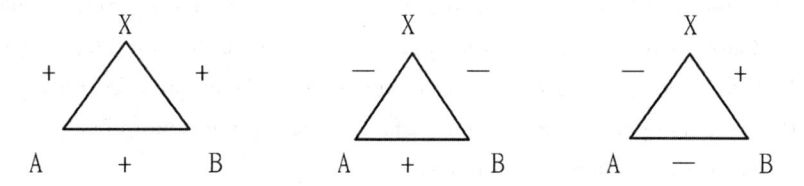

```
        X                 X                 X
      +   +             -   -             -   +
    A  +  B           A  +  B           A  -  B
```

Why should this be true? There are probably two major reasons. The first reason is suggested by balance theory (See figure 19.4). Balance theory states that people like to have an ordered, clear, and consistent view of their environment, where all the parts fit together. It seems natural or balanced that you will agree with your friends and disagree with your enemies. We expect good to go with good and bad with bad. Friends and agreement are good, enemies and dissent are not. Second, when people agree with us. they make us confident that our opinions are correct and that we are basically accurate in our view the world (Byrne, 1971).

Complementary Needs

Although attitudes similarity is important in a compatible relationship. another factor, which seems in some ways to be the opposite of similarity, has also been found to be important in long–term, intimate relationships between men and women. This is need complementary. It has been shown that in long–term relationships, people will get along best if their needs fit together or complement each other (Kerchoff & Davis, 1962; Winch, 1958). For example, A dominant person may be most compatible with someone who is submissive and needs direction. A nurturing person might get along better with someone who needs care and protection than with another nurturing person. Because it is much harder to measure needs and need complementarily than simple attitude similarity, research on this topic is less conclusive than is research on attitude similarity.

Romantic Love

As the beginning of this section, we distinguished liking, based on respect and feelings of similarity, from love, based on attachment, caring, and intimacy. What is involved in falling in love and in experiencing the emotional feelings of recent theory suggests that there are three conditions for experiencing loving feelings (Berscheid & Walster, 1974).

The first condition for feeling romantic love is some culturally based expectation that one will fall in love. Since the Middle Age, literature and art have made much of romantic love, and many people expect that they will experience this emotion. Second, there must be some appropriate person or "love object". The expectation that one will fall in love combined with meeting the right person often leads to "love at first sight." Berscheid and Walster (1974) report that fifty percent of adult males and females surveyed said that they have at least once fallen in love at first sight.

The third, and most complex, condition is that once one meets the appropriate person, emotional arousal felt in the presence of that person must be interpreted as love. Emotional arousal from a variety of different stimuli or events in the environment can be channeled into passionate feelings for a loved person if that person is frequently on your mind. Suppose, for example, that someone in your dormitory insults you. You are aroused and feeling angry and hostile. Then your thoughts turn to your lover. This theory suggests that the arousal due to the insult can be experienced as strong love or passion for your loved one. This explanation for romantic love grows out of Schachter's (1964) two-factor theory of emotion. This theory proposes that emotions are based on 1) some kind of physiological arousal, and 2) a labeling of that arousal as being a specific emotion, depending on cues in the environment.

There is evidence that supports the idea that arousal from other sources can be labeled as love and can lead to increased attraction. In a study by Dutton an Aron (1974), male subjectswho had walked across a bridge were stopped and interviewed by an attractive woman. Half the men met the women an a rickety and unsafe bridge which may have caused them to feel anxious. Others met her on a strong and perfectly safe bridge. The men who met the woman on the rickety bridge were more likely to call her for a date later on. Apparently the subjects' fear caused arousal, which was labeled as attraction to the woman.

More research is needed to determine just how arousal from other sources leads to increased feelings of love or attraction. For example, it may be that the attractive woman in the study above served to reduce the negative arousal of fear and thus served as a reinforcer (Kenrick & Cialdini, 1977).

第六节 从众与依从
(CONFORMITY AND COMPLIANCE)

Solomon Asch and Stanley Milgram are both social psychologists who subjected people to strong influence pressures. In one experiment subjects were pressured to conform to the judgments of other group members. In the other, subjects were pressured to obey the somewhat disturbing commands of an authority figure. The results of these studies have revealed a great deal about how human beings act and react to each other.

The Asch Experiments
How strong are the pressures in a group to make an individual conform to group ideas and standards for behavior? This is one of the foremost questions about group behavior. Can people think independently, make rational judgmentst and plan effective action in groups, or do they respond unthinkingly and irrationally to group pressures? When Solomon Asch became a social psychologist in the 1940s, a prevalent view was that people were as easily influenced as rats

by simple rewards and punishments. This view was influenced by Freud's claim that much of human behavior was irrational and by Watson's behaviorist perspective that conditioning could mechanically influence people to do or become anything. Asch, on the other hand, believed that people were rational and deliberative. Research that seemed to suggest otherwise was, he thought, open to alternative interpretations. In ambiguous situations individuals might easily follow other people's lead, but not when the truth was clear. To show that people would not be influenced by others when they could rely on their own good sense and judgment, Asch devised an experiment (1952).

In Asch's experiment, male subjects were told they would be participating in a study of "Visual discrimination". The experience of a typical subject is as follows. When he arrives at the laboratory, he finds several other subjects waiting for the experiment. When it is time to get started, the experimenter seats the subjects around a table and explains the purpose of the study. It concerns people's ability to make visual discriminations by matching one of three comparison lines shown on one board to a standard line shown on another(see Figure 19.5). The subjects' job will be to say which of the three comparison lines, A, B or C is the same as the standard.

Figure 19.4 Line–comparison cards used in Asch's experiment

Subjects were asked to state which of the three comparison lines (right) Matched the standard line(left). (Asch,1952)

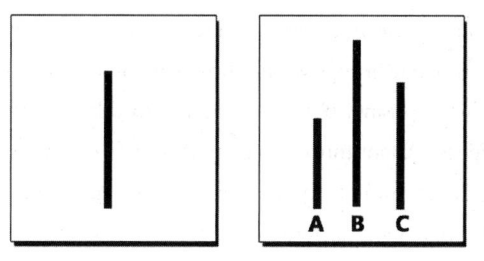

The experimenter remarks that, since the task is easy, he will save time and simply ask subjects to announce their judgments out loud in order of their seating position. Beginning on his left, the experimenter asks the first person for his judgment on the first trial. Our subject sees that he will be announcing his decision next to last and awaits his turn. The first trial seems easy, with line B clearly matching the standard line. The subject hears the first participant and all the others say line B, and when his turn comes, he calls out, "Line B". The second trial is routine, too, and the subject begins to settle back in his chair.

For the third trail, line C is obviously the correct answer. Much to our subject's surprise he hears the first subject announce line A. For a moment he can't believe his ears. He listens intently for the second subject's announcement: "Line A" The subject is completely baffled. He squints at the lines to see if he has made a mistake, but he feels positive that the right answer is line C. Suddenly it's his turn to state his decision. The five people on his right have all said line A. He experiences a momentary feeling of panic. He asks the experimenter if he should say what he thinks is really the right answer or just how it looks to him. The experimenter says just to say which line he thinks in the same as the standard. He blurts out, "Line C" The subject to his left then says, "Line A" the same as the others. The subject feels that he's sticking out like a sore thumb. He figures that the first person must just have made a mistake and that everyone else just followed along to avoid a contradiction.

On the next trial the subject looks carefully to form his own judgment before he hears anyone else say what they think. It's surely line B this time. But it happens again. The first subject says line C and the others calmly report the same. When it is the subject's turn, he wants to run away. He doesn't want to say line C when he's sure it's line B, but he doesn't want everyone to think he is playing games or losing his mind. He wishes he understood why the others were saying line C and that he could sit in their chairs or see the board differently. The experimenter is waiting for his judgment and he has to say something. If you were in this subject's place, what would you say?

Although our subject wasn't able to figure out why the other participants were giving such implausible answers. You might have guessed what was really happening. The subject we have been discussing was the only real subject in the entire experiment. The others were confederates of the experimenter and were instructed to give correct answers on the first two trials and then incorrect answers on twelve of the next sixteen trials. Asch's main concern was how many subjects would go along with the unanimous and incorrect majority on the "conformity trials". In a control group, where subjects had made judgments in isolation, there had been virtually no errors. Asch therefore had hypothesized the experimental groups would show very little conformity.

The results were quite surprising, both to Asch and to other people who had overestimated the individual's independence. About thirty-seven percent of the responses in the conformity trials agreed with the majority, even though these responses were incorrect. However, this does not mean that everyone conformed about a third of the time. There were large individual differences. About a quarter of the subjects were completely independent and never "yielded" to the majority. On the other hand, about a third of the subjects conformed on half the trials or more.

It is often tempting to conclude from these results that Asch's research identified two types of people, conformers and nonconformist. But as Asch discovered in interviews with subjects after the experiment, people conformed or defied the majority for many different reasons. Overall, Asch found a great deal more conformity than he had predicted, great variation in how people behaved, and even more variation in why the subjects acted as they did and how they felt about it.

Conformity, Nonconformity and Rejection

Asch's original experiments had a great impact on the field of social psychology. There seemed to be an unending series of questions about when and why people conformed in the line-judgment situation and what all this meant about human nature and social interaction. Subsequent research showed that majorities as small as three or four produced as much conformity as groups as large as sixteen, but conformity dropped sharply if the incorrect majority was not unanimous (Asch,1955). These and other follow-up studies quickly began to get at the basic questions of why people conform at all, what kinds of people are likely to conform more or less than average, and what kinds of situations elicit the most conformity. The issue of foremost importance was why people conform at all.

Asch's post experimental interviews and later research led social psychologists to consider two key motives for conformity (Deutsch and Gerard,1955). One is people's need to be correct. The other is their need to be accepted by others. Both of these needs operated in the original Asch experiment.

Because we are often not sure of the right thing to do, say or believe, we often rely on other people's judgments and actions to guide our own behavior. In the interviews after Asch's experiment, some of the conforming subjects reported they were so used to relying on others that they decided the others must be correct, no matter how the lines looked.

Still, analyses of Asch's interviews showed that the main reason subjects conformed in the line-judgment situation was that they were worried about what others might think of them for deviating from the majority. Additional evidence for this was that when subjects wrote their responses on a piece of paper rather than announcing their responses out loud, conformity-induced errors dropped drastically. During twelve conformity trials subjects averaged only 1.5 errors when the responses were written, when they were announced publicly, the average number of errors rose to 4.4.

Is the fear that others will reject, dislike, or mistreat us simply for holding different opinions actually warranted? A famous experiment by Stanley Schachter (1951) suggests it may be. Schachter investigated group reactions to individuals who conformed or deviated from the majority's opinion. In this study, groups of male college students read and discussed the case of a fictitious delinquent boy named Johnny Rocco. Johnny had a very difficult childhood, growing up in an urban slum, and he often got into trouble. Subjects in the experiment were asked to recommend that Johnny needed either lots of love and affection, harsh discipline and punishment, or some combination of both. The case was written to make subjects sympathetic to Johnny Rocco and to lead them to give lenient recommendations. To study the consequences of nonconformity, Schachter included in each discussion group a confederate who sometimes agreed with the real subjects that Johnny should be treated leniently and sometimes recommended that Johnny needed severe punishment. When the confederate took the deviant opinion, he maintained it and defended it as best he could. How did the majority treat this deviant confederate?

The result were quiet clear. The subjects' communications were immediately directed at the deviating confederate in an effort to get him to agree to a lenient recommendation. when it became clear that the deviant would stick to his position, communication dropped off sharply. He was largely ignored. After the discussion, when subjects had a chance to assign group members to tasks and to recommend who should be included in the group, the nonconforming confederate was clearly rejected. However, in groups where the same confederate took the majority opinion, he was viewed positively and not rejected. Thus, holding to an unpopular opinion even in a short discussion of a case study caused an individual to be ostracized. At least under some circumstances, fear of rejection due to nonconformity is justified.

Compliance with Authority

Conformity pressures within groups can lead to surprising changes in the opinions people express and the actions they take. Another important question is how much a person will agree to other people's direct requests or commands to behave in specific ways. Agreeing to such requests is called compliance.

To study the extent to which people will comply and why they comply, Stanley Milgram (1974) conducted some ingenious but highly controversial experiments on "obedience to authority".

The subjects in Milgram's experiments were adult men drawn from a variety of ages, occupations, and social positions in the area of New Gaven, Connecticut. They answered advertisements to participate in an experiment on learning. When each subject arrived at the laboratory, he was introduced to another gentleman who was also to participate in the study. The experimenter explained that one of the two would play the role of "learner" and the other "teacher". According to the experimenter, the focus of the experiment was the effects of punishment on learning, whenever the learner made a mistake, he was to be punished with an electrical shock. Then the subjects were shown the apparatus that was to be used to administer the punishment. This shock-generating machine had thirty switches on it, the first delivering 15 volts, the second 30, and so on up to 450 volts where the switches were labeled "Danger-Severe Shock-X X X". At this point names were drawn from a hat and one subject discovered he was to be the teacher and the other person the learner. The learner was taken to a different room, strapped into a chair, and wired with electrodes. The teacher then returned to the shock generator, where he could not see the learner, and was instructed to move up the row of switches every time the learner made a mistake, thereby giving the learner an increasingly severe shock.

Finally, the experiment started. It quickly became bizarre and frightening. The learner made many mistakes and the experimenter told the teacher to give increasingly severe shocks. At 75 volts the teacher could hear the learner grunting in the next room. At 150 volts the learner shouted, "Let me out" and said his heart couldn't stand the pain. He began to yell. He let out an agonizing scream at 285 volts and refused to answer after that. Then there was nothing.

Most teachers became very upset. Some asked the experimenter if they should continue, and others told him they wanted to stop. Sometimes they asked the experimenter to look in on the learner and sometimes asked if he would take complete responsibility for what happened. No matter what the teacher asked or how he protested, the experimenter only said, "The experiment requires that we go on," or "Please continue, teacher," or "Although the shocks may be painful, they are not dangerous," or "Go on to the next trial please," or "It is absolutely essential that you go on." No matter what the teacher said, the experimenter mechanically gave these replies, assuring the teachers that they would not be responsible. If the teacher adamantly refused to continue, the experimenter said, "You have no choice but to go on." Milgram wanted to know how many subjects would defy the orders of the experimenters and stop. How would you behave in this situation?

As you might have guessed, the "Learner" in Milgram's experiments was not a real subject but a confederate, and the shock machine did not really deliver shocks. After the experiment, the real subjects, the teachers, were told the truth. However, during the experiment they were convinced that the learner was another subject just like themselves.

Few people who knew about Milaram's proposed work before he started it felt that he would learn very much. They felt that no one would continue shocking the learner once it was clear he was suffering. In fact, forty psychiatrists at a leading medical school predicted that less than one tenth of one percent of the subjects would comply completely (Milgram, 1974).

We now know how wrong these experts were. In an earlier version of this experiment, the learner did not kick or scream. It never occurred to Milgram that this embellishment would be necessary to make some teachers stop. However, if the teacher was completely out of contact with the learner (the remote condition), obedience was nearly total. Milgram had to invent the voice feedback condition described above so that at least some subjects would break off. Even under these conditions, a solid majority was totally obedient: sixty-five percent of the teachers continued to the end.

What happens when the victim is brought even closer? In the proximity condition, the learner, portrayed by a professional actor who kicked and screamed, was seated only a foot and a half away. Here, forty percent of the subjects were fully obedient. Going one step further, Milgram conducted a touch-proximity condition, where the teacher actually had to push the learner's arm down on an electric grid. In this situation, obedience dropped to thirty percent.

How can we best explain the totally surprising degree of obedience in this research? Perhaps the key is the issue of responsibility. Subject after subject raised the issue of who would be responsible should harm come to the learner. Although the experimenter did not always discuss responsibility, when he did say, "I'm responsible for what goes on here," the subjects showed visible relief. Thus the idea that "I am not responsible" is crucial in getting subjects to obey. What is surprising is that subjects will so readily assign responsibility to someone else and deny it themselves. This process is called the diffusion of responsibility. Mailgram believed that diffusion of responsibility is crucial in understanding the murder of six million Jews in Europe during World War II. Individuals involved in this massacre often stated that they were just "caring out orders." Later we will see that diffusion of responsibility has been used to explain several other kinds of group behavior.

Compliance without Pressure

Milgrara's research shows us that people can be induced to comply with the directives of authority even when the behavior required is against their wishes and values. In our day-to-day experience, however, we are seldom exposed to such direct pressure to perform such disagreeable acts. More often, the pressure to conform or comply is more subtle. In this section we shall consider research on two subtle yet powerful techniques that can lead people to comply without feeling pressured.

The Foot-in-the Door Technique

One method of obtaining compliance sometimes used by salespeople is called the foot-in-the-door technique. This technique involves getting people to comply with small requests before asking them to comply with larger ones. For example, a life-insurance salesperson may ask you to discuss your financial plans, sign a form to make a small change in your policy or give some information. After you have agreed to these small requests, the salesperson may ask you to purchase more insurance. Are you more likely to buy after the salesperson has gotten a "foot in the door" by obtaining your compliance with these small requests?

An experiment designed to answer this question showed that people were more likely to agree to a large request after they had agreed to a small one (Freedman and Fraser, 1966). The subjects in this experiment were housewives who lived in a suburban area of California. There were two groups. Subjects in one group were simply asked to put up a small sign in a window of their home encouraging people to drive safely. Most complied. Whether or not they had complied, several days later they were asked to put up the large lawn sign.

Only 16.7% of the subjects in the first group, who were not asked to put up the small sign, agreed to put up the large sign. However, 76% of those in the second group, who were first asked to put up the small sign, put up the large one. Thus, complying with a small request made people more likely to agree to a large one.

One reason for this might be that agreeing to the first request makes people feel committed to being nice to the person making that request. A second reason might be that agreeing to the first request makes people feel committed to the specific cause of safe driving. However, Freedman and Fraser showed that neither of these reasons is a sufficient explanation. Even when people who had been asked to comply with a small request were later approached by an entirely different person to comply with an entirely unrelated large request, they were much more likely to agree to this large request than were people who had not been asked to agree to some small request.

What then is the explanation for the foot–in–the–door findings? Recent studies emphasize self–perception theory (Bem, 1972). Self–perception theory says that we infer our attitudes and traits from our behavior, as long as we feel that our behavior has been freely chosen. For example we know that we like spinach if we freely eat it. How does this work with the foot–in–the–door situation? When people agree to a small request, they come to see themselves as the king of person who helps out and gets involved in causes. To act consistently with this new self–image, they agree to the subsequent large requests. (Snyder Cunningham, 1975).

The Door–in–the–Face Technique

Foot–in–the–door research shows that people are more likely to comply with a large request if they have previously complied with a smaller one. Therefore it may surprise you to learn that people are also more likely to comply with a request if they have previously turned down a larger request.

Consider the following situation. A person collecting money for a charity you support asks you to make a one–hundred dollar donation. Most of us would probably gasp and say no. Suppose the person then said, "Well, all right, can you give us ten dollars?" What would happen then? You would probably sigh with relief and say yes. Here you have been caught by the door–in–the–face technique. Studies of situations similar to the one just described show that when people have refused to comply with a large request, they are more likely to comply with a small or moderate one (Cialdini, Vincent, Lewis, Catalan, Wheeler, & Darby, 1975). Later research has shown that this result occurs only when the same person makes the second request and when he or she makes it immediately (Cann, Sherman, & Elkes,1975).

This pattern of findings can be explained in terms of self-perceptions and considerations of fairness and equity (Walster & Berscheid,1978). By giving up on the large request and asking for a smaller favor, the asker has, so to speak, met you halfway. People usually feel that it only seems fair to agree to the small request since the asker has made a concession by not pushing them to comply with the big favor. These "equity" considerations operate only if the same person makes the second request. Furthermore, if several days go by, he asker's concession is forgotten, and self-perception (I am not the kind of person who agrees to this kind of favor) sets in.

Table 19.7 Percentage of Subjects complying with a Moderate Request Under Various Conditions.

This table illustrates both foot-in-the-door and the door-in-the-face phenomena. Compliance to a moderate request is increased if subjects have previously agreed to a small request. This is true whether or not there has been a seven-to-ten-day delay between request (foot-in-the-door effect).Compliance to a moderate request also increases after subjects have previously refused a large request, but only if there has been no delay between requests (door-in-the-face effect).

Size of initial request	Second, moderate request made immediately	Second, moderate request delayed
Small	78% comply (foot-in-the-door effect)	78% comply (foot-in-the-door effect)
Large	90% comply (door-in-the-face effect)	29% comply
No initial request (control)	50% comply	

After Cann,Sherman & Elkes. (*1975*)

第七节 攻击与利他主义
(AGGRESSION AND ALTRUISM)

In this section we will consider two kinds of behavior, aggression and altruism, in which the influence of other people is quite subtle and indirect but still profound. These less evidence forms of social influence may be the most important for you to understand.

Aggression can be defined as behavior that one person enacts with the intention of harming or destroying another person or object. Psychologists have debated the causes of aggression for many years. These debates have centered around the nature–nurture question: is aggression innate, that is, programmed into human beings from birth, or is it learned from various environmental influences? Older theories of aggression suggested in one way or another that aggressive behavior is innate. Later work has emphasized the way the environment influences us to be aggressive. We shall present both views and attempt to tie together some of the strands of evidence.

Instinct Theories of Aggression

Seventeenth–century political philosopher Thomas Hobbes argued that people are naturally competitive and hostile. They are interested only in their own power and in advantage over others. For this reason, they need government to prevent constant conflict and mutual destruction.

Sigmund Freud's theories echoed Hobes' pessimistic view of human nature. For many years Freud's Writings emphasized Eros, the human drive for pleasure. However, after observing the unprecedented and seemingly interminable carnage of World War? Freud postulated a second drive, thanatos, directed toward self–destruction and death. Freud felt that this drive, to return to an inanimate, lifeless state, conflicted with the pleasure drive and was satisfied by being turned outward. The result was aggression toward others. Unless there was a more acceptable way to express thanatos, Freud felt people would act aggressively from time to time. Thus Freud implied that people need to express hostile and destructive impulses periodically just as they need to eat, drink, and express sexual needs.

Freud was not the only person to propose that aggression is inborn. In his well–known book On Aggression (1966), Konrad Lorenz proposed that aggression in all animals' human beings included, is instinctive. He argued that because aggressive behavior is adaptive for animals; they evolved with an inborn tendency to aggress. He noted, however, that most animals also have rituals, such as exposing their throats, that signal submission and end conflicts. Thus most animals stop short of killing members of their own species. Humans. Lorenz noted, do not follow these submission signals and therefore may kill each other.

There are many difficulties with instinct theories of aggression. First, there is considerable evidence that learning plays a very important role in aggression. One classic study showed that kittens who were not permitted to observe their mothers hunting rats or who were raised with rats would not attack these animals (Kuo, 1930). Furthermore, it may be that animals are reinforced for aggressive behavior by gaining dominance and sexual privileges in their group. Thus their fighting could be explained by external rewards rather than internal drives. Finally, instinct theories do not explain why aggression is more prevalent in some situations than others. One approach that does try to explain when people will be aggressive is the frustration–aggression hypothesis.

The Frustration–Aggression Hypothesis

In the year of Freud's death, 1939, a book entitled Frustration and Aggression was published (bollard, Doob, Miller, Mowrer & Sears, 1939). This well–known work was influenced both by Freudian thinking and by developments in learning theory. The authors proposed that "frustration always leads to aggression" and that "aggression is always a consequence of frustration". Thus the authors argued that while aggression was an innate response, it would be elicited only in specific situations. Whenever an important need, such as for food, water, recognition, or achievement, is thwarted, the resulting frustration produces an aggressive response.

Research conducted soon after the publication of Frustration and Aggression showed some evidence that aggression does increase under frustrating circumstances. In one study, young children were shown an attractive set of toys but were prevented from playing with them. After an agonizing period of frustration, they were eventually allowed access to the toys, which they threw, stomped, and smashed. In comparison, children who had not been frustrated did not throw, stomp, or smash the toys. In this case, frustration did lead to aggression (Barker, Dembo & Lewin 1941).

The research on frustration and aggression suggested many hypotheses about both how and when people will aggress. For example, the aggressive response may not always be directed at the persons or objects causing the frustration. This may be too dangerous or inconsistent with moral values. Instead, the aggression may be temporarily held in and later displaced against someone or something else in a safe and socially approved way. The target of this displaced aggression is called a scapegoat. The concept of displaced aggression or scapegoat, is often used to account for racial or ethnic discrimination. People who are frustrated by economic or other circumstances, this viewpoint holds, will express their anger against certain groups who are powerless and who are deemed to deserve hostile treatment (Allport,1954). A correlational study of lynching's of blacks is consistent with this view. Hovland and Sears (1940) found that from 1882 to 1930 the number of lynching's per year in southern states was highly correlated with he price of cotton. When prices were low, indicating frustrating economic conditions, the number of lynching's increased.

Later research has qualified the frustration–aggression hypothesis. Berkowitz (1980) has suggested that frustration produces anger and a readiness to aggress. However, Berkowitz has also shown that certain cues are needed to convert this readiness into actual aggression. These cues are environmental stimuli associated either with aggressive behavior or with the frustrating object or person. In one study, for example subjects were insulted and berated by a confederate for failing to complete a jigsaw puzzle. Then the subjects watched a film in which the actor Kirk Douglas was brutally beaten. After the film the subjects were given an opportunity to show aggression by electrically shocking the confederate. By this time the subjects had learned that the confederate's name was either Bob or Kirk. Subjects used higher intensity shocks against the confederate if his name turned out to be Kirk. Because of its association with the brutality in the film, the name Kirk served as a cue to aggressive behavior (Geen & Berkowitz,1967).

Although the results of this and other studies lend powerful support to the frustration–aggression hypothesis, other research has revealed shortcomings. For example, some research has shown that frustration does not always lead to aggression (Gentry,1970). Other studies have shown that frustration can produce different responses in different people in different situations (Kulik & Browm,1979). These results led psychologists to develop a more comprehensive theory of aggressive behavior. This theory was social learning theory.

Social Learning and Aggression

Social learning theory is quite different from the instinct and frustration aggression approaches to aggression. First, social learning theory rejects the idea that aggressive behavior is inborn. Second. social learning theory attempts to specify how people learn aggressive behavior and which social conditions produce and maintain aggressiveness..

Social learning theorists have suggested that aggressive behaviors are learned through reinforcement and the imitation of aggressive models (Bandure, 1973). First, people may be reinforced or rewarded for aggressive behavior in a number of ways. Children who succeed in getting to the head of a line or in playing with the most desirable toys by being pushy will quickly learn to act aggressively. In this case, aggressive behavior is directly rewarded.

Children also learn through the process of imitation. This involves observing other people who serve as models for behavior. For example, an adult who is successful in being aggressive may become a model for a child, and the child's own aggressive tendencies will be strengthened through vicarious reinforcement. The child will come to expect reinforcement or reward for behaving like the aggressive model. In a classic study by Bandura, and Ross (1963) children observed models attack an inflated plastic Bobo doll Later, the children were allowed to play with the doll themselves. Those who had observed an aggressive model were aggressive toward the doll and directly imitated many of the model's specific behaviors.

One consistent finding in later research was that children will imitate the behavior of live models, filmed humans, and carton characters all to about the same degree (Bandure, 1973). These findings relate to a crucially important social issue: What are the effects of frequently watching televised violence? Is it possible that children are being taught to express aggressiveness? Over 1,500 research studies have tried to answer these questions.

Television and Aggression

In 1982, the National Institute of Mental Health released its analysis of more than ten years of research into the effects of watching television. The major conclusion is by now a familiar one. Watching violence on television causes children and adolescents to behave more aggressively. The response of the television networks is also familiar. They claim that the report is filled with inaccuracies and that NIMH's review of the 2,500 studies was biased and uncritical. We should recognize from the outset that people are of two minds about this issue.

First, let us consider some basic data about what is on television and how much people watch it. Since 1967, the percentage of television shows containing violent episodes has remained about the same, but the number of violent episodes per show has steadily increased. Prime−time shows that portray violence currently average about five violent acts per hour. On children's weekend shows, mostly cartoons, the count is eighteen violent acts per hour. In 1979 the networks agreed to a code limiting the amount of violence in cartoons. However, a recent study by Cramer and Mecham (1982) found no decrease in the amount of violence shown in cartoons. If anything, the newer cartoons are even more violent and less entertaining.

A steady increase in television viewing closed parallels the rising proportion of violence. In 1965−1966, the Nielsen ratings reported that the average American household watched television five hours and thirty minutes a day. By 1980–1981, the daily average had risen to six hours and forty–four minutes (Burger,1982). Children in the United States spend between fifteen and twenty–five hours every week watching television (Liebert, Neale, & Davidson, 1973).

It certainly is not implausible to think that people (adults and children) might be influenced by the violence they watch on television. In other domains, certainly, television producers claim that their medium does influence behavior. For example, they sell thirty–second segments of air time for many thousands of dollars, based on their claim that commercials influence behavior. But what evidence is there that televised violence influences children and adolescents to become aggressive?

Essentially, two kinds of studies address this issue. First are laboratory studies, whose crucial contribution is to show a causal relationship between watching televised violence and behaving aggressively. Subjects were randomly assigned to two groups. One group watched a violent television show, "The Untouchables". while a second group watched an equally engaging and arousing, but nonviolent, sports competition. Afterwards the children were allowed to play, while observers recorded their aggressive acts. The children who had watched the violent program behaved more aggressively than those who had watched the sports competition. This kind of study shows that televised violence does lead directly to aggressive behavior.

The second kind of study, the field study, tells us whether there is a correlation between televised violence and aggression outside the lab. Hundreds of these studies generally show the same results. Children who watch more televised violence at home are reported to behave more aggressively. One important study of this kind was conducted on several hundred subjects over a ten–year period (Lefkowitz, Eron. Walder & Huesmann, 1972). Lefkowitz and his colleagues showed that boys who watched more violent television in the third grade were rated as more aggressive by their peers and teachers at age nineteen–ten years later! These findings suggest the long–term effects of watching televised violence. Because they are correlation, however, they do not prove that televised violence causes aggressive behavior.

The reason the debate continues is that no study can combine the best features of both kinds of study, the demonstration of cause and effect found in the laboratory experiments, and the demonstration of a general, real–world relationship found in field studies. Just as no experimenter can ethically investigate the connection between smoking and lung cancer by randomly assigning some people to smoke two packs of cigarettes a day for fifteen years and others to abstain completely from smoking, the television watching habits of children cannot be controlled, Thus there will be continued debate. Eventually parents will have to decide if the results of laboratory experiments and field studies give sufficient support to the idea that violence on television is harmful. Then parents will have to decide whether they want to do anything about it. such as controlling the kind and amount of television their children watch.

In the meantime some other findings of the NIMH study (1982) can be pondered. People who watch television very frequently are more likely to view the world as a "mean and scary" place and often trust other people less. Also, children who watch more television than their peers have lower reading and IQ scores. In one town children's reading scores fell sharply two years after television was first introduced. Cause and effect have not been conclusively demonstrated. But these findings must give us pause.

Helping and Altruism

We have seen that people can be influenced to behave aggressively merely by observing other people behave aggressively. Can observing others' behavior also influence people to show altruism, the unselfish helping of others? Psychologists are interested in altruism partly because helping others is often seen as an ideal. But ironically, the modem study of altruism began with a depressing instance of people's failure to help.

In 1964, a woman named Kitty Genovese was brutally stabbed to death near her apartment in Queens, New York. At one point, the assailant ran away and then came back to stab her again to make sure she was dead. During the thirty minutes that the attack took place, Kitty Genovese cried out for help and begged for someone to intervene. Thirty-eight people looked on from their apartments. Not one even called the police. The incident gained national publicity. People wondered how the apparent indifference and apathy of so many people in our society could be explained. Are we really that uncaring?

Two social psychologists, John Darley and Bibb Latane, felt that the best way to understand situations like the Kitty Genovese murder is to find out why normally helpful people might not intervene and help in specific situations. One of the factors that Darley and Latane thought was important in the Kitty Genovese incident was the number of bystanders. While the news media focused on the number of people who didn't help as the most astonishing aspect of the case, Darley and Latane felt that perhaps Kitty Genovese was not helped precisely because there were so many bystanders. Their research has considered several ways in which the presence of other people can inhibit helping. The first is that other people's behavior can lead us to define an ambiguous situation as not serious or dangerous. The second is that the presence of other bystanders in an emergency situation can lead to the diffusion of responsibility.

Defining the Situation

When a potential emergency occurs, people must clarify what is happening. Is the situation dangerous? Does that person need help? These critical questions have a substantial impact on how people respond. Several studies by Darley and Latane have shown that people are less likely to define a situation as dangerous if other people are present.

In one study, subjects were shown into a room to fill out some questionnaires. In some cases they were alone; in other cases other subjects were present. Then, as part of the experiment, steam, which resembled smoke, began to pour through a vent in the wall. Darley and Latane measured how quickly subjects reacted to what was happening. They found that subjects reacted most quickly when they were alone. The more people in the room, the slower anyone was to act. Sometimes no one reacted until the steam was so thick that it was difficult to see the questionnaire (Latane & Darley, 1968). In another study, subjects heard a female experimenter fall, cry out, and moan for nearly a minute. Sometimes the subjects were alone, sometimes they were with one other person. Again, subjects were slower to respond and offer help when they were with another person (Latane

& Rodin, 1969).

How can we account for these results? Subjects unintentionally influenced each other to define the situation as not dangerous. In post-experimental interviews, each subject reported feeling very hesitant about showing anxieties and uncertainties. Thus, each subject looked to others to see if they seemed upset. Of course, the others were trying to conceal their own concerns. Thus they appeared calm. It looked as if they were not worried and did not think the situation was an emergency. Thus the individual defined the situation as safe. In this way each subject influenced the others to think there was no cause for alarm.

Diffusing Responsibility

Even if people define a situation as an emergency, they still may decide that they have no responsibility to take action. This is especially likely to take place if there are other people around who could help. People may reason that someone else should and probably will intervene. Thus no single individual feels responsible for helping. As we have seen before, the term for this phenomenon is **diffusion of responsibility**.

Darley and Latane (1968) conducted an experiment to see whether a large number of bystanders in an emergency situation can create diffusion of responsibility and thus reduce the frequency of help given to a victim in need. In this study, female subjects participated in a group discussion over an intercom system. One of the participants, who was actually a confederate of the experimenter, mentioned that he had epilepsy. Later in the discussion, this person began to have a mock seizure and begged for help. The independent variable in the study was the number of other people the subjects believed were involved in the discussion. Some women thought they were the only other person; others thought there was one other person besides themselves and the victim. A third group thought there was a total of six people; themselves, the victim, and four others. Darley and Latane measured the number of subjects who had responded by the end of the seizure and the average amount of time it took them to respond in each of the three conditions. The results are quite clearly, subjects generally responded and responded quickly. when they thought they were the only potential helper. Here there could be no diffusion of responsibility. If there was one or four other potential helpers, subjects responded neither as frequently nor as quickly.

Rewards and Costs in Emergencies

Even when a bystander defines a situation as dangerous and accepts responsibility, he or she may not necessarily take action. People typically weigh the rewards and costs of any potential behavior before going ahead with it. Naturally, this applies to the decision about whether or not to help.

What are the rewards and costs involved in helping or not helping? The rewards of helping would include good feelings about yourself and perhaps praise from others. The costs of helping might include getting involved in what could be an embarrassing, distasteful, or even dangerous situation. The reward of not helping would be the freedom to go about your normal business; the costs would be guilt or the disapproval of others. Psychologists have learned about the importance of rewards and, particularly, costs, in emergencies from several fascinating studies done on the subway systems of New York City and Philadelphia.

In the first study, student experimenters pretended to collapse in subway cars moderately full of people. They would simply fall to the floor and wait to see if they were helped. In some cases the student collapsing carried a cane, suggesting that he collapsed because he was lame. In other cases the student wore a jacket reeking of liquor and carried a bottle in a brown paper bag. In this case there was a different, but equally obvious, cause of the student's collapse. Observers who were part of the experiment watched to see what happened. As predicted by the reward–cost analysis, help was offered much less often in the "drunk" trials than in the "lame" trials. Ninety percent of the "lame" victims were helped within seventy seconds. Only twenty percent of the "drunk" victims were helped within seventy seconds. It is easy to see how passengers on the subway might think that the costs of not helping a drunk person would be low (who would really blame me for not getting involved with a drunk?) and the costs of helping as relatively high (he might get physically ill, make a fuss, or act violently) (Piliavin & Rodin,1969).

In two follow-up studies, the effect of other personal characteristics on helping was investigated. In one, the person who collapsed bit off a capsule of red dye resembling blood and let it trickle down his chin. Here the rate of helping was reduced from about ninety to sixty percent. People were much more likely to try to get someone else to help, perhaps someone who was more knowledgeable and competent in emergency situations (Piliavin, 1972). An interesting but depressing result emerged from a second follow-up study. When the victim had an ugly facial birthmark, help was significantly reduced, from about eight-six to sixty-one percent. Interacting with a stigmatized person is very costly for some individuals, which can lead them to ignore these people (Piliavin & Rodin, 1975).

The data from these and other studies suggest that the rewards and costs involved in specific emergency situations greatly affect whether help is forthcoming. Table19.8 suggests how these rewards and costs operate. When the costs of helping are low (there is no danger or difficulty) and the costs of not helping are high (others would blame and criticize you). people are likely to intervene directly and help. When the costs of both helping (this might be dangerous or this person seems very strange) and not helping (something needs to be done) are high, the most likely response is to help indirectly, usually by getting someone who is trained to act in such situations. An alternative response is to redefine the situation in ways that make it less costly not to help. When the costs of helping are high (this drunk might be violent) and the costs of not helping are low (no one will blame me for not helping this person), people generally will ignore the victim or leave the scene. When the costs of helping and not helping are low, the norms of the situation will determine what people do. Responses can vary greatly here.

What can we conclude about helping and altruism? When people do help, they usually feel very good about themselves. The anticipation of such feelings motivates the giving of assistance in many circumstances. Still, we have seen that often people do not help because they are unsure and afraid. They are fearful of acting inappropriately and they are fearful of getting involved in something that might be time-consuming, dangerous, or upsetting. As Maslow (1962) suggests, our need for safety taken precedence over our need for esteem.

We would rather be safe than a Good Samaritan. This does not mean that people have little capacity for goodness and kindness. It does mean that this capacity can be deflected by concerns with safety and, to some extent, convenience. The impulse to help does not flourish in a busy, demanding, and often threatening world.

Table19.8 Predictions of Typical Bystander's Response, Depending on Costs of Helping or Not Helping the Victim.

Cost of not helping victim	Response if cost of direct help low	Response if cost of direct help high*
High	(a)Direct intervention	(b)Indirect intervention or redefinition of the situation disparagement of the victim. etc.**
Low	(c)Varies, depending on the perceived norms of the situation	(d)Leaving scene, ignoring victim, using denial, et

There are some situations, generally those in which victims themselves are very likely to perish, such as sever fires, explosions, caveins, and ship accidents, in which the costs of helping become so high that they will be perceived as total, incalculable, or infinite. Under these limiting conditions, the actions and reactions of bystanders will deviate somewhat from these predictions.
**This lower the cost of helping, leading to(d).*
After PiliaVin, et al.,(1975)

词汇 (Vocabulary)

1. agonizing   adj. 使人极度痛苦的、折磨人的
2. alligator   n. 鳄鱼、短吻鳄鱼皮、水陆平底军车
3. complementary needs   n. 互补性需要
4. confederate   n. 同盟者、共谋者、共犯、南部联邦
5. consensus   n. 一致性、合意、一致同意、舆论、同感
6. consistency   n. 一致性、黏稠度、坚实、坚硬固守
7. covariation   n. 共变、协变
8. defensive mechanism   n. 防御机制
9. deflect   vt. 偏斜、转向、转移、引开
10. discerning   adj. 有眼力的、有辨别能力的
11. discount   vt. 折扣、低估、贴现
12. discrepancy   n. 不一致、差异、不相符之处

13. dispassionate　adj. 不带感情的、平心静气的、公平的
14. dissonance　n. 失调、刺耳声音
15. distraction　n. 精神涣散、注意力分散、心神烦乱
16. distill　vt. 提取精华、蒸馏、渗出
17. emulate　v. 同一竞争、努力仿效
18. fraternity　n. 友爱、博爱、大学生联谊会
19. harsh　adj. 严厉的、苛刻的、刺耳的、粗陋的
20. hypothetical　adj. 假设的、假想的、爱狂想
21. intervene　vt. 干涉、插入、调停
22. lenient　adj. 怜悯的、宽容的、温和的、仁慈的
23. massacre　n. 屠杀、残杀、裁员
24. menace　n. 威胁、恐吓、讨厌的人
25. necessitate　vt. 迫使、使成为必需
26. neutral　adj. 中立的、中性的
27. ostracize　vt. 排斥、放逐
28. penetrate　vt. 渗透入、刺入、深入了解、分辨
29. permeate　vt. 渗透、漫布、影响感染
30. primary effect　n. 首因效应
31. proximity　n. 近似、相似、大约
32. recency effect　n. 近因效应
33. reciprocal　adj. 相互的
34. revert　vi. 回复、归还、归属
35. salient　adj. 突出的、显著的、跳跃的、涌出的
36. sibling　n. 兄弟、同胞、民族成员
37. stigmatize　vt. 给……打上烙印、侮辱、污蔑
38. strand　n.（论据）组成部分、岸、绞、线
39. submissive　adj. 顺从的、服从的
40. thanatos　n. 死的愿望、自我毁灭的本能、桑纳托斯（希腊神话中的死亡之神）
41. thwart　vt. 挫折、反对、穿过、穿越
42. unconscious needs　n. 无意识需要

第二十章 心理学研究方法
（RESEARCH METHODS AND TECHNIQUES OF PSYCHOLOGY）

本章要点（Chapter Outline）
事件与变量（Happening and Variable)
实验法 (The Experimental Method)
观察法（Obeservation)
个案研究法（Case Study)
调查法 (Survey)
现场研究（Field Investigation)
跨文化研究（Cross-Culture Investigation)
相关法研究（Correlational Study)
研究范式的本质特征
(Essential Feature of Research Paradigms)
科学、方法论和理论 (Science，Methodology and Theory)

方法问题是人类在认识和改造世界的实践活动中产生的特有范畴。当代科学研究的方法体系从高到低可分为三个层次，即哲学方法论、一般科学方法论和具体的研究方法与技术。本章主要讨论心理科学研究中的具体方法技术问题。

心理学的研究方法很多，主要有实验法、观察法、个案研究、调查法、现场研究、跨文化研究和相关研究。在实际研究中要根据研究对象、研究内容及实际操作的可能性而选择不同的研究方法。每种方法各有其优势及不足，因此，使用时要扬长避短，多种方法的结合使用会使心理学的研究更为科学。

最后，本章还阐述了研究范式的本质特征和研究的新方向。

第一节 事件与变量
（HAPPENING AND VARIABLE）

Psychologists conducting research studies use the same tools and the same criteria as other scientists.

The happenings to be explained, however, are changes in human behavior. Like other scientists, psychological researchers first describe human happenings, then explain them, and ultimately hope to predict them.

Explaining human happenings is a complex task, for several reasons. The happenings themselves are often complicated or subtle changes in behavior that are sometimes difficult to observe. In many cases, it is difficult to distinguish the time sequence of related events and states. Another problem is that a great many events can occur in the sequence. Finally, there are so many unknowns associated with changes in human behavior that the task sometimes seems monumental. Since specifying cause–and–effect relationships for human events are extremely difficult, the knowledge base developed so far from scientific inquiry is limited. Much remains to be discovered and explained.

The first difficulty one encounters in a science of human behavior is the variability of the content itself. Human behavior varies from person to person and situation to situation. Even individuals in identical circumstances are almost certain to behave differently. This is true people's behavior is influenced by their make–up and experiences, which vary remarkably. To deal with individuality, the psychologist frames descriptions of happenings in terms of relationships between variables rather than between specific states and events. Even so, predictions about human outcomes always be stated in terms of probability rather than certainty.

The term variable, which comes from mathematics, indicates a measure that can assume more than one value. In the physical world, temperature is a variable, since temperature can have different numerical values. In human events, age, intelligence, and height, all of these are variables. Even experience is a variable, since individuals differ in the amount and nature of their past experiences. Actual behaviors can also be expressed as variables. Scores on a measure of reading skill, for example, that will vary across individuals: some will score very high, others will perform poorly. In attempting to explain human happenings, psychologists describe content in terms of variables.

A number of relationships can exist between two variables. In some cases, variables are not directly connected. Human noses, in instance, come in different sizes; nose size is a variable. Intelligence is a variable also, but the size of one's nose is unrelated to one's intelligence. On the other hand, some variables change together in a similar manner. During childhood, for example, height increases as age increases. These variables are called covary, or to change together. Other variables are causally related; changes in one variable are followed by changing in another. A change in diet, for example, may be followed by a change in weight. The latter two types of relationships, covariance, cause and effect, are the specific focus of psychological study.

Identifying relationships between variables is a reasonable way to approach the study of human behavior, but it is important to recognize that scientists' statements about relationships hold the most of time, not all of the time. Most children get taller as they increase in age, for example, but certain physical defects can prevent physical growth with increase age. In these cases, the specified relationship between age and size would not hold. Similarly most children who receive instruction in a specific skill will learn it, but some will not. Most of the conclusions we draw about relations between human variables hold most of the time, not all of the time. Psychologists' findings must therefore be expressed as probabilities.

Earlier in the chapter we listed the questions addressed by science: (1) What happened? (2) How does it happen? (3) Why did it happen? We can reexamine these questions in terms of variables. What questions are concerned with individual differences on a specific variable? If nose size is of interest, we can measure the noses on a group of people and describe the differences. Using different measurement devices, we can examine how children of a given age differ in mathematics proficiency, in the use of problem-solving strategies, in reading speed, and in innumerable other characteristics. In short, answering what questions involves describing differences on a given variable. How and why questions go beyond the description of a single variable to address the relationships between variables.

To find answers to questions about relationships between variables, psychologists must conduct research. Several different kinds of studies are possible, including (1) experimental studies, (2) correlational studies, (3) field studies, (4) case or clinical studies and so on. The studies vary in their settings, the types of information they yields, and their suitability to specific questions, but the goal of all of them is to discover something about causation.

第二节 实验法
(THE EXPERIMENTAL METHOD)

The approach closest to that used in nonsocial science research is the experimental paradigm. Experiments are conducted in laboratories or laboratory-like environments. The hallmark of the experiment is the experimenter's control over events. Precision and the careful use of procedures are also characteristic. Earlier in the chapter we suggested that a happening can be analyzed as a temporal sequence that suggests cause-and-effect relationships among events. In the experimental paradigm the experimenter decides in advance what the temporal sequence will be and controls the timing. To do this the experimenter creates a particular event and then carefully records its effects or results.

The investigator begins with a hypothesis about the relationship between two events, the "if A, then B" proposition discussed earlier. The "if A" part of the statement refers to an event the experimenter can create and control; this event is manipulable. The "then B" part is the outcome, which follows the manipulation and occurs because of it. The goal is to be able to conclude that A causes (or does not cause) B to occur.

Consider, for example, a hypothesis about human behavior: if children view violent television content, then their aggressive behavior will subsequently increase. A hypothesis similar to this one guided a number of laboratory studies in the 1960s (Bandura, 1969, 1977a). Another hypothesis behind an actual research effort (Pressley, 1976) was this: if children are provided with pictures when they read prose, then they will recall more prose content. These hypotheses are both statements about a possible causal link between two events, and the experimenter can create and control the first event when examining the plausibility of the statement. An investigator who has set up a study, created the prior event, and recorded the subsequent occurrence of another event has completed and experiment.

In psychological research, a hypothesis is a causal proposition about the relationship between two variables. It states essentially that changes in one variable (the "if" part) will be followed by changes in a second variable (the "then" part). Returning to the previous examples we see that viewing violent television is a variable because different values are possible. The programming could contain many violent acts, few violent acts, or none at all. The number of pictures accompanying a prose passage can also vary. These, then, are examples of variables.

The second half of the hypothetical statement also concerns a variable. The number of aggressive acts a child produces after watching violent television could change from a great many to few or none. In the prose-learning example, recall proficiency could also vary from near perfect to near zero. Resulting performances thus also involve variables.

Variables are given different labels depending on their role in the hypothesis. The prior event (the "if" part), is called the independent variable. The independent variable is the possible cause of the change in the second variable; it is thus the proposed causal variable. The outcome is the dependent variable. The dependent variable results from changes in the first variable and is thus dependent on those changes. The independent variable, then, is the cause, and the dependent variable is the effect. This relationship is depicted in Figure 20.1.

When we study human behavior in this manner, the independent variable is any event or situation that experimenters control so that the effects of the manipulation can be observed. The independent variable could involve providing individuals with a particular experience, a learning program, a strategy for problem-solving, or a set of instructions. The dependent variable is some aspect of human behavior, some action that the subject performs after receiving the experience provided by the experimenter. The experience is a possible cause of the performance.

If, after conducting a study like this, the experimenter gets positive results, the hypothesis is reformulated as a causal statement. The causal statement is a statement of a functional relationship. The TV-aggression hypothesis, for example, could be reformulated as: "Aggression is a function of watching violent television programs", or "Viewing violent television leads to increased aggression." The prose recall hypothesis could be restated as "Prose recall is a function of reading with pictures", or "Providing pictures with prose leads to better recall per-formance".

Figure 20.1 The Temporal Arrangement of Elements in a Hypothesis

The "if" part independent variable	Time	The "than" part dependent variable
Cause	Causal link	Effect

It is sometimes difficult to clearly demonstrate a functional relationship. Results tend to be equivocal, and many experiments do not permit us to make precise statements of this nature. This is true primarily because variables other than the independent one may influence the outcome. Suppose, for example, that Vern Victim views an aggressive television show, after which he goes to a room where his imitative aggressive behavior can slugs Vern. Once he is in the observation room, Vern behaves very aggressively, destroying and throwing toys. Is Vern's violent behavior a result of watching the aggressive show, or is it caused by Bernie's behavior? One cannot be sure, because two events rather than one occurred during the time span of the happening.

To draw cause–and–effect conclusions, the experimenter must control not just the independent variable, but all other events as well. The researcher may not be interested in manipulating some of these extraneous variables in the same time. but they, can affect the dependent variables. Research psychologists use many procedures to control extraneous variables. A laboratory setting is often preferred because control is easier to attain there. Less structured situations can present control problems.

Psychologists must also be concerned with the variability of individual subjects in an experiment. Characteristics of experimental subjects that may influence the study's outcome are called attribute variables. Different people may not react the same way when exposed to the same independent variable. Among the many attribute variables are such characteristics as age, sex, abilities, past learning, and past experience. The scientist examining human behavior must take such characteristics into account when identifying a functional relationship.

Unlike the independent and extraneous variables, attribute variables are not subject to the experimenter's complete control. These variables can be controlled to some extent through the selection of participants; the investigator may choose to study only girls or only high–ability individuals. However, people's characteristics cannot arbitrarily be changed. These characteristics are part of the existing conditions, the qualities that a participant brings to the experiment.

Consider once again, for example, the laboratory studies of the effect of violent television on children's subsequent behavior. Many studies show that aggression does increase following exposure to violent programming (Lesser, 1977). Some studies, however, yield more varied results: aggression increases in some children but actually decreases in others. Moreover, a child's reaction is influenced by past socialization experiences as well as by what is watched. Children who have been punished for aggression or taught that aggression is inappropriate may react differently. Violent programming may cause them to feel anxious; they may aggress less rather than more. Past socialization about aggression is something the child brings to the laboratory. Since it is out of the experimenter's direct control, it is an attribute variable, a condition existing before the experiment begins. Expanding our earlier diagrams to include attribute variables produces Figure 20.2.

The experimental paradigm or laboratory analogue as it is called sometimes, is a precise scientific approach to the study of human behavior. It has proved extremely useful in helping psychologists become more scientific and less philosophical. It has limitations, however.

First, many questions that might be asked about human events cannot be examined experimentally. Some variables are not subject to manipulation, and the experimental paradigm requires manipulation and control of an independent variable to demonstrate cause and effect. The effects of malnutrition in babies may be a legitimate scientific question, for example, but it would obviously be highly unethical to starve a group of babies for the purpose of collecting data. We might also want to study the relationship between an attribute variable, such as age, and an aspect of behavior, such as language skill, but attribute variables cannot be manipulated, so the experimental paradigm would be inappropriate in this study, too. There are many questions about human behavior that need asking; some cannot be answered in the laboratory.

Furthermore, some scientists (McCall, 1977) contend that the experimental paradigm is not always appropriate because it is artificial. The precise, controlled environment of the laboratory is very unlike the natural environment in which people actually behave. In non-contrived settings many variables work together to influence behavior, but this situation is hard to replicate in laboratories. Other techniques are needed for the study of human behavior occurring naturally in complex settings.

Figure 20.2 The Temporal Arrangement of Elements in a Hypothesis

Independent variable	Time	Dependent variale
	⟶ Attribute variable ⟶	
Cause	Causal link	Effect

第三节 观察法
(OBSERVATION)

Observation requires watching people and recording what happens. The psychologist does not meddle or interfere with what people are doing. Sometimes a one-way mirror is used because people often change their behavior when they believe they are being watched.

Recording of observations must be factual. Psychologists note what happens without making any interpretations or inferences. For example, if someone laughs, the psychologist records the laughter. No inference is made about the cause of the laughter. Whether the laughter was caused by something funny, a joyous feeling, nervousness, or an attempt to cover up fears cannot be determined through observation alone.

Caution! Beware of insinuations based on observation. Since inferences should not be made from observations, behavior cannot be explained. For example, suppose you observed that there were a large number of bearded men in a particular town. All you can conclude is that the town has a large number of bearded men. There are innumerable reasons for their beards. Perhaps beards are in vogue, or women prefer men with beards, or razor blades are expensive. Maybe the men are trying out for Santa Claus roles. The list of possible causes could be as long as this book. Suppose you saw a woman lift up papers and stare around the desk surface beneath them. Next she rubbed the desk with the palm of her hand. What can you conclude? Is she looking for a small object, brushing dust, or wiping a spot? If you are a cautious observer, you will not conclude anything. You will simply record her behavior.

Have you heard the joke about the psychologist and the frog? It seems the psychologist was observing a frog's response to a bell. The psychologist rang a bell. The frog jumped. The psychologist immediately wrote down that the frog jumped. The psychologist cut off one of the frog's legs and again rang the bell. The frog jumped. The psychologist noted that the frog jumped. A second leg was cut from the frog and the bell was rung. The psychologist again recorded her observation of the frog jumping. She then cut off the frog's third leg. The frog once again jumped in response to the ringing bell. The psychologist noted the behavior. Finally, the psychologist cut off the frog's fourth leg and rang the bell. The frog did not move. The psychologist wrote in her notes, "When frog's fourth leg is cut, frog becomes hard of hearing."

From what you know about the technique of observation, criticize the psychologist's conclusion.

第四节 个案研究
(CASE STUDY)

The case-study method is used primarily by clinical psychologists working with troubled persons. A case study is an in-depth examination of one individual. The purpose is to learn as much as possible about the person's problems. The technique is expensive and takes several sessions for completion.

Psychologists usually begin by acquiring biographical information that relates to the problem. In the case of a child, psychologists usually interview his parents and request reports from teachers and other significant people who know the youngster. They then interview the troubled person and begin extensive testing. Depending on the type of problem, intelligence, aptitude, achievement, perception, and personality tests may be administered. Based on the results of the tests, biographical information, and interviews, recommendations are made to alleviate the problems. Such recommendations may include therapy, a change in classes or jobs, a new direction in leisure activities, or improved communication with authorities.

Case study is conducted with one person or several persons. Sometimes this method involves merely describing an individual's behavior, but in other instances the procedure can be as precise and controlled as the laboratory experiment. It is sometimes possible to make cause-and-effect statements with this technique, but conclusions based on the behavior of a single individual may not hold for others, so generalizations must often be limited. On the other hand, the value of information about the behavior of a few subjects should not be minimized. Jean Piaget originally developed his highly influential theory of intellectual development by observing only three persons his own children (Gruber and Voneche, 1977).

第五节 调查
(SURVEY)

Have you ever received a call asking you which television program you were watching? Or perhaps you have received a questionnaire enclosed with an appliance or some equipment that you purchased. The questionnaire might have asked unusual questions from the number of bathrooms in your house to how much time you spend vacationing. In both instances, someone was conducting a survey. Think back on how you responded——or if you responded.

The purpose of a psychological survey is to determine the attitudes and behaviors of a large group of people. Usually everyone in the group cannot be questioned; thus, psychologists choose only a sample of the group. The sample might include half the group or as little as 5 or 10 percent of the group.

If only a small percentage of people are chosen for the sample, they must be selected carefully. Caution must be taken to be sure that the samples have the same important attributes in the population they represent. For example, suppose the officials of a college wanted to determine whether students felt that instructors were giving them higher grades than they deserved. They only want to survey 10 percent of the students. If the college is half male and half female, their sample should reflect that. Similarly, the sample should include the same distribution of subject majors and age groups as the total college population. Even more important, the sample s grades should reflect the distribution of the total college population.

Suppose grades were distributed on a normal curve. Indeed it would be unusual to have such a perfect assortment of grades, but assume for convenience that most students in the college have grades between 60 and 80. An equal number have grades between 80 and 90 and 50 and 60. Very few have grades above 90 or below 50. The sample must show the same distribution of grades if it is to represent everyone in the college.

After carefully selecting the sample, the college administrators would need to be accurate in wording their questions. Students may honestly feel that they are graded too leniently. However, they may fear their grades will drop if they admit their true feelings to college officials. Psychologists have found that people do not always respond honestly to surveys.

Now that the questions are written and a list of names has been carefully selected for a sample, how can you get the questions to the people in the sample? The cheapest method is the telephone. But you will be limited to people who have telephones and listed numbers; people without phones or with unlisted numbers will be left out. To be sure, they may have different attitude from the rest of your sample. You cannot assume that their thinking would be the same as the rest of the group.

Another alternative is to mail the questionnaires. Think about questionnaires you have received in the mail. If you are like most people, you neither completed nor returned them. Usually, less than 10 percent of the people return questionnaires received by mail. A 15 percent return is considered high by psychologists. Unfortunately, evidence from such a small percentage of a sample cannot be of much use. Those who took the time to answer questions are not neces-sarily typical of the people who chose not to respond.

The most accurate method for conducting surveys is through personal interviews. However, it is also the most time-consuming and costly method. As s result, surveys using the interview method are either overwhelmingly expensive or derived from samples that are too small to permit conclusions.

Caution! When reading the results of a survey, the first to note is the time that the survey was taken. World events change random! People do modify their thinking and make their minds with the change of time and events. American attitudes to ward Iran were relatively neutral until hostages were taken. Similarly, attitudes toward fashions, education, activities, and relationships constantly sway.

Read the results of surveys conscientiously. Check the size and representatives of the sample. If they are not stated, chances are good that the poll is hiding something. The conclusion that "three out of four housewives surveyed recommended Slowpoke baking powder" could mean that only four housewives were surveyed. All four housewives may be major stockholders in the Slowpoke Company. Conclusions should be based on a large representative sample.

第六节 现场研究
(FIELD INVESTIGATION)

The social psychologist that moves outside the laboratory to test a hypothesis is basically concerned with increasing the natural quality of the situation: naturalness of the behavior, the setting, and the treatment (Tunnell, 1977). Often the investigator's role in such a study is simply to observe what occurs, with little or no intervention. To test the hypothesis concerning deindividuation, one might therefore look for natural settings that would differ in the degree of anonymity they provided. For example, in a large urban center, we might expect anonymity to be much more pervasive than in a small university town where people are more likely to be acquainted .Thus, greater antisocial behavior could be predicted, on the basis of our hypothesis, in the large city than in the small town.

To test the deindividuation hypothesis in these circumstances, Zimbardo and Fraser bought a used car and left it on a busy street adjoining the Bronx campus of New York University. At the same time, a similar car was left on a street near the Stanford University campus in Palo Alto, California. Within 26 hours the car in New York was stripped of battery, radiator, air cleaner, radio antenna, windshield wipers, side chrome, all four hubcaps, a set of jumper cables, a can of car wax, a gas can, and the one tire worth taking. Meanwhile, in Palo Alto, the second car remained unharmed. In fact, one day when it rained, a passerby lowered the hood so the motor would not get waterlogged.

Although automobile-parts thieves and hooded students are obviously quite different, from the point of testing a hypothesis the conclusion remains the same: greater anonymity leads to a greater frequency of antisocial behavior.

Field studies, of which there are many varieties, are done in the natural environment rather than a laboratory. In some cases, independent variables are manipulated and cause-and-effect statements drawn. In others, the experimenter examines the effects of an event that occurs naturally. These studies lack the control found in laboratory investigations, but they have the advantage of realism.

第七节 跨文化研究
(CROSS-CULTURE INVESTIGATION)

What is true in industrialized countries may not be true in other parts of the world. Consequently, experimenters who want to determine the universality of their hypotheses may often look to other societies for a means of testing their ideas. One source for such tests is the Human Relations Area File (HRAF), a collection of information assembled by ethnographers on more than 200 kinds of culture throughout the world.

Watson (1973) used the material available in this file to test the anonymity/antisocial-behavior hypothesis in yet another context. He assumed that the extensive use of masks and of face and body paint by warriors serves as a guarantee of anonymity. Consequently, he hypothesized that societies in which use of paint and disguise was extensive would have a tradition of more aggressive and ferocious warfare than societies in which disguise was less frequent. To test the hypothesis, Watson simply categorized societies described in the HRAF on two dimensions: intensity of warfare (as indicated by reports of such practices as torture, sacrifice of prisoners, headhunting, and fighting to the death in all battles) and the presence or absence of paints and disguise as a prelude to battle. Once again, the hypothesis concerning anonymity and aggression was supported: those societies that engaged in more aggressive forms of warfare were also more likely to don heavy disguises than were the more peaceful cultures (see Table 20.1).

	Deindividuation	
	changed appearance	Unchanged appearance
Aggression		
High	12	1
Low	3	7

NOTE: N=23; X^2=7.12, df=1, p<0.01

Table 20.1 Relationship between changes in physical appearance before battle and extremity of aggression in warfare among 23 linguistically and geographically independent cultures

In Watson's study, it is more difficult to determine the direction of cause and effect than it is, for example, in the laboratory experiment. The correlational method (the study of the interrelationship between two sets of events) may tell us that two factors are associated, but we don't generally know which factor causes which. It could be, as hypothesized, that anonymity leads to aggression. However, it is also possible that aggressive people are more likely to seek anonymity. Or as a third possibility, perhaps some other factors, such as climate, leads both to aggression and to a desire for anonymity. In contrast, the experimenter in the laboratory first manipulated anonymity and then measured aggression, so that we are quite certain which factor came first and hence is the cause.

第八节 相关法研究
(CORRELATIONAL STUDY)

In correlational studies, researchers examine a relationship between attribute variables or between attribute variables and behavior. After measurements are collected, the data are examined to determine if and how strongly the variables are related. This approach is well-suited to the study of some questions. A psychologist interested in the relationship between age and language skill, between gender and behavior, or between intelligence and achievement could use a correlational approach. Independent variables are not manipulated. Correlational studies can only suggest, not prove, cause-and-effect relationships, but the information obtained is still very valuable.

第九节 研究范式的本质特征
(ESSENTIAL FEATURE OF RESEARCH PARADIGMS)

Regardless of the form of research paradigms, they have several features in common. All methods yield information about human behavior and help to explain it. Explanations permit us to help people with difficulties, predict what people will do, and teach effectively. A second shared feature is that all forms are based on scientific methods. Empirical science is public, so procedures must be described objectively. Replication is possible only if scientists do their job well and describe their studies fully.

The psychologist is no exception. Regardless of the type, psychological studies must also be public and thus objectively described. Objective description involves operationalization. In a research report the investigator must describe the operations performed in (1) creating the independent variable, (2) assessing attribute variables, (3) controlling extraneous variables, and (4) measuring the dependent variable.

Operationalizing the independent variable entails describing the experiences that the participants in the study were subjected to. The instructions used by the experimenter, the study's setting, the materials employed, and similar information should be included in this description.

If the experiment is done properly, a knowledgeable reader will understand exactly what took place and be able to replicate the study. The psychologists also describe the control of procedures and attribute variables taken into account.

Equally important is the process of operational zing the dependent variable. The investigator needs to develop a procedure to accurately describe not just what was done in the study, but what the subjects did as a result. The behavior of the subjects is stated in the form of an operational definition.

Creating a good operational definition for outcome performances is more difficult than you might suppose. It involves designing procedures to measure human performances, and the measurement must meet certain requirements. First, the measurement of performance must be logically related to the research hypothesis. A researcher concerned with learning outcomes will measure some aspect of learning. If the hypothesis pertains to memory, then performances involving memory processes must be assessed. This may seem like an obvious point, but it is often difficult to accomplish. Outcomes involving aspects of human behavior are often difficult to measure precisely. Human performances associated with such characteristics as cognitive skills, thinking processes, comprehension, learning, and understanding sometimes seem impossible to tap, but it is precisely these aspects of human behavior that are most important to those concerned with instruction and educational processes.

Suppose, for example, that a researcher hypothesizes that experience in role-playing activities (an independent variable) will enhance children's abilities to be empathetic about the experiences of other people (a dependent variable). What does the researcher mean by empathetic? How will empathy in a child's behavior be recognized and measured? The researcher's operational definition of empathy is determined by the operations or procedures used to measure empathy. Various investigators have used different measures of empathy in past research (Rosser, 1981). We may personally disagree with a particular investigator's operational definition, but it is important to know precisely what aspects of behavior were being measured and labeled.

A second requirement of operational definitions concerns reliability. Reliability, which you will learn much more about in other chapters, is an assessment of the consistency with which we measure behavior. In research, it often means that two individuals examining an incident of human behavior will classify it the same way. Suppose, for example, we observe two youngsters engaged in physical activity on a playground. They are in close physical contact, rolling on the ground, physically touching each other. Are they fighting? Engaging in healthy horseplay? Is it part of a sports activity? You would need clear guidelines for classifying a specific act in order to decide. Establishing those guidelines is part of devising a good operational definition. Armed with well constructed guidelines, two observers watching the youngsters should reach the same conclusion most of the time.

An important issue closely related to reliability involves externalization. Human behavior must be defined in terms of an external performance or action. Such internal performances as thinking, imagining, and self-verbalizing are not directly observable, nor are they always accompanied by observable signs. In the absence of clear outward signs of an internal event, we must make inferences about what we think is going on, but inferences are less likely to be reliable than direct observations. Suppose we give a child a three-dimensional puzzle, and the child sits quietly for several seconds without responding. Is the child thinking? Daydreaming? Is the child evolving a mental strategy? We cannot know for sure. We must guess: Inference involves guessing.

To reliably measure human phenomena, we need outward signs. These signs are external performances, observable actions. Operational zing the dependent variable is the process of obtaining those signs, collecting measurements of them, and reaching agreement about their meanings.

第十节 科学、方法论与理论
(SCIENCE, METHODOLOGY AND THEORY)

Explaining human happenings is an undertaking that requires skill, ingenuity, and the mastery of a set of tools. Even behavioral scientists need use their tools skillfully to face additional problems. What happenings most deserve study? In a particular happening, what key variables can be stated as hypotheses that will direct the investigations? Once data have been collected, how should they be interpreted? Choices made before the investigation will influence what is studied. How does the scientist make those choices? Selections are made primarily on the basis of theory.

Like any other event, scientific investigation is also a happening, and it does not occur in a vacuum. It is itself part of a temporal sequence: Every study has been preceded by some investigations and will be followed by others. Previous studies influence the choices and investigative procedures selected for a current study. In short, what will be done is related to what has been done. Research data from a number of investigations are compressed into systems that summarize previous findings. These systems also assess the implications and meanings of previous findings and suggest hypotheses that may lead to new discoveries. These Systems are the various psychological theories.

Theories are units of explanation about human behavior that cover more than a single experiment or set of experiments. Moreover, theories go beyond data, judging the relative importance of research findings and directing future examinations. Theory, then, influences what is studied and how it is studied.

For every human happening there is more than one theoretical explanation. We have several theories of learning, theories of personality, and theories of development. Each has its own system of explanation and its own body of empirical evidence. In the course of this book you will encounter many of them. Perhaps as psychology matures as a scientific discipline some of these theories of human behavior will emerge as clearly superior to others. At present, however, the discipline is in its infancy, or at best in early childhood. For this reason we must consider a number of perspectives and a varied body of evidence concerning how and why people act as they do. Despite their differences regarding human behavior, however, all of the theories have one feature in common. Theory may act as a guide, but empirical data are the evidence, evidence gathered on the assumption that people are an appropriate subject for scientific investigation.

New directions in research One facet of science fascinating to many is that it continually changes. Scientists make new discoveries, describe new phenomena, and explain old phenomena in more sophisticated ways. As the science changes, so too must the tools and methods of the science change to keep up with the cutting edge. Methodological innovations both reflect the state of the art and permit the art to evolve. In fact, one could propose that a science can progress only within the limits of the available tools. Psychology is no exception.

What we see happening in psychology right now is a shift in both theory and methodology toward greater complexity. Contemporary theories of behavior have a systems flavor—that is, the person is viewed as a complex network of interrelated components responding to multiple simultaneous influences.

The laboratory analogue is a good fit for breaking down complex phenomena into parts and testing, one at a time, the hypotheses associated with the parts. One might not, however, discover the nature of a system by studying the parts if breaking it into parts destroys the system. Instead, it may be wiser to test the system as a whole. In this way, single hypothesis testing is replaced by its extension, multiple hypothesis testing, or model testing.

Hypothesis testing and model testing are both based on the same basic tenets of science and are related. They differ in the size of the chunks studied. Traditionally, we examined the influence of one or two variables on one or two others while controlling for other factors—that is, a relatively small chunk. In model testing, we have multiple variables affecting another set of multiple variables. We want to specify all the relationships among the variables and test them as a unit a large chunk. The question is whether the full model, rather than the individual relations, is a good fit with human behavior. You thus test the model; in fact, the model becomes the hypothesis.

This level of analysis is not possible without a computer. What we see in contemporary psychology is a growth of sophisticated computer methodologies like those associated with causal modeling (Heise, 1975), confirmatory factor analysis (Joreskog & Sorbon, 1979), and computer simulation (Newell & Simon, 1972; Simon, 1979). These are the tools for testing systems.

The methods are new, and they are not without controversy. They may signal, however, a coming of age in psychology. In the near future testing theory rather than hypotheses that comprise the theory may become commonplace.

词汇 (Vocabulary)

1. alleviate   vt. 减轻、缓和
2. attribute variable   被试变量
3. covary   v. 协变

4. deindividuation 去个性化

5. disguize   vt. 把……装扮起来

6. entail   vt. 必需

7. equivocal   adj. 歧义的

8. extraneous   adj. 无关的、不重要的

9. ferocious   adj. 凶恶的

10. hallmark   n. 标志

11. hood   n. 车篷、罩

12. innovation   n. 革新、创新

13. insinuation   n. 暗示

14. legitimate   adj. 合理的

15. leniently   adv. 宽大的

16. malnutrition   n. 营养不良

17. meddle   vi. 干涉

18. monumental   adj. 巨大的

19. operational definition   操作定义

20. pertain   vi. 从属、关于

21. pervasive   adj. 弥漫的、遍布的

22. plausibility   n. 似乎有道理

23. proficiency   n. 熟练、精通

24. prose   n. 文章、文字

25. razor   n. 剃刀

26. slug   vt. 猛击

27. sophisticated   adj. 老于世故的、老练的

28. sway   v. 摇摆

29. tenet   n. 信条、宗旨

30. vogue   n. 时尚

附 录
（APPENDIX）

附录1：国外心理学文献撰写格式
（APA STYLE）

国外心理学文献标准格式为APA格式。APA格式是一个为大家广泛接受的研究论文撰写格式，特别针对社会科学领域的研究，规范学术文献的引用和参考文献的撰写方法，以及表格、图表、注脚和附录的编排方式。正式来说，APA格式指的就是美国心理学会（American Psychological Association）出版的《美国心理协会刊物准则》，目前已出版至第六版（ISBN 9781433805615），总页数272页，而此协会是目前在美国具有权威性的心理学学者组织。APA格式起源于1929年，当时只有7页，被刊登在《心理学期刊（Psychological Bulletin）》。其规范格式主要包括文内文献引用（Reference Citations in Text）和文后参考文献列举（Reference List）两大部分。APA格式强调出版物的年代（Time of the Publication Year）而不大注重原文作者的姓名。引文时常将出版年代置于作者缩写的名（the Initial of Author's First Name）之前。中国的外语类期刊（语言学刊物为主）及自然科学类的学术刊物喜欢使用APA格式。虽然有些作者对于APA格式中的一些规范感到不妥，但APA格式仍备受推崇。期刊采用同一种格式能够让读者有效率地浏览和搜集文献资料，写作时感到不确定的学者们发现这样的格式手册非常有帮助。譬如，手册中的"非歧视语言"章节明文禁止作者针对女性和弱势团体使用歧视的文字。不过使用APA格式的学术期刊有时也会为了让文章更有条理而允许作者忽略此规定。

APA格式要求

每一段的开头应当按一下键盘上的Tab键再开始写而不是直接空格Indent。首行缩进双倍行间距Double Space、字体要求Times New Roman、字体大小要求11~12号（教授的不同要求）。

需要有页眉。第一页的页眉要有Running head：（你的文章标题的简版，要求全部大写），页码要在页眉的最右边。而第二页的页眉内容不需要Running head，只需要你的文章标题的简版＋大写。

纸张的边距要求1英寸（2.54厘米），需要Title Page，上面要有文章名、作者名（你的）、指导老师、科目、学校、日期，甚至班级（这条不同的教授稍有不同的要求）。

标题、编辑：

根据APA格式，标题是用来组织文章，使得其有层次架构。APA格式规定了文章内"标题"的特定格式（1~5级），此详细内容可参阅《美国心理协会刊物手册》第五版的第113页，级数和格式如下：

第1级：居中大小写标题（Centered Uppercase and Lowercase Heading）

第2级：居中、斜体、大小写标题（Centered, Italicized, Uppercase and Lowercase Heading）

第3级：左对齐、斜体、大小写页边标题（Flush Left, Italicized, Uppercase and Lowercase Side Heading）

第4级：缩进、斜体、小写的段落标题，以句号结尾（Indented, italicized, lowercase paragraph heading ending with a period）

第5级：居中的大写标题（CENTERED UPPERCASE HEADING）

根据APA格式，若文章标题有：

1个级数：使用第1级标题
2个级数：使用第1和第3级标题
3个级数：使用第1、第3和第4级标题
4个级数：使用第1、第2、第3和第4级标题
5个级数：使用第5、第1、第2、第3和第4级标题

（按：2个级数以上以大标题→小标题方式使用）

注意：并无六级以上的标题规定。APA格式不允许"数字"和"单一字母"出现在标题之首。

文献引用、编辑：

文献引用是在一篇文章的段落或文字之中"参考来源"的标注。APA格式使用哈佛大学文章引用格式，通常来说，一个引用包含了作者名和发表日期，以括号夹注（有时会再加上页数），放在引用文字或句子之后。

详细的引用或参考资料则放在位于文章最后的"参考文献"或"Works Cited"部分。APA格式明确的定义"参考文献"只放入文章内容引用的来源，所以有些文章才会有"参考文献（Reference）"和"Bibliography"的分别。（Bibliography另外包含了作者背景知识的来源，不一定是直接被引用的文献。）

单一作者：

格式应为"（作者姓氏（非首字母），发表年份）"。若作者姓名在文章中已被提及，只需标出年份就好（若需要可加上页数），仍需使用括号。多位作者以上同理。

A recent study found a possible genetic cause of alcoholism (Pauling, 2005). Pauling (2005) discovered a possible genetic cause of alcoholism.

两位作者：

作者姓氏必须以他们的名字在其发表文章内的顺序来排序。若两个作者都在括号内引用，名字中间需加上"&"符号；若不在括号内则使用"and"。

A recent study found a possible genetic cause of alcoholism (Pauling & Liu, 2005). Pauling and Liu (2005) discovered a possible genetic cause of alcoholism.

3~5位作者：

第一次引用时需列举全部的作者，往后若引用相同的文献，只需举出最主要的作者，再加上"et al."。但是，在参考文献部分，全部作者的姓名皆须列举出来。

A recent study found a possible genetic cause of alcoholism (Pauling, Liu, & Guo, 2005). Pauling, Liu, and Guo (2005) conducted a study that discovered a possible genetic cause of alcoholism. Pauling et al. (2005) discovered a possible genetic cause of alcoholism. A recent study found a possible genetic cause of alcoholism (Pauling et al., 2005).

6位以上作者：

举出第一位作者即可，格式应为"（作者 et al., 年份）"。在参考文献部分，全部作者的姓名皆须列举出来。

Pauling et al. (2005) discovered a possible genetic cause of alcoholism.

多篇文献，同一作者：

若一作者有多篇你想引用的文献，只需用逗号来区隔作品的发表年份（最早到最晚依序排列）。若多篇文献在同一年内发表，请在年份后面加上a、b、c等标注。（abc的使用需与参考文献部分有所对应，而这些文献的编排以标题名称的字母来决定。）

A recent study found a possible genetic cause of alcoholism (Pauling, 2004, 2005a, 2005b). Pauling (2004, 2005a, 2005b) conducted a study that discovered a possible genetic cause of alcoholism

多篇文献，多位作者：

根据上一个的规则，使用分号隔开。排序先依照作者姓氏的字母，接着是发表年份。

A recent study found a possible genetic cause of alcoholism (Alford, 1995; Pauling, 2004, 2005; Sirkis, 2003)

直接引述：

格式与前述无不同，一样为"（作者，年份，页数）"。

When asked why his behavior had changed so dramatically, Max simply said "I think it's the reinforcement" (Pauling, 2004, p.69).

参考文献清单、编辑：

APA格式规定"参考文献"部分的人名必须以姓氏的字母顺序来排列，包括姓氏的前缀。譬如，Martin de Rijke应被改成"De Rijke, M."，Saif Al Falasi则应改成"Al-Falasi, Saif."。（阿拉伯文名字通常在姓氏和前缀之间加上连字号"-"，所以姓氏和前缀自成一体）。

纸本文献：

单一作者著作的书籍：

Sheril, R. D. (1956). The terrifying future: Contemplating color television. San Diego: Halstead.

两位以上作者合著的书籍：

Smith, J., & Peter, Q. (1992). Hairball: An intensive peek behind the surface of an enigma. Hamilton, ON: McMaster University Press.

文集中的文章：

Mcdonalds, A. (1993). Practical methods for the apprehension and sustained containment of supernatural entities. In G. L. Yeager (Ed.), Paranormal and occult studies: Case studies in application (pp. 42 - 64). London: OtherWorld Books.

期刊中的文章（非连续页码）：

Crackton, P. (1987). The Loonie: God's long-awaited gift to colourful pocket change? Canadian Change, 64(7), 34 - 37.

期刊中的文章（连续页码）：

Rottweiler, F. T., & Beauchemin, J. L. (1987). Detroit and Narnia: Two foes on the brink of destruction. Canadian/American Studies Journal, 54, 66 - 146.

月刊杂志中的文章：

Henry, W. A., III. (1990, April 9). Making the grade in today's schools. Time, 135, 28-31.

报纸中的文章：

Wrong, M. (2005, August 17). Misquotes are "Problematastic" says Mayor. Toronto Sol. p. 4.

政府官方文献：

Revenue Canada. (2001). Advanced gouging: Manual for employees (MP 65 - 347/1124). Ottawa: Minister of Immigration and Revenue.

线上文献：

针对电子文献、网站和线上文章，APA 格式的网站上有规定一些基本的规则，第一就是提供读者详细的文献内容来源，第二为提供其有效的参考来源。

网络文章的打印版本：

Marlowe, P., Spade, S., & Chan, C. (2001). Detective work and the benefits of colour versus black and white [Electronic version]。Journal of Pointless Research, 11, 123 - 124.

电子期刊的文章（只有网络版的期刊）：

Blofeld, E. S. (1994, March 1). Expressing oneself through Persian cats and modern architecture. Felines & Felons, 4, Article 0046g. Retrieved October 3, 1999, from 网页地址。

电子短信（newsletter）的文章：

Paradise, S., Moriarty, D., Marx, C., Lee, O. B., Hassel, E., et al.

(1957, July). Portrayals of fictional characters in reality-based popular writing: Project update. Off the beaten path, 7(3). Retrieved October 3, 1999, from 网页地址。

单篇线上文献（无作者及著作日期）：

What I did today. (n.d.). Retrieved August 21, 2002, from 网页地址。

从大学课程或系上网站取得的文献：

Rogers, B. (2078). Faster-than-light travel: What we've learned in the first twenty years. Retrieved August 24, 2079, from Mars University, Institute for Martian Studies Web site: 网页地址

从数据库搜寻的期刊文章的电子复制版本（3~5位作者）：

Costanza, G., Seinfeld, J., Benes, E., Kramer, C., & Peterman, J. (1993). Minutiæ and insignificant observations from the nineteen-nineties. Journal about Nothing, 52, 475 - 649. Retrieved October 31, 1999, from NoTHINGJournals database.

电子邮件或其他个人通讯（限定文字）：

(A. Monterey, personal communication, September 28, 2001).

储存于光碟的书籍：

Nix, G. (2002). Lirael, Daughter of the Clayr [CD]。New York: Random House/Listening Library.

储存于录音带的书籍：

Nix, G. (2002). Lirael, Daughter of the Clayr [Cassette Recording No. 1999-1999-1999]。New York: Random House/Listening Library.

附录2：国外主要心理学期刊及网站

国外心理学期刊
（JOURNALS）

一、总论

2《Psychological bulletin》（心理学公报）【美】

3《Psychological review》（心理学评论）【美】

5《Psychological reports》（心理学报告）【美】

17《Annual review of psychology》（心理学年度评论）【美】

25《Psychological science》（心理科学）【美】

41《American psychologist》（美国心理学家）【美】

42《Professional psychology, research and practice》（专业心理学，研究及实践）【美】

73《British journal of psychology》（英国心理学杂志）【英】

86《American journal of psychology》（美国心理学杂志）【美】

90《Scandinavian journal of psychology》（斯堪的纳维亚心理学杂志）【英】

二、实验

10《Journal of experimental psychology. Learning, memory, and cognition》（实验心理学杂志．学习、记忆和认识）【美】

14《Journal of experimental psychology. Human perception and performance》（实验心理学杂志．人类知觉与行为）【美】

38《Journal of experimental psychology. General》（实验心理学杂志．总论）【美】

74《Behavior research methods, instruments & computers》（行为研究方法、仪器与计算机）【英】

72《Journal of experimental psycholoy Animal behavior processes》（实验心理学杂志．动物行为过程）【美】

三、测量

50《Psychological assessment》（心理评价）【美】

70《Educational and psychological measurement》（教育与心理测量）【英】

四、个性与社会性

（一）社会心理

81《The Journal of social psychology》（社会心理学杂志）【美】

75《Social psychology quarterly》（社会心理学季刊）【美】
76《European journal of social psychology》（欧洲社会心理学杂志）【英】
64《Journal of experimental social psychology》（实验社会心理学杂志）【美】
（二）个性与社会性
1《Journal of personality and social psychology》（个性与社会心理学杂志）【美】
15《Personality and individual differences》（个性与个体差异）【英】
30《Personality & social psychology bulletin》（个性与社会心理学公报）【美】
53《Journal of personality assessment》（个性评估杂志）【美】
62《Journal of personality》（个性杂志）【美】

五、发展教育
12《Developmental psychology》（发展心理学）【美】
40《Journal of educational psychology》（教育心理学杂志）【美】
43《Child abuse & neglect》（虐待与忽视儿童研究）【英】
65《Journal of comparative psychology》（比较心理学杂志）【美】
58《Journal of experimental child psychology》（实验儿童心理学杂志）【美】
77《Infant behavior & development》（婴儿行为与发育）【美】

六、行为
（一）行为研究及应用
47《Journal of applied behavior analysis》（应用行为分析杂志）【美】
56《Ethology》（行为学）【德】
（二）认知行为学
4《Behavioral & brain sciences》（行为与大脑科学）【英】
80《Behavioral neuroscience》（行为神经科学）【美】

七、精神分析
66《The International journal of psycho-analysis》（国际心理分析杂志）【英】

八、认知
（一）认知总论
24《Cognitive psychology》（认知心理学）【美】
26《Cognition》（认知）【荷兰】
82《Cognitive science》（认知科学）【美】
（二）生物心理学
9《Journal of cognitive neuroscience》（认知神经科学杂志）【美】
16《Psychophysiology》（心理生理学）【英】

28 《Brain research》（大脑研究）【荷兰】

37 《Journal of psychosomatic research》（身心研究杂志）【美】

44 《Neuropsychology》（神经心理学）【美】

46 《Behavioural brain research》（行为大脑研究）【荷兰】

55 《Cognitive neuropsychology》（认知神经心理学）【英】

78 《Neuropsychologia》（神经心理学）【英】

84 《Biological psychology》（生物心理学）【荷兰】

85 《Psychobiology》（心理生物学）【美】

87 《Brain and cognition》（大脑与认知）【美】

（三）具体认知运用

7 《Perceptual motor skills》（感知与运动技能）【英】

21 《Journal of memory and language》（记忆与语言杂志）【美】

23 《Journal of affective disorders》（情感紊乱杂志）【荷兰】

29 《Perception & psychophysics》（知觉与心理学）【美】

31 《Vision research》（视觉研究）【英】

35 《Brain and language》（大脑与语言）【美】

36 《Memory and cognition》（记忆与认知）【美】

48 《Perception》（知觉）【英】

88 《Language and cognitive processes》（语言与认知过程）【英】

89 《Memory》（记忆）【英】

（四）社会认知与治疗

45 《Organizational behavior and human decision processes》（组织行为与人类决策过程）【美】

67 《Cognitive therapy and research》（认知治疗与研究）【美】

九、应用

（一）咨询与应用

6 《Journal of consulting and clinical psychology》（咨询心理学与临床心理学杂志）【美】

20 《Journal of applied psychology》（应用心理学杂志）【美】

52 《Journal of counseling psychology》（咨询心理学杂志）【美】

（二）临床

8 《Psychological medicine》（心理医学）【美】

13 《Psychosomatic medicine》（身心医学）【美】

18 《Behaviour research and therapy》（行为研究和治疗）【英】

19 《Pharmacology, biochemistry and behavior》（药理学、生物化学和行为）【美】

22 《The Journal of child psychology and psychiatry & allied

disciplines》（儿童心理学、精神病学及相关学科杂志）【英】
32《Psychopharmacology bulletin》（精神药理学公报）【美】
33《Journal of studies on alcohol》（酒精研究杂志）【美】
83《Journal of clinical child psychology》（临床儿童心理学杂志）【美】（临床）
79《Journal of pediatric psychology》（儿科心理学杂志）【英】
71《British journal of clinical psychology》（英国临床心理学杂志）【英】
68《Clinical psychology review》（临床心理学评论）【英】

（三）其他领域

11《Journal of abnormal psychology》（变态心理学杂志）【美】
51《Journal of abnormal child psychology》（变态儿童心理学杂志）【美】
27《Health psychology》（健康心理学）【美】
34《Psychology and aging》（心理学与衰老）【美】
39《International journal of eating disorders》（国际进食障碍杂志）【美】
54《Journal of traumatic stress》（创伤应激反应杂志）【美】
69《Journal of sport & exercise psychology》（运动与训练心理学杂志）【美】
63《Addictive behaviors》（成瘾行为）【英】
61《Journal of vocational behavior》（职业行为杂志）【美】
59《Law and human behavior》（法律和人类行为）【美】
60《Sex roles》（性别角色）【美】
57《Ergonomics》（人机学）【英】

国外心理学网站
（WEBS）

心理理论与实践　http://tip.psychology.org/
书评　http://www.apa.org/journals/bell.html
神经心理学中心　http://www.neuropsych.com/
Psychology Home　http://www.wadsworth.com/psychology_d/
国际心理学联合会　http://www.am.org/iupsys/
心理历史学会　http://www.psychohistory.com/
国际婴幼儿研究学会　http://www.isisweb.org/
澳洲心理学会网站　http://www.psychsociety.com.au/
比利时教育心理学网站　http://www.ulb.ac.be/bps
英国教育心理学网站　http://www.bps.org.uk/sub-syst/decp/default.cfm?action=home
英国心理医学学会　http://www.bspoga.ukgateway.net/
埃舍尔的世界（英）　http://www.worldofescher.com
大脑（英）　http://www.brain.com

加拿大教育心理学网站 http://www.cpa.ca
德国教育心理学网站 http://psychclassics.yorku.ca/
美国心理学会 http://www.apa.org/
APA 杂志网下设的心理学报刊杂志链接 http://www.apa.org/journals
心理学报刊链接 http://www.psycline.org/journals
国际心理分析杂志 http://www.ijpa.org/
注意与行为杂志 http://kramer.ume.maine.edu/~jmb/welcome.html
认知的风格 www.cognitivestyles.com
介绍神经科学发展及相关科学（认知，语言等方面） http://www.neuroguide.com
社会学方面 http://www.sosig.ac.uk/
学校心理资源在线 http://www.schoolpsychology.net/
心理学史经典著作 http://psychclassics.yorku.ca/
学校心理学家 http://www.school-psychologist.com/
社会心理学研究网络 http://www.socialpsychology.org/
社会心理学最新研究 http://www.uiowa.edu/~grppproc/crisp/crisp.html
思维网站 http://www.thinking.net/
心灵 http://psyche.cs.monash.edu.au/
自我心理 http://www.selfpsychology.org/
性格测验 http://www.queendom.com/tests/personality/index.html
心理问题 http://www.psychematters.com/
心理状态 http://www.moodstats.com/
大脑和认知实验室 http://lbc.nimh.nih.gov/
实验心理学会 http://www.eps.ac.uk/
加拿大行为科学杂志 http://www.cpa.ca/ac-main.html
psyche http://psyche.cs.monash.edu.au/
Perception on-line http://www.pion.co.uk/perception/
智商测验实验室 http://www.intelligencetest.com/
儿童焦虑网 http://www.childanxiety.net/
芝加哥大学心理学系 http://psychology.uchicago.edu/
格廷根大学心理学系 http://www.psych.uni-goettingen.de/
耶鲁大学心理学系 http://www.yale.edu/psychology
哥伦比亚大学心理学系 http://www.columbia.edu/cu/psychology/
斯坦福大学 http://www-psych.stanford.edu/
格拉斯哥大学心理学系 http://www.psy.gla.ac.uk/

附录 3：APA 格式范文

APA 格式范文（1）

Visualizing Minimal Ingroup and Outgroup Faces: Implications for Impressions, Attitudes, and Behavior

Kyle G. Ratner
The Ohio State University and New York University

Ron Dotsch, Daniel H. J. Wigboldus, and Ad van Knippenberg
Radboud University Nijmegen

David M. Amodio
New York University

More than 40 years of research have shown that people favor members of their ingroup in their impressions, attitudes, and behaviors. Here, we propose that people also form different mental images of minimal ingroup and outgroup members, and we test the hypothesis that differences in these mental images contribute to the well-established biases that arise from minimal group categorization. In Study 1, participants were assigned to 1 of 2 groups using a classic minimal group paradigm. Next, a reverse correlation image classification procedure was used to create visual renderings of ingroup and outgroup face representations. Subsequently, a 2nd sample naive to the face generation stage rated these faces on a series of trait dimensions. The results indicated that the ingroup face was significantly more likely than the outgroup face to elicit favorable impressions (e.g., trusting, caring, intelligent, attractive). Extending this finding, Study 2 revealed that ingroup face representations elicited more favorable implicitly measured attitudes than did outgroup representations, and Study 3 showed that ingroup faces were trusted more than outgroup faces during an economic game. Finally, Study 4 demonstrated that facial physiognomy associated with trustworthiness more closely resembled the facial structure of the average ingroup than outgroup face representation. Together, these studies suggest that minimal group distinctions can elicit different mental representations, and that this visual bias is sufficient to elicit ingroup favoritism in impressions, attitudes and behaviors.

Keywords: ingroup favoritism, minimal group paradigm, reverse correlation, face processing, mental representation

Intergroup biases are not always the result of long-standing rivalries. They may arise even in conditions where people do not know each other and have no conflicts of interest or any preexisting animosity toward each other. Indeed, mere identification with one of two distinct groups is sufficient to elicit a preference for one group over another (Tajfel, 1970; Tajfel, Billig, Bundy, & Flament, 1971; Tajfel & Turner, 1986). Once formed, a *minimal group* identity can influence a wide range of responses, including impressions, attitudes, and behaviors that have consequences for members of the ingroup as well as the outgroup (e.g., Ashburn-Nardo, Voils, & Monteith, 2001; Brewer & Silver, 1978; Locksley, Ortiz, & Hepburn, 1980; Otten & Wentura, 1999; Tajfel et al., 1971; Van Bavel & Cunningham, 2009).

In the last decade, researchers have begun to examine minimal group effects on visual perception and memory (e.g., Bernstein, Young, & Hugenberg, 2007; Hugenberg & Corneille, 2009; Ratner & Amodio, 2013; Van Bavel, Packer, & Cunningham, 2008, 2011). The recent focus on this topic reflects a broader recognition in social psychology that studying how people make sense of faces and other visual information provides insight into the nature of social interactions (Hassin & Trope, 2000; Macrae, Quinn, Mason, & Quadflieg, 2005; Todorov, Said, Engell, & Oosterhof, 2008;

Editor's Note. Kimberly Quinn served as the action editor for this article.

Kyle G. Ratner, Department of Psychology, The Ohio State University, and Department of Psychology, New York University; Ron Dotsch, Daniel H. J. Wigboldus, and Ad van Knippenberg, Behavioural Science Institute, Radboud University Nijmegen; David M. Amodio, Department of Psychology, New York University.

This research was supported by a National Science Foundation Graduate Research Fellowship, a New York University Dean's Dissertation Fellowship, and a Douglas and Katharine Fryer Thesis Fellowship to Kyle G. Ratner. This research was conducted as part of Kyle G. Ratner's doctoral dissertation at New York University under the sponsorship of David M. Amodio. We thank dissertation committee members Susan Andersen, Yaacov Trope, and Jay Van Bavel for their feedback during various stages of this project and Lisa Kaggen, Amy Krosch, and Petra Schmid for their comments on earlier drafts of this paper. A special thanks goes to Dustin Chien, Alexis Donovan, Manasa Kanthamneni, Tim Pasternak, Julia Schmidt, Bryan Tay, Danielle Troumouliaris, and Shelley Yang for their assistance with data collection.

Correspondence concerning this article should be addressed to Kyle G. Ratner, Department of Psychology, The Ohio State University, 1827 Neil Avenue, Columbus, OH 43210, or to David M. Amodio, Department of Psychology, New York University, 6 Washington Place, New York, NY 10003. E-mail: kyle.ratner@gmail.com or david.amodio@nyu.edu

Zebrowitz & Montepare, 2008). However, unlike other minimal group research that has focused on idealized representations of ingroup members as pleasant and trustworthy (e.g., Brewer & Silver, 1978; Tajfel et al., 1971), the work in visual processing has largely focused on how group membership may affect the degree of attention and perceptual resources allocated to the processing of ingroup as opposed to outgroup faces (e.g., Bernstein et al., 2007; Ratner & Amodio, 2013; Van Bavel et al., 2008, 2011; Young & Hugenberg, 2010). As a result, the literature has not addressed the question of how one's actual mental representation of an ingroup or outgroup member's face may be distorted by the top-down influence of mere group categorization or how such distortion might contribute to intergroup bias.

The Contribution of Facial Representations to Intergroup Responses

Facial representations are key to social interactions because they convey information about a person's intentions, reactions, and dispositions. Not surprisingly, people are highly attuned to facial information. Among both children and adults, faces receive preferential attention and processing over other objects (Birmingham, Bischof, & Kingstone, 2009a, 2009b; Goren, Sarty, & Wu, 1975; Johnson & Morton, 1991), and this preference is supported by the rapid encoding of faces in neural regions involved in high-level vision (Bentin, Allison, Puce, Perez, & McCarthy, 1996; Haxby, Hoffman, & Gobbini, 2000; Kanwisher, McDermott, & Chun, 1997). Neuroimaging findings suggest that mental images of faces are processed in much the same way as the direct perception of a face. Indeed, the same neural regions involved in direct face perception are also activated in response to an imagined face, suggesting that, as with perceiving actual faces, mental imagery of a face may profoundly shape the way information about a person is processed (Ishai, Haxby, & Ungerleider, 2002; Mechelli, Price, Friston, & Ishai, 2004; O'Craven & Kanwisher, 2000).

Given the weight afforded to facial cues during information processing, it is not surprising that information about appearance figures prominently in group-based knowledge structures. Kessler and McKenna (1978) reported that when people are asked to make gender inferences, they rely on physical characteristics to a larger degree than traits and behaviors. Furthermore, the inclusion of information about physical attributes increases the vividness and specificity of trait-based stereotypes (Andersen & Klatzky, 1987) and the likelihood that trait stereotypes will be applied during impression formation (Deaux & Lewis, 1984). Thus, representations of physical appearance promote the use of group-based stereotypes when making trait inferences.

The visual component of social group representations not only triggers trait inferences but also contributes to attitudes and behaviors. For instance, in the United States, Afrocentric features have been shown to activate negative attitudes toward Black individuals (Livingston & Brewer, 2002). In other work, White Americans who simulated the role of a patrolling police officer during a video game scenario were more likely to shoot unarmed Black men whose appearance was more prototypical of the Black stereotype (Ma & Correll, 2011). Furthermore, it has been shown that Black men accused of a crime receive harsher sentences when their appearance is closer to this stereotypical prototype (Blair, Judd, & Chapleau, 2004; Eberhardt, Davies, Purdie-Vaughns, & Johnson, 2006). Thus, visual representations constitute a powerful mechanism for conveying group-based prejudices.

Group identity is also related to the mental images people form of others, and these images have implications for social judgments and behavior. For example, Beaupré and Hess (2003) found that people were more likely to assume that targets portrayed in neutrally written vignettes were smiling if they shared the same ethnic group as the perceiver. Additionally, Dotsch, Wigboldus, Langner, and van Knippenberg (2008) observed an association between their Dutch participants' implicitly measured attitudes and the extent to which these participants formed mental images of Moroccan faces as appearing criminal and untrustworthy. In other work, Blair, Ma, and Lenton (2001) found that the strength of people's stereotypic associations could be weakened by asking them to engage in counterstereotypical mental imagery. Similarly, imagined contact with outgroups has been shown to reduce intergroup anxiety and improve attitudes toward several groups, including the elderly, homosexuals, and Muslims (Crisp & Turner, 2009; Turner & Crisp, 2010; Turner, Crisp, & Lambert, 2007). Together, the existing literature suggests that mental representations are important for guiding intergroup responses. However, the present question—of whether the simple act of categorizing others into the same or different social group as our own contributes to these mental representations and subsequent reactions—has not yet been directly addressed.

Clues That Mere Group Categorization Influences Visual Representations

Although most research on visual processing has focused on ingroup processing advantages (e.g., promoting perceptual accuracy), there are clues in the literature that ingroup favoritism under minimal group conditions can arise from distortions in facial representations, as we hypothesize. In the first wave of minimal group studies, Doise and colleagues (1972) examined whether anticipating a cooperative or a competitive context influences images of minimally generated groups and whether this effect on imagery could justify one's intended behavior toward the outgroup. In their study, they included evaluations of the groups on four physical trait dimensions: blond–dark, tall–short, fat–thin, colorful–quiet. Of importance for the present purposes, they also included a control group that consisted of minimal ingroups and outgroups with no anticipated interaction. Doise and colleagues did not conduct statistical analyses on differences between the ingroup and outgroup representations for the control group, but the data suggest that the ingroup was viewed to have physical traits deemed more favorable than the outgroup. A later study by Johnson (1981) investigated whether people have more favorable mental images of people belonging to their political party (a group with no clear perceptual basis). He found that when participants were presented with photographs of people who could be members either of their political party or of an opposing party, they selected more attractive people as belonging to their party. Most recently, Dunham (2011) reported that rapidly presented happy faces were more likely to be remembered as belonging to ingroup members. This link between happy expressions and the ingroup is consistent with the existence of a top-down expectation that ingroup faces comprise more favorable physiognomic information than outgroup faces.

On the basis of past work, we propose that mere membership in a social group has implications for the way faces of ingroup and outgroup members are represented in the mind and that differences in these mental representations can influence trait impressions, attitudes, and behaviors toward ingroup and outgroup members. In this way, mental representations of ingroup and outgroup members' faces may provide a mechanism through which mere group categorization contributes to stereotyping, prejudice, and discrimination. We tested this hypothesis across four studies.

Study 1

The objective of Study 1 was to test for differences in participants' mental representations of ingroup and outgroup faces and to assess whether these differences contribute to trait impressions formed by perceivers. This study was conducted in two parts, in which we (a) obtained visual renderings of participants' mental representations of minimally defined ingroup or outgroup members and (b) collected trait ratings of these renderings from a separate group of participants naive to the origin of the face images. This approach is described in more detail in what follows.

In Part 1, individuals were assigned to minimal groups and then categorized faces as belonging to either their ingroup or an outgroup. To capture the representational bias that we hypothesize can give rise to ingroup favoritism, we used a technique called *reverse correlation image classification*. Reverse correlation image classification belongs to a class of techniques that follow *reverse correlation* logic. Reverse correlation methods examine responses to many different stimuli and infer patterns in the stimuli that may have caused the responses. These patterns can be visualized and provide an approximation of the mental representations upon which participants based their responses. These techniques were developed over 40 years ago and have been applied to study a diverse range of topics, including auditory cognition (Ahumada & Lovell, 1971), neurophysiology (Ringach & Shapley, 2004; Victor, 2005), and low-level vision (Ahumada, 2002; Solomon, 2002). Recently, they have proved useful for investigating representations underlying face categorization (Dotsch & Todorov, 2012; Gosselin & Schyns, 2003; Mangini & Biederman, 2004; Martin-Malivel, Mangini, Fagot, & Biederman, 2006) and social cognitive biases in face processing (Dotsch et al., 2008; Dotsch, Wigboldus, & van Knippenberg, 2011; Imhoff, Dotsch, Bianchi, Banse, & Wigboldus, 2011; Jack, Caldara, & Schyns, 2012; Karremans, Dotsch, & Corneille, 2011; Young, Ratner, & Fazio, 2014). Thus, reverse correlation image classification provides a purely data-driven method for creating visual renderings of people's mental representations of faces that are resistant to experimenter bias (Mangini & Biederman, 2004; Todorov, Dotsch, Wigboldus, & Said, 2011).

In Part 2, we assessed whether these visual renderings could reveal biases that contribute to differential impressions of ingroup and outgroup members. To this end, we averaged together the visual renderings (also called classification images) generated for each participant to create grand-averaged ingroup and outgroup classification images. Then, an independent sample of participants was used to assess the impressions elicited by these grand-averaged ingroup and outgroup face representations. In order to determine the types of impressions people might discern from facial representations, we focused on trait dimensions that Oosterhof and Todorov (2008) have shown to be the most common types of impressions that people naturally draw from faces.

Study 1 was designed to test the role of facial representations as a mechanism involved in the effect of minimal group assignment on ingroup favoritism, in a manner analogous to a mediation pattern. Because much previous research has established the "direct path" between minimal group assignment and ingroup favoritism (e.g., Brewer & Silver, 1978), our design adopted the "experimental mediation" approach to examine a mechanism that contributes to this well-established effect (Spencer, Zanna, & Fong, 2005). We predicted, in line with the previously reviewed research and theory, that the ingroup facial representation would be rated more highly on traits signaling prosociality (e.g., trustworthiness, caring, sociality) and overall group fitness (e.g., intelligence, attractiveness, confidence) compared with the outgroup face representation.

Method

Part 1: Generating visual renderings of group-based facial representations

Participants. One hundred and seventy-six New York University students were recruited to participate in exchange for course credit. Up to four participants were run simultaneously in separate cubicle rooms.

Procedure. Upon arrival at the study session, participants were asked to complete a consent form and were told that they would perform several tasks on a computer. Next, a classic "dot estimation" minimal group procedure was used to assign participants to arbitrary, but believable, groups (Brown, Collins, & Schmidt, 1988; Gerard & Hoyt, 1974; Mussweiler, Gabriel, & Bodenhausen, 2000; Tajfel et al., 1971).

Numerical Estimation Style Test (NEST). Participants were led to believe that people vary in numerical estimation style, which was defined as the tendency to overestimate or underestimate the number of objects they encounter. To underscore the arbitrary nature of numerical estimation style, we told participants that approximately half the population are overestimators and half are underestimators, and that research has not related numerical estimation style to any other cognitive tendency or personality trait.

Participants were told they would categorize photographs of students from a previous semester whose numerical estimation style had been determined with a well-established task called the *Numerical Estimation Style Test*. They were then informed that past research had shown that people are able to reliably detect numerical estimation style from faces and that the purpose of the current study was to test whether people can determine numerical estimation style even when face images appear blurry. The instructions explained that the study was important because often people need to make judgments about others from far distances or at night, when perceptual information is not completely clear. It was crucial that participants accepted this aspect of the cover story, because the reverse correlation procedure requires that visually noisy images are used during the face categorization task.

Next, participants were told that in order to gain a concrete understanding of numerical estimation style and how it is measured, they should first complete the NEST themselves. In brief, the task consisted of estimating the number of dots in 10 rapidly presented dot patterns. At the end of the test, the computer program provided predetermined feedback (counterbalanced across participants), indicating that each participant was either an overestimator or an underestimator. The NEST was not actually used to assess any perceptual tendency; it simply provided a rationale for the manipulation of group assignment.

Several procedures were used to ensure that the novel group category was salient in participants' minds throughout the entire face categorization task. First, participants were prompted to report their numerical estimation style to the experimenter, which served as a public act of commitment to the group. The experimenter then wrote each participant's identification number and numerical estimation style in large letters on the cover page of a post-task questionnaire packet and placed the packet in the participants' line of sight to remind them of their group membership during the categorization task. Participants also typed their numerical estimation style group into the computer, in another behavioral act of association. These procedures served to keep participants' minimal group membership salient during the critical categorization task.

Face categorization. Following the NEST, participants completed a forced-choice face categorization task for 450 trials. On each trial, participants viewed two adjacent face images, each consisting of 211 × 270 grayscale pixels. Participants were told that on each trial one of the faces was an overestimator and the other was an underestimator, and that all the people whose faces they were viewing had completed the numerical estimation style test during a previous semester. According to a counterbalanced schedule, some participants were asked on every trial to choose which of the two faces was an overestimator and the other participants were asked on every trial to select the underestimator face. Thus, targets were ingroup members when their numerical estimation style was shared with the participant. Conversely, targets were outgroup members when their numerical estimation style was different from that of the participant.

Each face was actually derived from the same *base face* image: the grayscale neutral male average face of the Averaged Karolinska Directed Emotional Faces Database (Lundqvist & Litton, 1998). Noise patterns were layered on the images, to make each face look unique, distorting the various facial features and overall facial structure. The noise pattern added to each image consisted of 4,092 superimposed truncated sinusoid patches spanning two cycles in six orientations (0°, 30°, 60°, 90°, 120°, and 150°) × five spatial frequencies (1, 2, 4, 8, and 16 patches per image) × two phases (0, π/2), with random contrasts (amplitudes) as parameters.

On each trial, a random noise pattern was generated. This noise pattern was applied to one of the images in the pair, and the inverse of the noise pattern was added to the other image (see Figure 1). The image with the inverse noise was equally presented on the left and right sides of the screen in a random order. The same noise patterns were used for all participants.

It is important to note that because a response was required on each trial and participants were tasked with selecting on the basis of only one group (either overestimators or underestimators) for all the trials, an equal number of trials were used to generate visualizations of ingroup and outgroup representations

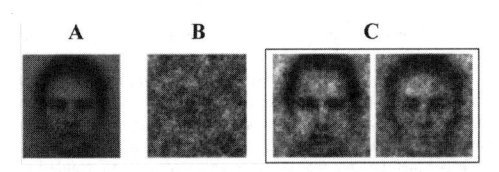

Figure 1. Example stimuli used in the Study 1 face categorization task. (A) Base face, (B) random noise pattern, (C, left) noise pattern superimposed on the face, and (C, right) inverse of the noise pattern superimposed on the base image.

(i.e., effects were not biased by the well-established tendency to exclude ambiguous individuals from the ingroup; Castano, Yzerbyt, Bourguignon, & Seron, 2002; Krosch, Berntsen, Amodio, Jost, & Van Bavel, 2013; Leyens & Yzerbyt, 1992; Quanty, Keats, & Harkins, 1975).

Face representation data processing. The logic of the reverse correlation method is that, on each trial, participants solve the task by comparing the two faces presented on the screen with their mental representation of ingroup or outgroup members, as defined by numerical estimation style. They presumably select whichever face best matches this mental representation. In order to create clear visualizations of social category representations, several hundred of these forced choice categorizations are averaged to form a classification image (Dotsch & Todorov, 2012; Dotsch et al., 2008, 2011; Imhoff et al., 2011). It is notable that if a participant categorized faces randomly, an average of the participant's responses would produce the base face image, because the counterbalanced visual noise would be canceled out (assuming enough trials are included in the average). If participants respond on some systematic basis (e.g., group membership), then systematic patterns in the pixel intensities will emerge that will reveal the mental representation. It is important to note that the visualization of the mental representation is dependent on the base face and type of noise that is used. Additionally, because there are limitations to the number of trials that can be presented, not all the noise will cancel out. However, averaging across participants provides adequate noise reduction for visualization.

Participant-level classification images. Custom MATLAB scripts were used to conduct the reverse correlation analysis. First, for each participant, a classification image was created by averaging together all of the parameters of the 450 noise patterns that he or she selected and superimposing the normalized average on the original base image. The images reflected participants' mental representation of faces belonging to the ingroup or outgroup, as a function of the counterbalanced numerical estimation style factor, the base face, group-specific features, and noise (i.e., error variance).

Group-level classification images. Because our theoretical interest concerned the effects of minimal group membership, and not numerical estimation style, ingroup ($n = 86$) and outgroup ($n = 90$) classification images were created by averaging the appropriate participant-level mean parameters and superimposing the normalized average on the original base image (collapsing across the numerical estimation style dimension; see Figure 2).[1]

Part 2: Assessing impressions of the ingroup and outgroup face representations. Having implemented the minimal group manipulation in Part 1, which produced visual images representing minimal ingroup and outgroup members, we tested in Part 2 whether ingroup face representations elicited more favorable impressions than outgroup representations, as hypothesized. To this end, an independent sample was recruited to measure trait judgments linked to the ingroup and outgroup face representations estimated during Part 1.

Participants. One hundred and nine participants were recruited through the Amazon Mechanical Turk website (www.mturk.com) to complete an online survey administered through Qualtrics (www.qualtrics.com). Participants were given 30 minutes to complete the study and were remunerated with $0.20. On average, participants finished the survey in approximately six minutes. Data from three participants were removed because, based on their Internet Protocol addresses, it appeared they had already completed the survey. Data from five other participants were excluded because their surveys were incomplete. The final data set included 101 participants. Past research suggests that the quality and reliability of data collected on Mechanical Turk are comparable to those of data collected in laboratory settings (Buhrmester, Kwang, & Gosling, 2011; Paolacci, Chandler, & Ipeirotis, 2010). All participants were naive to how the faces were generated—no mention was made of numerical estimation or any aspect of group membership.

Procedure. After providing informed consent, participants viewed the group-level ingroup and outgroup classification images and rated each on 13 trait dimensions (*trustworthy, attractive, dominant, caring, sociable, confident, emotionally stable, responsible, intelligent, aggressive, mean, weird,* and *unhappy*; Oosterhof & Todorov, 2008). The two group-level face images were presented adjacent to each other in the upper half of the screen, in counterbalanced positions, in order to draw attention to the comparison of the two images. Ratings were made on a 7-point scale. The order of the trait ratings was randomly determined by the Qualtrics stimulus presentation software.

Results

For each trait dimension, we conducted paired t tests comparing the ratings of the ingroup and outgroup classification images. The means, t values, and p values for each comparison are presented in Table 1. These tests revealed a striking pattern of results, such that the ingroup face was rated substantially higher than the outgroup face on all the traits considered to be desirable of an ingroup member (*attractiveness, intelligence, responsibility, confidence, trustworthiness, caring, emotional stability,* and *sociality*). By contrast, the outgroup face representation was judged as significantly more *weird* than the ingroup face. Ingroup and outgroup face ratings did not differ statistically on *dominance, aggressiveness, meanness,* and *unhappiness*.

Discussion

In Study 1, we investigated whether mere group membership can give rise to contrasting representations of ingroup and outgroup faces, and whether these can then lead to different social impressions. Our results indicate that sharing a minimal group membership with another person can indeed bias facial representations, in a manner that evokes more favorable impressions on a range of traits. Minimally defined ingroup and outgroup faces differed primarily on traits dimensions that signal whether a target should be approached or avoided, but they did not differ on traits found to signify dominance (Oosterhof & Todorov, 2008). This pattern comports with the broader literature on minimal group effects, whereby mere categorization evokes an ingroup preference but not necessarily competition or dominance hierarchies (Mummendey & Otten, 1998). Although past research has shown that people rely on appearance-related stereotypes when forming impressions (Deaux & Lewis, 1984; Kessler & McKenna, 1978; McArthur & Baron, 1983) and that information about a group member's behavior can trigger assumptions about appearance (Dotsch, Wigboldus, & van Knippenberg, 2013), this study is the first to suggest that even seemingly inconsequential group memberships can evoke facial representations that facilitate more favorable impressions of ingroup than outgroup members.

The use of a reverse correlation task was a particularly notable feature of the study because mental representations of faces are difficult to assess with traditional behavioral techniques. Because the reverse correlation approach, used in Part 1, allows all the features of the representation to vary freely and thus does not make strong assumptions a priori about the informational content of the face, it is able to generate estimates of participants' facial representations unbiased by the experimenters' preconceptions. Thus, reverse correlation methodology allowed us to create purely data-driven visualizations of ingroup and outgroup face representations. In Part 2, we then objectively ascertained the impressions elicited by ingroup and outgroup facial representations by asking a naive sample to rate the faces on traits that are highly relevant to face-based evaluations (Oosterhof & Todorov, 2008). It was important that we separated the image generation process from the impression formation stage, because without doing so it would have been difficult to mechanistically show that the facial representations can directly contribute to trait inferences.

Ingroup   **Outgroup**

Figure 2. Group-level ingroup and outgroup classification images from Study 1.

---

[1] The ingroup image was averaged across 44 overestimator and 42 underestimator participant-level classification images. The outgroup image was averaged across 42 overestimator and 48 underestimator images.

Table 1
Means and Paired t-Test Results for the Study 1 Trait Ratings

Trait	Ingroup mean [95% CI]	Outgroup mean [95% CI]	t	p
Attractive	**4.85 [4.57, 5.13]**	3.73 [3.42, 4.05]	6.17	**<.001**
Intelligent	**4.96 [4.70, 5.18]**	4.19 [3.93, 4.46]	5.17	**<.001**
Responsible	**4.69 [4.42, 4.96]**	3.92 [3.67, 4.19]	4.65	**<.001**
Confident	**4.78 [4.54, 5.03]**	4.09 [3.81, 4.37]	4.17	**<.001**
Trustworthy	**4.73 [4.48, 4.99]**	3.96 [3.68, 4.24]	3.89	**<.001**
Caring	**4.50 [4.23, 4.76]**	3.91 [3.64, 4.18]	3.44	**.001**
Emotionally stable	**4.58 [4.33, 4.84]**	4.12 [3.87, 4.37]	2.59	**.01**
Sociable	**4.53 [4.28, 4.79]**	4.15 [3.88, 4.42]	2.16	**.03**
Mean	4.32 [4.02, 4.61]	4.06 [3.77, 4.36]	1.35	.18
Dominant	4.26 [3.97, 4.55]	4.08 [3.78, 4.38]	0.95	.34
Aggressive	3.87 [3.55, 4.15]	4.03 [3.72, 4.34]	−0.80	.43
Unhappy	4.00 [3.67, 4.33]	4.29 [3.96, 4.60]	−1.40	.17
Weird	**3.86 [3.31, 3.86]**	3.96 [3.68, 4.24]	−2.33	**.02**

Note. Items are ordered from the largest positive *t* value to the most negative. Negative *t* values indicate that the means were greater for the outgroup than the ingroup. Bold type indicates items with significant effects. CI = confidence interval.

Although the reverse correlation approach provided a powerful method for probing the role of facial representations in the minimal group effect, some limitations of this approach should be considered. First, it is unclear whether this representational process occurs spontaneously and in all situations. In all likelihood, there are many situations in which visual representations are not generated or in which group-based preferences are not driven by such representations. Thus, the visual biases identified in Study 1 may represent one of multiple processes that may contribute to minimal group effects. Additionally, it is possible that participants in Part 1 of Study 1 spontaneously generated trait inferences and attitudes that influenced their mental representations of the minimal groups, suggesting a more dynamic interplay of impressions and visual representations. Nevertheless, our experiments showed that once these facial representations are formed, the differences in these representations are themselves sufficient to evoke intergroup bias in trait impressions.

Another potential limitation concerns the effect of the visual clarity of the images produced by the reverse correlation method. For example, it is possible that differences in the clarity of the ingroup and outgroup images contributed to the observed effects, beyond structural differences between these facial images. However, such an effect is difficult to discern from our data because the images used in this study were aggregated across participants. The clarity of the aggregated images could result from different across-group variability for ingroup and outgroup faces. It is additionally possible that image normalization of the noise influenced the pixel intensities across participants in a nonlinear manner complicating the interpretation of clarity differences in the images. Nonetheless, Study 1 served as an initial proof-of-principle that mere group categorization can distort mental representations of faces in a manner that leads to more favorable impressions of ingroup than outgroup members.

Study 2

Study 1 provided preliminary evidence that mental representations of faces elicited by minimally defined ingroup and outgroup members can vary and lead to trait impressions that favor the ingroup. The ingroup favoritism evident in these trait ratings suggests that differences in mental representations, based on minimal group membership, could also contribute to prejudiced attitudes (i.e., evaluative positions or associations that are not tied to a particular trait attribute; Amodio & Devine, 2006; Allport, 1954). Therefore, in Study 2, we tested whether the face representations computed in Study 1 on the basis of mere group assignment also elicit ingroup favoritism in attitudes. The strategy of Study 2 was similar to that of Study 1, except that instead of asking an independent sample to explicitly rate the face images on trait dimensions, we recruited an independent sample to complete an implicit measure of attitudes toward the ingroup and outgroup images generated in Part 1 of Study 1.

Additionally, instead of presenting participants with the aggregate ingroup and outgroup classification images, as in Study 1, we used individual participant-level classification images as stimuli in Study 2. Use of the participant-level images allowed for repeated measurements of attitudes associated with the ingroup and outgroup representations, which increased the likelihood that the attitude measure would provide stable effects. The use of participant-level images also precluded potential effects of face variability, which could affect clarity in group-level images, thereby addressing a potential limitation of Study 1.

Finally, given that social attitudes may be expressed without conscious deliberation (Devine, 1989; Dovidio, Evans, & Tyler, 1986; Fazio, Jackson, Dunton, & Williams, 1995), use of a measure that implicitly assesses attitudes provided an opportunity to test whether the minimal group effects on face representations can elicit pro-ingroup attitudes at an implicit level of processing.

Method

Participants. One hundred and one undergraduates from New York University participated in exchange for course credit and were run simultaneously in individual cubicles in groups of up to four participants.

Procedure and materials. After providing consent, participants completed an *Affect Misattribution Procedure* (AMP; Payne, Cheng, Govorun, & Stewart, 2005), an implicit measure of attitudes. Past work has validated the AMP's ability to implicitly assess evaluative associations, including those related to racial prejudice, addiction cravings, political ideology, and evocative images (Payne et al., 2005; Payne, McClernon, & Dobbins, 2007). The logic of the AMP is that if people are asked to judge an ambiguous target, their evaluation of this target will be biased by the attitudinal information associated with an image that directly preceded that target.

Before they began the AMP, participants were told that the purpose of the study was to measure their responses under distracting conditions and that, on each trial, two images would appear in sequence. The first image would be a grayscale picture and the second image would be a Chinese character. Participants were instructed to do nothing in response to the first image but to respond to the Chinese character by guessing how pleasant or unpleasant the symbol appeared on a scale of 1 to 4 (with 4 being very pleasant). Participants were also told that they should not let the first picture influence their judgment of the symbol. They then completed three practice trials, followed by 176 experimental trials, which used each ingroup and outgroup face image generated by the participants from Part 1 of Study 1 as primes. Trial order was determined randomly according to the DirectRT stimulus presentation software. Additionally, the Chinese characters were randomly chosen on each trial from a set of 200 characters that was downloaded from http://www.unc.edu/~bkpayne/materials.html.

Each trial began with a face (ingroup or outgroup) presented for 75 ms, followed by a blank screen for 125 ms, and then a Chinese character for 100 ms. The character was replaced with a mask consisting of grayscale visual noise, which remained onscreen until a response was registered (following Payne et al., 2005). At the conclusion of the AMP, participants were carefully debriefed. As part of this debriefing, participants indicated whether they could read Chinese characters. Eight participants reported being able to read these characters; their data were excluded from analysis, leaving data from 93 participants.

Results

We predicted that if faces representing minimal ingroup members trigger more favorable attitudes than those representing outgroup members, Chinese characters should be rated as more pleasant when preceded by an ingroup than an outgroup classification image. To test our prediction, we computed the average pleasantness rating associated with each participant-level classification image. We then conducted a paired t test to examine differences in the pleasantness ratings associated with the ingroup and outgroup images. Consistent with our hypothesis, Chinese characters that followed the ingroup faces ($M = 2.59$, $SD = 0.32$) were rated more positively than those that followed the outgroup faces ($M = 2.56$, $SD = 0.32$), $t(92) = 2.33$, $p = .02$, $d = .09$, 95% CI of difference [0.004, 0.056].[2]

Discussion

In Study 2, we tested whether differences in mental representations of mere ingroup and outgroup members are sufficient to create pro-ingroup attitudes. The results revealed that the visual renderings of ingroup faces did indeed evoke a more positive attitude than those of outgroup faces, suggesting that subtle differences in the way people visualize ingroup and outgroup members may be sufficient to produce prejudices that favor the ingroup. Although the effect of minimal group assignment on attitudes has been shown in much previous research, our findings show that this effect could, at least in part, be mediated through mental representations of faces.

Our findings also revealed that attitudes elicited by ingroup and outgroup face representations operate implicitly, complementing the observation of explicit impression effects in Study 1. This result is in line with previous research demonstrating that positive ingroup attitudes following mere group categorization can occur implicitly (Ashburn-Nardo et al., 2001; Otten & Wentura, 1999; Van Bavel & Cunningham, 2009). Furthermore, this finding is consistent with evidence that brief, even nonconscious, presentations of faces can elicit neural responses indicative of affect (de Gelder, Vroomen, Pourtois, & Weiskrantz, 1999; Morris, de Gelder, Weiskrantz, & Dolan, 2001; Whalen et al., 1998; see also Amodio, Harmon-Jones, & Devine, 2003).

From a methodological standpoint, it is notable that the results of Study 2 reflected responses to the participant-level images, as opposed to the two group-level images used in Study 1. This finding addresses the concern regarding variability effects on group-level aggregate images and provides converging evidence for the validity of the procedure (as in Dotsch et al., 2008). Furthermore, it is notable that the standard deviations of the AMP responses to ingroup and outgroup participant-level images were close to equivalent. Therefore, it is unlikely that differential variability between the ingroup and outgroup images could explain the observed difference in attitudes.

Study 3

Having demonstrated that mere group membership alters mental representations of ingroup and outgroup faces in a way that elicits differential trait impressions and attitudes, we aimed in Study 3 to assess the degree to which mental representations of ingroup and outgroup members can influence behavior. Here, we focused on trust behavior, because trust is a central dimension for evaluating faces (Oosterhof & Todorov, 2008) and a critical facilitator of harmonious interactions among ingroup members (Foddy, Platow, & Yamagishi, 2009; Kramer, 1999; Tanis & Postmes, 2005). To assess the degree to which trust is evoked by ingroup facial representations, in comparison with outgroup representations, we conducted a study in which participants completed an economic trust game with interaction partners represented by the ingroup and outgroup classification images from Study 1 (Berg, Dickhaut, & McCabe, 1995). As in Study 2, participants responded to the participant-level classification images.

Method

Participants. Eighty-one undergraduates from New York University completed the study in exchange for course credit. Up to four participants were run simultaneously in separate cubicles.
Procedure.
Trust game. After providing informed consent, participants completed a hypothetical trust game with people depicted by the ingroup and outgroup face classification images. Participants were instructed to imagine that they were given $10 on each trial, and that they could choose either to keep this money or to take the chance to increase their share by engaging in a hypothetical economic interaction with individuals who purportedly provided responses in an earlier session. On each interaction trial, participants were given the choice to share a portion of $10 (i.e., $0, $2, $4, $6, $8, or $10). Any money they shared would be quadrupled and given to the interaction partner. The partner would then have the option to return half of the sum to the participant who had

---

[2] We reported the results for a paired t test collapsing across the numerical estimation style dimension because we were interested in group differences. However, because our analyses for this study used the participant-level images, and we thus had information about the group and numerical estimation style for each image, we were also able to conduct a 2 (group: ingroup vs. outgroup) × 2 (numerical estimation style: overestimator vs. underestimator) repeated measures analysis of variance (ANOVA). Consistent with the results of our paired t test, this analysis produced a main effect of group, such that, irrespective of numerical estimation style, Chinese characters that followed the ingroup faces ($M = 2.59$, $SD = 0.32$) were rated more positively than those that followed the outgroup faces ($M = 2.56$, $SD = 0.32$), $F(1, 92) = 5.33$, $p = .02$, $\eta_p^2 = .06$. There were no numerical estimation style or interaction effects ($ps < .31$).

shared the money. In this way, it would be possible for the participant to make more money than if he or she had not shared. Hence, the amount of money shared indicates the degree to which the participants trusted the interaction partners.

Participants played the trust game with 176 different partners, represented only by a photograph. In actuality, these photographs were the participant-level classification images of the ingroup and outgroup faces, presented in a random order across trials. Participants were told that each partner's face was blurred to protect his or her identity.

Results

We predicted that participants would entrust more money to individuals depicted by the ingroup classification images than to those depicted by the outgroup classification images. As a test of this, the average amount entrusted to ingroup faces and outgroup faces was computed for each participant and submitted to a paired t test. This analysis indicated that ingroup face depictions ($M = \$3.01$, $SD = 1.62$) were trusted significantly more than outgroup face depictions ($M = \$2.77$, $SD = 1.62$), $t(80) = 6.64$, $p < .001$, $d = .15$, 95% CI of difference [0.17, 0.30].[3]

Discussion

In Study 3, we tested the hypothesis that representations of ingroup and outgroup faces formed on the basis of a minimal group distinction could elicit different patterns of behavior, in the form of trust decisions in an economic game. We found that participants acted in a more trusting manner toward faces reflecting mental representations of ingroup members, as compared with outgroup members, evidencing a pattern of ingroup favoritism in behavior. As in Study 2, the variance in responses to participant-level ingroup and outgroup faces did not differ, further suggesting that the effects were not driven by differential variability in representations of ingroup and outgroup faces. Thus, this study suggests that subtle biases in the way an individual mentally represents the face of an ingroup or outgroup member could result in a difference in trust decisions.

The results of Study 3 add to previous research on trust behavior under minimal group conditions by extracting the effect of minimal group assignment on facial representations and then showing that this information alone can cause differences in trust behavior. In past research (Foddy et al., 2009; Platow, Foddy, Yamagishi, Lim, & Chow, 2012), minimal group effects were examined in the absence of group-specific facial information. Given that ingroup favoritism, especially in zero-sum situations, can result in disadvantaging outgroup members, this work suggests a novel pathway through which group-based facial representations can contribute to prejudice, discrimination, and intergroup conflict.

It is important to mention that our conclusions are drawn from trust behavior during hypothetical transactions, in the sense that participants could not actually earn money during the game. Differences between hypothetical and real scenarios tend to occur because people risk more money and exhibit self-presentation concerns more strongly during hypothetical situations (Ajzen, Brown, & Carvajal, 2004). Although we cannot conclusively rule out the possibility that participants' behavior would have differed if real money had been exchanged, we believe it is unlikely. First, our procedure should have precluded any self-presentation concerns related to ingroup and outgroup membership, given that participants were unaware of the group-based origins of the face images. Second, although it is possible that participants would have risked less money in their decisions if the money had been real, our interest was in the relative difference in money entrusted to ingroup and outgroup representations rather than the mean amount.

Study 4

The aim in Study 4 was to examine, more directly, how facial cues signaling trust contribute to the observed effects of group membership. Because the reverse correlation procedure used to render the images in Study 1 allows for unconstrained representations of facial features, it is sensitive to the many possible ways in which group membership could be instantiated in the physiognomy of a face. For instance, it is possible that trust was conveyed primarily in the eyes or by the shape of the mouth (Schul, Mayo, & Burnstein, 2004; Zebrowitz, 1997). Thus, our goal was to objectively test the correspondence between ingroup (vs. outgroup) face representations and an independently produced representation of a trustworthy face. Insight into this physiognomic correspondence would clarify the mechanism underlying the results of Studies 1–3.

A second, related goal was to examine the extent to which the resemblance between trust and ingroup representations is distributed across the face. This analysis would shed light on whether the ingroup favoritism effects observed thus far are due to specific or gestalt differences between the ingroup and outgroup face representations.

To address these goals in Study 4, we recruited a new sample of participants to complete a face categorization task. Although similar to that used in Study 1, it pertained to whether a face appears trustworthy. The reverse correlation analysis method was then used to produce visual renderings of participants' mental images of a trustworthy face. Because people have a relatively strong notion of what a trustworthy face looks like (Dotsch & Todorov, 2012), a smaller sample was needed to generate a clear estimate of

---

[3] As with Study 2, the analyses for Study 3 used the participant-level images. Therefore, we were also able to conduct a 2 (group: ingroup vs. outgroup) × 2 (numerical estimation style: overestimator vs. underestimator) repeated measures ANOVA. In line with the results from the paired t test, this analysis produced a significant main effect for group, such that ingroup face depictions ($M = 3.01$, $SD = 1.62$) were trusted significantly more than outgroup face depictions ($M = 2.77$, $SD = 1.62$), $F(1, 80) = 44.02$, $p < .001$, $\eta_p^2 = .36$. Of interest, and unexpectedly, a significant main effect also emerged for numerical estimation style, indicating that overestimators ($M = 3.01$, $SD = 1.61$) were generally trusted significantly more than underestimators ($M = 2.76$, $SD = 1.63$), $F(1, 80) = 37.28$, $p < .001$, $\eta_p^2 = .32$. These main effects were qualified by a significant interaction, $F(1, 80) = 10.46$, $p < .01$, $\eta_p^2 = .12$, which revealed that the group effect was larger in response to faces representing underestimators ($M = .33$, $SD = .40$) than to faces representing overestimators ($M = .11$, $SD = .46$), $t(80) = 3.24$, $p = .002$, $d = .51$. It is notable, however, that the ingroup was trusted significantly more than the outgroup for both the overestimators, $t(80) = 2.14$, $p = .04$, $d = .07$, and the underestimators, $t(80) = 7.56$, $p < .001$, $d = .20$. Thus, our hypothesis about the effect of group membership was supported independently of the effect observed for the numerical estimation style factor.

physiognomic information associated with trust. We then compared the resulting classification image of a *trustworthy* face (collapsed across subjects) to the group-level classification images from Study 1 that were used to estimate ingroup and outgroup face representations.

Method

Participants. Fourteen undergraduates from New York University participated in exchange for extra course credit and completed the study in private cubicles, in groups of one to four participants at a time.

Procedure. The procedure and stimuli were identical to those in Study 1, except that there was no group assignment and, thus, no minimal group paradigm was used. Instead, during the face categorization task, participants were instructed to choose the face from each trial pair *that looks the most trustworthy.* As was predicted, a visual inspection of the aggregate trust classification image (see Figure 3A) indicated that a sample size of 14 participants was sufficient to generate a clear estimate of participants' mental image of a trustworthy face. This image closely resembled the trustworthy face classification image generated by Dotsch and Todorov (2012).

Data reduction. Participant-level classification images were first created by averaging the 450 faces selected as appearing trustworthy for each participant. A composite mental representation of a trustworthy face was then created by aggregating these participant-level classification images. The classification image depicting the trust representation is presented alongside the Study 1 ingroup and outgroup group-level images in Figure 3A.

To quantitatively test similarities between the trust- and group-based representations, we correlated the patterns of pixel intensities that composed these classification images. Before calculating the correlations, we removed the base face from all the images, leaving only pixel patterns representing the variation due to participants' mental images, as inclusion of the base face would have artificially inflated observed correlations between the images. Regions of the image outside the face, including the hair, were masked and excluded from analysis (see Figure 3B to see the masked noise patterns). Finally, for each image, the intensity values of the remaining 89,177 pixels were converted into a single vector and correlated with the other two vectors.

Results

Correlations between the trust and ingroup/outgroup images. We hypothesized that the pixel intensities of the trust classification image would be more highly correlated with the ingroup than the outgroup classification image, indicating a greater correspondence between the facial representations of trustworthiness and the ingroup face, as compared with the outgroup face. Supporting our prediction, the vectors representing pixel intensities for the ingroup and trust classification images were significantly correlated ($r = .46$, $p < .001$). The outgroup and trust classification images were also significantly correlated ($r = .23$, $p < .001$), but the magnitude of this correlation was significantly lower than that of the trust–ingroup correlation ($z = 55.56$, $p < .001$). This test confirmed that the resemblance of the ingroup and trust classification images was significantly greater than that of the outgroup and trust classifications.

Given the large sample size (i.e., number of pixels), the significance of the p value is not as notable as the fact that the ingroup classification image accounted for over four times as much variance in the trust classification image as did the outgroup classification image ($r^2 = .21$, 95% CI [0.205, 0.215] vs. $r^2 = .05$, 95% CI [0.047, 0.052]). Moreover, if partial correlations are considered to adjust for shared variance between the ingroup and outgroup images, the variance accounted for in the trust image is nine times as large for the ingroup image ($r^2 = .18$) as it is for the outgroup image ($r^2 = .02$). These results objectively demonstrate that the facial information associated with people's representation of an ingroup member overlaps more with a mental representation of a trust face than does their representation of an outgroup member.

Region of interest analyses. To assess whether the differences in the correspondences between the ingroup and outgroup faces with the trustworthy face representation were localized or distributed across the face, we conducted the same partial correlation analyses on pixels representing noise patterns within regions of interest (ROIs) covering the eye region, nose, and mouth (see Figure 4). The results from these analyses are summarized in Table 2. Of importance, for each of the regions of interest, the similarity between the trust classification image and the ingroup classification image was significantly larger than the trust classification image and the outgroup classification image. Consistent with research demonstrating that the eyes are especially important for trust judgments (Schul et al., 2004; Zebrowitz, 1997), the differences in correlations for the ingroup and outgroup were largest for the eye region, followed by the nose, and then the mouth.

Discussion

Study 4 examined the hypothesis that differences in facial representations of minimal ingroup and outgroup members could be attributed, at least in part, to the ascription of features associated with trustworthiness to the ingroup face. By comparing patterns in the pixel intensities of the ingroup and outgroup classification images to those of the trust classification image produced by an independent sample, this study provided an especially stringent and objective test of this hypothesis. These results support our

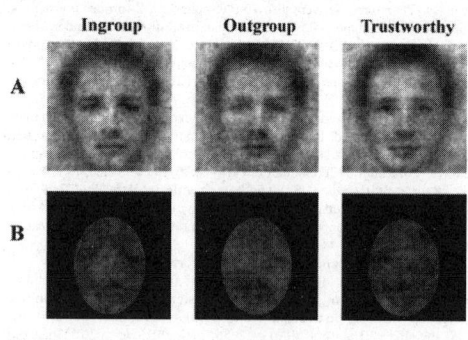

Figure 3. (A) Ingroup, outgroup, and trustworthy classification images. (B) Masked classification images with the base face removed used during the Study 4 analyses.

Eye region   Nose   Mouth

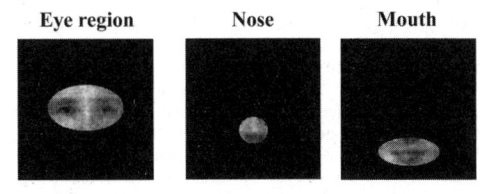

Figure 4. Masks used to conduct the Study 4 region of interest analyses, shown on the trust classification image. The number of pixels in each region of interest were 36,994 (eye region), 8,269 (nose), and 18,251 (mouth).

theoretical proposal that shared group membership can bias mental representations of faces toward a facial geometry that communicates affiliative signals, which would elicit more favorable impressions, attitudes, and behaviors from perceivers.

It is also noteworthy that the ingroup face representation was positively correlated with the trustworthy face presentation, but the outgroup face representation was not negatively correlated with the trustworthy representation. This is consistent with the existing minimal group literature, which has shown that merely separating people into groups increases ingroup favoritism but does not elicit outgroup derogation (Mummendey & Otten, 1998).

Finally, in Study 4, we also examined the ingroup favoritism effect in three regions of the face (the eyes, nose, and mouth). In all three regions, the trust image was correlated more highly with the ingroup image than the outgroup image. This finding suggests that the ingroup bias in mental representations is distributed across multiple regions of the face or, at the very least, is represented in different regions by different participants. Although trust information was communicated in multiple regions of the ingroup face, the effects were strongest for the eyes. This result is consistent with a growing body of research that suggests that the eyes are attended to when making decisions related to trust, possibly because they are assumed to act as a window into the unobservable mind (Schul et al., 2004; Zebrowitz, 1997).

General Discussion

Over four decades of research has demonstrated that mere group categorization alone is sufficient to cause discriminatory behavior. Simply assigning a person to an arbitrarily defined group produces behavioral and evaluative preferences for the ingroup over the outgroup (e.g., Ashburn-Nardo et al., 2001; Brewer & Silver, 1978; Locksley et al., 1980; Otten & Wentura, 1999; Tajfel et al., 1971; Van Bavel & Cunningham, 2009). In the past several years, numerous studies have investigated how sharing a group identity with others can influence the processing of and memory for their faces. Although this work has revealed that ingroup faces are processed more deeply and accurately than outgroup faces (Bernstein et al., 2007; Hugenberg & Corneille, 2009; Ratner & Amodio, 2013; Van Bavel et al., 2008, 2011; Young & Hugenberg, 2010), the present research investigated a different mechanism through which mere group categorization can influence face processing. That is, we proposed that mere group assignment can distort mental representations of faces in a way that leads to more favorable responses to ingroup than to outgroup members.

This hypothesis was examined across four studies. In Study 1, we showed that membership in a minimally defined group was sufficient to produce differences in the facial representations of ingroup and outgroup members and that, when shown to naive participants, a representation of an ingroup face elicited more favorable trait impressions than a representation of an outgroup face. The ingroup facial representation was judged to be more trustworthy, attractive, caring, sociable, emotionally stable, intelligent, responsible, and confident than the outgroup face representation: a pattern of ingroup traits signifying group fitness and affiliative tendencies. Furthermore, we found that ingroup face representations elicited more positive implicitly measured attitudes (Study 2) and trusting behavior (Study 3) than did outgroup face representations. Finally, Study 4 demonstrated that participants' representation of facial trustworthiness more closely resembled the information contained within an ingroup face representation than an outgroup face representation. Together, these results suggest that people form subtly different mental images of ingroup and outgroup members that can contribute to significant differences in trait impressions, attitudes, and behaviors and that the difference in mental images can be driven, in part, by the ascription of trust-related features to the ingroup face.

Inferring a Causal Influence of Facial Representations on Intergroup Responses

The overarching objective of our work was to study the effects of mere group categorization on facial representations as a means to understand how group memberships can lead to intergroup bias. Although several mechanisms likely contribute to the effect of minimal group assignment on intergroup bias, we examined internal representations of facial information as one causal pathway (cf. Bullock, Green, & Ha, 2010; Green, Ha, & Bullock, 2010). In order to provide inferential traction when multiple mechanisms might exist, methodologists have encouraged experimentally testing each step in a predicted causal path (Spencer et al., 2005). In line with this recommendation, we first manipulated the effect of mere group categorization on facial representations (Study 1, Part 1) and then independently assessed the effect of the resultant facial representations on trait impressions (Study 1, Part 2), attitudes (Study 2), and behavior (Study 3). This approach was built upon the already well-established "direct path" between minimal group induction and ingroup favoritism (e.g., Ashburn-Nardo et al., 2001; Brewer & Silver, 1978; Van Bavel & Cunningham, 2009). The use of this design suggests that facial representations can

Table 2
Study 4 Partial Correlations Between Trust and Ingroup/Outgroup Classification Images as a Function of Face Region

	Trust		
Group	Eyes	Nose	Mouth
Ingroup	0.48	0.55	0.47
Outgroup	−0.09	0.15	0.31

Note. All the correlation coefficients were significant ($p < .001$). Within each region, the two correlation coefficients were different from each other ($p < .001$).

contribute to minimal group effects on attitudes, inferences, and trust decisions.

To be clear, our results suggest that biased facial representations can operate as a mechanism leading to intergroup bias, but, like other mediation-based approaches, they do not rule out a role for other mechanisms at any stage of the process. For instance, our work does not preclude the possibility that participants in Part 1 of Study 1 explicitly generated trait inferences as a means to develop mental representations of the minimal groups. It is also possible that clarity differences in the mental images of ingroup and outgroup members contributed to downstream favoritism effects, although the results of Studies 2 and 3 suggest that this is unlikely to be the case. Some people might also use their self-image or prototypical features of other groups they belong to as a basis for discerning their image of a minimally defined ingroup member (see Gramzow, Gaertner, & Sedikides, 2001; Imhoff & Dotsch, 2013, for research consistent with these possibilities). Further research will be required to fully illuminate the range of facial representation mechanisms that contribute to the effects of minimal group distinctions.

Implications for Mental Simulations Involving Ingroup and Outgroup Members

Our research suggests that facial representations associated with ingroup favoritism may influence social relations. One way this may occur is by guiding mental simulation. Mental simulation refers to people's ability to transcend the here and now by role-playing past and future experiences (Schacter, Addis, & Buckner, 2007; Tulving, 1983). Functionally, mental simulation allows people to plan for and feel emotions associated with scenarios that they are not currently experiencing (Marks, 1999; Taylor, Pham, Rivkin, & Armor, 1998).

An implication for intergroup interactions is that mental representations of an ingroup face could result in self-fulfilling prophesies (Chen & Bargh, 1997; Darley & Fazio, 1980; Merton, 1948). For instance, when anticipating an interaction with an ingroup member, expectations that the target person will look trustworthy, responsible, and sociable could contribute to approach-related attitudes and cooperative behaviors during the interaction, which in turn could increase the likelihood that the ingroup member develops warm attitudes toward the perceiver and reciprocates affiliative behavior. Similar mental simulation effects could also emerge when people are interacting with an ingroup member over e-mail or in other situations that do not provide access to appearance information about the target individual. These self-reinforcing processes could perpetuate good will that promotes positive ingroup relations. Given that outgroup representations elicit less favorable impressions than ingroup representations, outgroup members may be less likely to receive the benefit of the doubt than ingroup members. This would put outgroup members at a further disadvantage.

Implications for Intergroup Face Perception and Self-Regulation

In most research on minimal group effects on face processing, the guiding assumption is that the ingroup is more motivationally relevant, which leads to deeper and more accurate processing of ingroup faces and relatively superficial processing of outgroup faces (Hugenberg & Corneille, 2009; Ratner & Amodio, 2013; Van Bavel et al., 2008, 2011; Young & Hugenberg, 2010). This work has been particularly useful for demonstrating the generality of the *other race effect* (i.e., the finding that same-race faces are remembered better than other-race faces; Malpass & Kravitz, 1969). However, as we have mentioned, in minimal group work outside of the domain of face processing, researchers have suggested that ingroup biases are driven by enhanced positivity toward the ingroup (e.g., Ashburn-Nardo et al., 2001; Brewer & Silver, 1978). Motivated in part by this apparent disconnect in literatures, the current work examined whether people see ingroup members through "rose-colored glasses" and whether these distortions in facial representations contribute to biased intergroup impressions, evaluations, and behaviors. In this way, the perceptual biases promoted by these mental representations provide a mechanism for facilitating one's goal to favor ingroup members (i.e., an example of how motivated perception serves self-regulation; Amodio, 2010).

Our findings also raise the possibility that internally generated representations of ingroup and outgroup faces influence bottom-up processes through which faces are attended to and perceived. Predictive coding theories state that expectations can guide the acquisition of visual information (Friston, 2005; Mumford, 1992; Summerfield et al., 2006). From this perspective, it is possible that if people expect an ingroup member to have certain facial characteristics but the person's appearance diverges from this prediction, this discordant information would receive more processing. As such, formal models could be developed that use visual renderings of ingroup and outgroup face representations as Bayesian priors for predicting the duration and location of endogenous attention and eye saccades allocated to processing attributes of a particular face. This type of an analysis could advance theories of how mere group knowledge biases the perceptual information that reaches the retina and is subsequently encoded in the visual cortex. Moreover, such work may lead to the development of strategies that protect against this type of bias by changing the predictive visual codes that people use to disambiguate facial information of group members.

Conclusion

Although the role of appearance cues in group-based processes had been emphasized in seminal theoretical articles (e.g., Brewer, 1988; Carlston, 1992; McArthur & Baron, 1983), until recently, the bulk of social cognition research overlooked the contributions of facial information (Macrae & Bodenhausen, 2006; Zebrowitz, 2006). Our studies contribute to the recent movement to reintegrate research on visual face processing into the social psychological understanding of intergroup responses (e.g., Dotsch et al., 2008; Hugenberg & Corneille, 2009; Ito & Urland, 2005; Kaul, Ratner, & Van Bavel, 2014; Ofan, Rubin, & Amodio, 2011, in press; Ratner & Amodio, 2013; Ratner, Kaul, & Van Bavel, 2013; Van Bavel et al., 2011).

In this spirit, our work provides evidence that mere group categorization can lead to ingroup favoritism through effects on mental representations of faces. Whereas past research had shown that simply separating people into novel groups triggers biases that favor ingroup members, it had not been previously established that representations of faces could contribute to this phenomenon. Given that facial representations are utilized to make sense of other people, this research provides insight into a previously underexplored route through which group-based biases can influence society.

References

Ahumada, A. J. (2002). Classification image weights and internal noise level estimation. *Journal of Vision, 2,* 121–131. doi:10.1167/2.1.8

Ahumada, A., & Lovell, J. (1971). Stimulus features in signal detection. *Journal of the Acoustical Society of America, 49,* 1751–1756. doi:10.1121/1.1912577

Ajzen, I., Brown, T. C., & Carvajal, F. (2004). Explaining the discrepancy between intentions and actions: The case of hypothetical bias in contingent valuation. *Personality and Social Psychology Bulletin, 30,* 1108–1121. doi:10.1177/0146167204264079

Allport, G. W. (1954). *The nature of prejudice.* Reading, MA: Addison-Wesley.

Amodio, D. M. (2010). Coordinated roles of motivation and perception in the regulation of intergroup responses: Frontal cortical asymmetry effects on the P2 event-related potential and behavior. *Journal of Cognitive Neuroscience, 22,* 2609–2617. doi:10.1162/jocn.2009.21395

Amodio, D. M., & Devine, P. G. (2006). Stereotyping and evaluation in implicit race bias: Evidence for independent constructs and unique effects on behavior. *Journal of Personality and Social Psychology, 91,* 652–661. doi:10.1037/0022-3514.91.4.652

Amodio, D. M., Harmon-Jones, E., & Devine, P. G. (2003). Individual differences in the activation and control of affective race bias as assessed by startle eyeblink responses and self-report. *Journal of Personality and Social Psychology, 84,* 738–753. doi:10.1037/0022-3514.84.4.738

Andersen, S. M., & Klatzky, R. L. (1987). Traits and social stereotypes: Levels of categorization in person perception. *Journal of Personality and Social Psychology, 53,* 235–246. doi:10.1037/0022-3514.53.2.235

Ashburn-Nardo, L., Voils, C. I., & Monteith, M. J. (2001). Implicit associations as the seeds of intergroup bias: How easily do they take root? *Journal of Personality and Social Psychology, 81,* 789–799. doi:10.1037/0022-3514.81.5.789

Beaupré, M. G., & Hess, U. (2003). In my mind, my friend smiles: A case of in-group favoritism. *Journal of Experimental Social Psychology, 39,* 371–377. doi:10.1016/S0022-1031(03)00012-X

Bentin, S., Allison, T., Puce, A., Perez, E., & McCarthy, G. (1996). Electrophysiological studies of face perception in humans. *Journal of Cognitive Neuroscience, 8,* 551–565. doi:10.1162/jocn.1996.8.6.551

Berg, J., Dickhaut, J., & McCabe, K. (1995). Trust, reciprocity, and social history. *Games and Economic Behavior, 10,* 122–142. doi:10.1006/game.1995.1027

Bernstein, M. J., Young, S. G., & Hugenberg, K. (2007). The cross-category effect: Mere social categorization is sufficient to elicit an own-group bias in face recognition. *Psychological Science, 18,* 706–712. doi:10.1111/j.1467-9280.2007.01964.x

Birmingham, E., Bischof, W. F., & Kingstone, A. (2009a). Get real! Resolving the debate about equivalent social stimuli. *Visual Cognition, 17,* 904–924. doi:10.1080/13506280902758044

Birmingham, E., Bischof, W. F., & Kingstone, A. (2009b). Saliency does not account for fixations to eyes within social scenes. *Vision Research, 49,* 2992–3000. doi:10.1016/j.visres.2009.09.014

Blair, I. V., Judd, C. M., & Chapleau, K. M. (2004). The influence of Afrocentric facial features in criminal sentencing. *Psychological Science, 15,* 674–679. doi:10.1111/j.0956-7976.2004.00739.x

Blair, I. V., Ma, J. E., & Lenton, A. P. (2001). Imagining stereotypes away: The moderation of implicit stereotypes through mental imagery. *Journal of Personality and Social Psychology, 81,* 828–841. doi:10.1037/0022-3514.81.5.828

Bodenhausen, G. V., & Macrae, C. N. (2006). Putting a face on person perception. *Social Cognition, 24,* 511–515.

Brewer, M. B. (1988). A dual process model of impression formation. In T. Srull & R. Wyer (Eds.), *Advances in social cognition* (Vol. 1, pp. 1–36). Hillsdale, NJ: Erlbaum.

Brewer, M. B. (1999). The psychology of prejudice: Ingroup love or outgroup hate? *Journal of Social Issues, 55,* 429–444. doi:10.1111/0022-4537.00126

Brewer, M. B., & Silver, M. (1978). Ingroup bias as a function of task characteristics. *European Journal of Social Psychology, 8,* 393–400. doi:10.1002/ejsp.2420080312

Brown, J. D., Collins, R. L., & Schmidt, G. W. (1988). Self-esteem and direct versus indirect forms of self-enhancement. *Journal of Personality and Social Psychology, 55,* 445–453. doi:10.1037/0022-3514.55.3.445

Buhrmester, M., Kwang, T., & Gosling, S. D. (2011). Amazon's Mechanical Turk: A new source of inexpensive, yet high-quality, data? *Perspectives on Psychological Science, 6,* 3–5. doi:10.1177/1745691610393980

Bullock, J. G., Green, D. P., & Ha, S. E. (2010). Yes, but what's the mechanism? (don't expect an easy answer). *Journal of Personality and Social Psychology, 98,* 550–558. doi:10.1037/a0018933

Carlston, D. E. (1992). Impression formation and the modular mind: The associated systems theory. In L. L. Martin & A. Tesser (Eds.), *The construction of social judgments* (pp. 301–341). Hillsdale, NJ: Erlbaum.

Castano, E., Yzerbyt, V., Bourguignon, D., & Seron, E. (2002). Who may enter? The impact of in-group identification on in-group/out-group categorization. *Journal of Experimental Social Psychology, 38,* 315–322. doi:10.1006/jesp.2001.1512

Chen, M., & Bargh, J. A. (1997). Nonconscious behavioral confirmation processes: The self-fulfilling consequences of automatic stereotype activation. *Journal of Experimental Social Psychology, 33,* 541–560. doi:10.1006/jesp.1997.1329

Crisp, R. J., & Turner, R. N. (2009). Can imagined interactions produce positive perceptions? Reducing prejudice through simulated social contact. *American Psychologist, 64,* 231–240. doi:10.1037/a0014718

Darley, J. M., & Fazio, R. H. (1980). Expectancy confirmation processes arising in the social interaction sequence. *American Psychologist, 35,* 867–881. doi:10.1037/0003-066X.35.10.867

Deaux, K., & Lewis, L. L. (1984). Structure of gender stereotypes: Interrelationships among components and gender label. *Journal of Personality and Social Psychology, 46,* 991–1004. doi:10.1037/0022-3514.46.5.991

de Gelder, B., Vroomen, J., Pourtois, G., & Weiskrantz, L. (1999). Nonconscious recognition of affect in the absence of striate cortex. *NeuroReport, 10,* 3759–3763. doi:10.1097/00001756-199912160-00007

Devine, P. G. (1989). Stereotypes and prejudice: Their automatic and controlled components. *Journal of Personality and Social Psychology, 56,* 5–18. doi:10.1037/0022-3514.56.1.5

Doise, W., Csepeli, G., Dann, H. D., Gouge, C., Larsen, K., & Østell, A. (1972). An experimental investigation into the formation of intergroup representations. *European Journal of Social Psychology, 2,* 202–204. doi:10.1002/ejsp.2420020204

Dotsch, R., & Todorov, A. (2012). Reverse correlating social face perception. *Social Psychological □ Personality Science, 3,* 562–571. doi:10.1177/1948550611430272

Dotsch, R., Wigboldus, D. H. J., Langner, □., & van Knippenberg, A. (2008). Ethnic out-group faces are biased in the prejudiced mind. *Psychological Science, 19,* 978–980. doi:10.1111/j.1467-9280.2008.02186.x

Dotsch, R., Wigboldus, D. H. J., & van Knippenberg, A. (2011). Biased allocation of faces to social categories. *Journal of Personality and Social Psychology, 100,* 999–1014. doi:10.1037/a0023026

Dotsch, R., Wigboldus, D. H. J., & van Knippenberg, A. (2013). Behavioral information biases the expected facial appearance of members of novel groups. *European Journal of Social Psychology, 43,* 116–125. doi:10.1002/ejsp.1928

Dovidio, J. F., Evans, N., & Tyler, R. B. (1986). Racial stereotypes: The contents of their cognitive representations. *Journal of Experimental Social Psychology, 22,* 22–37. doi:10.1016/0022-1031(86)90039-9

Dunham, Y. (2011). An angry = outgroup effect. *Journal of Experimental Social Psychology, 47,* 668–671. doi:10.1016/j.jesp.2011.01.003

Eberhardt, J. L., Davies, P. G., Purdie-Vaughns, V. J., & Johnson, S. L. (2006). Looking deathworthy: Perceived stereotypicality of Black defendants predicts capital-sentencing outcomes. *Psychological Science, 17,* 383–386. doi:10.1111/j.1467-9280.2006.01716.x

Fazio, R. H., Jackson, J. R., Dunton, B. C., & Williams, C. J. (1995). Variability in automatic activation as an unobstrusive measure of racial attitudes: A bona fide pipeline? *Journal of Personality and Social Psychology, 69,* 1013–1027. doi:10.1037/0022-3514.69.6.1013

Foddy, M., Platow, M. J., & Yamagishi, T. (2009). Group-based trust in strangers. *Psychological Science, 20,* 419–422. doi:10.1111/j.1467-9280.2009.02312.x

Friston, K. (2005). A theory of cortical responses. *Philosophical Transactions of the Royal Society B: Biological Sciences, 360,* 815–836. doi:10.1098/rstb.2005.1622

Gerard, H. B., & Hoyt, M. F. (1974). Distinctiveness of social categorization and attitude toward ingroup members. *Journal of Personality and Social Psychology, 29,* 836–842. doi:10.1037/h0036204

Goren, C. C., Sarty, M., & Wu, P. Y. K. (1975). Visual following and pattern discrimination of face-like stimuli by newborn infants. *Pediatrics, 56,* 544–549.

Gosselin, F., & Schyns, P. G. (2003). Superstitious perceptions reveal properties of internal representations. *Psychological Science, 14,* 505–509. doi:10.1111/1467-9280.03452

Gramzow, R. H., Gaertner, L., & Sedikides, C. (2001). Memory for ingroup and outgroup information in a minimal group context: The self as an informational base. *Journal of Personality and Social Psychology, 80,* 188–205. doi:10.1037/0022-3514.80.2.188

Green, D. P., Ha, S. E., & Bullock, J. G. (2010). Enough already about "black box" experiments: Studying mediation is more difficult than most scholars suppose. *Annals of the American Academy of Political and Social Science, 628,* 200–208. doi:10.1177/0002716209351526

Hassin, R., & Trope, Y. (2000). Facing faces: Studies on the cognitive aspects of physiognomy. *Journal of Personality and Social Psychology, 78,* 837–852. doi:10.1037/0022-3514.78.5.837

Haxby, J. V., Hoffman, E. A., & Gobbini, M. I. (2000). The distributed human neural system for face perception. *Trends in Cognitive Sciences, 4,* 223–233. doi:10.1016/S1364-6613(00)01482-0

Hugenberg, K., & Corneille, O. (2009). Holistic processing is tuned for in-group faces. *Cognitive Science, 33,* 1173–1181. doi:10.1111/j.15551-6709.2009.01048.x

Imhoff, R., & Dotsch, R. (2013). Do we look like me or like us? Visual projection as self- or ingroup-projection. *Social Cognition, 31,* 806–816. doi:10.1521/soco.2013.31.6.806

Imhoff, R., Dotsch, R., Bianchi, M., Banse, R., & Wigboldus, D. H. (2011). Facing Europe: Visualizing spontaneous in-group projection. *Psychological Science, 22,* 1583–1590. doi:10.1177/0956797611419675

Ishai, A., Haxby, J. V., & Ungerleider, L. G. (2002). Visual imagery of famous faces: Effects of memory and attention revealed by fMRI. *NeuroImage, 17,* 1729–1741. doi:10.1006/nimg.2002.1330

Ito, T. A., & Urland, G. R. (2005). The influence of processing objectives on the perception of faces: An ERP study of race and gender perception. *Cognitive, Affective, and Behavioral Neuroscience, 5,* 21–36.

Jack, R. E., Caldara, R., & Schyns, P. G. (2012). Internal representations reveal cultural diversity in expectations of facial expressions of emotion. *Journal of Experimental Psychology: General, 141,* 19–25. doi:10.1037/a0023463

Johnson, M. H., & Morton, J. (1991). *Biology and cognitive development: The case of face recognition.* Oxford, England: Blackwell.

Johnson, R. W. (1981). Perceived physical attractiveness of supporters of Canada's political parties: Stereotype or in-group bias? *Canadian Journal of Behavioural Science/Revue canadienne des sciences du comportement, 13,* 320–325. doi:10.1037/h0081203

Kanwisher, N., McDermott, J., & Chun, M. M. (1997). The fusiform face area: A module in human extrastriate cortex specialized for face perception. *Journal of Neuroscience, 17,* 4302–4311.

Karremans, J. C., Dotsch, R., & Corneille, O. (2011). Romantic relationship status biases memory of faces of attractive opposite-sex others: Evidence from a reverse-correlation paradigm. *Cognition, 121,* 422–426. doi:10.1016/j.cognition.2011.07.008

Kaul, C., Ratner, K. G., & Van Bavel, J. J. (2014). Dynamic representations of race: Processing goals shape race encoding in the fusiform gyri. *Social Cognitive and Affective Neuroscience, 9,* 326–332. doi:10.1093/scan/nss138

Kessler, S. J., & McKenna, W. (1978). *Gender: An ethnomethodological approach.* New York, NY: Wiley.

Kramer, R. M. (1999). Trust and distrust in organizations: Emerging perspectives, enduring questions. *Annual Review of Psychology, 50,* 569–598. doi:10.1146/annurev.psych.50.1.569

Krosch, A. R., Berntsen, L., Amodio, D. M., Jost, J. T., & Van Bavel, J. J. (2013). On the ideology of hypodescent: Political conservatism predicts categorization of racially ambiguous faces as Black. *Journal of Experimental Social Psychology, 49,* 1196–1203. doi:10.1016/j.jesp.2013.05.009

Leyens, J., & Yzerbyt, V. Y. (1992). The ingroup overexclusion effect: Impact of valence and confirmation on stereotypical information search. *European Journal of Social Psychology, 22,* 549–569. doi:10.1002/ejsp.2420220604

Livingston, R. W., & Brewer, M. B. (2002). What are we really priming? Cue-based versus category-based processing of facial stimuli. *Journal of Personality and Social Psychology, 82,* 5–18. doi:10.1037/0022-3514.82.1.5

Locksley, A., Ortiz, V., & Hepburn, C. (1980). Social categorization and discriminatory behavior: Extinguishing the minimal intergroup discrimination effect. *Journal of Personality and Social Psychology, 39,* 773–783. doi:10.1037/0022-3514.39.5.773

Lundqvist, D., & Litton, J. E. (1998). *The averaged Karolinska directed emotional faces—AKDEF—CD-ROM.* Stockholm, Sweden: Psychology Section, Karolinska Institutet.

Ma, D. S., & Correll, J. (2011). Target prototypicality moderates racial bias in the decision to shoot. *Journal of Experimental Social Psychology, 47,* 391–396. doi:10.1016/j.jesp.2010.11.002

Macrae, C. N., & Bodenhausen, G. V. (2000). Social cognition: Thinking categorically about others. *Annual Review of Psychology, 51,* 93–120. doi:10.1146/annurev.psych.51.1.93

Macrae, C. N., Quinn, K. A., Mason, M. F., & Quadflieg, S. (2005). Understanding others: The face and person construal. *Journal of Personality and Social Psychology, 89,* 686–695. doi:10.1037/0022-3514.89.5.686

Malpass, R. S., & Kravitz, J. (1969). Recognition for faces of own and other race. *Journal of Personality and Social Psychology, 13,* 330–334. doi:10.1037/h0028434

Mangini, M. C., & Biederman, I. (2004). Making the ineffable explicit: Estimating the information employed for face classifications. *Cognitive Science, 28,* 209–226. doi:10.1207/s15516709cog2802_4

Marks, D. F. (1999). Consciousness, mental imagery and action. *British Journal of Psychology, 90,* 567–585. doi:10.1348/000712699161639

Martin-Malivel, J., Mangini, M. C., Fagot, J., & Biederman, I. (2006). Do humans and baboons use the same information when categorizing human and baboon faces? *Psychological Science, 17,* 599–607. doi:10.1111/j.1467-9280.2006.01751.x

McArthur, L. Z., & Baron, R. M. (1983). Toward an ecological theory of social perception. *Psychological Review, 90,* 215–238. doi:10.1037/0033-295X.90.3.215

Mechelli, A., Price, C. J., Friston, K. J., & Ishai, A. (2004). Where bottom-up meets top-down: Neuronal interactions during perception and imagery. *Cerebral Cortex, 14,* 1256–1265. doi:10.1093/cercor/bhh087

Merton, R. K. (1948). The self-fulfilling prophecy. *Antioch Review, 8,* 193–210. doi:10.2307/4609267

Morris, J. S., de Gelder, B., Weiskrantz, L., & Dolan, R. J. (2001). Differential extrageniculostriate and amygdala responses to presentation of emotional faces in a cortically blind field. *Brain, 124,* 1241–1252. doi:10.1093/brain/124.6.1241

Mumford, D. (1992). On the computational architecture of the neocortex. *Biological Cybernetics, 66,* 241–251. doi:10.1007/BF00198477

Mummendey, A., & Otten, S. (1998). Positive–negative asymmetry in social discrimination. *European Review of Social Psychology, 9,* 107–143. doi:10.1080/14792779843000063

Mussweiler, T., Gabriel, S., & Bodenhausen, G. V. (2000). Shifting social identities as a strategy for deflecting threatening social comparisons. *Journal of Personality and Social Psychology, 79,* 398–409. doi:10.1037/0022-3514.79.3.398

O'Craven, K. M., & Kanwisher, N. (2000). Mental imagery of faces and places activates corresponding stimulus-specific brain regions. *Journal of Cognitive Neuroscience, 12,* 1013–1023. doi:10.1162/08989290051137549

Ofan, R. H., Rubin, N., & Amodio, D. M. (2011). Seeing race: N170 responses to race and their relation to automatic racial attitudes and controlled processing. *Journal of Cognitive Neuroscience, 23,* 3153–3161. doi:10.1162/jocn_a_00014

Ofan, R. H., Rubin, N., & Amodio, D. M. (in press). Situation-based social anxiety enhances the neural processing of faces: Evidence from an intergroup context. *Social Cognitive and Affective Neuroscience.* doi:10.1093/scan/nst087

Oosterhof, N. N., & Todorov, A. (2008). The functional basis of face evaluation. *Proceedings of the National Academy of Sciences, USA, 105,* 11087–11092. doi:10.1073/pnas.0805664105

Otten, S., & Wentura, D. (1999). About the impact of automaticity in the minimal group paradigm: Evidence from affective priming tasks. *European Journal of Social Psychology, 29,* 1049–1071. doi:10.1002/(SICI)1099-0992(199912)29:8<1049::AID-EJSP985>3.0.CO;2-Q

Paolacci, G., Chandler, J., & Ipeirotis, P. G. (2010). Running experiments on Amazon Mechanical Turk. *Judgment and Decision Making, 5,* 411–419.

Payne, B. K., Cheng, C. M., Govorun, O., & Stewart, B. D. (2005). An inkblot for attitudes: Affect misattribution as implicit measurement. *Journal of Personality and Social Psychology, 89,* 277–293. doi:10.1037/0022-3514.89.3.277

Payne, B. K., McClernon, F. J., & Dobbins, I. G. (2007). Automatic affective responses to smoking cues. *Experimental and Clinical Psychopharmacology, 15,* 400–409. doi:10.1037/1064-1297.15.4.400

Platow, M. J., Foddy, M., Yamagishi, T., Lim, L., & Chow, A. (2012). Two experimental tests of trust in in-group strangers: The moderating role of common knowledge of group membership. *European Journal of Social Psychology, 42,* 30–35. doi:10.1002/ejsp.852

Quanty, M. B., Keats, J. A., & Harkins, S. G. (1975). Prejudice and criteria for identification of ethnic photographs. *Journal of Personality and Social Psychology, 32,* 449–454. doi:10.1037/h0077093

Ratner, K. G., & Amodio, D. M. (2013). Seeing "us vs. them": Minimal group effects on the neural encoding of faces. *Journal of Experimental Social Psychology, 49,* 298–301. doi:10.1016/j.jesp.2012.10.017

Ratner, K. G., Kaul, C., & Van Bavel, J. J. (2013). Is race erased? Decoding race from patterns of neural activity when skin color is not diagnostic of group boundaries. *Social Cognitive and Affective Neuroscience, 8,* 750–755. doi:10.1093/scan/nss063

Ringach, D., & Shapley, R. (2004). Reverse correlation in neurophysiology. *Cognitive Science, 28,* 147–166. doi:10.1207/s15516709cog2802_2

Schacter, D. L., Addis, D. R., & Buckner, R. L. (2007). Remembering the past to imagine the future: The prospective brain. *Nature Reviews Neuroscience, 8,* 657–661. doi:10.1038/nrn2213

Schul, Y., Mayo, R., & Burnstein, E. (2004). Encoding under trust and distrust: The spontaneous activation of incongruent cognitions. *Journal of Personality and Social Psychology, 86,* 668–679. doi:10.1037/0022-3514.86.5.668

Solomon, J. A. (2002). Noise reveals visual mechanisms of detection and discrimination. *Journal of Vision, 2,* 105–120. doi:10.1167/2.1.7

Spencer, S. J., Zanna, M. P., & Fong, G. T. (2005). Establishing a causal chain: Why experiments are often more effective than mediational analyses in examining psychological processes. *Journal of Personality and Social Psychology, 89,* 845–851. doi:10.1037/0022-3514.89.6.845

Summerfield, C., Egner, T., Greene, M., Koechlin, E., Mangels, J., & Hirsch, J. (2006, November 24). Predictive codes for forthcoming perception in the frontal cortex. *Science, 314,* 1311–1314. doi:10.1126/science.1132028

Tajfel, H. (1970). Experiments in intergroup discrimination. *Scientific American, 223,* 96–102. doi:10.1038/scientificamerican1170-96

Tajfel, H., Billig, M. G., Bundy, R. P., & Flament, C. (1971). Social categorization and intergroup behaviour. *European Journal of Social Psychology, 1,* 149–178. doi:10.1002/ejsp.2420010202

Tajfel, H., & Turner, J. C. (1986). The social identity theory of inter-group behavior. In S. Worchel & L. W. Austin (Eds.), *Psychology of intergroup relations* (pp. 7–24). Chicago, IL: Nelson-Hall.

Tanis, M., & Postmes, T. (2005). A social identity approach to trust: Interpersonal perception, group membership and trusting behaviour. *European Journal of Social Psychology, 35,* 413–424. doi:10.1002/ejsp.256

Taylor, S. E., Pham, L. B., Rivkin, I. D., & Armor, D. A. (1998). Harnessing the imagination: Mental simulation, self-regulation, and coping. *American Psychologist, 53,* 429–439. doi:10.1037/0003-066X.53.4.429

Todorov, A., Dotsch, R., Wigboldus, D. H. J., & Said, C. P. (2011). Data-driven methods for modeling social perception. *Social and Personality Psychology Compass, 5,* 775–791. doi:10.1111/j.1751-9004.2011.00389.x

Todorov, A., Said, C. P., Engell, A. D., & Oosterhof, N. N. (2008). Understanding evaluation of faces on social dimensions. *Trends in Cognitive Sciences, 12,* 455–460. doi:10.1016/j.tics.2008.10.001

Tulving, E. (1983). *Elements of episodic memory.* New York, NY: Oxford University Press.

Turner, R. N., & Crisp, R. J. (2010). Imagining intergroup contact reduces implicit prejudice. *British Journal of Social Psychology, 49,* 129–142. doi:10.1348/014466609X419901

Turner, R. N., Crisp, R. J., & Lambert, E. (2007). Imagining intergroup contact can improve intergroup attitudes. *Group Processes & Intergroup Relations, 10,* 427–441. doi:10.1177/1368430207081533

Van Bavel, J. J., & Cunningham, W. A. (2009). Self-categorization with a novel mixed-race group moderates automatic social and racial biases. *Personality and Social Psychology Bulletin, 35,* 321–335. doi:10.1177/0146167208327743

Van Bavel, J. J., Packer, D. J., & Cunningham, W. A. (2008). The neural substrates of in-group bias: A functional magnetic resonance imaging investigation. *Psychological Science, 19,* 1131–1139. doi:10.1111/j.1467-9280.2008.02214.x

Van Bavel, J. J., Packer, D. J., & Cunningham, W. A. (2011). Modulation of the fusiform face area following minimal exposure to motivationally relevant faces: Evidence of in-group enhancement (not out-group disregard). *Journal of Cognitive Neuroscience, 23,* 3343–3354. doi:10.1162/jocn_a_00016

Victor, J. D. (2005). Analyzing receptive fields, classification images and functional images: Challenges with opportunities for synergy. *Nature Neuroscience, 8,* 1651–1656. doi:10.1038/nn1607

Whalen, P. J., Rauch, S. L., Etcoff, N. L., McInerney, S. C., Lee, M. B., & Jenike, M. A. (1998). Masked presentations of emotional facial expressions modulate amygdala activity without explicit knowledge. *Journal of Neuroscience, 18,* 411–418.

Young, A. I., Ratner, K. G., & Fazio, R. H. (2014). Political attitudes bias the mental representation of a presidential candidate's face. *Psychological Science, 25,* 503–510. doi:10.1177/0956797613510717

Young, S. G., & Hugenberg, K. (2010). Mere social categorization modulates identification of facial expressions of emotion. *Journal of Personality and Social Psychology, 99,* 964–977. doi:10.1037/a0020400

Zebrowitz, L. A. (1997). *Reading faces: Window to the soul?* Boulder, CO: Westview Press.

Zebrowitz, L. A. (2006). Finally, faces find favor. *Social Cognition, 24,* 657–701. doi:10.1521/soco.2006.24.5.657

Zebrowitz, L. A., & Montepare, J. M. (2008). Social psychological face perception: Why appearance matters. *Social and Personality Psychology Compass, 2,* 1497–1517. doi:10.1111/j.1751-9004.2008.00109.x

Received August 27, 2013
Revision received February 7, 2014
Accepted February 10, 2014 ∎

Members of Underrepresented Groups: Reviewers for Journal Manuscripts Wanted

If you are interested in reviewing manuscripts for APA journals, the APA Publications and Communications Board would like to invite your participation. Manuscript reviewers are vital to the publications process. As a reviewer, you would gain valuable experience in publishing. The P&C Board is particularly interested in encouraging members of underrepresented groups to participate more in this process.

If you are interested in reviewing manuscripts, please write APA Journals at Reviewers@apa.org. Please note the following important points:

- To be selected as a reviewer, you must have published articles in peer-reviewed journals. The experience of publishing provides a reviewer with the basis for preparing a thorough, objective review.

- To be selected, it is critical to be a regular reader of the five to six empirical journals that are most central to the area or journal for which you would like to review. Current knowledge of recently published research provides a reviewer with the knowledge base to evaluate a new submission within the context of existing research.

- To select the appropriate reviewers for each manuscript, the editor needs detailed information. Please include with your letter your vita. In the letter, please identify which APA journal(s) you are interested in, and describe your area of expertise. Be as specific as possible. For example, "social psychology" is not sufficient—you would need to specify "social cognition" or "attitude change" as well.

- Reviewing a manuscript takes time (1–4 hours per manuscript reviewed). If you are selected to review a manuscript, be prepared to invest the necessary time to evaluate the manuscript thoroughly.

APA now has an online video course that provides guidance in reviewing manuscripts. To learn more about the course and to access the video, visit http://www.apa.org/pubs/authors/review-manuscript-ce-video.aspx.

APA 格式范文（2）

ATTITUDES AND SOCIAL COGNITION

"I'll Have One of Each": How Separating Rewards Into (Meaningless) Categories Increases Motivation

Scott S. Wiltermuth
University of Southern California

Francesca Gino
Harvard University

We propose that separating rewards into categories can increase motivation, even when those categories are meaningless. Across six experiments, people were more motivated to obtain one reward from one category and another reward from another category than they were to obtain two rewards from a pool that included all items from either reward category. As a result, they worked longer when potential rewards for their work were separated into meaningless categories. This categorization effect persisted regardless of whether the rewards were presented using a gain or loss frame. Using both moderation and mediation analyses, we found that categorizing rewards had these positive effects on motivation by increasing the degree to which people felt they would "miss out" if they did not obtain the second reward. We discuss implications for research on motivation and incentives.

Keywords: categories, incentives, motivation, regret, fear of missing out

Researchers across the social sciences have long sought to understand how to foster individual motivation. Much of this research has highlighted mechanisms that either increase or make salient the monetary or nonmonetary benefits that people can obtain by applying effort. For instance, prior work has found that people become more motivated when the prosocial impact of their jobs is highlighted (Grant, 2007, 2008), when their work is imbued with task identity or task significance (Hackman & Oldham, 1976), or when they come to see the performance of a task as central to their own identity (Koestner & Losier, 2002). Setting concrete goals and providing meaningful rewards contingent upon the achievement of those goals can also increase individual motivation (Locke, 1968; Locke & Latham, 2002; see Sansone & Harackiewicz, 2000, for a review).

Drawing on research on the psychological principles of categorization (Rosch, 1973; Rosch & Lloyd, 1978; Rosch, Mervis, Gray, Johnson, & Boyes-Braem, 1976) and regret theory (Bell, 1982, 1983; Loomes & Sugden, 1982), we examine how categories of rewards influence individuals' motivation to exert task effort. We propose that grouping rewards into categories can increase the effort people apply toward goals, even when those categories are constructed arbitrarily, because categorizing incentives can increase the extent to which participants feel that they would be "missing out" on something if they failed to obtain a second reward. In illustrating this, our research goes beyond showing that people exhibit diminishing sensitivity to rewards in a single category and establishes a novel mechanism by which categorizing rewards enhances motivation.

Our investigation aims to establish that even factors that should not rationally affect the amount of effort people apply toward attaining incentives may in fact do so. By examining the effects of dividing rewards into meaningless categories on individual motivation, we contribute to research on the role psychological tendencies play in explaining the relationship between incentives and motivation. A more nuanced understanding of the impact of these psychological tendencies could benefit not only scholars interested in motivation but also parents, educators, managers, and anyone else who seeks to motivate others through rewards. Of course, such an understanding might also allow people to manipulate others into working more than they would otherwise deem optimal.

Incentives and Motivation

Motivation is defined as the driving force of directed activity that causes a person to act (Deci & Ryan, 1985; Lewin, 1935; Ryan & Deci, 2000). It is "the contemporary (immediate) influence on direction, vigor, and persistence of action" (Atkinson, 1964, p. 2). Several theories have been proposed to explain the process of motivation. Many of these theories assume that an individual's level of motivation depends directly on the expected consequences attributable to applying effort. Vroom's (1964) expectancy theory of motivation, for example, posits that people decide to behave in

---

This article was published Online First November 26, 2012.

Scott S. Wiltermuth, Marshall School of Business, University of Southern California; Francesca Gino, Harvard Business School, Harvard University.

We gratefully acknowledge comments on drafts of this article and helpful suggestions from Drew Carton, Nate Fast, Cassie Mogilner, and Don Moore.

Correspondence concerning this article should be addressed to Scott S. Wiltermuth, Marshall School of Business, University of Southern California, Los Angeles, CA 90089-0808. E-mail: wiltermu@usc.edu

• 507 •

a particular manner because they expect the consequences of that behavior to be more desirable than the consequences of alternative behaviors. The theory holds that people consider both the likelihood of attaining the desired consequence and the expected valence of the consequence when deciding to apply effort. Incentive theory (Killeen, 1979, 1982; McDowell & Kessel, 1979) also holds that the expected consequences of effort shape how motivated people are to work toward a goal. Indeed, most economic reasoning assumes that rewards can effectively motivate behavior (Laffont & Martimort, 2002).

While such theories explain much about how incentives affect behavior, their ability to predict how incentives affect behavior is far from complete. Indeed, numerous scholars have asserted that expected utility theory would more accurately reflect behavior if it accounted for regret (e.g., Bell, 1982; Loomes, 1988; Loomes & Sugden, 1982), which is a "negative, cognitively based emotion that we experience when realizing or imagining that our present situation would have been better, had we decided differently" (Zeelenberg, 1999, p. 94). Bell (1982) and Loomes and Sugden (1982) each put forth regret theory, which assumes that the expected utility depends not only on the pain and pleasure associated with the outcomes of a decision but also on the regret experienced (or anticipated) by comparing those outcomes to those that would have resulted from different decisions. Providing support for this enhancement of utility theory, scholars have repeatedly found that the anticipation of regret can lead people to behave in ways designed to minimize the potential for subsequent regret (Loomes, Starmer, & Sugden, 1992; Ritov, 1996; Zeelenberg & Beattie 1997; Zeelenberg, Beattie, van der Pligt, & de Vries, 1996; Zeelenberg, van Dijk, & Manstead, 1998; but see Battalio, Kagel, & Jiranyakul, 1991, and Harless, 1992).

Although scholars often draw upon regret theory to examine decision making under uncertainty (e.g., Larrick & Boles, 1995) and decision making in consumer contexts (e.g., Simonson, 1992), little research has drawn upon regret theory to explain how much effort people will apply in pursuit of incentives. Yet, the degree to which people anticipate feeling regret for foregone incentives may well predict motivation in ways not predicted by current theories of motivation—particularly when multiple incentives are available and people may construe these incentives as falling into different categories. The present research explores this possibility, examining specifically how the categorization of nonmonetary incentives may affect people's motivation by affecting their level of anticipated regret. We call this anticipated regret "fear of missing out."

Categories and Anticipated Regret

People cognitively construct categories using a basic level of processing (Rosch, 1975). This occurs because categories provide a great deal of information while allowing people to preserve their finite cognitive capacities (Rosch, 1978). In particular, categories allow people to identify differences between items very quickly (Heit & Rubinstein, 1994; Lassaline, 1996; Rosch, 2002; Sloutsky, 2003). Because categories allow people to quickly sort items into similar and dissimilar categories, and because people believe that every act of communication conveys information (Clark, 1985; Grice, 1975), people tend to assume that items labeled as belonging to the same category are more similar than are items labeled as belonging to different categories (Mogilner, Rudnick, & Iyengar, 2008).

We propose that the categorization of incentives has important implications for decision making and motivation. Mogilner et al. (2008) demonstrated that this phenomenon has implications for consumers' perceptions and behavior. Using both field and laboratory experiments, these researchers found that increasing the number of categories available at the moment of choice (e.g., categories that partitioned an assortment of magazines) led to greater feelings of self-determination, which is the degree to which people experienced a sense of choice when making their purchasing decision. In turn, these greater feelings of self-determination increased people's satisfaction with their purchase. The results were obtained even when the categories were completely arbitrary. While Mogilner et al. (2008) focused on how the presence of categories of items influence the choice people make when choosing one of the available items, here we examine how dividing potential rewards for performance into categories affects people's motivation to exert effort on the tasks that they are facing.

In this context, we argue, separating rewards into arbitrary categories is likely to increase the extent to which people fear they would be missing out by not attaining every category of reward. When rewards are uncategorized, people are unlikely to feel that they would miss out on the best reward available if they earned only one reward. Because people would not consider themselves to be missing out on obtaining the best reward available if they obtained only one reward, they would not likely anticipate that they would experience much regret from failing to obtain a second reward. However, when rewards are categorized into multiple categories, people may want to obtain a reward from each of the available categories in order to keep from feeling as if they are missing out on something. In short, they would anticipate greater regret. To avoid the negative emotional impact of failing to obtain a reward, people are likely to exert more effort when rewards are divided into multiple categories than when they are not. Fear of missing out can be a powerful motivating force. To wit, fear of missing out can motivate managers to work more hours than they otherwise would (Rutherford, 2001), college students to spend seemingly endless hours on the Internet (Kandell, 1998), athletes to return to competition prematurely after injury (Tracey, 2003), and investors to create speculative bubbles (Kindleberger, 1978/1989). We therefore propose that categorizing incentives increases people's motivation to obtain a second reward.

Distinct Reference Points as an Alternative Mechanism

Categorizing incentives may increase people's motivation to obtain multiple rewards because of an alternative mechanism that we account for in our research. It may lead people to consider multiple rewards as belonging to separate mental accounts (Thaler, 1985, 1990, 1999), which are defined as frames that specify "(i) the set of elementary outcomes that are evaluated jointly and the manner in which they are combined, and (ii) a reference outcome that is considered neutral or normal" (Tversky & Kahneman, 1981, p. 456). Considerable research (e.g., Thaler & Johnson, 1990) supporting Kahneman and Tversky's (1979) prospect theory has demonstrated that people's sensitivity to increases in gains or losses diminishes with the magnitudes of those gains and losses, such that the gain function is concave and the loss function is convex (see Figure 1).[1] If categorizing rewards leads people to view those rewards as belonging to separate mental accounts, it should also lead them to use separate reference points when evaluating those rewards. Given the concavity of the gain function, people should therefore be more sensitive to increases in gains that involve distinct mental accounts than they should be to increases in gains within a single mental account. As such, categorizing rewards should lead people to be more motivated to pursue a second reward. In our experiments, we test whether this alternative mechanism may explain the link between categorization and motivation.

In short, we propose that separating gains into categories increases the degree to which people feel as though they would be missing out if they failed to obtain rewards from each category. Specifically, we propose that simply labeling potential rewards as belonging to different categories can increase motivation, even when those categories do not objectively differ. For example, people might be more motivated to obtain both a box of candy and a box of popcorn if these items were said to be from different categories of goods than if they were said to be from a single category. Thus, we seek primarily to demonstrate how the simple act of categorizing incentives increases their impact on individual motivation, even when categorization does not increase the objective value of the incentives.

Overview of the Present Research

In six experiments, we tested the hypothesis that separating incentives into categories can increase the effort people exert to attain those incentives, even when those categories are arbitrarily constructed. Furthermore, we examined how fear of missing out explains the relationship between categorizing incentives and increased motivation. Finally, we ruled out alternative mechanisms that could potentially explain our effects. In Experiment 1, we examined whether splitting incentives into arbitrary categories leads people to apply more effort toward a goal. In the next two experiments, we replicated the results of Experiment 1 using a loss rather than a gain frame (Experiment 2) and a different measure of motivation, namely, self-reported task performance (Experiment 3). In Experiments 4, 5, and 6, we tested whether categorizing rewards increases motivation by creating a fear of missing out and ruled out the alternative mechanism of establishing distinct reference points. In Experiment 4, we examined whether the categorization-of-rewards effect is strongest when increased effort can largely eliminate the fear of "missing out" associated with failing to obtain a second reward. In Experiment 5 we demonstrated that fear of missing out mediates the link between categorization and increased motivation. Finally, in Experiment 6 we employed both mediation and moderation analyses to provide further evidence for the process by which categorization increases effort.

Experiment 1: Two Categories or a Single Category

In Experiment 1, we tested whether splitting incentives into arbitrary categories leads people to apply more effort toward a reward. We did so by manipulating whether items purchased from a local dollar store were portrayed as belonging to a single category or to two categories. The items available in the two conditions were the same. In testing our main hypothesis, we attempted to move beyond current research showing that people respond differently to financial and nonfinancial incentives (e.g., Heyman & Ariely, 2004) to show that the framing of nonfinancial incentives can and does affect individual motivation.

Method

Participants and design. Sixty-three undergraduate business students (56% female; mean age = 21.0 years) at a large, private university on the West Coast of the United States participated in the study in exchange for course credit. Participants were randomly assigned to one of two experimental conditions: categorization and no categorization.

Procedure. We instructed participants that they would be transcribing a number of sections of typewritten text to help us prepare for a future study in which we would examine how handwriting can affect the perceptions people form of others. Participants were told they could spend as much time or as little time transcribing the sections of text as they liked. They then examined their potential rewards, which were placed in two 55-quart storage containers. The rewards were not sorted into specific categories; rather, there was a mix of stationery and food items in each container. Thus, while in this study and most of the studies that follow the containers contained slightly different mixes of products, the differences in product mixes were not meaningful. Examples of rewards were boxes of hot cocoa, packages of pens, calculators, notebooks, and animal crackers. Participants then read about the rewards they would accumulate for spending at least 10 min and at least 20 min transcribing the sections of text. Participants then began transcribing the sections of text. After they decided to stop transcribing, participants selected their reward(s). As their last task, participants completed a short questionnaire.

In this and all following experiments except Experiment 5, the experimenter was blind to participant condition. In Experiment 5, it was not possible to keep the experimenter blind to participant condition; however, the experimenter in Experiment 5 was unaware of the study hypotheses.

Categorization manipulation. We manipulated whether participants perceived the rewards as belonging to two distinct categories or only one. In the categorization condition, participants read the following:

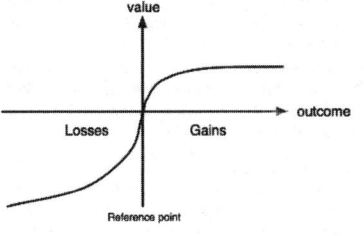

Figure 1. Value function.

---
[1] Prospect theory also holds that people are loss-avoidant, such that the loss function is steeper than the gain function. This aspect of the theory is not particularly relevant for our predictions.

There are two categories of rewards you can earn by spending time transcribing these sections of text. Category 1 is in the Purple Storage Container and Category 2 is in the Clear Storage Container. If you spend ten minutes transcribing these sections of text, you will be allowed to take home one of the items from either the Purple Storage Container or the Clear Storage Container. It will be your choice. If you spend twenty minutes transcribing these sections of text, you will also be allowed to take one of the items home from the other storage container. So, you will be able to take home an item from each of the two categories if you spend twenty minutes transcribing the sections of text.

In the no-categorization condition, participants read the following:

There are rewards you can earn by spending time transcribing these sections of text. If you spend ten minutes transcribing the sections of text, you will be allowed to take home one item. If you spend twenty minutes transcribing the sections of text you will be allowed to take home a second item. So, you will be able to take home two items if you spend twenty minutes transcribing these sections of text.

Thus, in the no-categorization condition, participants actually had more choice regarding the rewards they could take, as they could have chosen two rewards from the same container. Participants in both conditions visually inspected the rewards before starting the transcription task. The items in each storage container were of equal monetary value.

Measures. The likelihood of participants transcribing sections of text for a full 20 min served as the primary dependent variable. After the transcription task, participants indicated on a 7-point Likert-type scale (from $1 = $ *not at all* to $7 = $ *very much*) how motivated they were to earn the first reward, how motivated they were to earn the second reward, and how much they enjoyed the task.

Results

We first used a logistic regression to examine the effect of categorization condition on participants' likelihood of working for the full 20 min required to claim two rewards. Participants in the categorization condition were more likely to transcribe for the full 20 min (34.4%) than were participants in the no-categorization condition (9.7%), $B = 0.79$, $SD = 0.36$, Wald $= 4.96$, $\text{Exp}(B) = 2.21$, $p = .03$. They also reported that they were more motivated to obtain the second reward ($M = 4.22$, $SD = 2.21$) than did participants in the no-categorization condition ($M = 3.07$, $SD = 1.95$), $t(60) = 2.17$, $p = .03$, $d = .55$. We note that participants' self-reported motivation to obtain the second reward correlated significantly with their likelihood to transcribe for the full 20 min, $r(62) = .36$, $p < .01$.

Participants in the categorization condition also reported enjoying the task more ($M = 2.97$, $SD = 1.49$) than did those in the no-categorization condition ($M = 2.20$, $SD = 1.27$), $t(59) = 2.16$, $p = .04$, $d = .52$. However, task enjoyment did not mediate the link between categorization condition and likelihood of working for the full 20 min, nor did it mediate the link between categorization condition and self-reported motivation to obtain the second reward.

Importantly, we found no differences across conditions in likelihood to transcribe for the 10 min required to obtain the first reward ($p > .40$) or in motivation to obtain the first reward ($p > .35$).

Discussion

The results of Experiment 1 provide support for the categorization-of-rewards effect we hypothesized: Participants spent more time working on the transcribing task and reported feeling more motivated to obtain a second reward in the categorization condition than in the no-categorization condition, even though the categories of rewards created in this study were completely arbitrary. Interestingly, participants also reported enjoying the task more in the categorization-of-rewards condition.

Experiment 2: Loss Frame and Valuation of Rewards

Experiment 1 participants were more motivated and worked longer when their rewards ostensibly came from two categories rather than from a single category. As such, participants derived more subjective value from categorized rewards than they did from noncategorized rewards even though the objective value of the rewards was equivalent. To test the robustness of these findings, in Experiment 2 we employed a loss frame. Specifically, we examined whether participants would be willing to work longer to avoid losing rewards from two distinct categories than they would to avoid losing multiple rewards from a single category. Experiment 2 also examined whether the categorization effect persists when people actively calculate the value of the incentives before they engage in the given task. The valuation of the incentives may attenuate or eliminate the effect of categorization if it leads people to focus on the financial value of the incentive. We expected that it would not.

Method

Participants and design. ne hundred thirty-one business students (56% female mean age $= 20.6$ years) at a large, private university on the West Coast of the nited States participated in the study in exchange for course credit. Participants were randomly assigned to one of four experimental conditions from a 2 (categorization of rewards) $\times$ 2 (valuation of rewards) between-subjects design.

Procedure. Participants completed the same task used in Experiment 1. However, in this study, participants selected their potential rewards before embarking on the transcription task. Additionally, we introduced a second manipulation to examine whether categorization increases effort even when participants are first asked to estimate the monetary value of potential rewards. We varied whether participants calculated the monetary value of their rewards before they engaged in the transcription task. After the transcription task, participants rated how motivated they were to earn the second reward (on a 7-point scale ranging from $1 = $ *not at all* to $7 = $ *very much*).

Categorization manipulation. We manipulated whether participants perceived the rewards as belonging to two distinct categories or only one. In the categorization condition, participants first read the following:

There are two categories of rewards that you earn by doing this experiment. Category 1 is in the Purple Storage Container and Category 2 is in the Clear Storage Container. Please go to the front of the room and select an item that you would like to take home with you from each of these two categories.

They were then told the following:

> If you work for at least twenty minutes transcribing the sections of text, you will be able to keep an item from each of the two categories. If you spend between ten and twenty minutes transcribing the sections of text, you will have to return an item from one of the two categories but will be allowed to keep the item from the other category. If you spend less than ten minutes transcribing the sections of text, you will have to return the items from both categories. So, spending twenty minutes transcribing the sections of text would enable you to take home an item from each of the two categories.

In the no-categorization condition, participants read the following:

> There are rewards that you earn by doing this experiment. If you work for at least twenty minutes transcribing the sections of text, you will be able to keep both of the items you have selected. If you spend between ten and twenty minutes transcribing the sections of text, you will have to return one of the items but will be allowed to keep one of the items. If you spend less than ten minutes transcribing the sections of text, you will have to return both of the items you selected. So, spending twenty minutes transcribing the sections of text would enable you to keep both items.

We reminded participants in both conditions that they could spend as much or as little time as they liked on the transcription task. As in Experiment 1, the items in each storage container were of equal monetary value.

Valuation manipulation. Participants in the valuation condition estimated the monetary value of each of the items that they selected. Participants in the no-valuation condition did not.

Dependent variables. The primary dependent variable was participants' likelihood of transcribing sections of text for a full 20 min. We also examined participants' self-reported motivation to earn the second reward.

Results

We first conducted a logistic regression to examine the effect of categorization condition and valuation condition on participants' likelihood of working for the full 20 min required to retain two rewards. We found a significant main effect for categorization condition ($B = 0.70$, $SD = 0.36$, Wald $= 3.70$, Exp(B) $= 2.01$, $p = .05$). As Table 1 illustrates, participants in the categorization condition were more likely to transcribe for the full 20 min (49.3%) than were participants in the no-categorization condition

Table 1
Participants Effort and Motivation by Condition, Experiment 2

	% transcribing at least 20 min			ea n (SD) motivation to obtain the second item		
	Evaluate monetary value			Evaluate monetary value		
Condition	o	es	Total	o	es	Total
o categories	41	23$_a$	33$_a$	3.53 (1.99)	2.73 (1.44)$_a$	3.16 (1.78)$_a$
Categories	45	53$_b$	49$_b$	3.61 (2.29)	3.91 (2.28)$_b$	3.76 (2.27)$_b$

Note. ifferent subscripts within a column denote that means differ at $p < .05$.

(32.8%). The valuation condition did not significantly affect participants' likelihood of working the entire 20 min ($p > .70$).

Consistent with this finding, participants in the categorization condition reported being more motivated to obtain the second reward ($M = 3.76$, $SD = 2.27$) compared to participants in the no-categorization condition ($M = 3.16$, $SD = 1.78$), $t(127) = 2.02$, $p = .05$, $d = .29$. Participants' self-reported motivation to obtain the second reward correlated significantly with their likelihood to transcribe for the full 20 min, $r(130) = .36$, $p < .01$. Together, these results provide further support for our hypothesis regarding the effects of categorizing rewards on individual motivation.

We did not find significant differences across conditions in participants' likelihood to transcribe for the 10 min required to obtain the first reward, $p > .90$.

Discussion

Experiment 2 tested the robustness of the categorization effect by using a loss frame. Providing further support for our main hypothesis, participants exerted more effort when their rewards were split into meaningless categories than when they were not, indicating that their motivation was influenced by the categories of rewards. Importantly, this categorization effect persisted when participants estimated the monetary value of the incentives before engaging in the task.

Experiment 3: Getting One of Each

We suggested that categorizing rewards increases the extent to which people feel that they would miss out on something if they failed to obtain a second reward. To provide support for this mechanism, in Experiment 3 we tested whether the strength of the categorization effect differs depending upon whether increased effort could eliminate people's fear of missing out on something. We predicted that people who could expend effort to eliminate the fear of missing out on something would be more motivated than would participants whose efforts could not eliminate such fear. In essence, we propose that the opportunity to eliminate the fear of missing out on something provides motivation not present in conditions in which participants have no opportunity to eliminate the fear of missing out on something. Thus, if people could only choose two rewards out of more than two categories as compensation for their performance, we would expect them to be less motivated to exert effort in the given task than when they could choose a reward from each of two categories. In the latter case, we would expect the chance to eliminate the fear of missing out on something to result in higher motivation than would be evident in the former case. In Experiment 3, we consequently employed conditions in which people's increased motivation and effort could enable them to earn rewards from each possible category, and, in doing so, greatly attenuate the risk of regret caused by missing out on something.

In particular, we tested whether categorizing rewards increases performance when that increased effort can allow people to achieve all categories of rewards rather than only some of the categories. We reasoned that the relationship between performance and the attenuation of anticipated regret is stronger when the effort enables the person to obtain a reward from all available categories.

Experiment 3 also allowed us to test for the role of two alternative mechanisms that can explain the effects demonstrated in

Experiments 1 and 2. First, this third experiment included a measure of perceived variety to examine whether it influences motivation. Previous work has demonstrated that categorization can lead to increased satisfaction in consumer choices by increasing perceived variety (Mogilner et al., 2008). In a similar manner, categorization may lead to increased motivation through the same mechanism when the object of categorization is potential rewards for performance. That is, people may be more motivated when they perceive that there are a variety of rewards available to them than they may be when they perceive that the rewards available are all very similar. We tested this possibility directly in Experiment 3 by including a measure of perceived variety.

Second, this experiment allowed us to test for the role of establishing separate reference points, the alternative mechanism discussed in the introduction. According to this account, people treat rewards from different categories as belonging to different accounts, and so the rewards are separately motivating. People treat rewards from the same category as belonging to the same account, causing them to devalue the second of the two potential rewards due to diminishing sensitivity. To rule out this alternative account, in Experiment 3 we included three conditions (rather than just two as in our previous studies). Across conditions, we varied the number of rewards and categories of rewards available to participants. Specifically, in addition to a no-categorization condition, we included a two-of-two-categories condition (where the second reward was from a second category out of two available) and a two-of-four-categories condition (where the second reward was from a second category out of four available). We expected participants' effort to be higher in the two-of-two-categories condition than in both the no-categorization condition and the two-of-four-categories condition. Furthermore, we did not expect differences in participants' effort between the two-of-four-categories condition and the no-categorization condition. Such a pattern of results would be consistent with our main hypothesis by showing that categorizing rewards improves motivation most dramatically when participants' performance allows them to attain rewards from each available category. Instead, if diminishing sensitivity is the correct explanation for the categorization-of-rewards effect, we should observe greater effort in the two-of-four-categories condition relative to the no-categorization condition.

Method

Participants. One hundred seventy-two online participants (48.9% female; mean age = 33.3 years, SD = 11.2) recruited from Amazon.com's MTurk website participated in the experiment in exchange for $1 plus the chance to earn additional prizes.

Procedure. We instructed participants that they would be alphabetizing groups of three fruits (e.g., pomegranate, raspberry, and mango). Before beginning the alphabetizing task, participants were presented with the lists of rewards from which they could choose if they alphabetized more groupings of fruit than 70% of participants. We instructed participants that they would be able to earn a second reward if they alphabetized more groupings of fruit than did 90% of participants.

Categorization manipulation. We manipulated how the rewards were categorized across three experimental conditions: no categorization, two of two categories, and two of four categories. Participants in the no-categorization condition read that they could choose one reward if they alphabetized more groupings of fruit than 70% of participants, and two rewards if they alphabetized more groupings of fruit than 90% of participants. Participants in the two-of-two-categories condition read that they could choose a reward from either of the two groups of rewards if they alphabetized more groupings of fruit than 70% of participants and that they could choose a reward from the second group if they alphabetized more groupings of fruit than 90% of participants. Those in the two-of-four-categories condition read that they could choose a reward from one of the four groups of rewards if they alphabetized more groupings of fruit than 70% of participants and that they could choose a reward from a second group if they alphabetized more groupings of fruit than 90% of participants. Each group of rewards contained a mix of items similar to those used in our first two experiments, and participants were provided with a full list of the items in each group. We instructed participants in both the two-of-two-categories condition and the two-of-four-categories condition that we arbitrarily placed the items in each group and told them that, as a result, each group of possible rewards contained similar items.

The alphabetizing task. Participants were asked to estimate how many groupings of three fruits they would alphabetize. They were free to use a value between zero and 50 as their estimate. Participants then alphabetized groupings of fruit. The number of groups they alphabetized served as our measure of effort.

Measures.

Dependent variable. The primary dependent variable of interest was the number of fruit groupings participants alphabetized.

Perceived variety. We asked participants about variety because we wanted to ensure that categorizing items did not increase their motivation by increasing the amount of variety participants perceived in the available rewards. Participants used a seven-point Likert-type scale (ranging from 1 = *not at all* to 7 = *very much*) to respond to three items reflecting how much variety they perceived in the rewards (α = .71). The three items were as follows: "How much variety was there in the rewards you could earn?"; "How different would the second reward you choose be from the first reward you choose?"; and "How similar were the rewards available to you?" (reverse coded).

Results

Reported performance. A one-way analysis of variance (ANOVA) revealed that the effect of categorization condition (no categorization vs. two of two categories vs. two of four categories) on participants' reported performance was marginally significant, $F(2, 169) = 2.34$, $p = .10$.

Planned contrasts showed that participants in the two-of-two-categories condition alphabetized more groupings ($M = 31.7$, $SD = 17.1$) than did participants in the other two conditions combined ($M = 26.3$, $SD = 18.0$), $t(169) = 1.96$, $p = .05$, $d = .31$, and participants in the no-categorization condition alone ($M = 24.7$, $SD = 17.6$), $t(169) = 2.15$, $p = .03$, $d = .41$. The number of groupings alphabetized by those in the two-of-four-categories condition ($M = 27.8$, $SD = 18.4$) did not significantly differ from that of participants in the no-categorization condition, $t(169) = 1.24$, $p = .22$, $d = .17$, or in the two-of-two-categories condition, $t(169) = -0.91$, $p = .36$, $d = .22$.

Perceived variety. Categorization did not influence participants' perceived variety, $F(2, 169) = 1.83$, $p = .16$. Importantly, participants did not perceive greater variety in the two-of-two-categories condition ($M = 4.10$, $SD = 1.17$) than they did in the no-categorization condition ($M = 4.44$, $SD = 1.31$), $t(169) = 1.52$, $p = .13$, or the two-of-four-categories condition ($M = 4.49$, $SD = 1.10$), $t(169) = 1.76$, $p = .08$.

Discussion

As predicted, categorizing rewards increased the degree to which people anticipated they would miss out if they did not attain multiple rewards. When participants had the opportunity to obtain rewards from each of the available categories (i.e., in the two-of-two condition), their motivation increased, as indicated by their higher performance. However, their motivation was not enhanced when the presence of multiple categories of rewards was not accompanied by the possibility of receiving rewards from each of the available categories (i.e., in the two-of-four-categories condition). Thus, results were consistent with the idea that categorizing rewards increases effort by instilling anticipated regret about missing out on rewards. The results were consistent neither with the alternative account of increased variety nor with the notion that categorizing rewards establishes separate reference points.

Experiment 4: Mediation by Fear of Missing Out

In Experiment 3, we used multiple conditions to test for the role of the anticipated regret associated with missing out in explaining the link between categorization of rewards and individual motivation. In Experiment 4, we provided further evidence for the posited psychological mechanism by measuring fear of missing out directly. Specifically, we asked participants about feelings of missing out before they performed an anagram task that we used to assess their performance. We did so because we believe it is the anticipation of missing out that drives motivation. We therefore sought to show that a heightened fear of missing out mediates the relationship between categorization of rewards and increased motivation.

Method

Participants and design. One hundred thirty-nine online participants (65% female; mean age = 30.7 years, $SD = 10.3$) recruited from Amazon.com's MTurk website participated in the experiment in exchange for $2 plus the opportunity to earn additional prizes. We randomly assigned participants to one of two conditions: no categorization and categorization.

Procedure. We instructed participants that they would be forming words out of a series of scrambled letters, an anagram task we adapted from Schweitzer, Ordonez, and Douma. (2004). Specifically, participants saw an example consisting of the letters ISTEBOM and were told to write down, on a separate sheet of paper, as many words as they could form out of those letters in 1 min and then to report the number of words they formed. After the example, participants completed six experimental rounds. In each round, they were given a different set of seven letters and were asked to generate as many words as they could in the allotted 1 min. In both conditions, participants simply reported the number of words they formed. Because they were not required to list those words, they had an opportunity to overreport their performance.

Categorization manipulation. Before beginning the anagram task, participants viewed the lists of potential rewards from which they could choose depending on their performance, and they received instructions on how they could receive the rewards. Participants in the no-categorization condition read that they could choose one reward if their performance placed them in the top 30% of test takers and two rewards if their performance placed them in the top 10% of test takers. Participants in the categorization condition read that they could choose a reward from either of the two categories of rewards available if their performance placed them in the top 30% of test takers and that they could choose a reward from the second category if their performance placed them in the top 10% of test takers. Each category contained a mix of items similar to those we used in Experiments 1–3. We provided participants with a full list of the items in each category but, in contrast to Experiment 3, did not tell them explicitly that we assigned the items to the groups arbitrarily.

After viewing the potential rewards and before completing the anagram task, participants responded to the question "How much would you be missing out on something if you did not earn both rewards?" using a seven-point Likert-type scale (from $1 = not\ at\ all$ to $7 = very\ much$). This question measured fear of missing out.

Measures. Participants' reporting of how many words they formed served as the primary dependent variable. We used participants' self-reported fear of missing out as the mediating variable.

Results

As we expected, participants in the categorization condition indicated that they were more concerned about missing out on the second reward ($M = 3.42$, $SD = 1.70$) than were participants in the no-categorization condition ($M = 2.78$, $SD = 1.66$), $t(137) = 2.23$, $p = .03$, $d = .38$. They also reported creating more words in the anagram task ($M = 29.56$, $SD = 17.30$) than did participants in the no-categorization condition ($M = 24.68$, $SD = 12.15$), $t(137) = 1.94$, $p = .05$, $d = .33$.

We conducted a mediation analysis to determine whether fear of missing out mediated the relationship between categorization and higher reported performance on the anagram task. Participants in the categorization condition reported feeling greater fear of missing out than did those in the no-categorization condition, $B = 0.63$, $SE = 0.28$, $t(136) = 2.23$, $p = .03$. The fear of missing out correlated positively with reported performance, $B = 1.52$, $SE = 0.75$, $t(136) = 2.04$, $p = .04$. Accounting for the fear of missing out reduced the significant relationship between condition and reported performance, $B = 4.88$, $SE = 2.51$, $t(136) = 1.94$, $p = .05$, to nonsignificance, $B = 0.63$, $SE = 0.28$, $t(136) = 2.23$, $p = .12$. A bootstrap analysis revealed that the 95% bias-corrected confidence interval for the size of the indirect effect excluded zero 0.07, 4.13 , suggesting a significant indirect effect (Mac innon, airchild , ritz , 2007; Preacher Hayes, 2004). Thus, fear of missing out mediated the relationship between the categorization of incentives and increased reported performance.

Discussion

Experiment 4 provides further evidence for the psychological mechanism explaining the robust link between categorization of rewards and increased motivation. We found that when rewards were divided into arbitrary categories, participants reported higher levels of performance and that fear of missing out mediated this link.

Experiment 5: Further Evidence for the Mediating Role of Fear of Missing Out

In Experiment 4, we measured motivation through self-reported performance. It is possible that our categorization manipulation affected participants' motivation to inflate their performance on the anagram task (i.e., to cheat) rather than their motivation to exert greater effort on the task. Since we did not have data to compare actual to reported performance, we could not rule out this possibility in Experiment 4. To address this potential confound, we conducted another experiment in which we measured motivation to exert effort on a task. Furthermore, in Experiment 5, we used a different manipulation for categories of rewards to ensure that participants perceived the categories of rewards as meaningless. Specifically, we presented the categories of rewards to participants without referring to these categories explicitly. Instead, we placed the potential prizes in front of participants within either two or three containers.

Method

Participants. One hundred one students attending local universities in a city in the Southeastern United States (57% male; mean age = 21.72 years, SD = 3.21 years) participated in the study for $7. We recruited the participants through an advertisement on a university-wide website.

Procedure and design. The experiment used a job application cover-letter editing task developed by Grant et al. (2007). We informed participants that we were collaborating with a local career center to enrich our knowledge of how to improve students' effectiveness in their job searches. Participants were told that the career center had provided actual cover letters from students who were searching for jobs and that their task was to edit a student's cover letter and provide feedback on how to improve it.

The experiment employed one between-subjects manipulation with two experimental conditions: two containers of potential rewards versus three containers. At the beginning of the study, the experimenter placed either two or three containers on a table in the center of the room so that they were visible to all participants. As potential rewards, we used the same types of items as in our other studies. In this experiment, however, all items were initially in the same large basket. In both conditions, the experimenter dumped the rewards from the basket into the plastic containers (either two or three depending on the experimental condition) while saying, "Here are the potential rewards for completing the editing task, in addition to the monetary payment you received for participating in today's study." The experimenter then told participants that if they spent 10 min editing the cover letter, they would be allowed to take home one of the items of their choosing. If, instead, they spent 20 min or more working on the editing task, they would be allowed to take home two of the items of their choosing. Finally, the experimenter noted that the containers contained similar items and asked participants to walk close to the table so that they could view the items before they started working on the editing task.

Next, participants received a student's job application cover letter in Microsoft Word and were asked to introduce edits and provide feedback using the track changes feature. The experimenter informed participants that they could stop working on the task whenever they wanted or felt they were finished. The experimenter recorded the amount of time in minutes that participants spent on the task and informed them that we would use such information to calibrate future studies. Participants had timers on their individual desks so that they could easily keep track of time. The amount of time participants spent editing the cover letter served as our measure for effort (our dependent measure).

Before participants engaged in the editing task and after viewing the potential rewards, they completed a short questionnaire that included a two-item measure for fear of missing out ("How much would you be missing out on something if you did not earn both rewards?" and "How much would you fear missing out on something if you did not earn both rewards?"; α = .91). Participants indicated their answers for each item using a 7-point scale (ranging from 1 = *not at all* to 7 = *very much*). We used this measure as our mediator in the analyses we present below.

Results

We first examined the effect of our manipulation (i.e., the presence of two vs. three containers containing potential rewards) on participants' effort. As predicted, and consistent with the results of the previous studies, participants in the two-containers condition spent more time working on the editing task (M = 18.20 min, SD = 5.00) than did participants in the three-containers condition (M = 15.80, SD = 4.96), $t(99)$ = 2.42, p = .018, d = .48. Consistent with this result, a larger percentage of participants spent 20 min or more working on the editing task in the two-containers condition (62%) than in the three-containers condition (41.2%), χ^2 (1, N = 101) = 4.38, p = .036. In addition, participants indicated that they were more concerned about missing out on something if they did not earn both rewards in the two-container condition (M = 4.28, SD = 1.40) than in the three-container condition (M = 3.59, SD = 1.28), $t(99)$ = 2.59, p = .011, d = .51.

Next, we examined whether participants' fear of missing out mediated the effect of our manipulation on the amount of time participants spent working on the editing task. The effect of two versus three containers of rewards was reduced to marginal significance (from β = .24, t = 2.42, p = .018 to β = .17, t = 1.77, p = .08) when fear of missing out was included in the equation, and fear of missing out was a significant predictor of participants' effort (β = .25, t = 2.50, p = .014). A bootstrap analysis showed that the 95% bias-corrected confidence interval for the size of the indirect effect excluded zero 0.088, 1.68 , suggesting a significant indirect effect (Mac innon et al., 2007; Preacher Hayes, 2004).

esults examining participants' likelihood of working 20 min or more on the editing task were similar. The effect of the categories manipulation on likelihood of working for at least 20 min was reduced to nonsignificance, from B = 0.85, SD = 0.41, Wald = 4.32, Exp(B) = 2.33, p = .038 to B = 0.64, SD = 0.43, Wald = 2.27, Exp(B) = 1.90, p = .13, when we included fear of missing out as a mediator. Moreover, fear of missing out was a significant predictor, $B = 0.35$, $SD = 0.16$, Wald = 4.67, Exp(B) = 1.42, $p = .031$. Also in this case, a bootstrap analysis revealed that the 95% bias-corrected confidence interval for the size of the indirect effect excluded zero [0.02, 0.76], suggesting a significant indirect effect (MacKinnon et al., 2007; Preacher & Hayes, 2004). Together, these results show that fear of missing out mediated the relationship between categorizing rewards into meaningless categories and participants' enhanced motivation to exert effort on the editing task, even if there was no explicit mention of categories.

Discussion

The results of Experiment 5 further support our main hypotheses regarding the relationship between categorizing rewards and enhanced motivation and the role of fear of missing out in explaining this link. Using a procedure that assured that participants perceived the categories of rewards as meaningless, we found that participants worked longer on an editing task and more strongly feared missing out on a second reward for their performance when they could attain two rewards of their choosing among rewards placed in two rather than three containers.

Experiment 6: The Same Items in Each Container

We conducted a final experiment to further corroborate our hypothesis that categorizing incentives can increase motivation by instilling feelings of anticipated regret about missing out on incentives. In this experiment, we placed exactly the same items within each of the containers. As in Experiment 5, we also omitted the word *category* from the instructions to see if segregating rewards into categories would produce differences in effort even if we did not explicitly activate the construct of categories. Moreover, we asked all participants to note that the experimenter did not care how much time they spent on the transcription task. Finally, we included a condition in which participants could earn a reward from each of two of three available containers.

Method

Participants and procedure. One hundred thirty-one undergraduate students (51% female; mean age = 20.3 years, $SD = 2.5$) participated in the experiment in exchange for course credit plus the chance to earn additional prizes. Participants were randomly assigned to one of three experimental conditions: two of two containers of rewards, combined containers, and two of three containers. They completed the same transcribing task we used in Experiments 1 and 2. This time, however, participants received a reward for transcribing for 5 min and two rewards if they transcribed for at least 10 min.

Categorization manipulation. We manipulated the presentation of rewards across three conditions. In the two-of-two-containers condition, participants first read the following:

> If you spend five minutes transcribing these sections of text, you will be allowed to take home one of the items from either the Purple Storage Container or the Clear Storage Container. It will be your choice. They contain similar items and you are free to peruse the items before engaging in the task. If you spend ten minutes transcribing these sections of text, you will also be allowed to take home one of the items from the other storage container. So, you will be able to take home an item from each of the two storage containers if you spend ten minutes transcribing the sections of text.

In the combined-containers condition, participants read the following:

> If you spend five minutes transcribing these sections of text, you will be allowed to take home one of the items from the storage containers. It will be your choice. The storage containers contain similar items. You are free to peruse the items before engaging in the task. If you spend ten minutes transcribing these sections of text, you will also be allowed to take home a second item. So, you will be able to take home two items if you spend ten minutes transcribing the sections of text.

In the two-of-three-containers condition, participants read the following:

> If you spend five minutes transcribing these sections of text, you will be allowed to take home one of the items from either the Purple Storage Container, the Clear Storage Container, or the Gray Storage Container. It will be your choice. The storage containers contain similar items. You are free to peruse the items before engaging in the task. If you spend ten minutes transcribing these sections of text, you will also be allowed to take home one of the items from one of the other storage containers. So, you will be able to take home an item from two of the three storage containers if you spend ten minutes transcribing the sections of text.

The written instructions reminded participants in all conditions that they could spend as much or as little time as they liked on the task.

Measures.

Effort. The primary dependent variable was participants' likelihood of transcribing sections of text for a full 10 min.

Anticipated regret. Before participants began transcribing, we asked them to use a 7-point scale (ranging from 1 = *strongly disagree* to 7 = *strongly agree*) to rate their agreement with the statement that they would regret their decision if they had decided to work for 5 min and therefore did not receive the second reward item.

Perceived experimenter concern. To ensure that participants' inferences about experimenter concerns did not drive our effects, we asked participants how much they thought the experimenter cared about how much time they spent on the transcription task.

Results

Effort. We conducted a logistic regression to examine the effect of condition on participants' likelihood of working for the full 10 min required to retain two rewards. We used the two-of-two-containers condition as the baseline condition and used dummy variables to represent the combined-containers condition and the two-of-three-containers condition. Consistent with the results of our previous studies, participants in the two-of-two-containers condition were more likely to transcribe for the full 10 min (69.1%) than were participants in the combined-containers condition (46.5%), $B = -0.94$, $SD = 0.45$, Wald = 4.33, Exp(B) = 0.39, $p = .04$, or the two-of-three-containers condition (26.1%), $B = -1.4$, $SD = 0.47$, Wald = 15.17, Exp(B) = 0.16, $p = .01$. Participants in the combined-containers condition were significantly more likely to work for the full 10 min than were those in the two-of-three-containers condition, $B = -0.90$, $SD = 0.45$, Wald $= 3.94$, $Exp(B) = 0.41$, $p = .05$.

Anticipated regret. We conducted a one-way ANOVA to examine whether condition affected anticipated regret and found a marginally significant effect, $F(2, 127) = 2.40$, $p = .09$. Participants in the two-of-two-containers condition indicated that they would experience greater regret for their decision if they only worked for 5 min and therefore did not receive a second reward ($M = 4.22$, $SD = 1.49$) than did participants in the other two conditions ($M = 3.63$, $SD = 1.61$), $t(83.6) = 2.02$, $p = .05$, $d = .38$. Participants in the two-of-two-containers condition anticipated significantly greater regret than did participants in the two-of-three-containers condition ($M = 3.48$, $SD = 1.57$), $t(84.7) = 2.25$, $p = .03$, $d = .48$. The contrast between the two-of-two-containers condition and the combined-containers condition ($M = 3.79$, $SD = 1.66$) did not reach significance, $t(81.7) = 1.25$, $p = .22$, $d = .27$.

As shown in Figure 2, anticipated regret mediated the relationship between being in the two-of-two-containers condition versus being in the other two conditions and increased the likelihood of transcribing for the full 10 min (95% bootstrapping confidence intervals of indirect effects [0.002, 0.580]).

Experimenter concern. Our categorization manipulation did not affect how much participants thought the experimenter cared about how much they transcribed (all $ps > .55$).

Discussion

The results of Experiment 6 provide further evidence for the link between dividing rewards into categories and increased motivation, even when the categories are meaningless. Furthermore, this experiments shows that the anticipated regret associated with missing out on a reward explains the relationship between categorizing rewards and heightened effort in pursuit of those rewards. As in Experiment 3, the results are not consistent with a distinct reference point explanation for the link between categorizing rewards and enhanced effort.

General Discussion

Across six experiments, assigning incentives to distinct categories increased participants' motivation to exert effort on a variety of tasks. Even if we arbitrarily constructed the distinctions among categories of potential rewards, participants spent significantly more time working on tasks when they were told that the benefits of doing so would stem from multiple categories than they did when the benefits were not said to stem from multiple categories. These effects proved robust under various conditions. First, they occurred even though participants who worked to attain noncategorized incentives could obtain some or even every possible combination of rewards that participants in the categorization condition could obtain. Second, the effects also occurred despite the fact that participants visually inspected the items prior to working on the given task and, in Experiment 2, estimated their monetary value. Last, they also occurred when exactly the same rewards were present in each category and when there was no explicit mention of categories.

The results of our studies also provide evidence for the psychological mechanism explaining this categorization-of-rewards effect. We found that the regret participants anticipated that they would experience as a result of potentially missing out on a second reward mediated the effects of categorization on increased effort. Our results also indicated that categorization of rewards did not lead to enhanced effort if such effort did not allow participants to ameliorate their anticipated regret about missing out by obtaining a reward from each available category. Our findings are therefore consistent with a fear-of-missing-out mechanism and do not provide support for the alternative possibility that categorization could lead to enhanced effort by leading people to establish distinct reference points to be used in the evaluation of the utility derived from the reward.

Theoretical Contributions

The present research contributes to the extant literature on motivation, to psychology research on the effects of creating categories, and to behavioral decision research in several ways. First, our studies are the first empirical investigation that demonstrates a link between categories of rewards, anticipated regret, and motivation. n doing so, our work adds to the collective understanding of how dividing rewards into categories can affect when and where individuals are likely to invest their efforts, even when those categories are completely arbitrary. Our findings may thus offer people a novel way to motivate themselves and avoid procrastinating. y giving themselves rewards that they can classify into distinct categories, people may find the increased motivation they need to perform the tasks necessary to accomplish their goals.

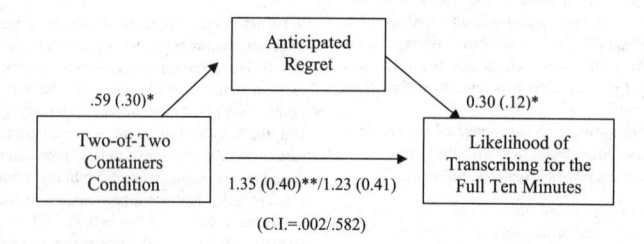

Figure 2. Anticipated regret mediates the relationship between categorized rewards and likelihood of transcribing text for the full 10 min (Experiment 6). Values are unstandardized regression coefficients (values in parentheses are standard errors). . . . = confidence interval. $^*p < .05$. $^{**}p < .01$.

Second, our results are unique in showing that mental segregation of rewards can increase the regret people anticipate they will experience by missing out on a potential reward. As we have shown through various analyses, people became more motivated to apply effort in pursuit of a second reward when their effort could ameliorate the regret they anticipate that they will experience from missing out on a reward.

Our research also suggests that fear of missing out may influence people's decisions to invest resources other than effort. Heath (1995) has found that people become hesitant to escalate their commitment beyond pre-set budgets unless they can escalate their commitment by drawing resources from a category of resources that was not initially budgeted. For example, after spending all of the money allotted to a project, those involved would be more likely to invest additional time than additional money. In contrast, if they were almost out of time, they would be more likely to invest additional money than additional time. In short, when the costs come from multiple categories, people can more easily ignore the fact that they are escalating their commitment beyond the level they initially intended. In contrast, our work focuses on the benefits of goal attainment. It suggests that a goal that comes with multiple categories of benefits may lead people to be more likely to escalate their commitment than would a goal that produces benefits that are not categorized. Future research could productively examine whether categorization of benefits systematically affects escalation of commitment.

Importantly, our findings also contribute to existing work on individual motivation. Prior work in psychology has examined the factors that increase motivation and the processes that underpin motivation from various perspectives. One theoretical approach has been particularly influential: the organismic approach (Deci & Ryan, 1985). This approach focuses on the contexts and dispositional orientations that affect motivation. For instance, according to one of the well-known models in this tradition, namely self-determination theory (Deci & Ryan, 1985), individuals are guided by two main types of motivations, controlled and autonomous, which are influenced by various environmental factors. Our work extends this body of research by focusing on a previously overlooked factor: creating categories of rewards. We demonstrated that simply dividing rewards into multiple categories increases the effort people exert on tasks. Across six experiments, we found that even when the categories of rewards are completely arbitrary, they enhance individual motivation to work harder on the given task.

The present research also contributes to extant behavioral decision research that demonstrates that the mere presence of seemingly irrelevant factors influences individual decisions and behaviors. For instance, prior work has identified a mere accessibility effect, by which making positive information easy to retrieve triggers more positive evaluations (Menon & Raghubir, 2003). Closer to the current investigation, Mogilner and colleagues (2008) have identified a mere categorization effect in consumer behavior, whereby the presence of category labels in an option display increased consumer satisfaction with a product. Extending this body of work, our research focused on the effects of categorizing rewards and investigated how such categorization, even when completely arbitrary and meaningless, can influence individual motivation to exert effort on tasks by heightening people's fear of missing out on potential rewards.

Limitations and Directions for Future Research

The contributions of our research must be qualified in light of several limitations. First, we did not investigate the effects of creating meaningful or meaningless categories on motivation when people face tasks that are clearly intrinsically interesting or when they have the opportunity to learn. The task that comes closest to these types of task is the editing task used in Experiment 5. Although we believe our results would generalize to those contexts (as suggested by the results of Experiment 5), future studies would benefit from examining how creating categories of rewards can stimulate motivation for tasks that are intrinsically motivating or that provide an opportunity for learning.

Second, we did not examine the role of dispositional factors as potential moderators for the effect of creating categories of rewards on individual motivation. For instance, need for achievement (McClelland, Atkinson, Clark, & Lowell, 1958) may moderate the categorization effect observed in our studies, as people who are high in need for achievement may feel particularly compelled to "tick off all the boxes" and obtain all categories of rewards. Future research could also investigate the moderating role of situational rather than dispositional factors. For instance, one could examine whether individuals are more sensitive to these categorization effects when they are working under time pressure or when they are competing with others who can obtain rewards from the same set of categories.

Third, our research has only focused on the effects of creating categories of incentives that serve as rewards for individual performance. Categorizing rewards may not reliably increase motivation in all types of relationships. Increasing the magnitude of compensation reliably increases effort in monetary markets but does not reliably produce the same increase in effort within relationships that are not based on monetary exchange (i.e., social markets) (Heyman & Ariely, 2004). Future work could therefore examine if categorizing rewards increases motivation in both social and monetary markets to the same degrees. Future studies could also explore whether categorizing rewards can, in some instances, transform people's conceptualization of an exchange relationship from a social market to a monetary market. If this is the case, then categorizing rewards could actually decrease effort, as the introduction of a monetary form of payment can sometimes reduce motivation relative to conditions in which no payment of any kind is offered (Heyman & Ariely, 2004).

In this research, we focused on how exogenously creating categories of rewards for performance influences motivation and effort. Future research could examine how endogenously creating categories of goals affects motivation and effort. Recent research has highlighted the important role of self-regulation in goal pursuit and motivation (e.g., Fishbach & Dhar, 2005; Fishbach, Dhar, & Zhang, 2006) and has demonstrated that the course of self-regulation over time depends on whether people are asked about commitment or about progress. Future work could investigate whether dividing goals into categories, even when arbitrary, can help individuals track their progress, and more easily achieve their goals.

Finally, our research has focused primarily on the beneficial effects of the presence of categories of rewards on individual motivation. Yet, categories of rewards may also lead to costly behavior or suboptimal decisions. For instance, people may continue engaging in the same course of actions because they are motivated to obtain a reward from a different category even when the course of action is not beneficial (as in the case of escalation of commitment or sunk costs). Our work has started investigating the powerful effects that meaningless categories can have on motivation. Future research extending our work to domains where the categorization effect may be costly could further our understanding of the effects demonstrated here.

Conclusion

In this paper, we proposed that separating rewards into categories increases motivation, even when those categories are completely arbitrary and meaningless. Across six laboratory experiments employing different categories of rewards, as well as different tasks and measures of effort, we found robust support for this prediction. Our results are important in light of the fact that fostering human motivation has been a topic of interest across disciplines over the last fifty years, and one of clear practical relevance. Our research suggests that taking existing possible rewards and splitting them into categories is a simple way to bolster individual motivation.

References

Atkinson, J. W. (1964). *Introduction to motivation*. Princeton, NJ: Van Nostrand.
Battalio, R. C., Kagel, J. H., & Jiranyakul, K. (1991). Testing between alternative models of choice under uncertainty: Some initial results. *Journal of Risk and Uncertainty, 3,* 25–50.
Bell, D. E. (1982). Regret in decision making under uncertainty. *Operations Research, 30,* 961–981. doi:10.1287/opre.30.5.961
Bell, D. E. (1983). Risk premiums for decision regret. *Management Science, 29,* 1156–1166. doi:10.1287/mnsc.29.10.1156
Clark, H. H. (1985). Language use and language users. In Gardner Lindzey and Elliot Aronson (Eds.), *Handbook of Social Psychology* (pp. 179–231). New York: Harper & Row.
Deci, E. L., & Ryan, R. M. (1985). *Intrinsic motivation and self-determination in human behavior.* New York: Plenum.
Fishbach, A., & Dhar, R. (2005). Goals as excuses or guides: The liberating effect of perceived goal progress on choice. *Journal of Consumer Research, 32*(3), 370–377. doi:10.1086/497548
Fishbach, A., Dhar, R., & Zhang, Y. (2006). Subgoals as Substitutes or Complements: The Role of Goal Accessibility. *Journal of Personality and Social Psychology, 91,* 232–242. doi:10.1037/0022-3514.91.2.232
Grant, A. M. (2007). Relational job design and the motivation to make a prosocial difference. *Academy of Management Review, 32*(2), 393–417. doi:10.5465/AMR.2007.24351328
Grant, A. M. (2008). The significance of task significance: Job performance effects, relational mechanisms, and boundary conditions. *Journal of Applied Psychology, 93*(1), 108–124. doi:10.1037/0021-9010.93.1.108
Grant, A. M., Campbell, E. M., Chen, G., Cottone, K., Lapedis, D., & Lee, K. (2007). Impact and the art of motivation maintenance: The effects of contact with beneficiaries on persistence behavior. *Organizational Behavior and Human Decision Processes, 103,* 53–67. doi:10.1016/j.obhdp.2006.05.004
Grice, H. P. (1975). Logic and conversation. In Peter Cole and Jerry L. Morgan (Eds.), *Syntax and Semantics III: Speech Acts* (pp. 41–58). New York: Academic Press.
Hackman, J. R., & Oldham, G. R. (1976). Motivation through the design of work: Test of a theory. *Organizational Behavior and Human Performance, 16*(2), 250–279. doi:10.1016/0030-5073(76)90016-7

Harless, D. W. (1992). Actions versus prospects: The effect of problem representation on regret. *American Economic Review, 82,* 634–649.
Heath, C. (1995). Escalation and de-escalation of commitment in response to sunk-costs: The role of budgeting in mental accounting. *Organizational Behavior and Human Decision Processes, 62,* 38–54. doi:10.1006/obhd.1995.1029
Heit, E., & Rubinstein, J. (1994). Similarity and property effects in inductive reasoning. *Journal of Experimental Psychology: Learning, Memory, and Cognition, 20,* 411–422. doi:10.1037/0278-7393.20.2.411
Heyman, J., & Ariely, D. (2004). Effort for payment: A tale of two markets. *Psychological Science, 15*(11), 787–793. doi:10.1111/j.0956-7976.2004.00757.x
Kahneman, D., & Tversky, A. (1979). Prospect theory: An analysis of decision under risk. *Econometrica, 47,* 263–291. doi:10.2307/1914185
Kandell, J. (1998). Internet addiction on campus: The vulnerability of college students. *CyberPsychology & Behavior, 1*(1), 11–17. doi:10.1089/cpb.1998.1.11
Killeen, P. R. (1979). Arousal: Its genesis, modulation, and extinction. In M. D. Zeiler & P. Harzem (Eds.), *Advances in analysis of behaviour: Vol. 1. Reinforcement and the organization of behaviour* (pp. 31–78). Chichester, England: Wiley.
Killeen, P. R. (1982). Incentive theory: II. Models for choice. *Journal of the Experimental Analysis of Behavior, 38,* 217–232. doi:10.1901/jeab.1982.38-217
Kindleberger, C. P. (1989). *Manias, panics, and crashes: A history of financial crises* (2nd ed.). NewYork, NY: Basic Books. (Original work published 1978)
Koestner, R., & Losier, G. F. (2002). Distinguishing three ways of being internally motivated: A closer look at introjection, identification, and intrinsic motivation. In E. L. Deci & R. M. Ryan (Eds.), *Handbook of self-determination research* (pp. 101–121). Rochester, NY: University of Rochester Press.
Laffont, J. J., & Martimort, D. (2002). *The theory of incentives: The principal-agent model.* Princeton, NJ: Princeton University Press.
Larrick, R. P., & Boles, T. L. (1995). Avoiding regret in decision with feedback: A negotiation example. *Organizational Behavior and Human Decision Processes, 63,* 87–97. doi:10.1006/obhd.1995.1064
Lassaline, M. E. (1996). Structural alignment in induction and similarity. *Journal of Experimental Psychology: Learning, Memory, and Cognition, 22,* 754–770. doi:10.1037/0278-7393.22.3.754
Lewin, K. (1935). *A dynamic theory of personality: Selected papers (D. E. Adams & K. E. Zener, Trans.).* New York, NY: McGraw Hill.
Locke, E. A. (1968). Toward a theory of task motivation and incentives. *Organizational Behavior and Human Performance, 3*(2), 157–189. doi:10.1016/0030-5073(68)90004-4
Locke, E. A., & Latham, G. P. (2002). Building a practically useful theory of goal setting and task motivation: A 35-year odyssey. *American Psychologist, 57,* 705–717. doi:10.1037/0003-066 .57.9.705
Loomes, G. (1988). Further evidence of the impact of regret and disappointment on choice under uncertainty. *Economica, 55,* 47–62. doi:10.2307/2554246
Loomes, G., Starmer, C., & Sugden, R. (1992). Are preferences monotonic Testing some predictions of regret theory. *Economica, 59,* 17–33. doi:10.2307/2555063
Loomes, G., & Sugden, R. (1982). Regret theory: An alternative theory of rational choice under uncertainty. *Economic Journal, 92,* 805–824. doi:10.2307/2232669
MacKinnon, D. P., Fairchild, A. J., & Fritz, M. S. (2007). Mediation analysis. *Annual Review of Psychology, 58,* 593–614. doi:10.1146/annurev.psych.58.110405.085542
McClelland, D. C., Atkinson, J. W., Clark, R. A., & Lowell, E. L. (1958). A scoring manual for the achievement motive. In J. W. Atkinson (Ed.), *Motives in fantasy, action and society* (pp. 179–204). New York, NY: Van Nostrand.

McDowell, J. J., & Kessel, R. A. (1979). A multivariate rate equation for variable-interval performance. *Journal of the Experimental Analysis of Behavior, 31,* 267–283. doi:10.1901/jeab.1979.31-267

Menon, G., & Raghubir, P. (2003). Ease-of-retrieval as an automatic input in judgments: A mere accessibility framework? *Journal of Consumer Research, 30,* 230–243. doi:10.1086/376804

Mogilner, C., Rudnick, T., & Iyengar, S. S. (2008). The mere categorization effect: How the presence of categories increases choosers' perceptions of assortment variety and outcome satisfaction. *Journal of Consumer Research, 35,* 202–215. doi:10.1086/588698

Preacher, K. J., & Hayes, A. F. (2004). SPSS and SAS procedures for estimating indirect effects in simple mediation models. *Behavior Research Methods, Instruments, and Computers, 36,* 717–731. doi: 10.3758/BF03206553

Ritov, I. (1996). Probability of regret: Anticipation of uncertainty resolution in choice. *Organizational Behavior and Human Decision Processes, 66,* 228–236. doi:10.1006/obhd.1996.0051

Rosch, E. (1973). Natural categories. *Cognitive Psychology, 4*(3), 328–350. doi:10.1016/0010-0285(73)90017-0

Rosch, E. (1975). Cognitive reference points. *Cognitive Psychology, 7,* 532–547. doi:10.1016/0010-0285(75)90021-3

Rosch, E. (1978). Principles of categorization. In E. Rosch & B. B. Lloyd (Eds.), *Cognition and categorization* (pp. 27–48). Hillsdale, NJ: Erlbaum.

Rosch, E. (2002). Principles of categorization. In D. Levitin (Ed.), *Foundations of cognitive psychology: Core readings* (pp. 251–270). Cambridge, MA: MIT Press.

Rosch, E., & Lloyd, B. B. (1978). *Cognition and categorization*. Hillsdale, NJ: Erlbaum.

Rosch, E., Mervis, C. B., Gray, W. D., Johnson, D. M., & Boyes-Braem, P. (1976). Basic objects in natural categories, *Cognitive Psychology, 8,* 382–439. doi:10.1016/0010-0285(76)90013-X

Rutherford, S. (2001). 'Are you going home already?': The long hours culture, women managers and patriarchal closure. *Time and Society, 10,* 259–276.

Ryan, R. M., & Deci, E. L. (2000). Self-determination theory and the facilitation of intrinsic motivation, social development, and well-being. *American Psychologist, 55,* 68–78. doi:10.1037/0003-066X.55.1.68

Sansone, C., & Harackiewicz, J. M. (2000). *Intrinsic and extrinsic motivation: The search for optimal motivation and performance*. Amsterdam, the Netherlands: Elsevier.

Schweitzer, M., Ordonez, L., & Douma, B. (2004). Goal setting as a motivator of unethical behavior. *Academy of Management Journal, 47*(3), 422–432. doi:10.2307/20159591

Simonson, I. (1992). The influence of anticipating regret and responsibility on purchase decisions. *Journal of Consumer Research, 19,* 105–118. doi:10.1086/209290

Sloutsky, V. M. (2003). The role of similarity in the development of categorization. *Trends in Cognitive Sciences, 7,* 246–251. doi:10.1016/S1364-6613(03)00109-8

Thaler, R. H. (1985). Mental accounting and consumer choice. *Marketing Science, 4,* 199–214. doi:10.1287/mksc.4.3.199

Thaler, R. H. (1990). Saving, fungibility and mental accounts. *Journal of Economic Perspectives, 4,* 193–205. doi:10.1257/jep.4.1.193

Thaler, R. H. (1999). Mental accounting matters. *Journal of Behavioral Decision Making, 12*(3), 183–206. doi:10.1002/(SICI)1099-0771(199909)12:3<183::AID-BDM318>3.0.CO;2-F

Thaler, R. H., & Johnson, E. J. (1990). Gambling with the house money and trying to break even: The effects of prior outcomes on risky choice. *Management Science, 36*(6), 643–660. doi:10.1287/mnsc.36.6.643

Tracey, J. (2003). The emotional response to the injury and rehabilitation process. *Journal of Applied Sport Psychology, 15*(4), 279–293. doi: 10.1080/714044197

Tversky, A., & Kahneman, D. (1981, January 30). The framing of decisions and the psychology of choice. *Science, 211,* 453–458. doi: 10.1126/science.7455683

Vroom, V. H. (1964). *Work and motivation*. New York, NY: Wiley.

Zeelenberg, M. (1999). Anticipated regret, expected feedback, and behavioral decision making. *Journal of Behavioral Decision Making, 12*(2), 93–106. doi:10.1002/(SICI)1099-0771(199906)12:2<93::AID-BDM311>3.0.CO;2-S

Zeelenberg, M., & Beattie, J. (1997). Consequences of regret aversion 2: Additional evidence for effects of feedback on decision making. *Organizational Behavior and Human Decision Processes, 72,* 63–78. doi: 10.1006/obhd.1997.2730

Zeelenberg, M., Beattie, J., van der Pligt, J., & de Vries, N. K. (1996). Consequences of regret aversion: Effects of expected feedback on risky decision making. *Organizational Behavior and Human Decision Processes, 65,* 148–158. doi:10.1006/obhd.1996.0013

Zeelenberg, M., van Dijk, W. W., & Manstead, A. S. R. (1998). Reconsidering the relation between regret and responsibility. *Organizational Behavior and Human Decision Processes, 74,* 254–272. doi:10.1006/obhd.1998.2780

Received June 28, 2011
Revision received August 27, 2012
Accepted August 28, 2012 ∎